# Legal Fundamentals

FOURTH EDITION

## for Canadian Business

FOURTH EDITION

# Legal Fundamentals
## for Canadian Business

RICHARD A. YATES Simon Fraser University

PEARSON

Toronto

**Vice-President, CMPS:** Gary Bennett
**Editorial Director:** Claudine O'Donnell
**Acquisitions Editor:** Megan Farrell
**Marketing Manager:** Jessica Saso
**Project Manager:** Kimberley Blakey
**Developmental Editor:** Lila Campbell
**Manager Content Development:** Suzanne Schaan
**Media Editor:** Lila Campbell
**Media Developer:** Tiffany Palmer
**Production Services:** Kailash Jadli, iEnergizer Aptara®, Ltd.
**Permissions Project Manager:** Joanne Tang
**Photo Permissions Research:** iEnergizer Aptara®, Ltd.
**Text Permissions Research:** iEnergizer Aptara®, Ltd.
**Interior Designer:** iEnergizer Aptara®, Ltd.
**Cover Designer:** iEnergizer Aptara®, Ltd.
**Cover Image:** © marekuliasz/Shutterstock

**Library and Archives Canada Cataloguing in Publication**

Yates, Richard, author
    Legal fundamentals for Canadian business/Richard
A. Yates, Simon Fraser University.—Fourth edition.

Includes bibliographical references and index.
ISBN 978-0-13-337028-7 (pbk.)

    1. Commercial law—Canada—Textbooks. I. Title.

KE919.Y38 2015      346.7107      C2015-900763-1      KF889.Y38 2015

ISBN 13: 978-0-13-337028-7

# CONTENTS

# PREFACE

I am very pleased to have the opportunity to write a fourth edition of *Legal Fundamentals for Canadian Business* but also feel some trepidation. It is difficult to resist adding a lot more information because certainly the law is constantly changing; there are new case decisions, new legislative enactments, and new challenges facing business people that are not clearly elucidated in the current law. The difficulty is that adding more threatens the primary purpose of the text—to make the information manageable in a one-semester undergraduate course and to cover the information essential for students to enter into the business environment with confidence. So in the process of revising, I have kept the original focus clearly in mind. I have implemented a number of recommendations from reviewers, modifying, increasing, and reducing content as appropriate. I have maintained a focus on intellectual property and information technology, as they are areas where there have been dramatic legislative changes and technological advancements in recent years. I always keep in mind that a risk-averse businessperson is perhaps the most astute, and so we have increased the suggestions and ideas on how legal complications can develop and have proposed ways and means to avoid them. As usual we have replaced many of the cases with newer decisions and commented on their impact on the laws that affect business decision making. Recognizing that judicial decisions are the essential guideposts to business activity, I give full recognition to their importance in this endeavour. I am grateful to students and instructors whose use of the text suggests that I am still on the right track.

## APPROACH

Although some may raise their eyebrows at yet another business law text in an already crowded field, I have observed that most of the texts currently used are too extensive or too detailed for some courses. In this text I have attempted to create a shorter book (only 10 chapters) without sacrificing essential content. I have also found that the text usually drives the course; and many instructors complain that they don't have enough time in a 14-week term to deal with all of the subjects they would like to cover. Sometimes instructors teach a course that must be delivered in an even more condensed time frame. Some teach specialized courses in marketing, computers, finance, and the like, and find that they have to spend so much time on a general introduction to business law that they don't have time to focus on the law that affects the specialized topic that is the primary objective of the course. This text gives business law instructors the flexibility to deal with all of the topics, to customize their course by supplementing it with additional material, and/or to concentrate on an area of specialization.

Many instructors feel a pressing need to deliver the introductory and foundation material efficiently so that there is enough time left to cover more advanced material. Hence, in this text there is only one introductory chapter setting out the history, institutions, and litigation processes used in Canada, only one chapter on torts, and three chapters on basic contract law. A great deal of effort has gone into making these chapters as efficient as possible, while still covering the essential concepts and rules. The remaining five chapters deal with more advanced and technical information—

everything from the legal issues regarding agency and employment to the timely issues of intellectual property—and have not been simplified to the same extent as the first five. Although somewhat condensed here, these topics don't really lend themselves to abbreviation.

## FEATURES

I've incorporated several features into the text to engage students. Throughout the text there are **Case Summaries** designed to illustrate the legal concepts under discussion. Such case studies are the heart of any business law course and create a dynamic, practical environment for a subject that, without them, would be dry and uninspiring at best.

For some topics I have also included **diagrams** that illustrate the legal relationships in the case. There are also a number of **figures** and **tables** included throughout the text; these are designed to clarify and summarize information so that it's easily accessible to students.

The **Questions for Student Review** are designed to help students review the chapter material. As they respond to the questions, referring back to the content of the chapter, students should develop a good grasp of the concepts and principles contained in the chapter.

Also at the end of each chapter, **Questions for Further Discussion** can be used in class or group discussions. They raise issues with respect to the topics discussed. There are no solutions provided, as they are intended to point out the dilemmas often faced by those who make or enforce these legal principles.

### Questions for Student Review

1. Why is it important for a business student to understand the law?
2. Define law and distinguish between substantive and procedural law.
3. Explain the origin and function of the *Constitution Act (1867)*, formerly the *British North America Act*, and its importance with respect to how Canada is governed.
4. Explain parliamentary supremacy and its place in our legal system.
5. Indicate the importance of the *Constitution Act (1982)*, and explain why it was important to the development of Canada.
6. How are individual human rights protected in Canada?
7. Explain the significance of the *Charter of Rights and Freedoms*, and identify three limitations on its application.
8. Describe the basic rights and freedoms protected in the *Charter*.
9. Describe the court structure in place in your province.
10. Contrast the nature and function of the provincial court and superior trial court in your province, and distinguish between the roles of trial courts and courts of appeal, including the Supreme Court of Canada.

### Questions for Further Discussion

1. Discuss the relationship between law, morality, and ethics. How does an individual determine what is ethical behaviour and what is not if one cannot use the law as the test? What would be the outcome if the courts tried to set a social or personal moral standard? What role should morality and ethics play in business decisions?
2. Canada has a tradition of parliamentary supremacy inherited from Great Britain. However, that tradition has been modified somewhat by the passage of the *Charter of Rights and Freedoms*. Explain how the *Charter* has limited parliamentary supremacy; how that affects the role of the courts, and whether these changes are advantageous or detrimental to Canada as a democracy.
3. The process leading to trial is long, involved, and costly. Most jurisdictions are trying to change the procedures to alleviate delays and costs. How successful are they, and what other changes would be appropriate? Keep in mind the benefits of the current system; do they outweigh the disadvantages? In your discussion consider the advantages and disadvantages of alternate dispute-resolution methods.

### Cases for Discussion

1. *Isen v. Simms*, S.C.C., 2006 SCC 41; [2006] 2 S.C.R. 349

   Isen was the owner of a 17-foot pleasure boat. After a day of boating on the lake and loading the boat on its trailer in preparation for transporting it on the highway, Isen was securing the boat with the help of Dr. Simms. Isen was stretching a bungee cord over the engine when it slipped and hit Dr. Simms, causing an eye injury. He and his wife sued in the Ontario Superior Court for $2.2 million. Mr. Isen brought an application before the federal court for a declaration that the federal maritime law applied and the *Canada Shipping Act* imposed a $1 million limitation on damages in this situation. Explain whether the limitation imposed in the federal statute should apply in this situation and why.

2. *Ramsden v. Peterborough (City)*, [1993] 2 S.C.R. 1094, 106 D.L.R. (4th) 233 (SCC)

   This is a classic case dealing with freedom of expression. The City of Peterborough had passed a by-law prohibiting the posting of any material on city property. The by-law prohibited the posting of "any bill, poster, or other advertisement of any nature," on any

Finally, the **Cases for Discussion** at the end of each chapter are based on actual court reports. I have not included the decisions so that the cases can be used in assignments or for classroom discussions. Instructors have access to the actual outcomes in the Instructor's Manual, or students can follow the reference to discover the outcome for themselves.

## SUPPLEMENTS

*Legal Fundamentals for Canadian Business*, Fourth Edition, is accompanied by a new comprehensive and exciting supplements package.

**Companion Website** The Companion Website is an online study tool for students. The Companion Website provides students with an assortment of tools to help enrich the learning experience, including, glossary flashcards, student PowerPoints, self-quiz, internet exercises, short essay exercises, cases with assessments, and hyperlinked URLs. This comprehensive resource includes provincial supplements for British Columbia, Alberta, Saskatchewan, Manitoba, Ontario, and the Atlantic provinces, covering special topics for each of these areas. These topics include a brief overview of business legislation specific to the province, along with links to relevant cases, legislation, and additional resources.

**Instructor's Manual** This manual includes a number of aids, including outlines of how lectures might be developed, chapter summaries, answers to review questions, and suggestions for conducting classroom discussions. The court decisions for the end-of-chapter cases are also provided, and sample examination questions are included for each chapter.

**MyTest** MyTest from Pearson Canada is a powerful assessment generation program that helps instructors easily create and print quizzes, tests, and exams, as well as homework or practice handouts. Questions and tests can be authored online, allowing instructors ultimate flexibility and the ability to efficiently manage assessments at any time, from anywhere. MyTest for *Legal Fundamentals for Canadian Business*, Fourth Edition, contains a comprehensive selection of multiple-choice, true/false, and short essay questions with answers. A link to the MyTest is available on the Pearson online catalogue. These questions are also available in Microsoft Word format as a download from the online catalogue.

**PowerPoint® Presentations** This supplement provides a comprehensive selection of slides highlighting key concepts featured in the text to assist instructors and students. The complete PowerPoint slides can be downloaded from the Pearson online catalogue.

**Image Library** Every image from the book is available to instructors in electronic format to use in lectures and presentations. The Image Library can be downloaded from the Pearson online catalogue.

**Technology Specialists** Pearson's Technology Specialists work with faculty and campus course designers to ensure that Pearson technology products, assessment tools, and online course materials are tailored to meet your specific needs. This highly qualified team is dedicated to helping schools and instructors take full advantage of a wide range of educational resources, by assisting in the integration of a variety of instructional materials and media formats. Your local Pearson Education sales representative can provide you with more details about this service program.

**CourseSmart for Instructors** CourseSmart goes beyond traditional expectations—providing instant, online access to the textbooks and course materials you need, at a lower cost for students. In addition, even as students save money, you can save time and hassle with a digital eTextbook that allows you to search for the most relevant content at the very moment you need it. Whether it's evaluating textbooks or creating lecture notes to help students with difficult concepts, CourseSmart can make life a little easier. See how when you visit www.coursesmart.com/instructors.

**CourseSmart for Students** CourseSmart goes beyond traditional expectations—providing instant, online access to the textbooks and course materials you need, at an average savings of 50 percent. With instant access from any computer and the ability to search your text, you'll find the content you're looking for quickly, no matter where you are. And, with online tools like highlighting and note-taking, you can save time and study efficiently. See all the benefits at www.coursesmart.com/students.

Navigate to the book's catalogue page to view a list of available supplements. See your local sales representative for details and access.

# ACKNOWLEDGMENTS

I would like to acknowledge the help of all those who have assisted in making the production of this work possible. My wife, Ruth, has helped, encouraged, and supported me in more ways than I can list. I wish to thank as well the reviewers whose suggestions and criticisms were invaluable as the text was honed and shaped into its final form, including:

Donna Boots, SIAST
George Allen, Red River College
Mary Gibbons, George Brown College
M. Linda Chiasson, University of Guelph

Also, my thanks to the firm, guiding hands of all those at Pearson, who supported me throughout the long gestation period of this text, including Gary Bennett, Vice-President; Megan Farrell, Acquisitions Editor; Lila Campbell, Developmental Editor; Kimberley Blakey, Project Manager; and Susan Adlam, Copy Editor.

# Chapter 1
## The Canadian Legal System

Creativa/Fotolia

## Learning Objectives

LO 1  Define what law is

LO 2  Identify the sources of Canadian laws and distinguish their components

LO 3  Describe the structure of the courts in Canada and illustrate the litigation process

LO 4  Outline the processes of trial and judgment

LO 5  Explain the function and use of alternative methods for resolving disputes

LO 6  Define administrative law and explain when and how it is used

LO 7  Describe the aspects of criminal law that should be of concern to a business person

Knowledge of law is vital for business

An understanding of law and the legal system in Canada is essential for the business person. Business activities, like other forms of human endeavour, involve significant human interaction. Whether you are a manager, a consultant, a professional, or a consumer, you must deal with suppliers, employees, creditors, lawyers, insurance agents, landlords, accountants, shareholders, and senior managers, as well as government agencies. All of these relationships carry with them important rights, responsibilities, and obligations. These rights and obligations take the form of legal rules, and to participate in business it is important to understand them. The objective of this text is to provide the business person with enough information about the law so that legal problems can be avoided; to know when he or she is involved in a situation where legal advice is needed; and to be a more informed and effective client when those services are required. The client must give the lawyer instruction and direction as to what to do, not the other way around. With a basic understanding of the law, the client is better able to give those instructions. Business people without such an understanding will often ignore the law or make the wrong decision in situations that have important legal consequences and thus make the situation much worse.

Perhaps the most important benefit to the student from the study of business law is the knowledge of how to reduce the legal risk of doing business. Risk avoidance with respect to physical facilities such as stores, restaurants, plants, showrooms, warehouses, and factories is easy to understand but often difficult to implement. We often see accidents waiting to happen. A plate-glass door polished to invisibility is an invitation for someone in a hurry to crash through it. A step down in a restaurant that is obscured by lighting set low for effect will likely result in a fall. Unlit stairwells, frayed carpets, improperly secured grab handles or railings, and balconies with low railings are just a few examples of physical dangers that should be removed or repaired. It is equally important to do everything possible to reduce legal risk with respect to business practices. A simple example is a restaurant server using a glass to scoop ice cubes instead of a metal or plastic scoop. The glass can chip or break and cause a serious injury. But the same principle applies to the more complicated aspects of doing business. Contracts must be carefully drawn to anticipate all eventualities. Intellectual property, including electronically stored data and electronic communications, should be protected. Checking references is important with respect not only to potential employees, but also to suppliers, service providers, and important customers. Even the lawyers providing legal advice should be carefully chosen. Risk avoidance is not simply a long list of things to avoid. Rather, it is a state of mind, where we try to anticipate what can go wrong and take steps to avoid that eventuality. Of course, to manage risk it is necessary to recognize the risks and to understand them. Employment, personal injury and contract disputes are most common in business. This text covers these and several other related topics and, encourages the development of a risk-avoidance attitude throughout. The first chapter examines the foundation of the legal system and some basic Canadian institutions upon which the commercial legal environment has been built.

## LO 1    WHAT IS LAW?

Law consists of rules enforceable in court or by other government agencies

Most people think they understand what law is, but in fact, an accurate definition is difficult to come by. There are serious problems with most definitions of law, including the following, but from a practical standpoint and for the purposes of this book, which is primarily about business law, **law** consists of rules with penalties that are likely to be enforced either by the courts or by other agents of government. While business people should avoid litigation as much as possible, it is hoped that understanding the rules discussed in this text will help you to avoid and resolve legal problems.

It is especially important for business people not to confuse law and morality. The impetus for any given legal rule can vary from economic efficiency to political expediency. It may well be that the only justification for a law is historical, as in "it has always been that way." Legal rules may express some moral content, but no one should assume that because they are obeying the law, they are acting morally. Ethics has become an important aspect of any business education. Recent high-profile incidents of corporate abuses have made the topic of ethics a major area of discussion at both the academic and practical levels. The law is an important consideration in this discussion, if only to stress that law does not define ethical behaviour, and that business people should rise above the minimal requirements of the law. For example, the huge bonuses executives of U.S. financial institutions took for themselves after the government bailout in 2008 may well be morally reprehensible, but it is doubtful that any law was broken. This text will not deal directly with such moral issues, but they will be raised in the Questions for Further Discussion at the end of each chapter.

Law and morality should not be confused

While this text is most concerned with **substantive law** (the rules determining behaviour, including our rights and obligations), we must also be aware of the other great body of law, **procedural law,** which is concerned with how legal institutions work and the processes involved in enforcing the law. Although there will be some examination of **public law**, where the dispute involves the government (including criminal law and government regulation), the main objective of this text is to examine the rules governing business interactions. **Private law**, or **civil law,** is composed of the rules that enable an individual to sue a person who has injured him or her. From a business point of view, any time a business person is dealing with a government official or regulatory body, such as a labour relations board or human rights commission, it is a matter of public law. It is a matter of private law when a business person is involved in a contract dispute with a supplier or customer. We also distinguish between domestic and international law, where **domestic law** refers to the rules governing interactions between persons in Canada, while **international law** applies to activities between individuals in different countries or the relations between those nations. A limited discussion of criminal law (an aspect of public law) is included, at least as it affects business. A criminal matter is usually offensive conduct considered serious enough for the government to get involved and punish the wrongdoer.

While only a small proportion of business disputes ever get to court, the cases that do establish the legal rules. Knowing that the principles established in court decisions will be enforced in subsequent judicial cases helps parties to resolve their disputes without actually going to trial. When a dispute is taken to court, the person suing is called the **plaintiff** and the person being sued the **defendant**. Note that in some special cases the person bringing the matter before a judge is referred to as the **applicant** and the opposing party the **respondent**. When one party is dissatisfied with the decision and appeals it to a higher court, the parties are then referred to as the **appellant** and the **respondent**. Be careful not to make a mistake about these parties. The appellant may be either the plaintiff or the defendant, depending on who lost at the trial level and is now appealing the decision, and the respondent is the party (usually the winner at the trial level) who is responding to that appeal. In a criminal action the prosecution is referred to as the Crown (indicated as Rex or Regina, but usually simply by the capital letter *R*) and the person defending is referred to as the accused.

An important relationship for any business to establish is the one with a lawyer. Whether it is to help construct corporation documents or to assist in the creation of contracts, discussions with a lawyer can prevent costly legal entanglements. But when there is a dispute, a lawyer who is already familiar with the business, its managers, and goals, can be a valuable asset. Lawyers, trained in universities are "called to the bar" in each province. This means they are certified to function in legal matters and represent their clients in court. Their role is to give their clients advice rather than make decisions for them. Lawyers often specialize in one area of the profession, and so it is important to choose one that is skilled in business transactions and dispute resolution. Notary publics or paralegals can also provide legal services but are much more restricted in what they can do.

*Choose a lawyer carefully*

## LO 2   SOURCES OF LAW

*Quebec uses the Civil Code*

Each province was given the right to determine its own law with respect to matters falling under its jurisdiction. Jurisdiction in this sense has two meanings. A province has a limited physical jurisdiction in that it can only make laws that have effect within its provincial boundaries, but it also has a limitation in what kinds of laws it can pass as determined by the *Constitution Act (1982)* and the *Charter of Rights and Freedoms* discussed later in this chapter. Since private law is primarily a provincial matter, it is not surprising that the English-speaking provinces adopted the law used in England— or the **common law**— while Quebec adopted the French legal system based on the Napoleonic Code. The French **Civil Code** is a body of rules setting out general principles that are applied by the courts to the problem before them. In this system the judge is not bound by precedent (following prior decided cases), but must apply the provisions of the *Code*. For example, when faced with the problem of determining liability in a personal injury case, the judge would apply section 1457 of the Quebec *Civil Code*, which states:

> Every person has a duty to abide by the rules of conduct which lie upon him, according to the circumstances, usage or law, so as not to cause injury to another. Where he is endowed with reason and fails in this duty, he is responsible for any injury he causes to another person by such fault and is liable to reparation for the injury, whether it be bodily, moral or material in nature. He is also liable, in certain cases, to reparation for injury caused to another by the act or fault of another person or by the act of things in his custody.

When a runner carelessly bumps into another and causes injury, a Quebec judge would apply this provision and order that the runner pay compensation. The decisions of other judges may be persuasive, but the duty of a judge in Quebec is primarily to apply the *Code*. Most other countries in the world use a variant of this codified approach to law, and it is this codification that makes the law predictable in those countries.

**Common Law**   The other Canadian provinces and the territories adopted a system of law derived from England, referred to as the common law (mentioned above). As a result, Canada is one of the few "bijural" countries in the world where the civil law and common law work side by side. The unique aspect of the common law system is that instead of following a written code, the judge looks to prior case law. When faced with a particular problem, such as the personal injury situation described above, a common law judge would look at prior cases (normally brought to the judge's attention by the lawyers arguing the case) and choose the particular case that most closely resembles the one at hand. The judge will determine the obligations of the parties based on that **precedent**. Of course, there is a complex body of rules to determine which precedent the judge must follow. Essentially, a case involving the same issue decided in a court higher in the judicial hierarchy is a binding precedent and must be followed. Thus, a judge in the Provincial Court of Saskatchewan is bound to follow the decision of the Court of Appeal of that province, but not the decision of the Court of Appeal in New Brunswick, which is in a different judicial hierarchy. That decision may be persuasive, but is not binding. Our judges will often look to decisions from other, similar judicial systems, including Great Britain, the United States, Australia, and New Zealand, but it must be emphasized that these decisions are not binding, only persuasive, on Canadian courts.

When the judge prepares a report of the case, a considerable portion of the decision is usually an explanation of why the judge chose to follow one precedent rather than another. This process is referred to as **distinguishing cases**. The system of determining law through following precedent in our legal system is referred to as *stare decisis*. Following prior decisions requires that judges and lawyers know and understand the implications of many cases that have been heard in the courts and have ready access to reports of those cases. Case reports are normally long and complex documents. To recall the significant aspects of the case quickly, students of the law use case briefs to summarize these reports. Table 1.1 describes the important elements of a case brief. Most of the cases summarized in this text will include these components, although because the cases are used primarily

> Other provinces use common law, which is based on cases

> Judges are bound to follow prior cases

---

### Table 1.1 Elements of a Case Brief

**Parties** This identifies the parties to the action and distinguishes the plaintiff from the defendant (appellant or respondent at the appeal level). When the letter *R* is used to signify one of the parties it refers to Rex or Regina, the king or queen, who symbolizes the state or government, meaning this is a public law case in which the Crown or state is prosecuting the defendant. When both parties are named as individuals or companies, it is a private law case where the plaintiff is suing the defendant.

**Facts** This is a brief description of what happened to give rise to the dispute between the parties. Only the facts necessary to support the decision are usually included in a brief.

**History of the Action** This lists the various courts that have dealt with the matter and the decisions at each hearing, that is, at the trial level, appeal level, and Supreme Court of Canada level.

**Issues** These are the legal questions that the court must consider to decide the case. (It is at this point that the student should consider the arguments that support both sides of the issue. This will do more than anything else to assist in the analysis of cases and foster appreciation of the unique way that students of the law approach such problems.)

**Decision** This is the court's decision, either in favour of or against the plaintiff or defendant, or in the case of an appeal, in favour of the appellant or respondent.

**Reasons** This is a summary of the reasons for the decision and is usually a response to the issues raised. In this text, this is the most important part of the judgment because the case will normally be used as an example illustrating the principle of law.

**Ratio** This is the legal principle established by the case and is usually only included when it will be binding on other courts. For our purposes, students could use this heading to summarize the legal principle the case was used to illustrate.

to explain a single legal principle and for interest's sake focus on the narrative of the case, we may not specify each of them. When you read the case summaries try to extract the information using the elements outlined below.

**Law of Equity**   The common law evolved from case decisions made in three common law courts set up under the king's authority during the Middle Ages in England. These courts were the Court of Kings Bench, the Court of the Exchequer, and the Court of Common Pleas—together referred to as the common law courts. This body of judges' decisions continued to develop in England, but eventually because of restrictions on the power of the king imposed by the nobles and because of what was essentially institutional inertia, the common law courts of England became harsh and inflexible. People seeking unique remedies such as an injunction (an order that an offender stop the offending conduct) or relief from some restrictive common law rule had only one recourse—to petition the king. Since, in theory, the king was the source of power for all courts, he also had the power to make orders overcoming individual injustices caused by their shortcomings. This task was soon assigned to others and eventually developed into a separate body known as the **Courts of Chancery**. The common law courts and the Courts of Chancery were often in conflict and were eventually merged in the 19th century, but the body of rules developed by the Courts of Chancery (known as the **Law of Equity**) remained separate. Today, when we talk about judge-made law in the legal systems of the English-speaking provinces, we must differentiate between common law and equity. The name we give the system of laws used in the English speaking provinces is the Common Law, which is named after this most significant component. This terminology sometimes causes confusion since it is not always obvious whether the speaker is referring to the common law system or this important component as distinguished from equity.

*Common law developed by common law courts*

*Equity developed by Court of Chancery*

## Case Summary 1.1 *R. v. Butchko*[1]

# Provincial Supreme Court Judge Must Follow Court of Queen's Bench Decision

R. (The Crown) v. Butchko (the Accused and also the Appellant) in an appeal before the Saskatchewan Court of Queen's Bench.

Facts: Mr. Butchko was stopped by the police in Saskatchewan after making an illegal U turn, and the officer smelled liquor on his breath. Butchko was asked several times to submit to a breathalyzer test and refused. He was then charged and later convicted in the provincial court with refusing to submit to a breathalyzer test under section 254(2) of the *Criminal Code*.

History of the Action: This is a Saskatchewan Court of Queen's Bench decision reversing the conviction of the

accused at trial in the provincial court. Note that the matter was further appealed to the Court of Appeal which reinstated the conviction.

Issue: Was the mere smell of alcohol on the breath of the accused sufficient to constitute reasonable grounds to demand a breathalyzer test resulting in the section 254(2) refusal charge? Was the judge right in choosing to follow an Ontario decision rather than the decision of the Saskatchewan Court of Queen's Bench?

Reasons: There was a Saskatchewan Court of Queen's Bench decision (*R. v. Arcand* unreported) stating that the mere smell of alcohol on a person's breath was not enough reason

[1]2004 SKQB 140 (CanLII), appealed 2004 SKCA 159 (CanLII).

to demand a breathalyzer test. But there was also a Court of Appeal for Ontario case (*R.v.Lindsay*) holding that the smell of alcohol by itself did constitute reasonable grounds to demand the breathalyzer test. The provincial court judge chose to follow the Ontario case on the basis that it better stated the law, resulting in Mr. Butchko's conviction.

That decision was appealed to the Court of Queen's Bench, where the judge held that even though the Ontario decision may be better law, under the rules of *stare decisis* the inferior provincial court was required to follow the *R. v. Arcand* decision made by a Saskatchewan Court of Queen's Bench judge. Only the Court of Appeal for Saskatchewan could overturn the *Arcand* case. In fact the prosecutor then appealed the matter to that court, and the Court of Appeal reinstated the conviction of Mr. Butchko, choosing to adopt the law as stated in the Ontario *R. v. Lindsay* case, overturning the *Arcand* decision.

Ratio: The operation of *stare decisis* requires that an inferior court must follow the decision of a superior court even where the judge thinks that decision is incorrect. The idea is that the matter can then be appealed until it gets to a level that can overturn the questionable decision (as happened here) and establish a new precedent case for the province.

To illustrate the difference between common law and equity, if someone erected a sign that encroached on your property, you could claim trespass and ask a court to have it removed. Monetary compensation is the normal common law remedy for trespass, but that would not solve this problem. An order to remove the sign would require an injunction, which is an equitable remedy developed by the Courts of Chancery. The common law then is a body of rules based on cases developed in the common law courts, whereas equity is a list of rules or principles developed by the Court of Chancery from which a judge can draw to supplement the more restrictive provisions of the common law. Note that while it looks like the common law developed independently, in fact those judges borrowed from several different sources as they developed the law. Thus, canon law (church law) influenced our law of wills and estates, Roman law influenced property law, and the law merchant (the body of rules developed by the merchant guilds that traded throughout Europe) that was adopted as a body into the common law gave us our law with respect to negotiable instruments (cheques, bills of exchange, and promissory notes).

The English-speaking provinces adopted the English legal system at different times in their history. British Columbia declared that the law of England would become the law of that province as of 1857, and Manitoba did the same in 1870. Ontario and the eastern provinces adopted English law prior to Confederation. Since adopting the common law of England, the courts of each province have added their own decisions, creating a unique body of case law particular to each province (see Figure 1.1).

**Statutes**    The third body of law used in our courts is derived from government **statutes**. As a result of the English Civil War, the principle of **parliamentary supremacy** was firmly established with the consequence that any legislation passed by Parliament overrides judge-made law, whether in the form of common law or equity. Today in Canada, most new law takes the form of statutes enacted by either the federal Parliament or the provincial legislatures. Since statutes override prior judge-made law, the judges will only follow them when the wording is very clear and specific, which goes some way toward explaining their complicated legalistic form. In any given case today, a judge will look to case law taken from the common law or equity for direction, but if there is a valid statute applicable to the dispute, that statute must be followed. It should be noted that Quebec also has enacted statutes to supplement the provisions of the *Civil Code* and so a judge in that province faced with a case could turn to both the *Civil Code* and statutes as the circumstances warrant.

Statutes are passed by Parliament or legislatures

Our law is based on statutes, common law, and equity

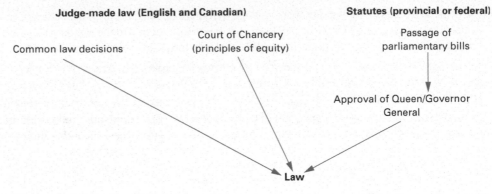

**Figure 1.1** Sources of Law

Law applied in courts today is derived from judge-made law (common law and equity) and from statutes, including regulations at both federal and provincial levels.

## LO 2 THE LAW IN CANADA

*BNA Act creates Canada with constitution like Britain's*

Canada was created with the passage of the *British North America Act* (*BNA Act*), which in 1867 united several English colonies into one confederation. The *BNA Act* declared that Canada would have a constitution "similar in principle to that of the United Kingdom." In contrast to the United States, which has one constitutional instrument, England has an unwritten constitution in the sense that it is found in various proclamations, statutes, traditions, and judicially proclaimed principles. Thus, the **rule of law** (the principle that all are subject to the law and legal process), the *Magna Carta* (the first royal proclamation of basic human rights), and parliamentary supremacy (the principle that everyone, even monarchs and judges, is subject to laws made by Parliament) are all part of the constitutional tradition inherited by Canada. The *BNA Act* itself—now called the *Constitution Act (1867)* —has constitutional status in Canada. This means its provisions cannot be changed through a simple parliamentary enactment; they can only be altered through the more involved and onerous process of constitutional amendment.

*Constitution Act (1867) (BNA Act) divides powers between federal and provincial governments*

Today the main function of the *Constitution Act (1867)* is to divide powers between the federal and provincial governments. Parliament is the supreme law-making body in Canada (parliamentary supremacy). But this constitutional principle, inherited from England, presented our founding fathers with a problem. In Canada there are now 11 sovereign governing bodies (10 provincial legislative assemblies and one federal Parliament). Which of these bodies is supreme? The answer is that each governs in its assigned area. Thus, the *Constitution Act (1867)*, primarily in sections 91 and 92, assigns powers to the federal and the provincial governments. Section 91 gives the federal government the power to make laws with respect to such areas as money and banking, the military, criminal law, and weights and measures, whereas other areas such as health, education, and matters of local commerce are assigned to the provinces under section 92. Because most of the business law we deal with is concerned with local trade and commerce, we will concentrate on provincial legislation and judge-made law. Still, there are many business situations where federal statutes will govern. The various categories listed in sections 91 and 92 are sources of power rather than watertight compartments, and as a result there can be occasional overlap. The business person may face both federal and provincial statutes that apply. When that happens and there is a true conflict (where it is not possible to obey both), the federal legislation takes precedence over the provincial. This is called the principle of paramountcy. The *Lafarge* case that follows illustrates what happens when valid provincial legislation conflicts with valid federal legislation. Sections 91 and 92 of the *Constitution Act (1867)* may be viewed online at www.canlii.org. Note that this website is extremely valuable to the law student as it provides access not only to provincial and federal legislation and regulations, but also to all important recent cases in the various provinces and in the federal courts. There are a number of other provincial websites that are helpful, but the author has found this to be the most complete and accessible free site.

*Federal law followed where provincial and federal laws conflict*

---

## Case Summary 1.2 *British Columbia (Attorney General) v. Lafarge Canada Inc.*[2]

## Federal Law Supersedes City By-laws

A Vancouver ratepayer's group, later joined by the Attorney General of British Columbia brought this application opposed by the respondent Lafarge. Lafarge is the appellant at the Supreme Court of Canada level.

A group of Vancouver ratepayers filed an application to require Lafarge to get a development permit from the city to build a cement plant on the Vancouver waterfront. This was opposed by Lafarge and the Vancouver Port Authority (a federally controlled organization). Lafarge lost at that level and appealed to the Court of Appeal for British Columbia. The Appeal Court decided in favour of Lafarge, and the ratepayers appealed to the Supreme Court of Canada. Note that the Attorney General of British Columbia joined the ratepayers as appellant, and several other provinces joined the action as interveners.

Lafarge felt that it was under the jurisdiction of the Vancouver Port Authority (a federal entity created under the *Canada Marine Act*) and didn't have to comply with provincial or municipal regulations. The court had to decide whether city zoning rules applied to this project and how the federal and provincial laws interrelate.

The Supreme Court first looked at the power granted to the province and thus to the city under the *Constitution Act (1867)* and decided that the municipal by-laws and zoning rules did apply to the Lafarge project. It is clear that under sections 92(8), 92(13), and 92(26) of the *Act,* the City of Vancouver's by-laws were constitutionally valid.

The court also found that the project was necessarily incidental to the exercise of federal power with respect to "debt and property" and "navigation and shipping" under section 91(1a) and section 91(10) of the *Act*. The Vancouver Port Authority was properly created under the *Canada Marine Act* and the Lafarge project fell within its mandate, so only its approval was required. There was a clear conflict between valid federal law and valid provincial law, and under the principle of paramountcy only the federal law applied.

This case illustrates not only how the powers of government are divided between the federal and provincial governments under sections 91 and 92 of the *Constitution Act (1867)*, but also what happens when the provincial law and the federal law are in conflict. When both cannot be obeyed the principle of paramountcy requires that the federal laws prevail and be followed.

---

Both the federal and provincial governments make law by enacting **legislation** (see Figure 1.2). Elected representatives form the House of Commons, while appointed members make up the Senate. Together those bodies constitute the Parliament of Canada. The provinces have only one level, consisting of elected members, which is referred to as the Legislative Assembly of the Province. The prime minister or premier and the cabinet are chosen from these members and form the federal or provincial government. The governments of the territories don't have the status of provinces, but remain under federal control, much as a city or municipality is subject to provincial control. Still, the Yukon, the

---

[2][2007] 2 S.C.R. 86; (2007), 281 D.L.R. (4th) 54 (S.C.C.).

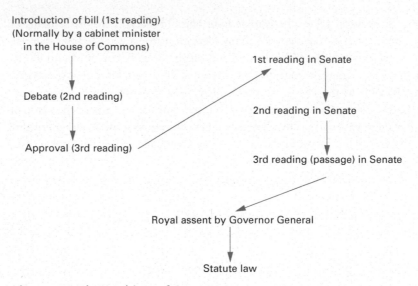

**Figure 1.2** The Making of Statutory Law

Northwest Territories and Nunavut have been authorized by the federal government to pass legislation much like the provinces. Note that other bodies also have the authority to make law, including cities and towns, as well as regional districts and First Nations communities, and the laws they create can be very important for businesses operating within their jurisdictions. But these bodies pass subordinate legislation (by-laws) and they must act within the limited authority granted under federal or provincial legislation.

In our democracy voters choose members to represent them in the federal Parliament and in the provincial legislative assemblies. These legislative bodies begin the law-making process when an elected member—usually a cabinet minister—presents a **bill** for the consideration of the House of Commons. Note that other members from both the government side and the opposition often introduce bills as well, which are known as private members bills. These bills are usually defeated since they don't have the support of the majority party, but every so often there is a groundswell of support, and a private member's bill is passed and becomes law. The introduction of the bill is referred to as first reading. Then, if it survives a process of debate known as second reading, where the general principles rather than the details are debated, the bill is referred to one of the various parliamentary committees where it is goes through a clause-by-clause examination with amendments being made. It is at this stage that witnesses may be called before the committee if appropriate. The committee then reports back to the House, reintroducing the bill with appropriate amendments, which are then debated. This is referred to as the third reading of the bill. A vote is then taken and, if passed, the bill becomes an enactment of parliament. Eventually the approved bill is presented to the Queen's representative (the governor general at the federal level or the lieutenant governor at the provincial level) to receive royal assent. With that assent the bill becomes law, and is then referred to as an **act** or statute. At the federal level the bill must also go through the same process in the Senate before receiving royal assent. There are variations, but this is the normal process whereby a bill is introduced and becomes law in Canada. Government enactments are published each year and are made available to the public in volumes referred to as the *Statutes of Canada (S.C.)*, *Statutes of Alberta (S.A.)*, *Statutes of Ontario (S.O.)*, and so on.

Every few years the statutes are summarized and are referred to as the *Revised Statutes of Canada (R.S.C. 1985)*, *Revised Statutes of British Columbia (R.S.B.C. 1996)*, and so forth. Today, the federal government, the provinces, and the territories have made unofficial versions of their current consolidated legislation available on the internet. You can access these statutes at www.canlii.org or at the respective government websites.

Statutes often authorize a cabinet minister or other official to create sub-legislation or **regulations** to accomplish the objectives of the statute. These regulations are published and available to the public. If the regulations have been properly passed within the authority specified in the statute (the enabling legislation), they have the same legal standing as the statute. Thus, the *Canadian Human Rights Act*[3] has nine different bodies of regulations associated with it, including equal wage guidelines, immigration guidelines, and regulations protecting personal information. The general rules would be set out in the statute, whereas the regulations set out the specific procedures to be followed, penalties for violations, or the fees to be charged for different services. Both the statute and the regulations passed under it have the force of law and can be enforced as specified in the statute and regulations.

Regulations have status as law

## THE *CONSTITUTION ACT (1982)* AND THE *CHARTER OF RIGHTS AND FREEDOMS*

Prior to 1982 the English Parliament in theory still had power to make law that could directly affect Canada, but that all changed with the simultaneous passage of the *Canada Act* in England and the *Constitution Act (1982)* in Canada. These acts cut our last ties to England, and the English Parliament can no longer pass legislation that affects Canada. Although our ties with the English government have been severed, our ties to the monarchy remain intact, and Queen Elizabeth II remains the Queen of Canada. The *Constitution Act (1982)* also included the *Canadian Charter of Rights and Freedoms*.

*Constitution Act (1982)* gives Canada independence

The beginning of the latter half of the 20th century saw an upsurge of interest in basic human rights, probably in response to the atrocities associated with the Second World War. Most jurisdictions enacted legislation prohibiting discrimination based on race, religion, ethnic origin, gender, and disability in areas such as accommodation, public services, and employment. All Canadian provinces and the federal government enacted statutes and established regulatory bodies to ensure that these basic human rights were protected. The *Canadian Human Rights Act*[4] applies in those areas where the federal government has jurisdiction and prohibits discrimination on the following grounds:

Federal and provincial statutes guarantee human rights

> **3.** (1) For all purposes of this Act, the prohibited grounds of discrimination are race, national or ethnic origin, colour, religion, age, sex, sexual orientation, marital status, family status, disability and conviction for which a pardon has been granted or in respect of which a record suspension has been ordered.

The *Act* also sets out a number of prohibited discriminatory practices, including the denial of goods, services, facilities, or accommodation that would normally be available to the public and the denial of access to commercial premises or residential accommodation on one of these prohibited grounds. Harassment and hate messages are also prohibited. Prohibited discriminatory practices with respect to employment are set out in considerable

---

[3]R.S.C. 1985, c. H-6.
[4]R.S.C. 1985, c. H-6.

detail and essentially cover all aspects of employment, including advertising, application forms, hiring, training, wages, promotion, transfers, termination, "or any other matter relating to employment." Typically harassment in the workplace and the requirement to accommodate people with special needs are also included in such legislation.

The specific laws in the provinces will vary, and some may not include the same grounds, but all have established strong enforcement bodies (human rights tribunals or commissions) that have been given the specific charge to enforce these provisions. They have the power to hear complaints, gather information, hold hearings, and provide remedies. In most cases the procedures are relatively user-friendly and encourage complainants to complete the process. From a practical point of view, a business person is much more likely to have dealings with provincial human rights bodies than with the *Charter* or other constitutional matters. They should therefore become well acquainted with their requirements and processes and be careful to avoid any practices that can give rise to such complaints. Careful training of employees should also be undertaken to eliminate the risk of any human rights violations. Still, an understanding of the *Charter* is important for a business person since governments at all levels regulate business through statutes and by-laws, which must comply with the *Charter* to be enforceable. In addition, all government regulators and officials must conform their conduct and decisions to the provisions of the *Charter*, or they can be challenged.

---

## Case Summary 1.3 *Fasken Martineau DuMoulin LLP v. British Columbia (Human Rights Tribunal)*[5]

## Prohibition Against Gender Discrimination and Retaliation

Fasken Martineau DuMoulin LLP (Petitioner/Appellant) v. British Columbia (Human Rights Tribunal), (Respondent/Respondent) in an appeal before the Court of Appeal for British Columbia.

McCormick was a lawyer working at Fasken Martineau DuMoulin LLP and a term of the partnership agreement required all partners to retire when they reached the age of 65. McCormick reached that age, and when he was required to retire, brought this complaint before the British Columbia Human Rights Tribunal claiming discrimination in employment on the basis of age. The problem was whether Fasken Martineau DuMoulin LLP could be considered a separate legal entity, like a corporation, for employment purposes and whether McCormick could be an employee of that firm for the purposes of the *Human Rights* Code. The Human Rights Tribunal found that the partnership was a separate legal entity for human rights purposes and that McCormick was an employee who had been discriminated against. The matter was appealed to the Supreme Court of British Columbia, which supported the decision, whereupon it was appealed again to the Court of Appeal for British Columbia.

The Appeal Court reversed the decision, finding that the law firm was a partnership, and although the *Human Rights Code* had to be interpreted broadly, it could not change the common law principle that a partnership is not a separate legal entity apart from its members. Therefore, the partners that make up a partnership cannot be employees of that partnership. The provision of the *Human Rights Code* dealt with discrimination in employment. Since there was no employment here, the Human Rights Tribunal did not have jurisdiction to hear the complaint.

Partnerships and corporations will be dealt with in Chapter 7, but this case serves as an introduction to the principle that while a corporation is treated as an individual, separate and apart from the shareholders and officers who make it up, the same is not true of a partnership. The case also illustrates the operation of a Human Rights Tribunal as it applies to the legislation protecting human rights in a particular jurisdiction. One of the areas where the Code prohibits discrimination is in employment. In the past the prohibition against discrimination on the basis of age was applied up to the age of 65, but that exception was removed and now age discrimination in employment is prohibited for anyone over 19.

---

[5] 2012 BCCA 313 (CanLII).

The problem was that none of these statutes had the power to remedy discrimination when it took place at the hands of government. The doctrine of parliamentary supremacy provides that, in Canada, the supreme law-making body is parliament. Thus, Parliament or the legislative assemblies in the provinces could simply pass legislation overriding the rights protected in these human rights statutes. The passage of the *Canadian Bill of Rights* in 1960 was the first attempt to overcome this problem, but it was largely ineffective because it was simply another act of parliament and was narrowly interpreted by the courts so as not to interfere with the power of parliament. What was required was a document with constitutional standing.

The *Charter of Rights and Freedoms*, which is part of the constitution of Canada, overcomes this problem. All constitutional provisions, including the *Charter*, are declared to be the "supreme law of Canada." Neither the federal nor the provincial governments can change the provisions of the *Charter of Rights and Freedoms* without going through the constitutional amendment process. Any statute enacted by any level of government that is inconsistent with the provisions of the *Charter* is void, and any action by a government official violating the provisions of the *Charter* is actionable under the *Charter*.

*Charter* protects from rights abuses by government

We have to be careful here, because there are limitations built into the *Charter* that give back to government some of the power that the *Charter* takes away. Section 1 allows for reasonable exceptions to the rights and freedoms set out in the *Charter*. It is only common sense to allow a person to be held liable for fraud or defamation despite the guarantee of free speech or to prevent prisoners in jail from claiming their mobility rights. These are simple examples, but the problems can be quite complex. When dealing with *Charter* questions today, much of the effort of the courts is directed at determining the reasonable extent of these exceptions. Look carefully at the *Alberta v. Hutterian Brethren of Wilson Colony* case (Case Summary 1.4) and *Greater Vancouver Transportation Authority v. Canadian Federation of Students—British Columbia Component* (Case Summary 1.5), which illustrate the application of section 1 of the *Charter* and the restrictions placed on its use.

Section 1 limitation allows for reasonable exceptions

Another limitation is found in section 33; it is known as the "notwithstanding clause." This provision allows both provincial and federal governments to pass legislation directly in contravention of specified sections of the *Charter* (section 2 and sections 7–15). While this clause seems to undo much that the *Charter* sets out to accomplish, a government choosing to exercise this overriding power must do so clearly, by declaring that a particular provision will be in force "notwithstanding" the offended section of the *Charter*. Note that such a declaration has to be renewed every five years. Those advocating for the inclusion of the clause knew that its use would come at a high political cost, and as a result section 33 would rarely be used. In fact, this has proven to be the case, and very few legislators have had the political will to use the notwithstanding provision of the *Charter*. The Quebec law requiring business signs to be in French only is one notable example of its use; that province's proposed law banning the wearing of religious symbols may also be passed using section 33, but the political risk of doing so is obvious. Excerpts from the *Constitution Act (1982)* appear on the Companion Website for this text. The *Constitution Act* may be accessed at www.canlii.org or at the federal government website.

Section 33 limitation allows opting out

The third limitation on the power of the *Charter*, set out in section 32, is that it only applies to government, including laws made by all levels of government, government institutions, and agents acting on behalf of government. Thus, the provisions of the *Charter* cannot be relied on to challenge other infringements on fundamental rights such as discrimination faced in normal nongovernmental situations, including employment, accommodation, or services, areas that are normally protected by federal or provincial human rights legislation.

## Case Summary 1.4 *Alberta v. Hutterian Brethren of Wilson Colony*[6]

# Required Photos Violate *Charter* Rights

Alberta (Defendant/Appellant) v. Hutterian Brethren of Wilson Colony (Plaintiff/Respondent) in an appeal before the Supreme Court of Canada.

In 2003 the Alberta government removed the exception allowing the Hutterite people not to have a photo of the holder included on their driver's licences. The Hutterites had religious objection to the inclusion of such photos and so the matter was challenged in the courts as a violation of their section 2a *Charter* right of freedom of religion. The Alberta government agreed that this was a violation of their section 2a religious freedom but claimed it was justified as a reasonable exception under section 1 of the *Charter*.

Both the trial court and the Court of Appeal for Alberta found in favour of the Hutterian Brethren, holding that this regulation could not be justified as a reasonable limit to freedom of religion. The matter was then appealed to the Supreme Court of Canada which reversed this decision.

The objective of the legislation was to reduce identity theft by creating a central photo database of driver's licence photos. Chief Justice McLachlin found that this goal was substantially important and pressing, and that this legislation was an effective way to accomplish it. She also found that the law went no further than necessary to accomplish the goal and that the interference was proportional in that it only minimally impacted the right of freedom of religion of the Hutterites. This satisfied the Oakes case test requirement that "[t]he government is entitled to justify the law . . . by establishing that the measure is rationally connected to a pressing and substantial goal, minimally impairing of the right and proportionate in its effects."

Note that although there were strong dissenting opinions, this case illustrates how careful the courts are when asked to override one of the rights set out in the *Charter* under the section 1 limitation and the stringent tests they apply when doing so. At the appeal level there are normally several judges deciding the case. When they do not all agree, those not in agreement with the majority are said to be dissenting.

---

*Charter* protects:
- Fundamental freedoms
- Democratic rights
- Mobility rights
- Legal rights
- Equality rights
- Language rights

The provisions of the *Charter* protect basic or **fundamental freedoms** (section 2), such as the freedoms of speech, religion, the press, and association. The *Charter* also protects **democratic rights** (sections 3–5) at both the federal and provincial levels, such as the right to vote, the right to run in an election, and the requirements that an election will be held at least every five years and that the elected government will sit every year. **Mobility rights** (section 6) include the right to live and work in any part of Canada, as well as to enter and leave Canada. The most extensive provisions relate to **legal rights** (sections 7–14), which include the rights to life, liberty, and the security of person; the rights to be told why you are being arrested and to have a lawyer; the right not to incriminate yourself; the right to be tried within a reasonable time; the right to a jury trial; and the right not to be exposed to any unreasonable search and seizure or cruel or unusual treatment. Perhaps the best-known provisions of the *Charter* relate to **equality rights** (section 15), as stated in subsection (1) "Every individual is equal before and under the law and has the right to the equal protection and equal benefit of the law without discrimination"; in particular, discrimination based on race, national or ethnic origin, colour, religion, sex, age, or mental or physical disability is prohibited. Note that this list does not exhaust equality rights. It only lists some of them. Others are protected through the general provision prohibiting discrimination in the first part of section 15 set out earlier. For example, there is no specific protection of "sexual orientation" rights, but the Supreme Court of Canada has found that these rights are protected under this general prohibition.

---

[6]S.C.C., 2009 SCC 37; 2009 CSC 37; [2009] 2 S.C.R. 567; 310 D.L.R. (4th) 193.

Finally, **minority language education rights** (section 23) are protected. Both the *Charter* and a separate part of the *Constitution Act (1982)* make it clear that **aboriginal rights** inconsistent with *Charter* provisions are not affected by it and are preserved. These treaty rights predate the *Charter* and, in many cases, predate Confederation itself. They include rights yet to be determined in the native land claims process.

---

Case Summary 1.5 *Greater Vancouver Transportation Authority v. Canadian Federation of Students—British Columbia Component*[7]

## Freedom of Expression Included Buses

Canadian Federation of Students (Plaintiff/Appellant) v. Translink (Defendant/Respondent) in an appeal before the Supreme Court of Canada.

The Canadian Federation of Students went to the Greater Vancouver Transportation Authority to arrange to put an advertisement on the side of buses (a common commercial practice in the city). The company refused to accept the advertisement because it considered the ad political in nature and stated it was their policy to refuse any ads with political content. The student federation brought this action claiming that their section 2b *Charter* rights (the right to freedom of expression) had been violated. The Supreme Court of British Columbia agreed with them, but that decision was overturned on appeal. The students then appealed to the Supreme Court of Canada, which held that in fact the freedom-of-expression right guaranteed by the *Charter* had been violated.

After finding that this was a valid means of expression with an historical foundation in expressions of opinions and commentary, the Supreme Court determined that BC Transit and Translink were agents of government or controlled by government and as a result the *Charter* applied to both. It held that the sides of buses are an appropriate place for public expression and comment, and the policies limiting such ads to commercial content and prohibiting any political content clearly infringed on the students' freedom of expression.

The Supreme Court of Canada also determined that the prohibition was not a reasonable limitation (section 1) on the freedom-of-expression *Charter* protection. The objective of the policy was to create a "safe, welcoming public transit system." But such advertising could not be said to create an unsafe or unwelcoming environment to bus users any more than commercial advertising. The court found that in any case, the prohibitions went much further than a minimal impairment of the right; they amounted to a blanket exclusion from a highly valuable form of public expression.

The case nicely illustrates not only what constitutes freedom of expression, but also the extension of that right even to individuals and organizations that are agents of government or controlled by government. It is also instructive in that it shows that to qualify as a section 1 limitation, a policy must be necessary to accomplish a reasonable objective and go no further than is necessary in reaching that objective.

---

The provisions set out in the *Charter* are general principles: what specific rights they actually convey in a practical sense has been the subject of a great number of judicial pronouncements since 1982. Thus, to understand just what "freedom of expression" means, for example, it is necessary to carefully examine the decisions of the courts, and especially those of the Supreme Court of Canada.

It must be emphasized that the *Charter* and its provisions only apply to our relations with government. Thus, legislation passed by all levels of government and the conduct of government officials must comply with the provisions of the *Charter*. As explained above, in other situations where discrimination is experienced, for example, in employment,

*Charter* limited to government actions

---

[7]S.C.C., 2009 SCC 31; 2009 [2009] 2 S.C.R. 295; 309 D.L.R. (4th) 277.

housing, or public services, individuals can make a claim to a human rights tribunal rather than the courts. Such tribunals act under separate provincial or federal human rights legislation, which in turn must be in harmony with the provisions of the *Charter*.

## LO 3   THE COURTS

The traditional means of resolving disputes in our culture is in a court of law. Under the *Constitution Act (1867)*, the actual structure of the courts is left to the provinces, resulting in some variation from province to province, although they are generally similar in nature and function. (See Figure 1.3 below.) Note that these provincial courts deal with both criminal and civil matters. The lower-level courts (provincial courts) are divided into various functions. The small-claims court deals with civil actions in which one person sues another for relatively small amounts of money (up to $50 000 depending on the province). Other specialized divisions of the lower-level provincial courts include youth courts dealing with juveniles; criminal courts dealing with the less serious criminal offences; and family courts that deal with family law matters, including the division of assets, awarding maintenance, and custody of children (but not the divorce itself, unless a specialized court has been established for that purpose presided over by a superior court judge; otherwise divorce must be handled by the superior trial court of the province). Note that Ontario's

Court structure varies between provinces

- Provincial court
- Small claims
- Family
- Criminal

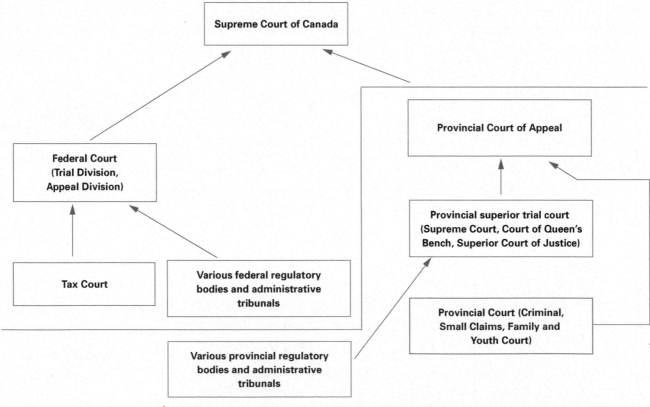

**Figure 1.3** Court Structure*

_____
*Provincial structure will vary.

small-claims courts and family courts are a division of the Superior Court of Justice, leaving the Ontario Court of Justice to deal primarily with criminal matters. Since 2002, the provinces of British Columbia, Alberta, Ontario, Quebec, and Nova Scotia have established specialized courts that deal with such matters as drug-related offences, domestic violence, and mental health–related problems. Other provinces, including Saskatchewan, Manitoba, and New Brunswick, have also considered establishing specialized courts for these types of cases. British Columbia created a Community Court in 2008, which deals with certain offenders who plead guilty and agree to terms of community service and/or rehabilitation in specified substance-abuse recovery programs. The goal is to reduce recidivism and increase opportunities to improve the health and well-being of repeat offenders. First Nations, in some areas, have established restorative justice courts concentrating on the restoration of the victim and accountability of the offender rather than crime and punishment.

The superior trial courts of the provinces are variously referred to as the Supreme Court, Court of Queen's Bench, or in Ontario, Superior Court of Justice. They are the highest-level trial courts of the provinces and deal with all serious civil and criminal matters. In the case of Ontario, the Superior Court of Justice is divided into a divisional branch, a small-claims branch, and a family branch. The Ontario Divisional Court is unique in that it hears appeals from Small Claims and Family Court trials and from various statutory administrative tribunals. Note that some jurisdictions still retain a separate probate or surrogate court to handle estate matters. These are special function courts presided over by a superior court judge.

*Superior trial courts in each province*

In all provinces the highest court is a court of appeal which deals with appeals from lower courts and some government regulatory bodies, such as human rights tribunals, labour relations boards, and worker's compensation boards. In Ontario appeals from regulatory bodies are generally heard in the Divisional Court but can be appealed further to the Court of Appeal for Ontario.

A matter tried in the lower courts can be taken to the appeal court of that province, which may be the final appeal for the case. Whereas at the trial level there is a single judge who is sometimes assisted by a jury, at the appeal level usually at least three judges hear the case. Juries are limited to the trial level and are rare in civil cases, with the exception being personal-injury cases under tort law. But in criminal matters, where the potential penalty is over five years, trial by jury is guaranteed if wanted under the *Charter of Rights and Freedoms*. Where a jury is involved, its function is to hear the evidence and decide **questions of fact** (what happened that gave rise to the action), whereas the **questions of law** (what are the legal obligations of the parties or what legal rules are to be applied to the case) are left to the judge, who instructs the jury on such matters before they retire to make their decision. Where no jury is involved, the judge deals with questions of both law and fact. Courts established in the territories have a similar structure. Note that P.E.I. and Nunavut have only two levels; a superior court and a court of appeal.

*Superior appeal court in each province*

The federal government has established the Supreme Court of Canada, located in Ottawa, as a court of last resort for Canadians. Nine judges, appointed by the governor general upon recommendation by the prime minister and cabinet, are chosen from the various regions of the country. The Supreme Court hears appeals from all of the provincial appeal courts, including Quebec's. There is no longer a right to appeal to the Supreme Court of Canada. The Supreme Court selects the cases to hear based on what it thinks is most important for the country. If it refuses to hear a particular case, it is not a comment

*Supreme Court of Canada highest court*

on the validity of the arguments or the lower court's decision. It means only that it has other more important cases to deal with. Usually seven or nine judges will sit to hear a case. The Supreme Court of Canada will also on rare occasions hear **references** (questions involving serious legal issues normally involving some urgency), directed to the court by the prime minister. A significant example was put to the court in 2004 on the question of same-sex marriage, which led to such unions being legalized in all provinces.[8] The federal government has also established a federal court with a trial division and an appeal division. These courts handle matters that fall within the federal jurisdiction, such as copyrights, patents, and trademarks, as well as matters brought from the federal tax court, military courts, and other federal government regulatory bodies such as the Immigration and Refugee Board and the Competition Tribunal. The Tax Court and military tribunals also have the status of federal courts with specialized functions.

At the present time the courts are basically paper based but the Supreme Court of Canada has recently permitted the tweeting of messages from the court during the hearing, and the Chief Justice has observed that it would be beneficial for the justices to have dedicated tablet computers so they could limit their paper load. Some lawyers are experimenting with paperless offices, and courts are becoming more inclined to accept electronic documentation and digital evidence. As the courts convert to electronic filing of documents, the use of paper will be considerably reduced.

Federal court, trial and appeal divisions handle federal matters

## LO 3    THE LITIGATION PROCESS

A civil action involves one person (the plaintiff) suing another (the defendant). The process is complex and time-consuming, but each step is designed to uncover more information, so that the parties will be encouraged to settle without going to trial. In fact, the vast majority of cases never make it to trial. But if a trial cannot be avoided, this pre-trial process also ensures that the actual issues to be decided on by the court are narrowed and refined. The following describes the traditional process used in a civil action in a superior court. Note that in small-claims courts, many of these steps have been eliminated altogether. There is also considerable provincial variation, and many provinces have introduced changes to increase efficiency and reduce delay. See Figure 1.4 for an outline of the initial stages of the litigation process. Provincial trial courts normally hear only matters that have taken place in or are closely connected to their area of jurisdiction. This connection can refer to a geographical limitation, as with various provincial courts, or to a subject matter limitation, as with different level courts or federal versus provincial courts. The matter of jurisdiction particularly the exceptions to this policy, will be addressed more specifically in other chapters.

In both the civil and criminal systems, people have the right to represent themselves. This is often the case in small-claims court, but where more serious matters are involved, professionals usually represent the parties. In Canada we call these professionals lawyers. In the United States they are sometimes referred to as attorneys. In England the trial lawyers are called barristers, and those looking after commercial contracts, estates, and other legal transactions are called solicitors When lawyers receive their official status (i.e., "called to the bar") in the English-speaking provinces of Canada, they are designated as both barristers and solicitors. Others who may provide legal services are notary publics

---

[8]Reference re Same-Sex Marriage, [2004] 3 S.C.R. 698; (2004), 246 D.L.R. (4th) 193; (S.C.C.).

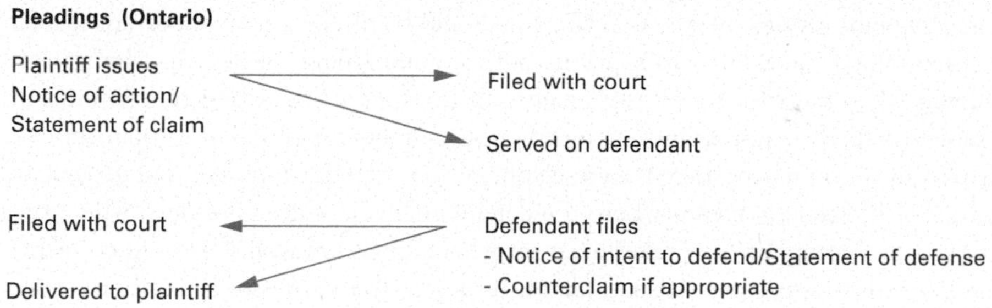

**Pleadings (Ontario)**

Plaintiff issues
Notice of action/
Statement of claim

Filed with court

Served on defendant

Filed with court

Delivered to plaintiff

Defendant files
- Notice of intent to defend/Statement of defense
- Counterclaim if appropriate

**Figure 1.4** Pre-Trial Litigation Process (Usually After Negotiation)

and paralegals. These are not lawyers, but, depending on the situation, they may be able to provide some limited legal services especially where estates and the transfer of land are involved. One of the reforms taking place in British Columbia and Ontario is the expansion of the services that notaries and paralegals can provide to facilitate access to justice and to lower costs.

In all provinces where a civil action is involved, that action must be commenced within a time limit specified in statute, known as a limitation period. The limitation period traditionally varies with the type of action being brought. For example, in most jurisdictions where personal injury is involved, the action must begin within two years of the accident. A failure to start the action within that period ends the plaintiff's right to sue. There is a movement in many provinces to rationalize these various limitation periods. For example, Ontario has imposed a two-year limitation period for most proceedings.[9]

*Action must be commenced within specified time period*

## Case Summary 1.6 *Castillo v. Castillo*[10]

# Expiration of Limitation Period Causes Loss of Right to Sue

Mrs. Castillo (Plaintiff/Appellant) v. Mr. Castillo (Defendant/Respondent) in an appeal before the Court of Appeal for Alberta

Mr. and Mrs. Castillo were in the process of moving their residence from British Columbia to Alberta when they were in a single car accident in California. Mrs. Castillo waited until she returned to Calgary before getting medical treatment for her injuries. In this action brought in Alberta, she is seeking compensation from her husband—the owner and driver of the vehicle—for her injuries. The problem was that she waited almost two years before bringing the action. The Alberta limitation period (the period within which an action must be brought) is two years, but the California limitation period is only one year. The question for the court was which limitation period applied.

After losing at trial, Mrs. Castillo appealed to the Court of Appeal for Alberta, which determined that both limitation periods applied, and she had to comply with both. Since the California period was shorter and had expired there was no actionable tort in that state. Since there was no actionable tort where the accident took place, there was nothing to sue for in Alberta "regardless of any longer limitation period."

This case illustrates not only how a limitation period operates but also how important it is to be aware of the limitation applicable to an action. The case also shows how a court, in one area (here Alberta) may take jurisdiction but still apply the law of another area (California in this case). Here, because the person being sued (the husband) also resided in Alberta, the court was willing to assume jurisdiction to try the matter.

---

[9]*Limitations Act*, 2002, S.O. 2002 c. 24, Sch B.
[10][2005] 357 A.R. 288; (2004); 244 D.L.R. (4th) 603; [2004] 9 W.W.R. 609; (2004), 30 Alta. L.R. (4th) 67.

From the point of view of risk avoidance it should be obvious how important it is to obtain competent legal advice so that any action commences within that limitation period. Even when negotiating for settlement, all leverage is lost when that limitation period has expired. The importance of jurisdiction may be less obvious. A plaintiff can only initiate an action where there is a close connection with the courts in that geographical location. That usually means where the defendant lives or does business, where the action or conduct complained of takes place, or where an action would be most convenient. The court may also consider such factors as where the witnesses and other parties reside and where the assets of the defendant are located, as in the Castillo case above. The jurisdiction problem can often be controlled by including it as a term of the original contract or the parties otherwise agreeing to the jurisdiction even after the complained-of event. Thus, having a matter heard where the laws are more favourable, or access to the courts is more convenient, can often be controlled by including it as a term of the original contract or the parties otherwise agreeing to jurisdiction even after the complained-of event. The question of jurisdiction is dealt with in more detail in Chapter 10.

Service of writ of summons or notice commences process

Once questions of jurisdiction and time limits have been decided, the traditional method for the plaintiff to initiate the action is by issuing a **writ of summons**, registering it with the court, paying a fee and serving it on the defendant. The writ contains a brief description of the nature of the complaint and the address where future documents related to the case can be served. Only adults with standing can initiate an action. **Standing** means that the person suing must be able to show that their rights have been affected in some way by the offending conduct. Children sue with the help of an adult. The defendant responds by filing an **appearance** at that same court registry. This is simply an indication that the matter will be disputed. It is unwise to ignore a writ of summons. If the defendant fails to file an appearance, the plaintiff can normally proceed to judgment without any further notification to the defendant. This is referred to as a **default judgment**. Again, knowing when to consult a lawyer is vital, and delay in doing so is often fatal to any defence that might have been raised.

Statement of claim identifies issues

The plaintiff then issues a **statement of claim**, which contains a summary of the allegations that support the **cause of action** (that is, a summary of what the plaintiff says happened) and the nature of the legal claim, such as a claim of negligence or breach of contract. It also contains an indication of the remedy requested and, where damages are claimed, the specific amount sought. Often the statement of claim is included with the writ of summons. Several provinces have made changes to this process. For example, in Ontario the action is commenced with the issuance of a **notice of action**, usually including the statement of claim, and in British Columbia with issuance of a notice of civil claim.

Statement of defence defines area of contention

Upon receiving the statement of claim, the defendant must respond with a **statement of defence**, or its provincial equivalent, stating what is agreed on and what is disputed in the statement of claim. The defendant can also issue a **counterclaim** that, in effect, initiates a counteraction on the defendant's behalf. It is similar to the plaintiff's statement of claim. These documents are referred to as the **pleadings**, and there may be further communications between the plaintiff and the defendant to clarify any uncertainty arising from them.

Discovery: discloses documents

Next comes the two-stage discovery process (see Table 1.2). First, each party has the right to look at and copy documents held by the other side, such as receipts and reports from experts, and even electronic documents that might later be used as evidence in the trial. The second stage involves the examination under oath of each party by the other

## Table 1.2 Litigation Process Continued

| Discovery Process | Payment into Court |
|---|---|
| • Plaintiff inspects documents in possession of defendant. | • Defendant may pay money to the court. |
| • Defendant inspects documents in possession of plaintiff. | • Defendant informs plaintiff, who may then accept payment. |
| • Plaintiff examines defendant under oath. | • Plaintiff may make an offer to settle. |
| • Defendant examines plaintiff under oath. | • Offer to settle is filed with the court. Defendant is informed of the offer and may or may not accept. |
| | (In some provinces both parties make offers.) |

side's lawyer. Where companies are involved, an officer or other employee who has direct knowledge of the matter must be made available to answer these questions. This is done before a court reporter, who puts the party to be examined under oath and records the process, making a transcript available to the parties for a fee. Transcripts can later be used as evidence at the trial.

*Discovery: produces statements under oath*

To further encourage the parties to settle, many jurisdictions require a mediation process and a pretrial conference often presided over by a judge, if not to accomplish a settlement, at least to narrow the issues for trial. Also, either party can make a formal offer to settle the dispute by paying or accepting a specific sum before trial, which is recorded. If the offer is not accepted and the judgment turns out to be less favourable than the offer, the party refusing the offer may be required to pay a penalty in the form of higher costs.

*Mediation and offers to settle encourage settlement*

Although pre-trial proceedings ease the burden on the court and encourage settlement, they also cause considerable delays and become frustrating for the parties. British Columbia, Alberta, Ontario, and Nova Scotia, with an eye toward increased efficiency and reduced costs, have made significant changes to their litigation procedure. One of the most important reforms has been to reduce the scope of discovery and time permitted for it, and where smaller claims are involved or where the facts are not in dispute, to eliminate it entirely. Some other innovations include summary trials, increased use of **affidavits** instead of direct testimony by witnesses, elimination of discovery, mandatory mediation before trial, and case management by a judge. That is when the assigned judge examines the pleadings and discovery documents, and, during the pre-trial proceedings, advises the parties what will be the likely outcome if the case does proceed to trial, thus encouraging them to settle. These changes are generally governed by the principal of proportionality, meaning that the time and effort spent in trial time and discovery will be proportional to the amounts involved and the importance of the issues. Thus, where lesser amounts are involved (under $100 000 in Ontario), a simplified procedure will be used. In British Columbia they will proceed with a summary trial.

*Reforms introduced to simplify and streamline the process*

In some situations, instead of just one or two plaintiffs, there are many. These are called **class action suits**, where a number of individuals have suffered the same loss as a result of the same conduct of a particular defendant. It makes no sense for each injured party to bring a separate action; consequently, most provinces have enacted statutes allowing the actions to be brought all at the same time. The result is that one action and decision will be applicable to all those represented in the class. The process is essentially

*Class actions involve many plaintiffs represented by one procedure*

the same, with the exception that an application must first be made to the court to have the matter certified as a class action and one individual designated as the representative plaintiff. The court may also be asked to decide whether a given individual is entitled to be a member of that class, or if his or her particular situation is different enough to merit a separate action. It should be emphasized that this litigation process can be very costly, and good business judgment should be exercised, not only whether to proceed in the first place, but also to budget carefully and keep track of the costs as they develop. Often the costs involved far outweigh any potential benefit.

## LO 4  THE TRIAL AND JUDGMENT

*At trial, the plaintiff goes first . . . then the defendant*

It is a fundamental democratic principle that trials, except in very rare circumstances, are open to the public. "Justice must be seen to be done." The burden of proof falls upon the plaintiff, meaning that it is up to the plaintiff to convince the court that it is more likely than not that what they are alleging actually happened and that those facts constitute the substance of the legal complaint, such as defamation or negligence. As a result, the trial usually begins with an opening statement by the lawyer for the plaintiff, followed by witnesses called by the plaintiff who respond to questions from the plaintiff's lawyer. This is called **direct examination** or examination-in-chief. As each witness testifies, the defendant's lawyer has an opportunity to cross-examine. The types of questions that can be asked are broader on **cross-examination** than on direct examination. Thus, the plaintiff's lawyer would not be permitted to ask the plaintiff "You were driving the car, were you not?" Leading questions, such as this, where the question suggests the answer, are permitted on cross-examination but not on direct examination. These kinds of restrictions are included in the rules of evidence, governing just what can be presented, usually based on how reliable such evidence is likely to be. For example, hearsay evidence is generally not permitted. This involves third party statements where the witness testifying did not hear the statement in question but was told about it by someone else. That someone else who actually heard the statement is the one who should be testifying. After the plaintiff has presented his or her evidence through the testimony of witnesses, the defendant responds by calling his or her witnesses. The defendant's lawyer questions them and the plaintiff's lawyer cross-examines. Finally, the lawyers for both the plaintiff and the defendant have an opportunity to summarize their cases and make their arguments.

*The case must be proved "upon balance of probabilities"*

In civil actions plaintiffs must establish their claim on the "balance of probabilities." This means that the judge need only be satisfied that the plaintiff's position is more likely correct than the defendant's. In a criminal matter the standard is much higher, where the prosecution must establish to the satisfaction of the decision makers that the accused is guilty "beyond a reasonable doubt." That is, even if the judge thinks the accused is guilty, if there is another reasonable theory that could explain what happened, there must be a verdict of not guilty.

*Judge instructs the jury in law, but the jury decides facts*

If the matter is heard before a judge alone, he or she will determine both questions of law and questions of fact and render a decision. As explained above, questions of fact relate to what happened, whereas questions of law refer to the legal principles that apply to those events and determine the rights of the parties. If a jury is involved, it must determine the facts, that is, exactly what happened. The judge instructs the jury, setting out the law to be applied to the matter before them, including the legal rights and obligations of the parties. Then the jury retires to consider the matter and renders a decision. In

Canada criminal juries consist of 12 people, although in specific cases 13 or 14 can be chosen to provide alternate jurors if some are disqualified or become sick during the trial. In civil cases juries are much less common, but when used (most often in personal injury cases), they typically consist of a lesser number (seven in Nova Scotia), and the decision does not have to be unanimous.

Once a judgment for **liability** is obtained in a civil action, the standard remedy is an order that the defendant pay the plaintiff a sum of money called **damages**. Damages are usually designed to compensate the victim for his or her loss. **Special damages** are those that can be accurately calculated, such as medical expenses or lost wages. **General damages** are estimates of losses that are not capable of being directly calculated, such as lost future wages or pain and suffering. **Aggravated damages** are also sometimes awarded where the victim has suffered unusual mental distress. Note that the Supreme Court of Canada has placed significant limitations on the availability of damages for pain and suffering.[11] This restriction on damages is just one of the reasons judgments in Canadian courts in civil matters are often considerably lower than in the United States. In rare circumstances where the conduct complained of was deliberate, **punitive damages** may also be granted, where the object is to punish the wrongdoer rather than simply to compensate the victim.

> Damages and other remedies awarded

Where a monetary award will not appropriately compensate the victim, the court may order one of the following equitable remedies: an **injunction**, which is an order, normally to stop the offending conduct, but can also be in the form of a mandatory injunction where the parties are ordered to do something, such as employees involved in an illegal strike being ordered back to work; **specific performance**, which is an order that one contracting party actually fulfill the terms of an agreement, for example, transfer title to his or her house; an **accounting**, where the defendant must pay over any profits he or she has made because of his or her misdeed (as opposed to compensating the victim for any loss); or other unique remedies associated with particular kinds of action. Several different types of injunctions are available. Interim and interlocutory injunctions are given before the ultimate determination of the matter at trial, usually to prevent greater harm to one of the parties during that period of delay. Of course, the judgment at trial may include an order for a permanent injunction. A **Mareva injunction** is a court order freezing the assets of the defendant to ensure they are available to satisfy an eventual judgment at trial. An **Anton Piller order** is similar and is often combined with the Mareva injunction; it authorizes one party without warning to the other to search and seize evidence, including assets and documents to ensure they are not destroyed.

In addition to these remedies, the court would also normally make an order for costs requiring that the losing party pay a substantial amount to compensate the winner for the expenses, such as for initiating the action, photocopying, producing transcripts, and fees paid to expert witnesses. These costs will also provide partial compensation for lawyers' fees. Traditionally these are called party and party costs. In rare cases where the judge determines it is justified, more substantial costs can be awarded that come closer to the actual fees the lawyer will charge for those services. These are traditionally referred to as solicitor client costs, but that terminology has been abandoned in several provinces. Today it is common for lawyers to provide services on a contingency fee basis. This means that no hourly fee is charged; rather the lawyer agrees to take a percentage of the eventual judgment (usually 23 percent–35 percent) and finance the process out of his own pocket.

> Costs usually awarded to winner

---

[11]*Thornton v. Prince George School District* No. 57 [1978] 2 S.C.R. 267.

Contingency fees usually are limited to those actions where the judgment is not in doubt, only the amount as in many personal injury cases.

Trial decision can be appealed

Once the court has rendered its judgment, the matter is not yet finished. Either party has the right to appeal the decision where they believe the trial court has made an error of law. This is not a rehearing of the matter. The trial court is in the best position to determine what actually happened, but sometimes the trial judge will make a mistake with respect to the law, such as allowing evidence to be heard that should have been excluded. These matters can be appealed, and the court of appeal can either sustain the decision, overturn it, or send the matter back for retrial if they do find an error of law has taken place that may have affected the trial court outcome. At this level the person bringing the appeal is referred to as the appellant and the person responding, the respondent.

---

### Case Summary 1.7 *Majormaki Holdings LLP v. Wong*[12]

## Contempt Warrants Jail Sentence

Majormaki Holdings LLP (Plaintiff/Respondent) v. Wong (Defendant/Appellant) in an appeal before the Court of Appeal for British Columbia

The plaintiff established a strong *prima facie* (on the face of it) case alleging that they had been fraudulently induced to pay the defendant $3.5 million to purchase a business. They were granted a Mareva injunction requiring the Wong's to account for the $3.5 million and to freeze their assets so that they would be available to satisfy an ultimate judgment. The defendant instead improperly spent $190 000 of the funds and provided the plaintiffs with an inadequate or misleading accounting of their assets. They were found in contempt of the court order, and despite an apology and settlement of the plaintiff's claim, Mr. Wong was still sentenced to 21 days in jail for contempt. He appealed that sentence in this action. The appellant argued in the Court of Appeal for British Columbia that the judge treated the matter as criminal contempt rather than civil contempt and that he failed to take into account the apology and settlement made. Note that for criminal contempt to be imposed there has to be an element of public defiance, and that element was not present here, as Mr. Wong tried to hide his conduct, not flaunt it. The Court of Appeal found that although the jail sentence imposed by the Supreme Court of British Columbia was unusual for civil contempt, it was appropriate in a serious case such as this. The court also noted that the judge considered whether the apology was sincere and found that it was not genuine. That finding was up to the chambers judge alone, and the appeal court upheld the contempt sentence. The case illustrates the appropriate use of the Mareva injunction and also shows the court's willingness to take serious action to enforce its orders even to the extent of imposing a jail sentence for civil contempt. Note that in order to acquire the Mareva injunction before the trial of the matter, the plaintiff had to establish a strong *prima facie* case so they would be successful at trial.

---

The plaintiff (now judgment creditor) must enforce judgment

The court cannot guarantee payment of damages. Where damages are awarded and the defendant, now referred to as the **judgment debtor**, fails to pay, the **judgment creditor** (plaintiff) must take extra steps to collect that money (see Figure 1.5). This may include a post-trial hearing to identify the judgment debtor's assets and what steps can be taken to execute against those assets. Bank accounts or wages may be taken (attached or garnisheed) by court order. Assets such as cars, boats, and other types of valuable equipment can be seized, pursuant to the court order, and sold to satisfy the judgment. Similarly, real property in the form of land and buildings can be required to be sold, and title transferred, to satisfy the judgment. Of course, if the judgment debtor has no assets or is bankrupt,

---

[12]B.C.C.A., 2009 BCCA 349; 97 B.C.L.R. (4th) 64.

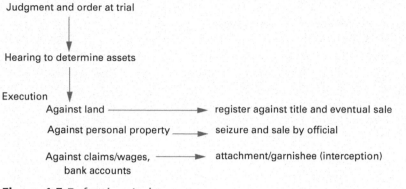

Figure 1.5 Enforcing Judgment

trying to collect may be a fruitless exercise. This risk must be taken into consideration when deciding to sue in the first place. Where specific conduct has been ordered under an injunction or specific performance, for example, and the defendant fails to comply, or when a judgment debtor tries to conceal assets or otherwise avoid payment, his or her conduct may amount to **contempt of court**, and the defendant can face stiff fines and even imprisonment as a result.

In the interest of risk management the question must be asked whether the litigation is worth the trouble it creates. The fees charged for court services, discovery transcriptions, and document reproduction can be high, but are nothing compared to the cost of expert witnesses and lawyers whose fees can range from a few hundred to thousands of dollars per hour. It has been reported that a single day in court in Toronto can cost up to $10 000. Since many trials last much longer than that, a plaintiff must be very certain of some return before risking litigation. Often taking some form of security at the outset, before any conflict arises, can avoid much of the risk associated with litigation. Depending on the type of transaction, it is often possible where a debt is created to take a claim against some asset as security. This might be anything from tangible to intangible property, such as shares, negotiable instruments, or accounts receivable. Alternatively, a third party can guarantee the debt. When such security is present, the claimant can usually take possession of it and resell it without a trial or even a court order.

It may also be possible to reduce some of the costs associated with litigation by obtaining legal aid, but this is only available in limited circumstances. Note that in some cities student-run legal clinics may be available. This can be an invaluable service for those who are hesitant to take their problems to a practicing lawyer. For those who have not already established a relationship with a lawyer, provincial branches of the Canadian Bar Association offer a lawyer referral service.

Is it worth it?

## ALTERNATE DISPUTE RESOLUTION

LO 5

Before taking a matter to court, it is vital to consider some alternatives to the litigation process—referred to as alternate dispute resolution (ADR). The object of turning to alternative methods is to avoid the delay, expense, lost productivity, and publicity normally associated with the litigation process. The first option, and one that results in a quick and

Alternatives to litigation provide advantages

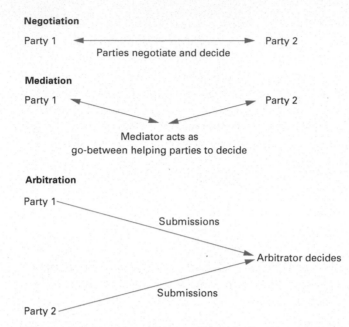

**Negotiation**

Party 1 ←——————————————→ Party 2

Parties negotiate and decide

**Mediation**

Party 1                    Party 2

Mediator acts as
go-between helping parties to decide

**Arbitration**

Party 1

Submissions

Arbitrator decides

Submissions

Party 2

**Figure 1.6** Alternate Dispute Resolution (ADR) Methods

cheap resolution, is for the parties in dispute to simply negotiate with each other, either directly or indirectly through their lawyers, until they reach a settlement. Where there is some degree of goodwill and the parties are willing to cooperate and compromise, **negotiation** should be the method of choice for resolving disputes. Sometimes, however, it is necessary to turn to the more structured methods of ADR that have been gaining prominence in recent times (see Figure 1.6).

*Negotiation avoids conflict*

**Mediation** is the process whereby some trusted third party acts as a go-between or facilitator and assists the parties to resolve their dispute. The job of the mediator is to communicate with both parties and try to find some area of common ground between them. This may include making suggestions to the parties, but it is still up to the parties themselves to make the final decision, not the mediator. When both parties agree to the settlement, it is more likely that they will live up to the obligations they have assumed and feel better about it. But if they fail to do so, the terms of the settlement taking the form of a contract will be influential in a court hearing or may even form the basis of the court-imposed decision. When a settlement is not reached, what happened in the mediation is normally kept confidential. Thus, a willingness to compromise will not weaken a party's position in subsequent proceedings. There are, however, exceptions as when fraud or other criminal activity is involved. Mediation is required in some situations, such as collective bargaining, before taking any action such as a strike or lockout. Mandatory mediation is also now required in many jurisdictions as part of the pre-trial proceedings in civil litigation. A mediated settlement is convenient, inexpensive, and private, and normally allows parties to resume their business relationship.

*Mediator helps parties to reach a decision*

**Arbitration** occurs when the decision making is surrendered to an arbitrator who is selected by both parties. This is often set out in the initial contract between the parties, or it can be agreed upon as the means of settling a dispute after it arises. The parties together

*Arbitrators make binding decisions*

choose an arbitrator, or they may choose to have the matter heard by a panel of three. Each side chooses a panel member, and those two recommend a third neutral person. The parties must agree in advance to be bound by the decision, but as part of that agreement can place limitations on the scope of the decision and what remedies can be imposed. Where arbitration of a dispute is a requirement in a contract and one party chooses to litigate instead, the courts will usually refuse to hear the case on the basis that it should have gone to arbitration. Arbitrators usually have expertise in the area under dispute, and this, along with the power to make a binding decision, makes them particularly effective. Arbitration is required by law in some areas, such as collective bargaining. Once a collective agreement is in place, it must include some mechanism whereby any dispute arising under the contract will ultimately be arbitrated rather than made the subject of litigation in the courts. Another good example is the Canadian Motor Vehicle Arbitration Plan (CAMVAP). Contracts between customers and dealers require that disputes arising in that industry be arbitrated before CAMVAP, rather than decided through court action. It is now a much more common practice to include contract provisions requiring arbitration of disputes in all sorts of business and consumer transactions.

## Case Summary 1.8 *Murphy v. Amway Canada Corporation*[13]

## Binding Arbitration Clause Applied in Private Dispute

Murphy (Applicant in class action proceedings) and Amway Canada Corporation (Respondent and Appellant in this action before the Federal Court of Appeal).

Amway sells personal care and beauty products through a multilevel marketing scheme, and Mr. Murphy was an "independent business owner" (IBO) within the umbrella of that operation. The *Competition Act* now permits individuals to bring private actions for violations of that *Act*. Mr. Murphy brought such a private action initiating a class action against Amway Canada Corporation and Amway Global claiming that they had failed to provide the required information with respect to remuneration as required of multilevel marketing schemes and had misled the participants. He also alleged that Amway was participating in an illegal pyramid scheme in violation of the *Act*. The Registration Agreement between Amway and IBOs such as Murphy contained a mandatory arbitration clause, as well as commitment to waive any right to bring a class action. Amway relied on these clauses in an application to have the action dismissed on the basis the dispute should have been settled through arbitration. The Federal Court of Appeal agreed that as a private matter it was possible to waive the right to a class action as had been done here and to be bound to have any disputes arbitrated. Mr. Murphy's claim was dismissed. The case is important in that it shows how important such arbitrations clauses can be.

There are many variations of negotiation, mediation, and arbitration, making flexibility one of the most attractive features of ADR (see Table 1.3). The parties are free, either at the beginning of their relationship or after the dispute arises, to individually tailor a dispute-resolution process to best suit their particular business needs. It can even include an appeal process to another level of private arbitrator. Although litigation is central to our legal system, a business person should turn to the courts only as a last resort. Keep in mind, however, that court decisions determine the law. Understanding the law facilitates the negotiation, mediation, or arbitration of disputes. Including such litigation alternatives in commercial dealings is a valuable cost-reducing tactic and should be

*ADR provides flexibility*

---

[13]2013 FCA 38 (CanLII).

| Table 1.3 Pros and Cons of Alternate Dispute Resolution (ADR) | |
|---|---|
| **Advantages** | **Disadvantages** |
| Lower cost | Does not deal with legal complexities |
| Flexible | Not appropriate when there is a power imbalance |
| Less time-consuming | No precedent set |
| Private | No pressure to satisfy public demands |
| Win-win resolution | Limited powers of enforcement |

included in a risk-avoidance strategy formulated for any business. Today, ADR is often required before litigation can take place. In some industries, such as the construction industry, arbitration is becoming more common than litigation. As a result, the process is becoming more structured and formalized losing some of its appeal. Another problem is that arbitrators usually apply the law developed in courts. With less court cases being decided there is a danger that the law will stagnate and fail to keep pace with modern requirements.

## LO 6 ADMINISTRATIVE LAW

Dealing with regulatory bodies

Government can be viewed as divided into three functions. The **judicial branch** consists of the courts, the **legislative branch** refers to the Parliament (and provincial legislative assemblies), and the **executive branch**, consists of the prime minister, the cabinet, and all of the government departments and officials that make up what we normally consider the bureaucracy as well as their provincial counterparts. Government regulation of business is an ever-increasing reality. Federal and provincial statutes control everything from building permits to environmental protection codes. The statute provides the power to administer its terms, and the government department will appoint officers to educate, enforce, investigate, conduct inquiries, and penalize offenders. Since the officials, boards, and tribunals are employees of the government, their extensive powers are used to apply and enforce the policies and the interests of the department that employs them. If, when they exercise those powers, they overstep their authority or act unfairly, the court may be asked to review the process and the decision. This whole area is referred to as government regulation or administration, and the body of law applied to it is called administrative law. Examples of bodies exercising statutory authority that students may be familiar with are landlord and tenant dispute tribunals, human rights tribunals, workers compensation tribunals, labour relations boards, and employment insurance appeal tribunals. Even the governing bodies of universities and colleges qualify as administrative tribunals.

## Requirement of Authority

Administrative decisions must be within jurisdiction and compliant with the *Charter*

Court may review process

When regulators make decisions affecting individuals or businesses they must act within their authority and follow specified procedures. The statute authorizing a process, or regulations passed under it, must deal with matters within its constitutionally mandated area and must not infringe on the rights set out in the *Charter*. Thus, when a provincial statute is not authorized under the *Constitution Act* (*1867*), encroaches on a federal area, or violates the *Charter* provisions, decisions made under it will be void. Similarly, the appointed decision maker must not overstep the powers authorized by the legislation or act outside of his or her jurisdiction. Thus, where a statute requires a decision in writing, the failure to provide one would be fatal to that decision. The courts will not tolerate an error of law associated with the documentation of the regulatory process and will overturn the decision if the error is serious enough. For example, if the written decision of a labour relations board made it clear that the board assumed the right of freedom of assembly under the *Charter* did not include the right to belong to a trade union, that error, if vital, would make the decision void.

## Procedural Fairness

The decision-making process must comply with the principles of procedural fairness, the first of which is a **fair hearing**. This means that a person appearing before the board or tribunal whose rights will be affected by their decision, must have received reasonable notice of the hearing and be made aware of exactly what the hearing is about so that he or she can prepare an appropriate response. The person must be given the opportunity to speak before the decision is made. In some situations the right to submit his or her position in writing may be sufficient. The persons making the decision must be present to hear all of the evidence. If a panel is involved and one person leaves for a short time and comes back or is replaced by another during the hearing, that constitutes grounds for challenging the decision. The decision maker must not be biased or have a personal interest in the decision. A fair hearing does not necessarily mean that a person has a right to legal representation or to cross-examine witnesses, or that the rules of evidence, common in a judicial hearing, will apply.

*Procedural fairness required in administrative hearing*

If any of the first four questions posed in Table 1.4 are answered negatively, suggesting that the tribunal may have made an error of law, acted beyond its jurisdiction, or failed to meet the requirements of procedural fairness, the decision of that tribunal can be challenged or reviewed by the courts. The courts will review the decision when it is clearly unreasonable. Even then it is important to remember that a review is not an appeal. The courts will normally not question the merits of the decision, only whether it was properly made. If they find an error they may order the matter to be reheard by a tribunal exercising proper authority and following the requirements of fair process. Of course, the challenge will be a waste of time and resources if the tribunal, this time being more careful,

### Table 1.4 Checklist for Action

Ask the following questions to determine if a complaint should be made:

- Is the decision authorized by properly enacted statutes and regulations?
- Has the decision maker acted within his or her power?
- Have the statutory procedures been followed?
- Have the rules of procedural fairness been complied with?
- Is there any benefit in seeking a court to review the decision?
- What is the appropriate remedy to request?

## Case Summary 1.9 *P.J.D. Holdings Inc. v. Regina (City)*[14]

# Fairness Vital Before at City Council Decision

P.J.D. Holdings Inc.(Applicant), Regina (City) (Respondent) in this application for judicial review before the Saskatchewan Court of Queen's Bench.

In 2010 representatives of P.J.D. Holdings Inc. appeared before the Regina City Council in support of an application to convert certain rental property into condominiums. During the presentation they were asked questions by the councillors; one noted that they had received some "very disturbing letters" and asked several questions with respect to them. The representatives of P.J.D. answered as best they could, not having access to them and not knowing their content. The Council, without providing a copy to P.J.D., moved that the letters "form part of the official record" and unanimously decided to reject the application for conversion of the properties. P.J.D. eventually obtained copies of two letters which contained very serious accusations against them, including claims of intimidation, bullying, bribery, and threats against the tenants.

In this application P.J.D. asked the Saskatchewan Court of Queen's Bench to overturn the decision of the Council and send the matter back to them on the basis that the Council breached the rules of procedural fairness. What constitutes procedural fairness varies with the circumstances. Here the use of the letters and the reliance on them in making the decision amounted to nondisclosure of relevant material upon which the decision was made denying P.J.D. an opportunity to properly respond. This failure to disclose amounted to a breach of procedural fairness that required the quashing of the Council's decision and the return of the matter for a rehearing before the City Council.

This is a good case to illustrate that procedural fairness requires disclosure of the materials upon which a decision will be based so that the other party can have an opportunity to answer those materials. It is the same principle as the requirement of notice. Without notice of the charges that have to be met, you cannot properly respond to them. Note as well that challenging such a decision is often an exercise in futility as is likely in this case; the same body will rehear the same matter making sure that they follow the procedures properly this time while making exactly the same decision.

reaches the same decision. The court exercises its review power with the option to apply the remedies listed in Table 1.5.

Naturally, the goal of the statute is to avoid having its terms and processes challenged, and so usually included in the statute are **privative clauses** designed to insulate tribunal decisions from judicial review. Although courts often find ways to ignore or avoid such restrictions on their authority, today considerable deference is given to such tribunals, especially where special expertise and complex matters are involved. It is important to keep in mind the benefits of having these matters decided outside of the courts.

We have already discussed the challenges of court processes. Regulatory boards and tribunals generally are more efficient, are usually made up of experts in the field under dispute, and can render decisions more quickly and cost-effectively than can the courts. They play an important role in enforcing the law, and business people need to be aware of their powers and how they are exercised. The Supreme Court of Canada in several relatively recent decisions has made it clear that considerable deference should be given to such regulatory bodies, and only rarely should the courts interfere with their decisions. The grounds for such interference have been reduced to "correctness" and "reasonableness." Correctness refers to the process described above and includes the tribunal having authority (jurisdiction) and to the fairness of the process. The reasonableness standard means essentially that where the board has several different choices, the choice made has to be reasonable.[15]

---

[14]2010 SKQB 386 (CanLII).

[15]*Dunsmuir v. New Brunswick*, 2008 SCC 9.

## Table 1.5 List of Available Remedies

- Court may order prohibition. Decision maker will be ordered not to proceed.

  This is done to stop a tribunal from acting before any decision can be made. Where a hearing is to be held before expropriating property, and the owner of the property involved hears about it indirectly but has not been given proper notice, an order of prohibition stopping the hearing would be appropriate.

- Court may order *certiorari*. Decision will be overturned.

  Where a hearing has been held and a decision made to expropriate property, but no notice of the hearing was given to the property owner, an order of *certiorari* would be appropriate to overturn the decision. Other remedies such as damages and an injunction could also then be ordered.

- Court may order *mandamus*. Decision maker will be ordered to decide.

  Where an application for a permit to build on the property has been applied for, but the decision maker is stalling for some reason, an order of *mandamus* requiring the decision to be made would be appropriate. Other remedies such as damages and an injunction could also then be ordered.

- Court may declare the law. Court will state the correct law applicable.

  Even where one of the above remedies may not fit, the court will still have the power to declare the law and then order further remedies such as damages or an injunction. Where a building was demolished pursuant to an improper process and the above remedies were not available or did not fit for some reason, the court would still have the power to declare the law and then award damages.

- Court may issue injunction. Combined with the above, the court will order offending conduct to stop.

  Where an order to demolish the building in the above situation has been given, but not yet implemented, an injunction to stop the demolition process would be appropriate.

- Court may award damages. Combined with the above the court will award monetary compensation.

  Where the building has been improperly demolished monetary compensation in the form of damages would likely be the only appropriate remedy.

- Court may make another order under section 24 of the *Charter*, where appropriate.

  Where a violation of the *Charter* is involved the courts have the discretion of awarding any appropriate remedy. This remedy might be damages, an injunction, specific performance, or any other appropriate remedy. Thus, if a person was improperly detained in violation of his *Charter* rights, a court could award monetary compensation if it thought it appropriate to do so.

# CRIMINAL LAW                                                    LO 7

Although this text focuses primarily on civil law, the topic of criminal law has become much more important for businesses in recent years. Corporations are commonly the victims of criminal activities such as shoplifting, employee theft, and fraud in its various forms. Increasingly, senior employees, directors, and executives run afoul of criminal law. It is, therefore, important to refer to the criminal process.

In a criminal action the state prosecutes the accused

First, we should define criminal law and distinguish it from civil law. In a civil action, one individual—the injured party—sues the party causing the injury, usually seeking compensation or other remedy. In a criminal matter the conduct is considered serious enough to offend the whole community, and it is the state that prosecutes the accused. The victim has the status of a witness only in this process and is unlikely to benefit from the outcome. The accused may be a corporation, which can be held criminally liable for offences committed by senior executives or those acting under their direction. Sometimes the senior executives can be charged. It is not uncommon for both criminal charges and a civil action to arise from the same incident. For example, when insider trading causes losses to investors, a criminal offence has taken place and those involved can be prosecuted. In addition, the shareholders who have been injured by such insider trading can sue civilly for compensation for their individual loss.

Power to make criminal law resides exclusively with federal government

To business, regulatory offences and criminal law very similar

Although the power to make criminal law is given exclusively to the federal government under the *Constitution Act (1867)* (section 91 (27)), provinces, as well as the federal government, have power to create and enforce statutes by creating regulatory offenses, the violation of which can result in serious penalties, including significant jail terms. From a business point of view there is little difference between these regulatory offences and violations of criminal law, since both can result in fines and/or imprisonment.

Federal criminal law found in *Criminal Code* and other federal statutes

Federally, the criminal law is found mainly in the Canadian *Criminal Code*, but other federal statutes such as the *Competition Act*, the *Controlled Drugs and Substances Act*, the *Copyright Act*, and the *Patent Act* also contain true criminal provisions. In this chapter, a few important criminal law principles will be set out, and in subsequent chapters other criminal rules and principles will be discussed as they relate to chapter topics.

Criminal standard beyond a reasonable doubt

Prosecution must prove intent as well as the act

In a criminal case the prosecutor must establish "beyond a reasonable doubt" that the accused is guilty of the offence. It is not enough to show that the offensive conduct (the *actus reas*) has taken place; it is also necessary to prove that there was an intention (the *mens rea*) to do the act. This intention is usually presumed once a person has been shown to have committed the offensive conduct, and so it is the defence that usually must try to show there was no intention present. Insanity is an example of a defence that may rebut that presumption. Intoxication is not a defence for most criminal charges, nor is ignorance of the law an excuse. The required intention, as it is used here, refers to an intention to do the act, not an intention to commit a crime or do harm to another. Thus, if you drink and drive and injure someone, it is no defence to the criminal charge to say you did not mean to cause harm.

Note *Charter of Rights and Freedoms* protections

Standards of proof and the rights set out in the *Charter of Rights and Freedoms* (primarily sections 7–14) are imposed whenever imprisonment is the potential outcome. Where only fines can be levied, it may be sufficient to prove that the offensive conduct took place. These are called **strict liability offences** and the only defence normally available is that the accused acted with **due diligence**. Essentially, due diligence can be established where the manager or executive involved is shown to have taken reasonable steps to ensure that the offensive conduct would not take place, including proper training of the employees involved, as well as the establishment of adequate procedures and safeguards that would reasonably be expected to prevent its occurrence.

Due diligence is the only defence to strict liability offence

Summary conviction for minor offences

Indictment for serious offences

**Summary conviction offences** are minor offences and usually involve lesser penalties, with a jail term limited to two years. An **indictable offence** is more serious with penalties involving heavy fines and sentences of up to life in prison, depending on the offence. These terms refer to the judicial process that is undertaken with each type of

## Case Summary 1.10 *R. v. MacMillan Bloedel*[16]

# Due Diligence Not Established

MacMillan Bloedel was the accused at the provincial court level (with the crown prosecuting). The company successfully appealed a decision against it to the British Columbia Supreme Court. The Crown then appealed to the Court of Appeal.

MacMillan Bloedel's underground pipeline located in the Queen Charlotte Islands leaked into a watercourse, and the company was charged under the federal *Fisheries Act* with allowing a deleterious substance to escape and contaminate water frequented by fish. This is a strict liability offence in that it is sufficient to prove that the offensive conduct took place to obtain a conviction. The only defence available is that of due diligence, which is the issue the court must decide in this case. Due diligence is established in two ways: first, if the event that constituted the offence was not reasonably foreseeable and so could not have been anticipated; and second, if the company had taken reasonable steps to prevent it. Although the pipes in question were old, the

company and a government inspector had recently inspected the pipeline and found it to be sound with no indication of trouble. It was discovered that microbiological corrosion caused the leak—something no one could have anticipated. At trial the company's due diligence defence was rejected. It was then appealed to the Supreme Court of British Columbia, which decided in favour of the company.

The Crown in turn appealed to the Court of Appeal. That court allowed the appeal and reinstated the conviction, rejecting the company's due diligence defence. It was true that the company could not have reasonably anticipated leakage caused in this particular way, but they could anticipate that the aging pipes could fail and so leakage in general was reasonably foreseeable. Second, while the company did have a good inspection process in place and their conclusion that the pipes were in good shape was reasonable, they had no plan in place to deal with the leakage when it did occur.

---

offence with the summary conviction offense involving a much simpler procedure and the matter tried at the Provincial Court level.

**Plea-bargaining** is also a common aspect of the criminal process. This involves giving the accused the opportunity to plead guilty to a lesser offence. This process offends some people, but it has advantages from the point of view of serving justice, ensuring a conviction, and avoiding the costs and uncertainty of a trial.

Plea-bargaining can avoid trial

A criminal trial is similar to a civil trial, with a prosecutor presenting evidence against an accused, who then presents his defence. When there is a jury, it will hear the evidence and then receive instructions from the judge as to the law. The jury then decides whether the defendant is guilty. If the jury cannot agree on a verdict, a new trial may be ordered. If the trial is before a judge alone, he or she will decide on the guilt or innocence of the accused and impose a sentence within the sanctions set out in the *Criminal Code* or other statute for the offence. The length of sentence will vary with the seriousness of the criminal conduct. In addition to a fine and imprisonment, the judge can make other orders, including confiscating the proceeds of the crime or requiring restitution or payment to compensate the victim for the losses incurred. A judge may also have the discretion to impose a suspended sentence. This is still a conviction, but with no penalty. Sometimes conditions are attached, such as community service or probation, rather than a fine or imprisonment. The judge may also order an absolute discharge, which does not involve a conviction.

Criminal trial similar to civil trial

Alternative sentences

---

[16](2002), 220 D.L.R. (4th) 173 (B.C.C.A.).

There are a number of offences that do not involve the direct commission of an actual crime. For example, it is an offence for someone to aid or abet another in the commission of a crime, to be an accessory before or after a crime, or to counsel the commission of a crime. A particular danger from a business point of view is conspiracy. When several people together plan the commission of a crime, this constitutes a conspiracy, and all are guilty even though they may not have directly participated in the offence.

Finally, note that individuals or corporations doing business in other countries are subject to the legal systems in those jurisdictions. Also, because of international treaties, conventions, and legal customs, conduct in this country that may violate the laws in place in other countries may have legal consequences here. This is a very complex area of law and will be discussed to a limited extent in the final chapter of this text.

## Key Terms

**aboriginal rights** (p. 15)

**accounting** (p. 23)

**act** (p. 10)

**affidavits** (p. 21)

**aggravated damages** (p. 23)

**Anton Piller order** (p. 23)

**appearance** (p. 20)

**appellant** (p. 3)

**applicant** (p. 3)

**arbitration** (p. 26)

**bill** (p. 10)

**cause of action** (p. 20)

*Civil Code* (p. 4)

**civil law** (p. 3)

**class action suit** (p. 21)

**common law** (p. 4)

**contempt of court** (p. 25)

**counterclaim** (p. 20)

**Courts of Chancery** (p. 6)

**cross-examination** (p. 22)

**damages** (p. 23)

**default judgment** (p. 20)

**defendant** (p. 3)

**democratic rights** (p. 14)

**direct examination** (p. 22)

**distinguishing cases** (p. 5)

**domestic law** (p. 3)

**due diligence** (p. 32)

**equality rights** (p. 14)

**executive branch** (p. 28)

**fair hearing** (p. 29)

**fundamental freedoms** (p. 14)

**general damages** (p. 23)

**indictable offence** (p. 32)

**injunction** (p. 23)

**international law** (p. 3)

**judgment creditor** (p. 24)

**judgment debtor** (p. 24)

**judicial branch** (p. 28)

**law** (p. 2)

**Law of Equity** (p. 6)

**legal rights** (p. 14)

**legislation** (p. 9)

**legislative branch** (p. 28)

**liability** (p. 23)

**Mareva injunction** (p. 23)

**mediation** (p. 26)

**minority language education rights** (p. 15)

**mobility rights** (p. 14)

**negotiation** (p. 26)

**notice of action** (p. 20)

**parliamentary supremacy** (p. 7)

**plaintiff** (p. 3)

**plea-bargaining** (p. 33)

**pleadings** (p. 20)

**precedent** (p. 5)

**private law** (p. 3)

**privative clauses** (p. 30)

**procedural law** (p. 3)

**public law** (p. 3)

**punitive damages** (p. 23)

**questions of fact** (p. 17)

**questions of law** (p. 17)

**references** (p. 18)

**regulations** (p. 11)

**respondent** (p. 3)

**rule of law** (p. 8)

**special damages** (p. 23)

**specific performance** (p. 23)

**standing** (p. 20)

*stare decisis* (p. 5)

**statement of claim** (p. 20)

**statement of defence** (p. 20)

**statute** (p. 7)

**strict liability offences** (p. 32)

**substantive law** (p. 3)

**summary conviction offences** (p. 32)

**writ of summons** (p. 20)

## Questions for Student Review

1. Why is it important for a business student to understand the law?

2. Define law and distinguish between substantive and procedural law.

3. Explain the origin and function of the *Constitution Act (1867)*, formerly the *British North America Act*, and its importance with respect to how Canada is governed.

4. Explain parliamentary supremacy and its place in our legal system.

5. Indicate the importance of the *Constitution Act (1982)*, and explain why it was important to the development of Canada.

6. How are individual human rights protected in Canada?

7. Explain the significance of the *Charter of Rights and Freedoms*, and identify three limitations on its application.

8. Describe the basic rights and freedoms protected in the *Charter*.

9. Describe the court structure in place in your province.

10. Contrast the nature and function of the provincial court and superior trial court in your province, and distinguish between the roles of trial courts and courts of appeal, including the Supreme Court of Canada.

11. Explain the purpose of the federal court and the role it plays in the Canadian judicial process.

12. How is a civil action commenced?

13. Explain the nature and role of a statement of defence, a counterclaim, and the discovery process.

14. Contrast the process and the requirements of proof in a civil as opposed to a criminal action.

15. Compare the roles played by a judge and a jury in a trial.

16. Explain how a judgment can be enforced.

17. Distinguish among negotiation, mediation, and arbitration, and indicate the advantages and disadvantages of alternate dispute resolution over litigation.

18. Explain the nature of regulations and their legal status.

19. Explain the nature of administrative tribunals and their relationship to our legal system.

20. Distinguish between criminal and regulatory offences.
21. Explain the difference between a criminal and a strict liability offence.
22. Distinguish between summary conviction and indictable offences, and explain the various options of the parties involved.

## Questions for Further Discussion

1. Discuss the relationship between law, morality, and ethics. How does an individual determine what is ethical behaviour and what is not if one cannot use the law as the test? What would be the outcome if the courts tried to set a social or personal moral standard? What role should morality and ethics play in business decisions?

2. Canada has a tradition of parliamentary supremacy inherited from Great Britain. However, that tradition has been modified somewhat by the passage of the *Charter of Rights and Freedoms*. Explain how the *Charter* has limited parliamentary supremacy, how that affects the role of the courts, and whether these changes are advantageous or detrimental to Canada as a democracy.

3. The process leading to trial is long, involved, and costly. Most jurisdictions are trying to change the procedures to alleviate delays and costs. How successful are they, and what other changes would be appropriate? Keep in mind the benefits of the current system; do they outweigh the disadvantages? In your discussion consider the advantages and disadvantages of alternate dispute-resolution methods.

4. Government boards and tribunals may be considered an appropriate form of dispute resolution. Is it appropriate for the courts to be able to exercise review powers over their decisions? Are there enough safeguards in place to protect the rights of people and businesses who are affected by administrative decisions?

5. Describe the essential difference between a criminal prosecution and a civil action, and discuss the advantages and challenges associated with each process. Consider when a business person might have to choose between them and what factors would affect that decision.

## Cases for Discussion

1. *Isen v. Simms*, S.C.C., 2006 SCC 41; [2006] 2 S.C.R. 349

Isen was the owner of a 17-foot pleasure boat. After a day of boating on the lake and loading the boat on its trailer in preparation for transporting it on the highway, Isen was securing the boat with the help of Dr. Simms. Isen was stretching a bungee cord over the engine when it slipped and hit Dr. Simms, causing an eye injury. He and his wife sued in the Ontario Superior Court for $2.2 million. Mr. Isen brought an application before the federal court for a declaration that the federal maritime law applied and the *Canada Shipping Act* imposed a $1 million limitation on damages in this situation. Explain whether the limitation imposed in the federal statute should apply in this situation and why.

2. *Ramsden v. Peterborough (City)*, [1993] 2 S.C.R. 1094, 106 D.L.R. (4th) 233 (SCC)

This is a classic case dealing with freedom of expression. The City of Peterborough had passed a by-law prohibiting the posting of any material on city property. The by-law prohibited the posting of "any bill, poster, or other advertisement of any nature," on any "tree . . . pole, post, stanchion or other object . . ." within the city limits. Ramsden put up advertising posters on several hydro poles to advertise an upcoming concert for his band.

He was charged with committing an offence under the by-law. It is not disputed that he posted the bills on the hydro pole. Indicate what other defence he might have to the charge, the arguments for both sides, and likely outcome.

3. *Lawton's Drug Stores Ltd. v. Mifflin* (1995), 402 A.P.R. 33, 38 C.P.C. (3d) 135, 129 Nfld. & P.E.I. R. 33 (Nfld. T.D.)

When Mifflin sold their business to Lawton's Drug Stores, the contract included a clause restricting them from opening a similar business in competition. Lawton's had paid extra for customer goodwill, which would be lost if Mifflin were to start up a business in competition and recapture that customer loyalty. Six months later Mifflin did open up a business in competition, and Lawton's sued for breach of contract. As part of the pre-trial discovery process, Lawton's demanded a copy of Mifflin's customer list. Such lists are extremely confidential and must be kept out of the hands of competitors at all costs, so Mifflin refused. Assuming the list was relevant to the proceedings, what rights do the parties have in these circumstances? What should Lawton's do? Is there any way to compromise in these circumstances?

4. *Consolidated Fastfrate Inc. v. Western Canada Council of Teamsters*, S.C.C., 2009 SCC 53; 2009; 313 D.L.R. (4th) 285

Consolidated Fastfrate operated a freight-forwarding business with branches across Canada. Their business consisted of picking up freight in one province, consolidating it into containers, arranging for transportation to the destination province, and distributing that freight to various locations in the province. The business was managed and rates set at a regional or national level. The branch employees did not cross provincial boundaries, and third-party carriers transferred the containers between branches. A union representing the employees in branches in Alberta, Saskatchewan, and Manitoba applied to the Canada Industrial Labour Relations Board for certification, and in this action the union was applying for a declaration whether the employees should be federally or provincially certified. Explain the arguments for both sides and the likely decision.

5. *Wong v. College of Traditional Chinese Medicine Practitioners and Acupuncturists of British Columbia*, B.C.C.A., 2005 BCCA 509, [2005] 260 D.L.R. (4th) 329

Mr. Wong was employed as the registrar for the College of Traditional Chinese Medicine Practitioners and Acupuncturists of British Columbia, an organization and position established pursuant to the statute in British Columbia. He had been hired to implement an accounting system and an audit determined that he failed to do so. He had also failed to record any of the financial transactions in the previous year. An accounting firm was hired to prepare financial statements as required by the by-laws and to investigate. The firm prepared a report showing that Wong had committed several irregularities, including improper overtime pay and expenses and diversion of property belonging to the college. Mr. Wong was not shown the report, rather the board sent him a letter terminating his employment. His solicitor sent a letter wishing to initiate negotiations, which was ignored. Explain any basis Mr. Wong might have to challenge the decision. Explain the likely outcome. Would it make any difference to your answer to know that the findings of misconduct in the report were accurate?

# Chapter 2
## Torts and Professional Liability

Burlingham/Fotolia

## Learning Objectives

LO 1  Define a tort and a crime and differentiate the two

LO 2  Identify several types of intentional torts

LO 3  List the elements required to establish negligent conduct

LO 4  Outline the defences available to someone who has committed a tort

LO 5  Consider the significance of the finding of a duty of care

LO 6  Trace the development of law related to product liability

LO 7  Apply tort principles to professional conduct

LO 8  Identify a number of business-related torts

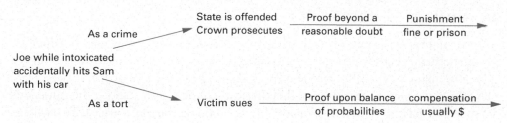

**Figure 2.1** Crime Versus Tort

Personal liability involves one person being held accountable when their conduct causes injury or loss to another. A tort is defined as a private wrong. If the wrongful act causes an injury, the injured person can sue the wrongdoer in a private or civil court action for compensation. Some common examples of wrongful conduct, or torts, that may be found in business situations are assault and battery, false imprisonment, trespass, defamation, deceit, nuisance, and negligence, with negligence being by far the most common and thus, for us, most important. A tort is committed when the conduct complained of is inherently wrong. When a contract is breached (contracts are discussed in following chapters), the conduct, or lack thereof, is unacceptable only because the agreement obligates them to do otherwise. However, when someone drives carelessly or defames another, the conduct itself is wrongful. Criminal conduct also must be distinguished from a tort. As discussed in Chapter 1, a crime is offensive conduct considered serious enough for the state to get involved and prosecute the offender. A tort is a civil wrong in the sense that it is the injured party, not the state, that is bringing the action, and the penalties, procedures, and standards of proof are different. Note, however, that specific conduct may be both a crime and a tort, and may result in two court procedures, one civil and one criminal (see Figure 2.1). Note as well that because the standards of proof are different in a civil action, the accused may be acquitted in a criminal trial and still be found liable in a subsequent civil action.

*A tort is a civil wrong*

*Wrongful conduct may be both a crime and a tort*

The reason that a business person has more than a passing interest in tort law is because of **vicarious liability**. An employer is responsible (vicariously liable) for torts committed by employees in the course of their employment. The employer, usually a company, is responsible for any injuries or damage caused by their employees while doing what they have been employed to do, even when the employees were doing it badly or improperly. The employee is liable as well, but usually only the employer has the resources to pay.

*Employer can be vicariously liable*

## INTENTIONAL TORTS

**LO 1/LO 2**

The listing of torts by category, as we are about to do, is thus somewhat misleading. It is only possible to list a few of the recognized categories of torts, and even where conduct does not fit into a well-defined category, the courts may still provide a remedy when rights have been violated. We use categories because it makes the concept easier to understand and because the courts apply different rules and award different remedies, depending on the type of tort involved. This first section deals with intentional torts involving deliberate conduct. The courts are more willing to impose harsher remedies such as punitive damages when intentional, reprehensible behaviour is involved. Note that the issue is not whether the injury was intended, but whether the conduct leading to it involves a deliberate act. Thus, walking onto someone's property not knowing where the property line is would still be a deliberate act and constitute an intentional trespass. (For a summary of the categories of intentional torts, see Table 2.1 on p. 47.)

*Intentional torts involve deliberate acts*

# Assault and Battery

Assault and battery (a form of trespass to person) involves intentional physical interference with another. A **battery** takes place when there is actual physical contact. An **assault** is a threat to harm another. If someone points a gun at a person, an assault has taken place because of the victim's fear of being shot. Even when the person pointing the gun knows there are no bullets, it is still an assault if the victim thinks the gun is loaded. To qualify as an assault, the threat of physical contact must be immediate and physically possible to carry out. If someone threatens to beat you up later, or shakes a fist while you drive off in your car, there is no assault. However, if someone steps out in front of you shaking his or her fist, the threat of violence is immediate and possible, and so an actionable assault has taken place. The threatened interference need not be harmful, just unwanted. Medical practitioners are sometimes sued for trespass to person (battery) because they failed to obtain proper consent before a surgical procedure. Even when that procedure is beneficial and the motive is benevolent, people have the right to decide what happens to their bodies, and a doctor cannot proceed without approval. Such consent can be implied when conditions are life threatening, the patient is unable to give instructions to the doctor, and no guardian is available. Nevertheless, no consent can be implied when there is a clear refusal from the victim. Note that a battery, in almost all cases, also includes an assault; therefore, it has become common practice to simply use the term *assault* even where physical contact is involved. Also, this type of physical interference can constitute a crime, and under the *Criminal Code* the term *assault* includes physical contact that in tort law would be referred to as a battery.

**Defences**   Consent is a valid defence to a claim of assault and battery. Kissing would be a trespass to another person, but is considered innocent when the two parties consent. Medical treatment is appropriate and not actionable when the patient consents to the procedure—even when unexpected damage results. In all cases practitioners must ensure that the medical treatment or other conduct goes no further than the informed consent allows. A hockey player might be protected from being sued by the principle of consent even for a hard check, but if a player were to charge that the other player intentionally speared him with his stick, the consent defence might well be lost. Such extreme contact is not part of the game. Another important defence for assault and battery is **self-defence.** When attacked, a victim can use reasonable force in response. Such an attack cannot be viewed as an invitation to respond with unrestrained violence. The victim can use only reasonable force, or as much force as is necessary to fend off the attack. If excessive force is used, that unreasonable response by the victim is actionable in its own right. Further, that reasonable force must be in response to an immediate threat, not one that has passed; then the response becomes revenge rather than self-defence, and is also actionable. Nor will provocation justify a violent response. When someone calls you insulting names and you respond violently, it is you, rather than your adversary, who has committed the assault and battery. Such provocation can be taken into consideration by the court, however, and may result in a reduced award of damages against you.

Conduct that amounts to assault and battery in tort law can also constitute several different criminal offences under the *Criminal Code* of Canada. These charges range from the actual use of force to the uttering of threats, intimidation, and making harassing phone calls. As in tort law, self-defence and consent will excuse the use of physical force but that force must be reasonable, and consent will not justify assisting a suicide or other specified types of prohibited criminal conduct. Reasonable force can also be used to accomplish a justified arrest or to defend property. A number of other offences such as robbery and homicide also include the prohibited use of physical force or the threat of such force.

---

## Excessive Force Overrides Defences

Ellis (Plaintiff) and Fallios-Guthierrez (Defendant) in a trial in the Ontario Superior Court of Justice.

Two friends had a falling out over a girl and after some time met at a bar. Together with a third friend they went to another bar and then eventually back to the defendant's basement apartment, where they continued to drink. At each of these locations there was some limited altercation between them, after which they made up. Finally, in the apartment the fight that was the subject of this action broke out. The defendant got the upper hand and forced the plaintiff to the ground. While straddling him, he continued to punch and bite the plaintiff causing severe damage, including the loss of over 25 percent of his lips. The plaintiff claimed for the cost of reconstructive surgery and for considerable psychological damage.

The court found that the plaintiff threatened the defendant, which provoked the defendant to throw the first punch. The physical contact (biting and hitting) clearly constituted a battery. The defendant claimed self-defence or, alternatively, that it was a consensual fight between the parties. The judge found that the plaintiff started the fight by threatening the defendant and his family, but that it was the defendant who threw the first punch. The judge also found that the defendant was not responding to the threat but was acting out of rage when he struck the

plaintiff. It was therefore not an act of self-defence. Even if he was defending himself, the nature of the response was unreasonable and out of proportion to the threat. By the time the face biting occurred the defendant had subdued the plaintiff by straddling him and holding both wrists. Any threat had ended, and the face biting was excessive.

The judge also determined that the fight was consensual. Both parties were drunk. Both had engaged in fighting earlier in the evening and both had acted aggressively. So long as they were wrestling and punching there was implied consent, but there could be no implied consent to having your lips bitten off. At that point the plaintiff committed an actionable battery. Also, when there is an intention to cause serious bodily harm, as a matter of policy, a victim cannot consent to that interference. "In other words, a defendant who both intends and causes serious bodily harm to a plaintiff cannot avoid civil liability for the intentional tort of battery by claiming and establishing that the plaintiff consented to their fight." The excessive force constituted a battery, and the defendant was held liable for the injuries. The case is helpful in that it shows what constitutes a battery, the nature of the defences of consent and self-defence, and when those defences are not available.

---

## False Imprisonment

Another type of intentional tort, also amounting to trespass to person, is **false imprisonment**. Business people dealing with the public will sometimes get into trouble when they suspect someone of shoplifting, or some other inappropriate conduct, and then restrain the person until the police arrive. This amounts to an imprisonment, and when it is done improperly or without authority, it is actionable as false imprisonment. Most people think of an imprisonment as involving a cell, handcuffs, or some other physical restraint, but an imprisonment may take place even where no physical restraint is present. When someone demands that another person accompany him or her, or even remain in a certain location, and the individual complies thinking he or she has no choice, that person is submitting to the other, and an imprisonment has taken place. Of course, not all such imprisonments are actionable. If the person really has committed a crime for which he can be arrested, and is caught in the act,

Complete restraint without authority is an actionable tort

Restraint can be physical or submission

No false imprisonment where authority to arrest

even a private citizen has the authority to arrest. Note that this power of a private citizen to arrest has recently been expanded in instances where the citizen is defending his property. Now, the arrest is authorized if it takes place within a reasonable time after the offence was committed.[2] Whenever a citizen makes an arrest, only reasonable force can be used and the arrested person must be delivered to a police officer without delay. Where no crime has taken place, the imprisonment is false and the victim can sue. Note that the police, border guards, and other security officials have significantly broader powers of arrest.

Shoplifting, or failing to pay for services, is a serious problem facing people in businesses such as retail stores, hotels, or restaurants. Managers of such businesses are sometimes driven to take decisive action. But they must take great care in doing so, as the potential loss from a false imprisonment allegation or from criminal charges can far outweigh the actual losses from the shoplifting. To reduce risk in this area, proper training of all employees is essential. The classic example, of a restaurant manager detaining a dissatisfied customer who refuses to pay his bill, is a graphic illustration of employee overreaction and lack of awareness of the limits of the employee's authority. One such incident cost a hotel $3500 in damages plus legal expenses in a dispute involving an $8 bottle of wine.[3]

---

## Case Summary 2.2 *Trew v. 313124 Saskatchewan Ltd.*[4]

## Suspicious Conduct No Defence for False Imprisonment

Trew (Plaintiff) v. 313124 Saskatchewan Ltd. (Defendant) in a trial before the Saskatchewan Court of Queen's Bench.

Larry Trew was a customer at the defendant's small grocery store in Moose Jaw. He was dressed in a full-length trench coat that was completely closed up, and several witnesses indicated that he was acting in a suspicious manner. One of the witnesses approached a store clerk and informed her that the customer was shoplifting. After selecting his items for purchase, Trew came to the checkout and paid for them. As he was about to leave, the supervisor asked him to show what he had in his pockets and he refused. He was asked to stay and wait for the police. He attempted to leave and was prevented from doing so. While he waited, he said several times that he would sue the store. When the police did come, he showed them his empty pockets. No unlawful conduct had taken place, and Trew sued.

The issues at trial were whether a false imprisonment took place, and if so, what were the damages. It came out at trial that Mr. Trew had been convicted of shoplifting in the past and that he had started actions for false imprisonment against other stores and settled before trial. The judge said he did not believe the plaintiff's testimony about being embarrassed and thought there was a real likelihood that this was a "setup" Even so, he found that a false imprisonment had taken place and awarded nominal damages of $750.

This case shows that even where the behaviour of a customer was suspicious and it was reasonable to suppose that shoplifting had taken place, if there was no unlawful conduct there is no authority to imprison. It is hard to imagine a more favourable case for the store than this, and yet they were found liable for false imprisonment.

---

## Trespass

Trespass involves voluntary conduct without authority

The tort of **trespass to land** involves someone coming on to another's land without permission or authority. A person can be a trespasser without even realizing he or she is on someone else's property. Someone wandering onto another's property, not realizing he or she had

---

[2]*Citizen's Arrest and Self Defence Act S.C. 2012, c. 9.*

[3]*Bahner v. Marwest Hotel Co.* (1969), 6 DLR (3d) 322 (BCSC).

[4]2005 SKQB 79 (CanLII).

crossed the boundary line, would still be a trespasser because the conduct was voluntary. By contrast, a person hit by a car and knocked on to another's property is not. Of course, someone with authority, such as a postal delivery person or meter reader, is not a trespasser. This is true even when that person is acting without permission, provided he or she does not go beyond that authority. The entrance of a meter reader would be authorized, but if the meter reader cut through the back yard to get to the next street, such an unauthorized shortcut would be a trespass. A trespass can also take place indirectly when someone throws something onto the land or where a permanent incursion takes place, as when a structure is built that encroaches on another's property. Customers can become trespassers when they overstay their welcome, cause destruction, or otherwise break the rules associated with the premises. In this case the proprietor has the right to eject them using reasonable force (no more force than is necessary). This requires that the proprietor first tell the person to leave and give him or her enough time to vacate the premises before having the individual forcefully ejected.

*Trespassers may be ejected using reasonable force*

There is also a *Criminal Code* offence of trespassing, where a person loitering on another's property at night by a dwelling house is liable to summary conviction. The *Criminal Code* also permits the use of reasonable force to eject a trespasser and to defend real or personal property. Where the trespasser resists, his or her conduct constitutes an assault against the property owner. Some jurisdictions have also made trespassing a provincial offence[5] so that the offender may simply be ticketed, much like a motor vehicle offence, rather than charged under the *Criminal Code*.

Trespassers are responsible for any damage they cause on the property. But no damage is actually necessary for the trespass to be actionable by the landowner. Most jurisdictions have passed legislation modifying the duty owed by occupiers to those using their land, but even then, the duty owed to trespassers is significantly less than the duty owed to others using the property. When a building encroaches on another's land, this is called a continuing trespass and, as with other forms of trespass, the remedy might be damages or an injunction. An injunction would pose a huge problem, requiring the building to be removed at great expense unless a settlement could be negotiated.

*Responsibility to trespasser modified by statute*

*Injunctions used to stop trespassers*

## Nuisance

**Private nuisance** involves one person using his or her property in such a way as to interfere with a neighbour's use of his or her property. This might involve fumes, odours, water, noise, or other substances, including golf balls, escaping from one property so as to interfere with a neighbour's enjoyment of his or her property. Remedies may include damages or an injunction. But the activity complained of must be an inappropriate use of that property. A person moving into an industrial area cannot complain about the noise from a factory next door unless it is unreasonable even for that area, and someone in a farming area cannot complain about normal barnyard smells. But a person in an urban area could complain about smoke from a neighbour's smokehouse drifting onto his property and making it impossible to use the backyard. Also, the interference with the use of the neighbour's property must have been reasonably foreseeable; the offender should have anticipated the result. Reasonable foreseeability will be discussed in greater depth under "Negligence" in this chapter.

*Nuisance involves unusual use of property interfering with neighbour*

---

[5]*Trespass Act*, RSBC 1996, c 462; *Trespass to Property Act*, RSO 1990, c T-21; *Trespass to Premises Act* RSA 2000, c T-7.

## Case Summary 2.3 *Balmain Hotel Group L.P. v. 1547648 Ontario Ltd. (Ménage)*[6]

# Noise at Night a Nuisance

Balmain Hotel Group L.P. (Applicant) and 1547648 Ontario Ltd. (Ménage) (Respondent) in this application for an injunction before the Ontario Superior Court of Justice.

The respondent in this case operated a premises with a restaurant on the main floor and a night club called the Ménage on the second floor with a patio area facing the back of the Balmain Hotel some 45 feet away. When the patio area was used, usually on Wednesday nights, the noise interfered with the sleep of guests staying in that part of the hotel. Even though the hotel triple glazed the windows, the noise was still loud enough to disturb the guests. Interim injunctions had been issued before, but the noise persisted and so this application for a permanent injunction to stop the noise was brought. The application was founded in tort claiming a nuisance was taking place and also that the Ménage was in breach of the City Bylaw. Even though there were other similar establishments in the area, it was found that the noise taking place between 11:00 PM and 9:00 AM was an unreasonable interference with the peace and quiet of the guests at the hotel and constituted a nuisance. Nuisance is an attempt to strike a balance between the opposing interests of the parties in the use of their land. To succeed, the interference has to be unreasonable. To make that determination the court will consider 1) the severity of the interference; 2) the character of the locale; 3) the utility of the defendant's conduct; and 4) the sensitivity of the use interfered with. A determining factor was that the noise took place after 11:00 PM., clearly interfering with the reasonable expectation of peace and quiet on the part of the hotel guests.

Since the harm done to the business of the hotel could not be calculated or compensated with money, it was appropriate to grant a permanent injunction prohibiting the issuing of any noise that could be heard beyond the boundaries of the club between those night time hours. It is interesting to note that the parties had reached a settlement just before this judgment that provided for the landlord to take steps to remedy the problem, but the court issued the injunction anyway, not having confidence that the owners of the club would follow through.

# Defamation

Defamation can also be a serious problem for the business person. It involves a false statement about someone to his or her detriment. The statement must not only reflect badly on the victim but also clearly refer to the person suing. If you said the workers in a particular office were slackers, an individual in that group could not claim defamation since that person could not prove that the statement referred particularly to him or her. When a radio host made disparaging remarks about Arab and Haitian taxi drivers in Quebec, the court of appeal dismissed the defamation action. As in the common law provinces, it was necessary to show that the racist remarks referred to specific individuals rather than a group, and this had not been established.[7] It is also possible to defame a corporation. Thus, circulating a false statement that a competing company is about to seek bankruptcy protection would qualify as defamation.

The derogatory statement must also be published to be actionable, which means it must be heard or read by someone other than the two parties involved. This might take the form of a newspaper article, a letter to the editor, or a radio or TV broadcast, but it also could be a letter to the other person's employer, or simply a conversation overheard at a restaurant. Sometimes a statement might appear innocent, but because of some special

*Defamation involves derogatory false statement*

*Defamation may involve innuendo*

---

[6]2009 CanLII 28199 (ONSC).

[7]*Métromédia CMR Inc. v. Bou Malhab*, [2008] J.Q. no 10048. Appeal to SCC dismissed [2011] 1 SCR 214, 2011 SCC 9 (CanLII).

knowledge held by the hearer, it becomes derogatory. A statement in a financial paper about a couple at a business convention might appear perfectly innocent, until it's combined with the knowledge on the part of some readers that both are married to other people. This is called an **innuendo**, and even where the statement is made in error, it is actionable as **defamation**. **Mistake** is no defence. **Libel** is written defamation, whereas spoken defamation is **slander**. Libel is treated much more seriously, on the theory that it takes a more permanent form and thus can do more damage. Essentially, libel is easier to prove although the distinction is becoming less important in many jurisdictions. Legislation has been passed in most jurisdictions that declares broadcasted (over radio or TV) defamation to be libel rather than slander. Communications over the internet are becoming an increasing problem, but there is no question that emails, social networking sites, and internet blogs now pose a great danger. It is so easy to thoughtlessly post inappropriate material on a blog, or to send hurtful emails to many different destinations, that this has become an important cause of defamation actions today.

Slander is verbal; libel is written and easier to prove

Broadcasted defamation is libel by statute

**Defences**    There are several important defences available to a defamation action, not the least of which is **justification**. So long as the statement is substantially true, this represents an effective defence. However, it is important to note that the defendant must prove the statement true rather than the plaintiff having to prove it false. Remember that it is the actual message being communicated (even if it is an innuendo) that must be true, not simply the bare words or the idea that was intended by the communication. Statements made on the floor of the legislature or Parliament, in senior government committees, and as part of trial proceedings are considered **absolute privilege**, and cannot form the basis of a defamation action. The free flow of information and the encouragement of debate and free speech are considered to be too important in these circumstances to be hindered by the threat of litigation. Statements made in the context of employment such as the evaluation of another employee's work habits or reports made to the police investigating a case are protected to a lesser extent. This lesser protection is also given to statements made with respect to some matter of mutual interest, as with members of professional bodies such as lawyers', accountants', doctors', or dentists' associations. This is called **qualified privilege**, and as long as the person made the statement thinking it was true, made it without malice, and did not communicate it to anyone other than those who needed to know, the victim cannot successfully sue, even if the communication was false and damaging. One of the dangers of using the internet or email is that the message may be communicated too broadly, and thus qualified privilege may be lost.

Derogatory statements made in Parliament or court are protected

Derogatory comments made pursuant to duty are protected

## Case Summary 2.4 *Shavluk v. Green Party of Canada*[8]

# Defences Effective Against Defamation Claim

Shavluk (Appellant/Plaintiff) and the Green Party of Canada and Elizabeth May (Respondents/Defendants) before the Court of Appeal for British Columbia.

Mr. Shavluk was a candidate for the Green party in the 2008 federal election when it was discovered that several years earlier his comment on a blog included the words, "*. . . attack on your shoddily built Jewish world bank headquarters. You know "the 2 towers."* This became public knowledge, and the Green Party responded by removing him as a candidate. The leader said, referring to the event,

[8]Trial 2010 BCSC 804 (CanLII), Appeal, 2011 BCCA 286 (CanLII).

*"We condemn anti-Semitism and our members work to encourage respectful dialogue, diversity, peace and cooperation."* She also said *"I apologize for the fact that John Shavluk initially passed screening."* And also *"[w]e believe in free speech but we draw the line . . . on things that are hate filled and we will never allow that to contaminate our dialogues."* Mr Shavluk sued for defamation, among other things. At trial the judge found that from the comments and press releases "the ordinary reader would conclude that Mr. Shavluk holds views that are anti-Semitic. Further, a reasonable person would understand from the press release that as a consequence of these views, Mr. Shavluk is unsuitable to hold an office of trust as a Member of Parliament."

The judge cited the definition of defamation from *Salmond and Heuston on the Law of Torts 21st ed.* Based on the principle that a statement is derogatory when it injures the reputation of another, lowering them in the esteem of right thinking people the judge determined that the statement was defamatory.

The defendant offered the following defenses. Justification was not established because there was no other evidence to show that Mr. Shavluk was anti-Semitic. Fair comment was also rejected. The matter was of public interest, and there was no proof of malice, but such an opinion must be clearly based on matters of fact that the hearer of the comments are aware of. Here, it was not clear that the comment was opinion, and, if it was, what facts the comment was an opinion about.

But both the trial judge and the Court of Appeal determined that the defence of qualified privilege did apply. This was a matter in which the public at large had an interest since it concerned qualifications of a candidate in a federal election. The case is unique—since all of the public had an interest, it could not be said to have been too broadly published. There was no proof of malice and so qualified privilege applied.

Interestingly, the court also considered the defence of "responsible communication" on a matter of public interest, a defence recently established by the Supreme Court of Canada. The comments made were clearly on a matter of public interest (the qualifications of a candidate in a federal election). But the person making the comment must also show a diligent attempt to verify the correctness of the comment. In fact, given the urgency of the situation, and the fact that several attempts were made to contact Mr. Shavluk, responsible communication turned out to be an effective defence as well. Note that the Court of Appeal upheld the defence of qualified privilege and so found no need to comment on the defence of responsible communication.

This case nicely sets out not only what constitutes defamation, but also when the major defences are—or are not—available.

---

**Derogatory comments made as fair comment on public matter are protected**

**Fair comment** is another important defence used mostly by the media. People are entitled to have and to express opinions on matters of public interest; therefore, commentaries on plays, exhibitions, sports, or even on the actions of politicians and other public figures are protected. As long as the expression of opinion is commentary based on true facts known to the public—even where the opinion is unpopular and most of the public disagrees—and as long as it is a possible conclusion based on the public facts and stated without malice, it is protected. For these reasons, harsh or derisive reviews of restaurants, plays, sporting competitions, and the like are not actionable. Politicians are also fair game, but great care must be taken to keep the statement an expression of opinion based on known facts. If the commentary involves statement that is not true, it is actionable as defamation. You can conclude that a politician's actions were incompetent, but your statement of what happened to lead you to that conclusion had better be accurate. It is interesting that fair comment also protects political cartoons that get their messages across by exaggeration.

The Supreme Court of Canada in a recent decision[9] made an extremely important change to the law of defamation with respect to the balance between freedom of speech and protection of reputation. The Court adopted the defence of "responsible communication," holding that so long as a publication was on a matter of public interest, was

---

[9]*Grant v. Torstar*, [2009] S.C.J. No. 61.

## Table 2.1 Intentional Torts

| Intentional Torts | Nature | Defences |
|---|---|---|
| Assault and Battery | Assault: threatened battery | Consent: must be informed and complete |
| | Battery: intentional hitting | Self-defence: must be reasonable force |
| | | Accident but not a mistake |
| False Imprisonment | Complete physical or mental restraint without authority | No actual confinement or submission |
| | | Had authority to imprison |
| Trespass | Coming on to or putting something on another's land without authority | Had authority to do so |
| | | Had consent |
| | | Accident but not a mistake |
| Nuisance | Use of property so that it interferes with neighbour's use | Appropriate use of property for area |
| | | Not foreseeable outcome |
| Defamation | A published false and derogatory statement: spoken (slander) or written (libel) | Truth, absolute privilege, qualified privilege, fair comment, and reasonable communication |

reasonable in the circumstances, and a diligent attempt was made to verify the facts, the publisher may be protected even where the comments were false and derogatory. This is now good law in all of Canada, giving journalists and others even greater protection than they enjoyed in the past. Note that in Canada the defence is not limited to journalists.

Legislation in place also limits the exposure of newspapers and other communications media by limiting the amount of damages that can be claimed by the victim if an appropriate apology is published. Still, remember that defamatory remarks can be extremely dangerous and cause serious damage to the victim. The courts have awarded significant damages. In *Hill v. Church of Scientology of Toronto*,[10] for example, the total damages awarded were $1.6 million, and in an Ontario case, a jury awarded $3 million to a pilot who was defamed with respect to his work and as a result lost his job and career. The latter decision was upheld by the Court of Appeal for Ontario.[11]

Defamatory libel can also constitute a criminal offence under the *Criminal Code* of Canada where the published words will injure a person's reputation by "exposing him to hatred, contempt, or ridicule." The usual defences discussed above apply, but the truth of the defamation will only justify its publication if it is also in the public interest. Note also that extortion by defamatory libel, or the threat of it, is also an offence. Publishers can also be liable unless they can show they had no knowledge of the inclusion of the offending words. In *R. v. Lucas*[12] a husband and a wife were charged with criminal libel when

*Responsible communication defence gives journalists greater protection*

*Libel may also be criminal*

---

[10][1995] 2 SCR 1130 (SCC).

[11]*Fennimore v. SkyService Airlines, Inc.*, 2009 ONCA 26 (CanLII).

[12][1998] 1 SCR 439 (SCC).

they picketed a provincial court building. Their signs suggested that a police officer investigating the sexual abuse of children failed in his duty and contributed to, or participated in, sexually abusive conduct himself. The Supreme Court of Canada found that although sections of the *Criminal Code* did interfere with freedom of expression, they were justified under section 1 of the *Charter of Rights and Freedoms* to protect the reputation of individuals so defamed. The original sentences imposed at trial were two years less a day for Mr. Lucas and 22 months for his wife, but these were reduced to 18 months and 12 months on appeal. These convictions were upheld by the Supreme Court of Canada.

Note also that false statements damaging the reputation of a product or service can also constitute a tort similar to defamation. Thus, circulating a false statement that a competitor's brand of beer is contaminated would qualify as tortuous conduct. All such false statements attacking another business product or service can constitute an injurious falsehood and be actionable.

## LO 3/LO 4/LO 5    NEGLIGENCE

Negligence involves inadvertent conduct causing loss

Of all the different ways of incurring liability in tort, negligence is by far the most important for the business person. **Negligence** involves inadvertent or careless conduct causing injury or loss to another. At the outset, it must be made clear that negligence is not a state of mind. We are not talking about someone being silly or stupid. Negligence involves the failure of one person to live up to a standard of care required in his or her dealings with others. The term *careless*, as it is often used, in this discussion refers to the failure to take proper care or the failure to live up to that required standard of care. When suing someone for negligence, several things must be established. First, that there was a duty of care. We do not owe a duty to be careful to everyone in the world or even to everybody in our community—only to limited classes or groups of people determined by legal test and social policy, as explained below. Second, once it is determined that a duty is owed, the next problem is to determine the nature of that duty. Just how careful does a person have to be? To succeed, the plaintiff must show that the conduct fell below a required standard or level of care. Third, it must be determined that there was some sort of injury or loss caused by the alleged conduct (see Table 2.2).

*Reasonable person* means better than average but less than perfect

At the outset it is vital to understand the concept of the **reasonable person** in law. While the conduct of average people might be more important in other disciplines, in law we set a standard of required behaviour somewhat higher than what would be expected of an average person. In effect, the court asks what a reasonable, objective bystander would have done in the same circumstances. This reasonable person test requires behaviour that is higher than average but less than perfect. A helpful comparison is the concept of par in a

| Table 2.2 Requirements of Negligence Action Plaintiff Must Establish | |
|---|---|
| Duty to Take Care | That injury or loss was reasonably foreseeable (sometimes limited by social policy based on the *Anns* case test) |
| Failure to Take Care | That the conduct complained of fell below the reasonable person standard (or other standard imposed by statute) |
| Causation and Damage | That the conduct complained of caused loss or injury to the plaintiff |

game of golf. Each hole on a golf course has a standard number of strokes associated with it called "par." An average golfer will require more strokes than this number to sink the ball, even though it is possible for a good golfer (or a lucky one) to do it in less. Par, then, is a higher standard or goal, designed to challenge the golfer. It reflects what a good golfer having a good day would likely be able to accomplish. The reasonable person standard in law is similar. It reflects a standard of behaviour we would expect from a prudent person being careful, and while it need not reach perfection, it is clear that average is not good enough.

## Duty of Care

One of the most significant civil cases in the 20th century is the famous "snail in the ginger beer bottle" case, *Donoghue v. Stevenson*,[13] which took place in Scotland in the 1930s. The decision made by the House of Lords is followed in most common-law jurisdictions. Mrs. Donoghue went to a café with a friend, who bought her a ginger beer float. The ginger beer was served in an opaque bottle, so it was not until the second serving that Mrs. Donoghue discovered it contained a decomposed snail. Mrs. Donoghue became violently ill, but she could not successfully sue the café for breach of contract, since her friend bought the ginger beer for her. (Contract law is a major area of discussion in the following chapters.) Instead, she sued the bottler of the product, Stevenson, in tort for negligence. The case turned upon whether the bottler, Stevenson, owed a duty to be careful to Mrs. Donoghue, the ultimate consumer of the product he produced. The case is famous because it established the test to be used when determining whether a duty of care is owed to another. It is also a good example of the dangers faced by manufacturers with respect to liability for their products. Product liability will be discussed in some detail below. This is the **reasonable foreseeability test**. Thus, we owe a duty to be careful to anyone we can reasonably foresee (anticipate) might be harmed by our conduct. In this case it was clear that Mr. Stevenson should have anticipated that if he was careless in the production of the ginger beer, an ultimate consumer, Mrs. Donoghue, might be injured. Therefore, a duty to be careful was owed to her. This reasonable foreseeability test has become extremely important in the development of the law of negligence and personal liability, although it has been modified in some circumstances. While in normal negligence cases it is clear that foreseeability still applies, the Supreme Court of Canada has made it clear that, today, when faced with a new or unique problems for which there is no precedent to follow, the courts are to apply the two-stage *Anns* case test.

*Negligence requires duty of care*

*Existence of duty determined by reasonable foreseeability*

The *Anns* case[14] test requires first that there be a degree of proximity or neighbourhood between the parties such that one person should have realized that his or her conduct placed the victim at risk. This is another way of expressing the reasonable foreseeability test developed in *Donoghue v. Stevenson*. The second part of the test, however, asks the question whether there is any good reason not to impose the duty, or to reduce the duty or the damages imposed. This second part of the *Anns* test allows the courts to modify the nature of the duty where circumstances warrant, based on social policy. The *Anns* case originated in England and has since been abandoned there, but in Canada our Supreme Court has made it clear on several occasions that the principle remains good law in this country. In Canada then, where an action in negligence takes

*In rare cases Anns case test may limit duty*

---

[13][1932] A.C. 562 (H.L.).

[14]*Anns v. Merton, London Borough Council*, [1977] 2 All E.R. 492 (H.L.).

place, and where it does not fall within a category of cases where a duty of care has previously been recognized, the two-stage test characterized as the *Anns* case test will be used to determine if there is a duty of care. The first stage determines if injury or damage was reasonably foreseeable, and the second stage asks whether there is any good reason to reduce or eliminate the duty of care. It must be emphasized that it is only in very rare circumstances where there is no preexisting precedent that the *Anns case* test will apply. Case Summary 2.5 illustrates the application of this test. In the vast majority of cases the reasonable foreseeability test developed in *Donoghue v. Stevenson* will be applied to determine if a duty of care is present.

*Unique new cases must satisfy two-stage Anns case test*

One recent expansion of the duty of care, and a serious problem for commercial hosts in restaurants and pubs, was to make them liable to patrons who drink too much and then are injured. It is now well established that these people are owed a duty of care by the commercial establishment, even though they are largely the authors of their own misfortune. This duty extends not only to the customers themselves, but also to others injured through their intoxicated conduct. For example, in *Laface v. Boknows Hotels Inc. and McWilliams*,[15] the hotel in question had served alcohol to the driver to the extent that it should have known that there was danger of an accident. After leaving the pub, the driver drove his car into a group of people on the roadway, causing serious injuries. The appeal court upheld the trial judge's decision to divide liability equally between the driver and the hotel. A similar obligation is imposed on employers who serve alcohol to employees at office parties and on other occasions. For example, in the *Hunt* case[16] an employer was liable for the injuries suffered by a receptionist who became intoxicated at an office Christmas party and was subsequently injured driving home. A more difficult question is whether a social host at a private party is liable when one of the guests leaves intoxicated and is injured or injures another. In the *Childs v. Desormeaux* case[17] the Supreme Court of Canada held that no duty was owed in such a situation. Here, the hosts did not supply the alcohol that their guest consumed, and there was no proof that they even knew that the guest was intoxicated when he left the party. Although it is clear that the Supreme Court was reluctant to extend the duty to such social hosts, the question is still open as to the extent of social hosts' liability when they do supply the alcohol that leads to an accident.

*Commercial hosts now owe duty to intoxicated patrons and others*

## Case Summary 2.5 *Design Services Ltd. v. Canada*[18]

## No Duty of Care Found for Subcontractors

Design Services Ltd. (Plaintiff/Appellant), Canada (Defendant/Respondent) in an appeal before the Supreme Court of Canada.

The Department of Public Works (DPW) (Canada) requested tenders on a building that was to be constructed. A number of tenders that conformed to the tendering requirements were submitted, but the DPW selected one that did not conform. Olympic Construction Ltd., a bidder that had complied and should have won the contract, sued. A number of their subcontractors also sued the DPW. Olympic settled but the subcontractors continued their action, claiming damages in tort for negligence. They were not partners, nor were they in any form of joint venture relationship with Olympic Construction Ltd.,

[15] 2006 BCCA 227 (CanLII).
[16] *Hunt (Guardian of) v. Sutton Group Incentive Realty In.*, (ONCA), 2002 CanLII 45019, 215 DLR (4th) 193).
[17] [2006] SCJ No. 18.
[18] [2008] 1 SCR 737, 2008 SCC 22.

and since there was no privity of contract (direct relationship) between them and the DPW they had to sue in tort claiming negligence. The question of whether the DPW owed them a duty to be careful became the main issue in this action.

At trial the federal court determined that there was a duty of care but that was reversed in the Federal Court of Appeal. The subcontractors then appealed to the Supreme Court of Canada.

This is a case where the only damage suffered was economic, and there was no historical precedent for such economic loss. Because this was a unique case, the Supreme Court of Canada applied the *Anns* case test and found that even if a duty was found to exist under the first part of the test, it would be negated under the second part due to policy reasons. The court reasoned that the subcontractors could have joined into a joint venture or partnership relationship with Olympic and chose not to. Had they done so they could have sued in contract and had a remedy. They were suing in tort for negligence to get around the fact that they had no contractual relationship. If the court had found a duty, the result would have been to ignore the intentions of those contracting parties and to impose a result not intended by any of them. There were, therefore, sound policy reasons for not finding a duty in this case, and the appeal of the subcontractors was dismissed.

The case illustrates the importance of finding a duty of care owed to the plaintiff as well as how the *Anns* case test is applied in this kind of unique situation. It also contrasts the rights of the parties in a contract action with those in a tort action and introduces the concept of privity of contract.

## Standard of Care

In most negligence cases the existence of a duty of care is self-evident, and the problem is to determine whether there was a failure to live up to the appropriate standard of care. As a general rule, our law does not impose a duty to act and so omission (nonfeasance) is not generally actionable unless there is some special relationship imposing a duty. Examples would include roles such as a lifeguard or guardian, or where there is a duty to warn of some danger, as is the case with the occupier of property or the manufacturer of a dangerous product. In most examples of actionable negligence, inappropriate conduct or misfeasance is involved. The question remains, therefore, how careful does a person have to be? The general answer in Canadian law is that a person is required to live up to what would be expected of a reasonable person in the same circumstances. As long as that standard is maintained or surpassed, there has been no negligence even where serious harm has taken place. This is the second major application of the reasonable person test as used in the law of negligence, and it is the most significant application of this test in our legal system. Remember that reasonable care is not average but is what is expected of a prudent person being careful. In determining reasonable conduct, the courts will look at several factors. The risk of potential damage will be taken into account. Thus, in a desert where torrential rains are rare, extensive waterproofing of a building would not be expected, especially where the costs of protecting against such an unlikely occurrence would be high. Risk, cost, and potential loss, therefore, are important factors to be taken into consideration in determining reasonable conduct.

*The standard of conduct required is determined by reasonable person test*

*Reasonable conduct is determined by risk, cost, and potential of loss*

In situations where high risk is involved, with great potential for damage, the duty to be careful is extremely high. When food handlers and motor vehicle operators cause injury, for example, negligence is easier to prove since the required standard of care is extremely high.

In rare circumstances when someone brings something dangerous onto his or her property and it escapes, causing injury to a neighbour, liability may be imposed, even where the owner of the property has not caused the escape and where he has taken all reasonable steps to avoid it. This is called **strict liability**, or the rule in *Rylands v. Fletcher*.[19]

*Expertise claimed affects reasonableness of conduct*

Another important factor in determining the duty of care is the expertise claimed by the person being held to a standard. Doctors, accountants, engineers, and other professionals are expected to have the skills and abilities associated with their profession and to exercise those skills in a reasonable manner. Accordingly, the standard expected is that of a reasonable doctor or a reasonable engineer. While it would likely not be negligent for an average person to misdiagnose a person having a stroke or a heart attack, it could well be negligence for an attending physician to make such an error.

*"Careless" conduct can be presumed from circumstances*

It is often difficult to determine just what caused a loss or injury. Some situations, however, such as a snail in a soft drink, a piano falling from a building, or contaminated food leads one to the conclusion that someone must have been careless. Canadian courts can look at such circumstantial evidence, and, if it is strong enough, conclude that a presumption of negligence has been established. Then it is up to the defendant to produce evidence that he or she was not negligent. If the defendant cannot do so, the presumption is confirmed and liability for negligence determined. In the past, this was treated under the principle of *res ipsa loquitur*, but the Supreme Court of Canada has decided that these matters are better dealt with by applying the more flexible principle of circumstantial evidence.[20]

## Case Summary 2.6 *Kripps v. Touche Ross and Co.*[21]

## Accountant Negligent Despite Following Rules

Kripps (Plaintiff/Respondent), Touche Ross (Defendant/Appellant) in an appeal before the Court of Appeal for British Columbia.

The defendants were a firm of accountants that audited the books of Victoria Mortgage and Housing from 1980 to 1983. The audited statements were used to issue a prospectus and sell debentures to the public. The auditors' refusal to approve the 1984 statements of the company led to its collapse. The debenture holders, who had relied on the previous statements, lost a considerable amount in the collapse and sued the defendant auditors. The debenture holders claimed the auditors had been negligent in providing a favourable audit for the prior years. The problem related to a number of mortgages held by Victoria Mortgage that were in default. They amounted to one-third of the mortgages held by that company. The bad mortgages had been capitalized as valuable assets along with the unpaid interest, instead of being treated as uncollectible losses.

The auditors defended their actions by stating that this was consistent with the rules that they followed (GAAP, Generally Accepted Accounting Principles, and GAAS, Generally Accepted Audit Standards), and so long as they acted within those rules, they could not be acting negligently. The trial judge agreed, but on appeal the court found the auditors negligent. Professionals cannot hide behind the rules they make themselves and claim that they are following the appropriate standard, no matter what the consequences. "GAAP may be their guide to forming this opinion, but auditors are retained to form an opinion on the fairness of the financial statements, not merely on their conformity to GAAP." The auditors knew the mortgages were in default at the time, thus making their audited statements clearly misleading. Note that these rules were changed afterward to avoid this kind of problem.

This case illustrates the high standard of care required of professionals and the fact that simply adhering to standard practice or rules of conduct set by a professional association may not always be good enough to escape liability.

---

[19](1868), L.R. 3 (H.L.) 330.

[20]*Fontaine v. British Columbia (Official Administrator)*, [1998] 1 SCR 424 (SCC).

[21]1992 CanLII 923 (BCCA); 94 DLR (4th) 284; 69 BCLR (2d) 62.

Historically, special rules were applied to some unique situations. For example, occupiers (the people in possession of property as opposed to the landlord) had a particular responsibility to people using the land and premises, depending on their status. The occupier had to protect an invitee from any unusual danger. Invitees were people on the land for some business purpose. Licensees, who were there out of sufferance or with permission, had to be warned of any hidden danger, but the only duty owed to a trespasser was not to intentionally or recklessly harm him or her. Most jurisdictions have enacted occupier's liability acts, which modify these traditional obligations. Typically, the distinction between invitees and licensees has been abolished, requiring the occupier to take reasonable steps to protect all visitors and their property. The obligations to trespassers remain minimal. If the trespasser is a child, however, the obligations on the occupier are typically greater. The principle is that various features on a property can be an attraction to children and extra care must be taken to keep the children out of and away from danger. In *Tutinka v. Mainland Sand and Gravel*[22] the operator of a gravel pit was aware that it was being used by dirt bike riders but continued to work the property. In the process, they dug away a section just over a hill used by the riders, creating a cliff, which an unsuspecting 15-year-old motorcyclist went over. The motorcyclist was seriously injured. Even though the plaintiff had not been given permission to be there, the operator was found to be 75 percent responsible under the *Occupiers Liability Act* of British Columbia. Note that it is the occupier, not the owner, of property that is liable under these statutes. Only the person in possession and in control of the premises qualifies as the occupier. In commercial relationships it is the tenant that is in possession and control of the premises and responsible for those injured on the property not the landlord. However, in residential tenancies the landlord and tenancy acts (*Residential Tenancies Acts)* place a particular responsibility on the landlord to ensure that the property is safe and in good repair. The landlord cannot contract out of this responsibility and therefore may also be considered an occupier in control of the premises under the *Occupier's Liability Act*. In *Taylor v. Allard*,[23] the Court of Appeal for Ontario found that the landlord's failure to keep the property safe supported the imposition of tort liability under the *Ontario Occupiers' Liability* Act. In that case a visitor at a party fell over some cinder blocks into a fire pit and was seriously injured. The court found these cinder blocks constituted a danger. Under the Ontario legislation an occupier is a person who is in physical occupation of the property or a person who has responsibility and control over the condition of the premises and the activities there carried on. The landlord's failure to keep the property safe gave him sufficient control to make him an occupier under the *Occupiers' Liability Act* and liable.

> Duty of occupiers is now based on legislation.

There are other examples where legislation has been used to change the standard of care required of certain classes. The unique obligations owed by innkeepers to their guests and common carriers to their customers have been modified by statute in most jurisdictions. However, it is important to realize that not every time a statute imposes a duty on someone is a new category of tort created. For example, human rights legislation and privacy legislation both impose duties and rights, but they are not tort obligations unless specifically made so by statute, and the remedies available are limited to those set out in the legislation that creates them. Note that insurance is a method of avoiding the risks associated with tort liability. In business, of course, insurance becomes a very important aspect of risk avoidance,

> Special statutory standards override common law

---

[22](1993) 110 DLR (4th) 182 (BCCA).

[23][2010] ONCA 596.

duty owed ──────► duty breached ──────► causation ──────► loss ──────► no defences

**Figure 2.2** Negligence

and the cost of acquiring the various forms of insurance required to operate a business successfully must be factored into the overall cost of doing business. In many jurisdictions certain types of insurance coverage is mandatory, such as automobile insurance.

## Causation and Damage

Finally, to succeed in a negligence action, the plaintiff must demonstrate **causation**, that the conduct complained of was the cause of the injury or damage (see Table 2.2 on p. 48). With intentional torts such as assault and battery, false imprisonment, or trespass, it is not necessary that actual damage be shown. The commission of the tort is enough to warrant payment of damages, although compensation for losses will also be included in any judgment. However, with negligence there must be some sort of resulting injury or damage before compensation can be sought from the defendant. Almost getting hurt is not good enough. It follows that the damages must be the direct result of the negligent conduct complained of. Figure 2.2 illustrates the chain of events leading to liability caused by negligence. The test applied is the "but for" test. The plaintiff must establish that "but for" the conduct complained of there would have been no injury or damage. If it were established that the driver involved in an accident knew his or her brake lights were not working, the plaintiff would still have to demonstrate that the lack of brake lights caused the accident. If the accident involved a head-on collision, it would be very unlikely that this failure contributed to the collision. The defendant may have been careless for driving without brake lights, but that failure did not cause the accident. In some situations it can be a very difficult and complex problem for the court to determine just how much of a causal connection is needed for liability for negligence to be imposed. This will be discussed below under the heading "Remoteness."

*Conduct complained of must have led to loss or damage*

## Defences

Table 2.3 summarizes defences that the defendant can raise to eliminate or reduce liability in a negligence action.

| **Table 2.3** Defences That the Defendant Can Raise to Eliminate or Reduce Liability in a Negligence Action | |
| --- | --- |
| Contributory Negligence | Where the plaintiff is also negligent, the court will apportion the damages. |
| Voluntary Assumption of Risk | Where the plaintiff has voluntarily put him- or herself in danger—and thus has assumed the legal as well as physical risk—this will be a complete bar to recovery. |
| Remoteness | Where the causal connection is indirect or consequences are out of proportion to expectations, liability may be reduced. |

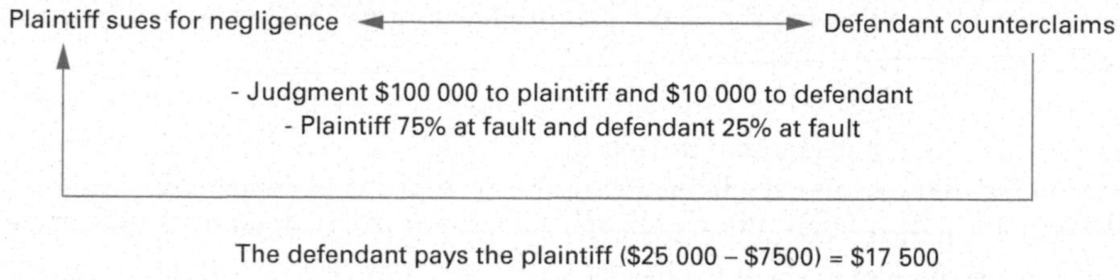

Plaintiff sues for negligence ⟷ Defendant counterclaims

- Judgment $100 000 to plaintiff and $10 000 to defendant
- Plaintiff 75% at fault and defendant 25% at fault

The defendant pays the plaintiff ($25 000 − $7500) = $17 500

**Figure 2.3** Negligence Action

**Contributory Negligence**   Traditionally, if it could be shown that the person who was suing had also contributed to the loss, he or she would receive no compensation from the defendant. This was first modified to a limited extent in common law and, subsequently, by legislation. Statutes such as Saskatchewan's *Contributory Negligence Act*[24] now allow the court to assign proportional liability, making both parties responsible for the loss (see Figure 2.3). For example, when both drivers are held equally responsible for an automobile accident, people often expect that both parties would simply pay for their own loss, but it doesn't work that way. If the driver of one car suffered only vehicle damage ($5000) but the other suffered major personal injury ($100 000) the uninjured driver would be required to pay half of the other driver's loss ($50 000) minus half of his own loss ($2500). So even though both are equally to blame in these circumstances, the uninjured driver would be required to pay the other $47 500. The courts will often determine fault differently; for example, finding one party 25 percent to blame and the other 75 percent. This would change the amounts awarded based on the appropriate mathematical calculation. Thus, when **contributory negligence** is present, the court reduces the amount of compensation paid to a victim of negligence based on the proportion the victim's own carelessness contributed to the loss.

> Where the victim is also negligent, loss is now apportioned

**Voluntary Assumption of Risk**   People who deliberately put themselves in harm's way are disqualified from suing for the injury or loss that results. Unlike contributory negligence, this is a complete bar to recovery of loss. This used to be a much more important aspect of negligence law, but to raise this defence today, the defendant must show not only that the injured party voluntarily put himself or herself in danger, but also that he or she did it in such as way as to absolve the defendant of any legal responsibility for the consequences. It must be established that not only did the victim assume the physical risk, but also the legal risk as well. This is difficult to prove; consequently, when people act foolishly—taking risks that they shouldn't—the courts usually deal with it as contributory negligence. The courts can then apportion the loss between the parties based on their percentage of fault. This is a much more satisfactory result. Thus, when a drunken individual participated in a tubing race at a winter resort and was seriously injured, contributory negligence was applied rather than **voluntary assumption of risk**, because it could not be established that he had assumed both the legal risk and the physical risk. This was the case even though he had signed a waiver form before commencing the activity.[25] Still, in extreme cases where people knowingly

> Where victim voluntarily assumed the legal risk, there is no remedy

---

[24]*Contributory Negligence Act*, RSS 1978, c C-31.

[25]*Crocker v. Sundance Northwest Resorts Ltd.*, [1988] 1 SCR 1186 (SCC).

put themselves in harm's way, the court may find voluntary assumption of risk and completely bar recovery.

Rescuers who put themselves into dangerous situations are treated differently. If a person is negligent and puts another at risk, he or she also owes a duty to be careful to someone coming to the rescue. If a bystander pushes a child out of the path of a speeding car, and is injured in the process, she can sue the negligent driver without fear that a claim of voluntary assumption of risk will bar recovery.

**Remoteness**    Another argument that is sometimes raised in defence of a negligence action is that the injury or loss was too remote. The test used for **remoteness** is the same reasonable foreseeability test used to determine duty of care, but there it applied to the foreseeability of injury generally. Here, the question is whether the particular injury in question was reasonably foreseeable. The *Mustapha* case[26] decided by the Supreme Court of Canada is a good example. Mr. Mustapha was changing a water bottle when he saw a fly in the bottle. This caused him great anxiety, eventually seriously affecting his health. He developed a phobia with respect to drinking water. He suffered from nightmares and an inability to sleep, was unable to drink water, and became seriously depressed. In these product-liability cases a duty of care is clearly established on the manufacturer based on the reasonable foreseeability test established in *Donoghue v. Stevenson*. The trial judge determined that there was a breach of that duty of care because of lax inspection procedures. That failure caused the real, although unusual, injuries and Mr. Mustapha was awarded a total of $341 774 in damages.

The Court of Appeal overturned that decision, and the Supreme Court of Canada dismissed the appeal. The reasons given are instructive. The chief justice found that while there was a duty to be careful and a breach of that duty, and that the damages suffered were the result of that failure, the injuries in question were too remote. Therefore, there was no liability. Physically the injuries were caused by the breach of duty, but legally they were too remote. The court found that such injuries have to be reasonably foreseeable to an ordinary person. They must be a real risk and not one that a normal prudent person would consider to be far-fetched. In this case the court found that if the manufacturers had put their minds to it, they would not have concluded that what happened due to their conduct was a real risk, and so no liability was imposed. Basically, the court said that Mr. Mustapha's susceptibility to injury was so unusual that it would have been unreasonable to impose a duty on the defendants to avoid the harm. Legal causation will only be established when there is reasonable foreseeability of such an injury to a person of "ordinary fortitude."

Thus, there must be a sufficient causal connection between the conduct complained of and the resulting injury. If that connection is considered to be too remote or too indirect, the requirement of causation will not be met, and there will be no liability imposed.

Note that once the causal connection is found, when personal injury is involved, we take our victims the way we find them. Once an injury is foreseeable, the plaintiff will be liable even if the degree of injury is unusual. Thus, if the person whose hand I negligently injure is a concert pianist, I will be responsible to pay much greater compensation than if the person is a lawyer or accountant. This is called the thin skull rule. I will not normally be able

Responsibility imposed even where unusual occupation or condition causes victim greater loss than normal

---

[26]*Mustapha v. Culligan of Canada Ltd.*, 2008 SCC 27 (CanLII).

to claim that because of the unusual occupation of the victim his loss is too remote, or that the damages should be limited only to what a normal person would lose. If damage to the hand was foreseeable, I must take my victim as I find him and pay the greater compensation. Of course, if the hand was becoming more and more arthritic, and my negligent conduct just sped up the process, the damages would be reduced accordingly. This is referred to as the crumbling skull rule. In the *Mustapha* case, the basic legal causation connection was not found in the first place (the connection was too remote), and so there was no question of taking the victim as found.

It should also be mentioned that as in contract law there is a duty to mitigate damages in a negligence action. This means that plaintiffs have to take all reasonable steps to keep their damages as low as possible. If they fail to do this, their damages will be reduced to the amount they would have received had they properly mitigated. In addition, where potentially dangerous activities are involved, such as sports or a medical procedure, the contract will normally include a provision restricting any such action or the patient will be required to sign a release. People can contract out of the right to sue in tort, and as a result such provisions, if worded correctly, can be an effective defence.

## PRODUCT LIABILITY

LO 6

The *Mustapha* case indicates some of the difficulties faced by both parties in product liability cases. As discussed in *Donoghue v. Stevenson*, when use of a particular product injures a person, there is normally a choice. The purchaser can sue the seller of the product for breach of contract and/or sue the manufacturer for negligence. Contracts will be discussed in the following chapters, but it is important to note at this stage that an action in contract has the distinct advantage of imposing strict liability where the product was defective and caused the injury. There is no need to prove fault on the part of the defendant. However, such a breach of contract action may not be available to the injured party, either because he or she was not the person who purchased the product or because the contract was with the retailer who sold the item, not the manufacturer. The principle that only the parties to a contract have obligations under it is referred to as **privity of contract**. When there is no contractual relation between the parties, the only option is to sue for negligence. The problem is that in a tort action fault must be demonstrated in addition to showing that the defective product caused the injury. The plaintiff must show that the defendant was negligent, having failed to live up to the standard of a reasonable manufacturer in the circumstances. This can be very difficult to do and is one of the situations where the courts are willing to look at the surrounding events and find that a *prima facie* (clear on the face of it) case of negligence has been established from circumstantial evidence. For example, finding a decomposed snail in a can of soda speaks loudly that someone must have been careless. Either the production process has not been properly designed to avoid this type of thing from happening, or someone made a mistake by failing to follow those proper procedures. Once the presumption of negligence has been established through circumstantial evidence, the onus then shifts and the manufacturer must face the daunting task of showing that it did everything reasonable to ensure that this type of injury would not happen. Once it is established that some aspect of the product was defective, it caused the injury complained of, and the manufacturer was careless, liability to compensate for that injury will be imposed.

When a manufacturer is sued, negligence must be established

Note the use of circumstantial evidence in these negligent cases

## Case Summary 2.7 *Bain v. Black & Decker Canada (1989)*[27]

# Defective Hair Dryer Causes Injury

Bain (Plaintiff) and Black and Decker Canada (1989) (Defendant) in trial before the Ontario Superior Court of Justice.

In 2002 Mrs. Bain was hurt when the hair dryer she was using emitted a spark seriously injuring her hand. The cause was a faulty manufactured strain relief boot where the dryer chord came out of the plastic housing of the hair dryer. Constant flexing caused the copper strands within the cord to fray and break. The boot was designed to reduce the natural flexing of the cord and stop the cord from deteriorating with use. However, the boot was poorly designed so it cracked or split over time. The split allowed the flexing and fraying to take place, which eventually caused the product to malfunction. This in turn caused the spark, consisting of molten plastic and copper, to escape injuring Mrs. Bain. This injury resulted in pain and deterioration in her ability to use her hand, which interfered with her work and her athletic activities and caused her pre-existing symptoms of anxiety to reoccur.

It is now well established that a manufacturer owes a duty of care to the ultimate user of the product. It is clear that the defective boot caused the chord to fail and inflict the injury. The defect that caused the injury constituted a failure to live up to the appropriate standard of care in the circumstances due to the poor design of the boot, improper materials used, or the failure to provide adequate warning of the danger. The defence argued that the injury suffered was too remote since it could not have been anticipated by the parties. The court held, however, that the injury suffered was just what should have been anticipated. The reoccurrence of Mrs. Bain's anxiety problems, however, was not a reasonably foreseeable result of the defective boot and so was too remote and not recoverable. The judge awarded damages of over $35 000 to Mrs. Bain and a further $1500 to her husband and each of her children for loss of guidance, care, and companionship.

The case illustrates the nature of the duty of care owed by a manufacturer to the ultimate user of their product, the standard of care required, as well as the concept of remoteness, which in this case reduced the amount of damages owed to Mrs. Bain for the reoccurrence of her anxiety.

The product liability area is where class-action suits are particularly important. Whether defective automobiles or tires, ruptured breast implants, or drugs that cause deformities or heart attacks are involved, when many people are injured as a result of the same complaint against the same manufacturer, a class-action approach to the problem is an attractive way to proceed.

In the United States, if a person can show that the product was defective and it caused his or her injury, usually that is enough to establish liability. This is called strict liability. Some jurisdictions in Canada have moved away from the traditional approach of requiring the demonstration of negligence in product liability cases. Other provinces have moved in that same direction by imposing contractual warranties on a manufacturer guaranteeing fitness and quality, and extending those rights to anyone who uses the product. This, in effect, eliminates the requirement in a breach of contract action that the victim be the purchaser of the product, as discussed above. Courts in other jurisdictions have found that because of advertising, specifications, and other literature, including manufacturers' warranties, a subsidiary contract exists between the manufacturer and the purchaser, making the manufacturer directly liable to the purchaser (see Figure 2.4). Remember that where contractual liability can be established, there is no need to show the existence of a duty or a failure to live up to the standard of a reasonable person.

*In some jurisdictions manufacturers may be sued in contract*

---

[27]2009 CanLII 26598 (ONSC).

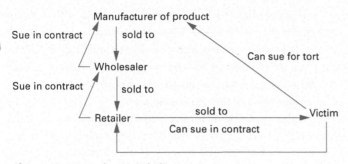

**Figure 2.4** Product Liability

## PROFESSIONAL LIABILITY                                                LO 7

A similar situation exists when professionals are involved. They have a direct contractual
liability to their clients and are liable, even without showing fault, when they make errors
that cause loss to those clients. However, as they carry out their professional duties, the
damage incurred often goes beyond their direct relation to their clients and causes economic or even physical loss or injury to third parties. Those injured claimants then must
sue in tort for negligence, and the question for the court to determine is just how far they
want to extend such **professional liability** in these circumstances. Historically, the courts
refused to provide a remedy where the loss was purely economic, especially where it was
caused by words rather than conduct. This changed in Canada in 1965 with the case of
*Haig v. Bamford*,[28] where investors suffered losses because of a misleading financial statement and successfully sued the negligent accountant who prepared them. In that case the
Supreme Court of Canada did not adopt the reasonable foreseeability test, but required
that the accountants have actual knowledge that investors would rely on the erroneous
statements. For the next 25 years there was some confusion as to when a duty would exist
and when it would not. The eventual solution was to supplement the reasonable foreseeability test developed in *Donoghue v. Stevenson* with a Canadian application of the *Anns*
case discussed above, which resulted in a much more straightforward and simple approach.

When an accountant prepares such financial statements for a company they are normally used by the shareholders to review the performance of the managers at an annual
shareholders' meeting. Sometimes, however, they are meant to be used in a prospectus to
attract new investors. The law as developed by the Supreme Court was that a duty was
owed when the accountants knew that investors would use the statements, but no duty
existed to investors when they were prepared solely for the shareholders to evaluate the
management of the corporation.

But a problem arose with the *Hercules* case.[29] Auditors prepared financial reports for
a company as part of the normal annual auditing process. These reports were prepared for
the shareholders to use in their evaluation of the performance of management. Instead,
the shareholders invested further funds in the company on the strength of the audited
reports. The invested funds were lost because of errors in the reports, and the investors/
shareholders sued the auditors for negligence. The Supreme Court of Canada applied the
two-stage *Anns* case test and held that, while damage to the shareholders was clearly

Duty may now be modified or
eliminated on policy considerations

---

[28](1976), 72 DLR (3d) 68 (SCC).

[29]*Hercules Management Ltd. v. Ernst & Young* (1997), 146 DLR (4th) 577 (SCC).

Court unwilling to expose
professionals to unlimited liability

reasonably foreseeable, there was a good policy reason to deny the existence of a duty in this case. The Supreme Court made it clear that it was reluctant to expose accountants and other professionals to open-ended liability where they would be liable for an "indeterminate amount for an indeterminate time to an indeterminate class." Applying this policy, the Supreme Court decided that because the erroneous reports were used for a purpose other than intended, there was no duty and no liability.

Professional liability to clients
based on contract

Today this approach will be used in any new or unusual situation when duty of care must be determined. This applies even when the careless conduct results in physical injury or loss, such as in a case of a bridge falling because of a design mistake. Just how extensive should the liability be to the people using the bridge? What about those who suffer a loss because they can no longer use the bridge? Once reasonable foreseeability has been determined, the court can then apply the second half of the *Anns* case test and impose limits on the basis of social policy considerations. But even with this limited approach to duty of care, professionals must always remember that not only are they required to be careful in their dealings with their clients, but they also may be held responsible for damages their conduct causes to others with whom they are not dealing directly.

Professional liability to others based
on negligence and *Anns* case test

Higher standard of conduct
required of experts

When professionals are involved, there are also some unique problems in determining the standard of care to which they must adhere. Just how careful must the professional be? The general principle is that the professional, like anyone else, must live up to the standard of a reasonable person in the circumstances. Thus, the standard imposed becomes what is expected of a reasonable lawyer, doctor, accountant, engineer, architect, teacher, or consultant. Whenever a degree of expertise is claimed, that expert or professional is required to have the level of skill and expertise expected of a normal person in that profession. Inexperience is no excuse. Further, the professional is required to exercise that expertise and skill in a reasonable manner. Showing that an expert adhered to the standard practice in a particular profession is usually good enough. The rationale is that professionals will generally act reasonably as they practise their profession. Even this may not always be sufficient. If the court can be convinced that the standard practice in a particular instance is shoddy or inappropriate, liability for negligence will still be imposed. As illustrated in *Kripps v. Touche Ross*[30] described above (Case Summary 2.6), strict adherence to professional rules will not always avoid liability for negligence.

Standard practice of profession
may not be good enough

If the victim can establish that a duty was owed by the professional—satisfying both parts of the *Anns* case test—that there was a failure to live up to the appropriate standard and that failure caused the injury complained about, liability for negligence will be imposed.

Fiduciary duty requires good faith
and clients' interests to be put first

Professionals and other experts also have a fiduciary duty to their clients. This means they have a duty to act in the best interests of their clients, even to the point of putting their clients' interests ahead of their own. Fiduciary duty will be discussed extensively in this text, especially with respect to agency, partnership, and corporations. It is sufficient to say at this point that the nature of a fiduciary duty involves loyalty and good faith. All information that comes to the professional that relates to what is being done for that client is the property of the client. The professional must not

---

[30] 1992 CanLII 923 (BCCA); 94 DLR (4th) 284; 69 BCLR (2d) 62.

disclose it to others or make use of it for any personal gain. Similarly, if the other interests of the professional are in conflict with those of the client (where the professional could serve his or her own interests at the expense of the client), those conflicting interests must be disclosed, and the professional must step back from any decision-making process where that conflict exists. For example, if a director of Company A has shares in Company B, and the directors of Company A are considering the acquisition of Company B or placing a large order with company B, that director must disclose his or her interest and not participate in or influence the decision.

Often the professional will have in his or her possession funds from various transactions involving clients. These are trust funds and must be kept scrupulously separate from the professional's other moneys and must never be used for any purpose other than the client's business. A breach of trust action is a very serious matter, and it will usually result in the professional being disqualified from practising his or her profession. This is a particular problem for lawyers, accountants, financial planners, and real estate and insurance agents. Often criminal penalties are also imposed.

Professionals are also answerable to various professional organizations that authorize them to practise their professions. These may be law societies, medical associations, teachers' associations, various accounting organizations, and others, depending on the profession involved. Their powers vary, but often these bodies have the authority to determine who can practise the profession and to set the standard of education, ethics, and skills required. Most bodies can also discipline members and disqualify them from practice or limit a member's right to practise in the profession if the complaint against the member is serious enough. Remember that these bodies are subject to law and must adhere to basic human rights legislation: where their decisions violate basic rules of due process, human rights, or other valid regulations, those decisions can be challenged in the courts.

Disciplinary bodies subject to rules of "due process"

Finally, it should be noted that the risks associated with tort liability can be avoided or significantly reduced for the professional and nonprofessional as well, simply through the acquisition of appropriate insurance. Insurance has become an essential aspect of doing business. Liability insurance (sometimes called errors and omissions insurance) will protect professionals and others when they make mistakes that cause loss to clients and other people. The insurer not only will compensate the victim for the injury but also will provide appropriate legal representation to cover the insured during the process of the claim. Insurance, however, will not usually protect the insured where the wrongful act was deliberate or fraud was involved. The victim may, in fact, be entitled to compensation in these circumstances, but the insurance company will normally demand repayment from the insured, including any legal expenses incurred. One serious problem with insurance today is the ever-increasing cost of premiums. With the huge awards that are being ordered by the courts for malpractice in all professions, the premiums are generally increasing to the point of becoming unbearable. Consequently, many professionals and business people are simply taking their chances and, where possible, not carrying insurance at all. Some professional bodies, however, require insurance coverage as a condition of practice. They sometimes provide that insurance, often at a high cost, as one of the services provided to their members. Some of these organizations are self-insured, incorporating substantial fees to cover potential losses. Even then there will usually be backup arrangements for insurance coverage for extraordinary claims. Insurance will be discussed in more detail in Chapter 8.

Professional risk is reduced by insurance

## Case Summary 2.8 *Davidson v. Noram Capital Management Inc.*[31]

# Financial Advisor Liable for Negligence and Breach of Fiduciary Duty

Davidson, (Plaintiff), Noram Capital Management (Defendant) in a trial before the Ontario Superior Court of Justice.

Mr. Willman was the principal and directing mind behind Noram Capital Management Inc. and made all of the investment decisions for that financial management business. The plaintiffs were clients of Noram and had invested large sums of money with that company. They had signed a standard "wrap" agreement that set out guidelines as to how their money was to be invested. These were to be very conservative investments designed to be safe, to preserve capital, and to provide a steady income. They were to include secure investments such as government and corporate bonds. The plaintiffs were for the most part older retired people with very little investment experience.

Instead of investing these funds conservatively, Mr. Willman invested in more risky securities and made further purchases on the margin (borrowed money) that resulted in the loss of a substantial portion of the investment. Mr. Willman had also charged a higher management fee (3.5 percent) than was common for the industry (1.5 percent), and this fee was calculated, not just on the invested funds but on the unauthorized borrowed funds as well, making the actual fees paid much higher than expected. When the plaintiffs understood that they had actually lost a substantial portion of their capital, they sued.

Mr. Willman admitted that he had improperly managed the portfolios involved and failed to deal honestly and in good faith with the clients. He had misled his clients and failed to disclose that he was making more risky investments than authorized. The court found that Mr. Willman and his company owed a duty of care to the plaintiffs to provide services that met the standard of a prudent investment advisor and that he had failed to live up to that standard. The court also determined that because the clients were vulnerable and relied on Mr. Willman to act in their best interests he owed them a fiduciary duty that he had breached. The court ordered that compensation for these losses be paid, and damages in excess of $1 million were awarded.

This case dramatically illustrates how a professional can face direct liability not only for his own negligence, but also for breach of a fiduciary duty. It is also interesting to note that Mr. Willman and his company had their registration terminated, and the Ontario Securities Commission permanently prohibited them from trading securities.

---

**Negligence may also be criminal**

Negligence can also constitute a crime under the *Criminal Code* of Canada, where a person in the performance of a duty does or neglects to do something that "shows wanton or reckless disregard for the lives or safety of other persons." This includes failure to ensure that the safety provisions in the workplace and in their sphere of operation are adequate to protect the workers, customers, and the public. If the negligent conduct causes bodily harm the accused is liable for imprisonment of up to 14 years, and for life when a death results. These *Criminal Code* provisions extend such liability to corporations and similar organizations as well as to those managing them. There are many other provisions of the *Criminal Code* relating to specific kinds of conduct that also provide a penalty for negligence. Note that organizations, including companies, can also be convicted under these provisions, usually with the imposition of significant fines. An example of a typical sentence imposed for criminal negligence is found in *R. v. Jeffery*.[32] The accused was a truck driver who, while intoxicated, caused an accident that resulted in two deaths. The court

---

[31] 2005 CanLII 63766 (ONSC), 13 BLR (4th) 35.

[32] Ont. Dist. Ct. 1987, as reported in *Lawyers Weekly Consolidated Digest*, Vol. 7.

sentenced the driver to three and a half years, and extended a driving suspension for over 10 years. This case indicates that the primary consideration in such alcohol-related cases should be deterrence.

Of course, criminal penalties are also imposed where deliberate acts are involved. For example, fraud committed by a British Columbia lawyer resulted in a sentence of seven years and an order to pay $2 million in restitution to the British Columbia Law Society (the Law Society had to pay out about $42 million in compensation to the lawyer's victims.)[33] It is interesting to note that this all started with one relatively small infraction, which then grew and grew as one fraud and forgery was used to cover another.

## OTHER BUSINESS TORTS

Negligence is by far the most important tort for the business people or professionals. However, they should be aware of several other related torts. When a person intentionally misleads another, cheating him or her out of money or obtaining some other advantage, this is a **fraud** or **deceit**. Of course, such fraud can also amount to criminal conduct, as was the case of lawyer professional misconduct discussed above. For more detail, see Chapter 4, where fraudulent misrepresentation is discussed as part of the discussion on contract law. Also, defamation has many different forms, and one way it can take place is when false information is intentionally spread to harm the sales of a particular product. This is called injurious falsehood or product defamation.

When one person persuades another to breach a contract with a third person, this may constitute **inducing breach of contract**. Often, one employer "steals" an employee from another employer, persuading that employee to breach his or her employment contract in the process. Whether it is done to obtain the unique skills of that employee or just to weaken a competitor, the employer usually thinks that the only one who has committed a wrong is the employee. In fact, there is considerable danger for the one inducing the breach. This is because the value of that employee to the business may be much greater than is reflected by the salary, and consequently the person inducing the breach can be held liable for the loss. This tort can also take place when one person persuades a potential client or customer to breach his contract with a competitor and to deal with his business instead. Even customers can induce breach of contract. An interesting example took place where a customer company (Cogeco) refused to let the employee of the service providing company (Mastec) work on one of their projects. This forced Mastec to breach the contract of employment dismissing that employee. The employee sued Cogeco which was found to have induced the breach of the employment contract and was liable to pay damages of $200 000.[34]

In the area of intellectual property there is nothing so valuable as a good name and reputation. Sometimes, by using a similar name, logo, or other identifying characteristic of a brand, one business will try to take advantage of another by misleading people into thinking they are associated with or are part of that reputable business, when in fact they are not. This is an attempt to mislead and is actionable as a **passing-off** action. For example, when a retailer sold a handbag line that was a copy of the Hermes line, Hermes Canada

**LO 8**

Other business torts include:
■ Fraud and deceit

■ Inducing breach of contract

■ Passing off

---

[33]*R. v. Wirick*, 2009 BSSC 1714 (CanLII).

[34]*Drouillard v. Cogeco Cable Inc.* (2007), 282 DLR (4th) 644 (OCA) 25.

sued, claiming the tort of passing off. Although there was no name on the handbag, it was only on close inspection that the name of a different manufacturer was apparent. This was a clear example of passing off where the customers were deceived into thinking they were purchasing a genuine Hermes handbag when in fact they had obtained a copy.[35] This passing-off action is in addition to the remedies provided under the *Trade-marks Act* and may even be available where the requirements of a trademark are not met.

■ Trespass to chattels and conversion

**Trespass to chattels** takes place when someone damages or otherwise interferes with some item of personal property, such as a vehicle or other equipment. Slashing a tire would be an example. Taking a car without authority may be a crime, but it is also a tort called **conversion**. Conversion is broader than simple theft and can take place in any situation where one person intentionally deprives another of the possession or use of his personal property. It would even constitute conversion when a person mistakenly took property he thought was his own. Thus, conversion can take place by someone taking control of another's property by taking it as their own, but also by hiding it, moving it, destroying it, or locking it up.

The normal remedy when a tort has taken place is damages, which is the awarding of a monetary payment, usually designed to compensate the victim for his or her loss. In rare circumstances, where the conduct was deliberate, punitive damages may also be granted when the object is to punish the wrongdoer rather than simply to compensate. Where a monetary award would not be appropriate, as is usually the case where a passing-off action is involved, the court will sometimes award an injunction ordering the offending conduct to stop. Sometimes an accounting will also be ordered, requiring that a wrongdoer disclose any profits made and pay them over to the victim.

Note that there are some other non-tort areas where the business person has a duty to maintain a certain standard of conduct in relation to others. Federal and Provincial Human rights acts prohibit discrimination in employment and other areas, but such discrimination cannot be the basis of a tort action unless specifically so stated in the statute. Such a complaint can only be enforced by the board of commission set up for that purpose and is not actionable in the courts. Breaching federal and provincial privacy legislation will also impose serious statutory penalties and several provinces have provided in their statutes that such breach of privacy will amount to an actionable tort. Also, the Court of Appeal for Ontario has recognized for the first time a breach of privacy tort independent of statute in *Jones v. Tsige*.[36] The defendant in that case was in a common law relationship with the plaintiff's former husband, and was found liable in tort for improperly accessing the plaintiff's banking records hundreds of times over several years. This case may point the direction for the development of tort liability for breach of privacy in Canada.

Finally, it should be emphasized that the most effective method of avoiding being the defendant in such a tort action, whether the target is the individual business person or the corporation, is a good understanding of the law and a vigilant effort to ensure that the situation or conduct giving rise to such legal actions does not occur. This usually involves careful selection of potential employees, vigorous training and safety programs,

---

[35]*Hermes Canada Inc. v. Henry High Class Kelly Retail Store*, 2004 BCSC 1694 (CanLII).
[36]2012 ONCA 32 (CanLII).

internal and external audits, as well as simply keeping an observant attitude. No matter how many programs or training sessions take place, the key to avoiding such legal problems is to create a corporate environment where everyone, from executives to clerks, is alert to the risks that may be present and is encouraged to remove them or report them to others who will.

Some companies have resorted to a much more aggressive response when threatened by such legal action. Often they will launch their own lawsuits, usually claiming defamation with the object of reducing criticism and disabling potential plaintiffs. By tying them up in court, causing significant expenditure of assets, and generally harassing them through the legal system, they hope to discourage people from pursuing their lawsuits. These are called SLAPPs (strategic lawsuits against public participation), and in some circumstances they can be effective. Still, the ethics of these SLAPPs are questionable and there is an effort across Canada to curb their use through legislation, thus preventing what is considered a significant abuse of the legal system.

The use of SLAPPS considered abusive.

## Key Terms

| | |
|---|---|
| **absolute privilege** (p. 45) | **negligence** (p. 48) |
| **assault** (p. 40) | **passing off** (p. 63) |
| **battery** (p. 40) | **private nuisance** (p. 43) |
| **causation** (p. 54) | **privity of contract** (p. 57) |
| **contributory negligence** (p. 55) | **professional liability** (p. 59) |
| **conversion** (p. 64) | **qualified privilege** (p. 45) |
| **deceit** (p. 63) | **reasonable foreseeability test** (p. 49) |
| **defamation** (p. 45) | **reasonable person** (p. 48) |
| **fair comment** (p.46) | **remoteness** (p. 56) |
| **false imprisonment** (p. 41) | **self-defence** (p. 40) |
| **fraud** (p. 63) | **slander** (p. 45) |
| **inducing breach of contract** (p. 63) | **strict liability** (p. 52) |
| **innuendo** (p. 45) | **trespass to chattels** (p. 64) |
| **justification** (p. 45) | **trespass to land** (p. 42) |
| **libel** (p. 45) | **vicarious liability** (p. 39) |
| **mistake** (p. 45) | **voluntary assumption of risk** (p. 55) |

## Questions for Student Review

1. What is a tort? Distinguish between a tort and a crime, and explain when a tort can also constitute a crime.
2. Explain vicarious liability and any limitation on its availability.
3. Distinguish between intentional and inadvertent torts.
4. Explain what is meant by a reasonable person and the reasonable person test.
5. Distinguish between assault and battery, and explain any defences.
6. Explain what is required to establish a false imprisonment.

7. Why is trespass to land considered an intentional tort? Under what conditions does a trespass occur? What is a continuing trespass?

8. Explain the obligation of an owner or occupier of land for injuries suffered by a trespasser and others using that land.

9. Under what circumstances might one neighbour sue another for nuisance?

10. What is meant by defamation? What is an innuendo?

11. Distinguish between libel and slander. Why is the distinction important?

12. Explain the difference between absolute and qualified privilege, and discuss when these defences would be used. What is fair comment?

13. Explain the role of fault with respect to the tort of negligence.

14. What must be established to successfully sue for negligence?

15. Explain the role of the *Donoghue v. Stevenson* and the *Anns* cases in determining duty of care.

16. Explain what is meant by strict liability and when it might be imposed on an occupier of property. Explain how the standard of care imposed on occupiers has been modified by statute.

17. How have the principles of contributory negligence and voluntary assumption of risk been modified in recent times?

18. Explain how the problems with remoteness in a negligence action have been substantially resolved in recent times.

19. If I were to carelessly injure the hand of a musician, on what basis would damages be determined, given the victim's occupation?

20. Why are manufacturers usually sued for negligence rather than for breach of contract? Why is an action in contract preferable for the victim?

21. Explain when a professional's liability will be based on contract and when it will be based on tort. How is the standard imposed with respect to tort determined?

22. Explain what is meant by fiduciary duty and when such a duty arises.

23. Explain the nature of the following torts: deceit, product defamation, inducing breach of contract, passing off, trespass to chattels, and conversion.

## Questions for Further Discussion

1. Individuals are sometimes convicted of a crime and then sued in tort for the same conduct. Is it fair or just for one person to face trial twice for the same thing?

2. Is the reasonable person test appropriate for determining what standard of behaviour should be imposed in a negligence action? Would it be more appropriate to determine negligent conduct on the basis of the average person or some other test?

3. In Canada, when someone produces a defective product or performs an imperfect service, he or she must be shown to have been careless—to have fallen below a community-established standard of behaviour (the reasonable person test)—before he or she can be found liable for negligence. When a person is suing for breach of contract, it is unnecessary to establish fault; the breach is enough. Consider whether the requirement to establish fault where someone's conduct causes injury to another ought to be abandoned in a tort action. In other words, should it be enough to show that one person caused the injury for him or her to be liable?

4. Our constitution guarantees freedom of expression. Yet when people criticize public officials and other public figures, they can be sued for defamation, even if they believe what they say is true. Do you think we should adopt an approach similar to that in the United States and take the position that it is more important to have a frank debate with respect to such matters, a debate free of the chill imposed by the threat of legal action? Should the protections of privileged communications be applied to all such discussions of matters of public interest, whether the statements are accurate or not? Should the media enjoy special protection in such matters? Consider the appropriateness of the new "responsible communication" defence in your discussion.

## Cases for Discussion

1. *Epstein v. Cressey Development Corp.* (1992), 89 DLR (4th) 32 (BCCA)

   Cressey Development Corporation excavated a lot next to property owned by Mr. Epstein and asked permission to drive supports under Epstein's property to support that excavation. Epstein refused. After unsuccessfully trying other methods to shore up the excavation, Cressey drove the supports under the property anyway. When Epstein found out, he sued for trespass. Does this conduct constitute a trespass? What defenses are available to Cressey? What else could Cressey have done? Explain the likely outcome.

2. *Resurfice Corp. v. Hanke*, 2007 SCC 7, [2007] 1 SCR 333 (SCC)

   Hanke was the operator of an ice-resurfacing machine and was filling it with water when an explosion injured him. The water tank and the gasoline tank were similar and located in close proximity and he made the mistake of filling the gasoline tank with water from a hose. When the water filled the tank, the gasoline escaped and an overhead heater ignited the resulting fumes. Hanke sued the manufacturer and distributor of the machine for negligence. Explain the arguments available on both sides and the likely outcome, including the calculation of damages, if appropriate. Would it make any difference to your answer to know that Hanke testified that the two tanks did not confuse him?

3. *Kralik v. Mount Seymour Resorts Ltd.,* 2008 BCCA 97 (CanLII) 78 BCLR (4th) 313

   Kralik was skiing on Mount Seymour when he fell from a ski lift. He was about to get on the chair when he found ice on it and tried to remove it as the chair moved onto the boarding ramp. As it started to leave, he grabbed onto the chair, but realizing he couldn't get on he let go and in the process fell about three metres, causing him serious injury. There was a lift attendant present whose job was to ensure that the skier mounted the chair properly. Kralik sued, claiming that the lift attendant had failed in his duty and that the employer was also liable. Explain what arguments the defendants could raise, and indicate the likely outcome and how damages, if appropriate, would be calculated.

4. *Babiuk v. Trann* 2005 SKCA 5 (CanLII), (2005) 248 DLR (4th) 530. (Sask. CA)

   Shawn Babiuk and Cory Trann were on opposing teams in a rugby league. At one point in the game Trann's teammate was on the ground and Babiuk, an opposing player, was stepping on his face. Trann stepped forward and struck Babiuk in the face breaking his jaw. This action was brought by Babiuk seeking compensation for those injuries. Explain what tort Babiuk is claiming was committed by Trann, what defences Trann might raise, and the likely outcome of the case.

5.   *McGarrigle v. Dalhousie University* 2007 NSSC 85 (CanLII), [2007] N.S.J. No. 10

Mr. McGarrigle, the coach of the Dalhousie University basketball team, had improperly allowed an academically ineligible player to play in five basketball games in violation of the CIS rules governing the sport. When this happens, there is an obligation upon the institution to disclose the violation by submitting an appropriate letter to the governing sports body Canadian University Sports (CIS), with the result that the games involved would be forfeited. The letter was also sent to the officials of *Atlantic University Sports,* which had no direct role in the disciplinary process but did need to know why Dalhousie was forfeiting the specified games. Assuming some of the words in the letter were defamatory, what would be the best defense for Dalhousie in these circumstances? Explain why or why not that defence would be effective.

# Chapter 3
## Formation of Contracts

Alphaspirit/Fotolia

## Learning Objectives

LO 1  List the essential elements of a contract

LO 2  Describe the process for reaching consensus

LO 3  Identify what constitutes a valid offer and an effective acceptance

LO 4  Explain the principle of consideration

LO 5  Consider gratuitous promises and the effect of promissory estoppel

LO 6  Recall the requirements of capacity

LO 7  Compare insanity and infancy defences with respect to contracts

LO 8  Consider the element of legality in a contract

LO 9  Define the element of intention

LO 10  Determine when a written document is required

The process of carrying on business involves transactions, agreements, arrangements, consultations, services, employment, and other forms of interaction—all based on contracts between the parties. Everything from the purchase of a pencil or a bus ticket to an order for an ocean liner or passenger jet is based on contract law. An examination of contract law is fundamental to any study of business law, and most of the other topics that will be examined in this text are founded largely on contract law principles.

*Contract: an exchange of promises enforceable in court*

A **contract** can be defined as a voluntary exchange of promises or commitments between parties that are legally enforceable in our courts. When people enter into such contracts, they create a world of law unto themselves. They can create new obligations and responsibilities, but they can also modify or remove obligations and responsibilities. When a ticket to an event contains a provision stating that patrons "enter at their own risk," or that the "management is not responsible for injuries or damage," an attempt is being made by contract to remove the risk of liability for negligence that would otherwise be present. Contract law developed in the courts, and there has been little statutory interference with these common law fundamentals. As we will see in subsequent chapters, however, there are a myriad of examples of statutory modification of contract laws in specific situations, including the sale of goods and consumer protection, both of which will be discussed in the first half of Chapter 5. Not all promises or arrangements between parties are contracts. There are several requirements that must be met for such agreement to be contracts. This chapter will examine the formation of a contract and qualifications that must be met, including consensus obtained through offer and acceptance, the exchange of consideration, capacity, legality, and intention. Note that although it is prudent practice, in most situations there is no requirement that a contract be in writing.

From the point of view of managing risk, it should be obvious that business people should be extremely careful to understand fully what they are agreeing to do. Typically, the transaction proceeds as agreed and the legal technicalities don't matter, but when problems do arise, the parties are often surprised to find that some eventuality was not anticipated and so is not covered in the agreement. Or, they may find that it has been anticipated by the other party, who has included an exemption clause that limits their liability. There are risks in most business transactions, and it is common practice for contracts to include such exemption clauses to reduce the risk significantly. The extent of exposure to liability if things do go wrong should be a major factor in calculating the costs and compensation terms to be included in all contracts. The courts tend to enforce such exemption clauses on the assumption that the reduced risk was included as a factor in calculating the value of the benefits to be exchanged in the original contract. Exemption clauses will be discussed in more detail below. Even when something does go wrong, it does not necessarily mean that litigation will follow. That depends on such factors as the chance of success and the weighing of what may be recovered against the costs and damage to reputation and good will, or the breakdown of the ongoing business relationship between the parties.

## LO 1/LO 2/LO 3   CONSENSUS

*Consensus reached through bargaining*

*Offer and acceptance leads to agreement*

Reaching an agreement is at the heart of the formation of a contract (see Figure 3.1). **Consensus** is normally achieved through a process of **offer and acceptance**, which results in a shared commitment when both parties clearly understand the obligations and responsibilities they are assuming. The bargaining process includes enticements, offers,

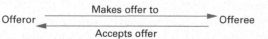

**Figure 3.1** First Element of a Contract

questions, arguments, and counter-offers, until the parties eventually reach an agreement, when a valid offer is accepted. This is often referred to as the meeting of minds. While we look at the traditional requirements of offer and acceptance here, it is important to remember that a court may find that a consensus exists (even when no specific offer or acceptance can be identified) by looking at the subsequent behaviour of the parties. If no specific offer or acceptance can be identified, yet the parties have obviously come to common understanding (with all the other elements of contract present), it is likely that the court would still find that a contract exists. Nor is it necessary for both parties to have a complete understanding of what they have agreed to. The only requirement of consensus is that the terms are clear and unambiguous. A basic principle of contract law is that the courts will give effect to the reasonable expectations of the parties. If one of them fails to read those terms or misunderstands them, it is not usually an excuse to get out of a contract. However, they must have reached an agreement. The court will not bargain for them. When a party leaves important terms out, or plan to negotiate them later, without having implied them, there is no contract. Still, mistakes with respect to the nature, terms, or some other aspect of the contract do take place, and the courts have developed a structured approach to dealing with them. The court usually interprets and enforces those terms, rather than finding there is no agreement. The way courts deal with such mistakes will be dealt with under "Mistake" in the following chapter (see pp. 96–97).

---

Case Summary 3.1 *West End Tree Service Inc. v. Danuta Stabryla*[1]

## The Courts Will Give Effect to Reasonable Expectations

West End Tree Service Inc. (Plaintiff/Appellant), Danuta Stabryla (Defendant/Respondent) in the Divisional Court-Ontario.

Mrs. Stabryla approached West End Tree Services to remove a tree. Mr. Di Marco representing the West End responded, and he gave an itemized estimate of $950.00 to remove the tree leaving everything on the site, an additional $400 to dispose of the debris, and another $400 to dispose of the logs, and $100 for the arborist's report, and $100 for a city permit. Mrs. Stabryla paid $214.00 and the balance was to be $1658.50. The invoice that was submitted to her was to be paid upon completion unless otherwise prearranged. Mr. Di Marco obtained the arborist's report and the city permit and then he cut down the tree and removed it.

Mrs. Stabryla refused to pay, claiming that she only contracted for the procurement of the permit and the arborist's report. Mr. Di Marco claimed that he never would have agreed to the job if all that was required of him was to obtain permits, as it would not have been economical for his business. West End Tree Service would have only taken on that job if it was contracted to remove the tree. Mrs. Stabryla claimed, however, that she had planned to have her husband take down the tree.

At trial the judge found in Mrs. Stabryla's favour. In these circumstances there would have been two separate contracts, one for securing the permit and the other one for cutting down the tree, and Mrs. Stabryla only agreed to the first. West End appealed and the trial decision was

---

[1] 2010 ONSC 68 (CanLII).

overturned. The appeal judge agreed that as it would have been uneconomical for West End Tree Service, it was unreasonable to expect that Mr. Di Marco, representing the company, would have agreed to only obtain the permit and report. It was in fact all one contract and Mrs. Stabryla was bound by it.

This case is interesting because it demonstrates that the terms of a contract are not determined by what the party thought they were agreeing to. Rather the test is objective. The appeal judge stated, "A party may be bound even when they did not intend to be bound when a reasonable person would believe, based on the contract and words, that she was assenting to the terms proposed by the other party." In other words the courts, when looking at consensus and intention, will give effect to the reasonable expectations of the parties to the contract.

## Offer

*An offer is a tentative commitment containing essential terms*

The **offer** creates the first legal consequence. It is a tentative promise that contains the terms of the anticipated contract. It is tentative in the sense that the other party need only indicate a willingness to be bound by the stated terms (to accept) to create a binding contract. Before this stage is reached, however, a significant amount of communication can take place between the parties. Bargaining usually involves considerable negotiation between the parties before an agreement is ultimately reached. Pre-contract communications, whether they take the form of advertising or provide product or service information, do not create contractual obligations. They are referred to as invitations to deal or **invitations to treat** and sometimes are confused with offers. It is often difficult to determine at what point we are dealing with an offer rather than an invitation. Most media advertisements, catalogues, brochures, window and floor displays, and even clearly marked and priced goods set out on shelves in self-service situations are invitations to treat rather than offers. There is some controversy over this last point, but it was the subject of a decision of the English court of appeal in the *Pharmaceutical Society* case[2], where certain drugs had to be sold under the supervision of a pharmacist. In this case the drugs in question were displayed with the prices marked in the back of the store while the pharmacist was at the front near the check out. Was that display of the drugs an offer and picking them up an acceptance? The court held no. The offer was made by the customer as the product was brought to the front and the sale, therefore, took place at the front under the supervision of the pharmacist as required. Although the reasoning of the judge in this case is suspect, the decision has been followed and is thus good law in Canada, making goods displayed in such self-service situations invitations and not offers. The case is of interest because it is one of the few that makes it clear when an invitation ends and an offer begins.

*Invitations do not create legal obligations*

Such an invitation has no legal effect in contract law. The actual offer that leads to an acceptance and eventual contract depends on subsequent communications between the parties. It only takes place when all of the important terms are present, and it is clear that the person making the **offer** has reached the point where he or she is serious and expects to commit to those terms.

For the communication to be an offer, it must contain all of the important terms of the contract. This usually requires, at a minimum, the identification of the parties to the agreement, the subject matter, and the price to be paid (parties, price, and property). If the parties have added other important terms, they too must be clear. Thus, if the goods

---

[2]*Pharmaceutical Society of Great Britain v. Boots Cash Chemists (Southern), Ltd.*, [1953] 1 All E.R. 482 (C.A.); aff'g. [1952] 2 All E.R. 456 (Q.B.).

are to be purchased on credit, the payment schedule and interest payable should be clear. An agreement to enter into an agreement is not a contract. If Joe agreed to sell his car to Sam for $5000, "credit terms to be arranged later," there would be no contract, since no final agreement had been reached. All of the important terms of the agreement must be set out or be implied in the agreement. It is possible to make a term such as the price, based on some calculation such as the market price at a given time. The key is for that term to be certain and not subject to further negotiation. It must be emphasized that putting a contract in writing is always good practice. However, except for a few specific instances that will be discussed below, a written contract is not a legal requirement. Because of this, it is possible for parts, or even the whole contract, to be implied from the circumstances, including the past history of dealings between the parties.

Note that the object is to reach a consensus, and so the offer must be communicated before it can be accepted. The offeree (the person to whom the offer is made) cannot accept an offer that he or she does not know about. The problem of communication sometimes arises when the offeror (the person making the offer) wants to include an **exemption clause** that restricts or limits his or her liability in the transaction. This must be brought to the attention of the other party at the time the contract is created. For example, a sign at a parking lot may state, "Not responsible for lost, stolen, or damaged vehicles." To be a binding part of the contract, the clause must be communicated to the customer at the time he or she enters into the contract. Sometimes this is done by including it on the receipt issued at the time the contract is made, or by clearly posting a sign where the ticket is obtained. If it is only communicated after the fact, such as on a bill sent later, or on a sign located in a part of the business where the customer is not likely to see it, that exemption clause will not be a part of the contract. Where that exemption clause appears on the back of the ticket or receipt, there must be something on the front directing the party to the terms on the back. Where an exemption clause is included in a written contract it must not be embedded in such a way as to disappear in the "small print" of the document. Today the practice is to boldface or otherwise emphasize such provisions so they are drawn to the attention of the parties.

*Offer/contract need not be in writing*

*Exemption clauses must be brought to the other party's attention*

## Case Summary 3.2 *Brownjohn v. Pillar to Post*[3]

## Exemption Clause May Not Be Binding

Brownjohn (Plaintiff), Pillar to Post (Defendant) in a trial before the British Columbia Provincial Court.

Pillar to Post (PTP) provided house inspection services in Kelowna, British Columbia, and sent an inexperienced inspector to provide such a service for Janet Brownjohn. In the inspection Mrs. Brownjohn claimed that the inspector, Mr. Averil, missed a number of important defects, and because of this she suffered considerable losses in her purchase. The judge examined the claims and, while dismissing most as trivial or omissions that Mrs. Brownjohn

should have seen for herself, he did find several significant errors on the part of Averil, including the age of the furnace and a termite infestation. PTP countered by pointing out the exclusionary clause in their contract limiting their liability for any cause to the inspection fee of $240. The issue before the court was whether the limitation clause in the contract was binding on Brownjohn.

The judge found that this was such an all-encompassing limitation clause that it had to be brought to the attention of the client at the time the contract was signed. This had

[3]2003 BCPC 2 (CanLII).

not been done; moreover, the last thing the inspector wanted to do, the judge suggested, was to bring the client's attention to such an expansive limitation clause when trying to attract her business. Significant damages were awarded over what would have been permitted by the exemption clause.

The case illustrates the general requirement that any term must be brought to the attention of the parties to be part of the agreement at the time of the contract. Even though this term was included in the contract, it was so important that it had to be underlined or in some other way made to stand out to attract the attention of the client.

Offer will end:
- At end of a specified time
- At end of reasonable time
- Upon death or insanity of offeror
- Upon revocation

**End of an Offer** Consistent with the bargaining model for the creation of a contract, a number of rules determine when an offer will end (see Table 3.1). Where the offeror states a specific time for expiration, such as "at noon on May 12, 2009," the offer ends when specified. After that time it is too late to accept the offer. If no expiration time has been specified, the offer will end after a reasonable time. What is reasonable depends on the circumstances. If ripe fruit is being offered, a few hours might be appropriate. If land is involved, or heavy-duty equipment, the offer might last a few weeks. The offer will also automatically end with the death or insanity of the offeror. Because the offer is only the first step in the creation of a contract, it imposes no legal obligation on the offeror, who is free to withdraw the offer any time before acceptance, even when he or she has indicated it would remain open. This is called revocation, and so long as the revocation has been communicated to the offeree before acceptance has taken place, it is then too late to accept. There can be no valid acceptance after the offeree learns that the offeror has changed his or her mind. This power to revoke can be given up in a separate option agreement, which is explained below.

- Upon rejection
- Upon counter-offer
- Selling item does not end offer

The conduct of the offeree can also cause the offer to end. If the offeree communicates a rejection of the offer to the offeror, the offer ends. The offeree cannot later change his or her mind, accept, and hold the offeror to the deal. A **counter-offer** by the offeree has the same effect, and if that counter-offer is rejected, he or she cannot turn around and

### Table 3.1 Bargaining

| | | |
|---|---|---|
| Invitation | Not an offer; not capable of being accepted to form a contract | |
| Offer | After expiration of specific time | Original offer ends |
| Offer | Where not specified, after a reasonable time | Original offer ends |
| Offer | After communicated revocation | Original offer ends |
| Offer | After counter-offer or rejection | Original offer ends |
| Offer | After death or insanity of offeror | Original offer ends |
| Offer | Where option agreement has been purchased | Original offer continues for specified time despite above |
| Offer | Sale to another | Original offer continues unless revocation |
| Offer | Qualified acceptance | This is a counter-offer; original offer ends |
| Offer | Effective acceptance | Results in a binding contract |

force a contract by accepting the original offer. The offeree would have to make another counter-offer, embodying the original terms, and hope that they are still agreeable to the other party. Thus, if Joe offered to sell his car for $5000 and Sam responded by saying, "I'll give you $4500," Joe's original offer ended with Sam's counter-offer. If Joe said, "No," and Sam responded with, "Okay, I'll give you the $5000," that constitutes a new offer from Sam, not an acceptance of Joe's original offer, which ended with the counter-offer. Even if Sam's response had been "I accept. I'll pay you the $5 000 next week," that would have been a counter-offer since Sam had added a new term, delayed payment. This may seem somewhat complicated, but it has the advantage of eliminating confusion as to just what offer is being accepted to form the basis of the contract. Of course not all communications from the offeree are counter-offers. If Sam had just asked, "Will you take less?" this would simply be an inquiry and have no legal effect. A common mistake is to assume that selling the subject matter of an offer to someone else automatically ends that offer. This is incorrect. If anything, it would be a revocation of the offer by conduct and would have no effect on the offer, unless the other party learned of the sale before accepting. This is a dangerous situation, and the offeror should make sure that the original offeree knows that he or she changed his or her mind before concluding the sale to another. Of course, if the offeree finds out the goods have been sold to someone else, that communicates the revocation indirectly, and it is too late to accept. There can be no meeting of the minds when the offeree knows that the offeror has changed his or her mind before the acceptance is made.[4]

## Case Summary 3.3 *Roma Construction (Niagara) Ltd. v. Dykstra Bros. Roofing (1992) Limited*[5]

## A Rejection of an Offer Before Acceptance Ends That Offer

Roma (Plaintiff), Dykstra (Defendant) in a trial before the Superior Court of Justice (Ontario).

Dykstra did several roofing jobs for Roma, which ended in litigation. Several attempts were made to resolve the matter, and shortly before the trial an offer was made by Roma to settle the matter "all inclusive" for $96 000. The defendant's lawyer rejected the offer orally. Shortly after this the defendants learned of additional problems with other roofing jobs they had done for Roma and quickly made a formal acceptance of Roma's offer to settle the matter for $96 000 "all inclusive." Roma refused to honour the agreement and Dykstra brought this action to enforce the settlement. The issue facing the court was whether the offer to settle was still open when the acceptance was given.

The court first determined that there were no technical court rules involved and that this offer was simply a common-law offer. Since it was rejected, that ended the offer and there was no longer an offer open to be accepted when Dykstra purported to accept the offer. No settlement agreement had been reached.

The case illustrates an important feature of the process of offer and acceptance. A rejection or counter-offer after an offer ends that offer. There was no outstanding offer to accept.

The right of the offeror to change his or her mind and revoke the offer anytime he or she wants is often an impediment to doing business. Therefore, it is possible to create a situation where the offer cannot be revoked and must remain open until expiration at a specified time. This is called an **option agreement**. In effect, a separate contract is entered into where the offeree pays the offeror, usually a small sum, to hold the offer open for the

Option keeps offer open

---

[4]*Dickinson v. Dodds* (1876), 2 Ch. D. 463 (C.A.).
[5]2007 CanLII 44827 (ON S.C.).

designated time. The offeror is now bound in a separate contract to hold the offer open. Thus the offeror is bound, but the offeree is free to accept or reject the original offer. This gives the offeree some time without the worry that the offer will be revoked or the deal taken up by someone else. Placing the offer under seal will have the same effect. The seal will be discussed below.

A similar relationship is created in the tendering process. When one company wants to advance a project, which requires the services of others, they often put out a request for bids on the job. This is referred to as putting a job out to tender and is especially common in the construction industry. This looks simply like an invitation to treat but is more than that. When a bid is submitted, a special contractual relationship is created called the tender agreement, which is independent of the ultimate contract to do the job. The party requesting the bid has committed to follow certain rules as set out in the tender such as:

- disclose all relevant information affecting the project
- accept only bids that are compliant with the terms of the tender
- not accept bids submitted after the specified closing date
- to accept the most competitive bid (in most cases)
- to treat all parties equally and in good faith.

*Submitted bids create obligation even before acceptance*

When a bidding party submits their bid, they are accepting that subsidiary offer binding both parties to the rules set out in the bidding process, and the resulting obligations are enforceable in court. Note that it is not only the party requesting bids that is bound here, the party submitting the bid is also bound not to change that bid once submitted. The Supreme Court of Canada confirmed the binding nature of this subsidiary contract in 1981.[6] This is like an option agreement since without such a subsidiary agreement, the bidding party would normally have the right to withdraw or change their offer any time before its ultimate acceptance.

### Standard Form Contracts

We do not always have the choice to bargain. In some businesses, standard form agreements are in place, which create a "take it or leave it" situation. Often one-sided terms are present, including exemption clauses that favour the offeror. It must be emphasized that when such a standard contract is accepted, it is just as binding as any other contract. The only adjustment made for the lack of bargaining is that any ambiguity in a term favouring just one of the parties is interpreted in favour of the other party. Also, some statutory protection has been provided, especially where consumer contracts are involved, as will be discussed under "Consumer Protection Legislation" in Chapter 5 (see p. 135).

Even where the parties are bargaining equally, standard phrases are used. When lawyers create legal documents, including contracts, they use standard phrases and clauses with known legal effects so that the interpretation of the legal agreement can be certain from the outset. Only minor changes will be made to accommodate the particular transaction in question. This is true with insurance contracts, securities, and with any other type of transaction that is not unique. Such certainty justifies the complexity of the documents and is the reason lawyers resist taking the time and incurring the risk of changing and simplifying the documents used in these common transactions. Today, software is available

---

[6]*R. v. Ron Engineering & Construction (Eastern) Ltd.* [1981] 1 S.C.R. 111.

to assist lawyers in drawing up most contracts making the process extremely efficient and much less time consuming.

## Acceptance

Once a valid offer has been made, there is a tentative commitment to be bound on the part of the offeror. The offeree then must make a similar commitment for a contract to be formed. Since the terms of the agreement are embodied in the offer, the offeree's commitment consists merely of an indication of a willingness to be bound by those terms. This may consist of something as simple as a handshake or a signature. Such an acceptance must be total and unconditional. Sometimes an offer will involve several different aspects. The offeree cannot pick and choose which part to accept unless that was the intention of the offeror. You have to accept all of the terms of an offer or none. Similarly, a conditional acceptance does not qualify. If Joe offers to sell his car to Sam for $5000, and Sam responds, "I accept, providing you fix the rust on the fender," this is a counter-offer rather than an acceptance. Sometimes a supplier will provide the customer with an order form but the customer will respond using his or her own order form, which has different, terms and conditions. That new order form is in reality a counter-offer, and, by delivering the product, the supplier has accepted those new terms and conditions often unwittingly.

*Acceptance is a commitment by the offeree to terms of offer*

*Acceptance must be complete and unconditional*

The general rule is that an acceptance must be communicated for it to be effective. A contract requires a meeting of the minds: there is no contract until the offeror is notified of the offeree's acceptance. This can be important since it determines when and where the contract comes into effect. When Joe in Vancouver offers to sell his car to Sam in Montreal by phone, and Sam accepts, also by phone, the acceptance is effective when and where Joe hears the acceptance—in Vancouver. Where the contract is formed can be an important consideration in determining what court has jurisdiction and which province's law should be applied to the transaction.

*General rule: acceptance is effective when and where communicated*

The offeror may require the offer to be accepted by some specified conduct. When this happens, the conduct required must be something unique, not part of a person's normal routine, and the offeree must respond as directed. If the specified acceptance requires the offeree to "go to work tomorrow as usual," going to work would not constitute acceptance. But if the direction is to put a red ribbon on the front door, doing so would amount to acceptance of the offer. Usually the offer and acceptance process involves an exchange of promises. In some situations however, the nature of the contract itself requires the actual performance of the contract as the method of acceptance. This is called a **unilateral contract**. The offering of a reward is a good example. When someone places an ad offering a $100 reward for the return of a lost dog, the method of acceptance is the actual return of the dog.

*Acceptance by conduct*

Sometimes marketers will send unsolicited goods to a prospective customer, stating that if they do not send it back, they have bought it. The general rule is that silence by itself will not be construed as acceptance, and a person in receipt of such goods is not required to go to the trouble to return them. Note that care should be taken not to use such goods, as this would affirm the contract. Only when there is a pre-existing business relationship will silence be an appropriate acceptance. If you have been receiving a regular supply of a product from a business, it is quite appropriate for that business to send a note: "If we don't hear otherwise, we will renew your order as of May 20, 2015." Because of the already established relationship, there is a duty to communicate a cancellation in these circumstances. A few years ago a company providing cable services notified their customers that they would be

*No acceptance by silence*

supplying them with extra channels at an added cost unless the customer notified the company that they did not want the additional service. Because of the pre-existing service relationship, silence in these circumstances would have affirmed the new arrangement. The public was outraged, however, and the company was forced to back off. This is the danger of joining a CD- or book-of-the-month club. Once the relationship is established, it is hard to terminate it. Note that Manitoba recently amended its *Consumer Protection Act* (Part XXI), imposing fines of up to $300 000 for the use of such negative option schemes.

**Exception: Where use of mail is reasonable, acceptance is effective when and where posted**

There is one important exception to the rule that an acceptance must be communicated to be effective. This is the **post-box rule**. As contract law developed, the postal service was the accepted method of doing business at a distance. The inherent delay in communications created uncertainty as to what point a contract actually came into existence. The solution was the rule that if it was appropriate to respond by mail, the acceptance was effective when and where it was posted. In the example above of selling a car, if the mails, instead of the phone, were used—with Joe in Vancouver sending a letter to Sam in Montreal offering to sell his car for $5000, and Sam responding with a letter of acceptance—that acceptance would be effective when it was mailed in Montreal. If Joe had required acceptance before Saturday, and the letter was mailed on Friday, there would be a valid contract, even though Joe would not know of it until the letter was actually received by Joe—likely sometime in the following week. In addition, since the contract was formed in Quebec, this could be an important factor in determining what court would have jurisdiction and what provincial law would apply to the contract. Note that the post-box rule only applies where it is reasonable to respond by mail and no other method has been specified. There is usually no problem posting an acceptance when the offer is sent by mail. However, where the offer is presented in some other way, such as in person, past dealings between the parties, as well as the nature of the subject matter of the contract, will be important factors in determining if response by mail was reasonable. If ripe fruit were offered, a response by mail would likely be unacceptable. To avoid the problem, the appropriate means of acceptance should be specified in the offer.

## Case Summary 3.4 *Eastern Power Ltd. v. Azienda Communale Energia and Ambiente*[7]

## Post-Box Rule Not Applied to Fax

Eastern Power (Plaintiff/Appellant), Azienda (Defendant/Respondent) in an appeal before the Court of Appeal for Ontario.

Azienda, an Italian company, negotiated a cooperation agreement with Eastern Power Ltd., which was based in Ontario. When Azienda terminated the agreement and refused to pay the bill for costs submitted by Eastern Power, the Ontario company brought this action against Azienda in an Ontario court. In determining if they had jurisdiction, the Ontario court had to decide, among other things, where the contract was made. The issue before the court was whether the post-box rule applied to a fax.

Negotiations took place by facsimile. The final acceptance of the offer was also sent by fax by the Ontario company to Azienda in Italy. Claiming the post-box rule exception applied, Eastern Power argued that acceptance was effective when and where the fax was sent in Ontario. The court rejected this argument, stating that the use of facsimile transmissions involved instantaneous communication, much like a telephone, and so there was no justification for applying the post-box exception. Since the fax was received in Italy, the contract arose in Italy. Consequently, Ontario was an inappropriate place to sue.

---

[7](1999), 178 D.L.R. (4th) 409 (Ont. C.A.).

| **Table 3.2** Acceptance | | |
|---|---|---|
| Offer | Acceptance, general rule | Acceptance is effective when and where offeror hears of acceptance |
| Offer | Acceptance by performance | Unilateral contract accepted upon performance of contract term |
| Offer | Acceptance, post-box rule | Acceptance effective when and where posted, if use of post was appropriate |

In recent times there has been a profound change in the nature of business communications. The mail is still used to a significant extent, but fax, email and courier service have become commonplace. An important question faced by the courts was whether the post-box rule should be extended to other forms of communications. It has been extended to the use of telegrams, but should it be extended further? The question was answered in the *Entores* case,[8] where the English court of appeal held that when telex (similar to a modern fax) and other forms of instantaneous communication were used, there was no need for the post-box rule. Thus, when fax is used, the acceptance is only effective when and where it is received by the offeror, as was applied in the Eastern Power case discussed above. Although there may be some small delay when email is involved, it is not likely that any court would expand the rule in that direction. These modern forms of communication are discussed in some detail in Chapter 10. Today the post-box rule is restricted to the use of the postal service, telegrams, and possibly couriers. It must be emphasized that the post-box rule is an exception to the requirement that an acceptance be communicated before it is effective. There is no indication that the rule will be applied to other forms of communications between the parties as they bargain. In fact, in the English case of *Henthorne v. Fraser*,[9] which was important in establishing the rule in the first place, the court made it clear that the rule did not apply to a mailed revocation, which was not effective until received. See Table 3.2 for a summary of the rules of acceptance. Several provinces have passed legislation specifically directed at transactions using electronic means of communication such as the internet. British Columbia, for example, has legislated that documents communicated in this way are deemed to be sent when entered into the system and outside of the control of the sender, and deemed to be received when they are in the system and could have been accessed by the addressee.[10]

*The post-box rule will not apply where a fax is used*

*Exception only applies to an acceptance*

## CONSIDERATION

LO 4

The second qualification that must be met for the formation of a contract is the exchange of **consideration** (see Figure 3.2). In keeping with the bargaining model, both parties must get some benefit from the deal. This may take the form of money, service, goods, or some other type of benefit. Note that it is not necessary for the consideration to actually change hands at the time of the acceptance; rather, both parties must make a commitment to give

*Exchange of promises/benefits required*

---

[8]*Entores Ltd. v. Miles Far East Corp.*, [1955] 2 All E.R. 493 (C.A.).
[9][1892] 2 Ch. 27 (Ch.D.).
[10]*Electronic Transactions Act*, S.B.C. (2001) c.10 s.18.

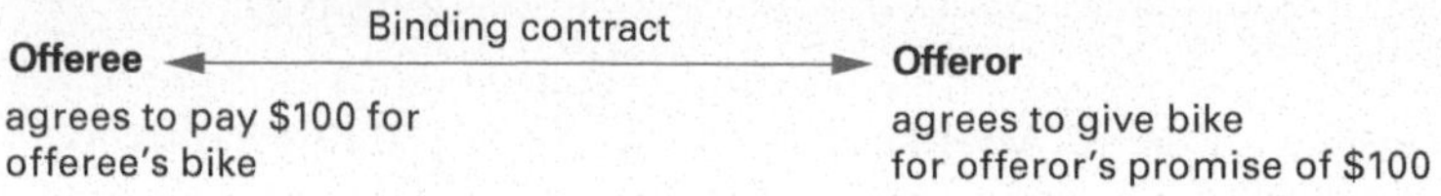

Offeree ◄————— Binding contract —————► **Offeror**

**Offeree**
agrees to pay $100 for
offeree's bike

**Offeror**
agrees to give bike
for offeror's promise of $100

**Figure 3.2** Consideration Involves an Exchange of Commitments

the other some form of consideration pursuant to the agreement. This is often referred to as the exchange of promises.

**Gratuitous promises are unenforceable**

People sometimes promise to give a gift or do something for someone else and expect nothing in return. Such one-sided promises (called **gratuitous promises**) are not legally enforceable. Of course, once a gift has been given, the giver cannot force its return; rather, it is the promise to give such a gift that cannot be enforced. If I give you a fur coat, it's yours. But if I promise to give you a fur coat and then change my mind, there is nothing you can do about it legally.

**Consideration must be specific**

In business it is sometimes difficult to tell whether there has been an exchange of consideration or not. While the court will not normally worry about whether the consideration is reasonable (that would be interfering in the bargaining process), the benefit must be specific. A promise to pay "something" or a "reasonable price" is generally not good enough, as there is no specific commitment and the matter will require further negotiation in the future. The exception is when services are requested. Then, based on the equitable principle of *quantum meruit*, the requester is obligated to pay a reasonable amount for the services delivered. If you ask a plumber to fix a leak in your basement, and after the leak is fixed the plumber hands you a bill, you will have to pay it if it is reasonable, even though you did not agree to a price beforehand.

**Consideration need not be reasonable but must be legal, possible, and have some value**

What is promised must also be possible, legal, and of some value. A commitment to bring a pet dog back from the dead for $1000 would not be legally enforceable because, at least in the eyes of the law, it is not possible to bring a dog back to life. A promise to pay someone $500 to perform an illegal act, such as buying drugs or assaulting someone also fails to qualify, because a promise to commit an illegal act is not valid consideration. Nor would a promise to return friendship or love and affection normally constitute valid consideration, as no value can be put on such affection. As mentioned above, it is not necessary that the consideration be fair, only that there be some consideration on both sides. However, if the transaction is grossly one-sided, it may support an allegation of fraud or the claim of incapacity.

To determine if there is consideration it is often much easier to look at the price to be paid rather than the benefit to be received. If I promise to pay $50 to John to mow my aunt's lawn, it is hard to identify what specific benefit I will get out of the deal. However, if we look at it from the point of view of what is to be paid (in the sense of what is being given up, not just money), it is clear that both of us are paying a price. By agreement, we both have changed our legal position in relation to each other. John is now obligated to mow the lawn, which he was not obligated to do before the agreement, and I am obligated to pay the $50. There has been an exchange of commitments, which constitutes consideration.

**Both parties must pay a price**

For example, in business one person is often required to sign a **guarantee** before a financial institution will loan money to a debtor. What does the guarantor get out of it? It is better to look at the commitments. The guarantor is now responsible for paying the loan if the debtor defaults. His or her legal position has changed in accordance with the agreement.

In return the bank commits to advance the funds to the debtor, something they otherwise would not have done. They also have changed their legal position pursuant to the deal, and so there is consideration on both sides. Both have paid a price in the sense that they have assumed obligations that they did not have before. However, if the money is advanced before the guarantee is extracted, as sometimes happens, it may well be a gratuitous promise and not binding. The guarantor has made a commitment, but the bank does not change its legal position, since it has already advanced the money. This is an example of past consideration. Where the benefit has been given before the deal is struck, it cannot be part of an exchange and hence the expression "past consideration is no consideration." Another area where consideration is not always apparent is where the parties settle their dispute out of court. Here they enter into a contract where the suing party agrees not to pursue the matter in exchange for a partial payment. What if later the plaintiff learns he would have won? Where is the consideration? Since both parties have given up their right to have the matter dealt with in court, both have paid a price. There is consideration on both sides and the settlement is binding.

*Past consideration is no consideration*

## Case Summary 3.5 *Mackenzie v. Mackenzie*[11]

## Past Consideration Is No Consideration

Linda MacKenzie (Plaintiff), Hanford MacKenzie (Defendant) in a trial before the Supreme Court of Prince Edward Island.

Linda MacKenzie and her husband built a house on land given to her husband by her mother. Her father-in-law assisted in the construction and paid for some of the materials. He also claimed to have loaned his son considerable funds before the house was constructed. Shortly before the house was completed, Linda and David MacKenzie signed a mortgage in favour of her father-in-law for $25 000 at 10 percent interest. She claims she didn't understand what she was signing. No money changed hands and the father-in-law stated at that time that he had "already advanced the $25 000 to his son." This mortgage was not registered until three months after the son died, 14 years after it was made. (Note that before the house had been completed Linda and her husband had been separated for six months.) The issue

before the court was whether there was any consideration to support the mortgage in question. The father-in-law is claiming on the mortgage, which has accumulated to $112 000. The judge, in finding that there was no consideration to support the mortgage, found that any monies given to the son had been given before the mortgage was signed and therefore past consideration. Past consideration is no consideration and will not support the contract. He found that any money that had been given to the son prior to the building of the house was a gift given out of love and affection. The mortgage that was created after the separation was to ensure that the wife would not get the property if the marriage failed.

The case illustrates the bargaining nature of the contract, which requires consideration on both sides. Here there was no such bargain as any consideration had been given before the agreement was entered into.

**Gratuitous Promises**   Sometimes there is an existing legal relationship or obligation that the parties want to change. In general, any obligation created by contract can be changed by agreement, but there has to be consideration on both sides to support the change. If a builder had a contract to finish renovating your house by June 10 and fell behind, you might well agree to pay an extra $2000 to hire more help to get the job done on time. At first glance, it looks like there is consideration on both sides, but in

## LO 5

A change in a contract should be supported by additional consideration

---

[11]1996 CanLII 3698 (PE S.C.T.D.).

fact there is not. You have made a commitment to pay more, but the builder is in exactly the same legal position that he was in before you made that promise—to finish the job by June 10. He has made no new commitment and so this is a one-sided or gratuitous promise not binding on the promisor. It is true that the builder has agreed to hire extra help and this will cost him more, but he would have had to do that anyway to fulfill the original agreement. The commitment has not changed. You would not be obligated to pay the $2000 promised, unless the builder agreed to do something extra for it. If, however, it was a tenant that agreed to pay the extra $2000 so that the renovation would be finished on time this promise would be binding on that tenant. Before the promise the contractor was only obligated to the owner but now he is obligated to the tenant as well hence both parties have changed their legal positions and there is consideration on both sides.

Taking less in satisfaction of a debt made binding by statute

Paying less to satisfy a debt is a similar problem. If I owe you $1000 and I offer to pay you $800 if you will take it in full satisfaction of the debt, the reduction of the debt is one-sided. You get nothing out of it. Yes, you will be paid, but I was obligated to do that before you agreed to take the lesser payment. So unless I agree to do something extra such as pay early, after getting the $800 you should still be able to sue me for the other $200. However, this is another one of those situations where the necessities of business overshadow the logic of the law. It is often better to settle debts this way—with certainty. As a result, many jurisdictions have passed legislation to the effect that if a creditor agrees to take less in full satisfaction of a debt, and in fact takes the money, he or she cannot turn around and sue for the remainder. The debt is settled.[12]

Reliance upon one-sided promise may be used as a defence

**Exceptions**   There are two exceptions to the unenforceability of gratuitous or one-sided promises (see Table 3.3). **Promissory estoppel** (often referred to as equitable estoppel) is a difficult concept, best understood by example. In the example above, when you agree to pay a builder an extra $2000 to get the renovation of your house done by June 10 as originally agreed, that promise is clearly gratuitous, as the builder's legal position has not changed. Even if he hires extra help, he is only doing what he was already committed to do—finish the job by June 10. He cannot sue to enforce that promise. But what if you had actually paid the extra $2000 and then read this text and realized that the promise was gratuitous? Could you sue to get the $2000 back from the builder? To do so you would have to deny the validity of your own promise and you are estopped, or prevented, from

**Table 3.3 Consideration and Alternatives**

| A makes promise to B | Under seal without consideration | B can sue A to enforce promise |
| A makes promise to B | With mutual consideration | Result is a binding contract, so B can sue A to enforce promise |
| A makes promise to B | Bare promise without consideration | Promissory estoppel; B can defend if A sues and thus ignores promise, but B cannot sue A |

[12]Examples are British Columbia's *Law and Equity Act*, R.S.B.C. 1996, c. 253, s. 43, and Ontario's *Mercantile Law Amendment Act*, R.S.O. 1990, c. M-10, s. 16.

doing so. The builder can show that he has relied on your promise by hiring extra help and can raise the defence of promissory estoppel.

This defence is rarely available since it is the person who made the promise who has to sue, and that only happens when there is some pre-existing obligation, usually a contract that is being modified by the gratuitous promise. Promissory estoppel, then, will only be used where there is a gratuitous promise, and then only where it can be used as a defence. The expression is that promissory estoppel can only be used "as a shield and not as a sword." Perhaps the easiest case that illustrates the principle is the *Gilbert Steel* case that happened in Ontario in 1973[13] and is discussed below.

The second exception is the use of the **seal**. The use of the seal predates the requirement of consideration and was used to indicate a person's commitment to the deed or transaction in question. That historical recognition of seals continues, and today when a design is pressed into wax on the document itself or a wafer is affixed, it has a similar effect. Contract law and the need for consideration never replaced the sanctity of the seal, and today where a seal has been affixed to a document containing a promise or commitment, there is no need to establish consideration. Financial institutions will usually affix seals to credit transactions involving a guarantor to avoid any possible question of lack of consideration. Note that the presence of a seal does not replace the need for consensus or any other requirement of contract law, only consideration. In some jurisdictions specialized corporate documents must be under seal to be effective, and some specialized documents prepared by lawyers and notaries are also placed under seal. But generally, the seal is not a requirement in modern contract law.

*Where there is a seal, no consideration is required*

---

## Case Summary 3.6 *Gilbert Steel Ltd. v. University Construction Ltd.*[14]

## Promise to Pay Higher Price Not Supported by Consideration

Gilbert Steel (Plaintiff/Appellant), University Construction (Defendant/Respondent) in an appeal before the Court of Appeal of Ontario.

Gilbert Steel agreed to supply steel at a specific price to University Construction for the construction of a number of buildings. The cost of steel went up, and upon request, University Construction agreed to pay Gilbert a higher price than previously agreed for the steel it supplied. University made regular payments as the job progressed, but not enough to cover the increase in price. When the job was completed, Gilbert Steel sued University Construction for the shortfall. The issue before the court was whether sufficient consideration was present to support the promise to pay the extra cost. University Construction claimed they were not obligated to pay the agreed-upon increase based on the lack of consideration supporting the change. The court agreed. University Construction had agreed to pay a higher price, but Gilbert Steel had not agreed to do anything in return for the change. Note that promissory estoppel was raised by Gilbert Steel. This was rejected by the court, since promissory estoppel can only be "used as a shield, not as a sword," and Gilbert Steel was suing to enforce the gratuitous promise. Had University Construction made the higher payments and then sued to recover the excess paid, it could well be that Gilbert Steel could have used University Construction's promise to pay the higher amount as a defence on the basis of promissory estoppel.

---

[13]*Gilbert Steel Ltd. v. University Construction Ltd.* [1973] 3 O.R. 268 Ontario High Court of Justice. Appeal, (1976), 67 D.L.R. (3d) 606 (Ont. C.A.).

[14][1973] 3 O.R. 268 Ontario High Court of Justice. Appeal, (1976), 67 D.L.R. (3d) 606 (Ont. C.A.).

## LO 6/LO 7   CAPACITY

As a rule the courts do not interfere with the parties' freedom to contract. There are, however, some people who are considered incapable of negotiating a contract.

### Infants

The age of majority at common law used to be 21 years. In Canada this has been reduced to 18 or 19 years, depending on the province. Anyone under that age is considered to be an infant and is protected to the extent that the contracts they make with adults are binding on the adults, but voidable (not binding) on the infant. The terms *void* and *voidable* will come up throughout the discussion of contract law (see Figure 3.3). Void means there never was a contract, and both parties are free from any obligation under the agreement. A voidable contract is valid, but one of the parties, because of some problem, has the right to escape if he or she chooses to do so. This is the case with infants. The adult is bound by the contract, but the infant can escape if he or she so chooses. Of course, the infant cannot have it both ways and must return any goods obtained under the agreement. If the infant purchases a car on credit from a merchant and then stops making payments, he or she has no further obligation with respect to the payments, but must return the car. Notice that in some jurisdictions where the contract had been completed and price paid (an executed contract), the infant could not get his money back unless what he received was worthless. There are significant exceptions to the infant's right to escape from contracts. Infants are bound to pay a reasonable price when they contract for necessities. Such necessities include food, clothing, lodging, and transportation. Infants are also bound by their beneficial contracts of service. These contracts are determined to be in the infant's best interest such as employment or an apprenticeship arrangement.

> Infants not bound by contracts but adults are

> Infants are bound by beneficial contracts of service and for necessities

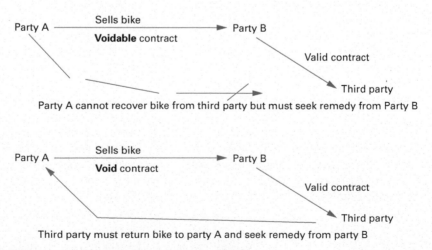

**Figure 3.3** Void and Voidable Contracts

Case Summary 3.7 *Mosher v. Benson*[15]

# Car Is Not a Necessity, Contract Voidable

Mosher (Plaintiff), Benson (Defendant) in a trial before the Small Claims Court of Nova Scotia.

Kyle Mosher was only 17 years old when he purchased a car from Peter Benson. The issue before the court was whether or not that contract could be set aside on the grounds that the plaintiff was a minor.

In this action, Mosher asked to have the transaction reversed on the basis that he was a minor at the time of the contract. He also claimed that the car was not roadworthy and that he had been charged an excessive price considering the condition. The judge found that there were no expressed or implied warranties with respect to the physical condition of the vehicle, given the fact that it was a private sale.

Since the age of majority in Nova Scotia is 19 years, the contract of sale was with an infant. It was therefore voidable unless it was for a necessity. The judge then considered whether the sale of a car qualified as a necessity.

The judge referred to the *Law of Contract in Canada*,[16] which stated concerning necessities, "Curiously enough, a car has been held not a necessary, even in these days, even as in *Pysett v. Lampman* where the car was used by the minor in the business of selling fish by which he earned a living."

In this case as there was no claim that the car was needed for any special use, there was no question that it could be considered a necessity. The contract was with an infant for a non-necessity and was therefore voidable. Therefore, the judge ordered that the parties be restored to their original positions. The seller was required to return the purchase price paid, as well as the filing fee for bringing this action, and Mr. Mosher was ordered to return the car.

This case illustrates the way contracts with infants are treated and indicates the appropriate remedy when a contract is determined to be voidable.

The British Columbia *Infants Act*[17] is unique in that it declares that *all* contracts with infants are **unenforceable** against the infant, except those specifically made enforceable by statute, such as student loans. In British Columbia even contracts for necessities and beneficial contracts of service are unenforceable against the infant. An unenforceable contract only prevents the adult from suing the infant to enforce the contract; it does not empower the infant to get out of the deal once he or she has performed as required in the contract. The infant has done only what he or she agreed to do, and the courts will stay out of it. The legislation then prevents the adult from suing to enforce the contract against the infant, but not the infant from suing to enforce the contract against the adult. Of course, this can lead to an unfair result, and the court has the power to give relief to both the adult and the infant when appropriate. The British Columbia Act goes further, stating that an infant's representative can apply to the court for a declaration that a contract is binding on that infant. The process involves the public trustee who safeguards the infants interests. These provisions have particular importance for the entertainment industry and have created more certainty in British Columbia than in other provinces with respect to infants' contracts.

In every jurisdiction, if the infant ratifies the contract after becoming an adult, he or she is bound by it. Such ratification requires the infant to do something to indicate that

*Infant can ratify when adult*

---

[15]2008 NSSM 72 (CanLII).

[16]Gerald Fridman, *The Law of Contract in Canada*, 5th ed., (Toronto: Thompson Carswell, 2006).

[17]R.S.B.C. 1996, c. 223.

he or she considers the contract binding. This may be done directly in writing or by implication, such as receiving some further benefit or making additional payments.

Note that this protection of infants in contract law does not extend to tort liability. Infants are as liable for torts committed by them as anyone else, subject of course to what reasonable standard of behaviour could be expected of that infant. The adult cannot get around the protection provided to an infant in contract law by suing in tort instead. For example, if an infant damages a rented car, the rental company could not sue in contract, but may try to sue in tort claiming negligence on the part of the infant. This would not be allowed.

Parents, as a general rule, are not responsible for the contracts entered into by their children unless they have authorized that contract, or they have agreed to be a guarantor or co-debtor. Nor are parents responsible for the torts committed by their children. Only when the adults themselves are negligent, as would be the case if they allowed a child access to a loaded gun, will they be held personally liable. In fact, this has been changed by statute in several jurisdictions where parents have not only been made responsible for torts, but also in some cases responsible even for the criminal conduct of their children.

## Insanity and Intoxication

A contract supposedly involves a meeting of the minds, but when one of those minds is insane or intoxicated, the individual may be able to escape the contract. The person, or his or her representative, trying to escape a contract for a non-necessity—something other than food or lodging—on the basis of diminished mental capacity must be able to establish three things. First, it must be shown that the contracting party did not understand the nature of the transaction that he or she entered into. Anything short of this, and the contract is binding. Second, it must be shown that the other party knew, or should have known, of the insanity. A central principle in contract law is that the courts will enforce the reasonable expectations of the parties. So if a person has no idea that he or she is dealing with someone whose mind is gone, and there is nothing in the situation that should have alerted him or her to that fact, that contract will be enforceable. In the case of *Hardman v. Falk*,[18] after terms for the sale of a property were negotiated with two daughters, the women introduced the purchasers to their elderly and sickly mother, the owner of the property. The terms were then explained to the woman and she signed the documents with an X. The daughters explained that their mother was too feeble to sign her name. Later the daughters tried to get out of the deal on the basis of their mother's insanity at the time of the contract. The court found that her mind was gone at the time of the contract, but even though she was visibly old and sickly, there was nothing to alert the purchasers to her insanity, and so the contract for the sale of the property was valid. Third, if a person regains his or her sanity, that person must take steps to repudiate the agreement quickly. If the person has bought shares, for example, he or she cannot wait to see if those shares have gone up or down in price before repudiating.

This latter requirement is more important when the mental impairment is caused by intoxication, since sobriety usually follows. Whether drugs or alcohol causes the intoxication, the requirements for escaping liability under the contract are the same: that the person was so impaired that he or she did not understand the transaction; that the other person knew or ought to have known of the intoxication; and that the agreement is

Infants are liable for their own torts.

Parents may be made liable by statute

Person must be so incapacitated as to not know what they are doing

Where one party is insane or intoxicated, there is no contract if the other person should have known

---

[18][1953] 3 D.L.R. 129 (B.C.C.A).

repudiated quickly upon becoming sober. Insanity will be a defence to a criminal charge where the accused did not understand what he or she was doing or that it was wrong. Intoxication, however, in most cases will not constitute a defence to a crime. Note that where a person has been committed to a mental institution, a trustee is appointed to look after his or her affairs. The person may be given an allowance, and any contracts he or she enters into beyond that are simply not binding—not even contracts for necessities.

There are several other situations where the **capacity** to contract might be a problem. Where corporations and societies are involved, the extent of their capacity to contract depends on the legislation that creates them. This is not a problem where ordinary corporations are involved, but when dealing with Crown corporations, government agencies, universities, municipalities, trade unions, and societies and associations their powers are often limited. Any doubt should be resolved by checking the appropriate statute. A different problem exists when dealing with foreign governments and their representatives. Because governments are sovereign, they may be immune from criminal prosecution or civil action in our courts. Note, however, that when the foreign government is acting as a commercial entity it will be bound by its contracts in the same way as any other contracting corporation. Finally, it should be noted that the capacity of status Indians (First Nations peoples) while living on a reserve is also limited to some extent under the provisions of the *Indian Act*.[19] These provisions were intended to protect them from exploitation and is a right that remains despite the provision of the *Charter of Rights and Freedoms*. When dealing with First Nations people, especially the bands themselves, it would be prudent to review the relevant provisions of the *Indian Act* and any other legislation in place that relates to the transaction.

*Statutory bodies may have limited capacity*

*Diplomats protected*

*First Nations people are protected*

## LEGALITY

**LO 8**

Contracts that have an unlawful objective or an illegal consideration are void and unenforceable. Examples are contracts to commit a crime or tort; contracts involving an immoral act, including prostitution; contracts to sell government secrets or to bribe officials; and contracts that obstruct justice, such as paying someone to go to jail and thus defeating the deterrent nature of a jail sentence. Such agreements may be illegal because they are against public policy or because they violate the terms of a specific statute. Where a statute prohibits a certain act, the terms of the statute itself must be examined to determine the consequences. The prohibited agreement may or may not be void, depending on the provisions of the statute. Gambling was illegal according to common law but now is permitted, providing the terms of appropriate statutes, such as obtaining permits, are complied with. Without such permits, there are significant penalties under the *Criminal Code* for gambling in various forms, for placing bets for others, and for operating the premises involved in such activities.

*Contracts to commit a crime or other illegal acts are void*

Insurance arrangements also face the danger of being illegal contracts—a form of wagering—unless they are intended to cover a loss. To collect you must demonstrate that you have an **insurable interest** in what was insured, meaning that the insurance payout must compensate for a loss and not constitute a windfall. Contracts where merchants agree to sell their merchandise at a common price (price fixing) also raise questions of **legality**. Under the federal *Competition Act*, a number of specified activities that have the effect of limiting competition are controlled or prohibited. The *Competition Act* imposes significant

*Valid insurance contracts require insurable interest*

---

[19]R.S.C. 1985, c. 1–5.

criminal penalties for various forms of agreements between businesses that have the effect of unduly injuring or limiting competition, including conspiracy and bid-rigging.

Perhaps the most important business situation in which the legality of an agreement may arise occurs when a business is sold and a provision is included prohibiting the seller from carrying on a similar business. Such a provision is permissible only where it is reasonable within the context of the agreement, meaning that it goes no further than is necessary to protect the goodwill of the business being sold. If Joe sells Sam a barbershop, and a term is included that prohibits Joe from carrying on the trade of a barber, this would be void. It goes too far. The rationale is that if Joe were to immediately start up a new business near the old one it would defeat the goodwill of the one sold because he would attract all of his old customers. However, if Joe opened up a barbershop in another province or five years later, this would pose no danger. Such a contract should include a time limitation and an area limitation that goes no further than is necessary to protect the business being sold from such unfair competition. In this example, the limitations of not opening up another barbershop within two years and within 40 kilometers of the original business might be more appropriate. In fact, such restrictive covenants often take the form of non-competition and non-solicitation clauses. In a recent Supreme Court of Canada case,[20] it was made clear that when a non-competition clause is involved, both a time limitation and a territory limitation are required. Where a non-solicitation clause is involved, only a time limitation is required since the non-solicitation is much narrower as it prohibits actual communication with current or former customers. Thus, it is not necessary for such a territory limitation to be included. It must also not harm the public interest. If only one barber were left, who then could charge exorbitant prices, this might be sufficient reason to void the contract. A similar problem arises when employers impose such terms on their employees that require them not to work in a similar industry after termination. This condition may be necessary to protect trade secrets or special customer relations, but the term should also be reasonable and not go further than necessary to prevent the anticipated evil. It should be noted, however, that the courts are less inclined to enforce such restrictive covenants against employees, especially when they are prevented from carrying on their trade or profession.

*Restrictive covenants must be necessary and reasonable*

Case Summary 3.8 *Martin v. ConCreate USL Limited Partnership*[21]

## Uncertain Restrictive Covenant Void

Martin (Appellant/Defendant), ConCreate (Respondent/Plaintiff) in the Court of Appeal for Ontario. (Note that the facts have been simplified.)

Martin had worked as a labourer for ConCreate since his youth and eventually rose to a responsible position in the company. He also had a substantial minority holding in both ConCreate and SDF, an associated company. Eventually, ConCreate and SDF were sold to another company. Martin sold some of his interest but retained an indirect interest in the operation and continued as an employee. As part of the sale of his interest, Martin signed a restrictive covenant, which included a non-competition covenant, a restriction on soliciting customers, employees, agents, dealers and distributors, and a prohibition on the use of any confidential information. The area covered was all of Canada, and the duration was to be for 24 months after Martin disposed of his remaining indirect interests in the operation.

The problem was that to dispose of his interest, which took the form of units in a limited partnership, he had to have permission of the other unit-holders and also of anyone who had loaned funds to that partnership. Also the

[20]*Payette v. Guay Inc.*, 2013 SCC 45 (CanLII).
[21]2013 ONCA 72 (CanLII).

non-solicitation clause covered past, present, and future customers. Martin was dismissed and shortly after started a new business in competition with ConCreate, where he employed several of ConCreate's former employees.

At trial the judge found that the restrictive covenant was not ambiguous and found it valid and binding. The appeal judge disagreed.

The time frame was uncertain because the other partners and those loaning money to the partnership had to give permission for Martin's units to be sold or surrendered, and there was no certainty that they would do so. This made the duration of the restrictive covenant uncertain and

therefore void. With respect to the non-solicitation clause, it also covered future customers, which also made it too broad and therefore void. However, the third requirement that Martin not make use of any confidential information was enforceable.

This case is interesting in that it shows how careful parties must be in drafting restrictive covenants. Any time they are uncertain or unreasonable as to subject matter, duration, and area they will be void. In this case the area restriction (all of Canada) was reasonable, but the duration and non solicitation clauses were unreasonable and void.

## INTENTION

LO 9

The parties must intend to be legally bound by their agreement, but a person cannot get out of an agreement just by saying he or she was only kidding. As mentioned above, the court will give effect to the reasonable expectations of the parties. Therefore, the question is not so much whether you intended to be bound, but whether the other party reasonably thought he or she was entering into a legally binding agreement. In some situations, such as family and social arrangements, it would not be normal for the arrangements to be legally binding. Thus, where such domestic relations are involved, there is a presumption that there was no **intention** to be legally bound. This means that unless the other party can produce evidence to rebut or overcome this presumption, indicating that the parties truly did intend to produce a legally binding contract, there is no legally enforceable agreement. An agreement by a parent to pay a child an allowance in exchange for performing chores would be such an arrangement. Similarly, if a friend failed to show up for a planned fishing trip, he could not be sued for breach of contract even though you incurred considerable inconvenience and some expense in the preparation. Business agreements are the opposite. There is a presumption that business and commercial contracts are legally binding, and to get out of one you would have to produce evidence that indicated an opposite intention. Sometimes people in business enter into understandings that they do not want to be legally enforceable. But to overcome that presumption, they must clearly state that the arrangement is not intended to be a binding contract or have any legally enforceable effect on the parties.

Business and family affairs may intersect, or the agreement may involve exaggerated terms. For instance, during a golf game a person might say, "I'll give you a million dollars if you make that putt." Each situation must be looked at separately, and the reasonable person test must be applied. The question is: Was it reasonable for the other contracting party to have expected legal consequences to flow from the agreement? Only if the answer is yes, and the other elements necessary to form a contract are present will a legally enforceable contract exist.

> Parties must intend legal consequences to result from contract

> In domestic or social relationships there is presumption of no intention

> In commercial transactions there is a presumption of intention

> Presumptions may be rebutted

## FORMAL REQUIREMENTS

LO 10

Historically, the form of the document was important in determining whether it was binding. The use of the seal as discussed above is an example, but today these formal requirements have largely been removed.

> Formal requirements generally no longer required

# Writing

Writing may be required by statute

It must be emphasized that it is always good practice to put an agreement into written form. It is surprising how even the best-intentioned people will remember the same agreement differently. Referring to a written memorandum can overcome this difficulty and will constitute evidence of the actual terms agreed upon. A handshake may show trust and understanding, but put the agreement into writing for future reference. Still, people are usually surprised when they find out that a verbal contract is every bit as binding as a written one. The writing is important because it is evidence of the contract. There are a few situations, however, where a contract will not be enforceable unless it is evidenced by writing. Several statutes are in place requiring writing for specific types of transactions. The most important is the *Statute of Frauds*, originally passed in England in the 17<sup>th</sup> century. This statute originally required evidence in writing for contracts dealing with interests in land, such as the purchase and sale of land, including easements, leases, and so forth, as well as agreements where one person assumes responsibility for the debt of another. Other less common provisions include contracts not to be completed within one year, a personal commitment of an executor to pay the debt of the estate, and agreements where someone promises another something if they get married. In some jurisdictions the sale of goods acts require that items sold over a given amount be accompanied by writing (a receipt). In Canada most provinces have either repealed or severely limited the application of their versions of the *Statute of Fraud*. In most provinces it is expected that agreements dealing with land—except for a short-term lease of less than three years—and agreements to be responsible for the debt of another, such as a guarantee, will require written evidence. We must distinguish between a guarantee and an indemnity. A guarantee involves a promise to pay if the debtor does not; it is a contingent liability. But an indemnity makes the promisor equally liable for the debt along with the co-debtor. British Columbia requires both to be evidenced in writing, whereas most other jurisdictions require only a guarantee to be written. Note that Alberta also requires a guarantee to be notarized by a notary public. To satisfy the requirement, the writing must be made by the person trying to avoid the contract and must be consistent only with the existence of that contract. Thus, a receipt for money paid is generally not good enough since it could have been paid for anything. (Note that the British Columbia statute does make such a receipt for money paid sufficient evidence.) Most jurisdictions have passed electronic documents acts that give electronic documents and signatures the same status as written ones and have passed consumer protection statutes requiring that the consumer receive a written copy of some agreements, especially if that agreement is for services or goods to be delivered in the future.

*Statute of Frauds* requires evidence in writing in specific situations

Sale of goods act requires writing in some jurisdictions

Where writing is required but absent, the contract is unenforceable

When written evidence is not present, such agreements are unenforceable. As discussed above, this means that without such writing one party cannot sue in court to force the other to perform. However, if a party has already performed his or her obligations under the contract, he or she has done only what he or she should have and cannot use the courts to get out of the deal. Also, if there has been partial payment or partial performance (providing that it is only consistent with the existence of the agreement), as a rule that will take the place of the writing requirement, and the contract will be enforceable.

Partial performance satisfies writing requirement

## Case Summary 3.9 *Steinberg v. King*[22]

## A Guarantee Must Be Evidenced by a Written Memorandum

Steinberg (Plaintiff), King and Marlow (Defendants) in the Ontario Superior Court of Justice.

Steinberg is a lawyer who represented Mark King in a criminal action. As the action proceeded it became clear that Steinberg would not be paid. He threatened to withdraw from the case, and King's mother, Janine Marlow, stated that if he were not paid by King, she would pay his fees. This was repeated at a later stage in the proceedings. Steinberg continued to represent King with the result that King was acquitted of 9 criminal charges. Still Steinberg was not paid fees now amounting to $37 000.

He initiated this action against both King and his mother, but King became bankrupt and so the action was continued against Mrs. Marlow. She defended her continued refusal to pay on the basis that this was in effect a guarantee and as such under section 4 of the Ontario *Statute of Frauds,* which provides that any, "promise to be responsible for the debt, default or miscarriage of any other person," is unenforceable if it isn't evidenced by writing. There was no writing in this case. Steinberg argued that part performance was sufficient, but the judge found that there was no precedent for such part performance being applied against anything but interests in real property. And even if it was applied here, there was no conduct that was consistent with the existence of the contract.

The case is interesting in that it shows the operation of the *Statute of Frauds* applied to a guarantee. It is also interesting to note that even a lawyer can get caught out in this way.

In summary, where there has been consensus in the form of offer and acceptance, consideration has been exchanged, both parties have capacity to contract, the agreement is legal, and there was intention to be bound, a legally enforceable contract has been created.

## Key Terms

capacity (p. 87)

consensus (p. 70)

consideration (p. 79)

contract (p. 70)

counter-offer (p. 74)

exemption clause (p. 73)

gratuitous promises (p. 80)

guarantee (p. 80)

insurable interest (p. 87)

intention (p. 89)

invitations to treat (p. 72)

legality (p. 87)

offer (p. 72)

offer and acceptance (p. 70)

option agreement (p. 75)

promissory estoppel (p. 82)

post-box rule (p. 78)

*quantum meruit* (p. 80)

seal (p. 83)

unenforceable (p. 85)

unilateral contract (p. 77)

---

[22]2011 ONSC 3042 (CanLII).

## Questions for Student Review

1. Explain consensus, its importance in contract law, and how such consensus is reached.
2. Distinguish an offer from an invitation to treat.
3. What must be contained in an offer for it to form a binding contract?
4. What role does the requirement of writing play in the formation of a contract?
5. What is an exemption clause and how is it treated by the courts?
6. Under what circumstances can an offer end before acceptance?
7. Explain the requirements for an option agreement to be binding.
8. What is required for acceptance of an offer and how can such acceptance be accomplished?
9. When and where is an acceptance effective?
10. What is the effect of the post-box rule and when does it apply? To what forms of communications does it apply?
11. When a unilateral contract is involved, how is acceptance accomplished?
12. When will an acceptance sent by email or fax be effective?
13. Explain what is meant by consideration and the contract rule associated with it.
14. Explain what is meant by past consideration and why the designation is important.
15. What is the effect in most jurisdictions of a creditor taking less in full satisfaction of a debt? Why?
16. Explain what is meant by promissory estoppel and why it is important.
17. What is the relationship between a sealed contract and the requirement of consideration?
18. Explain the effect of a contract between an infant and an adult on the parties to it. When will infants be bound by their contracts?
19. What must be proved to escape liability of contracts on the basis of insanity or intoxication? List other situations where capacity may be a problem.
20. What is required for a restrictive covenant to be enforceable?
21. Explain what constitutes intention on the part of parties to a contract.
22. Explain the provisions of the *Statute of Frauds* and when a contract must be in writing.
23. What is the effect if the requirements of the *Statute of Frauds* are not met? Will anything else other than actual writing satisfy the requirements of the *Statute of Frauds*?

## Questions for Further Discussion

1. Consider the creation and use of the post-box rule in terms of its original purpose, whether it met that objective, and whether its continued use can be justified today. In your answer consider whether the rule ought to be applied to communications between the parties other than acceptance and to different forms of communications, such as email and the internet generally.
2. It is arguable that the requirement of consideration in a contract serves no other purpose than to indicate that the parties intend their agreement to be binding. Do you think that the continued requirement of consideration in contract law serves any valid purpose today? What about the separate requirement of intention?
3. Consider the fact that in most jurisdictions only some forms of contracts have to be evidenced in writing to be enforceable. Many jurisdictions have made important changes to these requirements. What do you think? Should only written contracts be enforceable in

court? Should writing ever be required? In your answer consider the costs and use of legal resources as well as whether the purposes of justice in a broad sense are served by your recommendations.

4.  People who are insane are given special treatment with respect to the contracts they enter into. If they are so insane they don't know what they are doing, the contract isn't binding unless the other party knew or ought to have known of the insanity. Should the only question be whether there was insanity? Would that be fair to merchants? Why don't we treat contracts with infants the same way and allow the infant to escape the contract only if the adult with whom they were dealing knew they were contracting with an infant?

## Cases for Discussion

1.  *Williams v. Condon,* 2007 CanLII 14925 (ON S.C.)

    Steven Williams was a pedestrian when he was struck and seriously injured by the defendant. The driver's insurance company was State Farm Insurance, and for payments of $2400 and $5300 he signed a complete release of all claims. He claimed the he did not even read the documents. Some time later, while still in pain and having difficulty working, he approached State Farm for further benefits but was refused. State Farm took the position that the releases he had signed were final and the matter was ended. Williams testified that he had been consuming significant amounts of alcohol on a regular basis since the accident to mask the pain, and that he had been taking prescription and non-prescription medicines as well. He stated that on the date when he signed the releases he had consumed five or six king-size cans of beer and a couple of painkillers and that he was, according to witnesses, visually intoxicated. Also, he had been chewing gum to disguise the smell of liquor on his breath when he signed the release.

    Explain the issues before the court, the arguments of the parties and the likely outcome.

2.  *Shafron v. KRG Insurance Brokers (Western) Inc.* 2009 SCC 6, [2009] 1 S.C.R. 157, (2009) 301 D.L.R. (4th) 522 • [2009] 3 W.W.R. 577

    Morley Shafron worked through his incorporated company Morley Shafron Agencies Ltd. and then sold his shares in that company to KRG Insurance Brokers (Western) Inc. He continued to work for them and as a term of his employment contract agreed, upon leaving, not to work in the same industry for a period of three years "within the metropolitan City of Vancouver." In 2000, Mr. Shafron left KRG and went to work for an insurance company in Richmond, British Columbia, a city immediately to the south and adjacent to the City of Vancouver. KRG sued claiming a breach of the restrictive covenant. Explain what arguments are available to Mr. Shafron to escape this restrictive covenant. Explain the likely outcome. In your answer consider whether this was an employment or a business relationship, and what difference that would make to the decision.

3.  *Stone v. Polon,* 2006 CanLII 24712 (ON C.A.)

    Stone and Polon were partners in an accounting firm that was dissolved when they both joined a larger firm. Eventually Stone left that firm and this action was brought to settle the accounts between the parties. The matter was submitted to the court, and the judge accepted Stone's calculations as accurate with respect to the early years of the partnership. They could not agree on the calculations for the final years and agreed to submit the matter to arbitration. The arbitrator accepted Polon's position that all of the accounts, even those dealt with by the courts, should be reviewed. Solon disagreed and withdrew from the arbitration. This action is brought to determine whether Stone was bound to proceed with the arbitration on those terms or not. What do you think? What are the arguments that both parties could raise and the likely outcome of the matter? Did they ever have an enforceable agreement to arbitrate the dispute?

4. *Atria Networks LP v. AboveNet Communications Inc.* 2007 CanLII 33115 (ON S.C.)

Atria Networks LP wanted to acquire access to cable to establish a fibre-optic cable network with its partner throughout Ontario. They negotiated with MFN, which had a lease agreement with Telus, for the assignment of that lease giving them access to the Telus fibre-optic network in Ontario. But they also needed consent of MFN's parent, the American company AboveNet. Serious negotiations took place between Atria and AboveNet, with Atria thinking that an agreement had been reached. An important aspect of the deal for Atria and its partner was some sort of protection if something should go wrong, such as the lease with Telus being terminated. AboveNet took the position that they wanted a "no strings attached" deal with no such built-in obligations. AboveNet took the position that no agreement had been reached and refused to honour the contract. Explain the issues before the court, the arguments of both parties, and the likely outcome.

5. *Ontario (Minister of National Revenue) v. Sunset Recreational Vehicles Ltd.* 2003 CanLII 30337 (ON S.C.)

Curtis Jutzi, the sole director and officer of Sunset, claimed to have entered into an oral contract with McGlynn Lumber for the sale of some land that McGlynn needed for access to certain woodlots for $35 000. Jutzi understood they would sell the property back to him when they were finished harvesting the trees from the adjacent lands and so retained title. The Minister of National Revenue was a creditor of Sunset and executed an order under the *Excise Tax Act*. When the Minister proceeded to sell the land, it was discovered that McGlynn Lumber had registered their interest against the title, preventing the sale. This action is brought by the Minister for a declaration that McGlynn Lumber has no interest in the property and should be removed from the title. McGlynn takes the position that they are the rightful owners of the property pursuant to the oral agreement. What problem does McGlynn face in arguing his position? Is there any alternative position he can put forward? Explain the likely outcome.

# Chapter 4
## Enforcing Contractual Obligations

Pixsooz/Fotolia

## Learning Objectives

LO 1   Identify the various mistakes that can end or otherwise affect a contract

LO 2   Describe and contrast the different forms of misrepresentation

LO 3   Explain the effects of duress and undue influence on a contract

LO 4   Consider the implications of privity and assignment for a contract

LO 5   Explain the difference between assignment and negotiation of a negotiable instrument

LO 6   List the events that can bring a contract to an end

LO 7   Describe how a contract can be breached or otherwise ended

LO 8   Summarize what constitutes a frustrating event and its effect on a contract

LO 9   Outline the remedies that are available for breach of contract

LO 10  Explain what is meant by damages and any limitation on their availability

LO 11  Compare equitable remedies to other remedies available for breach of contract

At the heart of most business dealings is the understanding that in the event of a dispute, the courts will enforce the contractual agreement. When both parties are happy with the outcome, it is not necessary that the contract be legally enforceable. It's only when the parties think the agreement is not being honoured that the legal validity of such arrangements and their enforceability in court becomes an important issue. Those disputes can revolve around the existence of the contract, complaints about the conduct of the parties at the time of agreement, or the performance of the obligations arising from it. The prior chapter dealt with what was needed for a legally enforceable contract to exist. This chapter looks at disputes that arise with respect to the start of the contractual relationship, including mistakes as to the nature, terms, or other aspects of the agreement; misrepresentation; duress; and undue influence. The concept of privity and the assignment of contractual obligations are examined. The chapter concludes by examining problems related to the proper performance of the terms of the agreement.

## LO 1  MISTAKE

One of the most effective ways of reducing risk in business transactions is to exercise great care to ensure that the parties being dealt with are honourable, reliable, and solvent. Of equal importance is to ensure that there is complete and accurate documentation of all aspects of that transaction. The actual contract is, of course, of utmost importance, and extreme care should be taken over the choice of words and phrases used in the resulting document. Not only is it important to ensure that there is no ambiguity in those words and phrases, and that they say what is intended, but also great care should be taken to ensure that the document is complete, with all eventualities anticipated and provided for. Still, disputes will arise. Often costs can be considerably reduced by including provisions for all disputes to be handled through mediation and arbitration. When contracts are challenged, the argument often revolves around the interpretation of particular terms. Often the parties have a different understanding of the wording or effect of the terms of an agreement. Such mistakes can take place in three ways (see Figure 4.1). Note that the term, mistake, as it is used here refers to an error with respect to the actual terms or effect of the agreement itself, and not simply an error in judgment with respect to the outcome. You may have made a mistake buying certain shares in a company when they go down in price rather than up, but that has nothing to do with the actual contract of purchase. You simply misjudged the market.

The first type of mistake occurs when only one of the parties is in error. Such **one-sided mistakes** (often referred to as unilateral mistakes) will normally not affect the existence of the contract, unless the mistake is obvious to the other party. This is where the principle of *caveat emptor* (let the buyer beware) is applied. When one party has been

One-sided mistakes usually have no effect on contract

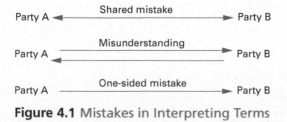

**Figure 4.1** Mistakes in Interpreting Terms

induced to make the mistake by misleading statements made by the other, this is an actionable misrepresentation, as discussed below. But when that person misleads himself or herself, normally he or she has no recourse. On rare occasions a person might sign a document by mistake, thinking it is about something different than it actually is. If that mistake is so profound that it goes to the nature of the agreement in its entirety, not just some aspect of it such as the price, the document may be void. The principle is **non est factum** (it is not my act), and while it used to be very important, the Supreme Court of Canada has now determined that negligence may block such a claim.[1] The problem is that it is difficult to make an error about the essential nature of a document, for example, mistaking a mortgage for a guarantee, unless you haven't read it—and not reading it qualifies as negligence that may block the claim. Today such a claim would likely be restricted to someone who couldn't read the document because of illiteracy, unfamiliarity with the language, blindness, or a mental disability.

But *non est factum* can cause void contract

When both parties have made the same serious error, the resulting **shared mistake** (often referred to as common mistake) may destroy consensus and result in no contract between them. The contract is said to be **void** in such circumstances. For example, where both parties think they are dealing with one parcel of land when in fact they are dealing with another, or where both parties share a belief that an event has taken place when it hasn't, or even when both believe a particular law or regulation applies to the situation and it doesn't, the contract may be void. If this kind of shared misapprehension is not the fault of one of the parties and is serious enough to actually destroy the basis of the agreement, it can cause the contract to be void for lack of consensus. Such shared mistakes are rare. Sometimes, when a mistake is made in recording the agreement, the courts will respond to a request to **rectify** the document so that it corresponds to the original understanding between the parties. But for rectification to take place, the actual terms of the agreement must be clearly understood by both parties at the time of contract and the error must be simply in the recording of that agreement. Thus, if the parties agreed to sell and purchase a boat for $50 000, and it was mistakenly written down as $5000, the court may be willing to supply the missing zero.

Parties making the same mistake may destroy consensus

Court may correct mistake through rectification

The third type of mistake occurs when both parties have a different understanding of the terms of a contract. Such **misunderstandings** (often referred to as mutual mistakes) are the most common disputes in contract litigation and are usually resolved by the court imposing the most reasonable interpretation of those terms on the parties. For example, if I thought the terms of the contract required that you include the sheepskin seat covers with the sale of your car, and you refused to supply them, the court would look at the terms of the contract and the surrounding circumstances to determine whether they were included. The court would determine the most reasonable interpretation of the terms. If the car was originally shown to me with the seat covers on, it is likely they would be included. It is only when the court finds both interpretations equally reasonable that the mistake will destroy the contract. Thus, two British merchants who agreed on the sale and purchase of the cargo of the ship *Peerless*, on route from Bombay, India, to Liverpool, England, ran into difficulty when it was discovered that there were two ships of that name making that passage but at different times. The purchaser intended the cargo to be sent on one ship and the seller intended it to be sent on the other. Both positions were equally reasonable; consequently, the court found that there was no contract.[2]

When parties disagree, court will apply reasonable interpretation

Terms may be implied into contract

---

[1]*Marvco Colour Research Ltd. v. Harris*, [1982] 2 SCR 774.
[2]*Raffles v. Wichelhaus* (1894), 2 H. & C. 906, 159 E.R. 375 (E.D.).

## Contract Interpretation

As explained above, when there is a disagreement over the meaning of a term used in a contract, the normal approach taken by the courts is to apply the most reasonable interpretation. Remember that the preference of the court is to give effect to the reasonable expectations of the parties to the agreement. If the term is clear and there is no ambiguity, the court simply applies the literal meaning of the term. In determining that meaning, the courts will often look not only to dictionaries but also, more importantly, to the common usage of the industry involved.

Parol evidence rule excludes extrinsic evidence

Where there is ambiguity, the courts will look to the rest of the document to try to discern the intention of the parties. In some circumstances they will also look to other dealings between the parties, but the **parol evidence rule** requires that where the terms of the agreement are clear and unambiguous, no outside extrinsic evidence will be considered that contradicts those clear terms. But there are some exceptions. Evidence of fraud, duress, or of a subsequent agreement ending or changing the contract in question will all give reason to abandon the operation of the rule. Even evidence that the written document was not intended to embody all of the terms of the agreement will support the introduction of extrinsic evidence.

It must also be noted that in some instances the courts will imply terms into the agreement that the parties have left out. The practice is to include such a term where it is clear that the parties would have done so had they thought of it. But the courts will not renegotiate the contract for the parties. Nor will they supply missing terms that are necessary for a contract to exist. If the parties have neglected to state a price, the courts will normally not supply it for them. However, if the parties have not stated when the price is to be paid the court will normally imply into the agreement that the price is to be paid upon performance or within a reasonable time, depending on the nature of the agreement. Some statutes also imply terms into contracts. The whole purpose of *Sale of Goods Act*, discussed in the following chapter, is to supply such missing terms when goods are being sold.

## Case Summary 4.1 *Performance Industries Ltd. v. Sylvan Lake Golf & Tennis Club Ltd.*[3]

## Written Contract Corrected by Rectification

Performance Industries (Appellant/Defendant) and Sylvan (Respondent/ Plaintiff) in this appeal before the Supreme Court of Canada.

Sylvan (owned by Bell) operated an 18-hole golf course and entered into a joint venture agreement with Performance (owned by O'Conner) to exercise an option held by Sylvan for the purchase of additional land. The joint venture agreement contemplated a residential housing development around a cul-de sac along the 18-hole fairway. Both parties agreed that a width of 110 yards was needed to accommodate a double row of houses.

However, when the oral agreement was put into writing, the length was correct at 480 yards but the width was written as 110 feet instead of 110 yards. When Performance decided to start the development Sylvan insisted on the written terms, claiming they were an accurate representation of the oral agreement. The case went all the way to the Supreme Court of Canada, which found that the oral agreement was for 110 yards, not feet, and Sylvan (O'Conner) knew it. There were many other sources and witnesses that determined the 110 yard finding. In addition to finding O'Conner, the principal of Sylvan, had

[3]2002 SCC 19 (CanLII).

committed a fraudulent misrepresentation, the court also found that this was an appropriate situation to rectify the written contract and changed the 110 feet to read 110 yards, as the parties had originally intended.

The case is helpful in that it shows the operation of the equitable remedy of rectification at the highest level. It was argued that Performance should not be awarded an equitable remedy because it had failed to exercise due diligence.

The Court found that due diligence was not a prerequisite to obtain a remedy of rectification and that, in any case, Mr. O'Conner was in no position to claim such a failure because of his own fraud. At the trial level damages were awarded for breach of the rectified contract based on loss of profits and $200 000 in punitive damages. The punitive damage award was overturned. Only in exceptional cases will punitive damages be awarded, and this one didn't qualify.

# Exemption Clauses

As mentioned in Chapter 3, an area where disputed contract terms often arise is over exemption clauses, sometimes referred to as exculpatory, exclusion, or limitation clauses. These are provisions that favour one side, usually exempting or limiting the liability of that side for failure to perform some aspect of the contract. It is important to understand that the courts base their approach to all such terms on the principle of freedom of contract. The parties are free to agree to whatever they want, and once they have done so they are bound by the terms. The courts are generally reluctant to interfere with such terms, even when they may appear unfair, because the benefits and obligations agreed to by the parties to a large extent will have been calculated on the basis of the risks each faces, and such risk-reducing clauses are very important in that calculation. Still, when the courts do apply such clauses, they usually do so very narrowly. Any ambiguity will be interpreted at the expense of the party favoured by the clause. If a hotel has a sign saying that it is "not responsible for lost or stolen goods," and those goods were destroyed by fire, the hotel would not be protected. It is vital, then, for the parties to take great care in composing such a clause. It must be clear, cover only the situations intended, and be capable of no other interpretation.

Exemption clauses must be brought to the attention of the other contracting party. Today it is generally accepted that any unusual clause like this should be highlighted in some way and not buried in the general language of the contract. The language used should be concise and easily understood and be capable of no other interpretation. Where possible it is wise to have the other contracting party initial the clause. If the notification is by sign, as would likely be the case in a parking lot or restaurant, that sign must be at a location where it is clearly visible to the customer.

**Standard-form contracts** usually contain such exemption clauses. Contract law is based on a bargaining model, but, in fact, parties are often in unequal bargaining positions. Try bargaining with an airline over the terms included in a ticket or a car dealer over the terms included in the warranty. In those circumstances the courts are particularly vigilant in interpreting such exemption clauses as narrowly as possible.

The Supreme Court has made it clear that the parties to a contract are free to contract out of even fundamental obligations.[4] Still, especially in consumer transactions, the court will generally exercise their discretion to interpret the words used very narrowly in favour of the consumer. To overrule such a clause, whether in commercial or consumer transactions, the courts will first look at the construction of the contract to determine

*Exemption clauses limit liability*

*Exemption clauses strictly interpreted*

*Exemption clause must be brought to other part's attention*

---

[4]*Tercon Contractors Ltd. v. British Columbia (Transportation and Highways)*, 2010 SCC 4, [2010] 1 SCR 69.

whether the wording of the clause catches the situation or whether terms should be implied into the contract. As in the example above, if the clause refers only to "lost or stolen goods," and the goods are destroyed in a fire, the clause will not be broad enough to cover the situation. Sometimes, however, the courts will find a duty of good faith overriding even a clearly worded exemption clause. Second, the courts will determine whether the clause is valid in terms of there being no undue influence, or whether both parties were in equal bargaining positions at the time of the creation of the contract (see discussion below). And finally, the courts will consider whether there is some misconduct, such as fraud or criminality on the part of the person seeking to hide behind the exemption clause, or whether that exemption clause should be ignored because of other public policy considerations.

---

## Case Summary 4.2 *Boutcev v. DHL International Express Ltd.*[5]

## Exclusion Clause Not Properly Brought to the Attention of Customer

Boutcev (Plaintiff), DHL International Express Ltd. (Defendant) in a trial before the Alberta Court of Queen's Bench.

When two boxes that were supposed to contain computers arrived empty at their destination, the plaintiff, Boutcev, sued the shipper, DHL International Express Ltd., for compensation. The shipper refused to pay and denied all liability, referring to an exemption clause contained in very small print on the back of the waybill. The judge found that the clause was illegible, saying it was "painfully small and defied reading with the naked eye." He refused to enforce it, holding in favour of the plaintiff. Parties to an agreement are only bound by the terms that are reasonably brought to their attention, and to ensure that such exclusion clauses are enforceable, the party drawing up the contract should put them in bold type or otherwise highlight them in some way.

---

## LO 2   MISREPRESENTATION

Misrepresentation involves false and misleading statements

If a false statement is a term of contract, the remedy is to sue for breach

False statements that induce a contract are also actionable

Misrepresentation involves false and misleading statements that induce a person to enter into a contract. Note that the term *false* includes half-truths, where what is *not* mentioned makes the statement misleading. Telling a prospective investor that a finance company has several million dollars in assets in the form of outstanding loans is misleading if the investor is not also told that half of those loans are unsecured and unrecoverable. The matter is simplified if the false statement becomes a term of the contract and, consequently, the injured party can sue for breach of contract. Breach of contract will be discussed as a separate topic below. Often, however, these misleading statements never become part of the contract, even though they are persuasive and the very reason the person enters into the agreement in the first place. If you purchase property because the vendor told you that a new resort is being built nearby, the purchase agreement would normally make no reference to the new resort. Still, if you relied on that false information

---

[5][2001] A.J. No. 297 (Alta. Q.B.).

to persuade you to purchase the property, you would likely have recourse under the law of misrepresentation.

For a statement to be an actionable misrepresentation, normally it must be a statement of fact, not a statement of opinion or a prediction of some future event. You are entitled to have the opinion that you are selling a "great little car in good shape." It is only when an expert makes the statement that the opinion can be an actionable misrepresentation. When a mechanic says the car he is selling is a "great little car in good shape," the statement had better be true. But in most cases the false statement must be a statement of fact to be an actionable misrepresentation. Even the non-expert will be liable if he falsely claims as a fact that the engine of the car he is selling has recently been rebuilt or replaced. When marketing products or services, legislated advertising standards must be followed. Even when those standards are adhered to, if the message is false or misleading, individual customers may be able to sue for misrepresentation. Consumer protection legislation, which is in place in all jurisdictions, broadens the responsibility of employers for misleading statements made by their salespeople. Even when the contract declares that there are no other representations express or implied outside of that contract, consumer protection legislation will usually still hold the seller liable for such misleading statements. Consumer protection legislation will also be discussed under "Consumer Protection Legislation" in Chapter 5 (see p. 135).

Silence will not normally be misrepresentation. Only when there is a legislated duty, or some special relationship between the parties requiring disclosure, will failure to make such a disclosure constitute misrepresentation. A recent development in contract law is the recognition in a growing number of relationships that there is a **duty of good faith** between the parties. Where such a duty is present, there is an obligation to disclose pertinent information. The failure to do so may well be considered misrepresentation and can be challenged in court. Even in a business transaction where someone withholds information that would lead the other party to change his or her mind, the person withholding information could be violating the duty to act in good faith. Of course, where a misleading statement was made and it did not induce the other party to contract, there is no remedy. Suppose the vendor of a property told you that a company had purchased nearby property to build a resort and you purchased your property to build a home or for some other purpose not affected by that claim. You will have no complaint if the statement later turns out to be false, since it did not induce you to enter into the contract in the first place. When the false statement does induce a person to enter a contract, the misrepresentation may be considered innocent, fraudulent, or negligent (see Table 4.1 for a summary of the types of misrepresentation and their remedies).

> To be actionable, a false statement must be a statement of fact, not an opinion

> Silence is not misrepresentation except where duty of good faith or relationship

> The misleading statement must have induced the person to contract to be actionable

## Table 4.1 Remedies

| | |
|---|---|
| Innocent misrepresentation | Rescission only |
| Fraudulent misrepresentation | Rescission and/or damages (tort) |
| Negligent misstatement | Rescission and/or damages (tort) |
| Misstatement—becomes a term of the contract | Rescission, damages, and other breach of contract remedies |

# Innocent Misrepresentation

A distinction has to be drawn between someone who intentionally misleads and **innocent misrepresentation**. When a person misleads another without knowing, and he or she is otherwise without fault, the misrepresentation is said to be innocent. The recourse is limited to the equitable remedy of **rescission**. Rescission involves the court attempting to restore the parties to their original positions. Thus, if a seller had misrepresented the year of production of a car sold to you, honestly believing it to be true, and this was important enough to induce you to enter into that transaction, you could seek to have the contract rescinded on the basis of innocent misrepresentation. You would return the car, and the seller would be required to return the purchase price as well as any incidental costs you may have incurred, such as repair and maintenance expenses. Note that these are not damages (discussed below under remedies) but simply incidental payments designed to keep the appropriate balance between two innocent parties.

A problem arises when the goods have been destroyed, resold, or are otherwise not available to return to the other party. Rescission is then not possible. Where the misrepresentation has been innocent, no other remedy is available. Damages are not available. The remedy of rescission will also be refused where the victim of the misrepresentation has in turn done something inappropriate, such as causing unreasonable delay or having cheated or misled the other party. To obtain an equitable remedy such as rescission, the person seeking it must "come with clean hands." Rescission will also be refused where the contract has been affirmed. This means that the victim has done something to acknowledge the validity of the contract after learning of the misrepresentation, such as trying to resell the goods to someone else.

## Case Summary 4.3 *Samson v. Lockwood*[6]

## Rescission Not Available Where Contract Affirmed

Samson (Plaintiff/Respondent), Lockwood (Defendant/Appellant) in an appeal before the Court of Appeal for Ontario.

The defendants produced a brochure advertising property that stated that a building of 150 000 square feet could be built on it. Unknown to the defendants, because of a change in local by-laws, a building of only 30 000 square feet could be built. The plaintiff, after having read the brochure, agreed to purchase the property and put a substantial deposit down on the transaction. Before the actual transfer of that property, land values in the area dropped significantly. The plaintiff tried to sell the property, and when this proved impossible, he refused to go through with the transaction, claiming misrepresentation and demanding the return of the deposit. The court held that the plaintiff was not permitted to rescind the contract in this case. He knew of the error six months before the agreed-upon date for the completion of the transaction, and yet he still indicated a willingness to complete. The plaintiff also attempted to sell the property to others long after learning of the error and before land values dropped. This amounted to affirmation of the contract after he already knew of the innocent misrepresentation. The result was that the purchase agreement was binding on him, despite the innocent misrepresentation in the brochure. The plaintiff was required to forfeit all of the deposit that he had paid.

---

[6](1998), 40 O.R. (3d) 161, 39 B.L.R. (2d) 82 (Ont. C.A.).

## Fraudulent Misrepresentation

**Fraudulent misrepresentation** takes place when one person intentionally and knowingly misleads another and induces him or her to enter into a contract. If it can be shown that you didn't believe that what you were saying was true, you have committed a fraud and the remedies available to the defendant are expanded. Where the misrepresentation is fraudulent, the victim can seek rescission of the contract, or he or she can seek a remedy of damages for the tort of deceit, or both.

As mentioned earlier, damages involve the wrongdoer paying money to the victim to compensate for his or her losses. Because this is a tort remedy, the objective is to put the victim into the position he or she would have been in had the misrepresentation never taken place. In rare circumstances where the fraud is serious enough, the court will award punitive damages, which is an attempt to punish the wrongdoer rather than to compensate the victim. In such cases, the victim will be awarded more money than he or she has actually lost. Victims will often sue for innocent misrepresentation, even though the presence of fraud is apparent. This can be confusing until you appreciate the strategy involved. Establishing fraud and intention is much more difficult. Where the remedy sought is only rescission, the victim will usually take the easier route of suing for innocent misrepresentation. Note also that an innocent misrepresentation can become fraud if the person who made the statement later learns it is false and fails to correct the false impression left with the victim. Finally, it should be emphasized that a contract induced by fraudulent misrepresentation is voidable not void. The term **voidable** means that the victim can get out of the contract unless a third party has become involved. If goods that were the subject of the fraud get into the hands of a third party, the victim cannot get them back; however, she will still have a remedy of damages against the fraudster if he has any assets.

*Fraudulent misrepresentation occurs when a person knowingly misleads*

*Remedy for fraud can be damages and/or rescission*

*Innocent misrepresentation is easier to prove than fraud*

## Negligent Misrepresentation

Historically, there was no difference between innocent and **negligent misrepresentation**. Since the victim was not knowingly misled, the only remedy available was rescission. In recent years, however, the courts have also awarded damages where it can be established that the wrongdoer should have been more careful. In such cases negligence is established. The legal rules associated with the tort of negligence were discussed in Chapter 2. To summarize, the remedy of rescission is available whether the misrepresentation is innocent, fraudulent, or negligent. However, the remedy of damages is restricted to circumstances where it can be established that the misrepresentation was fraudulent, negligent, or where the misleading term became part of the contract.

*Damages also available where misrepresentation was negligent*

---

### Case Summary 4.4 *Ramdath v. George Brown College*[7]

## Damages Awarded for Negligent Misrepresentation

Ramdath (Designated Plaintiff), George Brown College (Defendant) in this class action before the Ontario Superior Court of Justice.

This class action was brought against George Brown College by a group of business students who claimed they had been the victims of misrepresentation. It was clear

---

[7] 2012 ONSC 6173 (CanLII).

from the evidence that one of the main reasons for choosing and attending George Brown was, as advertised in the course calendar, that completion of the International Business Management post graduate program "provides students with the opportunity to complete three industry designations/certifications" (CITP, CCS, and CIFF). The calendar went on to list the required courses needed for each of the industry designations in addition to what they needed for the George Brown College Post Graduate Certificate. The business students were led to understand that no further course work was required, only examinations. This proved incorrect. All they received upon completion was the George Brown Certificate. In fact the college had no arrangements or understanding with those industry organizations, and much more was needed to obtain the industry designations, including significant time, course work, examinations and monetary commitment.

When the problem came to light the college changed the offending statements and removed the course requirements from the calendar. The court found that the statement "an opportunity to complete" would be reasonably understood by the students to mean there would be no further course work or on-the-job training required to obtain these certificates. This misleading statement in the calendar, although not becoming a term of the contract with the students, did amount to negligent misrepresentation on the part of the college. It was also clear that the students had been induced to attend the college and take the course by relying on that misleading statement. The remedy of rescission was not available because the students had finished their programs and so significant compensation damages were awarded. Note that the court also found that the students qualified as consumers under the *Ontario Consumer Protection Act* and were entitled to compensation under that statute as well. Consumer protection will be discussed in the following chapter.

## Criminal Fraud

Inducing someone to enter a transaction through intentionally misleading statements can also constitute a crime with potentially significant penalties. There are many specific provisions where various forms of fraudulent activity are prohibited, but for this discussion the most significant are sections 361–365 of the *Criminal Code*, which prohibit knowingly making false representations that are intended to induce someone to act on that representation. These provisions include obtaining credit, the extension of credit, or some other benefit for himself or herself or someone else under false pretences, including misleading statements about the financial condition of the applicant or others. Knowingly paying with a cheque without sufficient funds to back it (N.S.F.) or executing some other valuable security by making false representations are also specifically prohibited. Obtaining food, beverages, or accommodation by false pretences is also included. Section 380 contains provisions generally prohibiting fraudulent activities that cheat the public "of any property, money, or valuable consideration or service." This is followed by a number of specific offences, including using the mails to defraud and fraudulent manipulation of stock exchange transactions. There are a number of other related offenses set out in the *Criminal Code* and other federal legislation. The violation of these provisions will subject the offender to significant fines and substantial periods of imprisonment.

## LO 3   DURESS AND UNDUE INFLUENCE
### Duress

Duress and undue influence also involve disputes related to the formation of contract. **Duress** occurs when the free will to bargain is lost because coercion, involving threat of violence, imprisonment, scandal, damage to property, or even inappropriate financial pressure is exercised by one of the parties. If someone threatens to harm your family or vandalize your business to force you to enter into a contract, the agreement would be voidable (not void) because of duress. If you sold your car to A under threat, you could sue to have it returned because you sold it under duress. But if A had already resold the car to B, you can't force B to give it up. Your only recourse is against A, the person who threatened you for damages. Historically, duress was only available where the threats were threats of violence or imprisonment to the contracting party or his family. In Canada this has been expanded and duress can also be claimed where the threats are against property or take the form of economic duress. A classic example of such **economic duress** took place when a landlord put inordinate pressure on a tenant to sign a lease with unfavourable provisions. The tenant had taken over a prior lease from a tenant who had left several months' rent unpaid. She did so with the understanding that she was not obligated to pay that back rent. However, the rent remained unpaid, and the landlord insisted that she was responsible for it. She was completely committed to carrying on her business at that location and so, under tremendous pressure, she signed a new lease where she assumed the back-rent obligation. The court held that the landlord knew she had to sign to avoid "catastrophic financial losses." This economic duress made the transaction unconscionable and released her of her obligations.[8]

Uttering threats of physical violence to a person, to his or her property, or even to his or her animals can also amount to the criminal offence of assault. Obtaining some advantage from people by threats or intimidation can constitute the criminal offence of extortion with serious penalties. Duress, as discussed above, may constitute criminal harassment or intimidation, which are also offences under the *Criminal Code*. These offences are also punishable by indictment up to 10 years in prison or by summary conviction up to two years in prison. The *Criminal Code* also makes it a summary conviction offence for an employer to threaten or intimidate an employee with respect to his or her trade union activities.

Note that where one person compels another to commit an offence by threats of death or immediate bodily harm, that can constitute a valid defence except where the crime involves very serious crimes such as high treason, murder, abduction, sexual assault, or robbery.

## Undue Influence

**Undue influence** is more common. It also involves the loss of free will to bargain, causing the resulting contract to be voidable. Instead of force, the unique influence of the other contracting party takes away the free will of the victim. In certain types of relationships, undue influence is presumed. Examples include professionals such as lawyers, doctors, and trustees taking advantage of their clients, as well as guardians contracting with wards, religious advisors with parishioners, and adults with infant children or aging parents. The presumption of undue influence means that in the absence of other evidence to the contrary, simply showing that the relationship exists is enough for the court to allow the victim to escape the contract on the basis of undue influence. Professionals doing business with their clients often find themselves in such relationships, and they are well advised to ensure that the client obtains independent legal advice before committing to

Undue influence involves abuse of a trusting relationship making a contract voidable

Undue influence presumed in some situations

---

[8]*Canada Life Assurance Co. v. Stewart* (1994), 118 D.L.R. (4th) 67 (NSCA).

the transaction. That will normally provide sufficient evidence to overcome the presumption of undue influence. There are other situations, however, where undue influence can arise based on the unique circumstances involved. For example, in the Manitoba case *Francoeur v. Francoeur Estates*, when Oscar Francoeur learned he was dying of cancer, he transferred some of his estate to his nephew. When his brother, Arthur, found out, he got angry and demanded that Oscar transfer the rest of his estate to him and his wife. Arthur's yelling at his brother and pressuring him to go to the lawyer to change his will the next day was clear evidence of undue influence, and the transactions and will were set aside.[9] Where there is no legal presumption based on the relationship between the parties, the person trying to escape the contract must produce evidence of actual undue influence. This is much harder to do.

## Unconscionability

**Unconscionable contract when vulnerable people taken advantage of**

The principle of **unconscionability** is related to undue influence. This is also a recently developed area of contract law that allows the court to set aside or modify the contract on the basis of vulnerability, such as poverty or mental impairment (short of incapacity) that has allowed one party to unfairly take advantage of the other. In effect, it must be shown that because of these factors the bargaining position of the parties was unequal, resulting in an unjust contract that was grossly unfair to the victim. Note that simple economic advantage will not create an unconscionable transaction. If you are charged a high rate of interest on a loan because you are a high risk, this is not an unfair or unconscionable contract. Most provinces have statutes regulating unconscionable transactions involving loans or mortgages, but unconscionability has now been expanded into contract law generally. A finding of unconscionability will sometimes persuade a court to disregard the terms of an exemption clause that limits the remedies of the disadvantaged party.

## LO 4   PRIVITY AND ASSIGNMENT

### Privity

**Privity means only the parties to contract are bound by it**

The problems of privity and assignment are concerned with determining who has rights and claims under the contract and who can sue to enforce those claims. Privity of contract is a basic principle of contract law under which only the parties to a contract have rights. Strangers to the contract are not bound by it, nor can they enforce its provisions. In the example used in Chapter 2, *Donoghue v. Stevenson*,[10] Mrs. Donoghue, after finding a decomposed snail in her ginger beer, could not sue the seller because she was not privy to the contract. Her friend bought the drink for her. Her only alternative was to sue the bottler/manufacturer for negligence. The same principle of privity prevents shareholders or investors in corporations from suing accountants or others who negligently do business for that corporation, such as providing incorrect audited financial statements. The corporation is considered a separate person, and the contract is between the accountant and that company—not the shareholder or investor. The only option for the shareholder is to sue in tort for negligence.

---

[9]*Francoeur v. Francoeur Estates*, 2001 MBQB 298 (CanLII).
[10][1932] A.C. 562 (H.L.).

There have always been some specific exceptions to the privity rule. Three important exceptions are: 1) interests in land that go with the land—thus a lease will bind not only the original owner and tenant but also any person to whom that land was sold during the term of the lease; 2) trust arrangements—where a person puts property in trust with a trustee for the benefit of some third party, that third party can enforce the trust though a stranger to the contract; and 3) life insurance—where the beneficiary is able to enforce the policy taken out by the deceased. Note as well that in some jurisdictions the restrictions of privity have been removed by statute, allowing, for example, the consumer of a product to sue the manufacturer for breach of contract, even though the original contract was with the dealer.

Privity exceptions:
- Interests in land
- Trusts
- Life insurance

## Case Summary 4.5 *Ragoobir v. RGK Wheelchairs, Inc.*[11]

## Only Parties to the Agreement Can Sue in Contract

Ragoobir (Plaintiff), RGK Wheelchairs, Inc. (Defendant) in a trial before the Superior Court of Justice (Ontario).

Anthony Ragoobir had lost a leg and needed a wheelchair. With the help of several support programs that supplied most of the funds, he approached Niagara Mobility, a dealer in St. Catharines in the business of selling wheelchairs. Niagara in turn referred him to RKG Inc. in Ottawa. A representative of that company (Mr. McClellan) attended at his home taking his measurements, which were then sent to RKG Wheelchairs Ltd. in England, which then proceeded to assemble a custom-made wheelchair for Mr. Ragoobir and supplied it to Niagara Mobility, who in turn sold it to Mr. Ragoobir.

He was satisfied with it at first but things then started to go wrong. Eventually the wheelchair fell apart and when the frame collapsed, it caused him to fall in front of a vehicle, with the result that he suffered serious injuries. There was a warranty supplied by the English company, but in this action Mr. Ragoobir sued the Ottawa company (RKG Inc.) for breach of contract.

At trial that company was found to be liable for the loss but on appeal that decision was overturned. The court held that there was no contract between Ragoobir and the Ottawa company. The contract was between Ragoobir and Niagara Mobility and with the English company (RKG Ltd.) under the warranty. There was no privity of contract between Ragoobir and the Ottawa company (RKG Inc.) The seller was Niagara Mobility and the manufacturer/supplier was RKG Ltd. in England. The court also noted that there may well have been an action against RKG Ltd. (England) under the warranty and against RKG Inc. (Ottawa) in negligence but because the Ottawa company was not a party to the contract of purchase, RKG Inc. (Ottawa) could not be successfully sued for breach of that contract.

This case is relatively simple but strongly illustrates the operation of the principle of privity of contract. Only the parties to a contract are bound by it and have rights under it. It also shows how important it is to make sure you are suing the right person and for the right reason.

Note that when agents act for principals in dealings with third parties, the principle of privity does not enter into the situation, since the resulting contract is between the principal and the third party, and the agent is merely a go-between. Similarly, when one person takes over the obligations of another in a contractual relationship with a third party (called a **novation**), there is no privity problem since that new relationship requires a complete new contract between the newcomer and the original contracting parties. All three must agree to the change substituting a new contract for the old one. Note that such a new contract can be implied from the conduct of the parties. For example, where Jones

Agency and novation do not violate the privity principle

---

[11]2009 CanLII 22803 (ON S.C.).

has a business delivering baked goods to various supermarkets there is a contract between Jones and those individual supermarkets. If Jones sells the business to Smith (assuming Smith and Jones are sole proprietors and no corporation is involved), and Smith started making the deliveries, the supermarkets would not have to accept, since their contract was directly with Jones, not Smith. The change between Jones and Smith could not be imposed on them. They must agree. But if they did permit Smith to make the deliveries, by implication they have consented to the change and a novation has taken place. Their contract is now with Smith, not Jones.

In addition to the statutory exceptions mentioned above, the courts have also shown a willingness to move away from the privity rule. For example, in the case of *London Drugs Ltd. v. Kuehne & Nagel International Ltd.*[12] Kuehne & Nagel was storing valuable goods for London Drugs, and there was an exemption clause in that storage contract that limited any liability for loss to $40. Employees of Kuehne & Nagel caused considerable damage by careless handling of goods, and London Drugs sued them directly for the loss. Even though the employees were not party to the contract limiting liability to $40, the Supreme Court of Canada extended that protection to those employees treating them as third party beneficiaries of the limited liability clause, thus ignoring the rule of privity that normally would have applied.

*Privity rules are changing*

## LO 5   Assignment

*Contract benefits can be transferred or assigned to a non-party*

Perhaps the most significant area where the rules of privity have been modified involves the **assignment** of contractual rights (see Figure 4.2). Assignment involves the assignor transferring a benefit to which they are entitled under a contract to a third party, called the assignee. In effect, they are selling an entitlement or claim to someone else. For example, if a debtor owes money to a creditor, that creditor can assign the claim to a third party. Merchants selling goods on credit, such as car dealerships, often do this. Their business is selling cars, not extending credit, so they assign the credit transaction they have entered into with their customer to a finance company for a fee, and the payments are then made to the finance company. Such assignments are also used as a method of securing debt. The merchant makes an assignment of his accounts receivable to the creditor conditionally so that if he defaults on the debt owed, that creditor then has the right to step in and collect those receivables. Secured transactions such as these will be discussed

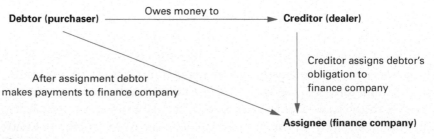

**Figure 4.2** Assignment

---

[12][1993] 1 W.W.R. 1 (S.C.C.). See also *Fraser River Pile & Dredge Ltd. v. Can-Dive Services Ltd.*, 1999 CanLII 654 (SCC), where the Supreme Court extended a "waiver of subrogation" provision in an insurance contract to a third party.

more extensively in the following chapter. Note that an assignment can also take place involuntarily where the person dies or becomes bankrupt.

The problems arise when the person owing the obligation that has been assigned fails to perform. Because of the rule of privity, the assignee cannot sue directly; the assignor and assignee must join together to sue the debtor. This is a cumbersome process, and most jurisdictions have enacted statutes that allow the assignee to sue directly if certain criteria are met. This is called a **statutory assignment**, and to qualify the assignment must be absolute. This means that it must be complete and unconditional; it must be in writing; and proper notice of the assignment must be given to the person owing the obligation that has been assigned. In the example above, the car dealership would make the assignment of the original debt owed by the purchaser to the finance company in writing. The finance company would then send a copy of that assignment to the debtor, asking that all future payments be made to it. In the event of default, the requirements for a statutory assignment have been met, and the finance company can sue the debtor directly. A further problem arises if an unscrupulous creditor assigns his claim to more than one assignee. Who does the debtor pay? The answer is that priority is based on the order of assignment as noticed to the debtor. The first in line has first claim.

Finally, it should also be noted that only benefits can be assigned, not obligations. In this example, if a car were defective, the dealership would still be responsible for its breach of contract, no matter what their agreement with the finance company said. The dealership cannot assign such obligations. For that reason, in any assignment, the assignee is said to take "subject to the equities." Thus, if the car dealership doesn't honour the warranty when something goes wrong, the purchaser would have an excuse not to continue paying the finance company. The assignee can be in no better position with respect to the contract than was the assignor. Of course, the assignor could normally have an employee or subcontractor do the work, but if it is not done, or done improperly, the assignee remains responsible.

*Statutory assignments can be enforced directly*

*Only benefits can be assigned, not obligations*

## Case Summary 4.6 *Trans Canada Credit Corp. v. Zaluski et al.*[13]

# Promissory Note Enforceable Despite Salesman's Fraud

Trans Canada Credit Corp. (Plaintiff), Zaluski (Defendant) in a trial before the Ontario County Court.

Green was a salesman representing Niagara Compact Vacuum Cleaner Company when he persuaded and pressured the Zaluski family into signing a conditional sales agreement and promissory note for the purchase of a vacuum cleaner. Niagara, in turn, assigned their interest in the transaction to Trans Canada Credit. When Zaluski made no payments, Trans Canada Credit sued Zaluski on the strength of the assigned conditional sales agreement and on the promissory note.

The court found that Green was guilty of fraud, which tainted the sale, thus giving Zaluski a good

defence against Green and his principal Niagara. This defence also extended to Trans Canada Credit, which, as the assignee of the conditional sales agreement, could be in no better position than Niagara. But Trans Canada had sued on the promissory note, and this led to a different result. Once a negotiable instrument, such as a promissory note, gets into the hands of an innocent third party (called a *holder in due course*), they can enforce it independently of any failure on the part of the original party. Trans Canada Credit, as such a holder in due course, was in a position to enforce the promissory note, and therefore Zaluski had to pay. Negotiable instruments are extremely dangerous, and people should be careful

---

[13](1969), 5 D.L.R. (3d) 702 (Ont. Co. Ct.).

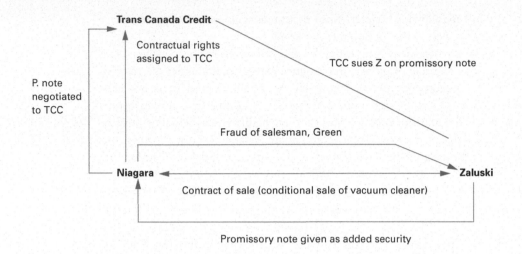

when they enter into them. A more detailed discussion of negotiable instruments follows. Zaluski, in turn, successfully sued Niagara for the return of the money he had to pay Trans Canada Credit. Note that today, because of statutory amendment, this note would have been stamped "consumer purchase" and the result would have favoured Zaluski even with respect to the promissory note.

## Negotiable Instruments

The position of a third party can be quite different when a negotiable instrument is involved. **Negotiable instruments** have an ancient origin but are now controlled by the federal *Bills of Exchange Act*.[14] These instruments are passed between people or institutions and represent claims for funds owing. The key to understanding negotiable instruments is to appreciate their free transferability from party to party. To facilitate this they have to be enforceable at face value. This is accomplished by first allowing the holder to collect on it even though no notice of the various transfers that may have taken place has been given to the original debtor. Secondly, and more importantly, they are made enforceable at face value by giving the innocent third party (called a **holder in due course**) who acquires possession without notice of any defect, the right to collect on it whether the original contractual obligations have been met or not—short of outright fraud or forgery with respect to the instrument itself. This must be contrasted with assignment, where the assignee takes subject to any claims between those initial parties to the transaction. That's why Trans Canada Credit couldn't sue on the strength of the original debt it had been assigned in the *Zaluski* case, above. The transaction was tainted by the fraud of the salesman, Green. But Zaluski also signed a promissory note, which is a negotiable instrument, and because Trans Canada qualified as a holder in due course with respect to that promissory note, they could enforce it directly against Zaluski. (This is an old case from a minor court but I have found no modern case that better illustrates the principle.) The defences with respect to assignment do not apply when a negotiable instrument and a holder in due course are involved. For this reason, most credit transactions include a promissory note so that the position of any third party acquiring rights under it can be protected. It is the existence of this third

*Holder in due course gets better rights than parties*

---

[14]RSC 1985, c. B-4.

**Figure 4.3** Promissory Note

party holder of the instrument that makes negotiable instruments so unique. If he is innocent in the sense of not being a party to or having notice of any wrongdoing, he qualifies as a holder in due course and can collect from the original maker despite any problems with the instrument. Today, because of an amendment to the statute in consumer transactions, when a negotiable instrument, usually a promissory note, is used to advance credit it must be stamped "consumer purchase" and then even a holder in due course will be subject to the same defences available to the original contracting parties.

Thus, when a purchaser gives a cheque in payment for a car and there has been misrepresentation, he or she can stop payment on the cheque as long as it is in the hands of the person to whom it is made out. However, if that cheque is transferred to an innocent third party, including the payee's bank, the purchaser/drawer will have to pay, even though there has been misrepresentation, if that payee qualifies as a holder in due course. Note that the "consumer purchase" provision described above would not apply in that case since the cheque was given as payment and not as a tool to advance credit.

Negotiable instruments include cheques, bills of exchange (sometimes called drafts), and promissory notes, which can be used to advance credit and to transfer funds.

A **promissory note** is a signed, written instrument whereby one person promises another unconditionally to pay a specific sum of money at some future date or on demand (see Figure 4.3).

A **cheque** involves three parties. The drawer in writing unconditionally orders a bank where he or she has an account to pay a specific sum of money to a third party, who is called the payee. The drawer delivers the cheque to the payee, who normally then takes it to the bank and presents it for payment (see Figure 4.4). When the bank certifies the cheque, the bank has added their guarantee of payment and the drawer cannot then countermand it.

A **bill of exchange** or a *draft*, which also involves three parties (drawer, drawee, and payee), is similar but broader. A cheque must be drawn on a bank, but the bill of exchange can be drawn on any person or business. Also, the bill of exchange can be made payable at some future time, whereas the cheque must be payable on demand (see Figure 4.5). It is

*Holder in due course must be innocent*

*Negotiable instruments take the form of:*

- Promissory notes
- Cheques
- Bills of exchange or drafts

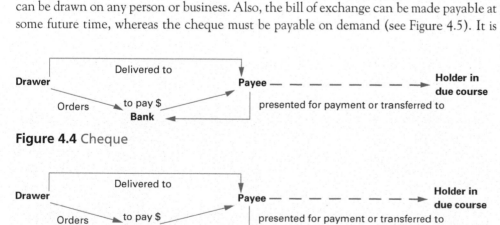

**Figure 4.4** Cheque

**Figure 4.5** Bill of Exchange

normal for the payee or holder of such an instrument to present it to the drawee for acceptance, especially where it is made payable at some future date. When it is a accepted in this way, the holder is guaranteed payment by the drawee, much like a certified cheque.

It must also be emphasized that when one of the persons in possession of the cheque or other negotiable instrument endorses the back before transferring it, he or she can also be held liable for the amount of the cheque if the original drawer fails to pay. There are several different types of endorsement, but where the holder merely signs his or her name (a blank endorsement), it becomes a bearer instrument negotiated simply by passing it from one person to another. When the holder adds the words "pay to the order of" it is an order instrument and the next person must also endorse it before transferring. In both cases the endorser has added his or her credit to the instrument and must be prepared to pay if the drawer fails to do so. Still, the use of a negotiable instrument does not guarantee payment. If the drawer of the cheque has insufficient funds in the account, or the maker of a promissory note can't pay, you will be out of luck. For this reason the person entitled to payment will often insist on receiving a certified cheque. In this case the bank has accepted the obligation in effect adding their credit and guaranteeing payment.

Today with the growth of electronic banking and the common use of internet banking and credit and debit cards, negotiable instruments, especially cheques, are not used as much as in the past. But they are still commonly used and important to understand especially in commercial transactions.

*Normally, the endorser adds credit to a negotiable instrument*

## LO 6/LO 7/LO 8    DISCHARGING CONTRACTUAL OBLIGATIONS

### Performance

Most disputes with respect to contracts arise because of incomplete or improper performance of contractual obligations (see Table 4.2). This is called **breach of contract**, and there is a significant problem in determining just how imperfect performance has to be before it becomes a serious enough breach to discharge the other party's obligations. A contract is **discharged by performance** once both parties have performed as required under the agreement and there are no further outstanding obligations. The terms of an agreement can be characterized as major terms, called **conditions**, and minor terms, called **warranties**. Be careful not to confuse the term *warranty*, as it is used here, with the assurance given by a manufacturer with respect to the quality of a product produced by them and sold to consumers (a manufacturer's warranty). That is a specialized use of the term. The more formal use of warranty refers to any term of lesser importance (a minor term) in

*Contractual obligations can be ended by performance*

| Table 4.2 How to End Contractual Obligations | |
|---|---|
| Performance | Discharge by performance takes place where there is complete performance or where failure to perform is minor |
| Breach | Breach of a condition can discharge the victim of his or her obligations under the contract |
| Frustration | Discharge by frustration takes place where performance is made "impossible" by some outside event |
| Agreement | Obligations can be modified or ended by a new agreement |

all contractual relationships. You can tell if a term is a condition or a warranty by applying the reasonable person test. Ask yourself whether, if the contracting party had known ahead of time that the term was going to be breached, he would still have entered into the contract. If he would have walked away, the term is a condition, but if it is likely that the contracting party still would have entered into the contract, with possibly some minor adjustment to the consideration to be paid, the term is of lesser importance or a warranty.

If a condition is breached after the contract is in place, the victim can elect to treat the contract as discharged. He or she doesn't have to perform their obligations under the agreement since the contract has been discharged by breach. However, if a warranty is breached, the failure is not considered serious enough to discharge the contract or end the obligations of the non-breaching party. Thus, the contract is still in effect, and the non-breaching party must still perform his or her side of the agreement. There has been a breach, however, and the non-breaching party does have the right to seek compensation in the form of damages from the breaching party.

*Breach of warranty still considered performance*

A similar result takes place when a condition is breached in some minor way. Even though a major term has been breached, the failure is so minor that the contract is considered substantially performed and the non-breaching party is still required to perform his or her obligations under the agreement. This is referred to as **substantial performance**. Of course, here there is also a right to seek compensation for the loss from the breaching party. If you were to order a new car from a dealership and it was delivered with regular wheels rather than the racing rims you specified, this would be a breach of warranty. You could not refuse to take delivery of the car and would have to pay the agreed-upon price, reduced by what it would cost to replace the wheels. If the car was delivered without an engine or a different model altogether was sent, this would be a breach of condition, and you could refuse delivery and would not have to pay for the car. If you operated a fleet of cars and ordered 1000 cars from the dealership and only 999 were delivered, this would be substantial performance of a condition of the contract (the delivery of 1000 cars). You would still have to pay, but only for the 999 delivered cars. Of course, if you contracted with your mechanic to fix the engine in your car and after working on it for weeks it wasn't fixed even though he had done substantial work there is no substantial performance. Here only complete performance, fixing the engine, will do. It is good practice for the parties to such agreements to specify the various terms as conditions if they are important to that party. This is especially true where it may appear as only a minor term to an outsider. Thus, if you were to order a car in a particular shade of yellow and it was delivered in orange, that would normally be a breach of a warranty. But if you were in a franchise business where all of the franchisees drove vehicles of that colour, getting a vehicle in the same colour would be a vital part of the purchase transaction. You would be protected if you had specified that shade of yellow as a condition of the contract.

*Substantial performance still considered performance*

When money is involved, there are some special rules. A cheque, even a certified cheque, is not the same as cash. If the contract calls for the payment of a specified amount of money, that means Canadian legal tender unless otherwise specified. Cheques can be used if their use has been agreed to or has been the accepted method of doing business in the past. When in doubt, make sure that actual Bank of Canada bank notes are delivered. Even Canadian coins do not qualify as legal tender over a specified amount. For example, under the *Currency Act*[15] anything over 25 pennies is not considered legal tender. All

*Proper tender is considered performance except with money*

---

[15]RSC 1985, c. C-52.

coins have restrictions in this way; the amount that can be used varies with the denomination of the coin. However, there is no similar limitation on bills.

It should also be noted that one party can't prevent the other from performing and then claim to be relieved of his or her obligations because the other party has failed to properly perform his or her contractual obligations. As long as the performing party is ready, willing, and able to perform and has attempted to do so, that **tender of performance** is considered equivalent to proper performance of the contract. Suppose I agree to paint your house and arrive at the time specified with the appropriate paint and brushes, and you refuse to let me in. I have lived up to my contractual obligation. If you fail to pay me, you are the one in breach, not me. Again, money is treated differently. If I owe you money and come ready to pay it at an appropriate time and place, and you refuse to take it, I still owe you the money. But there is one significant change in my obligation. Normally, it is the debtor's obligation to seek out the creditor to make payment. But I have done that, and now the obligation will be upon you to seek to collect the money from me. You must bear any expenses (including court costs) arising in that process.

## Breach

As noted, a serious breach of contract can discharge the other party of his or her obligations under the contract. This breach of contract could take place by incomplete or improper performance of the contractual obligations. The breach can also occur through **repudiation**. This involves one of the parties informing the other that he is refusing to perform his contractual obligations, or doing something that makes proper performance impossible (implied repudiation). When the repudiation takes place before performance is due, it is called **anticipatory breach**, and the victim of that breach has two options. He can either ignore the repudiation and continue to demand performance, or treat the contract as discharged and make other arrangements. Treating the contract as ended allows the victim to make other arrangements and to sue right away rather than waiting for the actual failure before suing. If the victim must hire someone else to do the job, for example, any higher costs can be recovered in that action. On the other hand, if the victim continues to demand performance, the damages eventually recovered may be higher, but there is also the danger that some unexpected event such as a fire, natural disaster, or even sickness may make the contract impossible to perform. Such an event would discharge both parties of their obligations by frustration (discussed below). Worse, the victim of the repudiation may find that he is no longer in a position to perform, making him the one in breach. The victim is bound by whichever choice he or she made.

If the refusal to perform comes after performance is due, this is just another form of breach through failure to properly perform contractual obligations. The remedies available for such a breach will be discussed below. Of course, it takes both parties to end a contract and where one party breaches a condition the other is discharged from their obligations only when they choose to treat the contract as ended. If the victim of the breach still wants to go through with their side of the agreement, they may do so where it is still possible to perform. If I were to purchase an antique automobile from you in running condition, and you were to deliver it without an engine, I would be entitled to refuse to go though with the transaction because of your breach of condition, but if I still wanted the car I could take it, either by ignoring the breach or reserving the right to sue you for compensation at a later date.

As discussed earlier in the chapter, parties to contracts will often include terms limiting their liability when breaches do occur. Because parties are free to include in their bargains whatever they want, such exemption clauses are an important part of doing business. In the absence of other forms of misconduct or interfering legislation, how successful they are at limiting liability will depend on how carefully those clauses are worded or in rare circumstances on public policy considerations (see Chapter 5).

---

### Case Summary 4.7 *BP Global Specials Products (America) Inc. v. Conros Corporation*[16]

## Anticipatory Breach by Conduct Gives Right to Terminate Contract

BP Global Special Products (America) Inc. (Plaintiff), Conros Corporation (Defendant) in a trial before the Superior Court of Justice (Ontario).

Conros was in the business of producing fire logs, and an essential ingredient in the manufacturing process was slac wax. BP was in the business of supplying this product and entered into a contract with Conros to supply a specified amount of slac wax at a given price. However, over the term of the agreement Conros failed to make the contracted purchases at the rate agreed. During that period there was evidence that Conros was purchasing slac wax on the open market and not ordering from BP as agreed. There was also evidence that during slow sales periods Conros was not purchasing from BP as a tactic to negotiate a lower price.

Because BP had put infrastructure in place in the form of shipping arrangements and storage, receiving no orders from Conros put significant pressure on BP to lower its price, which in effect was tantamount to blackmail. When BP did deliver the product to Conros, it refused to take delivery unless the price was reduced. The court found that this clearly showed by conduct that Conros considered itself no longer bound by the contract. This was not agreed to or waived by BP and so amounted to repudiation of the contract in the form of anticipatory breach. Accordingly, BP refused to make any further deliveries. The court found that BP was justified in terminating the remainder of the contract and suing. Note here that Conros' conduct amounted to an anticipatory breach, and BP had a choice: it could elect to demand performance of the contract or to treat it as terminated. The court found that by conduct BP communicated to Conros an election to terminate. BP was thus entitled to sue. Instead of compensation for damages suffered, BP was awarded an amount sufficient to put it in the position it would have been in had the contract been properly performed.

---

Finally, it should be noted that under rare circumstances a breach of contract can amount to a criminal offence with serious penalties. For such a breach to constitute a crime under section 422 of the *Criminal Code*, the breaching party must know, or have reasonable cause to believe, that the breach will result in danger to human life, serious bodily injury, or serious property damage; or that the breach will delay a train; or even deprive a city (or a significant part of it) of light, power, gas, or water. See Table 4.3 for a summary of the types of performance and breach.

## Frustration

A contract discharged through **frustration** is a recognition that the parties should not be penalized when events happen that are out of their control. Frustration usually takes place when after the contract has been entered into, performance becomes impossible, such as

*Frustration ends contractual obligations*

---

[16]2010 ON S.C. 1094 CanLII.

## Table 4.3 Performance and Breach

| Performance and Breach | | Options of the Other Party |
|---|---|---|
| Repudiation | | |
|   Before performance is due | Election | Can treat obligations as ended and sue or wait for performance |
|   After performance is due | Breach | Can treat obligations as ended and sue |
| Failure to perform | Breach | Can treat obligations as ended and sue |
| Partial performance | | |
|   Serious failure | Breach | Can treat obligations as ended and sue |
|   Minor failure | Performance | Must perform obligations, but can sue for compensation |
| Complete performance | Performance | Must fulfill contractual obligations |
| Performance tendered but refused | | |
|   Goods and services | Performance | Must fulfill contractual obligations |
|   Money | | Money still owed, but no obligation to seek out creditor |

when the subject matter of the contract is destroyed before performance through no fault of the parties. A contract can also be frustrated when performance is still technically possible, but would lead to a completely different result because of the changing circumstances. For example, if you were to rent a room to view a parade and the parade was cancelled for some reason that would likely frustrate your contract. It would be possible to still occupy the room, but the whole basis for the contract would be gone; to require you to go through with it now would be something essentially (or fundamentally) different from what you intended, especially when you consider the higher rental rate you would likely be paying.

> **Frustration involves impossibility of performance or fundamental change**

The kinds of situations that can lead to a contract being frustrated are personal illness, destruction of the subject matter, an event the contract was based on being cancelled or changed, and interference by government (such as changing the law, refusing permits and licences, or expropriating property). For a contract to be frustrated, the changing events leading to frustration must be unforeseen and outside the control of either party and prevent the proper performance of the contract. Such events destroy the foundation of the contract and make performance impossible or something completely different from what was contemplated. Suppose that Jones contracted to build a house for Smith, but was denied a permit due to a change in government regulation. That would likely be frustration. But if he was denied that permit because of his failure to supply necessary plans or other documentation, that would be breach of contract, since the matter was within his control. This is referred to as *self-induced frustration*, which is simply a breach of contract. Also the frustrating event must be fundamental. If the job simply became uneconomical because of rising prices, Jones would still be obligated to build the house.

> **Self-induced frustration is breach of contract**

Sometimes a provision will be put into the contract such as stating what will happen and who will bear the loss in the event of such frustrating events. If that is the case, the provisions of the contract will prevail. For example a *force majeure* clause is often included sometimes referred to as an "act of god" clause freeing both parties from any liability should such an event such as war or natural disaster take place. This is a good risk-reducing practice. It illustrates that it is vital when drafting contracts to carefully set out the obligations of the parties to avoid any ambiguity but also to anticipate what can go wrong and provide for that eventuality. Similarly, when ongoing obligations are involved, a term specifying under what conditions those obligation will end will often be included in the contract, thus avoiding a problem. This is an example of a *condition subsequent*, discussed below.

---

### Case Summary 4.8 *KBK No. 138 Ventures Ltd. v. Canada Safeway Limited.*[17]

## Zoning Change Frustrates Contract

KBK (Plaintiff/Respondent), Canada Safeway (Defendant/Appellant) in this appeal before the Court of Appeal for British Columbia.

In this case KBK paid a first installment of $150 000 towards the purchase of property from Canada Safeway for a total purchase price of $8.5 million. The property was advertised as a "prime Development opportunity", with a zoning of C-2, and KBK made it clear that the purpose of the purchase was to develop a mixed commercial and residential condominium project. Unexpectedly, the director of planning for the city made a successful application to reduce the zoning of the property from CD-2 to CD-1 which had the effect of reducing allowable building square footage from 231 800 to 30 230 making the condominium project impossible. KBK refused to complete the purchase and brought this action for the return of the $150 000. The court had to decide whether the contract

was frustrated. At trial the judge held that this was not a situation where the contract just became more inconvenient, difficult or less economical. Rather an intervening unexpected event took place that was out of the control of either party, that "radically altered" the contract transforming it into something fundamentally different from what the parties originally intended. This amounted to frustration. The Court of Appeal agreed, dismissing the appeal.

This case nicely illustrates what constitutes frustration and its effect on a contract. Here it was still technically possible for KBK to complete the purchase even after the unexpected and unforeseeable intervening event, but to do so would have led to a result fundamentally different from what the parties originally intended. Note that since KBK had received nothing under the *Frustrated Contracts Act* it was entitled to the return of the deposit.

---

Historically, the effect of a frustrated contract was simply to "let the loss lie where it falls." Both parties were discharged of any further obligations, keeping any benefits and bearing any losses that had been incurred to that point. But that was seen to be unfair, and today all jurisdictions have enacted frustrated contracts acts that overcome much of this unfairness. Essentially, if either party has benefited from a partially performed contract, he or she will have to pay for that benefit. If a deposit has been paid and no benefit has been received, the deposit must be returned. Note that a portion of that deposit can be retained to compensate for costs incurred in preparing to perform the contract. The British Columbia *Frustrated Contracts Act* goes further by requiring the parties to share equally any costs incurred, even where no deposit has been paid. Note that the *Sale of Goods Act* states that where goods have perished the contract is avoided, placing the risk on the seller who must return any money paid unless the parties have otherwise agreed.

*Frustrated contract acts require payment for benefits received and the return or apportionment of any deposit*

---

[17]2000 BCCA 295 (CanLII).

## Agreement

Changing legal relationships through agreement is the basis of contract law. Just as contractual obligations are created by agreement, they can be modified or ended by agreement as well. But for a **discharge by agreement** to take place, all of the elements necessary to form a contract must be present. The problems usually arise with respect to the requirements of consensus and consideration. One party cannot impose such changes on the other without his or her consent. If one party decides to pay less, or not go through with the contract without the agreement of the other party, that is simply a breach of contract.

The lack of consideration is a more difficult problem. Where both parties are relieved of some obligation—or get something more by the change—there is no problem. This is normally the situation where the parties agree to end a contract that has not yet been performed. Both are relieved of their obligations and so both get a benefit from the change. The contract is said to be rescinded. Where the parties agree to discharge the old contract and substitute a new one with different major terms or parties, the same principle applies. This is called a novation. Sometimes the parties agree to changes to end or modify a contract that benefits only one side. In these circumstances the party benefited must agree to do something extra for the changes to be binding. This is referred to as the process of **accord and satisfaction**. In the absence of such an arrangement, the person benefiting from the gratuitous promise cannot enforce it. Still, where the person making the gratuitous change to the agreement changes his or her mind and then brings an action to enforce that original provision, the other party, who has relied on the change, may be able to raise promissory estoppel as a defence. It should be noted that in almost all instances where promissory estoppel has been applied by the court, the gratuitous modification of a prior contractual obligation was involved. Consideration and promissory estoppel are discussed in detail in Chapter 3.

Finally, it should be noted that the original contract might include conditions that will end or modify the obligations. In some circumstances where there are ongoing obligations such as employment or rental, the contract may include an option for one of the parties to terminate upon giving proper notice. Since the obligations of both parties will end there is sufficient consideration. More commonly, there will be a condition precedent or a condition subsequent included. A **condition precedent** is a term requiring that some event or circumstance must take place first before the obligations set out in the contract become binding on the parties. When someone buys a house subject to selling his or her old one or subject to arranging financing at a particular rate, that is a condition precedent. Until it is met, there is no obligation under that contract. Conditions precedent are most commonly found in purchase and sale agreements involving real property, but they can be included in any contract where something is required to happen before the obligations assumed by the parties are to be binding on them. Contracts involving continuing obligations will sometimes include terms specifying when that obligation will end; this is called a **condition subsequent**. A contract to supply food services until a particular construction project is finished is an example of a condition subsequent. Again, good practice requires great care in drafting such clauses to ensure their proper operation, especially when things don't go as planned.

# Remedies for Breach

**LO 9**

When a dispute arises over the formation of a contract, judicial remedies are designed to put the parties in the position they were in before the contract was entered into. Thus, where there has been misrepresentation or the contract is void or voidable, the court will usually grant rescission and attempt to put the parties back to their pre-agreement positions. But when the dispute relates to improper or incomplete performance, the remedies attempt to put the injured party in the position he or she would have been in had the contract been performed properly. In the first case the courts look back, and in the second case they look forward.

---

## Case Summary 4.9 *Tang v. Zhang*[18]

# Deposit Forfeited Despite No Damages

Tang (Appellant/Plaintiff), Zhang(Respondent/Defendant) in this appeal before the Court of Appeal for British Columbia.

Tang agreed to sell and Zhang to purchase residential property for $2 030 000. Zhang paid a $100 000 deposit to be "... absolutely forfeited to the seller... on account of damages." Zhang notified Tang that they would not be going through with the purchase and requested the return of the deposit. Tang refused and after some time sold the property to a third party at a higher price. This action was brought by Tang in order to retain the deposit claiming that since the property was sold at a higher price, there were no damages and the deposit should be returned. Note that the deposit would be in the trust account of the lawyer or real estate agent until the matter was resolved.

The trial judge agreed, finding the vendor was only allowed to keep the deposit if it was applied against damages. Since there were no damages, Tang had to return the deposit. On appeal that decision was overturned. Here the court found that a true deposit was to be forfeited if the purchaser failed to go through with the purchase. The term was not enough. There had to be an indication that the deposit was to be forfeited upon non-completion of the contract, as was the case here. The statement that the deposit was to be applied against damages had effect only if there were damages. It had no effect on the fact that it was to be forfeited if the purchasers repudiated the contract.

The case is valuable in that it shows that a true deposit is to be forfeited upon repudiation. There must be clear indication that it is to be forfeited and reference to damages does not take away from the fact that a true deposit can be lost. Also the amount involved must not amount to an unreasonable penalty. In this case it was not.

---

**Damages**   The primary remedy for a breach of contract is the awarding of damages. This is an order for the breaching party to pay a monetary award to the victim of the breach in an attempt to put him or her in the position he or she would have been in had the contract been performed properly (expectation damages). When someone agrees in contract to sell his yacht to one person for $100 000 and then sells it to another, he might well be sued for breach of contract. If the victim of the breach had to pay $110 000 to obtain a similar yacht, the damages awarded would be the difference ($10 000) plus any costs incurred. When the loss can be calculated, such as where wages already lost are involved or where more money had to be paid to accomplish the contractual purpose, as in the example above, this is referred to as special damages. But where the damages have to be estimated, as in compensation for pain and suffering, lost enjoyment of life, or even

**LO 10**

Remedy of damages involves money payment

---

[18]2013 BCCA 52 (CanLII).

an estimate of lost future earnings, this is referred to as an award of general damages. These amounts are usually given to compensate for monetary loss, but in some cases, when appropriate, the courts today are also willing to provide monetary compensation for emotional stress or pain. For example, in medical malpractice actions and in wrongful dismissal cases, the courts will often take into consideration any pain and mental upset in the damage award. A classic example where damages for mental distress were awarded involved a hospital that in breach of contract improperly disclosed confidential information that implied the plaintiff may have been infected with AIDS.[19] Normally, punitive damages designed to punish the breaching party rather than compensate the victim for the loss are not available for breach of contract. They are sometimes awarded where a tort such as fraud is also involved, or in other special circumstances. For example, in the case of *Whiten v. Pilot Insurance Co.*[20] the Supreme Court of Canada reinstated a jury award of $1 million punitive damages to a couple whose fire insurance claim was refused by the insurance company on the completely discredited grounds that the family had torched their own home. The family had found themselves out in the street in winter conditions in their bedclothes as a result of the fire, and the fire chief and the insurance company's own investigators and experts all said there was no evidence of arson. The company, knowing the family was in financial distress, cut off their benefits without explanation and continued with protracted litigation, refusing to honour their contractual obligation. This conduct caused the jury, to make, in addition to normal damages, a $1 million award of punitive damages. The Court of Appeal for Ontario recognized the outrage of the jury, but clearly stated the objective of avoiding "uncontrolled and uncontrollable awards of punitive damages in civil actions" when it reduced the award of punitive damages to the more reasonable amount of $100 000. This result was appealed to the Supreme Court of Canada, which reinstated the $1 million punitive damage award, agreeing with the jury that a "powerful message of denunciation, retribution, and deterrence had to be sent."

Punitive damages usually only available where separate wrong

In general, punitive damages are to be awarded only in exceptional cases involving "malicious, oppressive, and high-handed misconduct that offends the court's sense of decency."[21] In a breach of contract case for punitive damages to be awarded, there must also be stand-alone wrongful conduct present. Usually, this will be some tort such as fraud or breach of fiduciary duty, but in rare cases that stand-alone wrongful conduct need not constitute an independent tort. In the above breach of contract case that independent wrong consisted of the insurance company's breach of their duty to act in good faith, and while that did not constitute an independent tort, it was sufficient to support an award of punitive damages.

Liquidated damages are pre-agreed payments for breach in contract

The parties can agree in the contract to limit the amount of damages to be paid in the event of a breach. We have discussed exemption and limitation clauses above where one party limits the damages for which it will be responsible. Similarly, a contract will sometimes specify just what will have to be paid in the event of a given breach. These are called **liquidated damages**. For example, an electrician may have a term in his contract that he loses $50 per day for every day he is late on a contract. A prepaid **deposit** is a form of liquidated damages. When someone purchases a new car, he or she will usually be required to pay a certain amount as a deposit before delivery. If the purchaser fails to go

---

[19]*Peters–Brown v. Regina District Health Board*, 1996 CanLII 5076 (SK CA); [1996] 1 W.W.R. 337 (Sask. Q.B.).
[20]*Whiten v. Pilot Insurance Co.*, 2002 SCC 18, [2002] 1 SCR 595.
[21]*Hill v. Church of Scientology of Toronto*, [1995] 2 SCR 1130 (SCC).

through with the deal, that amount will be forfeited as a pre-estimation by the parties as to what damages will be paid in the event of breach. Another form of prepayment that must be distinguished is a **down payment**. This is simply the first payment of the purchase price and is not forfeited in the event of breach. The terms used are not conclusive, but where the contract does not provide that the prepaid amount is to be forfeited upon breach, it is a down payment and is not directly available as damages. For such a liquidated damages clause to be enforceable, it should be an honest attempt by the parties to pre-estimate what damages would be suffered in the event of a breach and not to unreasonably penalize the breaching party. Limitation and exemption clauses, discussed above, have a similar effect.

There are significant limitations on the availability of damages in contract law. First, the victim must mitigate his or her loss. That means the victim must take all reasonable steps to minimize that loss. Failure to do so will reduce the damages awarded to what should have been lost had there been proper **mitigation**. For example, when someone is wrongfully dismissed from his or her employment, he or she has an obligation to mitigate by trying to find another job. Any damage award for wrongful dismissal will be reduced by what the person earns (or should have earned) from that alternate employment. Second, the victim of the breach can only receive compensation in an amount that was reasonably foreseeable by the breaching party at the time they entered into the agreement. This means that unreasonable or unexpected losses are too remote and cannot be claimed. In one case, a victim of fraudulent misrepresentation was induced to enter a franchise agreement to purchase and service soft drink and food dispensers. The court awarded compensatory damages, including the recovery of the initial investment, and also awarded punitive damages for the fraud. But the plaintiff had also put a deposit down on a van to be used to service the dispensers, which had to be forfeited when the franchise arrangement failed. He also sought compensation for the loss of his deposit on the van. The court held, however, that the purchase of the van was not part of the franchise agreement and was therefore too remote and could not be recovered.[22]

> Mitigation requires victim to keep damages low

> Damages only payable where reasonably foreseeable

## Equitable Remedies

**LO 11**

> Equitable remedies require good behaviour of victim

Sometimes monetary compensation will not sufficiently compensate the victim of a breach. The Courts of Chancery developed several remedies that are still available when a contract is breached. Note, however, these equitable remedies are not available when money damages would provide adequate compensation, when there has been wrongdoing on the part of the person seeking the remedy (including unreasonable delay), and when some innocent third party would be adversely affected.

**Specific Performance**    This is an equitable remedy that requires the breaching party to perform his or her part of the contract. Where the goods involved are unique, such as a painting by a famous artist, no amount of money will compensate if the seller changes his or her mind. A specific performance remedy involves the court ordering the breaching party to actually transfer the painting to the buyer. Land transactions are often remedied by an order for specific performance because each plot of land is unique.

> Specific performance requires carrying out original contractual obligation

---

[22]*Lapensee v. First Choice Industries Ltd.* (1992), 46 C.P.R. (3d) 115 (Ont. Gen. Div.).

**Injunction requires the end of conduct that is breaching a contract**

## Injunction

An injunction is used in contract and in tort to stop a person from doing something that is wrong. If the party breaching a contract is involved in some activity inconsistent with the proper performance of the contract, the court may order him or her to stop doing it. If I rented a hall from you to put on a concert and you changed your mind, I could seek an injunction to prevent you from renting that hall to anyone else. I could also seek an order of specific performance forcing you to let me use it as per the original contract. It should also be noted that just as it can be good practice to include liquidated damages clauses in a contract, so too it may be helpful to set out in the actual contract other appropriate remedies for a breach. For example, one could put in a clause stating "in the event of breach it is acknowledged that irreparable harm to the victim will result, that monetary compensation would not provide adequate compensation, and therefore the victim of the breach will be entitled to relief by way of preliminary injunction or other remedy." Such a provision should make it easier to obtain that injunction.

**Accounting requires disclosure of profits and their surrender to victim**

## Accounting

There are other types of specialized equitable remedies. An accounting is available when profits have been diverted and it is difficult to determine just what injury has taken place. The court can order the breaching party to disclose financial records and dealings, and to pay any profits obtained through their wrongdoing to the aggrieved party.

**Quantum meruit requires reasonable payment for services given**

## Quantum Meruit

This remedy is applied when the contract is breached before all work has been done or when no specific consideration has been agreed upon for services rendered. Here, the court orders a reasonable amount to be paid for what has been done. If you seek help from a plumber or mechanic, often you don't agree on a price ahead of time. You are then required to pay a reasonable price on the basis of *quantum meruit*, which is what you are billed, unless you immediately protest and dispute the amount claimed. See Table 4.4 for a summary of the remedies for a contract breach.

---

Case Summary 4.10 *Alumitech Architectural Glass & Metal Ltd. v. J.W. Lindsay Enterprises Ltd.*[23]

## Payment Owed for Work Done with or Without a Contract

Alumitech Architectural Glass & Metal Ltd. (Plaintiff/ Defendant in Counterclaim), J.W. Lindsay Enterprises (Defendant/Plaintiff in Counterclaim) in a trial before the Nova Scotia Supreme Court.

Examining only the counterclaim, both Alumitech and J.W. Lindsay Enterprises bid on a job at Dalhousie University and Alumitech got the job. J.W. Lindsay Enterprises made a separate deal with Alumitech to do some of the work, but eventually a dispute arose as to how Lindsay Enterprises was to be paid. One thought there was to be a flat-rate price, and the other thought the payment was to be based on a unit price per square foot completed. The court found that there was no consensus between the parties, the price being a very important term of the agreement. With no consensus there was no contract, but since there had been a considerable amount of work done, the court awarded a remedy to Lindsay Enterprises based on the principle of *quantum meruit*. Applying this remedy, the court then determined a fair and reasonable price for the work that had been done, and the award was based on that. This amounted to a calculation based on the costs incurred plus a small allowance for profit. *Quantum meruit* is an equitable remedy where someone receiving a benefit is required to pay a reasonable price for that benefit received, even in the absence of a binding contract.

---

[23]2006 NSSC 14 (CanLII).

## Table 4.4 Remedies

| Remedies | Type | Nature |
| --- | --- | --- |
| Damages | Common law | Money compensation limited by mitigation and remoteness |
| Liquidated damages | Contract | Deposit forfeited or contract terms specify damages to be paid |
| Specific performance | Equitable | Order to perform contract terms |
| Injunction | Equitable | Order not to act inconsistent with contract terms |
| Accounting | Equitable | Order to disclose and pay over profits to victim |
| *Quantum meruit* | Equitable | Order to pay reasonable amount for services supplied |

## Key Terms

**accord and satisfaction** (p. 118)

**anticipatory breach** (p. 114)

**assignment** (p. 108)

**bill of exchange** (p. 111)

**breach of contract** (p. 112)

**cheque** (p. 111)

**condition precedent** (p. 118)

**condition subsequent** (p. 118)

**conditions** (p. 112)

**deposit** (p. 120)

**discharge by agreement** (p. 118)

**discharge by performance** (p. 112)

**down payment** (p. 121)

**duress** (p. 104)

**duty of good faith** (p. 101)

**economic duress** (p. 105)

**fraudulent misrepresentation** (p. 103)

**frustration** (p. 115)

**holder in due course** (p. 110)

**innocent misrepresentation** (p. 102)

**liquidated damages** (p. 120)

**misunderstanding** (p. 97)

**mitigation** (p. 121)

**negligent misrepresentation** (p. 103)

**negotiable instruments** (p. 110)

***non est factum*** (p. 97)

**novation** (p. 107)

**one-sided mistake** (p. 96)

**parol evidence rule** (p. 98)

**promissory note** (p. 111)

**rectify** (p. 97)

**repudiation** (p. 114)

**rescission** (p. 102)

**shared mistake** (p. 97)

**standard-form contracts** (p. 99)

**statutory assignment** (p. 109)

**substantial performance** (p. 113)

**tender of performance** (p. 114)

**unconscionability** (p. 106)

**undue influence** (p. 105)

**void** (p. 97)

**voidable** (p. 103)

**warranties** (p. 112)

## Questions for Student Review

1. Distinguish between a shared mistake, a misunderstanding, and a one-sided mistake and explain how a court would deal with each of these problems. What other terms are used to refer to such mistakes?

2. Distinguish between innocent, fraudulent, and negligent misrepresentation, and indicate the remedies available for each.

3. Explain why it is easier to succeed with an action for innocent misrepresentation than for fraudulent or negligent misrepresentation.

4. Distinguish between a void and voidable contract. Why is this important to the discussion of duress and undue influence?

5. Explain what is meant by a presumption with respect to undue influence, the effect of such a presumption, and under what circumstances those presumptions will occur.

6. When will the courts find a contract to be unconscionable? What effect will that have on the position of the parties?

7. What is meant by privity of contract? Indicate any exceptions.

8. Explain what is meant by assignment in contract law, and indicate any limitations on what can be assigned.

9. What is necessary for an assignment to qualify as a statutory assignment? What is the importance of such a designation?

10. What does it mean to say the assignee is "subject to the equities"?

11. Define a negotiable instrument and distinguish between a cheque, a bill of exchange, and a promissory note.

12. Explain the position of an endorser of a negotiable instrument.

13. What is necessary for a person to qualify as a holder in due course? Why is that designation significant?

14. Distinguish between conditions and warranties, and explain how this can affect the discharge of contractual obligations.

15. Explain what is meant by substantial performance and how that can affect the discharge of contractual obligations.

16. Explain what is meant by repudiation and, in particular, the effect of anticipatory breach on the position of the parties to a contract.

17. What will cause a contract to be discharged through frustration and what are the consequences?

18. How has the effect of a frustrated contract been modified by statute?

19. What is necessary for a contract to be discharged or modified by agreement?

20. Explain the role promissory estoppel sometimes plays in the discharge or modification of a contract by agreement.

21. Distinguish between a condition precedent and a condition subsequent.

22. Explain the nature of an exemption clause in a contract and how the courts deal with such a provision.

23. Explain the remedy of damages as it applies to breach of contract.

24. Explain how damages for breach of contract are calculated and any limitations on their availability.

25. How are equitable remedies treated differently from an award of damages for breach of contract?

26. Distinguish between specific performance, an injunction, an accounting, and *quantum meruit*.

## Questions for Further Discussion

1. The law of contract is, to a large extent, based on the barter model. The guiding principle of this model is that the parties are in an equal bargaining position negotiating balanced

terms with which the courts shouldn't interfere. However, in recent years the courts have been showing an increasing willingness to overturn terms such as exculpatory clauses, or have been stepping in to protect individuals on the basis of good faith or unconscionability. Consider whether, in the process of attempting to ensure fairness in contract law, the courts and legislatures have unduly interfered with the underlying principle of the parties' freedom to contract as they wish. Should the guiding principle that the parties are in an equal bargaining position be abandoned and the courts take on more of a protective role?

2. Discuss the principle of privity of contract and whether it has any place in modern law. In your answer consider the problems it presents when the person injured by products or services supplied under contract is not the party who originally contracted for that product or service. Also look at the growing number of exceptions, including assignment of contractual rights and negotiable instruments, and consider whether the retention of privity causes more harm than it overcomes.

3. Consider the discharge of a contract through frustration. There are several restrictions on the application of frustration, such as the fact that the interfering event must be unexpected and out of the control of either party. In addition, legislation has been passed modifying the common-law position of "let the loss lie where it falls." Consider whether anyone should be allowed to escape his or her contractual obligations on the basis of frustration. Should the application of the principle be broader so that there are not so many limitations involved? Does the statutory interference reduce the problem or make it worse? Is there any place for the doctrine of frustration in modern contract law?

4. Whether they were misled intentionally or innocently will not affect the nature of the injury suffered by the victims of false statements. However, it makes a significant difference to the remedies available to the victims if they were misled intentionally or innocently. The victims of intentional misrepresentations can sue for damages, whereas the victim of an innocent misrepresentation can ask only for rescission. Should a distinction be drawn between fraudulent and innocent misrepresentation in determining the availability of damages as a remedy? Does the recognition of negligent misrepresentation solve the dilemma?

## Cases for Discussion

1. *Miller Paving Limited v. B. Gottardo Construction Ltd.* 2007 ONCA 422 (CanLII); 285 D.L.R. (4th) 568

   Miller supplied materials (aggregate) to the general contractor, Gottardo Construction, which was building a road extension for SLF. After supplying the material, Miller would invoice Gottardo, which would check the invoice against deliveries and then pay by cheque. At the end of the job Miller submitted the final invoice, which Gottardo paid, and then Miller and Gottardo signed a contract entitled "Memorandum of Release." This document was an acknowledgement by Miller that it had been paid in full and indicated that it was binding on all parties. Unfortunately, Miller discovered that a number of invoices for over $400 000 had been missed and subsequently submitted them to Gottardo for payment. The construction company refused to pay, and this action was brought seeking the outstanding payments. What would be the basis for their action? Explain the arguments on both sides and the likely outcome.

2. *Harrity and Northeast Yachts 1998 Ltd. v. Kennedy* 2009 NBCA 60 (CanLII)

   Robert Harrity, the principal of Northeast Yachts, acted as an agent in the sale of a Bayliner boat owned by Malcolm Clark and sold to Margaret Kennedy. As Kennedy looked over the boat, Harrity stated that it had a new motor, a new drive, and a painted hull. The boat was purchased after having the boat surveyed by a marine surveyor. Unfortunately, after five hours of use the motor broke down with several things going wrong. It turned out that the engine was not new but rebuilt and Kennedy sued. Harrity claimed that when he stated that the engine was new he meant it was new to that boat. What is the basis for Kennedy's complaint, the arguments for the parties and the likely outcome? How would it affect your answer to know that after the sale when the bill of sale was drawn up a paragraph was added. This document stated that the boat was inspected, that the boat was bought "as is, where is," and that there were no other representations from the agent with respect to the transactions.

3.  *968703 Ontario Ltd. v. Vernon*, 2002 CanLII 35158 (ONCA)

    Vernon agreed to have the assets of his business sold at auction with the proceeds to be deposited in a bank account. Vernon was to get the first $450 000, the auctioneer was to get the next $150 000, and anything else was to be split 70/30. But after two days the auctioneer made no bank deposit, keeping the entire $100 000 proceeds for himself. Vernon refused to let him back on his property to complete the auction. The auctioneer sued and Vernon countersued. Explain the arguments for both parties, who breached the contract, and their resulting responsibilities. How would it affect your answer to know that the auctioneer had sold some of the assets belonging to Vernon at a lower price than agreed, to a company with which the auctioneer was associated?

4.  *Cassidy v. Canada Publishing Corp.* 1989 CanLII 2864 (BC S.C.)

    Ms. Cassidy had a contract to work as part of an authoring team to produce a social studies text to be used in the public schools. Her contribution, among other things, was to provide a chapter on criminal law. Unfortunately, the Ministry of Education changed the curriculum requirements, and her contribution could no longer be used. She was dropped from the writing team with no compensation for the work she had done. She sued. Explain the arguments raised by both sides and the likely outcome. Note that this is a province where the *Frustrated Contracts Act* requires compensation to be paid for work done benefitting one of the parties.

5.  *Rodrigues v. Walters (Cole)* 2009 CanLII 62056 (On S.C.)

    Mr. and Mrs. Rodrigues entered into a contract to sell their home to Elizabeth Walters in July of 2004. Mrs. Walters paid a deposit of $10 000, with the agreement conditional upon Mrs. Walters being able to obtain financing for the purchase. On 4 August 2004, the agent presented a waiver of the condition precedent, indicating that Mrs. Walters had arranged financing for the purchase. On the strength of the now-firm contract, Mr. and Mrs. Rodrigues entered into a contract to purchase another home from James Barclay, putting down a substantial deposit. When the time came to complete the transaction, Mrs. Walters told Mr. and Mrs. Rodrigues that she did not have the financing in place and that she would not be going though with the purchase unless they lowered the price. This forced the Rodrigues to terminate their contract for the Barclay home, forfeiting the deposit paid. They also were threatened with a substantial lawsuit and had to pay an additional amount to settle the matter. The Rodrigues sued Mrs. Walters. Explain the basis of their complaint. What is the likely outcome and what would be included as a remedy? What difference would it have made if Mrs. Walters had not waived the subject to financing clause?

6. *Hix v. Ewachniuk,* 2010 BCCA 317 (CanLII)

Mrs. Ewachniuk had a son and two daughters. In 2006 at the age of 90 she died leaving a $2 million estate. In 2004 she had changed her will and left everything to her son. He had once practiced law and drew up the will for her and had it executed. Prior to this she had left her estate to be divided equally between her three children. The two daughters brought this action challenging the will. What would be the basis of their argument and the likely outcome? Would your answer be any different with the knowledge that the son had been responsible for preserving the family fortune from serious tax problems back in the 1960, and it was this fortune that had supported Mrs. Ewachniuk and her deceased husband over the years? There was no evidence of anything happening in the years immediately prior to the changed will that would have given her a reason to change it.

# Chapter 5
## Legislation in the Marketplace

Odua Images/Fotolia

## Learning Objectives

LO 1  Describe the function and form of the *Sale of Goods Act*

LO 2  Outline the duties of sellers and buyers

LO 3  Describe the nature and purpose of consumer protection legislation

LO 4  Review securities regulation in terms of consumer protection

LO 5  Discuss the role of federal legislation in controlling competition in the marketplace

LO 6  Consider the various methods for securing transactions

LO 7  Outline the legislation and its purpose in regulating securities

LO 8  Describe the process and objectives of bankruptcy

Our economic system is, to a large extent, based on a free market system, which in turn depends on the capacity of contracting parties to bargain freely. The courts, as a rule, will not interfere with people's freedom to make whatever bargain they want. Still, there are a number of situations where statutes have been passed to modify or interfere with that process. This chapter will examine some of the special situations where legislation controls or imposes special rules on sales transactions. The *Sale of Goods Act* applies to all contracts where goods are sold, whether they involve consumer or business transactions. **Consumer protection legislation** in its various forms is aimed at policing the marketplace, adjusting the balance between the bargaining position of the consumer and merchant, and establishing recourse for the worst abuses. An examination of the protections given investors with respect to the sale of various forms of securities and the stock market has been added in this edition. A significant portion of business and consumer transactions involves some form of security to ensure payment, and a significant portion of this chapter sets out the general principles involved in such **secured transactions**. Unfortunately, businesses fail and individuals often find themselves overwhelmed by debt. A brief discussion of the *Bankruptcy and Insolvency Act*, which provides relief for the debtor and protection for the creditor, is the final topic of this chapter. It is in this area of government interference, especially where that interference amounts to close regulation, that risk avoidance in the form of managerial vigilance is vital to a successful business enterprise. In this chapter the area of consumer protection legislation, particularly federal competition regulations, must be thoroughly understood, and practices and procedures implemented to ensure compliance. As will be seen, failure to do so can result in significant fines and other penalties, including extensive terms of imprisonment. Careful vigilance is especially important to ensure that regulations are strictly adhered to when dealing with the selling of shares and other securities to the public. The regulations discussed in this chapter often create strict liability offences where the only defence available is due diligence. As was explained earlier, a due diligence defence requires the accused to show that they had taken all reasonable steps to ensure that the offending conduct would not take place. This includes having proper procedures and safety programs in place as well as a broad training program for management and employees. The risks associated with sale of goods and secured transactions are not associated with government, but failure to appreciate the impact of legislation in these areas can be devastating to a business.

*Statutes modify business law*

## THE *SALE OF GOODS ACT*

**LO 1/LO 2**

In the 19th century several statutes were passed in England codifying the great volume of case law in an attempt to make the law more efficient. The *Sale of Goods Act* was one of those statutes and has been adopted with only minor differences in all common law provinces in Canada. The primary purpose of the sale of goods acts is to imply missing terms that the parties didn't think to include in their contract of sale. Because of this, unlike most other statutes, the parties can override the legislated provisions by clearly providing for a different result in their agreement. Remember, the *Sale of Goods Act* applies to all transactions where goods are sold, not just retail sales; therefore, it has important implications for all levels of business.

*Sale of Goods Act supplies missing terms*

## Goods or Services

For the *Act* to apply, goods must be transferred/sold

It must be emphasized that for the *Sale of Goods Act* to apply, there must be an actual sale where the goods are transferred from a seller to a purchaser. In our system, the title or ownership of the goods can be separated from possession, and in a sale, both the title and possession of the goods themselves must be transferred. Often the title of the goods will be transferred to a creditor as security for a loan. This sometimes involves the use of a bill of sale, but the nature of the transaction is for the loan to be repaid, with the debtor at all times retaining possession of the item used as security, unless there is a default. Only where the credit transaction involves a conditional sale will the *Sale of Goods Act* apply. In a conditional sale, the creditor is also the seller, and both possession and the title to the goods are eventually transferred to the purchaser.

The *Act* only applies where goods are sold. This requires that money be paid and that goods, as opposed to land or services, are involved. Goods or chattels are tangible, movable forms of property such as computers, cars, boats, furniture, and even locomotives or other heavy equipment. Where mixed goods and services are involved, if the transaction is primarily for a service such as an artist painting a portrait, the *Act* will not apply. The *Act* will apply, however, when that painting is resold. Where the service is incidental to obtaining the goods, as when a meal is supplied at a restaurant, the *Sale of Goods Act* will apply to the transaction. Where the service and goods can be separated, as with a mechanic repairing a car, the *Act* applies to the parts supplied but not to the labour.

---

### Case Summary 5.1 *Gee v. White Spot Ltd.; Pan et al. v. White Spot Ltd.*[1]

## Contaminated Food Covered by *Sale of Goods Act*

Gee (Plaintiff), White Spot Ltd. (Defendant) in a trial before the Supreme Court of British Columbia. Note that the same issues were involved in *Pan v. White Spot,* and so they were tried at the same time.

Two customers sued after suffering botulism poisoning from consuming food they obtained at the White Spot restaurant in Vancouver. They relied on section 18 of the British Columbia *Sale of Goods Act* that requires goods to be of merchantable quality and fit for normal use. The restaurant claimed it provided a service—not a good—and that the *Act* did not apply. The issue before the court was whether this constituted the sale of a service or the sale of a good covered by the

*Sale of Goods Act.* The judge, however, agreed with the plaintiff:

I agree with counsel's submission that an item on the menu offered for a fixed price is an offering of a finished product and is primarily an offering of the sale of a good or goods and not primarily an offering of a sale of services.

The contaminated food was not fit for the purpose for which it was sold and was not of merchantable quality. The contract of sale, therefore, had been breached, and the White Spot was liable for the injuries. This case shows how important the implied terms of the *Sale of Goods Act* can be, especially since the damages awarded were substantial.

---

[1](1986), 32 D.L.R. (4th) 238 (BC S.C.).

## Title and Risk

It is important to determine which party will bear the risk of damage to those goods while the transaction is proceeding. Under the *Sale of Goods Act* "risk follows title," meaning that whoever has the title to the goods when they are damaged must bear the loss. This area is often overridden by the parties in the agreement by including such phrases as CIF, FOB, or COD. With **CIF** (cost, insurance, and freight) contracts, one party is designated responsible for arranging the insurance and the transportation of the goods, thus assuming the risk. In **FOB** (free on board) contracts, the parties specify that title and risk will transfer at a specific place, for example, FOB the seller's loading dock. **COD** (cash on delivery) contracts require the purchase price to be paid and title and risk transferred when the goods are delivered to the purchaser. **Bills of lading** can also be used to control risk and title. When the goods are given to a common carrier, such as a bus line or other public freight carrying service, the carrier issues a receipt in the form of a Bill of Lading and it is a common practice for the seller to designate himself to receive those goods at their destination, thus retaining control over them during transport.

> Under the *Act* risk follows title, except . . .

> . . . in the case of CIF, FOB, COD, and bill of lading

In situations where such provisions are not made, risk will follow title and the transfer of title (the property in the goods) will be determined by the operation of five rules set out in the *Sale of Goods Act* (see Table 5.1).

**Rule #1** Where the goods sold are specific and identified, and nothing further has to be done to them, title transfers immediately upon the contract of sale being made. The purchaser bears the risk even though payment or delivery may take place at some later date and the goods continue in the hands of the seller.

> Five rules determine when title transfers

**Rule #2** If something has to be done to those goods to put them in a deliverable state, such as fixing a scratch or adjusting a part, title transfers when the repair is made and the customer is given notice that the goods are ready.

**Rule #3** If the goods have to be weighed or measured to determine price, title will transfer once that has been done and notice given.

### Table 5.1 Title and Risk

| Situation | Rule | Result |
|---|---|---|
| The sale of specific goods in a deliverable state | #1 | Title transfers immediately upon creation of the contract of sale |
| The sale of specific goods needing repairs, etc. | #2 | Title transfers when work is done and the purchaser is notified |
| The sale of specific goods needing to be weighed or measured | #3 | Title transfers when this is done and the purchaser is notified |
| The sale of goods on approval | #4 | Title transfers to the purchaser with<br>- Notification to seller of approval<br>- Passage of a specified or reasonable time<br>- Treatment of goods as the purchaser's own |
| The sale of goods that are not yet selected (from many) or not yet made at the time of contract | #5 | Title transfers when goods are unconditionally committed to contract with assent (expressed or implied) |

**Rule #4**  When goods are taken on approval or sale with the right to return them if the purchaser is not satisfied, title and risk transfer when the purchaser notifies the seller of his or her acceptance. If a time has been set to return the goods, title passes at the expiration of that time, and if no time is set, at the expiration of a reasonable time. Title will also pass when the purchaser acts towards those goods in a way consistent with having accepted them. For example, if cloth is involved and you make a dress out of it, the cloth is yours. You no longer have the right to return it.

**Rule #5**  When goods have not yet been made, or where a sample is relied on but the specific goods have not yet been selected, title only transfers after the particular goods to be purchased have been made (or selected and committed to the transaction) with the assent of the other party (usually the purchaser). In rules #2 and #3, actual notice is required, but the wording in #5 is broader; therefore, assent or approval can be implied. Suppose I were to leave my car at a tire store, specifying that four new tires were to be installed while I was shopping in the mall. Title would not transfer immediately. But when the seller chose the four tires and installed them on my wheel rims, they would be committed unconditionally to the transaction. My assent would be implied, since I left the merchant to make the choice and to install the tires on my car.

## Obligations of the Seller

Some of the most important provisions in the *Sale of Goods Act* relate to the seller's responsibility for the goods sold. Although the *Act* varies to some extent from province to province, there are usually four sections imposing conditions and warranties on the seller with respect to the nature of the goods supplied. As was the case with contracts generally, warranties are less important terms, and conditions are major terms, the breach of which will free the purchaser from his or her obligation to go through with the contract. This may make the difference between the right to return the goods to the seller for a refund or only to have the goods repaired or replaced. Note that the parties are free to designate a provision as a condition, thus making it important, when otherwise it would only be a warranty. All provinces have similar terms.

Obligations of seller under the Act: are
- To deliver good title (Condition)
- To deliver quiet possession (Warranty)
- To deliver goods free of liens (Warranty)

**Title**  There are several implied terms with respect to title. There is an implied condition that the seller must deliver **good title** to the goods to the purchaser. If it turns out later that the goods were stolen before the seller obtained them, whether the seller knew it or not, the purchaser can get his or her money back. There is an implied warranty requiring the seller to provide **quiet possession** with respect to the goods supplied. This means that the goods have to be usable as intended without interference. For example, if you purchased a cell phone but it could not work on any of the available networks, that would be a breach of quiet possession. Finally, there is an implied warranty that the goods will be free of any **charge or encumbrance**. This refers to a lien that gives a creditor the right to seize the goods upon default when the goods have been used as security for a loan. A wise purchaser will check for such liens when buying a car. If a valid lien is present, the purchaser will have the right to pay it off and seek reimbursement from the seller.

Case Summary 5.2 *Muskoka Fuels v. Hassan Steel Fabricators Limited*[2]

# Failure to Supply Goods of Merchantable Quality

Muskoka Fuels (Plaintiff/Respondent) and Hassan Steel Fabricators Limited (Defendant/Appellant) in this appeal in the Court of Appeal for Ontario.

Muskoka Fuels purchased a tank to store diesel fuel from Hassan Steel Fabricators Limited. It was established by experts that the fuel tank should have a life expectancy of at least ten years. However, it failed, causing a serious diesel spill after only 5 months of use with the result of over $71 000 in damages. The tank was made of stainless steel, and while it had an exterior lining the interior was bare metal. The spill was caused by a 3/16 hole that developed in the tank. It was clear that the hole was not there when purchased or installed and was not caused by any act of the purchaser. The likely cause was some unknown microbial action. In suing Hassan Muskoka relied on section 15(2) of the *Sale of Goods Act*, requiring that goods purchased "by description" must be of merchantable quality and free from any hidden defect. Although the exact cause of the failure was unknown, there was information in the industry about such failures, and Hassan should have know about the problem.

The manufacture of the tank without an interior coating was common practice and approved by the certifying agent for use in the province (Underwriters Laboratories of Canada). The lack of an interior coating was not the defect, although having one might have eliminated the problem. The defect was the susceptibility to the internal corrosion that led to the hole and made the tank unmerchantable. This constituted a breach of section 15(1) of the *Sale of Goods Act*. What caused the defect was unknown, but that there was a defect that caused the loss is clear from the facts.

This case shows the operation of section 15 of the *Sale of Goods Act*, especially that goods purchased from a dealer must be of merchantable quality. The goods must be free from hidden defects. Note that because this was a commercial purchase, a limitation clause could have been included by the seller to avoid the operation of this section of the *Sale of Goods Act*.

**Description or Sample**   If the goods are bought by **description** or by **sample** and what is delivered does not match the description or sample, the *Sale of Goods Act* implies conditions into the contract that permit the purchaser to refuse delivery. A purchaser buying a truckload of apples based on a sample Spartan would be able to refuse delivery if Macintosh apples were delivered. Sale by description not only covers situations where goods are bought through a catalogue or ordered from an advertisement, but also includes any purchase of goods that have been mass-produced. Since you do not choose one particular item over another, as they are all the same, you are relying on specifications (description) to make the purchase, and the goods must match that specification, picture, box, pamphlet, etc.

*Goods must match description or sample (Condition)*

**Quality**   Perhaps the most important implied obligation of the seller relates to the **fitness and quality** of the goods sold. The *Sale of Goods Act* requires that when goods are sold by description (which now is taken to mean all mass-produced goods), those goods must be of merchantable quality. This means essentially that the goods must be free of any defects that would render them unusable or interfere with their effectiveness. If they are defective in some way or fail earlier than expected, a condition of the contract has been breached, and a refund can be demanded. British Columbia has taken this even further, requiring the goods to be "durable for a reasonable period of time," and applies this protection to leased goods as well.

*Goods must be of merchantable quality (Condition)*

---

[2]2011 ONCA 355 (CanLII).

### Table 5.2 Implied Conditions and Warranties

| | | |
|---|---|---|
| Seller's obligations with respect to title | Seller must deliver property/good title | Condition |
| | Seller must deliver quiet possession | Warranty |
| | Goods must be free of charge or encumbrance | Warranty |
| When goods bought by description | Goods must correspond to description | Condition |
| Purchaser relies on advice of seller | Goods must be reasonably fit for purpose required | Condition |
| When goods bought by description | Goods must be of merchantable quality | Condition |
| When goods bought by sample | Goods must correspond to sample and be free of hidden defects | Condition |

**Goods must be fit for the purpose purchased (Condition)**

The *Act* also provides that when the purchaser relies on a seller's recommendation for goods that will do a specific job, the goods must be fit for that purpose. If you go to a paint store asking for a product suitable to cover a concrete floor and the product supplied then peels off the floor, a condition has been breached and you can recover not only the purchase price but also any costs you incur in stripping and repainting the floor.

**Limited warranties try to override these obligations**

Sellers often attempt to override these implied conditions of fitness and quality (see Table 5.2). A new product warranty is an attempt by the seller and manufacturer to limit the liability that would otherwise be implied by the provisions of the *Sale of Goods Act*. These warranties usually limit the time of the obligation to 90 days for electronic products, for example, or to a few years for automobiles. They also typically restrict the remedy available to repair or replace the product, and specifically exclude all other warranties, express or implied.

**Exemption clauses may limit liability**

In commercial transactions such limitation or exemption clauses will generally be enforced where they are clear and unambiguous. However, in consumer transactions most jurisdictions in Canada, and many in the United States, have included in their consumer protection legislation provisions that prohibit such all-encompassing limitation provisions. For example, if you check a manufacturer's warranty for a new automobile or electronic product, it will likely include a statement to the effect that "some states or provinces do not allow limitation on how long an implied warranty lasts or the exclusion of incidental or consequential damage, so the above limitation or exclusion may not apply to you." If you purchase a new car and the transmission breaks down or some other significant problem arises just after the warranty period expires, check the consumer protection legislation in your province. You still may have a right to have the problem corrected under "warranty."

In commercial transactions, the importance of such clauses as well as the extensive application of the *Sale of Goods Act* is illustrated by *Hunter Engineering Co. v. Syncrude Canada Ltd.*[3] In this case massive gears were sold as vital components of the huge conveyor belts used to convey the oil sands as they were extracted in the tar sands project of northern Alberta. The gears were defective, and the court held that the fitness and quality

---

[3][1989] 1 SCR 426 (SCC).

provision of the *Sale of Goods Act* applied, making Hunter Engineering liable to Syncrude for the defective parts. They had failed to contract out of that provision by including a carefully worded, limited warranty. It is interesting to note that another supplier of identical defective gears, Allis Chalmers, was not responsible because they had effectively limited their liability. It is, therefore, vital for a manufacturer or supplier of equipment or other services to take extreme care to include such exemption clauses in their transactions and to ensure that the wording goes no further than to cover the limitations in liability intended. The courts approach such clauses as being part of the negotiated terms of the contract with the liability assumed calculated into the consideration paid, and are, therefore, reluctant to overturn such clauses when they are clear and contain no ambiguity.

The *Act* implies many other important terms in sale of goods transactions. We can only mention a few here. Where no purchase price is stated, a reasonable price is implied. Where no date is specified, payment is due at a reasonable time, which is normally taken as the time of delivery. If the purchaser defaults and fails to take delivery of the goods or fails to pay for them, the seller is entitled to the normal contractual remedies, including damages, specific performance, and injunction discussed in Chapter 4. In addition, the seller has the right to **stoppage in *transitu***. This means that if the goods are in the hands of a transporter and being delivered to the purchaser at the time of default, the seller can intercept those goods and recover them from the transporter. Even if they do get into the hands of the purchaser, the seller has a limited right to recover them in the event of the purchaser's bankruptcy under the federal *Bankruptcy and Insolvency Act*. Where title has transferred and the full price is due and payable, even where delivery has not yet taken place, the seller can sue for the whole price in the event of a default—not just for lost profits and costs—a much more attractive remedy. Also, in some provinces, the *Sale of Goods Act* requires that there be evidence in writing if the sale is for over a certain amount ($50 in Alberta, $40 in Nova Scotia). Finally, it should be mentioned that each province has passed an international sale of goods act covering international sales transactions. This is essentially the adoption of the *United Nations Convention on Contracts for the International Sale of Goods*. International business transactions are a specific topic discussed in Chapter 10.

*If the purchaser defaults, the seller can stop goods in transit*

*If bankruptcy, seller has limited right to recover goods*

# CONSUMER PROTECTION LEGISLATION

**LO 3**

*Both federal and provincial consumer protection legislation*

As we use the term here, **consumer** refers to someone purchasing a product for his or her own use, not for resale, and normally not for use in a business activity. Historically, the common-law approach to consumer transactions has been *caveat emptor*, sometimes translated as "let the buyer beware." However, this is one area where many abuses have prompted governments at both the federal and provincial levels to enact legislation designed to protect the consumer.

## Provincial Legislation

While the legislation varies substantially from province to province, in the next few pages we will highlight some of the basic principles that the different provinces' legislation has in common.

Consumer goods must be of
minimum quality

**Quality and Fitness**   One of the most important protections provided relates to the quality of products and services supplied. As mentioned above, the *Sale of Goods Act* implies certain conditions and warranties related to title, fitness, quality, and nature (description) of goods supplied. Normally, the parties can override these provisions by including exemption clauses in the form of limited warranties, but where consumer transactions are involved, many provinces and territories have prohibited any attempt to do so. British Columbia's *Sale of Goods Act* includes these prohibitions, but in other provinces they are included in special consumer protection legislation. Thus, products must be fit for their purpose and of an acceptable quality, and sellers are liable for any failure, no matter what other provisions may be included in a limited warranty or other limitation clause in the contract. In Saskatchewan, these provisions not only apply to retailers but also to manufacturers giving people in that province the right to sue the manufacturer of the goods in contract, as well as in tort, for negligence. As mentioned in Chapter 4, where the product is dangerous and the seller breaches while knowing there is a risk to health or injury to property, criminal prosecution may result.

Case Summary 5.3 *Prebushewski v. Dodge City Auto (1984) Ltd.*[4]

## Breach of Warranty on New Truck

Prebushewski (Plaintiff/Appellant), Dodge City Auto (1984) Ltd. (Defendant/Respondent) in appeal before the Supreme Court of Canada.

Shawna Prebushewski purchased a new top-of-the-line Dodge Ram 4×4 truck. She also purchased an extended warranty. She borrowed $43 198.80 from the bank to finance the purchase. About 16 months later, she parked her truck near her place of employment, where it caught fire and was destroyed. It was determined that the cause of the fire was a defective daytime running light module. Ms. Prebushewski made a claim against the seller of the vehicle and the manufacturer (Dodge City Auto (1984) Ltd. and Chrysler Canada Ltd.) under the warranty agreement, claiming the fire was the result of a manufacturing defect. The dealer and the manufacturer refused the claim and simply told Ms. Prebushewski to make a claim to her insurer. She did this, but after the claim was paid out the proceeds were not enough to cover what was still owed the bank, which was $11 383.65. She then sued the manufacturer and the dealer.

The issue before the court was whether the damage caused by the defective light was covered under the *Consumer Protection Act* and whether it was a case for exemplary damages. At trial the manufacturer's representative admitted that they had been aware of these faulty daytime running light modules for several years and had not informed customers, nor had they issued a recall. The trial judge determined that the statutory warranty provisions of the Saskatchewan *Consumer Protection Act* had been breached, awarded general damages to Ms. Prebushewski to replace her truck and other expenses in the amount of $41 969.83 and also ordered exemplary damages (punitive damages) of an additional $25 000 on the basis that the violation of the *Consumer Protection Act* had been willful. The award of exemplary damages was overturned on appeal, but was reinstated at the Supreme Court of Canada level. The case illustrates how powerful and effective such consumer protection provisions can be.

Misleading and deceptive trade
practices are controlled

**Business Practices**   Consolidated consumer protection acts, or in some provinces separate specialized statutes, include provisions to protect consumers from unacceptable practices. They prohibit misleading and deceptive practices generally, and then list a

---

[4]SCC, [2005] 1 SCR 649; (2005) 253 D.L.R. (4th) 209.

number of unacceptable practices specifically. All involve different ways that merchants may deceive the consumer, whether intentionally or by mistake. These statutes also control unconscionable transactions where the consumer is taken advantage of because of factors such as undue pressure or some other vulnerability that results in the victim paying an unfair price, or some other harsh or adverse terms that are imposed in the contract. Such unconscionable transactions are unenforceable against the consumer. Some jurisdictions limit this unconscionability protection to mortgage contracts, where the courts have been given the power to modify, limit the obligations of, or otherwise change the terms of the agreements to make them more equitable. In most provinces, legislation also makes any false or misleading statement made in the course of the sale, whether in advertising or by the salesperson, a term of the contract, thus making it actionable as a breach, with all of the normal remedies available. Other remedies against the merchant engaging in unacceptable business practices include injunctions and damages, fines, and other penalties. These provincial statutes aimed at consumer protection are typical examples of statutes creating provincial offences.

*Unconscionable transactions are controlled*

**Specific Businesses Controlled**    These statutes also include provisions to control specific types of businesses that are prone to abuse. Where door-to-door sales (direct sales) are involved, cooling-off periods, as well as other protections, are provided giving the consumer the option of rescinding the contract within a specified number of days. Some provinces apply cooling off periods in other situations as well. Where **executory contracts** are involved (contracts to be performed in the future), a written contract is required and the consumer's obligations, before performance, are limited. Referral selling and the delivery of unsolicited goods are also controlled. Referral selling involves giving a discount when the purchaser provides a list of names for the seller to contact. Responsibility for unsolicited credit cards, and for lost and stolen credit cards, is also severely restricted. Legislation that requires that the true cost of borrowing be disclosed in all loan transactions is also in place. Sometimes the practice of including bonuses or using different methods of calculating the effect of compounding interest will lead people to pay much more for their loans than they expected. Now the actual rate and costs associated with the transaction, including the total amount to be paid, must be made clear at the outset. The practice of buying income tax returns and making short-term loans before payday are also controlled. These practices often involve huge interest rates exceeding the rate permitted under federal or provincial legislation. Most jurisdictions also control organizations that supply their customers' credit information to others, as well as debt-collecting practices. Some provinces, including Manitoba and Saskatchewan, have also included provisions controlling or prohibiting negative option schemes. (This is where the seller makes changes to an existing contract or sends unsolicited goods or services without the approval of the consumer, imposing an obligation to pay unless the seller is notified otherwise.) These are just some of the provisions that are typically included in such consumer protection statutes. These acts also control businesses such as prepaid funeral services and burial plots, food plan sales, future service contracts such as gym memberships, and so forth.

*Cooling-off period is provided for door-to-door sales*

*True cost of borrowing must be disclosed*

**Consumer Bureaus**    Provincial statutes aimed at consumer protection are typical examples of statutes that create provincial offences. Government agencies are set up to investigate abusive practices and to resolve disputes. Typically, such organizations have the power to investigate, to search and seize records, to assist the consumer to obtain

*Powerful government agencies enforce rules*

remedies, and to impose fines and other penalties in their own right. Large fines can be effective, but these bodies also often have the right to take away a licence and put the offender out of business. In many cases these consumer protection statutes provide for dual enforcement. The consumer, or even the designated government official, is given the option of proceeding in a civil action seeking damages and/or seeking an injunction to stop the offending conduct. But that government official will usually also have the power of treating the offending conduct as an offence punishable by fine and imprisonment. Although these offences are not criminal in a technical sense (only the federal government can pass criminal law), they can have the same impact and are referred to as **quasi-criminal offences** or **provincial offences**. The procedure involved for prosecution is set out in provincial legislation such as Ontario's *Provincial Offences Act*.[5] Because there is the potential of a significant fine and imprisonment, the *Charter of Rights* protections relating to legal process (sections 7–14) and other criminal prosecution requirements, including the "presumption of innocence" and "proof beyond a reasonable doubt" discussed in Chapter 1, generally apply. Each province provides an internet site to assist consumers needing information or to make complaints. For example, see Ontario's Ministry of Consumer Services (http://www.sse.gov.on.ca/mcs/en/pages/default.aspx).

**New Directions**    In 2002 Ontario enacted a comprehensive consumer protection statute, the *Consumer Protection Act*,[6] which likely points the way that consumer statutes will go in other jurisdictions as well. It not only ensures that warranties for fitness and quality set out in the *Sale of Goods Act* cannot be overridden in a consumer purchase agreement by a limited warranty, but also extends that protection to leases and services. The *Act* includes the provisions previously found in the former *Consumer Protection Act* and *Business Practices Act* of that province. Thus, there is a list of specified unfair practices that are prohibited (including unconscionable representations), as well as the remedies and procedures to follow when these provisions and others are violated. Extensive powers are given under the *Act* to search, seize, make orders, create offences, and so on. The current *Consumer Protection Act* also sets out regulations and prohibitions with respect to specific businesses and business activities, including agreements requiring future performance (such as the payment of price); time-share agreements; personal development agreements such as those provided by fitness clubs; agreements made over the internet; the repair of motor vehicles and other goods; and credit transactions in general. The current *Consumer Protection Act* and regulations also have extensive provisions to govern internet consumer transactions. Other jurisdictions, including British Columbia, Newfoundland and Labrador, and the Territories, have adopted similar comprehensive consumer protection statutes.

Non-government agencies also help consumers

There are other nongovernment, consumer-oriented organizations, both for-profit and nonprofit, that can be helpful to the disadvantaged consumer. The Better Business Bureau (BBB) is a unique organization consisting of and supported by member businesses. The idea is that reputable businesses are served by weeding out unscrupulous businesses that damage other members of the business community. The BBB issues reports, but also provides a service directly to the public where they can inquire about specific businesses to learn of any complaints that have been made. Other online services are also available to provide

---

[5]RSO 1990, c. P. 33.
[6]2002, S.O. 2002, c.30, Sch. A.

information and links to services and lawyers practicing in specific areas of the law, including the Canadian Legal Information Institute (CanLII), often referred to in this text. Most provinces also have some form of legal aid services staffed by lawyers and law students.

The increasing use of online shopping by consumers offers new challenges to lawmakers. While the legislation discussed here applies to those transactions as well, additional problems arise, such as jurisdiction, which complicate enforcement. Private companies are moving in to fill the gap. For instance, PayPal has developed a system to ensure that consumers get what they pay for. Credit companies such as Visa offer similar guarantees. These matters will be discussed in more detail in Chapter 10.

In addition to the consumer protection legislation discussed above, there are consumer protection provisions included in other acts such as the personal property security acts discussed below in this chapter. Also, each province has specific statutes designed to provide consumer protection in specialized industries. The residential tenancy acts are good examples and will be discussed in some detail in Chapter 8. Another important area where such protection is provided is with securities regulation. When corporations (discussed in Chapter 7) go public they sell securities in the form of shares, bonds and derivatives, usually in the stock market. There is great potential for abuse here, and each province has enacted statutes designed to regulate the industry. In this respect, Canada is very different from the United States where the securities industry is controlled federally. Although there have been attempts to create a federal securities regulator in Canada, at the time of writing the jurisdiction remains with the provinces resulting in separate regulating bodies for each province and territory, although there is considerable cooperation through a national organization called the Canadian Securities Administrators. Still the basic principles are the same between provinces and are summarized below. Note that an agreement in principle is in place as of September 2013 between the federal government, British Columbia and Ontario to create a common securities regulator, but Alberta has stated that they have no intention of joining and Quebec has threatened to challenge the arrangement in court on constitutional grounds.

> Securities regulation in Canada takes place provincially rather than federally

**Securities Regulation**    The main purpose of securities regulators is to ensure that the marketplace works efficiently. All participants (buyers and sellers) must have the same, complete and accurate information with respect to the securities being sold. It also requires that all corporate officers, marketers, investors, underwriters, dealers and brokers act honestly and with integrity. The idea is to create a level playing field so that the market is efficient, fair and free from manipulation. This is accomplished in several ways. First the structure of the corporation itself must meet certain qualifications if it is to sell securities to the public. The qualifications are outlined in Chapter 7 and include the requirement that an annual shareholders' meeting be held, that audited financial statements be produced, and that there be a functioning auditing committee independent of management to oversee the financial affairs of the corporation.

# LO 4

> The object is to ensure that all players have complete and accurate information

> Corporation must meet structural standards to issue shares to public

In order to distribute securities to the public, the corporation must first issue a **prospectus**. This is essentially a public disclosure document and must "provide full, true and plain disclosure of all material facts relating to the securities issued or proposed to be distributed."[7] (Thus, a prospectus will contain not only audited financial statements, but also information with relation to the rights included in the security being sold, the nature

---

[7]*Securities Act* RSO 1990, c S.5, s. 56 (1).

of the business, any major undertakings, what assets are held, information about directors and officers of the corporation, and any other material information that might affect the value of the securities. There is also a requirement that the prospectus be certified by the chief executive officer, chief financial officer and directors of the corporation, as well as by promoters, guarantors, and underwriters if involved, making them responsible and subject to penalty if the prospectus contains any inaccurate or misleading information. Even where that misleading statement is corrected, those individuals listed above may be subject to civil liability to anyone suffering loss by relying on it before it was corrected.

**Prospectus is a public disclosure document**

A preliminary prospectus is first filed with the securities commission and if the commission is satisfied, a receipt for the prospectus will be issued and the sale of securities to the public can then take place. If there were deficiencies with the preliminary prospectus, they must be corrected before the prospectus and securities can be distributed. Even then the obligation of disclosure continues. Any material event taking place that will affect the accuracy of the information in the prospectus or any subsequent material changes in the corporation's affairs that may have an impact on the value of the securities must also be disclosed in the form of a news release and filed with the commission. Also, audited financial reports must continue to be filed at least annually. As can be seen, this creates an atmosphere of continuous disclosure of information so that, at least as much as reasonably possible, all parties dealing in securities have the same accurate information.

## Case Summary 5.4 *Kerr v. Danier Leather Inc.*[8]

# Importance of Proper Disclosure in Prospectus

Kerr (Plaintiff/Appellant), Danier Leather Inc. (Defendant/Respondent) in an action brought in the Ontario Superior Court of Justice, then appealed to the Court of Appeal and then to the Supreme Court of Canada.

To support an issue of shares to the public, Danier issued a prospectus to that end. The information in it was correct at the day of issue, including a forecast of earnings, but because of an unexpected change in actual performance, that forecast was misleading by the date the public offering closed. Section 57 (1) of the Ontario *Securities Act* required that the issuer of a prospectus disclose any "material changes" that take place after the prospectus is issued. No such disclosure was made, and a class action was brought on behalf of investors who purchased shares relying on that prospectus, claiming the misrepresentation caused them a loss.

The case hung on the definition of a material change. The *Act* states that a material change includes "a change in the business, operations or capital of the issuer that would reasonably be expected to have a significant effect on the market price or value of any of the securities of the issue."

There was no such change here, rather what changed was a "material fact," that is, the fluctuation of sales. Such facts have to be correct as stated in the prospectus at the time of issue, but not corrected as they change after that. On appeal to the Supreme Court of Canada, the class action failed.

The case illustrates how careful a corporation must be to ensure that any important information is disclosed and correct in a prospectus before selling shares and also illustrates the technical nature of the rules. It also demonstrates the potential effectiveness of being able to bring a class action representing many shareholders. Although it failed here, such a class action can be a very effective method of enforcing shareholder rights. Also note that while this is a class action, the successful defendant, Danier Leather, was also entitled to its costs, which were very substantial. Those costs were awarded against the representative client who had to pay personally. That was within the discretion of the court, and it exercised that discretion in this case.

---

[8][2007] 3 SCR 331; 286 D.L.R. (4th) 601.

The danger is that certain parties, privy to undisclosed information, may take advantage of that privileged information by buying or selling securities to the disadvantage of other traders who do not have access to that information. This is referred to as **insider trading** and is strictly controlled both through provincial legislation and the *Criminal Code*. Insiders include directors and officers of companies, shareholders holding over 10 percent of the shares (in Ontario), others designated as insiders by the legislation and all those in a special relationship to the company who are aware of confidential information not available to the public because of their position, including bankers, lawyers, accountants and the like. Insiders are not prohibited from buying or selling shares in the corporation, but they must not do so using privileged information. To ensure that they don't, insiders are required to file a report with the commission showing what trades they have made over the designated period. Later when information becomes public those trades can be reviewed to see if large blocks of shares were traded, indicating such misuse of privileged information. Tipping, where the insider tells a relative or other person the privileged information who then unlawfully relies on that information to trade in the company's shares, is also prohibited. Insiders who misuse confidential information in this way, as well as tippers and the tippees, are subject to serious penalties.

Insiders prohibited from using confidential information in trading Tipping also prohibited

Finally, the legislation empowers the securities commissions to register participants in the industry, including underwriters, advisers, investment fund managers and various types of dealers. The commission sets guidelines as to who can be registered and what qualifications and standards they must meet. Any misbehaviour on their part will subject them to penalties, including deregistration prohibiting them from further participation in the industry. Note that some persons involved in the industry may be exempt from such registration because they belong to other professional bodies such as lawyers or mortgage brokers but their conduct will be subject to the same type of supervision within the professional body to which they belong. Penalties for infringement in Ontario can be up to $5 million (or up to triple the profit made or loss avoided) and up to 5 years imprisonment. They can also be ordered to make restitution or pay compensation to their victims and still be subject to civil remedies and criminal penalties.

Misbehaviour subject to severe penalties

Steps have been taken to provide for internet filing of information and cooperative dealings between the securities commissions of the various provinces, but a new problem has arisen. Crowdfunding, which occurs primarily on the internet, involves the opportunity to raise funds for new, small business enterprises by posting information about the business idea. Interested investors are then invited to participate in its development by donating funds, often for a perk that may include a gift, the first opportunity to use or take advantage of the proposed product, or even a share of the business. In many instances the process has been successful in raising significant amounts of funds for the budding entrepreneur. Unsophisticated investors have the opportunity to support what they feel might be worthwhile projects without undertaking more risk than their small investment. Like most undertakings on the internet, there are few regulations and wide open opportunities for fraudulent schemes to separate people from their money. In theory, the securities regulations and other consumer protection provisions discussed above apply to these transactions as well, especially where a share of the business is involved. However, this is one more area where modern communication technology has outdistanced regulation and created basically a freewheeling unregulated environment. It will be interesting to see what steps are taken in this area in the future.

Crowdfunding and the internet creating new challenges

## LO 5    Federal Legislation

The federal government also has significant consumer protection legislation enforced by government departments. These agencies control hazardous products, govern the bankruptcy process, and control anticompetitive business practices. They also investigate and resolve consumer complaints. They have considerable power and funds to support research, investigation, hearings, and education.

### The Federal *Competition Act*

A free market system is considered vital to our economy. It benefits business by making businesses more efficient as they become more competitive and benefits consumers with lower prices and better selection in the marketplace. But there is a tendency for businesses to try to manipulate that market to their advantage. The federal *Competition Act* is designed to prevent that manipulation. The stated purpose of the *Act* "is to maintain and encourage competition in Canada."[9] The *Competition Tribunal Act*[10] is supportive legislation that creates a tribunal to hear appeals from certain decisions made by the Competition Bureau. The Competition Bureau is the body responsible for the administration and enforcement of the *Competition Act*, the *Consumer Packaging and Labelling Act* (nonfood products), the *Textile Labelling Act*, and the *Precious Metals Marking Act*.

*Competition Act* controls mergers and abusive practices

The anticompetitive practices controlled by the *Competition Act* range from mergers and acquisitions designed to create monopolies and reduce competition to direct interference in the marketplace in the form of price fixing or false advertising. The tools used to prevent such conduct range from persuasion and pressure to the imposition of civil or criminal penalties. Note that the kinds of offensive conduct outlined below are intended not to be a comprehensive review of the *Act*, but only to set out significant examples of the kinds of activities and practices controlled. Throughout the discussion, always remember that economic principles, not technical legal rules, usually determine the outcomes.

Prohibited practices lessen competition

**Interference with Competition**    Conspiracies that lessen competition are prohibited. Note that until recently only those conspiracies that "unduly lessened" competition were prohibited, but this has been changed as a result of recent amendments that make any conspiracy that lessens competition an offence, even where such an agreement might make an industry more efficient. A **conspiracy** involves businesses getting together and, through agreement, trying to control the market and prices. The basic principle here is that any agreement or arrangement between businesses that has the effect of restricting competition constitutes an offence. When merchants agree not to sell a product below a certain price, or agree not to open a store or compete in a given area, their conduct is prohibited, and substantial penalties can be imposed. When these agreements attempt to increase prices by restricting production, transport, storage, or supply, or by increasing the price of insurance, the businesses have committed an

---

[9]*Competition Act*, RSC 1985, c. C-34 (1.1).
[10]RSC 1985 c. 19 (2nd Supp.).

indictable offence. Any attempt at **bid rigging** is also an indictable offence. This involves competitors conspiring together to control the bids on a particular project so that they can control the winning bid and charge a higher price. With respect to banks and other financial institutions, any agreement to fix rates of interest and prices charged for services also constitutes an indictable offence. The penalties have also been increased with fines "in the discretion of the court" (a $30 million fine was awarded recently) and up to 14 years imprisonment or both for bid rigging and up to $25 million and 14 years for other offenses.

Perhaps the most common form of conspiracy in restraint of trade is simple **price fixing**. This involves two or more parties agreeing not to sell products below a specified price. In 2005 a settlement was made involving several separate class actions for price fixing. The cases involved a complex conspiracy of price fixing and market sharing of the sale of vitamins in Canada. The settlement involved a consent order for $140 million.[11] Representations made to the public that are false or misleading are also offences under this section of the *Act*. This includes false and misleading statements made with respect to the labeling of the product or with respect to its promotion. Penalties for false or misleading statements made in association with telemarketing and with respect to contests and prizes are also set out here. **Double ticketing**, where two prices are placed on an item and the merchant sells at the higher price, is also prohibited under this part of the *Act*.

*Offences include manipulating the market through the control of the resale price or credit*

*Telemarketers must disclose all pertinent information*

### Pyramid Selling

When people pay a fee to participate in a multilevel organization that is not based on the sale of a product, it is an offence with substantial fines and jail terms. Under the *Competition Act* (section 55.1), the fine is at the discretion of the court and may include a penalty of up to five years' imprisonment. Under the *Criminal Code* (section 206(1)e), such schemes constitute a summary conviction offence. See Table 5.3 for a summary of offences against competition.

*Multilevel schemes must also make full disclosure*

*Pyramid selling is prohibited*

---

**Table 5.3 Offences Against Competition (Part VI of the *Act*)**

- Conspiracies that involve fixing prices, including restricting supply production, storage, and transportation of goods
- Bid rigging
- Banks controlling interest rates and service charges
- Giving one customer, but not others, a better rate, discount, or advantage
- Suppliers controlling the resale price to consumers (retail)
- False and misleading representations
- Double ticketing
- Telemarketers not disclosing required information or misleading the consumer
- Multilevel schemes not disclosing required information
- Pyramid selling schemes

---

[11]*Ford v. F. Hoffman-La Roche Ltd.* (2005), 74 O.R. (3d) 758.

## Case Summary 5.5 *R. v. Friskie*[12]

# Pyramid Sales Scheme Violates *Criminal Code*

Mrs. Friskie (Accused/Appellant), Her Majesty the Queen (Prosecutor/Respondent) in an appeal before the Saskatchewan Court of Appeal.

Mrs. Friskie started to market the Skybiz 2000 product in September 1999. The product was an internet website leased for one year to be used by businesses and families. The product was useful and had value, but the scheme for selling it was multilevel. The agents would make sales by making referrals of purchasers to Skybiz, which retained 70 percent of the price to distribute to the sales force in the form of commissions. Each associate would bring in more recruits by selling them websites, and these recruits would in turn gather more recruits to which to sell more websites. Each level would obtain a portion of the sales of the levels below (through the commissions from Skybiz), thus recouping their own investment and making a further profit as more websites were sold down the line. Mrs. Friskie had earned $130 000 within the first nine months. She was charged under section 206(1)(e) of the *Criminal Code*. The Court of Appeal had to determine whether this conduct amounted to a pyramid scheme as prohibited under the *Criminal Code*.

Multilevel marketing is permitted as regulated under the *Competition Act,* but a pyramid scheme is prohibited both in the *Competition Act* and in the *Criminal Code*. The difference is that all proceeds and commissions in a multilevel scheme must be from the sale of a product, and there must be no payment associated with joining or belonging to the scheme. Here, many of the recruits purchased multiple websites that would otherwise be useless to them just to enhance their position in the scheme.

The Court of Appeal determined that although the websites involved a useful product for some individuals, in most instances the 70% retained by Skybiz was a fee paid by a recruit to join which in turn was distributed to the various levels creating an incentive to get more recruits to join. Although some of the sales were legitimate, because part of them constituted a pyramid scheme, the whole scheme was illegal.

The amounts paid to the associates by Skybiz were a sham, since they were paid out of the 70 percent fund created from the amounts paid substantially by new recruits. The conviction of Mrs. Friskie was upheld, as was the $20 000 fine imposed on her. Although she did not know she was participating in an illegal act, she did know that her income was generated by the payments made by the new recruits buying into the pyramid. The line between a multilevel and pyramid scheme is a fine one, and this case crossed that line. Note that it was argued that this fell under the multilevel marketing regulation in the *Competition Act,* but the judge here observed that this did not affect the *Criminal Code* provision, and whether it was an offence under the *Competition Act* was irrelevant with respect to whether the conduct constituted an offence under the *Criminal Code*.

**Deceptive Marketing Practices**   Table 5.4 provides a list of deceptive marketing practices. These prohibitions against deceptive and misleading practices are designed to protect the consumer. Any false or misleading representation made to the public with respect to the promotion of a product is reviewable. Any claim with respect to life expectancy or performance of a product that is not based on proper testing, and any misleading warranty promises that are not likely to be carried out, constitute reviewable conduct. Testimonials or tests used to promote a product must only be used where such a test or testimonial has been published and permission has been given to use it. When goods are being sold at a "bargain" price and a regular price is referred to as the one normally offered by that particular retailer or others, they must be able to show that a reasonable volume of the product was sold at that higher price. The *Sears* case is a good example.

---

[12]2003 SKCA 72 (CanLII).

**Table 5.4** Deceptive Marketing Practices (Part VII.1 of the *Act*)

- False and misleading representations to the public
- Warranty or performance claims not supported by tests
- Unsupported tests and testimonials
- Bargain prices not supported by goods sold at regular prices
- Selling at a higher price than advertised
- Bait-and-switch selling
- Failure to disclose chances and value of prizes in a contest
- Failure to base contests on skill or random chance

Deceptive Marketing Practices include
- False and misleading representations
- Warranty or performance claims not supported by tests
- Unsupported tests and testimonials
- Bargain prices not supported by goods sold at regular prices
- Bait-and-switch tactics

Sears advertised a particular brand of tires as being on sale. The ad said, "Save 45%," when in fact Sears regularly sold only about 2 percent of those tires at the posted price. The ad inflated the regular cost of the tires, making the sales price appear more attractive. This constituted misleading advertising, which could bring "harm to consumers, business competitors, and competition in general." The penalty included a payment of $500 000 and a commitment not to do it again.[13] Note that the *Competition Act* requires a court, when determining whether an advertisement is false or misleading, to not only look a the literal wording but also the general impression of the ad. Merchants must be very careful when approving such adds to consider the general message in order to avoid running afoul of the act. Note also that current penalties being assessed with respect to misleading advertising make the Sears fines look insignificant.

The practice of **bait and switch** is also prohibited. This is where a product is advertised at one price, but not enough of the product is supplied so that the customer can be persuaded to buy a higher-priced alternative.

Where there are attempts to manipulate the market using "deceit, falsehood, or other fraudulent means," such actions are indictable offences under the *Criminal Code* with a potential penalty of up to 14 years' imprisonment.

**Full Disclosure**   The *Act* requires that merchants make full disclosure of all relevant information in many situations. For example, where games or contests are involved, the number of prizes and chances of winning must be disclosed and the winners must be chosen at random or based on a skill. Telemarketing operations must disclose such information as the identity of the seller and the nature and true price of the product being sold. Where multilevel marketing schemes are involved, representations as to earnings and sales (both actual and expected) must be fair and accurate. Of course, in all situations any false or misleading representation is an offence.

**Other Matters Reviewable by the Tribunal**   Often a supplier will manipulate the sale of a product at the retail level by restricting the supply of their product to only merchants that will sell at the suggested retail price, or by tying the sale of one product to another. If such a practice may have an adverse effect on competition in the market, the tribunal can order that the conduct stop. Where a supplier sells a product below

Schemes that tie the sale of products to other products or restrict who can buy are reviewable by tribunal

---

[13]*Commissioner of Competition v. Sears Canada Inc.* Comp. Trib. No. CT-2002-004.

Predatory pricing is also reviewable by tribunal

cost or uses other means to drive out a competitor or otherwise restrict competition, that is **predatory pricing** and is also reviewable. Under the *Act* this is referred to as abuse of dominant position.

The goal is to balance the loss of competition against increased efficiency

Tribunal can review mergers and acquisitions

**Mergers and Acquisitions**   There is a growing trend today towards mergers and acquisitions. This can lead to less competition on the one hand but can also, through economies of scale, create a more efficient business. A main objective of the *Competition Act* and its supporting legislation is to balance these considerations. Where businesses of any size have merged through the acquisition of assets or the purchase of shares so that competition is substantially lessened, the Competition Tribunal has the power to review the acquisition and order, among other things, the dissolution of the resulting corporation. When the merger is with a supplier, a competitor, or a customer, the merger will be in more danger of being disallowed as substantially lessening competition than if the merger is with an unrelated business. Table 5.5 provides a summary of matters reviewable by the Competition Tribunal.

---

## Case Summary 5.6 *R. v. Mitsubishi Corp.*[14]

## Indirect Involvement in Price Fixing Also an Offence

Mitsubishi (Accused), Her Majesty the Queen (Prosecutor) in a trial before the Ontario Superior Court of Justice.

This case involves a conspiracy by representatives of several corporations to restrict production and fix the price of graphite electrodes in world markets. These electrodes are important components used in steel foundries. One of the major corporations involved in Canada was UCAR, and Mitsubishi Corp. owned 50 percent of UCAR US. A representative of Mitsubishi was seconded to UCAR US and participated in meetings and otherwise was involved in the conspiracy. UCAR US sent memos and instructions to its Canadian subsidiary setting out policies and instructions with respect to the implementation of the agreement. The companies that were the major conspirators in violation of section 46(1) of the *Competition Act* were UCAR and SGL AG, and they were fined $11 million and $12.5 million after making guilty pleas, but this action is against Mitsubishi for violation of section 21(1) of the *Criminal Code*, which makes it a crime to aid or abet the commission of such a crime. The court had to determine whether the conduct of Mitsubishi and its representative violated this section of the *Criminal Code,* and also what an appropriate penalty would be.

Although it was clear that Mitsubishi itself did not sell the graphite electrodes in Canada, was not a principal party in the conspiracy, and had no direct involvement in it, its representative was at the meetings and had knowledge of the conspiracy. That knowledge is imputed to the representative's employer, Mitsubishi. The American affiliate sent instructions to its Canadian subsidiary with respect to the implementation of the agreement. Although the company willingly submitted to the Canadian courts and cooperated with the investigation, the conspiracy in question had a serious impact on the Canadian economy, and the company was found guilty of aiding and abetting the commission of that offence. Mitsubishi was fined $1 million. The fine imposed was economically significant and calculated to send a message to others that such anticompetitive behaviour would not be tolerated.

This case illustrates not only that such conspiracies in restraint of trade, while tempting in a business sense, will not be tolerated in Canada, but also that even those only marginally connected with the offence may still be guilty of aiding and abetting and be subject to significant fines. Even being aware of the conspiracy and implementing policies that support it, while not directly participating, will still result in significant penalties.

---

[14]2005 CanLII 21873; 40 C.P.R. (4th) 333, (ON S.C.).

---

### Table 5.5 Matters Reviewable by the Competition Tribunal

- Suppliers only selling goods to some retailers
- Suppliers setting a minimum price for resale
- Selling of one product tied to the sale of another
- Abuses of power
- Selling products below cost to defeat a competitor
- Mergers and acquisitions that affect competition
- Predatory pricing

---

Other federal statutes include the *Food and Drugs Act*, which regulates dangerous food and pharmaceuticals. For example, mandatory nutritional labeling has been established for prepackaged food products and beverages under food and drug regulations. There is also a *Hazardous Products Act*, which regulates dangerous products, prohibits some products, and requires appropriate warnings on others. The *Canada Consumer Product Safety Act* was passed into law in 2011, which, in addition to giving regulators the power to force immediate recalls of dangerous products, requires manufacturers to report incidents of products causing injury, and to keep detailed records so that sold products can be traced. The passage of this *Act* also involved major changes to the *Hazardous Products Act* so that these statutes would be compatible. These federal statutes also create specific criminal offences for certain kinds of prohibited conduct, and the new *Act* increases the potential penalty to $5 million for violations under that *Act*.

Of course, the *Criminal Code* protects consumers by setting out several serious offences, especially with respect to fraud. A fraud involves any situation where deception is used to cheat a person out of money or property. There are many different sections of the *Criminal Code* setting out penalties for different ways that fraud can be committed. One prominent example of a serious fraud committed on investors is the largest **Ponzi scheme** in U.S. history, committed by Bernard Madoff. A Ponzi scheme is an investment program where the early investors are paid out returns on their investments, not from earnings but from funds supplied by later investors, thus deceptively sustaining the myth of the success of the investment. The fraudster skims any money remaining until there is nothing left for the other investors. This is similar to the pyramid scheme discussed above. Mr. Madoff was able to keep his Ponzi scheme going for over 40 years and defrauded investors of over $50 billion. Similar Ponzi schemes have taken place in Canada.

## SECURED TRANSACTIONS

**LO 6/LO 7**

Security arrangements assure creditor of repayment

As a general rule, the simple promise embodied in a contract to repay debt is not good enough for a creditor to loan money. Whether in the consumer world or in arranging business financing, some extra assurance is required to ensure that the creditor will be repaid. This is usually accomplished by the debtor providing security, by giving the creditor first claim on some asset at least equal to the value of the debt. In the event of default, the creditor has first claim on that asset (see Figure 5.1). Any form of property can be used to create such security. Real property (land and permanent structures built on that land) is

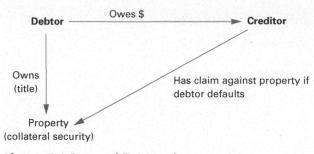

**Figure 5.1** Secured Transactions

Real property and personal property are used as security

normally the preferred form of security, but other forms of property can also be used. The use of real property as security will be discussed in a subsequent chapter.

Personal property, both tangible in the form of goods or chattels and intangible in the form of a right or claim one party has against another, can also be used as security. Share certificates, bonds, and negotiable instruments such as cheques and promissory notes are examples of intangible personal property. The documents involved merely represent the actual claim or right. The *Personal Property Security Acts* (*P.P.S.A.*) in place in all English-speaking provinces control secured transactions involving personal property. Historically, there were separate statutes in place for the different ways that personal property could be used as security. **Conditional sales, chattel mortgages,** and **assignment of book accounts** each had their own statute. Today these separate statutes have all been replaced by the *P.P.S.A.*, but it should be noted that there still has to be a contract creating the secured transaction, and these often take the form of those traditional agreements (conditional sales, chattel mortgages, and assignment of book accounts). A significant advantage of the *Personal Property Security Act* is to bring all transactions involving personal property as security under one statutory umbrella, with one consistent approach—no matter what form the security takes. A second advantage is that the *Act* allows any form of personal property—tangible or intangible—to be used. This flexibility creates a much more comprehensive system. An important change under the *Act* involves title. Historically, with a conditional sale, the title remained with the seller/creditor until full payment. With a chattel mortgage title was transferred to the creditor then transferred back upon full payment. Today, under the PPSA, title now stays with the borrower no matter what the contract says, but the rights given to the creditor remain the same.

Conditional sales, chattel mortgages, and assignment of book accounts are now under *P.P.S.A.* . . .

. . . but these standard forms of contract are still often used in credit transactions

*P.P.S.A.* accommodates all forms of personal property as security

Now title remains with the borrower

A security is created by giving the creditor first claim against the assets used as security. This is accomplished in a unique way under the *Act*. The transaction should be viewed in three stages—first the agreement; second, attachment; and third, perfection (see Figure 5.2). In fact, these steps often take place simultaneously, but conceptually distinguishing among the stages makes it easier to understand. When the contract is entered into it sets out the rights and obligations between the parties and designates the

| Creation of contract | Attachment | Perfection |
| --- | --- | --- |
| Contents of agreement determine rights of parties | Value given for security taken | 1. By registration or<br>2. By taking possession of property (security) (not repossession) |

**Figure 5.2** The Process

asset (such as a vehicle) to be used as security. The creditor still has no claim against the car, having provided no actual benefit to the debtor at this stage. **Attachment** takes place when value is given under the contract to the debtor. At that point the creditor obtains a claim against the asset. If money is involved, attachment takes place when the money is provided to the debtor. But what happens when the debtor wrongfully resells those assets to some third party or uses them as security in another transaction? The whole idea of security is to give the creditor a first claim in these circumstances. It would be unjust to allow the creditor to retake those goods from the third party, who has no way of knowing of the creditor's claim to the asset. To solve this problem, a registry has been created so third parties dealing with the assets can check to see if someone else has a claim against them. There is, therefore, an obligation on the creditor with the secured interest in the asset to register that claim in the appropriate registry, which perfects the security.

*Attachment gives the creditor rights against the debtor*

This final stage is called **perfection**, which is primarily accomplished through **registration**. Anyone dealing with such goods is well advised to search the registry before purchase. Perfection gives the creditor a prior claim to the property that is good against any subsequent holder or claimant. If Jones, through a chattel mortgage agreement that uses his car as security, borrows money from Ace Credit Union, the credit union has no claim against the car until they advance the funds. At that point their security attaches. In the event of default, this gives them a claim against the car while it is in Jones's possession, but not if it is resold. The credit union then perfects its secured interest by registering the claim. This is accomplished by filing a simple, standard form at the appropriate registry. Now anyone interested in buying or taking the vehicle as security in another transaction can search the registry to determine if there are any prior claims (called liens or charges). Finding such a claim should dissuade the buyer from the transaction or cause him or her to make sure the creditor is paid first, because the credit union's registered claim now has priority. When someone buys a vehicle, especially a used vehicle, he or she should always "search the title." That is the process described above.

*Perfection is accomplished by registration*

*Perfection gives the creditor rights to security that are good against all subsequent claimants*

Perfection can also take place by the creditor taking possession of the property used as security. This is usually done when intangible claims, such as stock certificates, bonds, or negotiable instruments, are used to secure the debt. However, the original document, not a photocopy, is required to accomplish perfection by possession. The creditor's security is established by the fact that the possession of the original document prevents it from being used to support another transaction. The key to understanding the *Personal Property Security Act* is to understand the process of attachment and perfection: Attachment gives the creditor a claim to the property or goods against the debtor, and perfection gives the creditor a claim to the property or goods against all others.

*Perfection can take place by possession*

## Case Summary 5.7 *Doran, Re,*[15]

## All Leases with Option to Purchase Must Also Be Perfected

This case concerned the bankruptcy of Mr. Doran before the Supreme Court of Nova Scotia and Easyhome, a creditor in that action.

Mr. Doran and his wife rented furniture from Easyhome in November 2003. The terms of the rental agreement provided for payment by the week and an option to purchase the furniture. The contract also made it clear that this was not a conditional sale or a credit transaction. Almost two years later, after making regular payments, Mr. and Mrs. Doran made an assignment in bankruptcy,

[15]2006 NSSC 123 (CanLII) (2006); 243 NSR (2d) 139.

transferring their assets over to a trustee in bankruptcy. Easyhome claimed that they were the true owners of the furniture and demanded its return. The trustee in bankruptcy refused, claiming that this was a credit transaction where personal property in the form of the furniture was used as security, and the *Personal Property Security Act* of the province required that Easyhome's interest in the furniture be perfected by registration, which it wasn't. Easyhome took the position that this was not a lease for credit situation but a true lease arrangement where Easyhome retained ownership and had never given it up. As such, the *Personal Property Security Act* did not apply and its interest in the furniture did not have to be registered.

The judge found that, although it was arranged on a weekly basis, this was a long-term lease, and because there was an option to purchase the subject matter, it was the kind of lease contemplated under the *Personal Property Security Act*. Since it had not been perfected through registration, the trustee in bankruptcy had priority, and Easyhome lost its claim to the furniture. It is interesting to note that some forms of assets, including furniture, can be retained by the bankrupt, but that did not apply in this case because at the time of the assignment in bankruptcy the Dorans did not actually own the furniture; they just had an option to purchase it.

Not only does this case illustrate the difference between a true lease and those with an option to purchase, which are covered by the *Personal Property Security Act*, it also illustrates that the danger of failing to perfect even applies when the property is assigned to a trustee in bankruptcy. The case also introduces the topic of bankruptcy, which will be dealt with subsequently in this chapter.

**Creditor has the right to repossess and resell upon default**

In actual practice the operation of the *Personal Property Security Act* can be quite complicated, especially where a variety of claims are involved. But once attachment and perfection, described above, are understood, the basic principle is relatively straightforward. In the event of default, the essential right of the creditor is to obtain and resell the property used as security. Where the tangible personal property involves goods that are not in the possession of the creditor, this process entails repossessing those goods from the debtor. It must be emphasized that when the contract gives the creditor this right upon default, there is no need to get a court order or otherwise involve official government services. Repossession is usually accomplished through employees or the services of a private agent called a bailiff. It is important to note that no force or violence can be used. When a car is locked in a garage or furniture is in a house and no permission is forthcoming, a court order must be obtained to get it. But when a debtor is in default and her car is parked on the street, she should not be surprised to return to it one day and find it gone. No notice or other process is necessary; the default authorizes the repossession.

**Court order is not needed to repossess . . .**

**. . . but force cannot be used**

Once possession has been gained, the goods can be sold to recover the debt. But anyone who has an interest, including the original debtor, must be notified of the sale and given a chance to redeem the goods by making appropriate payment. The seller must make an effort to obtain a fair price upon sale. This is usually done at public auction, although it can be done by private sale, provided the process is "commercially reasonable." Any excess obtained from the sale over the amount owed, less the costs of the process, must be paid to the debtor. If there is a deficit or shortfall, that amount is still owed by the debtor. If the sale was done properly, further steps can be taken to collect the remaining debt. Note that in some provinces, where consumer sales are involved, such a shortfall is not recoverable. Thus in British Columbia, when a consumer defaults on a car loan, the finance company has a choice. It can ignore the security and sue the debtor, or it can seize the car, but it cannot do both. Once the company has repossessed the car, that is the end of the remedy; it can seize or sue, but not both.

**Creditor must give the debtor notice and the opportunity to redeem the goods before resale**

**If resale is properly handled, creditor has the right to sue for deficit**

## Other Forms of Security

A problem has always existed in the construction industry where suppliers of labour and materials deal with contractors. Because the contractor normally does not own the property, the suppliers of goods or subcontractors have nothing to claim against if they are not paid. This has been remedied in all common law provinces and the territories with builders' lien/construction lien/mechanics' lien acts, which give suppliers and subcontractors a claim against the property if they are not paid (see Figure 5.3). A subcontractor can now register a lien against the property, which can eventually force the sale of the property if the subcontractor is not paid. The property owner is protected from this possibility by retaining an amount variously referred to as a **holdback, lienfund** or amount retained (7–20 percent of the amount owing to the contractor, depending on the province or territory) and making this available to satisfy the claims of the subcontractors or suppliers. Upon payment of the funds held back, an application can be made to the court to have the liens removed, and thus the property owner will have no further obligation even when the amounts claimed exceed the amount of the holdback. Where the payment is disputed, the property owner can pay the holdback amount into court, and the court will hold the funds until the matter is determined by the court or otherwise resolved.

*Builders' liens protect contractors, sub trades, workers, and suppliers*

The guarantee is another way to create security. It involves three parties—the creditor, the debtor, and the guarantor (see Figure 5.4). Instead of some property being put up as security, the guarantee involves someone else (the guarantor) agreeing to be responsible for the debt if the debtor defaults. Note that the guarantor has no obligation under this agreement until the debtor actually defaults. When the party co-signs the debt, this is known as an indemnity, and the debtors stand side-by-side, both obligated under the contract, in contrast to a guarantee, where the guarantor stands behind the debtor and only has an obligation when there is a default. Note that the guarantee is one of the forms of contract discussed in Chapter 3 that must be evidenced in writing to be enforceable. In most provinces, written evidence of an indemnity is not required. British Columbia, however, requires any promise by one person to be responsible for the debt of another to be evidenced in writing, thus catching both an indemnity and a guarantee. Often these agreements are put under seal to avoid any problem with consideration. Note that in Alberta such a guaranty must also be notarized.

*Guarantee: One person agrees to pay if debtor does not*

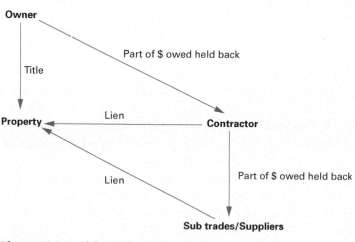

**Figure 5.3** Builders' Liens

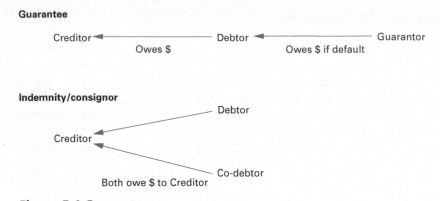

**Figure 5.4** Guarantee

Guarantor has the same defences as debtor

It should be noted that any defence that the debtor has against the creditor is also available to the guarantor, with the exception of bankruptcy and infancy. Thus, if the debtor purchases a car on credit and there is a default, the creditor can turn to the guarantor for payment. But if the car is defective or there has been fraud on the part of the vendor, the creditor/seller cannot demand payment from the guarantor instead of the debtor. Both can claim the defective product or fraud as a defence.

Guarantor steps into the shoes of the creditor upon payment

If the guarantor is called upon to pay the creditor, he or she steps into the shoes of the creditor and assumes the rights of the creditor. If, for example, there is some additional form of security involved, such as a charge against the debtor's car, the guarantor assumes the creditor's right to repossess that car from the debtor. It is also important to note that if the creditor and debtor get together and change the terms of the agreement to advance more credit, change the interest rates, or otherwise modify the agreement without the permission of the guarantor, the guarantor will not be bound by the new terms and will also be released from the original obligations provided he has not contracted out of this protection in the original guarantee. Thus a creditor must always remember to involve the guarantor in any arrangements made with the debtor that may affect the agreement. People often think that signing a guarantee is a mere formality, but it must be emphasized that to do so makes the guarantor responsible for the debt. The reason the guarantee is necessary in the first place is usually because the credit of the debtor is not very good and the creditor requires additional security. In other words, there is a good chance that there will be a default, and when that happens the guarantor will be required to pay. We should always take care not to sign a guarantee for any more than we are willing to assume as a debt.

Case Summary 5.8 *Guinness Tower Holdings Ltd. et al. v. Extranic Technologies Inc. et al.*[16]

## Changes to Contract Release Guarantor from Obligation

Guinness Tower Holdings Ltd. (Plaintiff), Extranic Technologies Inc. (Defendant) in a trial before the Supreme Court of British Columbia. Note that this summary deals with the position of Mr. Hsiao as guarantor of the defendant's lease.

The plaintiff landlord entered into a lease agreement with Extranic Technologies Inc. for the purpose of teaching English as a second language (ESL) to students on the premises. Mr. Eric Hsiao guaranteed the lease. The contract

[16]2004 BCSC 367 (CanLII).

provided for a five-year lease with an option to renew and to extend the leased premises to a larger area. In June 2002, Extranic started their ESL classes, but soon found they needed more space. They exercised their option to amend the lease and expand the premises. This involved signing a lease-amending agreement with the landlord, but because of complaints, this new agreement prohibited them from teaching ESL classes, which was a major part of their business. It also introduced a clause giving the landlord the right to cancel the expansion portion of the lease with only 30 days' notice. This amendment agreement was signed by representatives of the landlord and Extranic, but was not signed by the guarantor, Mr. Hsiao, who was not notified of the change.

The issue before the court was whether this change without the consent of the guarantor released him from the guarantee.

The business failed, and Extranic abandoned the premises. The landlord was claiming damages from Mr. Hsiao as guarantor on the lease. But Mr. Hsiao took the position that the lease terms were changed without his consent, and according to common law and equity, because his position was weakened by the change, he was released from the guarantee. The right to cancel the expansion portion of the lease on 30 days' notice and the prohibition of ESL classes on the premises were serious changes that weakened the position of the guarantor. The judge agreed. It was pointed out that parties were free to override this right for a guarantor to be released by changes by so stating in the original contract, but they had to do this clearly, and it had not been done in this instance. Mr. Hsiao was released as guarantor and had no further obligation under the lease.

This case points out how careful a creditor must be to ensure that the position of the guarantor is not weakened by any further dealings between the creditor and debtor without including the guarantor in the process.

## BANKRUPTCY AND INSOLVENCY                                    LO 8

No discussion of creditor/debtor relationships would be complete without an examination of the law of bankruptcy. People often confuse the terms *bankruptcy* and *insolvency*. When a person is **insolvent**, it simply means that he or she is unable to pay his or her bills as they become due. **Bankruptcy**, on the other hand, involves a process whereby the debtor's assets are actually transferred to an official, who then distributes them to the unpaid creditors. During 2012 there were 118 000 personal bankruptcies or consumer proposals filed, which were considerably less than the 152 000 filed the year before. The number of corporate bankruptcies was also considerably less.[17] The federal *Bankruptcy and Insolvency Act*[18] provides a uniform process of bankruptcy across Canada. The object of the legislation is to preserve as much of the assets of the bankrupt debtor as possible for the benefit of the creditors. At the same time, where personal bankruptcies are involved, the intention is to promote rehabilitation of the debtor so that he or she will have an insurmountable burden of debt removed and will again become a productive member of society.

There are two ways that bankruptcy can be accomplished. When a debtor voluntarily transfers his or her assets to a **trustee in bankruptcy** (a private professional authorized to act in the area), it is called an **assignment in bankruptcy**. When the debtor is forced into bankruptcy by his or her creditors, they must obtain a **receiving order** from the court to forcibly transfer those assets to the trustee. To obtain a receiving order the debtor must owe at least $1000 and have committed an act of bankruptcy such as a fraudulent preference (paying one creditor in preference to another), a fraudulent conveyance (transferring property to a spouse or friend to keep it out of the hands of a creditor), or fleeing the jurisdiction to avoid debts. These also constitute bankruptcy offences and are discussed

*Assignment is voluntary, but bankruptcy may also be forced by a receiving order*

---

[17]http://bankruptcy-canada.com/bankruptcy/bankruptcy-canada-statistics/
[18]RSC 1985, c. B-3.

below. However, the most common act of bankruptcy is insolvency, where the debtor has simply been unable to pay debts as they come due.

The function of the trustee, in addition to counselling individual debtors, is to look after the assets and preserve them, doing whatever is necessary to protect their value. This may involve making repairs, doing maintenance, or, where an operating business is involved, actually managing that business. But usually a trustee will determine the priorities among the creditors, sell assets where necessary, and distribute the proceeds to those creditors on the basis of their entitlement.

**Secured creditors**, as discussed above, retain their privileged position with respect to the assets taken as security. The trustee must surrender the asset to the secured creditor or pay out the valuation amount the creditor has estimated for the security. This way the onus is on the creditor to place a fair valuation on the security. If the valuation is low, the trustee will pay out that amount; if it is high, the trustee will surrender the security. When there is a shortfall and the valuation amount does not cover the debt, the secured creditors will become unsecured creditors for the remaining amount owed. In such cases, they usually only obtain a percentage of that amount, along with the other unsecured creditors. Sometimes a trustee will consider an outstanding debt not worth the trouble to go after considering the risks of collecting the debt balanced against the likely costs to be incurred. When the trustee abandons such a claim, the unpaid creditors can apply for a court order to assign that debt to them and pursue the claim on their own behalf. **Preferred creditors** are paid next. Some examples include funeral expenses, costs of the bankruptcy process itself, some taxes, and other fees such as employment insurance and workers' compensation. Also included are a limited amount of unpaid wages of employees and up to three months' back rent owed to a landlord. Recently, new federal legislation in the form of the *Wage Earner Protection Plan Act* (*WEPPA*) put employees and agents in a much better position to recover unpaid wages, commissions, vacation pay, and so on. Finally, any amount left over is distributed to the **unsecured creditors**. Each receives a percentage of what was originally owed. Often the amount the unsecured creditors receive is a very small portion of the actual debt; this underlines the wisdom of taking security when a debt is created, as discussed above. The trustee will often allow the bankrupt to keep certain assets that are difficult to sell and some assets such as tools and furniture, as well as pensions and RRSP investments, that are exempt from seizure. Other assets may be exempt depending on the province. Also, where a supplier before the bankruptcy has delivered goods to the bankrupt, that supplier can repossess those goods if a demand for repossession is given within 15 days of the bankruptcy and the goods are still in the same identifiable form.

Bankruptcy and insolvency are important for a business person in two ways. The first, of course, is to avoid your own business becoming insolvent and bankrupt, and the second is to avoid the negative consequences of doing business with those that become bankrupt. The most effective way to ensure the latter, after careful vetting of who you are doing business with, is to make sure that all such transactions are protected by taking security or a personal guarantee from parties with substantial assets. With respect to your own insolvency problems, steps can be taken to protect against the devastating effects of bankruptcy. For example, the shareholders of the company might ensure that any funds they have loaned to the operation are secured as well, and make sure that the corporate structure is firmly in place, ensuring limited liability (see Chapter 7). On the other hand, all efforts should be made not to disable such protections by signing personal guarantees to

**Assets are distributed:**

- First to secured creditors
- Then to preferred creditors
- Finally to unsecured creditors

Some possessions are exempt

support a company's indebtedness. If you are acting as an officer or director where there is the danger of personal liability, you should make sure that mechanisms are in place to ensure all required deductions from wages such as tax, CPP, and employment insurance premiums are deducted and forwarded to the government, and sufficient funds are in place to pay unpaid wages, including vacation pay. It is also possible to obtain insurance coverage to protect yourself while serving in one of these positions.

If the bankrupt commits a **bankruptcy offence** such as failing to disclose information, lying, or transferring property to a spouse or friend, this is a punishable offence and may ultimately interfere with him or her being discharged from the bankruptcy. The listed offences under the *Bankruptcy and Insolvency Act* are criminal offences with fines up to $10 000 or three years in jail, if treated as indictable offences. False claims made by creditors face similar penalties. The fraudulent transfer of real property with the intent to defraud creditors is also an indictable offence under section 387 of the *Criminal Code*, with a maximum term of imprisonment of two years.

*Bankruptcy offences are prohibited and penalized*

When the bankrupt is an individual, after nine months an application is automatically made to the court for the **discharge** of the bankrupt. If it is the first bankruptcy, the individual will automatically be discharged, unless the discharge is opposed by one of the creditors or there has been a bankruptcy offence committed. If less than 50 cents on the dollar is paid, the court will sometimes impose a **conditional discharge**, requiring the bankrupt to make some further payments. For a second bankruptcy, these times have been increased significantly. But usually once a person has been discharged, and has fulfilled any conditions imposed, he or she is then free of any former indebtedness. This means that even if that person were to win a lottery worth millions, those former creditors would have no claim, since the debts would have been discharged through bankruptcy. Note that some debts survive the bankruptcy process and will not be eliminated by a discharge. These include student loans less than seven years old, family maintenance obligations, child support, and court-imposed fines. Also "any debt or liability arising out of fraud, embezzlement, misappropriation or defalcation while acting in a fiduciary capacity" will not be discharged.[19]

*Discharge ends obligations*

*Note exceptions*

A corporation can also go through the bankruptcy process, but will not be ultimately discharged. After the bankruptcy process, all assets are distributed and the corporation is left as an empty shell or dissolved, although this is normally not worth the expense. Creditors, shareholders, and others may have other recourse against the directors, principals, and officers of the corporation. This will be discussed in Chapter 7.

*Corporations do not survive bankruptcy*

## Case Summary 5.9 *Orion Industries Ltd. v. Neil's General Contracting Ltd. and Keith G. Collins Ltd. v. Canadian Imperial Bank of Commerce*[20]

## Where a Debtor Pays One Creditor in Preference to the Others

Orion Industries made a payment to a creditor when it was insolvent and shortly before becoming bankrupt. In this action the trustee in bankruptcy is challenging that payment as a fraudulent preference favouring one creditor over the others and prohibited under the *Bankruptcy and Insolvency Act*. The lower court judge

---

[19]*Bankruptcy and insolvency act RSC 1985 c B-3 s.178(1)(d).*

[20]*Orion Industries Ltd. v. Neil's General Contracting Ltd.,* 2013 ABCA 330 (CanLII); *Keith G. Collins Ltd. v. Canadian Imperial Bank of Commerce* 2011 MBCA 41 (CanLII).

refused to invalidate the payment and did not require return of the money and that decision was upheld on appeal. The reasons are instructive. The payment was made to a storage facility so that the insolvent company could get access to and sell a valuable piece of equipment being stored at that facility. The payment had to be made to obtain the equipment so that it could be sold in an attempt to stay in business; therefore, the payment was not a fraudulent preference but a legitimate payment necessary for the continued operation of the business.

Compare this to *Keith G. Collins Ltd. v. Canadian Imperial Bank of Commerce*. Here the bankrupt made a payment to CIBC and the TD to pay off credit card debts out of a mortgage he obtained on his house. This was done one month before going bankrupt and clearly had the effect of favouring one creditor over the other. This was a fraudulent preference prohibited under the *Bankruptcy and Insolvency Act*, and the Banks were required to return the money paid to the trustee.

The cases clearly distinguish between a legitimate business expense and a prohibited fraudulent preference.

There are alternatives to the bankruptcy process, the most obvious consisting of simply negotiating alternative arrangements with creditors, including consolidating one's obligations. Where that fails, the *Bankruptcy and Insolvency Act* provides a formal alternative to the bankruptcy process. If individual debtors owe less than $250 000 not including a mortgage held on a primary residence (recently raised from $75 000), they can make a proposal to their creditors to pay less than the full amount owed, and/or over a longer time. If the offer is accepted and properly fulfilled, a certificate is issued and the debtor is then released from those obligations without having gone through bankruptcy. Failure to live up to such an accepted proposal will automatically result in bankruptcy. Debt counseling is involved, and the arrangements are usually made through the trustee/administrator. This is a **Division Two proposal**.

> Division Two proposal is an alternative for individuals

The arrangements for companies and larger debtors owing over $250 000 is more formal and complex; they involve more oversight and fall under a **Division One proposal**.

> Division One proposal is an alternative to bankruptcy for a company

A singular advantage for both Division One and Division Two proposals is that any action being taken to seize property is stopped until the time allotted for the proposal process has been completed. Even then, an application can be brought to the court to extend this time. This has led to some abuses. Large corporations with very large debt obligations (over $5 million) often proceed using a different federal statute, the *Companies' Creditors Arrangement Act* (C.C.A.A.),[21] which has a similar effect and allows some additional flexibility. Note that one of the objects of the recent amendments to the *Bankruptcy and Insolvency Act* was to bring the procedures followed under these two acts into closer harmony and create more flexibility with respect to proposals, allowing more efficient restructuring of the business.

> C.C.A.A. also provides alternative to bankruptcy for company

Usually secured creditors of large corporations will include terms in the original contract that give them the right to take over the management of that corporation in the event of default. This is called **receivership** and is often confused with bankruptcy. Receivership eliminates the need to go through the bankruptcy process, but the effect can be just as devastating on the business. A professional receiver is appointed by the creditor and literally takes over the business, displacing the directors and other managers in the process. No court order or formal process is required, just default on the debt triggering the receivership option. Table 5.6 provides a summary of the consequences of bankruptcy.

> Receivership is not bankruptcy

---

[21]RSC 1985, c. C-36.

## Table 5.6 Consequences of Bankruptcy

| Debtor | Options | Result |
|---|---|---|
| Debtor owing under $250 000 | Voluntary assignment<br>Receiving order (forced)<br>Division Two proposal | Loss of assets and ultimate discharge<br>Loss of assets and ultimate discharge<br>Payment as agreed; no bankruptcy |
| Debtor owing over $250 000 | Voluntary assignment<br>Receiving order (forced)<br>Division One proposal | Loss of assets and ultimate discharge<br>Loss of assets and ultimate discharge<br>Payment as agreed; no bankruptcy |
| Corporations | Receiving order (forced)<br>Division One proposal<br>Receivership (forced) | Loss of assets but no discharge; corporation dies<br>Payment as agreed; no bankruptcy; corporation survives<br>No bankruptcy, but creditors take over company |

## Key Terms

**assignment in bankruptcy** (p. 153)

**assignment of book accounts** (p. 148)

**attachment** (p. 149)

**bait and switch** (p. 145)

**bankruptcy** (p. 153)

**bankruptcy offence** (p. 155)

**bid rigging** (p. 143)

**bill of lading** (p. 131)

**charge or encumbrance** (p. 132)

**chattel mortgages** (p. 148)

**CIF** (p. 131)

**COD** (p. 131)

**conditional discharge** (p. 155)

**conditional sales** (p. 148)

**conspiracy** (p. 142)

**consumer** (p. 135)

**consumer protection legislation** (p. 129)

**Crowdfunding** (p. 141)

**description** (p. 133)

**discharge** (p. 155)

**Division One proposal** (p. 156)

**Division Two proposal** (p. 156)

**double ticketing** (p. 143)

**executory contracts** (p. 137)

**fitness and quality** (p. 133)

**FOB** (p. 131)

**good title** (p. 132)

**holdback** (p. 151)

**insolvent** (p. 153)

**insider trading** (p. 141)

**lienfund** (p. 151)

**perfection** (p. 149)

**Ponzi scheme** (p. 147)

**predatory pricing** (p. 146)

**preferred creditor** (p. 154)

**price fixing** (p. 143)

**prospectus** (p. 139)

**provincial offence** (p. 138)

**quasi-criminal offence** (p. 138)

**quiet possession** (p. 132)

**receivership** (p. 156)

**receiving order** (p. 153)

**registration** (p. 149)

**sample** (p. 133)

**secured creditor** (p. 154)

**secured transaction** (p. 129)

**stoppage in *transitu*** (p. 135)

**trustee in bankruptcy** (p. 153)

**unsecured creditor** (p. 154)

## Questions for Student Review

1. Explain the role played by the *Sale of Goods Act* and the qualifications that must be met for the *Act* to apply to a particular transaction.

2. How is the person who bears the risk determined under the *Sale of Goods Act*? Explain how this can be modified by the parties.

3. Explain the five rules that determine when title will pass under the *Sale of Goods Act*.

4. Explain the obligations imposed on a seller with respect to title, sale by sample and description, fitness and quality, and merchantable quality.

5. Discuss the nature of limitation or exemption clauses and their effect on the provisions of the *Sale of Goods Act*.

6. Describe the abusive business practices that are controlled by trade practices or business practices statutes. Describe how the statutes' provisions are enforced.

7. Explain what is meant by a cooling-off period, and explain how pyramid and referral selling schemes are controlled under consumer protection legislation.

8. Explain the purpose of a prospectus, how it is issued and what must be included.

9. Explain who are insiders, what controls are placed on them, and why.

10. Explain the purpose of the federal *Competition Act,* and list five competition offences.

11. Explain what is meant by bid rigging, double ticketing, and predatory pricing.

12. List and explain five deceptive marketing practices, and explain how they are treated differently from offences against competition.

13. What kind of matters are reviewable by the Competition Tribunal? What is the purpose of such a review?

14. Indicate other federal statutes that have a consumer protection aspect to them.

15. Explain what is meant by a secured transaction, indicating the special position of the creditor. Who holds the title under the Personal Property Security Act?

16. Distinguish between attachment and perfection, and describe how perfection can be accomplished.

17. Describe the rights of the creditor when there is a default under the *Personal Property Security Act*. What must the creditor do to protect his or her right to sue for a deficit?

18. Explain the significance of a holdback under the builders' lien or construction lien statutes.

19. Distinguish between an indemnity and a guarantee.

20. Explain the position of a guarantor with respect to the debtor's obligations and how those obligations are affected by subsequent dealings between the parties.

21. Distinguish between insolvency and bankruptcy, and between an assignment and a receiving order, and explain the role of a trustee in bankruptcy.

22. Distinguish between an act of bankruptcy and a bankruptcy offence.

23. Explain the positions of secured, preferred, and unsecured creditors in the event of a bankruptcy.

24. Explain the effect of a discharge on the bankrupt.

25. Explain the difference between the provisions of the Division One and Division Two proposals.

## Questions for Further Discussion

1. The purpose of the *Sale of Goods Act* is to imply terms into any contract of sale where the parties have not specifically agreed otherwise. In some provinces a few of these terms are imposed and any attempt to override them is void. Some other provinces accomplish the same result through separate consumer protection legislation. Consider whether the parties should be able to contract out of any of the terms of the *Sale of Goods Act*. Should such restrictions apply to both consumer and business transactions? Should there be any provision of the *Sale of Goods Act* that the parties cannot limit in this way? Should there be a distinction made between consumer and commercial transactions? Consider also consumer legislation generally. Should such legislation ever interfere with the parties' rights to have whatever terms they deem appropriate in a contract, whether it relates to a consumer transaction or not? Do such restrictions unduly interfere with the commercial process?

2. In Canada the regulation of the securities industry is provincial, whereas in the US it is federal. Would we be better off with a federal securities regulator? The purpose of such regulations is to create a level playing field. This is done by controlling the use of insider trading. Is this an interference with the marketplace? Would it be better to reduce the control of the use and disclosure of such information and restrict control to fraud, market manipulation, and misleading information?

3. Does the process of taking collateral security unfairly assist secured creditors over unsecured creditors? Does the requirement of registration sufficiently answer any criticism? In your answer, consider the process of bankruptcy and how secured creditors are given preferred treatment, often leaving an unsecured creditor with nothing.

4. Competition lies at the heart of the capitalist enterprise. Is government regulation necessary, and does it achieve its intended aims? What are some of the negative impacts of regulating competition? What other methods of controlling competition might be more effective?

5. Consider the bankruptcy process. It seems to be inconsistent with every principle of fundamental contract law and commercial relations. Is it fair to the creditors and to the debtor? What about discharge? Should debtors be allowed to escape their obligations in this way? Can you come up with a better alternative? Why prohibit student loans from being discharged through bankruptcy? Should there be other exceptions?

## Cases for Discussion

1. *Mustapha v. Culligan of Canada Ltd.*, 2008 SCC 27 (CanLII), (2008), 238 O.A.C. 130

   Mr. Mustapha suffered considerable trauma when, in the process of replacing a used jug of water with a new one, he discovered dead flies in his sealed jug of water. He had a particular sensitivity to this and suffered an unusual reaction. When he complained to the water producer, they offered him a few free water bottles and the cleaning of his dispenser as settlement. He was offended and sued. Explain the basis of his complaint and the likely outcome. What do you think should be the remedy Mr. Mustapha should receive, if anything? How would it affect your answer to discover that Mr. Mustapha suffered an unusual reaction, becoming argumentative and edgy, losing his sense of humour, and becoming unable to drink bottled water?

2.  *Royal Bank of Canada v. Head West Energy Inc.,* 2007 ABQB 154 (CanLII), 75 Alta. L.R. (4th) 263

    Harrison Western Canadian Inc. leased several trailers from Wells Fargo Equipment Finance Company. These leases were registered as secured transactions under the Alberta *Personal Property Security Act* in April and May of 2004 against Harrison Western Canadian Inc. at the appropriate registry. In July of that year Harrison Western changed its name to Head West. Subsequently, Head West became indebted to the Royal Bank, which secured that indebtedness with a general claim against the company's assets and registered that secured claim under the *P.P.S.A.* at the appropriate registry. Head West became insolvent and was taken over by a receiver, and the trailers were sold for $401 760. Both Wells Fargo and the Royal Bank claimed those funds. Which creditor was entitled to the funds and why?

3.  *Royal Bank of Canada v. Samson Management & Solutions Ltd.,* 2013 ONCA 313 (CanLII)

    Brasseur operated a business (Sampson Management and Solutions) in need of financing. He arranged a line of credit with the Royal Bank for $150 000. Both he and his wife (Cusack) signed guarantees in support of the loan. The amount was raised to $250 000 for which new guarantees were signed by both Braseur and his wife. Additional loans were arranged first for $500 000 and then $750 000. These new lines of credit were guaranteed by Brasseur, but not by his wife; nor did she consent to them. The Samson business failed in 2011 and the Royal Bank demanded payment from both Brasseur on the basis of his $750 000 and from his wife Cusack for her $250 000 guarantee. Explain what arguments she could raise in her defence.

    Would your answer change if the wording of the guarantee she signed allowed for further indebtedness and she had received independent legal advice?

4.  *R. v. Clarke Transport Canada Inc.* 1995 CanLII 7327 (ON SC); 130 D.L.R. (4th) 500 (Ont. Gen. Div.)

    A group of five companies provided freight forwarding services through container shipments in the Toronto area. They would take orders from customers, charge on the basis of weight, fill a container with those orders, and transport the goods by rail. All five agreed to control prices. They exchanged information and promised not to undercut each other's prices. Explain how their conduct would be viewed under the *Competition Act*. What arguments might they raise in their defence?

5.  *Jen-Zam Enterprises Inc. v. Mehrabian,* 2006 CanLII 17753 (ON S.C.)

    Mehrabian traded in a Toyota 4Runner on a new Subaru Legacy, receiving a $14 000 credit. It turned out later that the 4Runner was stolen. This action is brought by the automobile dealer (Jen-Zam) to recover the $14 000 from Mehrabian. Mehrabian takes the position that he is completely innocent, knowing nothing of the vehicle being stolen. Assuming that he is innocent and sold the vehicle not knowing it was stolen, explain the arguments available to the parties as to their respective legal positions and the likely outcome of the action.

# Chapter 6
## Agency and Employment

Poulsons Photography/Fotolia

## Learning Objectives

LO 1  Explain the roles and limitations placed on agents

LO 2  Discuss the liability of principals and agents

LO 3  Describe the fiduciary duty of agents and principals

LO 4  List appropriate processes for disciplining and terminating employees

LO 5  Create a list of best practices that would reduce the risk of an employee suing for unjust dismissal

LO 6  Discuss the role of unions in employment

LO 7  Outline the obligations of employers in providing a safe work environment

LO 8  Consider the impact of criminal activity on businesses

Essential aspects of any business activity are the various relationships through which business transactions are accomplished. These relationships may involve owners, managers, employees, agents, and independent contractors. They may also include consultants, lawyers, and accountants, as well as those who carry out the various functions associated with corporations, such as directors, officers, and shareholders. Each of these relationships involves unique responsibilities, rights, obligations, and benefits, all of which should be taken into consideration when a person makes decisions with respect to his or her business. These decisions start with choosing whether that business should be carried on through a proprietorship, a partnership, a corporation, or a combination of these methods. The functions and relationships associated with the different methods of carrying on business (proprietorships, partnerships, and corporations) will be the subject of the following chapter. In this chapter, we will look at agency and employment.

It is important to distinguish between independent contractors, employees, and agents. An **independent contractor** performs a specific service described in a contract. Normally, this is not an ongoing obligation. The contractor does the job and moves on. Essentially, a contractor works for himself or herself, as when a builder agrees to build a house for someone or a lawyer incorporates a company for a client. Consultants and auditors are other examples of independent contractors who provide a contracted service to a business. The general rules of contract law discussed in prior chapters govern the nature of these relationships.

An **employee**, on the other hand, commits to an employer in an ongoing relationship and is subject to more control from the principal and to specialized rules governing employment. A **dependant contractor** operates a separate business, but is more like an employee operating in an ongoing dependent relationship with one employer. The distinctions between employees, dependent contractors, and independent contractors will be discussed below, but the first topic to be examined in this chapter is the law of agency.

| | |
|---|---|
| An independent contractor works for him- or herself | |

An employee works for the employer in an ongoing relationship

## LO 1/LO 2/LO 3 AGENCY

The study of agency law is important because most business activity is carried on through agents, and agency forms a significant component of the law of partnership and corporations to be discussed in Chapter 7. It can't be emphasized enough that the selection of the individuals who will act as agents for a business will likely determine the success or failure of that business. An **agent** is someone who represents another person (the principal) in dealings with a third party (see Figure 6.1). Employees and dependent and independent contractors can find themselves acting as agents depending on the nature of their duties. For example, a plumber may be acting as an agent when he or she orders fixtures in the name of the property owner, but not when installing those fixtures into the building. Travel and insurance agents are examples of independent contractors acting as agents, whereas a store clerk or a restaurant server are examples of employees acting as agents. A consulting firm offering services exclusively to another firm over a period of years would likely qualify as a dependent contractor, and when those services involve arranging contracts with others they, too, are acting as agents. Of course, not all employees are agents, nor are all dependent or independent contractors agents. It depends on the duties they have been given. The agency relationship is usually created by contract, but in rare cases it can be created gratuitously where the agent acts as a volunteer. The important thing is to find that there has been a granting of authority to act on behalf of the principal. These duties usually consist of the agent entering into contracts on behalf of their principal, but this is not always the case. Lawyers will often file documents and account-

An agent represents a principal in dealings with a third party

An agent may be an employee or a dependent or independent contractor

Agency is usually created by contract

Agency depends on granting of authority

Agents usually enter into contracts on behalf of their principals

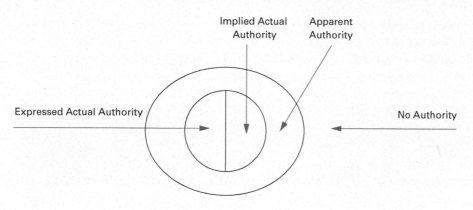

Implied Actual
Authority

Apparent
Authority

Expressed Actual Authority

No Authority

(An agent may have actual authority [expressed or implied] or apparent authority)

**Figure 6.1** Agent's Authority

ants file tax returns for clients. They are representing their clients but are not entering into contracts on their behalf.

## Principal/Third-Party Relationship

The unique aspect of agency law relates to the relationship between a principal and a third party, created when an agent functions as an intermediary. The primary consideration is to determine under what circumstances the third party will be able to hold the principal responsible for the conduct of the agent in contract law and/or in tort law.

**Authority**   In contract law the answer is deceptively straightforward. The principal and third party will be bound in contract when the agent has authority to bind the principal. The problem lies with respect to how that authority is obtained. When the principal has directly granted the authority to act, it is called **expressed authority** and will support the contract. But authority to act can also be implied from the surrounding circumstances. For example, a gas station attendant would have the **implied authority** to sell gas whether the employer has specifically stated he has such authority or not. Of course, there is no implied authority to sell the gas station itself. Such expressed or implied authority is referred to as an agent's **actual authority**.

The extent of an agent's **apparent authority** is a little more difficult to understand. Sometimes the principal may make it clear to an agent that his or her authority is limited, but not make that limitation clear to a third party. If the principal has done something to lead a third party to believe the agent has authority, even when he or she does not, the third party can rely on that representation and so the agent is said to act within his or her apparent authority. For example, where a clerk in an auto supply store has been told she cannot make any sale over $100 without the manager's express approval, she has a limitation on her authority. If, despite such instructions, the clerk sells an engine manifold for $300 without getting approval, the contract is still binding on the store. There is no expressed authority, and you cannot imply authority where there have been express instructions to the contrary. Rather, this is an example of apparent authority or agency by **estoppel**. Where the principal has led the third party to believe the agent has authority, the principal cannot later deny that authority. The principal put the clerk in a position where it would appear to a customer that she had the authority to make such a sale based

*Principal also bound where agent acts within apparent authority*

*Agent has apparent authority when principal leads another to that belief*

on the usual authority one would expect such a clerk to have in this situation. The principal is thus estopped from denying the agent had authority. Be careful not to confuse this with promissory estoppel discussed in Chapter 3. The latter involves a promise, whereas this involves the assertion of some fact indicating the agent has authority to act.

---

## Case Summary 6.1 *Financial Management Inc. v. Planidin*[1]

## The Consequences of Allowing Others to Believe Someone Is Your Agent

Financial Management Inc. (FMI) (Plaintiff/Respondent), Dennis Planidin and Associated Financial Planners Limited (Defendant). This action was brought in the Alberta Court of Queen's Bench and appealed to the Alberta Court of Appeal of Alberta. FMI and Associated settled the matter, so the appeal deals only with Mr. Planidin's personal liability.

Mr. Planidin was the branch manager of Associated and entered into an agreement with Mort Wayne, the manager of FMI, whereby the employees of FMI would sell certain financial products of Associated and earn a commission of 70–75 percent. In addition, FMI would get a further payment of 5-10 percent of those sales (called an override.) The commissions were paid, but the overrides to FMI were never paid. This action is brought by FMI, claiming those override payments from Associated and from Planidin personally. If Planidin was acting as agent only the principal (Associated) would be liable, but if he had no authority to act or if he was acting in his personal capacity, he would be personally liable to FMI.

The authority of an agent can be based on actual authority (expressed or implied) or on apparent authority.

In fact, Planidin never told Associated's head office about the arrangement and so there was no expressed authority here. It was not clear whether there was implied authority for Planidin to act, but there is no doubt that he did have the apparent authority to do so. As branch manager he was the agent of Associated, and it was common in the industry for branch managers to have this kind of authority. By making him their branch manager, Associated had held him out to be their agent and now was estopped from denying he had the authority. When Mort Wayne, the manager of FMI, made this arrangement with Planidin, he thought Planidin was acting as agent for Associated. And so the court determined that Planidin was acting as agent with apparent authority in the transaction and was therefore not personally liable.

The case not only illustrates the difference between actual authority (expressed or implied) and apparent authority, but also indicates that when an agent is acting with authority, either actual or apparent, that agent may be personally liable for transactions they enter into. Note that it was also argued that Planidin had a fiduciary duty to FMI, but he was the agent of Associated, not FMI, and since this was a commercial relationship there was no other "exceptional circumstances to justify the imposition of a fiduciary duty."

---

**Ratification**   There is an obvious overlap between apparent authority and implied authority. The distinction is only important where there have been express instructions to the agent not to act and he or she does so anyway. Of course, where the agent exceeds both his or her actual and apparent authority the principal is not bound. Still, if the principal likes the deal he or she can ratify the agreement, making it a binding contract. This can be done intentionally by the principal expressly ratifying the transaction, or it can be done inadvertently by the principal taking some benefit under the agreement. In effect, the principal is giving the agent authority to act after the fact, and that grant of authority works retroactively as if the agent always had authority. This is confusing but it is really the only way such **ratification** could create a binding contract.

In fact there are some restrictions on when a contract can be ratified. First, it must have been possible to enter into the contract at the time of ratification. For example, you cannot

*Agent can be given authority by ratification either intentionally or by implication*

*Ratification works retroactively*
*Restrictions on ratification*

[1]2006 ABCA 44, 384 A.R. 70; 56 Alta. L.R. (4th) 207.

ratify a contract of insurance after the house has burned down. Second, it must have been possible for the principal to enter into the contract at the time the agent purported to act. You cannot ratify a contract if you were insane at the time the contract was entered into by the agent. The ratification must take place within a reasonable time of the agent's unauthorized conduct. Also the agent must have identified the principal to the third party at the time he entered into the contract. The agent can't enter into a contract on behalf of some unidentified principal and then search around for a someone to ratify the contract.

### Vicarious Liability

Remember that the agent or employee will be personally liable to the third party victim for any torts that they commit. This discussion is to determine any additional responsibility the principal has for the torts committed by the agent. Where the agent is also an employee, the liability of the principal for the agent's conduct is based on the principles of vicarious liability as discussed in Chapter 2. Essentially, when the conduct of the employee is closely related to the job he or she is employed to do, the employer/principal will be liable as well as the employee (see Figure 6.2). If a company's purchasing agent negligently struck a pedestrian on her way to a meeting with suppliers, she would be liable, but so would her employer. She was acting within the scope of her employment when she committed the tort in question. However, if she were driving home or had diverted to do some personal chore, she would be on a "frolic of her own" and the company would not be responsible for her conduct.

The question is not always clear, and the Supreme Court of Canada has determined that the answer is usually based on the application of policy considerations. Chief Justice McLachlin stated, "The fundamental question is whether the wrongful act is sufficiently related to conduct authorized by the employer to justify the imposition of vicarious liability."[2] This leaves room for those acting outside their actual job responsibilities to still impose vicarious liability on the employers. These same obligations will likely apply when the agent is a dependent contractor. The more difficult question relates to when a principal will be liable for torts committed by an agent who is independent. Liability for the acts of independent contractors such as lawyers, accountants, insurance agents, and real estate agents is much more restricted. The principal will be liable only if the tort causing injury took place during the actual exercise of the authority that the principal gave the agent. The agent has to be in the process of transacting the business he or she was authorized to do. Usually this is restricted to the tort of fraud and negligent misstatement associated with the negotiation or enactment of the contract itself. Where my real estate agent negligently runs over someone on the way to show my house, I would not be held vicariously liable for her tort, but if she fraudulently or negligently misrepresented some aspect of the

*Vicarious liability will be imposed where an agent is also an employee and . . .*

*Where employee/agent commits tort in course of employment*

*Liability where agent is a dependent contractor is similar to employment*

*Liability of principal for agent's torts are limited where the agent is an independent contractor*

```
Vicarious liability
Principal/Employer  ◄──────────  Agent/Employee

Third-party victim
sues agent/employee              Agent/employee commits
and employer through agent       tort while performing
                                 duties

                    Third Party
```

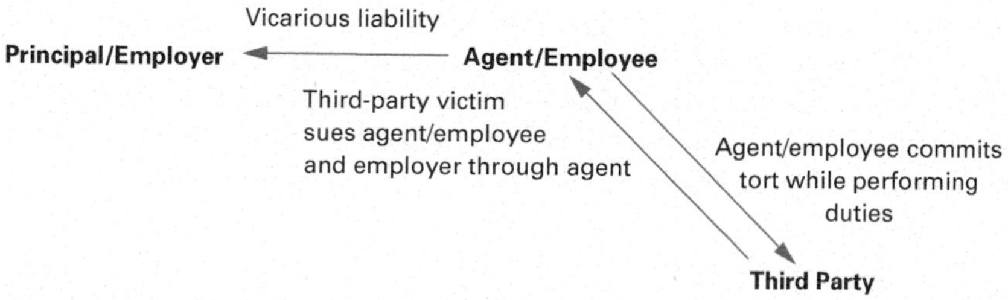

**Figure 6.2** Vicarious Liability

2*Bazley v. Curry*, [1999] 2 S.C.R. 534, (1999), 174 D.L.R. (4th) 45 (SCC).

**Principals will be responsible for their own torts committed through the agent**

house to a customer, I could be held vicariously liable for that tort. Of course, if the principal gave the false information to the agent, who then innocently passed it on, the agent would be completely innocent and it would be the principal alone who would be directly liable for the fraud or negligent statement. Be careful here. The agent may be found to have a duty to the third party to make sure the information provided by the principal is correct and be found negligent where he failed in this duty.[3]

Note that in the statutes of many jurisdictions the owner of a motor vehicle is vicariously liable when she loans out her vehicle.[4] Essentially, if you loan your car to someone and he gets into an accident that is his fault, you are responsible along with the driver.

## The Agent/Third-Party Relationship

**Normally, the agent can neither sue nor be sued under the contract**

**Exception: Agent may be sued for breach of warranty of authority**

As a general rule, the third party has no claim against the agent since the agent simply acts as an intermediary. The resulting contract is between the principal and a third party, and if not satisfied, the third party must look to the principal for a remedy. For the same reason, the agent has no claim against the third party and must look to the principal for any payment for services rendered. It is only when the agent has exceeded all authority to act that the third party can sue the agent for claiming authority not possessed. This is a tort action for "breach of warranty of authority," and gives the third party the right to obtain compensation from the agent for what was lost because of the unauthorized transaction.

---

### Case Summary 6.2 *Maple Engineering & Construction Canada Ltd. v. 1373988 Ontario Inc.*[5]

## Make It Clear When You Are Acting for a Company

Maple Engineering & Construction Canada Ltd. (Plaintiff), 1373988 and Peter Bisson (Defendant) in this action before the Ontario Superior Court of Justice.

The plaintiff, Maple Engineering, was a general building contractor and had successfully bid on the construction of a building in the municipality of Muskoka. The defendant, Peter Bisson, was the owner, director, and sole shareholder of 1373988 Ontario Inc. (doing business as ACI). Using the letterhead of ACI, Bisson had submitted a bid as a subcontractor but failed to go through with the contract. Maple had to turn to another supplier and sued Peter Bisson and 1373988 Ontario Inc. for breach of contract and damages for the extra amount it had to pay the other subcontractor.

The court found that a contract had been breached and damages for $50 000 were awarded. The problem was just who should pay. 1373988 Ontario Inc. was a properly

incorporated Ontario company, but Maple thought it was dealing with ACI through its agent Bisson. The court determined that Bisson had misled Maple, albeit innocently, into believing it was dealing with ACI. ACI in fact did not exist and so Bisson did not have the authority he claimed to represent it. Bisson was liable personally for the damages because he did not have the authority to act for ACI, which he led Maple to believe he had. This is an example of breach of warranty of authority.

Note that Bisson thought he was acting through the legitimate 1373988 Ontario Inc. throughout. He thought that ACI was simply the trade name of the company. This is a common error; had Bisson informed Maple of that fact he would have avoided personal liability. The point is that if you represent yourself as acting for a specific principal you had better have the authority to do so.

---

[3]*Krawchuk v. Scherbak*, 2011 ONCA 352.
[4]*Motor Vehicle Act*, R.S.B.C. 1996 c. 318, s. 86 (1).
[5]2004 CanLII 46655 (ON S.C.).

When an agent doesn't disclose to the third party that he or she is acting as an agent, or refuses to disclose who he or she is acting for, it is referred to as an **undisclosed principal** situation. For example, a developer may be reluctant to disclose that he or she is behind a particular project for fear that the information would push up the price of the land being acquired. The developer or principal would then employ an agent to make the purchase without disclosing whom he or she is acting for or the full nature of the project.

Exception: Agent may be sued where acting for undisclosed principal

If things go wrong, the third party has to sue the agent, not knowing the principal. In that process the identity of the principal is normally disclosed and then a choice must be made to continue the action against the agent or to sue the principal instead. After choosing, the third party is bound by the choice and cannot change her mind, even if it turns out that the party being sued has no funds. Note that there are some situations where a contract entered into by an agent for an undisclosed principal will not be binding—in contracts where identity is important, for instance. Thus, a famous tenor cannot agree to perform a concert and then send an understudy claiming he was acting as an agent for an undisclosed principal.

Third party can sue agent or undisclosed principal, but bound by choice

Third party not bound where identity of undisclosed principal is important

## The Agent/Principal Relationship

The contract that creates the relationship governs the relationship between the agent and the principal. Such contracts will usually specify the nature of the agent's duties, provide for payment for those services, reimbursement for expenses incurred by the agent and specify limits on the agent's authority amongst other things.

**Fiduciary Duty**    Although the principal has some obligations to the agent, such as the payment of expenses, salaries, and any fees already agreed to in the contract itself, the more interesting obligations in this relationship rest on the agent, who has a fiduciary duty to the principal (see Table 6.1). A **fiduciary duty** is basically an obligation to act in the best interests of the principal. This is referred to as an "utmost good faith relationship" and arises where trust has been placed in another by someone particularly vulnerable if that trust is broken. As a fiduciary, the agent cannot take advantage of a business opportunity that comes to him or her because of her position. That business opportunity belongs to the principal. A real estate agent engaged to find property for a client upon finding a good deal cannot purchase that property for himself unless the client after being fully informed declines to make the purchase. Where there is a conflict

Agent has fiduciary duty to principal

Agent must exercise utmost good faith to principal

### Table 6.1 Agent's Fiduciary Duty

- Must not take advantage of principal's business opportunities
- Must submerge his or her own interests in favour of principal's
- Must disclose conflict of interest
- Must not take benefit from both parties
- Must disclose information to principal
- Must not compete with principal
- Must not make profit at expense of principal

Agent must put principal's interest ahead of his or her own

between the agent's personal interests and that of the principal, the agent must disclose it and put his or her own interest aside. If the agent has an interest in the property being offered to the principal, he or she must fully disclose that fact and not make a profit on the deal without the consent of the principal. Similarly, any information the agent acquires with respect to transactions he or she is involved in belongs to the principal and must be communicated to the principal. A real estate agent selling a house for a client should communicate any offers received to that client even if she thinks a higher offer will come if they wait. An agent must act for only one principal and cannot take a benefit from both sides. These are called kickbacks, and for an agent to take even a small gratuity such as liquor, a trip, or some other benefit from a supplier would be a violation of this fiduciary duty.

Agent must make full disclosure to principal

The agent cannot make a personal profit from the deal, other than the commission or other payment coming from the principal. For example, if a real estate agent finds an unsophisticated principal willing to sell a house at a low price, he cannot purchase the property himself, even if done through a partner or a company. The agent's duty is to get the principal the best price possible and that duty would conflict with his own interests in this situation. Also, the agent cannot compete with the principal. If the agent is selling one particular product for the principal, he cannot promote his own product or someone else's product instead, unless the principal consents. To continue with the real estate example, if the real estate agent is selling a house for a principal and finds an interested buyer, the agent will be in violation of his fiduciary duty if he tries to sell the prospective purchaser his own property instead. A recent Supreme Court of Canada decision[6] has narrowed when such a fiduciary duty is present, but it is likely that agents will continue to have a fiduciary duty to their principal in all situations where it is clear that they have agreed expressly or by implication to act in the principal's best interests.

It is a criminal offence for an agent to accept secret benefits

Where such a fiduciary duty is breached, the principal can demand an accounting. She can require the agent to disclose any profits made personally from the transaction and then to pay those profits to the principal. The agent would also be deprived of any commission in these circumstances. Section 426 of the *Criminal Code* makes it a criminal offence for agents or employees to accept a secret commission or other benefit (or indeed for anyone to pay or offer such a secret commission), to act against the interests of their principal or employer, or to show favour or disfavour to a particular party in the business dealings of their principal. This is an indictable offence, and the penalty imposed can be up to five years in prison, with both the agent/employee and the person making the offer subject to be charged. In addition, there are specific offences related to agents involved in unique activities such as fraudulently dealing with minerals; title documents to land; or participating in, acquiring, or operating premises used for gambling or other prohibited activities. Thus, these agents not only face civil action, including the loss of their commissions for such breaches of fiduciary duty, but may also face criminal prosecution in certain circumstances.

Agent must also exercise reasonable competence and appropriate skill

In addition to a fiduciary duty, the agent also has an obligation to act competently in carrying out those duties. An employee or agent who carelessly performs his or her responsibilities, causing the employer or principal losses, may be required to pay

---

[6]*Galambos v. Perez*, 2009 SCC 48, [2009] 3 S.C.R. 247.

compensation in a negligence or breach of contract action brought by the principal or employer. Note that it is the agent's job to carry out the responsibilities assigned to him or her. As a rule the agent cannot delegate those responsibilities to others. There are many exceptions to this rule, usually based on industry practice. Thus, it is common for real estate agents to use sub-agents to fulfill their responsibility. Accountants and lawyers will also normally involve others in fulfilling their responsibilities to their clients.

*In general, an agent cannot delegate*

---

### Case Summary 6.3 *DeJesus v. Sharif*[7]

## An Agent Must Disclose Information to the Principal

Mr. and Mrs. DeJesus (Plaintiff/Respondent), Omar Sharif (Defendant/Appellant) in this action before the Court of Appeal for British Columbia.

Mr. Sharif was a real estate agent and had dealt with Mrs. DeJesus in the past, acting as agent in the sale to her of a rental property. In this instance, however, Mr. Sharif sold Mrs. DeJesus his own property, acting as a dual agent for both himself and for her. She intended to use the property which cost her $895 000 as a care home. Unfortunately, it was in need of considerable repair that she could not afford and she resold it.

The problem here was that Mr. Sharif failed to tell her that he had bought the property several months before having paid only $438 000, less than half the price of the sale to her. In addition, he failed to tell her that the actual market value of the property at the time of sale was only $760,000. Mrs. DeJesus claimed that Mr. Sharif breached his fiduciary duty to her and asked the court to award her the profit he made on the deal and deny him his commission. The court agreed that even though she was aware that he was selling his own property, he was still acting as a real estate agent and had a fiduciary duty to her which he had breached. He was denied any commission on the deal and had to pay her $135 000, the difference between the fair market value at the time of the sale and the $895 000 she had paid.

The case nicely illustrates the fiduciary duty owed by an agent to a principal. The court said that the agent's duty to the principal was even greater since he was selling his own property. Note that the court refused to award her the profit he made on the deal which would have been $438 000. It is interesting to note that when Mrs. DeJesus finally sold the property she sold it for $1 040 000 because of fluctuations in the market.

---

## Ending the Agency Relationship

An agent's actual authority to act for the principal will normally terminate when the job is finished, when the agent receives different instructions from the principal, or when the employment or agency relationship is changed or terminated. The authority to act will also end when the project involved becomes illegal or the principal dies, goes bankrupt, or becomes insane. Although an agent's actual authority may be terminated in this way, there is still the problem of apparent authority. This is one reason the principal should avoid the creation of such apparent authority in the first place. Where that is not possible, the employer must take steps to notify all customers and suppliers who would normally deal with the agent that the relationship has been terminated.

*Agency ends with termination of authority*

*Death, bankruptcy, or insanity terminates authority . . .*

*but apparent authority may continue*

---

[7] 2010 BCCA 121 (CanLII).

Most jurisdictions now permit a power of attorney to be created that will continue after the principal becomes mentally incapacitated, thus allowing a trusted friend or relative to manage the incapacitated principal's affairs. This usually must be done under the supervision of a public trustee or some other government official. These enduring powers of attorney (EPAs) are sometimes abused and all jurisdictions are taking steps to ensure that such abuse is limited as much as possible.

Note that in addition to these general comments about agency, there may be specific statutes imposing additional rules and responsibilities on the agency relationship. For example, real estate agents, travel agents, stock brokers, insurance agents and mortgage brokers have special statutes that govern their industry imposing additional responsibilities and disciplinary processes on them.

## LO 4/LO 5

Contract law applies to employment

## EMPLOYMENT

Employment is based on a special relationship that is historically recognized under the common law as one of master and servant. That term catches the essence of this special relationship, which involves unique obligations of commitment, duty, and loyalty. Today, the employment relationship is based on contract, and normal contract law applies—especially to the employment's creation, the duties to be performed, the consideration, and the terms of termination.

Three main areas are of concern regarding employment. First, the common law of master/servant applies in those areas that are not covered by collective bargaining and where no unions are involved. It deals primarily with the law of termination and wrongful dismissal. Second, we will look at those special relationships where collective bargaining determines the workplace environment, and where unions and management must comply with the law set out in specialized statutes. Third, there has also been a considerable amount of legislation passed that deals with employee rights and benefits, and this will be the final topic of discussion in this section. Federal legislation applies where employees of the federal government are involved and in industries that are federally regulated. Otherwise, appropriate provincial legislation will govern the employment relationship.

Specialized statutes have own definitions of employment

Vicarious liability based primarily on employment

Employer liable for torts of employee within scope of employment

The first question to be determined is whether an employment relationship exists. Today there are many statutes in place that provide a definition of employment, such as the *Employment Standards Act*, the *Workers' Compensation Act*, and the *Employment Insurance Act*. These are important, but the definition given is restricted to the operation of the particular statute within which it is found. No general statutory definition of employment is provided. One reason it is important to determine whether an employment relationship exists outside of these statutes is usually to determine the extent of the employer's liability for wrongful acts committed by their employees. As discussed above, such vicarious liability is usually restricted to the employment relationship, with the employer being responsible for wrongful acts of employees when the act committed is closely connected to the employment. The injured victim can seek redress from both the employee who caused the injury and the employer who profited from the work being performed. Since the employer is usually in a much better position to pay such compensation, it is vital, from the point of view of the victim, that an employment relationship is established. Employment also must be established for an employee to have access to those rights associated with master/servant law, including reasonable notice or pay in lieu of notice when terminated.

Historically, the test used to determine employment was based on the degree of control exercised. Independent contractors work for themselves, doing the job agreed to in the contract. They control their own hours and how they do the work. Employees, on the other hand, work for and under the direction of the employer and can be told not only what to do, but how to do it. If a painter was hired as an employee to paint an apartment building, he would be expected to come to work at a specified time, take limited breaks during the day, and leave for the night when instructed. He could also be told which rooms to do first and even the length of brush stokes to use in the process, whereas a painter hired as an independent contractor would have agreed to do the job and to meet certain specifications such as colour, number of coats, and quality of paint. But since the painter would be working for himself, he would determine the hours of work and process used. So long as the painter finishes according to the contract specifications, and does an adequate job, the owner of the property would have no complaint. Thus, the employee is subject to rules and control whereas the contractor is independent of those controls (see Figure 6.3).

> Employment exists when employee can be told what to do and how to do it

Sometimes this **control test** is not adequate for determining employment, and so a supplemental test has been developed based on an employee's relationship to the business. This is called the **organization test**. If the individual is found to be an integral and essential part of the business organization, he or she is an employee for purposes of vicarious liability and termination requirements, even though the actual control exercised over him or her is limited. Such an employee may exhibit many of the characteristics of an independent contractor, such as being paid as an independent, being declared as independent in the employment contract, and even operating his or her own operating company. But the court will still look at the relationship and may find such a worker is an employee, especially where the worker works exclusively for the employer and has little control over what they do and how they do it.

> Employment exists when employee is an essential element of employer's organization

A salesperson may look like an independent contractor selling by commission only, supplying his or her own car, and determining his or her own hours. But if he or she can only sell for that one business, must report to it for sales meetings, has an office or desk located at the business, and is part of the main sales force, then he or she can be said to be an integral part of that organization and will be treated as an employee of the business. The employer will be held vicariously liable for wrongful acts committed in the process of this employment. However, remember that the employer will only be responsible for conduct that takes place that is closely related to the employment, and not when the employee is "on a frolic of her own."

The employer will also have significantly greater obligations to an employee, as opposed to an independent contractor, if that salesperson's employment is terminated. Even when the court determines that the relationship is truly a contractual one, it may

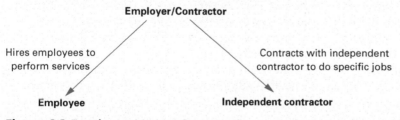

Hires employees to perform services

Contracts with independent contractor to do specific jobs

**Employer/Contractor**

**Employee**

**Independent contractor**

**Figure 6.3** Employee Versus Contractor

find that the worker is a dependent contractor rather than an independent one, again usually based on the long-term and exclusive relationship with the employer. The consequences of such a finding would be that the dependent contractor would be treated more like an employee for vicarious liability purposes and for termination rights, although the notice period requirement could be somewhat less. See discussion in Case Summary 6.5 below.

**Employment Duties**    In general, an employer has an obligation to provide a safe workplace, appropriate direction, tools where necessary, wages, and reimbursement for expenses, as well as any other specific obligations set out in the employment contract. The employee must be reasonably competent, have the skills claimed, and must also be honest, punctual, loyal, and perform the work agreed to. Where the employee is a manager or key to the business, there may be a fiduciary duty owed to the employer, but generally, at least in common law provinces, there is no fiduciary duty owed by an ordinary employee. Still, there may be a duty of confidentiality imposed because of the particular nature of the job performed, or because of a confidentiality agreement included in the contract of employment. This duty of confidentiality imposed on employees is discussed in detail in Chapter 9.

> Only managers or key employees have fiduciary duty

It is extremely important to include such provisions at the outset in an employment contract. Failure to do so can cause serious problems later, especially when dealing with long-term employees. Such a contract can include not only terms of pay and statement of duties but can also include provisions with respect to confidentiality, what happens when duties change, provisions for retirement, and notice requirements upon termination. Where restrictive covenants such as non-competition and non-solicitation clauses are included, they must be very carefully worded so as to go no further than necessary to protect the employer's business. Any ambiguity will generally be interpreted in favour of the employee and be void. See Case Summary 6.8 below.

> Employment contract can be used to avoid future problems

## Case Summary 6.4 *RBC Dominion Securities Inc. v. Merrill Lynch Canada Inc.*[8]

## Manager Breaches Fiduciary Duty to Employer

RBC Dominion Securities (Plaintiff/Appellant), Merrill Lynch and the former employees of RBC Dominion Securities (Defendants/Respondents). The case was brought in the Supreme Court of British Columbia, appealed to the Court of Appeal, and again to the Supreme Court of Canada.

Don Delamont was the manager of the Cranbrook office of RBC Dominion Securities. The Merrill Lynch manager in the area persuaded him to leave and come to work for them. When he left, he orchestrated the move of almost all of the staff working in that office to come with him. They also took information allowing them to bring their various clients with them. The issue here is whether there is a general duty of good faith implied into their

employment contracts that prohibits them from competing after they leave in such a way. The court determined that there was no such general duty of good faith and that the individual employees were free to compete as soon as they left. Note that they did have an obligation not to take confidential papers and other property of their employer and that they were required to give reasonable notice of their departure, which they failed to do and damages were awarded accordingly. Note that the client lists taken were returned within a few days and were not an important factor here.

The main problem, however, was whether the award of $1 483 239 against the manager, Mr. Delamont,

---

[8]2008 SCC 54, [2008] 3 S.C.R. 79, 2008 SCC 54 (CanLII) • 298 D.L.R. (4th) 1.

for violating his implied contractual duty of good faith, which had been overturned on appeal, should be reinstated by the Supreme Court of Canada. Those damages were the direct result of the almost complete collapse of the Cranbrook office caused by the mass departure of the employees and the subsequent movement of clientele. The Court of Appeal found that these lost profits were too remote and not reasonably foreseeable, but the Supreme Court of Canada reinstated them, finding that had the parties put their minds to it, they would have realized that this was exactly the type of consequence to be expected from a breach of this nature. Delamont had breached his duty of good faith as a manager of the Cranbrook office to run it to the benefit of his employer and was liable for that breach.

This case emphasizes that an ordinary employee has no duty of good faith nor duty not to compete once they leave, but that a manager has a duty of good faith and the violation of that duty, especially if done while still employed, can have serious consequences.

## TERMINATION

For our purposes the most important aspect of the law of master/servant relates to the termination of that employment and the notice that must be given, usually by the employer (see Figure 6.4). The employment contract itself sometimes contains terms with respect to the ending of the employment relationship, including duration and how much severance is to be paid if any. Otherwise, under the common law an employer must give the employee **reasonable notice** of the termination, unless there is just cause, which is discussed below. Most of the litigation with respect to wrongful dismissal involves disputes over the adequacy of the notice to terminate given to the employee. Note at the outset that it is notice, or pay in lieu of notice, that must be given. In appropriate circumstances working notice can be given where the employee must continue to work during that notice period. These disputes may involve other issues, including harassment, human rights abuses, defamation, and even assault, but these arguments almost always arise after termination and are included as part of the litigation associated with that termination and the amount of compensation to be paid.

The Supreme Court of Canada in the *Keyes* case discussed below stated that notice requirements in employment should be based on the following factors:

> The reasonableness of the notice must be decided with reference to each particular case, having regard to the character of the employment, the length of service of the servant, the age of the servant and the availability of similar employment, having regard to the experience, training, and qualifications of the servant.[9]

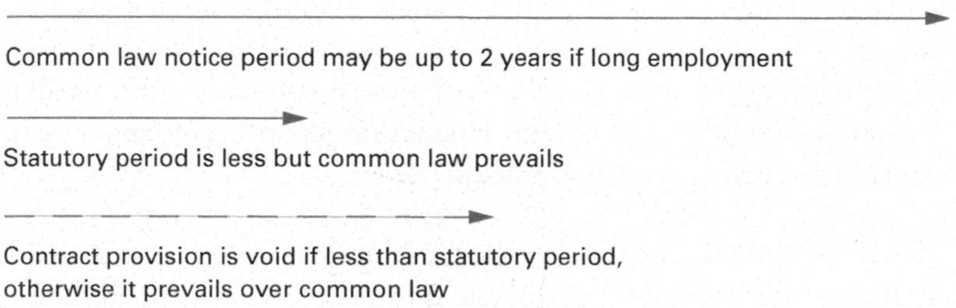

**LO 4/LO 5**

Employment contract may be for specific period or specify notice

Reasonable notice or pay in lieu of notice required

Common law notice period may be up to 2 years if long employment

Statutory period is less but common law prevails

Contract provision is void if less than statutory period, otherwise it prevails over common law

**Figure 6.4** Notice of Termination of Employment

---

[9]*Honda Canada Inc. v. Keyes*, 2008 SCC 39 (CanLII) (2008), 66 C.C.E.L. (3d) 159. Paragraph 28.

The longer the service and the more important the job, the longer the notice period must be although the nature or status of the employment becomes less important in the mix. Where long-term employment is involved, the required notice can approach two years although there is no set upper limit. A very rough rule of thumb is one month for every year of employment, but remember that other factors may affect the amount of notice required and there are several cases where courts have required significant notice period, even where relatively short periods of employment were involved. The employment standards acts in place in most Canadian jurisdictions set out a minimum amount of notice that must be given by an employer when terminating an employee. This ranges usually from one week up to a maximum of eight weeks in British Columbia and Ontario, for example, depending on the length of employment. However, those statutes make it clear that if there are higher standards, either in other statutes or at common law, those higher standards will prevail. Note as well that the amount that must be paid in lieu of notice is more than just the actual wages that would have been earned; it also includes benefits such as dental, medical, and disability insurance premiums; pension contributions; and even bonuses when they are normally paid to all employees and are not based on merit.

**Good practice to negotiate termination**

**Notice requirement may be set out in contract but must be more than statutory minimum**

It would be a mistake for an employer to assume that the higher common law amounts must be offered to all terminated employees. Often the employee will be willing to settle for less, since he or she will get the money right away, avoid the costs of litigation and lawyers' fees, and will avoid having his or her payout reduced by income from other employment (the obligation to mitigate). Still, if the matter does go to court, it is important to consider that judgments involving considerable amounts are a potential outcome. Of course, the best way to deal with termination of an employee, including the amount of compensation or notice to be given, is to specify the entitlement in the employment contract. So long as the amount specified is clear and greater than the minimum specified in legislation (the *Employment Standards Act*), the contractual agreement will prevail. This is the essence of the decision of the Supreme Court of Canada in the *Machtinger* case, where it was determined that the contractual notice period of two weeks was void, as it was in conflict with the statute, which required four weeks. Then, since the contractual notice period no longer applied, and since the common law notice (reasonable notice) was higher than the statutory minimum, the Supreme Court applied the higher standard, restoring the trial court's award of 7 months' notice for Machtinger and 7 1/2 months' for Lefebvre.[10] The case illustrates how important it is to at least exceed the statutory minimum in the employment contract. Had that been done that provision would have been applied with considerably less expense to the employer. It is also important to make the parting of an employee as painless as possible, not just to avoid confrontation and potential lawsuits, but because it is the right thing to do. Great care should be taken not to add to the trauma of the terminated employee, but to provide assistance in counselling, upgrading, and in finding alternate employment. Human resources departments today should have specialists in place to assist in this process.

**Just Cause**   An employer is not required to give any notice of termination where there has been **just cause** on the part of the employee. If the employee has stolen from or otherwise been dishonest with the employer, has acted immorally, or has been convicted of some crime that will interfere with his or her ability to perform the job or otherwise

---

[10]*Lefebvre v. HOJ Industries Ltd.; Machtinger v. HOJ Industries Ltd* (1992), 91 D.L.R. (4th) 491 (S.C.C.).

harm the employer, has disobeyed a lawful instruction, or has committed some actionable wrong while on the job, such actions can amount to just cause supporting immediate dismissal without notice or other compensation. Where an employee lies on a résumé and the employer finds out, that destroys trust and also amounts to just cause. Even a conflict of interest such as taking gifts from clients or suppliers can constitute just cause. Remember that accusations are not enough, and before termination the employer should investigate such claims of wrongful conduct, making sure that the employee is given an opportunity to explain his or her side of the matter. Terminating an employee on unsubstantiated allegations can result in expensive litigation and substantial damage payments for wrongful dismissal. Note also where such wrongful conduct has been ignored in the past without reprimand, there is less likelihood that that a renewed occurrence will constitute just cause.

The employer also has to be careful to make sure the conduct complained of actually does amount to just cause. Not every falsehood, argument, or immoral act will constitute just cause. The wrongful conduct must be egregious, and a single lapse committed by a long-term employee will not generally be enough to amount to just cause. It has been said that termination is akin to "capital punishment in employment law" and such punishment must be proportional to the wrong committed. For example, in *Asurion Canada Inc. v. Brown and Cormier*,[11] two employees were found to have received pornographic emails on their computers at work. These had not been solicited by them nor were they distributed to others. Still, the company had a zero tolerance to pornography and terminated their employment claiming just cause. Both employees had worked for the company for over eight years and had an unblemished record. The trial court and court of appeal found that this single incident was not enough to constitute just cause.

*No notice required where just cause*

Employee incompetence can also constitute just cause, but employers often lose the right to dismiss an employee on this ground because of their own past conduct. For example, where they have given annual raises or bonuses to the employee, they have led that employee to believe that the level of performance was adequate. In the process employers lose the ability to claim incompetence. Before such a problem arises, employers should establish a clear policy that when faced with such a problem, the manager will clearly inform the employee of his or her shortcomings with respect to the job and give the employee a chance to improve before proceeding to termination. Hopefully, some form of regular employee evaluation will identify problems before they become too serious. The employee will then be invited to participate in making a plan to overcome that problem or shortcoming, including making concrete attainable goals such as taking courses, sensitivity training, and the like. When the employee follows through and overcomes the problem, the business has regained a valuable employee. But when that employee fails to meet the goals after being given the opportunity and help to improve, the employer is on much more solid ground when the employment is terminated.

*Regular evaluations used to establish pattern of incompetence*

The same principle applies where a person has committed some less serious form of unacceptable conduct such as minor theft, lying to supervisors, erratic behaviour, and the like. Often the conduct, while serious, may not be enough to constitute just cause and a cautious employer, after carefully determining the exact nature of the inappropriate conduct, will provide for some program of **progressive discipline**. Providing a reprimand or other form of discipline and counselling after a first offence, and in the process making sure the employee understands what is and is not acceptable, should be part of such a

---

[11]2013 NBCA 13 (CanLII).

program. Giving the employee a second chance will often produce a better employee. With each repeated offence the discipline can become progressively harsher, eventually leading to termination. The repeated offences establish a pattern of wrongful conduct that will support a much stronger case of just cause for termination. Of course, very serious misconduct may support immediate termination.

Historically, illness that prevented an employee from working also constituted just cause for dismissal. Although this is not the fault of the employee, if he or she can no longer do the job, the employment contract has been frustrated. Today, human rights legislation requires that the employer make all reasonable efforts to accommodate a disabled employee. If that employee can do some work, the employer should find the individual a job that he or she can do—even if it is part time—providing it doesn't place an unreasonable burden on the business. If the disability causing the interruption in the employee's ability to work is only temporary, this will not support termination of employment. Only where the disability results in a permanent incapacity to return to work will the employment contract be terminated by frustration. Today, long-term disability plans and pensions go a long way to overcome the dilemma posed by sick employees who can no longer work. Lack of work because of a downturn in the economy does not amount to just cause for dismissal. That is not to say that an employer cannot terminate employees when the need arises, but the employer must provide reasonable notice and satisfy other statutory requirements. Often such conditions prompt a layoff where the employment is suspended until there is more work to do. Note that the employee may be entitled to treat such lay-offs as constructive dismissals, which triggers the above-mentioned employer obligations of notice and severance pay if permitted in the applicable employment standards legislation. Note, however, that in Ontario at least if the temporary layoff is done in accordance with the provisions of the *Employment Standards Act*, no claim for constructive dismissal will be considered.

*Reasonable accommodation required for disabled workers*

*Lack of work is not just cause*

## Wrongful Dismissal

A wrongful dismissal action in Canada almost always involves a dispute over whether an adequate amount of notice or pay in lieu has been given by the employer to the employee. Either the employer is claiming just cause and has given no notice at all, or the employee is claiming that although he or she received some notice or severance, it was not enough. When just cause is present, even if discovered after the termination has taken place, the employee will fail in his or her wrongful dismissal action.

---

Case Summary 6.5 *McKee v. Reid's Heritage Homes Ltd.*[12]

## Wrongful Dismissal of Employee/Dependent Contractor

This case was brought by Elizabeth McKee and Bribet Holdings Inc. (Plaintiff/Respondent) to the Superior Court of Justice, Ontario, and appealed by Reid's Heritage Homes Ltd. (RHH) (Defendant/Appellant) to the Court of Appeal for Ontario.

Mrs. McKee had sold homes for the defendant for 18 years when that relationship was terminated without cause by RHH, which after restructuring had tried to impose a different and unacceptable arrangement on her.

---

[12] 2009 ONCA 916 (CanLII).

Throughout the relationship she had worked through her own corporation and at times had employed her own sub-agents to help her carry out those responsibilities. The issue at trial was whether she was an independent (or dependent) contractor and whether the original contract entitling her to only 30 days notice was binding, or whether she was an employee entitled to considerably more notice or pay in lieu. The judge examined the factors to be taken into consideration in determining an employment relationship, including the exclusivity and control involved, and concluded that she qualified as an employee and was entitled to 18 months notice. Both the trial and appeal judges considered the matter vary carefully, but their decision is summed up in the statement quoted with the approval of both courts.

"In many ways, the question posed at the end of the fifth principle—whose business is it?—lies at the heart of the matter. Was the individual carrying on business for him or herself or was the individual carrying on the business of the organization from which he or she was receiving compensation?"

Here the relationship clearly involved her selling homes provided by RHH, using their stationary and forms, and attending meetings at their direction. They controlled what she was to sell, where she was to sell it, when she was to sell it, and how much it was to be sold for. They controlled the method of promotion and evaluated her performance. All of these factors qualified her as an employee and not as a contractor whether dependent or independent.

It is interesting that the court carefully considered the distinction between an independent and dependent contractor and then the distinction between a contractor and an employee and still found that she was an employee in this situation and entitled to considerably more notice (now damages) as a result.

When an employee does sue for wrongful dismissal, the compensation claimed is usually based on what should have been earned, given the difference between the amounts of notice the employee was given and what he or she should have been given. The idea is to make the employee whole, putting her in the same position she would have been in had the wrongful dismissal not taken place. Thus, if the employee received two months' notice and should have been given ten, the employee will claim an amount of damages equivalent to what she would have earned in that extra eight months. The compensation may also be increased on the basis of how that termination took place. Employers sometimes try to justify the termination on the basis of just cause, such as theft or lying, when there is none. The employer may also degrade the employee or otherwise harm her reputation, publicly causing further mental anguish. Today, the courts will take these aggravating factors into consideration but only where the employee has suffered actual psychological harm and some additional damage as a result, and not simply the hurt feelings which normally accompany such a termination. This is stated by the Supreme Court of Canada in the *Keyes* case discussed below. The Supreme Court also made it clear that punitive damages should not be added to this mix except where a separate tort has been committed (such as defamation) and where the award of punitive damages does not duplicate any aggravated damages already awarded.

Note that in some jurisdictions legislation establishes a separate class of wrongdoing supporting a separate action and punitive damages. The *Human Rights Code of Ontario*[13] allows such separate claims, including racial discrimination and sexual harassment. Additional damages may be awarded for violation of these rights in a wrongful dismissal action.

*Wrongful dismissal damages based on what notice should have been given*

---

[13]*Human Rights Code Amendment Act*, S.O. 2006, c.30.

## Case Summary 6.6 *Honda Canada Inc. v. Keyes*[14]

# Award of Punitive Damages Overturned

Keven Keyes (Plaintiff/Respondent), Honda Canada Inc. (Defendant/Appellant) in this action. The case was first heard in the Superior Court of Justice, Ontario, then appealed to the Court of Appeal and eventually to the Supreme Court of Canada.

After working for Honda for 14 years, Mr. Keyes became ill with chronic fatigue syndrome. Honda required Keyes to provide doctor's notes to support each of many absences and to be assessed by their doctor before he was eventually terminated. Keyes alleged that there was a conspiracy to force him out and successfully sued for wrongful dismissal. At trial the judge concluded that there was considerable wrongdoing on the part of Honda in the dismissal process and extended the notice period from 15 to 24 months because of "egregious bad faith" on the part of Honda (commonly referred to as Wallace damages). The trial judge also awarded punitive damages for discrimination and harassment of $500 000. On appeal the punitive damages were reduced to $100 000 and on further appeal to the Supreme Court of Canada the award of punitive damages was eliminated entirely.

The Supreme Court found that there was no evidence of harassment or discrimination. While there was some wrongdoing on the part of Honda, it fell far short of what was necessary to award punitive damages, which should only be awarded where conduct amounts "to advertent wrongful acts that are so malicious and outrageous that they are deserving of punishment on their own." The Supreme Court also reversed the trial judge's decision to extend the notice period from 15 to 24 months (Wallace damages) because the trial judge had been mistaken in finding such bad faith present.

Because of the Supreme Court reversal this case isn't as significant as once thought, but it is instructive of how the courts should be extremely reluctant to award punitive damages and that bad faith ("Wallace damages") should only be awarded in serious cases where some additional actual loss that stemmed from the manner the dismissal took place.

Excerpt from *"Honda Canada Inc. v. Keyes."* Published by the Court of Appeal for Ontario, © 2008.

---

**Terminated employee must mitigate loss**

A terminated employee must make a reasonable effort to mitigate his or her losses. The main purpose of the notice period is to give the employee an opportunity to find another job. If that is successful, damages will be reduced by whatever he or she earns from other employment during the notice period. The employee who should have received ten months' notice and only received two would have a right to claim for the difference. But if the employee found other employment after three months at the same rate of pay or higher, he would be entitled to only one month's additional compensation, making the wrongful dismissal action a waste of time and resources. Reinstatement is not generally an option in a wrongful dismissal action. It is a possibility, however, where a statutory requirement has been breached, such as dismissing an employee because of pregnancy or some other human rights violation. Also, where collective bargaining is involved, the grievance procedure often gives the arbitrator the power to reinstate. Even in these situations, there is usually a reluctance to order reinstatement because of animosity between the parties. Still in *Evans v. Teamsters Local Union No. 31*,[15] the Supreme Court of Canada found that where an employee had been wrongfully dismissed and the employer offered to reemploy him for the remainder of the notice period, his refusal to go back amounted to a failure on his part to mitigate and the damages awarded were reduced accordingly. Note that the court determined that he was not returning to a hostile working environment.

**Reinstatement not normally an option**

---

[14]2008 SCC 39 (CanLII); (2008), 66 C.C.E.L. (3d) 159.

[15][2008] 1 SCR 661; 2008 SCC 20 (CanLII).

**Constructive Dismissal**   Sometimes, by demoting, transferring, or otherwise changing the employment conditions, an employer will try to make an employee so uncomfortable that he or she will quit, thus avoiding the requirements of notice and termination. Whether it was done intentionally or simply as part of the restructuring of the business, it is the employer who has created a situation that makes it difficult or impossible for the employee to continue. Workplace violence, including harassment and bullying by other employees or supervisors, can also force the employee to quit work. This may also amount to constructive dismissal. Consequently, it is the employer who has breached the employment contract when the employee refuses the change or quits. The employee can successfully sue for wrongful dismissal in such circumstances. When changes do take place involving a change in the employee's duties or salary, the employee's obligation to mitigate will often require the employee to continue working during the notice period he should have been given. If this is the case that employee should be careful to indicate that he is doing so under protest otherwise he may be taken to have voluntarily accepted the change and have no further claim to compensation. This obligation to mitigate may also require him or her to take an alternate position when offered, unless the atmosphere has been so poisoned or the potential harm to his or her reputation makes such an option impractical. Examples of constructive dismissal include dismissal of an employee for refusing to relocate when that was not included as a term of the contract when hired; forcing an employee to retire by changing his or her duties; termination upon refusal of a foreman in a paper mill to be on call without pay; and the refusal of an employee to take a lower-paying position because of company downsizing. Even the practice of laying off a non-union employee for a period of time because of lack of work can constitute constructive dismissal, although this may depend on the employment standards legislation in place in that jurisdiction.

> Constructive dismissal is wrongful dismissal

Often if the employer consults with the employee before the changes are made, they can avoid the problems associated with constructive dismissal. An understanding of the employee's personal situation and needs will often present other options, and direct communication may overcome the employee's reluctance to make the change. An opportunity for the employee to try out the new arrangement before a permanent commitment is made may also reduce the fear of change.

This is also a situation where a carefully drawn employment contract can avoid any employee complaints about the change in their situation that otherwise would support an action for constructive dismissal. Such a contract could include provisions that anticipate changing economic times so that the company could temporarily lay off the employee, reduce compensation, or change benefits without triggering the right of the employee to claim constructive dismissal. Often the employer will think about such accommodation well after employment has commenced and force such an agreement on the employee. Remember that there must be real consideration present to support the change, not simply a continuation of employment.

> Problem may be avoided in carefully worded contract

Finally, it is becoming more common for disgruntled employees to base their complaint in the form of some other action. For example in *McNeil v. Brewers Retail Inc.*[16] the employer fired the employee and brought charges against him for theft based on incomplete evidence. The employee successfully sued the employer for the tort of malicious prosecution. In *Piresferreira v. Ayotte and Bell Mobility*[17] the employee who was harassed

---

[16]2008 ONCA 405 (CanLII).

[17][2008] O.J. No. 5187. *Appeal Piresferreira v. Ayotte*, 2010 ONCA 384 (CanLII).

and demeaned sued an abusive supervisor and the employer based on vicarious liability. The court found that she had been the victim of the tort of battery but her claim for intentional infliction of mental suffering was rejected on appeal. Where it can be established that a separate tort has been committed that isn't simply another face of the wrongful dismissal claim, that separate tort will support additional damages, even punitive damages in the right circumstances.

---

Case Summary 6.7 *Power v. Unique Chrysler Plymouth Ltd.*[18]

## Manager Constructively Dismissed

Frank Power (Plaintiff), Unique Chrysler Plymouth Ltd. (Defendant) in an action in the Ontario Superior Court of Justice, claiming wrongful dismissal.

Power was hired by the dealership in 1997 as service manager and eventually became general manager responsible for all of its operations. In 2003 the dealership ran into financial difficulties and in 2004 his duties were changed. His responsibility for sales was removed and he was then asked to move his office into the service and parts area with no private office. Many other changes took place, effectively isolating him from other managers and employees. He suffered diminished status. The changes made it clear to all that he was no longer func-

tioning as general manager. This constituted constructive dismissal and he was entitled to 10 months pay in lieu of notice.

In a similar case, Mario Evangelista (Plaintiff/Appellant) worked for Number 7 Sales Ltd. (Defendant/Respondent) as its used car manager for 15 years. He was approached by the employer and informed his compensation would be reduced from 30 percent of gross profits to 18 percent. He reluctantly agreed to this, but a year later this was further reduced to 9 percent. He refused to accept this and brought an action for wrongful dismissal. He was found to have been constructively dismissed and was awarded 15 months pay in lieu of notice.[19]

---

## Termination by the Employee

**Employee can quit where just cause or pursuant to contract provision**

Finally, we should look at termination of employment by the employee. The employee has a right to quit for cause when he or she is given dangerous or illegal instructions, is not properly paid, is put into dangerous situations, can no longer perform his or her duties because of disability or illness, or where important terms of the employment contract are otherwise breached. Where the employment contract or other subsequent agreement provides for notice from the employee or has other terms relating to termination, those provisions will prevail.

**Otherwise employee must also provide reasonable notice**

Usually, however, there is no such provision and the employee is required to give reasonable notice of termination. What constitutes reasonable notice on the part of the employee, however, is considerably less than reasonable notice on the part of the employer, unless that employee plays some special role so that his or her leaving on short notice would be particularly damaging to the employer. This might be the case where the employee is a manager or salesperson having exclusive dealings with the company's customers or where the employee had some particular skill or expertise that would be difficult to replace. Even then, it is unlikely that lengthy periods of notice would be required.

---

[18]2007 CanLII 54279 (ON SC); 62 C.C.E.L. (3d) 151.

[19]*Evangelista v. Number 7 Sales Ltd.*, 2008 ONCA 599 (CanLII); 240 O.A.C. 389; 68 C.C.E.L. (3d) 165.

Employees may be liable to their employers for wrongful or inappropriate conduct when leaving. When they leave to work for a competitor they sometimes take with them confidential customer lists, secret formulas or practices, or other information, the disclosure of which causes harm to the former employer's competitive position. Sometimes employees, while still employed, will approach the customers and try to persuade them to accompany them to their new business. Such activities may amount to a breach of trust, a breach of fiduciary duty, or a violation of the duty of confidentiality and could be the cause of legal action by the employer. When another employer has persuaded that employee to leave there also may be an action for inducing breach of contract or interfering with economic relations.

*Employees liable for misuse of confidential information or other wrong*

Often an employment contract will contain a restrictive covenant preventing an employee, upon termination, from working in a similar industry for a period of time. Such provisions are designed to prevent unfair competition by those employees or the disclosure or misuse of confidential information to competitors. Sometimes employers require long-term employees to enter into restrictive covenants long after the initial hiring. When this happens, there may be a problem with consideration. Clearly the employer should provide some added inducement for the employee to sign, but simply the promise of continued employment will not be sufficient unless there is a clear intention on the part of the employer to terminate the employment if he doesn't sign. Of course, if the employment is terminated, all of the requirements discussed above with respect to reasonable notice will apply. As discussed in Chapter 3, such restrictive covenants must be reasonable in that they must be necessary to protect a valid interest of the employer and go no further than necessary to accomplish that goal. In determining the reasonableness of the provision in the employment contract, the court will also look at the effect it has on the employee. If it prevents the employee from working in his or her profession, it is less likely to be enforced. The covenant must also be reasonable in that it sets out a limited geographical area for it to apply and has a reasonable time limitation. This applies to a term that restricts where the employee carries on a similar business or takes a job with another employer. Where a non-solicitation clause is involved there need only be a reasonable time limitation. The Supreme Court of Canada in *Payette v. Guay Inc.*, (see Case Summary below) has made it clear that there need be no geographical limitation where a non-solicitation clause is involved. Since it involves specific targeting of the customers or employees of that former employer it can apply worldwide. The case set out in Case Summary 6.8 illustrates the reluctance of the court to enforce such restrictive provisions in employment contracts.

*Restrictive covenant must be clear and reasonable*

## Case Summary 6.8 *Payette v. Guay Inc.*[20]

# Non-Solicitation Clause Without Spatial Limit Valid

Application by Guay for injunction rejected in Quebec Superior Court, injunction granted in the Quebec Court of Appeal. Further appealed to the Supreme Court of Canada by Payette.

Payette operated a crane business in Quebec that he sold to Guay. As part of that deal a non-competition clause and a non-solicitation clause for five years duration was included. As part of the deal, Payette agreed to work

[20]2013 SCC 45 (CanLII).

for Guay for a period of six months. This later became full employment with no specified duration. The employment contract also contained the five-year non-competition and non-solicitation clauses. Several years later, Payette was dismissed without cause. After several months he obtained a job with a competitive crane operation business, and Guay brought this application for an injunction to enforce the restrictive covenants against him.

The Court held that the non-competition clause did not apply since there was no reasonable geographical limitation as required. However, the Court did find the non-solicitation clause valid and binding and issued the injunction. Given that today in our global economy business can take place all over the world, and the non-solicitation clause was targeted specifically at clients of his former employer, the non-solicitation clause was appropriate and not too broad. Also, the five-year limitation was reasonable because of the specialized nature of the services provided.

This is a Quebec case, and there is a unique provision in the *Civil Code* of Quebec providing that such restrictive covenants will not apply to employment contracts where the employee has been dismissed without cause. The Court, however, found that the restrictive covenants were associated with the sale of the business rather than the employment contract. They were therefore commercial in nature and the *Civil Code* provision did not apply. Although that specific provision does not apply in the other provinces of Canada, it is clear that such restrictive covenants in employment are given a much more limited application because of the inequality of the bargaining relationship between employer and employee.

We learn from this case that a non-solicitation clause, while needing a reasonable time limitation, need not have any geographical limitation. This is a significant change in the law. Also where the sale of the business involves the seller becoming an employee of the purchaser or the business the court will be more likely to apply such a restrictive covenant.

## LO 6

Certification process reduces confrontation

Canada follows American approach

## COLLECTIVE BARGAINING

Low wages and poor working conditions prompted workers to band together in the 19th century in an effort to improve their lot. The resulting trade unions were initially resisted, sometimes violently, but throughout the 20th century they managed to achieve respectability and acceptance. The passage of the U.S. *National Labor Relations Act* (the *Wagner Act*) of 1935 (after which Canadian labour legislation was patterned) was designed to put an end to labour strife. The *Act* recognized the employees' right to organize collectively, but required the union to show they had the support of a majority of the workers. Once majority support was established, the union was certified as the exclusive bargaining agent for the employees, and the employer could then deal only with the union and not make special arrangements with individual employees. In all jurisdictions in Canada labour relations boards have been established to handle disputes arising with respect to collective bargaining and related labour matters. See Table 6.2 for a summary of the types of disputes and their consequences.

## Organization

All Canadian jurisdictions recognize that there is a general right for employees to be members of a trade union and to bargain collectively through a bargaining agent. The Supreme Court of Canada has confirmed this as a right under the *Charter of Rights and Freedoms*.[21] Management, usually defined as anyone who has supervisory or disciplinary responsibilities, is normally excluded from the bargaining unit, and some categories of

---

[21]*Health Services and Support-Facilities Subsector Bargaining Assn. v. British Columbia*, [2007] 2 SCR 391; (2007), 283 D.L.R. (4th) 40.

## Table 6.2 Types of Disputes and the Consequences

| | | |
|---|---|---|
| Recognition dispute | To get the employer to bargain with the union instead of individual employees | Certification process |
| Jurisdictional dispute | Rival unions contend over who should do what job or who should represent workers | Certification process or application to board |
| Rights dispute | Disagreement over the meaning of terms in the collective agreement | Grievance procedure and ultimately arbitration |
| Interest dispute | Disagreement over what should be included in the next collective agreement | Mediation and ultimately strike, lockout, and picketing |

employees such as police, firefighters, and health workers, who provide essential services, will usually have only limited rights to take job action.

A trade union seeking recognition as the bargaining agent for a group of employees must make application to the labour relations board for **certification**. It must show that it has a certain portion of the designated workforce signed up as members of the union; for example, 45 percent in British Columbia and 40 percent in Ontario, and similar percentages in other provinces. The process usually begins with disgruntled employees approaching a union such as the Teamsters, or union organizers approaching the employees to sign them up as members. In most cases this won't take place on the employer's premises or during working hours, although an employer will sometimes allow it to keep on good terms with the union and to be aware of what is happening. Note that some jurisdictions have specifically recognized the right of dependent contractors, including those who work through their own companies, to be certified under their legislation, including the federal government, British Columbia, and Ontario.

Historically, most of the violence took place when the union first tried to deal with the employer. This is known as a **recognition dispute**. The current certification process largely eliminates such confrontation. Often a company will have several different categories of employees, and different unions will represent them. Disputes can arise between the different trade unions as to which body should represent a particular group of workers or which union's members ought to be doing a particular job. For example, should the member of the carpenters' union install the new metal studs in a building or should a steelworker? This is called a **jurisdictional dispute** and is also resolved as part of the certification process or by subsequent application to the labour relations board.

Once the particular bargaining unit has been identified and the requisite number of employees signed up, an application is made to the board for certification of the union as the bargaining agent for that group of employees. In some jurisdictions, if the union can show they have signed up a large number of employees (over 50 percent federally and 55 percent in Ontario[22]), the union can be certified without a vote. But in most jurisdictions the next step requires that a government-supervised certification vote take place.

Certification requires signing up members and making an application

Recognition disputes reduced through certification process

Jurisdictional disputes also resolved through certification or by application to board

Union signs up members and applies to board

Followed by government-supervised vote

---

[22]*Canada Labour Code*, RSC 1985, c. L-2, ss. 28–29. And the *Ontario Labour Relations Act*, 1995, S.O. 1995 ch. 1 Sch. A, s. 128.1 (13).

There are some jurisdictional differences, but normally if a majority of those voting support union representation, the union is then certified as the official bargaining agent for those employees. The result is that the employer from that point on must deal with the union exclusively, and can no longer make separate deals with individual workers.

Even though it is a right for employees to be represented by a union and to bargain collectively, some employers will attempt to interfere with the process. Trying to intimidate or threaten employees, creating employer-dominated bargaining units, or even changing pay or conditions of work to undermine the certification drive are usually considered **unfair labour practices** and prohibited. Firing employees for their union activities is not only a violation of labour legislation but under section 425 of the *Criminal Code*, it is a criminal offence for an employer to fire or refuse to hire someone because of his or her trade union activity or to threaten or otherwise intimidate employees to keep them from joining a trade union. It is also a criminal offence for employers to conspire together to do those things. This refers to the past practice of creating a blacklist of employees in a particular industry. These acts are punishable as summary conviction offences with the potential of up to a two-year prison term. In the face of such unfair labour practices, in some jurisdictions (including federally), the board can certify the union without a vote if it is convinced that it is no longer possible to determine the true feelings of the workforce through a representative vote.

Still, freedom of speech is guaranteed in the *Charter of Rights and Freedoms* and the employer retains the right to make comments and express opinions with respect to the organization process and its effect on the business, providing those comments don't amount to threats or intimidation. But there are limits. An employer who played messages on loudspeakers repeatedly throughout the workday requiring employees to listen went too far — it amounted to intimidation and interference with an employee's free choice about union representation.[23]

While it may be a criminal offence to fire a worker because of union activities, it is interesting that in Quebec at least it is not an offence to close down a whole plant because the workers have chosen to join a union. A Wal-Mart store in Jonquiére, Quebec was closed down five months after certification of the union and on the same day as the matter was referred to an arbitrator for the imposition of a first contract. The Supreme Court of Canada held that the closure was within the rights of the Wal-Mart chain and did not violate the Quebec *Labour Code*. The same result can be expected in jurisdictions that have similar statutes in the rest of Canada.

In some jurisdictions it is possible for a group of employers to band together and be certified as an association for bargaining purposes. An example in British Columbia is the Forest Industrial Relations (FIR), an association of forest companies that bargain with the forestry unions through a common bargaining agent.

## Bargaining

Once certified, the process of collective bargaining begins. Either party can serve notice on the other to commence bargaining. Then representatives from both parties meet and negotiate with the object of reaching a collective agreement. When they do reach an agreement, it must be presented to the members of the union—the employees—for **ratification**. If

**Certification granted with majority vote**

**Intimidation and coercion prohibited**

**But employer free to express honest opinions**

---

[23]*RMH Teleservices International Inc. (Re)* ([2003] B.C. L.R.B.D. No. 345); 2003 CanLII 62921 (BC LRB).

there is an employer association involved, they too must ratify the contract, and once ratified there is a binding collective agreement in place. Often, however, there is a deadlock. One of the important developments in Canadian law has been the imposition of mediation, sometimes referred to as **conciliation**, into the process. Either party or the government can request the intervention of a mediator who will assist the parties in their efforts to reach an agreement. The mediator acts as a go-between, trying to find common ground between the parties. During this mediation process neither party can take any further job action. If mediation is successful, a collective agreement will result, but if the mediator feels that his or her efforts are no longer helpful, the mediator will "book out" of the dispute. The parties are then free to take further job action. An important requirement is that the parties bargain in good faith, but that does not mean that either party must compromise their position to reach an agreement. An Alberta Court of Appeal case illustrates this good faith requirement. Essentially, there should not be a change in working conditions during the bargaining process. In *Finning v. International Association of Machinists and Aerospace Workers, Local Lodge No. 99,*[24] even before the old collective agreement expired, the employer made arrangements to contract out some of its warehousing operation without informing the union, even though they were bargaining for a new contract. When the contract came into force, there were immediate layoffs, and the court found this to be a change in the terms of employment and a breach of the good faith requirement.

*Mediation available to assist bargaining*

*Parties must bargain in good faith*

If the parties do reach an agreement, there are some mandatory provisions that must be included. For example, any dispute that arises after the agreement is in place (called a **rights dispute**) must be handled through a grievance process set out in the contract itself and culminate in arbitration of the dispute. Strikes and lockouts are not permitted to resolve disputes with respect to current collective agreements, and in most cases individual employees must submit complaints to arbitration rather than seek a remedy in a civil action. When such a strike does take place, it is illegal and the court has little hesitation in issuing an injunction to bring it to an end. A collective agreement must last for a period of at least one year. Normally, a prior agreement will expire before serious bargaining takes place. As a result, when a new agreement is finally reached, it will normally be applied retroactively to the expiration of the prior agreement. Thus, even with the minimum one-year requirement, the parties can find themselves back into bargaining almost immediately, which makes contracts of longer duration much more attractive.

*Contract must provide for arbitration of rights dispute*

*Agreement must last at least one year*

Once an agreement is in place and the parties have become used to bargaining with each other, subsequent collective bargaining will often be accomplished in a more orderly fashion. However, often reaching the first agreement poses difficult, if not insurmountable, obstacles. Because of this, in most jurisdictions the labour relations board retains the right to impose a first contract. Often, just the threat of imposing a contract will encourage the parties to be reasonable and conclude an agreement without the need for such intervention.

*First contract can be imposed*

Unions will often insist that a **union shop** clause, which requires any future employees to join the union, be included in their agreements. Note that an exception is made for individuals who have religious objections. Sometimes the contract will require hiring

*Employees can be required to join a union, with the employer collecting dues*

---

[24]*Finning v. International Association of Machinists and Aerospace Workers, Local Lodge No. 99,* 2009 ABCA 55 (CanLII); 2009 AB C.A. 55.

union members only. This is called a **closed shop** agreement. Dockworkers, who are sent out to a job from a union hiring hall, are an example of this arrangement. A compromise where employees do not have to join the union is referred to as a **Rand Formula** agreement. In this form of collective agreement employees need not join the union, but they must pay dues and are subject to the terms of the collective agreement negotiated. Most collective agreements will also have a clause requiring the employer to deduct union dues directly off the employees' pay (a **check-off provision**). This has the advantage of saving the union from the trouble of collecting dues directly from their members, some of whom may not be enthusiastic about contributing.

## Job Action

If the parties cannot reach an agreement, normally a strike or lockout will follow. Such actions are only permitted where there is an **interest dispute**, which is a dispute over the terms to be included into the new collective agreement. After the parties have bargained in good faith, and all mediators involved have booked out without an agreement being reached, each party is free to serve **notice** (72 hours in British Columbia) on the other of a strike or lockout. A **strike** involves the employees withdrawing their services by stopping work, although this may not involve closing down the whole operation. Often, only some workers will be pulled off the job in different locations for study sessions, rotating strike actions, or escalating strike actions, all designed to cause increasing disruption for the employer. Although this is not a full-scale strike, it is still a withdrawal of services and so in most cases qualifies as strike action under the legislation. Working to rule, where the employees do no more than the minimum required in their contracts, is also considered a form of withdrawal of services or a strike. A **lockout** involves the employer closing down the operation and denying work to the employees. This is often done to control the timing of the work stoppage, so that it will have the least possible impact on the business, for instance, when stockpiles of products have been accumulated or when market demand is down.

Note that once one of the parties has served notice, the job action need not commence at the expiration of the notice period. Often the continuing threat of immediate job action will be used as a pressure tactic at the bargaining table during negotiations. Employee benefits such as health, dental, and insurance coverage will normally continue while the strike or lockout continues, but the employees will have to pay the entire amount. Employers will usually try to keep the business running with management personnel doing all of the essential jobs or, or in those jurisdictions where it is permitted, with replacement workers.

Aside from the strike, one of the strongest weapons in the union arsenal is **picketing**. This involves the employees (and often other sympathetic union members) posting themselves at strategic entrances to a job site or marching around the job site carrying signs. The signs display their grievances and try to persuade customers, suppliers, and other workers not to deal with the employer. The idea is to shut the business down completely during the duration of the strike or lockout.

In several jurisdictions where public employees are involved, the legislation in place prohibits strikes or lockouts, requiring all such disputes (including interest disputes) to be dealt with through binding arbitration. This is especially true where essential services are involved such as police, firefighters, and health workers. In other jurisdictions workers designated as essential must continue working during a strike.

**Interest dispute may lead to strike or lockout**

**Parties must give notice of strike or lockout**

**Union members can picket during lawful strike**

## Case Summary 6.9 *Glasrock Products Inc. v. United Steelworkers, Local 1005*[25]

# Injunction Granted in Case of Irreparable Harm

This is an application for an injunction brought in the Ontario Superior Court of Justice by Glasrock Products Ltd.

A labour dispute between the employer (U.S. Steel) and the union (United Steelworkers, Local 1005) culminated in a lock-out in November 2010. At first the union permitted employees of Glasrock Products Ltd. to cross the picket lines to maintain the coke ovens that were in need of constant maintenance. Otherwise, they would deteriorate and cause additional pollution. The union stopped this practice and refused to let the Glasrock personnel cross on August 14, 2011, fearing that they were performing the work normally done by the steelworkers. The employer denied that they were performing such work. Glasrock in this action is applying for an injunction to prevent the Steelworkers from denying them admittance to work on the coke ovens.

In issuing the injunction, the court looked first at whether there was a serious issue to be tried and determined that the "obstruction of lawful entry and vehicular traffic" was a serious matter. Next, the court looked at whether Glasrock would suffer irreparable harm if the injunction was not granted, and this, too, was found to be the case. If the coke ovens were left without maintenance serious damage could be done to them, and Glasrock could lose their contract with U.S. Steel. Finally, the court looked at the balance of convenience. Who would be hurt, the union or Glasrock, if the injunction was or was not granted? It was clear that the union would suffer little, if any, loss, while Glasrock could suffer irreparable harm for which it could not be compensated with a monetary award. In addition, the likelihood of damage to the environment if the coke ovens were allowed to deteriorate also supported the decision to issue the injunction to prevent the union from interfering with the employees of Glasrock from entering the premises to maintain the coke ovens.

The case illustrates what the court takes into consideration when issuing an injunction and the fact that there is legal a right to cross a picket line.

Note that people have the right to cross a picket line if they want to. However, this will sometimes lead to frustration on the part of the striking workers, and violence or intimidation may take place. Courts and labour boards usually will not tolerate this, and upon application by the employer, they will order the number of picketers limited to a reasonable amount. Because there is a strong tradition among union members never to cross a picket line, truck drivers, rail workers, and other union members who would be picking up or delivering will normally not cross a picket line, effectively cutting the business off with the possibility of preventing its continued operation. That is the strength of the strike and picketing process. It is usually very difficult in most jurisdictions for a company to continue its operations once a picket line has been established. In some jurisdictions only the location where the particular group of employees on strike works can be picketed. In others the union can picket anywhere the employer carries on business.

*Public has right to cross a picket line*

*Strong tradition of honouring picket line*

Note that trade unions must be democratic and free of discrimination and other human rights violations. They are also required to properly represent their employees in dealings with the employers. If they fail to do so, the legislation permits the dissatisfied employee/union member to bring an action against the union itself for compensation.

*Trade unions must be democratic, not discriminate, and properly represent members*

[25]2011 ONSC 5021 (CanLII).

## LO 7   OTHER LEGISLATION

Trade unions represent only a fraction of workers, and so a considerable body of employee welfare legislation has been passed in all jurisdictions to protect employee rights and curb abuses by employers. There are many examples of statutes passed to assist workers, both on the job and with social issues. Some of these provisions apply whether the workforce is unionized or not, while in some situations the collective agreement is allowed to override the statute.

**Workers' compensation statutes compensate injured workers**

The original factory conditions that employees found themselves working in during the industrial revolution were often dangerous and unhealthy in the extreme. Employees who became sick or were injured because of conditions on the job were simply terminated and left without recourse or compensation. Workers' compensation statutes were designed to overcome those problems and they apply to both unionized and non-unionized workplaces. Employers are required to contribute to a fund that works like no-fault insurance, providing compensation to workers who become ill or are injured due to work-related activity or to their families in the event of death. Sick or injured employees make a claim against the fund for compensation. Workers injured on the job cannot normally sue the employer or a fellow employee who causes them injury. Rather, their recourse is to seek compensation under the **workers' compensation** legislation. It is in the employers' interests to keep such claims to a minimum since the occurrence of job-related accidents would push the employer into a higher risk classification, requiring them to pay a higher fee for the mandatory coverage. In some jurisdictions where the injury is caused by a third party, employees have a choice to seek compensation from the fund or to sue that third party for damages in a civil action. For example, this choice would exist when an employee making a delivery was struck by another vehicle.

**Occupational health and safety statutes ensure worker safety**

A second aspect of workers' compensation legislation, often contained in a separate statute, authorizes a government-appointed body to set and enforce health and safety standards in the workplace. These standards include rules with respect to matters such as ventilation, workplace safety, and the use of safety equipment. This can include the use of hard hats, safety shoes, railings, harnesses, hearing protection, and the like. The rules also relate to safe practices and procedures by workers in the use of dangerous tools and equipment, chemicals, and other processes. Inspectors have authority to levy penalties and even close the job down where necessary to enforce these standards. The trend today is to impose more significant fines and penalties for violation of these safety rules and in some cases to make corporate officers and directors personally liable where serious injury or death is involved. Some jurisdictions have introduced "creative sentencing" for offences in this area. The offending company is charged and then, instead of a trial, an agreement is reached, usually including a fine that is then directed to charities involved in safety promotion, such as safety courses in local high schools. Such a cooperative approach, contributing to the promotion of occupational health and safety, is often attractive to all parties.

In reaction to the Westray mining disaster in Nova Scotia where 26 men died, the criminal negligence provisions of the *Criminal Code* have been broadened, making organizations more criminally responsible for the negligent action of their representatives that cause injury to others. A Quebec company was the first offender convicted under this section. There an employee was crushed by heavy machinery and the company was fined $110 000. A safety device on the machine had been "neutralized" and the employee had not been properly trained to operate the machine. The fine was lower than it would have been because the company was a relatively small family operation and immediately implemented higher safety standards than required so that this type of accident would never happen again.[26]

Note that as the practice of outsourcing workers has become more common, the responsibility for their health and safety has also been extended. Thus, where other employers provide cleaning, security, catering, and similar services, the business to which those services are provided is as responsible for their health and safety as it is for their own employees. Remember that these standards may apply to all workers, including temporary workers and dependent or independent contractors. From an employer's point of view, maintaining these standards is one of the most important aspects of good management. Failure to live up to these workplace safety standards will not only result in significant added expense and possible personal liability, but may also result in more frequent inspections, which interfere with production, and, in extreme cases, recurring workplace closures.

**Employment insurance** legislation is designed to provide a soft landing for those who are laid off. Both the employer and employees contribute to a fund. When laid off, the employee makes a claim and receives a set payment for a designated number of weeks to help bridge the gap until he or she finds other work. Other benefits such as payments for absences due to pregnancy and adoptions are also administered through the *Employment Insurance Act*. Note that under most circumstances, a person who voluntarily leaves his job or is on strike or locked out is not entitled to benefits.

The **human rights legislation** discussed in Chapter 1 has its greatest application in the field of employment. Discrimination based on race, religion, ethnic origin, gender, disability, and sexual orientation with regard to hiring, promotion, or any other aspect of employment is prohibited, as is sexual harassment. In the past, all complaints had to go to human rights boards, which have broad powers of investigation and enforcement. The remedies awarded by these tribunals can be significant, but the courts have shown an increased willingness to consider such violations in awarding compensation in other actions such as wrongful dismissal. Some provinces have changed their human rights legislation to support this new direction (such as the *Ontario Human Rights Code*[27]).

An important obligation imposed on employers by human rights legislation is the duty to accommodate. Put simply, where an employee has a disability, the employer must make a reasonable effort to do whatever is necessary to accommodate that disability. Thus, elevators and wider spaces between workstations would be required to accommodate a worker in a wheelchair. A better chair would be needed for a person with a back problem. Signs in Braille or audio signals would be used to accommodate the visually impaired. Still, this duty to accommodate is not unlimited. It does not extend to placing an undue hardship on the business. This is especially true where the business is small and the cost of accommodation unreasonably great. And, of course, where there is no way to accommodate the worker, that employment can be terminated. For example, if a taxi driver loses his sight, and the owner of the taxi has no other place for the now-blind worker, that employee could be terminated. Hopefully, there would be some sort of disability insurance in place to provide compensation.

Employer's obligations may extend to outsourced workers

Employment insurance statutes help workers between jobs

Human rights statutes protect workers discriminated against in employment

---

[26]*R. c. Transpavé Inc.*, [2008] J.Q. No 1857.
[27]RSO 1990, c. H.19.

A particular problem for employers is how to deal with employees with a substance abuse problem, especially where there are safety concerns. Should mandatory drug testing be allowed? Is this discrimination? Remember that a drug or alcohol addiction is considered a disability, and the employer has a duty to accommodate. Even in a dangerous workplace random drug and alcohol testing is not permitted, and reasonable cause such as a prior indication of a problem will likely be required to support such testing. Where there is addiction, the employer has a duty to accommodate and, to the point of suffering undue hardship, find other work for the employee and provide other help. It is interesting to note that an employee who violates a company's no-drug policy as a recreational user can be disciplined, but the addict has a disability and must be accommodated.

Note that an instance where sexual harassment or bullying has taken place may qualify as a violation of the employer obligation to provide a safe and healthy workplace or be a violation of the *Human Rights Code*, with the employer being held vicariously liable. The employer then is required to ensure that correction of the situation takes place. Remember, however, that the perpetrator has rights as well. Where the fellow employee doing the harassing or bullying is the source of the problem, simply disciplining or terminating his employment may just lead to more litigation. That employee is also entitled to a fair hearing and progressive discipline. It is much better to avoid the problem where possible by establishing clear workplace policies and proper training, which will ensure that everyone is aware of what is expected and the consequences of failing to adhere to those standards.

*Allowing harassment may violate employees rights*

## Case Summary 6.10 *Alberta (Human Rights and Citizenship Commission) v. Kellogg Brown & Root (Canada) Company*[28]

## No Duty to Accommodate Where No Addiction

This matter was heard before the Alberta Human Rights and Citizenship Commission. The decision was reviewed by the Alberta Court of Queen's Bench and that decision was appealed to the Alberta Court of Appeal. John Chiasson was the complainant before the Alberta Human Rights and Citizenship Commission and Kellogg Brown & Root the respondent. At the Alberta Court of Appeal John Chiasson was the appellant along with director of the Alberta Human Rights Commission and Kellogg Brown & Root the respondent.

John Chiasson applied for a job in the construction industry with Kellogg Brown and Root, which required a pre-employment drug test for safety reasons. He started work in the Fort McMurray area, but when the results of the test returned they were positive for cannabis. Chiasson had smoked marijuana five days prior to the test but thought that it would have cleared his system by the time

of the test. He was fired and brought a complaint of discrimination on the basis of physical and mental disability before the Alberta Human Rights and Citizenship Commission. The company policy was that all prospective employees would be drug tested before employment for safety reasons. Impairment because of alcohol or controlled substances could pose a serious safety hazard in the construction industry. In fact, Chiasson was a recreational user of marijuana and neither he nor his employer thought of him as addicted.

Because of this, the human rights panel found that there was no disability and no discrimination. They also found that had he been addicted, the drug testing policy would have been discriminatory and the company's zero-tolerance policy would have violated their obligation to accommodate the disabled person. He appealed that decision and in the Alberta Court of Queen's Bench the judge

---

[28]2007 AB C.A. 426 (CanLII), 425 A.R. 35; 289 D.L.R. (4th) 95, (AB C.A.).

overturned it, finding that he had been the victim of discrimination. The judge agreed that there was no actual disability but also found that because the employer treated all marijuana users as if they were addicted there was a perceived disability and so their actions were discriminatory. But at the court of appeal level the court reinstated the original panel decision, agreeing that because Chiasson was a recreational user only, and all parties didn't think he was addicted, there was no disability and no perception of disability in his case; therefore, there was no discrimination. The policy was no different from a trucking company requiring an employee to restrain from the use of alcohol for a period of time before driving. It was a valid safety provision and not discriminatory.

The case has the interesting implication that the employer's policy allowed the firing of someone who is a casual or recreational user of drugs but would be discriminatory against an addicted person.

Most jurisdictions have incorporated a number of different statutes setting out various standards for the workplace into one comprehensive statute (called the **Employment Standards Act** or *Employment Standards Code* in most jurisdictions in Canada). The federal government has taken this one step further and included workplace health and safety standards, as well as these employment standards provision into the *Canada Labour Code*. The acts set up standards that apply to all employees and cannot be waived by contract. The only exception is where a higher standard exists in common law or has been agreed to in a collective agreement. These statutes cover such areas as the amount of notice or pay that must be given in the event of termination; the number of hours to be worked in a day, a week, or a month; the amount of overtime to be paid if these figures are exceeded; pay for statutory holidays and annual vacation; the minimum wage that must be paid; and specified leaves for pregnancy, bereavement, parenting, emergencies, and the like. For example, where the family member of an employee experiences a medical emergency requiring the support of that employee, the *Ontario Act* provides for non-paid leave of up to eight weeks with a doctor's certificate. For pregnancy the *Ontario Act* provides for a maximum of 17 weeks of non-paid leave, but under the parental leave section this can be up to 35 weeks.[29]

> Employment standards statutes provide for holiday pay, leaves, overtime, termination, etc.

These statutes also set up government boards that have the power to hear complaints, investigate, enter the workplace, gather evidence, inspect records, impose penalties, and otherwise enforce the legislation. This discussion intends to give just a summary of the kinds of provisions that have been enacted. For specifics you should look up the particular statutes that apply in your jurisdiction. Note that contravention by employers of the provisions and standards established under these statutes can constitute a provincial offence and expose the offending party to significant penalties. For example, in the Ontario *Workplace Safety and Insurance Act*, fines of up to $25 000 can be imposed on an individual and $100 000 on a corporation. In Alberta under the new *Employment Standards Code* the potential fines are $100 000 for a corporation and up to $50 000 for an individual.

# SUPERVISING EMPLOYEES

LO 7/LO 8

At the outset it is important to emphasize that nothing will substitute for creating a good relationship with employees to foster loyalty and respect. Like any business activity it is important to develop clear and comprehensive employment policies that are known by managers and employees alike and carefully followed by all. Those policies should include

---

[29]*Employment Standards Act 2000*, S.O. 2000, c. 41, sections 46–49.

not only rules that are consistent with fair employment practices, but a system of education for the employees and managers, as well as a fair disciplinary process that is clearly understood and consistently applied. As much as possible these provisions should be included in the original contract of employment so that the employee understands what is expected of him or her right from the beginning. Many of the problems discussed below can be avoided with proper and in-depth pre-employment screening. Careful background checks should be initiated, including the requirement of references and the checking of those references. Checking for criminal convictions, drug or alcohol addictions, credit checks, and the like should be done with great care; go no further than necessary; and with the prospective employee's consent to avoid human rights or privacy violations.

developing comprehensive
employment policies vital

In this section we will examine some of the common workforce problems with legal implications that such policies should be designed to prevent. We have already dealt with wrongful conduct that constitutes just cause for termination. Often such conduct is obvious; however, at other times although it may be known that wrongful conduct such as theft has taken place, the culprit may remain unknown. Unfounded accusations based on rumour or suspicion leading to precipitous action such as termination may cause the employer more grief than the inappropriate conduct. The theft or other wrongful conduct may be minor and not enough to constitute cause for termination. Large corporations usually have security sections that can investigate suspected wrongdoers within the workforce and human resources departments that deal with hiring and firing employees as well as other disciplinary processes. They should be carefully trained to understand employee rights so that they will not violate those rights in the investigation and disciplinary processes.

Employers must take care not to
infringe the rights of employees

It is usually the owner or managers in smaller businesses that are left to do such investigations, but the same principles apply. They must take great care to respect the rights of the employee in the process. Often the manager, upon hearing an allegation of wrongful conduct, will terminate the employee immediately. But it is now clearly established that the employee has the same right to due process as we find in dealing with any disciplinary body. That means that the employee must be told the nature of the allegations and evidence against him and be given an opportunity to explain or refute them.

Regular performance reviews
important

Regular performance reviews should be a part of all employment relationships. A written summary should be kept that can be referred to and used as a bench mark should problems develop later. Termination should not automatically be the outcome in all cases of wrongful conduct or violation of company policies. For a minor infraction it may be appropriate to reprimand the employee, write the employee up, or even in more serious instances suspend the employee without pay for a period. Be careful here, as this might constitute constructive dismissal, especially where senior staff or long-term employees are involved. The process of reprimanding, writing up, and suspending creates a process of progressive discipline. Good employees who make mistakes are retained and made better employees. Incompetent, disruptive, or dishonest employees are identified and weeded out. This process of progressive discipline will identify problem employees and create a paper trail of evidence establishing a pattern of behaviours that may, when taken together, constitute just cause for termination. The same process is involved with incompetent employees. An evaluation review should be performed regularly with problems clearly identified to the employee. Together goals are set and promises made, such as to take courses to update skills or overcome weaknesses, or in the case of addicted employees, to commit to complete treatment programs. These commitments are subsequently reviewed and new goals set. If the employee fulfills the promises and reaches the goals, a more productive employee results. Where the employee fails to meet these goals or live up to the promises, it establishes a pattern of unsatisfactory performance, which may justify termination or demotion. The disciplinary processes must always be well documented with the view of these records being available for subsequent litigation.

---

Case Summary 6.11 *Backman v. Maritime Paper Products Ltd.*[30]

## Misuse of Computer Justifies Termination

Gregory Backman (Plaintiff/Appellant), Maritime Paper Products (Defendant/Respondent) in this action brought before the Court of Queen's Bench of New Brunswick and appealed to the Court of Appeal of New Brunswick.

Maritime Paper Products hired Gregory Backman shortly after graduation, and he worked there for 14 years before being terminated by the employer. He had received regular raises and a promotion despite the offending conduct that eventually led to his dismissal. When he was hired he was informed of the company policy against misuse of company computers and viewing offensive material over the internet. In 2002 after an audit it was determined that he had viewed pornography using company computers and was warned that it violated company policy and that continued behaviour could result in disciplinary action, including dismissal. In 2003 he engaged in similar behaviour and another letter of reprimand and warning was issued against him. In 2005 he was suspected of similar inappropriate behaviour, but because of lack of evidence nothing was done.

Finally, in 2006 he was again found to have viewed pornographic material using company computers and his employment was terminated for cause. He sued for wrongful dismissal and lost. He then appealed to the Court of Appeal where he again failed, the court finding that there was just cause for his dismissal. The only serious argument in his favour was that the company had condoned his behaviour by doing nothing about it and

so could not use it to justify the termination now. The court rejected that argument. If an employer ignores inappropriate behaviour, leading the employee to believe it did not matter or was not considered important enough to take action, it cannot use the behaviour later to justify disciplinary action. But here the situation was different.

The actions were not tolerated or condoned, and warnings were issued. Even if the actions were condoned, that tolerance would be based on the assumption of good conduct to follow. Here there were recurring instances of inappropriate conduct, and each time the prior conduct would be "added to the scales." The conduct of 2006 together with similar past behaviour with appropriate warnings was a clear violation of company policy and taken together justified the dismissal.

The employer made clear the company policy at the outset and tried to work with the employee over the years. It gave clear indications as to inappropriate behaviour with the warning that such conduct in the future could result in dismissal. Managment even tried to determine if the employee needed help to overcome his problem. The employer escalated the response to the problem, giving the employee sufficient warnings and time to correct the conduct. By the time of the dismissal, it was clear that the employer had tried to work with the employee and given him every chance to correct the behaviour. This shows a good managerial approach to this kind of disciplinary matter.

---

One of the greatest challenges to many businesses is to deal with shoplifting and employee theft. Theft is set out in section 322 of the *Criminal Code*. There are also a number of similar listed offences, all providing for significant penalty. Fraud is similar but involves cheating people out of their valuables through deceit and falsehood. Employees also sometimes sabotage the business by causing some form of physical damage to tools and equipment; interfering with software, data, or computer equipment; or contaminating

Examples of theft and theft-like activity

Employee training vital to avoid litigation

---

[30]2009 NBCA 62 (CanLII); 349 N.B.R. (2d) 171.

information or goods. This constitutes mischief (section 430) or one of the various property-related offences discussed in Chapter 8. Most of these theft-like offences expose the perpetrator to a maximum term of imprisonment of 10 years where the amounts involved exceed $5000 and the Crown proceeds by way of indictment. Fraud is set out in section 380 with a penalty of up to 14 years where amounts over $5000 are involved. Shoplifting by customers is also theft, but it usually involves lesser amounts and is punishable by indictment or summary conviction with a term of imprisonment of up to two years.

The challenges for businesses relate to detection, prevention and discipline. All businesses have to balance the costs of security, surveillance, and enforcement against the losses incurred. Of course, too tight security can also have the negative effect of destroying employee morale and loyalty and damaging customer goodwill. No one likes going into a store and having his or her bags searched, and the presence of security cameras and other forms of surveillance are sometimes taken by employees as an invitation to try to beat them. It is likely that the best counter to employee theft is the promotion of employee loyalty, but this will depend on the nature of the business. Where small valuable items are involved, such as precious jewels, watches, electronic and computer components, or valuable tools, most employees and customers would expect and tolerate a reasonable amount of surveillance and security, providing it is not too intrusive.

In all cases where surveillance is involved, it is important that employees are made aware of it from the outset; otherwise, there is not only the danger of losing employee loyalty but also of being accused of violating that employee's right to privacy. When countering shoplifting, well-trained security people and other employees are vital. A business will often lose much more as a result of a judgment for assault, defamation, or false imprisonment brought on by an overzealous or misguided employee than from the shoplifting itself.

Employee theft and fraud have to be treated somewhat differently. Often the existence of the theft is discovered before anyone in particular is suspected. At this stage the police can be brought in to investigate, but sometimes it is better for internal security people to investigate first. Again, the rights of employees have to be respected. There is no general right to search employees, their lockers, or computers unless there are reasonable grounds to suppose that a particular employee committed the theft. Police can obtain a search warrant, but that option is not available to managers or even their security services without involving the police. If it is made clear when employees are first employed that there is surveillance in place and that telephones and computers will be monitored, there is little likelihood of infringing on an employee's rights, providing the business owns the phones and computers. However, it is doubtful that such notice will entitle an employer to search an employee or his or her locker without police involvement.

Of course, where shoplifting or employee theft is involved, prosecution is often not effective due to the high standard of proof that must be established by the prosecution. Another serious disadvantage is the disruption to the business caused by the investigation, evidence gathering, and prosecution process; the long delays; and the damage that the publicity can bring to the business. Often it is better where employees are involved to simply terminate the employee, assuming enough evidence has been gathered to establish just cause. Unless the amounts for a particular individual are significant, it is generally not worth the trouble, time, and expense to pursue theft or frauds by customers in a civil action. For this reason, businesses often simply include such shoplifting, customer fraud,

Careful supervision, security, and surveillance can avoid problems

Improper process can have serious repercussion to business

Legal pitfalls when legal advice or police involvement is lacking

Termination often only effective remedy for employee theft

and employee theft as a cost of doing business, and add it to the cost of the merchandise or service provided. This, of course, is entirely unsatisfactory but does drive home the importance of putting the emphasis on prevention rather than enforcement. Note that fidelity insurance is available to compensate the employer where they suffer direct loss due to such theft or fraud.

If a decision is made not to involve the police, there is the danger that the business itself, the managers, or the owner who made that decision will be charged with the criminal offence of obstructing justice. This comes with the potential of 10 years' imprisonment when treated as an indictable offence. For example, suppose an employee has been stealing for some time. When he is found out, the employer promises not to tell the police if that employee agrees to repay the money by working longer hours. Or suppose a youthful shoplifter is caught, and the parents promise to repay the amount and a fee for overhead if the police are not brought in.[31] This is likely an obstruction of justice, as it amounts to withholding evidence of a crime from the police. Similarly, where an ad is placed in a newspaper offering a reward for the return of stolen goods "no questions asked," both the person who placed the ad and the business that published it have likely committed a summary conviction offence under section 143 of the *Criminal Code*.

While prevention is important, detection of fraud is vital. Often such crimes, committed by trusted employees, go on for years because there is no structure in place for detection. Proper processes of supervision and control, including appropriate security and surveillance, serve the double purpose of discouraging crime and detecting it when it takes place. Here again, care must be taken not to infringe on the privacy rights of employees. The rights to privacy will be discussed as a separate topic in Chapter 9. Whether there is simple abuse by an employee who makes personal use of a company's tools, equipment, or other facilities, or whether these resources are being used to commit a criminal act or to defraud the company, the practice will likely be reduced with proper surveillance. A business is more likely to have the right to monitor an employee's use of company equipment such as computers, phones, and other telecommunications equipment if it informs the employees that they are subject to such monitoring at the outset. It is also helpful to include a pop-up notification on the computer screen every time it comes on that the communications on it are not confidential and are subject to inspection. Employers also have the right to use closed-circuit TV to monitor various plant and office locations, again with appropriate pre-notification. In fact, such notification should be made a term of the contract of employment. This might be more difficult where a union is involved, and its agreement and cooperation are required. It is likely that anything beyond normal supervision of unionized employees will be considered a breach of an employee's privacy rights, unless there are reasonable grounds for launching an investigation. Note that such privacy legislation varies from province to province. While such close monitoring of an employee's activities and use of equipment may be taken as distrust and reduce loyalty, if the expectation is made part of the corporate culture from the outset, it will likely be more readily tolerated by all levels of employees.

Even when no crime has been detected, there are often telltale clues that should alert management to a potential problem. When an employee shows a marked change in personality or there is evidence of a serious drinking problem or drug abuse, this should at least trigger concern for the employee's welfare, but it may also indicate a serious problem

Notification to employees of surveillance will help avoid litigation.

---

[31]B.(D.C.) v. *Arkin* (1996), 138 D.L.R. (4th) 309, [1996] 8 W.W.R. 100 (Man. Q.B.).

with reference to his or her job performance or some criminal activity. High debt load or other financial difficulties, gambling problems, and even an employee avoiding taking a vacation may also be symptoms of a serious job-related problem, especially if the opportunity is present for the misappropriation of funds.

Expert help should be obtained when a crime is suspected

When an individual employee is suspected of criminal activity or other wrongdoing, great care must be taken in the investigation and punishment process. The first stage is usually a forensic audit to determine the extent of the fraud and find evidence of the wrongdoing. Lawyers should be brought in at this stage to ensure that evidence is preserved and the investigation does not interfere with the rights of the employee. Overenthusiastic investigators have been known to breach privacy rights, defame individuals, and trespass, putting at risk any further action and subjecting the corporation to a wrongful dismissal action. Such obnoxious behaviour by an investigator or supervisor may also expose the employer to vicarious liability for that tortious conduct. Sometimes a gentler, less threatening approach will be more productive.

A decision has to be made at this stage whether the goal is simply to dismiss the employee, to recover what has been lost, or to initiate criminal prosecution. If the goal is simply to get rid of the employee, there is the danger of a wrongful dismissal action or even an action for defamation if the grounds for the dismissal are theft or fraud and that is made public. Such an unfounded accusation can significantly increase the damages awarded. The employee should be given an opportunity to respond to any charges against him or her, and any other employees involved must be made to understand that everything associated with the investigation is completely confidential. The dismissal process itself should be done privately, preserving the dignity of the terminated employee so as to avoid defamation by innuendo.

If the goal is to recover what has been lost, great care must be exercised not to intimidate or coerce the employee by threats of prosecution. Any agreement not to inform the police in return for the employee's cooperation and the return of the item is an indictable offence under sections 141 and 142 of the *Criminal Code* and is punishable with imprisonment up to five years. Also, if there is any chance of recovering the items, action must be taken immediately to preserve them and any evidence of the wrongdoing. This may include police involvement, obtaining *ex parte* injunctions and court orders to freeze assets.

Employer should move quickly when fraud discovered

Where internal fraud or theft is involved, the corporation often will not be interested in pursuing a criminal prosecution because of damaging publicity, the disruption of the business, time-commitment of key personnel, the disclosure of confidential corporate information, the lengthy legal process, and the difficulties of getting a conviction. Still, it may well be that for the preservation of the company's reputation or as a deterrent to others, criminal prosecution will be appropriate. In this case it is advisable to involve the police at the earliest stage. Police have greater powers of investigation and greater investigatory expertise. They can obtain search warrants and are more likely to ensure that the process followed is correct and does not interfere with the rights of the suspected wrongdoer. While the primary focus of criminal prosecution is conviction and punishment, the prosecution process also has the potential of a restitution order in the event of a conviction. If the matter can be settled with the cooperation of the prosecutor before that stage, the restoration of the funds taken can be a condition of the settlement. The threat of jail might be a stronger inducement to return the funds, since doing so can significantly reduce any sentence imposed by the court.

Police have more power

One considerable problem with involving the police is that the corporate crime specialists are often overextended and overworked, and may not have the resources to properly investigate the complaint in a timely manner. The corporation can hire private professional legal and forensic experts to investigate. They then provide information to the police, thus overcoming this problem to some extent. However, in some cases the police simply do not have the resources and will refuse to get involved, especially where there is a civil remedy available. Still, insurance policies usually require that, at minimum, a police report be filed.

Police involvement and prosecution can have beneficial results

## Key Terms

**actual authority** (p. 163)

**agent** (p. 162)

**apparent authority** (p. 163)

**certification** (p. 183)

**check-off provision** (p. 186)

**closed shop** (p. 186)

**conciliation** (p. 185)

**control test** (p. 171)

**dependent contractor** (p. 162)

**employee** (p. 162)

**employment insurance** (p. 189)

**Employment Standards Act** (p. 191)

**estoppel** (p. 163)

**expressed authority** (p. 163)

**fiduciary duty** (p. 167)

**human rights legislation** (p. 189)

**implied authority** (p. 163)

**independent contractor** (p. 162)

**interest dispute** (p. 186)

**jurisdictional dispute** (p. 183)

**just cause** (p. 186)

**lockout** (p. 186)

**notice** (p. 186)

**organization test** (p. 171)

**picketing** (p. 186)

**progressive discipline** (p. 175)

**Rand Formula** (p. 186)

**ratification** (p. 164)

**reasonable notice** (p. 173)

**recognition dispute** (p. 183)

**rights dispute** (p. 185)

**strike** (p. 186)

**undisclosed principal** (p. 167)

**unfair labour practices** (p. 184)

**union shop** (p. 185)

**workers' compensation** (p. 188)

## Questions for Student Review

1. Explain why the topics of agency and employment are important with respect to the study of business law.

2. Distinguish between independent contractors, dependant contractors, employees, and agents. Explain why that distinction is important.

3. Distinguish between actual, apparent, and implied authority.

4. Explain what is meant by ratification, how ratification may arise, and its effect on the contracting parties.

5. Explain under what circumstances a principal will be responsible for the wrongful acts committed by an agent who is an employee and by an agent who is an independent contractor.

6. Explain what is meant by an undisclosed principal. What options are available to a third party when an agent acts for such an undisclosed principal?

7. Explain the nature of an agent's obligations to the principal, and what is meant by fiduciary duty.

8. Define employment and distinguish between the control test and the organization test.

9. Explain under what circumstances an employer will be vicariously liable for the torts committed by an employee and bound by contracts entered into by an employee.

10. Explain how the employment relationship may be terminated. In the absence of contractual provisions, how much notice is required? Include a discussion of constructive dismissal and what effect that will have on the requirement of notice.

11. Define just cause. Give examples, and explain what effect it has on the requirement of notice.

12. What are an employer's obligations with respect to disabled workers?

13. How are damages assessed in a wrongful dismissal action, and how is that award affected by bad faith on the part of the employer or an employee's failure to mitigate?

14. Explain the employee's obligations with respect to notice to quit, fiduciary duty, and confidential information.

15. Describe the certification process in your jurisdiction.

16. Distinguish between recognition, jurisdiction, interest, and rights disputes. Indicate how each of these types of disputes must be resolved.

17. Explain what is meant by unfair labour practices and how they are dealt with in Canadian law.

18. Explain what is meant by the obligation for the parties to bargain in good faith and the role mediation plays in the collective bargaining process.

19. Distinguish between a strike and a lockout, and indicate how much notice must be given and any other restrictions or requirements on strike or lockout in your jurisdiction.

20. What is meant by picketing? Why is it so effective and what limitations on the right to picket are there in your jurisdiction?

21. Explain what is meant by a union shop, a closed shop, and the right of "check-off."

22. Explain the purpose and effect of workers' compensation legislation, occupational health and safety statutes, employment insurance statutes, and human rights statutes with respect to employment.

23. List the standards imposed by employment standards statutes in your jurisdiction.

24. Describe effective strategies to avoid or deal with unlawful and inappropriate behaviours by employees.

25. What dangers does a business face with respect to the investigation and enforcement aspects of employee crime?

## Questions for Further Discussion

1. A principal who enters into a contract that specifically limits the agent's authority to act still faces the possibility of being bound by acts the agent performs outside that actual authority. This is because of the agent's apparent authority. Why should the principal bear responsibility to the third party when it was the agent who violated the authority limitation? Would it not be more appropriate for the third party to turn to the agent for

compensation for any losses suffered when the agent violates his or her authority? In your discussion consider the matter from the point of view of the principal, the agent, and the third party.

2. Employers are held vicariously liable for torts committed by their employees in the course of their employment. Some have questioned the fairness of this process, since it is the employee who is committing the wrongful act, not the employer. This is an example of holding the employer strictly liable for the employee's wrongdoing even though the employer is completely innocent. We don't even impose that kind of liability on parents for the wrongful acts committed by their children. Discuss the appropriateness of holding one person, such as an employer, responsible for the acts of another. Look at the question from the point of view of all parties involved and also consider the public interest. Consider as well that the Supreme Court of Canada has broadened when an employer will be vicariously liable for the acts of employees. The test now is not whether he was doing his or her job but whether the act was closely enough connected to his or her employment to impose liability.

3. In Canada we have developed the practice of requiring employers to give employees extensive notice or pay in lieu of notice when terminating without cause. Most provinces have enacted employment standards acts where the required statutory notice is much less than the common law requirement. But these statutes also provide that the longer term (in either the statute or the common law) should prevail. Is it appropriate or fair to employers to impose such lengthy notice periods? Should the declared statutory period simply override any prior common law approach, as would normally be the case with statutes? On the other hand, do you think that when a term is included in the employment contract that reduces this notice period, it should be allowed to stand? Think about the relative bargaining positions of the employer and the employee at the time of hiring, when these special terms are normally agreed to.

4. Do you feel that unions have too much power today? Look at the legislation in place in your jurisdiction and discuss whether it accomplishes a balanced approach between the needs of employees and their right to bargain collectively, and the freedom of action required by an employer to carry on its business.

## Cases for Discussion

1. *Doiron v. Devon Capital Corp.* [2002] 10 W.W.R. 439; 2002 ABQB 664 (CanLII) (Alta. Q.B)

   The plaintiffs wanted some short-term investments and turned to Mr. Demmers, who had looked after their pension fund and insurance matters as a representative of Manulife. He persuaded them to invest in Devon, calling the corporation "a no-risk investment." This proved to be bad advice and the plaintiffs lost all of their funds. They unsuccessfully sought compensation from Demmers, who had become bankrupt. In this action the plaintiffs sought compensation from Manulife. It was clear that the plaintiffs thought Demmers was an employee of Manulife and that the Devon investment was one of Manulife's products, which it was not. Indicate the arguments that could be raised by both parties and the likely outcome. Would it make any difference to your answer to know that even though Demmers was required to work for Manulife exclusively, Manulife had taken pains to set out in their contract that Demmers was not an employee, but was an independent contractor? What if you were told that Demmers' offices were located in the Manulife Building, that his calls were directed through the Manulife operator, and that when asked he was encouraged to present himself as a Manulife representative?

2. *Krasniuk v. Gabbs,* 2002 MBQB 14 (CanLII), [2002] 3 W.W.R. 364 (2002), 161 Man. R. (2d) 274

   The plaintiffs contracted with Donna Gabbs, a real estate agent, to sell their home. They made it clear to Ms. Gabbs that they needed $137 000 from the sale to pay off their debts. The house was listed for $149 900, but it didn't sell. The price was reduced to $144 450 and then to $139 500, and eventually sold for $130 000. The problem was that Mr. and Mrs. Balgobin, the ultimate purchasers, were seriously interested in the house and had verbally offered $135 00 and then $137 000 for it. However, Gabbs had failed to inform the Krasniuks of these offers. Explain the nature of the complaint against Gabbs and the likely options of the court if the plaintiffs were successful in their action. Would it make a difference had that offer been in writing?

3. *Wilmot v. Ulnooweg Development Group Inc.* 2007 NSCA 49 (CanLII) (2007), 283 D.L.R. (4th) 237

   The plaintiff had been employed by Ulnooweg Development group for 12 years when that employment was terminated because of numerous absences caused by illness. Before that time Ms. Wilmot had a history as an excellent employee, conscientious and diligent, who had never been disciplined for misconduct of any kind. Her sickness took the form of depression and panic attacks. There was no question about Ms. Wilmot's condition, but her absences had made a negative impact on the company and on the other people working with her. The company finally told her that she could only come back if she was prepared to work on a full-time basis. She could not do this and her employment was terminated. She sued for wrongful dismissal. Explain the arguments on both sides and the likely outcome.

4. *IT/NET Inc. v. Cameron,* 2003 CanLII 10653 (ON S.C.)

   IT/NET Inc. did consulting work for various government departments. The practice was for such government departments to publish a request for proposals (RFP) and the consultant company would respond by finding someone to fulfill the position and submit a proposal, including that person's résumé. In this case Leonard Cameron was contracted by IT/NET Inc. to fulfill such a service contract with the Department of National Defence (DND). The position was that of a UNIX system administrator and it was extended because of DND needs. The DND wanted to extend it again, but because of a dispute as to how long his contract with IT/NET would run, Cameron informed the DND that he would not extend it beyond May 31. He left at that time. The DND again posted the position to start on June 1. In the meantime, Cameron contacted FPC, a competitor of IT/NET, allowing it to use his résumé when applying for the contract. FPC was successful, and Cameron resumed his position with the DND, only now working for FPC instead of IT/NET. However, his contract with IT/NET contained a non-solicitation and a non-competition restrictive covenant. This action was brought to determine whether these provisions were binding. Note that there was a time limit but no geographical limitation stated. Indicate the likely outcome.

5. *Fisher v. Lakeland Mills Ltd.* 2005 BC S.C. 64 (CanLII), 2008 BCCA 42 (CanLII)

   Mrs. Fisher had worked for Lakeland for 15 years when she turned 65 in 2002. She asked and received assurance that she could work for the company for as long as she wanted. In 2003 she was required to do extra training and acquire computer skills. She had difficulty with the new demands and felt great pressure to retire and finally did so. She stated that she felt her immediate supervisor "wanted to get rid of her because she couldn't do the job." When she talked to the president of the company, he did nothing to change this impression. After retiring she considered what had happened and sued for wrongful dismissal. State the arguments supporting each position and the likely outcome.

6.  *United Food and Commercial Workers, Local 1518 v. Kmart Canada Ltd. et al.,* (1999), 176 D.L.R. (4th) 607 (SCC)

Employees lawfully on strike at one Kmart department store decided to pass out leaflets at another Kmart location. This was determined to be secondary picketing, which was prohibited in British Columbia. There was no intimidation or physical confrontation here, which was often present with normal picketing, but just the communication of accurate information persuading people not to deal with the store. An injunction was issued prohibiting the practice, and the union appealed all the way to the Supreme Court of Canada. Consider any constitutional arguments that could be raised and the likely decision of the Court.

7.  *Kelly v. Linamar Corporation,* 2005 CanLII 42487 (ON S.C.)

Kelly had worked for Linamar Corp. for 14 years. The company was the largest employer in the town and had a reputation as a good corporate citizen. Kelly was working as a materials manager supervising 12 other employees when he was arrested after the discovery of child pornography on his personal computer (at home). He had a good employment record; nevertheless, upon learning of the arrest, the company immediately terminated his employment. He sued for wrongful dismissal.

Do you think that the actions of the corporation were justified in these circumstances? How could they have handled the termination differently? Would it make a difference to your answer if it turned out that eventually he was acquitted of the charge? How would it affect your answer to learn that the corporation had a good reputation in the community especially because of charity work done to support children?

# Chapter 7
## Methods of Carrying on Business

Kablonk Micro/Fotolia

## Learning Objectives

LO 1  Distinguish the three basic methods of carrying on business

LO 2  Compare the advantages and disadvantages of sole proprietorship, partnership, and corporations

LO 3  Explain how a sole proprietorship, partnership, and corporation are formed and how they are governed

LO 4  Explain how a sole proprietor or partner might limit his or her legal risks

LO 5  Distinguish between three types of partnership and the importance of the distinction.

LO 6  Consider the risks associated with the failure to plan how a business will evolve

LO 7  Understand the methods and objectives of incorporating

LO 8  Consider the duties and obligations of directors, officers, and shareholders and how the business is controlled

LO 9  Indicate the importance of partnership and shareholder agreements and what should be included in them

LO 10  Understand the nature of shares and alternate methods of funding corporate activities

LO 11  Review ethical business practices

Choosing a method for doing business is one of the most important topics in this text. The methods have been developed to facilitate the commercial needs of society by spreading the control and risk of doing business among those involved. People should exercise great care when starting a business to ensure that the structure chosen is the best one for their particular needs. It must be stressed at the outset that a person can start a business with very little formal organization and expense. Partnerships can come about automatically and corporations can now be purchased off the shelf. This may seem acceptable when the business starts, but later this lack of planning will often come back to haunt the participants. Getting good advice from accountants, bankers, and lawyers at this stage may avoid serious difficulty later on. If business people and their advisors take the objectives of the business and the risks associated with it into account, and consider the particular needs of each participant, the structure of the business entity will better serve its purpose.

Although there are other business models, we will look primarily at sole proprietorship, partnership, and incorporation. The sole proprietor involves one person operating a business alone without going through the process of incorporation. A partnership involves two or more people carrying on business together without going through the process of incorporation. And the corporation involves any number of people going through the process of incorporation, where documents are filed with a government agency and a certificate is issued, thus creating a new entity—the corporation—which is the vehicle for carrying on the business. Although the most popular it should not be assumed that a corporation is the best way to carry on a business. Each structure has its advantages and disadvantages, but it is important to point out that often what is a disadvantage to one person is an advantage to another. As a result, we discuss business structures, except in a few instances, more in terms of their characteristics than their advantages or disadvantages. In this chapter we will first examine the general characteristics that apply to all business structures and then we will look at the most common methods of carrying on business. We will also examine the rights and obligations of those involved in the business and those who do business with them.

*Take care in choosing method to carry on business*

**LO 1**

## COMMON ELEMENTS

Each one of these structures is designed for the purpose of carrying on business and making profits for those involved. Government regulations present a series of hurdles that all businesses must face. For example, both federal and provincial income taxes must be paid, and business people must keep sufficient records of their dealings to account for those tax obligations. There may also be property taxes owed to a city or municipality. Where services or products are offered, federal and provincial sales taxes (GST, PST, or HST) must be collected from customers, depending on the jurisdiction. Those funds must then be remitted to the appropriate level of government. A certain portion of employees' pay must be retained for income tax purposes, and employers must pay employment insurance, workers' compensation, and Canada Pension Plan premiums. In some cases, depending on the nature of the business, it may be necessary to obtain a provincial or municipal licence and adhere to the regulations associated with that licence. For example, most businesses dealing with the public will need a municipal business licence, and some businesses, such as real estate, insurance, and travel agencies, will need a provincial licence to operate. Professionals such as lawyers, doctors, dentists, accountants, and real estate agents must also meet stringent qualifications and maintain membership in good standing in their respective professional organizations.

In addition, there are privacy and confidentiality obligations, human rights regulations, pollution controls, and health and safety standards that must be complied with. Carrying on business today is a highly regulated activity and an understanding of the regulations that affect a business is crucial to its success.

## LO 1/LO 2    THE SOLE PROPRIETOR

Sole proprietor works for himself or herself

No formal process required

A **sole proprietor** works for himself or herself (see Figure 7.1). The only formal requirement is that the business name be registered, if it is different from the sole proprietor's. When a child opens a lemonade stand, he or she is a sole proprietor. Sole proprietor then is the term used to describe an individual who starts up a business on his or her own without going through any formal process such as incorporation.

As a general rule the sole proprietor has control of the business. There is no one else to tell a sole proprietor what to do, and he or she is answerable to no one. The record and reporting burden is lighter and there are fewer government regulations. Any profits made from the business belong to the sole proprietor, and any obligations of the business also belong to the sole proprietor. Thus, the sole proprietor and the business are one. It is interesting to note that in the case of *R. v. AFC Soccer*[1] criminal charges were brought against AFC Soccer for certain copyright violations, and AFC Soccer was convicted. But AFC Soccer was simply the business name that Arree Arunkiet had properly registered for his sole proprietorship and the Appeal Court overturned the conviction, finding that AFC Soccer did not exist. It was not an incorporated body and since all charges had been dropped against Mr. Arunkiet the conviction against the non-existent company could not stand.

Sole proprietor has unlimited liability

Personal assets are at risk for business debt

The main problem with a sole proprietor is that there is **unlimited liability**. While all the profits belong to the sole proprietor any debts associated with the business also belong to the sole proprietor, and his or her personal assets will be vulnerable to creditors. There is no separation made between the sole proprietor and his or her business activities. In addition to his or her own debts and liabilities, the sole proprietor will be vicariously liable for an employee's wrongful conduct that takes place within the scope of the employment. It is usually this unlimited liability that discourages people from carrying on business as a sole proprietor. Unlimited liability adds significantly to the risks associated with carrying on business as a sole proprietor but this risk can be reduced greatly by acquiring adequate insurance coverage.

Perhaps the primary disadvantage of operating a business alone is also its greatest advantage. While others can invest in the business they become creditors not participants in the business. This gives the sole proprietor complete control but also limits the alternatives available for financing the business.

**Sole proprietor** ←— works directly with —→ **Client**

**Figure 7.1** Sole Proprietor Relationship

---

[1] (2004) 240 D.L.R. (4th) 178 Man CA.

In some jurisdictions professionals don't have the option of incorporating their practice and so must carry on their practice as a sole proprietor or as partners. A dentist may incorporate a company to hire the staff, and supply the office space and equipment, but the actual practice itself must be performed as a sole proprietor or partner. Many jurisdictions now provide alternatives such as allowing professionals to form professional corporations, but in most cases, because these are unlimited liability corporations they retain personal responsibility for their professional activities, significantly reducing the advantage of incorporation.

*Some professionals can't incorporate*

Another great disadvantage to a sole proprietor involves income tax. Since the income of the business and that of the person owning it are one, it is considered personal income and taxed at that rate. There may be ways for a corporation to defer taxes by leaving the profits in the corporation and when the funds are distributed to redirect that income to spouses and others. Such income splitting allows the parties to take advantage of the lowest personal tax rates. While it is clear that there may be significant tax advantages to carrying on a business through a corporation it is also true that a sole proprietor may be able to take advantage of any business losses by setting them off directly against personal income. These tax rules are continually changing, and it is important for a business person to get proper tax advice from an accountant.

*Less tax flexibility with sole proprietor*

Most sole proprietorships fall into the class of small businesses. They are often found in the construction and forestry sectors where one-man or small operations subcontracting with larger general contractors are common. They are also found in the service area, especially where individual professionals in small offices deal directly with the public.

## Case Summary 7.1 *Metroland Printing, Publishing & Distributing Ltd. v. Isabella*[2]

## Sole Proprietor Personally Liable for Business Debt

Metroland (Plaintiff), Isabella (Defendant) in this action before the Superior Court of Justice, Ontario.

Metroland had provided advertising and printing services to a business known as Liquidation Event and was owed $140 807.05 when this action was brought. The question for the court was whether the defendant, Isabella, was responsible for that debt. Her defence was that her deceased husband ran the business and he was the only one who had dealt with the plaintiff. In fact, she was registered as the sole proprietor of a business carried on in the name of Liquidation Event. She claimed that the registration had been done by her husband over the internet, but admitted that she opened the business bank account and over $50 000 in cheques had been made payable to her with respect to the business. She claimed she was doing the banking because her husband couldn't open a bank account. The judge referred to several authorities, making it clear that while a sole proprietor owns all the assets and is entitled to all the profits of the business, it is also true that the sole proprietor is personally responsible for all of the debts, no matter how careful he is to keep the business separated from other activities.

Although there was no written contract for the services, the verbal agreement was binding, and there was no doubt the debt was owed. The registry exists to provide notice to others and since the defendant was registered as the sole proprietor carrying on business as Liquidation Event, she was bound by that notice and liable for the debt. The case emphasizes the nature of a sole proprietor

[2]2009 CanLII 14793 (ON SC).

and how there is no separation between that sole proprie- tor and the business, making that proprietor responsible for all business debts. It also shows how dangerous it can be to allow yourself to be registered as a sole proprietor. Often this may be presented to you as just a formality, but it is one that can have devastating legal consequences.

## LO 2/LO 3/LO 5

### PARTNERSHIP

No formal process needed to form a partnership

A **partnership** is defined as "the relation between persons carrying on a business in common with a view to profit."[3] Essentially, partnerships are groups of sole proprie- tors who have agreed to carry on their business together without going through the incorporation process (see Figure 7.2). No formal process is needed other than, in some cases, registration with the appropriate government agency. This describes a general partnership. Limited partnership and a limited liability partnership are statu- tory creations and described below. Each province has a *Partnership Act*, and although there are some variations, the major provisions are the same in all common law provinces. While today there are often alternatives, it is still the norm for profession- als such as doctors, lawyers, dentists, and accountants to carry on business as sole proprietors or in partnerships. Note that there are some common law obligations that, while not included in the *Partnership Act*, still apply. Examples include both the con- tract law applied to partnership contracts, and the fiduciary duty owed by one partner to another.

### Creation

Partnership should be created by contract

Some provisions of partnership can be modified by contract

Partnership acts govern relations between partners where there is no contract

Partnerships should be created by express contract where the parties clearly indicate in writing the nature of the rights and obligations between them. Many of the provisions of partnership acts that deal with the relationship between the partners can be modified by such an agreement. Considerable deliberation and negotiation should be devoted to determining just what terms should be included in such a contract. For example, under the *Partnership Act* all partners have an equal share of the decision-making power, and are entitled to an equal share of the profits. This can be modified to create different classes of partners, with the senior partners having more control and receiving a greater share of the profits. The provisions of the *Partnership Act* will apply, unless the partners have agreed otherwise.

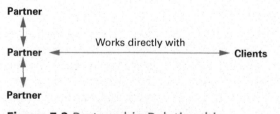

**Figure 7.2** Partnership Relationship

---

[3]*Partnership Act*, R.S.O. 1990, c. P.5, s.2.

Case Summary 7.2 *Tremblett v. Tremblett*[4]

# Partnership Formed Despite Lack of Contract

Doug Tremblett (Plaintiff), Bill Tremblett (Defendant) in a case heard in the Supreme Court of Newfoundland and Labrador Trial Division (General).

Doug and Bill Tremblett worked together in a fishing business for 17 years before their business and family relationship fell apart. This action deals with a dispute between them as to who owned the assets of that fishing enterprise. Although there was no contract or even acknowledgement of a partnership, Doug Tremblett claimed that the brothers operated as a partnership. He therefore wanted the court to declare that all of the business assets, including boats and gear were the property of that partnership and to be split equally between them. The main asset at issue was the ownership of a lucrative crab licence.

The court found that the brothers carried on their business together, sharing profits and satisfying all other requirements of a partnership, and it ordered the division of the assets, including the crab licence.

One of the assets of the partnership was a boat, which was damaged and sold in 2004, adding to the dissension between the brothers. The court held that that was the date that the partnership dissolved. The court found that at that time Bill bought another boat and converted the crab licence for his own use. He hired Doug, but at a fraction of what he was earning before. The court held that since the crab licence was part of the partnership assets, Doug was entitled to a share of any profits made from that partnership asset since dissolution. The case illustrates not only that parties can be in partnership without a contract and without actually knowing they are in such a relationship, but also the entitlement of the partners to share equally in the partnership assets upon dissolution.

---

A contract, whether it is expressed or implied, is not necessary for the creation of a partnership. The definition in the *Act* simply requires that the parties work together in some business where they are trying to make a profit. Such a relationship can be created inadvertently. What has to be determined is what constitutes carrying on business and when is that done in common. Normally, one event, such as a group of students getting together to put on a dance or party, will not constitute carrying on a business. But if that group of students promotes a series of dances and they do it for profit, then they are engaged in the business of promoting dances, and a partnership has been created. This has important consequences in terms of liability for those students. Note that when large companies band together to participate jointly in a particular project, such as developing a mine or an oil well, that may be enough to constitute carrying on a partnership, even though it is only for the one project.

A court will usually find that individuals are carrying on the business in common where it can be shown that the parties have contributed to the capital necessary to carry on the business, and where they each participate and have a say in the management of the business, or where they will share in any profits from the enterprise. **Profit**, as used here, means the net proceeds of the business after expenses have been deducted. Sharing payments or fees (gross receipts) is not enough. For example, if a lawyer were to kick back a given percentage of what she was paid for transferring property to the real estate agent who referred a client to her, this might be unethical, but it would not by itself establish a partnership. But if the lawyer paid a given percentage of the profits (after deducting

*Partners work together to earn a profit*

*Partnership can be created inadvertently*

*Carrying on business together can create a partnership*

*Sharing profits indicates partnership*

---

[4]2012 CanLII 67443 (NL SCTD).

expenses), that would be strong evidence of a partnership. The *Partnership Act* specifically lists a number of activities that by themselves will not establish a partnership. Thus, sharing rental profit from a jointly owned property, an employee commission or bonus based on the performance of a business, or repayment of a loan based on a percentage of business profits will not cause the person being paid to be considered a partner in the business. For example, when a person sells a business they will often base part of the price on payment for the goodwill of the business, and that payment will often be paid out by the purchaser as a portion of the subsequent profits. But if the seller does more and actually helps in the business activity he may well cross over the line and become a partner involved in carrying on a business together with the purchaser.

Note that the liability of a partnership will be imposed on a person who represents him- or herself or allows him- or herself to be held out as a partner. If an accountant introduces his friend to a client, referring to him as his partner in circumstances where it is reasonable for the client to believe that there is a business relationship between them, and the friend does not correct the statement, that friend will not be able to deny it later if the client sues him as a partner. This is an example of the principle of estoppel, which was explained in the previous chapter in the discussion relating to the apparent authority of an agent (see p. 163). Note that this does not create a partnership; it simply prevents individuals called partners from denying it for liability purposes. Such liability for "holding out" has been incorporated into statutes in several jurisdictions, including the Ontario *Partnerships Act*.[5] Finding yourself in an inadvertent partnership is a serious risk of doing business with others. Even clearly stating that there is no partnership in a contract will not protect you from liability to third parties. There is no substitute to being aware of the danger and avoiding any situation where profits are to be shared or where the business activities are being carried on in common unless, of course, the partnership is intended.

## Case Summary 7.3 *Brown Economic Assessments Inc. v. Stevenson*[6]

## Allowing Yourself To Be Called a Partner Imposes Liability

Brown Economic Assessments Inc. (Plaintiff), Robert Louis Stevenson and others (Defendants) in an action brought in the Saskatchewan Court of Queen's Bench.

Cara Brown, the president of Brown Economic Assessments Inc., was in the business of providing economic consulting services. This included estimates of lost income with respect to accident victims and the like. She met with R. L. Stevenson in Edmonton and he represented himself as a senior partner and litigator in the firm of "Stevenson Gillis Hjelte Tangjerd, Barristers and Solicitors" of Saskatoon and he showed her a letterhead and business card to that effect. There was also subsequent correspondence between them under that letterhead.

Ms. Brown agreed to and did provide her consulting service to him but was not paid and brought this action against all of the partners for an amount outstanding of $23 242 plus costs and interest. By the time of the trial Stevenson was bankrupt and so the question dealt with the liability of the other partners for the services Stevenson had obtained. However, the alleged partners all claimed that there was no partnership.

The judge found that in fact there was no partnership, but that these individuals had allowed themselves "unwittingly" to be held out as partners by Stevenson because of the letterhead. In fact they were a group of lawyers sharing office space, but they maintained separate

[5]*Partnerships Act*, R.S.O. 1990, c.P5 s.15 (1).
[6][2003] 11 W.W.R. 101; 2003 SK QB 149 (CanLII).

trust accounts, did not carry on their business in common, and did not share any profits, net or gross. But the judge also found that both at common law and under the relevant section of the *Saskatchewan Partnership Act* these individuals had allowed themselves to be held out as partners based on the letterhead and other communications between the parties. They were therefore estopped or prevented from denying that they were partners and were liable to pay the debt incurred by Stevenson.

Even if there is no partnership between individuals, this case shows the danger of allowing yourself to be called a partner. As was the case with agency, when you knowingly permit someone to think that a person is your partner, you cannot later deny that he was your partner.

## Liability of Partners

**LO 4**

Each partner is responsible for the debts and obligations of the partnership. This includes obligations based on tort, breach of trust, or contract. Each partner is vicariously liable for the torts of employees and other partners that are committed in association with the partnership business. If one partner carelessly injures a pedestrian while delivering documents, the other partners will also be responsible for those injuries. When one partner misuses client funds the other partners are also liable. And with respect to contracts, each partner is considered an agent of the other partners, so that any contract entered into by one partner with respect to the partnership business is binding on them all. If one partner in a flower store business purchases flowers from a distributor, the other partners are parties to that contract as well and liable under it, even though they may not have authorized the purchase and have no knowledge of the transaction. This liability is unlimited. Just as with the sole proprietor, the debts of the partnership are the debts of the individual partners.

*All partners are liable for all debts and obligations of partnership*

*Liability of partners unlimited*

---

**Case Summary 7.4** *McDonic et al. v. Hetherington et al.*[7]

## Other Partners Are Liable for Their Partner's Negligence

McDonic (Plaintiff/Appellant), Hetherington (Defendant/Respondent) in an action brought in the Ontario Supreme Court and appealed to the Court of Appeal.

Watt was a partner in a law firm and lost money on several imprudent investments he made for two elderly sisters. When they died, their estate sued all of the partners for the money lost.

Watt had used the firm's trust accounts to transfer the money. The partners were aware of the investments; the other partners sometimes signed the cheques, and some of the money was loaned to employees and their relatives. As a result the court found that the investments were made as part of the partnership business and all partners were liable for the loss.

---

If the resources of the partnership business are not enough to meet its obligations, each partner will be required to pay them out of his or her personal assets. If the business fails, the partners will not only lose their business but may lose their homes, cars, and other personal assets to satisfy the claims of the creditors. In the example where a partner injures a pedestrian while carrying out company business, if the injuries are significant and there is inadequate insurance, it is quite likely that all the partners would have to pay from their personal assets. If there are several partners and only one of them has assets, that

*Personal assets are at risk for partnership debts and liabilities*

*Insurance can alleviate unlimited liability problem*

---

[7](1997), 142 D.L.R. (4th) 648; 1997 CanLII 1019 (ON CA).

partner will be required to pay the entire claim and will be left with the hollow hope of collecting from the others as their circumstances improve. Thus to reduce this risk, it is vitally important that business people exercise great care in choosing partners who are trustworthy and financially sound. The great danger about unlimited liability in partnership is that one partner will not only be liable for his or her own mistakes but also completely responsible for the mistakes of the other partners and employees as well.

Unlimited liability unaffected by partnership agreement

While many of the provisions of the *Partnership Act* can be modified by the partners, terms that relate to their liability to outsiders cannot be changed. Thus, the partners could set out a term in their partnership agreement that a particular partner would only be responsible for 15 percent of any losses. But if a customer, creditor, or outsider had a claim of, for example, $50 000 against the partnership, and the other partners had no funds, that partner could be required to pay the entire $50 000, despite the provision of the agreement to the contrary. That partner would then be able to seek contributions from the other partners according to the contract, but that would be an empty remedy since those other partners have no funds. Again, choose your partners well.

A new partner coming into the partnership will not be responsible for prior debts and obligations unless he agrees to take on that responsibility. But a retiring partner is not in as favourable a position. As a general rule, he or she will not be responsible for debts incurred after he or she ceases to be a partner. However, as long as people dealing with the partnership still think that person is a partner, he or she will be liable to them on the basis of apparent authority. Every partner is an agent of every other partner. For this reason it is

Retiring partners should notify customers and public

vitally important that the retiring partner provide notification to others upon leaving the partnership. This usually requires specific notification to current customers, suppliers, and clients as well as a public notice of the retirement published in a newspaper or trade publication. Even then, if there are ongoing obligations that continue after he or she leaves, that retiring partner is still obligated. A lease with a term extending beyond his or her retirement is a good example. It is a good idea to get the remaining partners to agree to indemnify the retiring partner for any obligations that arise after he leaves.

It is usually this threat of unlimited liability that persuades business people to avoid the increased risk associated with the partnership model of doing business and to incorporate. But as was the case with sole proprietorships, much of the liability risk associated with partnership can be overcome by acquiring sufficient insurance coverage. As will be seen below, often the advantage of limited liability found in corporations is more of a myth than a reality. Also, there is a growing trend to use limited partnerships and the newly developed **limited liability partnerships** to overcome this liability problem. These modified partnerships will be discussed below.

It should also be noted that changes to the *Criminal Code* in response to the Westray mining disaster in Nova Scotia where 26 men were killed, increased the exposure of the partnership and thus the partners themselves to significant fines for criminal negligence. The changes broaden the application of these provisions making "organizations," including partnerships and corporations, more responsible for the negligence of their employees and representatives when such negligence causes injury or death.

**LO 3**    **The Partner Relationship**    Even though some terms of the *Partnership Act* can be modified in a partnership agreement, it is the relationship between the partners and their rights and obligations to each other as set out in the *Act* that makes partnership unique.

Majority vote governs day-to-day activities

With respect to the day-to-day operation of the business, a majority vote prevails, but one of the most significant features of a partnership is that no major decisions can be made that affect the nature of the partnership business itself without unanimous agreement of the partners. Where a decision must be made to admit a new partner, to borrow or invest money, to dissolve the partnership, or to embark on some new business venture—even if only one partner out of ten opposes the decision—that one veto will prevail. All partners are equal. They share the profits equally; they have equal access to the partnership books and records; and they all share in the management of the partnership with an equal say in its operation. Because partners carry on business together, they cannot earn a salary from the business. Each partner is entitled to an equal share of the profits, and arrangements are usually made so that they will take a monthly draw against those profits. An end-of-the-year adjustment is then made so that the draws equal each partner's profit entitlement. Any expenses incurred should also be repaid before the profits are determined. Of course, if business has not been good, or other liabilities have been incurred, this adjustment can be negative and should be planned for by the partners.

> Major decisions require unanimous consent

> Partners share equally in profits

> Partners don't get a salary but can take a draw against the profits

One of the most important features with respect to partners' obligations is the special duty owed by each partner to the others. Partners are agents of each other and as such owe a fiduciary duty to their principal (the other partners) as was discussed in Chapter 6. They must act in the best interest of the partnership, even to the extent of putting the interests of the partnership business ahead of their own. Thus, they can't take advantage of business opportunities that come to them because of their position, but must make them available to the partnership. If a partner in a real estate agency learns of a particularly good deal on commercial property, she must bring it to the partnership rather than make the investment alone. If she fails to do this and makes a profit on the deal, she may be required to pay over that profit to the partnership. If she loses money, the losses are hers alone.

> Partners owe fiduciary duty

Similarly, the partner must disclose any **conflict of interest**; avoid competition with the partnership; not use any partnership property for his or her own purposes; and properly account for all expenses, income, and benefits received. Of course, where one partner sets out to cheat others, he or she will be subject to damages and other civil remedies. In serious cases of intentional fraud, he or she may also be subject to criminal prosecution and the imposition of significant fines or imprisonment. This applies whether he or she commits that fraud against a fellow partner or a client. Often the fiduciary duty is breached inadvertently and so a partner, agent, or anyone who might be in a fiduciary relationship should be careful to learn what the fiduciary duty entails so that they can take steps to avoid breaching the duty.

Case Summary 7.5 *McKnight v. Hutchison*[8]

## Consequences of Breaching Fiduciary Duty to Partnership

Donald Dale McKnight (Plaintiff), John Michael Hutchinson (Defendant) in a matter tried before the Supreme Court of British Columbia.

Mr. Hutchinson was a partner in a law firm with Mr. McKnight. The partnership ended when McKnight learned that Hutchinson who had acted as director for one of their clients also accepted shares in that company. The shares paid substantial dividends, and Hutchinson failed to disclose the fact or pay over the funds to the partnership. He had also taken a position on a government

[8]2002 BC SC 1373 (CanLII).

board and failed to disclose he was receiving an honorarium and pay those funds over to the partnership. Mr. Hutchinson claimed this was private income but the court held that both sources of income came about because of his position in the partnership and that his failure to pay over the funds to the partnership was a breach of his fiduciary duty. Therefore, an accounting was ordered, and the funds were paid over to the partnership as partnership income.

Note that a partnership agreement allows the holding of shares and other business activities unrelated to the partnership, but in this case the shares held and the directorship were the direct result of the partnership

business, the company being one of their clients. And with respect to the service on the government board, it was clear that partnership assets and time that could have been used in the practice of law were spent carrying out that responsibility, thus making it an activity related to the partnership business. Partners owe a fiduciary duty to their partners, and as such Mr. Hutchinson was required to pay over the undisclosed funds that were earned through partnership related business. Note that the partnership agreement permitted similar outside business activities but did not go so far as to allow these activities that related directly to the partnership business.

*Relations between partners can be modified by agreement*

This is the default position as set out in the *Partnership Act*, but it is often modified by agreement. The importance of a carefully negotiated partnership agreement cannot be overemphasized. **Partnership agreements** are often used to create different classes of partners so that they are no longer equal. Senior partners will have a greater say in the operation of the business. Also, a partner's right to an equal share of profits may be modified by agreement. In a partnership of eight, for example, the two senior partners may be entitled to 20 percent of the profits each, while the six junior partners would only be entitled to 10 percent. Partnership agreements often contain terms restricting a partner's authority to act on behalf of the partnership and limiting their responsibility for losses. It is important to remember that these provisions give rights to compensation from each other only after claims by outsiders have been satisfied. The partnership agreement will not affect the rights of the people with whom the partners are dealing. Other provisions often included in partnership agreements establish the contribution expected from each partner in terms of capital and service, the maintenance and access to books and accounts, how disputes between the partners are to be resolved, provisions relating to the retirement of partners, and the dissolution of the partnership.

Note that the same tax considerations apply to the partnership as to the sole proprietor. Because the income of the partnership business is also the income of the partners, they must pay taxes on it at their personal rate. This is why many professionals create separate corporations to provide services to the practice. While they may not be able to incorporate the actual practice of their profession, they create a corporation to handle the rental or ownership of property; to employ secretaries, managers, and other staff; and to rent or purchase the equipment needed. The partnership pays a fee to the corporation for these services. The shareholders of the service corporation can be the partners' spouse or other family members, thus effectively splitting income for tax purposes.

## LO 4/LO 6/LO 9   Dissolution

Under the partnership acts a partnership is dissolved automatically upon the death or bankruptcy/insolvency of a partner. Where there are more than two partners this can have disastrous consequences for the business. This is one of the areas where the provisions of the partnership acts vary from province to province. For example, in British

Columbia, when there are more than two partners and one of them dies or becomes bankrupt, the partnership only dissolves with respect to that one partner, but the firm continues unless they have agreed otherwise.[9] In Ontario, where there are more than two partners the whole partnership dissolves in the event of the "death or insolvency of a partner unless they have agreed otherwise in the partnership agreement."[10] In fact, just what will cause a partnership to be dissolved is one of the most important provisions of the *Partnership Act* that is normally modified in a partnership agreement. Usually, the partners will agree that the partnership will not dissolve except with respect to that one partner, and they will arrange sufficient insurance to pay out the claims of that partner or his or her estate. The partnership agreement will also normally specify under what conditions the partnership will dissolve, how much notice should be given when one partner wants to leave or retire, and what are the rights and obligations are of the partner who is leaving.

*Partnership dissolves upon death or bankruptcy*

---

## Case Summary 7.6 *Ellerforth Investments Limited v. Typhon Group Ltd.*[11]

## Partnership Dissolved Due to Changing Circumstances and Mistrust

Ellerforth (Applicant/Respondent), Typhon (Respondent/Appellant) in a matter first brought before the Superior Court of Justice, Ontario and then appealed to the Court of Appeal for Ontario.

Ellerforth was an incorporated company formed by a group of physicians that was in partnership with Typhon, a medical laboratory; Ellerforth had a 75 percent interest in the partnership and Typhon held a 25 percent interest. The business of that partnership was the ownership of a building with a medical clinic as its primary tenant. Unfortunately, the medical clinic decided not to renew its lease, which left the partnership without a tenant for its building. It was also determined that a considerable amount of further investment would be needed for renovation before another medical clinic could be attracted as a new tenant. The physicians (Ellerforth), who were now retired, were unwilling to invest the required funds for the renovation and wanted to sell the building, but Typhon refused, wanting to hold onto the building indefinitely. Typhon also refused to sell its share to Ellerforth or to purchase their share from them, resulting in a stalemate.

This application was brought by Ellerforth for a court order that the partnership be dissolved. With one party wanting to hold onto the property and renovate and the other wanting to sell, the partners had a dramatically different view of where the partnership was going and this amounted to a fundamental disagreement about the future of the partnership.

The court made the order, finding that there had been a material change in the circumstances, effectively frustrating the purpose of the partnership. The court also found that the necessary trust needed to continue a partnership had also been lost. The principals of Typhon had accused the physicians of breaching their fiduciary duty and also, in the course of the litigation, of misleading the court. They also accused them of being responsible for the loss of the medical clinic tenant. In light of these accusations, any trust between the parties had been lost. Because of these factors, the fundamental change of circumstances, and the mistrust that had developed, the judge determined that the partnership should be dissolved. The Court of Appeal agreed with that decision.

This case is instructive in that it shows under what circumstances a partnership can be dissolved by court order. The partnership contract required agreement between the parties to dissolve the partnership and sell the building, but the court found that mistrust and changing circumstances justified the intervention of the court. It also illustrates that both partners can be incorporated companies as was the situation here.

---

[9]*Partnership Act*, R.S.B.C. 1996, c. 348, s. 36.1.b.

[10]*Partnership Act*, R.S.O. 1990, c. P. 5, s. 33.1.

[11]2010 ON CA 275 (CanLII).

**Partnership dissolves upon notice**

**Partnership dissolves upon court order**

**Assets first go to pay off liabilities and expenses**

**Assets are then divided equally or as per the agreement**

The normal way for a partnership to dissolve is simply by one partner serving appropriate notice to that effect on the others. Of course, if the partnership was created for a specific period of time or for a particular project, the completion of the specified time or project will also cause the partnership to dissolve. It will also dissolve if the activity becomes illegal or a court orders it to be dissolved. This normally happens where there has been misconduct, breach of the partnership agreement, or where one partner becomes incapable of fulfilling his or her partnership obligations. Partnership agreements will often state that a certain amount of notice must be given or that dissolution will only take place with the agreement of all partners. When one disgruntled partner wants to leave with shorter notice and that is not allowed in the agreement, the only way to do this without the consent of the other partners is to have the court dissolve the partnership. However, the courts are reluctant to interfere with partnership agreements in the absence of some other wrongdoing or incapacity and so the parties should provide for an alternative in their partnership agreement.

When the partnership is dissolved, all of the firm's resources must be devoted to paying the debts and liabilities of the partnership. If there are not enough funds, the individual partners will be required to use their own personal resources to meet those obligations. Where there are excess funds, they are first used to pay back expenses incurred by the partners. Then the partners will divide the capital, assets, and excess profits equally among them or according to the terms of the partnership agreement.

Partnership can be a very effective way for two or more individuals to carry on their business especially where professionals are involved. But caution should be exercised when embarking on such a venture. There is no substitute for taking great care in selecting who your partners will be. That person's competency, financial stability, honesty, and integrity should be primary factors when determining whether to go into business with him or her. Once the choice is made a wise business person will have a professional carefully draw up a partnership agreement covering such matters as;

- the name of the firm and of the partners;
- the nature of the business;
- what each partner will contribute with respect to capital;
- what role(s) each partner will be expected to perform in the business, including who will act as manager in the day to day operations of the business;
- the creation of different share structure if the partners are not to share equally in the profits;
- how control will be shared between the partners;
- how disputes between the partners will be resolved, for example, by arbitration;
- how the partnership will be brought to an end, including how much notice should be given to do so.

In addition, sufficient insurance should be obtained to help overcome the unlimited liability associated with this method of carrying on business. And of course, ongoing vigilance, keeping and reviewing proper records, being constantly aware of the activities of employees and partners, and keeping aware and reacting to changing circumstances and risks are all essential to the operation of any successful business.

# Limited Partners

LO 5

An important similarity between a partnership and a corporation is that both can sue or be sued in the name of the business, but unlike a corporation, each partner is individually responsible for the debt. It is this characteristic of unlimited liability that separates partnerships and sole proprietorships from corporations. Still, there are two ways that limited liability can come about in a partnership arrangement. Note that this is one area where there is some variation between provinces. For example, in Ontario there is a separate *Limited Partnership Act*[12] whereas in British Columbia the topic of Limited Partnerships is included in the *Partnership Act* as Part 3.[13]

**Limited liability** refers to an investor's risk of losing only the amount invested. Thus a shareholder in a corporation can lose what he or she has paid for shares, but is not responsible otherwise for the debts and liabilities of the corporation. This same protection is available to a limited partner. Limited partners are essentially investors (as opposed to creditors) in the partnership who don't actually take part in the partnership business. If they do participate in the management or provide services to the partnership, they will lose their status as limited partners and risk the same unlimited liability as the other general partners.

> Limited liability given to limited partners if:
> - The name of the limited partner is not included in the firm name
> - The limited partnership is registered
> - There is one general partner
> - They don't take part in management or provide services

The following requirements must be met for such a limited partnership to be created:

- there must be at least one general partner in the firm,

- the limited partnership must be registered as such with the appropriate government agency,

- the name of the limited partner must not be listed as part of the name of the partnership business, but the firm name must end with "Limited Partnership," and

- the limited partner must not participate in management or in the partnership business or otherwise provide services to that partnership.

This allows individuals to invest in the partnership business without assuming any responsibility other than the risk of losing what they have invested. But limited partners are in a precarious position and can easily lose their limited liability status by participating in the partnership or failing to meet one of the other qualifications. Often, through carelessness, the limited partnership will not be properly registered. Also, when the business gets into trouble there is a great temptation for the limited partner to get involved. By doing so the limited partner becomes a general partner with unlimited liability.

> Limited partner can become general partner with unlimited liability

Typically, limited partnerships will involve one general partner, often a corporation, and several limited partners, each holding shares (called units) in the business. When the business fails the general partner will be liable for all debts and obligation that are not satisfied by the assets of the partnership. The limited partners will only lose what they have invested unless they have assumed other obligations such as signing as a guarantor or signing a promissory note. Investing as a limited partner involves considerable risk and only a careful and experienced business person should consider investing in this way. Great care should be taken to read the contract carefully before investing, obtain

---

[12]R.S.O. 1990 c. L.16.
[13]R.S.B.C. 1996, c 348.

independent legal advice, and then be careful to avoid the pitfalls that could change the status of a limited partner to a general partner. To that end the limited partner should ensure that it has been properly registered as such and then keep an arm's length relationship with the business.

A limited partnership can be a very effective method of carrying on business for even large projects. A few years ago PWA (the parent of Canadian Airlines), Air Canada, and Covia (an affiliate of United Airlines) entered into a partnership as limited partners with Gemini as general partner. Gemini was a corporation owned by the limited partners. This was set up to create an automated joint booking operation, which unfortunately was not successful, but does illustrate that even large operations can be constructed this way.

---

Case Summary 7.7 *Haughton Graphic Ltd. v. Zivot et al.*[14]

## When Limited Partners Lose Their Protection

Houghton Graphic Ltd (Plaintiff), Zivot (Defendant) in an action brought in the Superior Court of Justice, Ontario. Note the application of the Alberta *Partnership Act* in this Ontario action.

Zivot and another individual were limited partners in Printcraft (a new magazine) with Lifestyle Magazine Inc., which had been incorporated so that it could be the only general partner. Zivot was also the president of Lifestyle Magazine Inc. and as such played an active role in controlling the business of Printcraft. Houghton was an unpaid supplier and sought payment directly from Zivot.

The court held that under the Alberta *Partnership Act,* Zivot lost his limited partnership status when he participated in the Printcraft business. It did not matter that he was acting as an employee of Lifestyle or even if he had informed the suppliers that he was a limited partner. Because he was taking part in the control of the Printcraft business, he lost his status as a limited partner and was liable as a general partner. This case shows the nature of a limited partner and how easily that status can be lost.

---

## LO 5   Limited Liability Partnership

Professionals such as accountants and lawyers often deal with large business operations and in the process face the potential risk of much more extensive liability for their mistakes. Because of this, legislation has been passed reducing the unlimited liability feature of some partnerships by allowing them to form a limited liability partnership. To create such a firm, the partners need only enter into an agreement designating the relationship as a limited liability partnership and stating that the act relating to limited liability partnerships governs the agreement. Also, the name of the partnership must be registered and must end with the words "Limited Liability Partnership" (LLP). It must be stressed that only members of professional organizations governed by a separate statute, such as Ontario's *Certified General Accountants Act 2010,*[15] are eligible and then only where the organization permits its members to carry on business as limited liability partnerships. Those organizations must also require their members to maintain a minimum amount of liability insurance.

Most provinces allow limited liability partnership

Must be registered and use LLP designation

Must be permitted by professional organization and have insurance

---

[14](1986) 33 B.L.R. 125 (Ont. H.C.).
[15]SO 2010 c 6, Sch A. s 24.

Carrying on business as a limited liability partnership eliminates a partner's liability for the mistakes of their partners, but does not relieve that partner from liability for his own mistakes. Where one partner, or a person supervised by him, acts negligently, that partner will still be personally liable to compensate the victim. And that liability is unlimited. All of his personal assets are exposed to risk as are any assets of the partnership, but the other partners will not be responsible for that partner's negligence. In this sense their liability is limited to the loss of their investment in the firm and for their own negligence. They are not responsible for the wrongdoing of their partners. Thus, if one accountant makes a mistake with respect to an audit and causes significant losses to investors, only that one partner, along with his insurers, will be required to compensate the victims. In some provinces this protection is limited to tort liability, but in others it extends to liability arising from contracts as well. In this way the risk faced by professionals doing business in professional partnerships is considerably lessened. Thus, limited liability partnerships have become much more common in the business world.

*Negligent partner retains unlimited liability*

*But other partners are not liable*

Finally, in some provinces professionals have been given the right to incorporate, but these professional corporations (PC) normally do not grant the professional the limited liability that would be present in a standard corporation. However, they do allow the professional all of the tax and other benefits associated with the incorporation process.

*Where professional corporations allowed, they don't give limited liability*

## CORPORATIONS

The essential thing to remember about corporations is that they are artificial creations of government, which have no existence in reality. A corporation is merely a convenient legal fiction that is properly referred to as "the corporate myth." A sole proprietor consists of one legal personality—the sole proprietor. Likewise, a partnership is not a legal person separate from the partners. But if there are 10 shareholders in a corporation there are 11 legal personalities—the 10 shareholders and the corporation itself. The corporation is considered a legal person, separate and apart from the shareholders that make it up. It is in that last legal personality—the corporation—that we find the corporate myth or the legal fiction. It is an artificial legal personality recognized by the courts and all other official bodies as well as the various elements of our business communities, but in reality it has no existence separate from its parts, hence its characterization as a fiction or myth (see Figure 7.3). There are examples of other legal entities incorporated by government such as towns, universities, hospitals, and other institutions incorporated under special statutes such as banks, trust companies, and the Canadian Broadcasting Corporation (CBC). Also nonprofit societies such as the Red Cross and religious organizations are common, but we will restrict our discussion to corporations created for the purpose of carrying on business. Still, much of what is said here is applicable to all of these various legal entities.

**LO 1/LO 2/LO 6/ LO 7**

*A corporation is a legal fiction*

*But recognized by the courts as a separate legal person*

*There are other forms of incorporated entities*

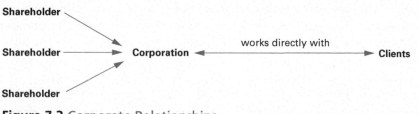

**Figure 7.3** Corporate Relationships

## LO 3   Creation

Incorporation creates federal or provincial companies

Creation by registration

Creation through letters patent

Creation through articles of incorporation

In Canada corporations can be created either under the federal (*The Canadian Business Corporations Act* (CBCA) or various provincial and territorial statutes. Historically, two different methods of incorporation were used in Canada, the **registration** and the **letters patent** methods. In most provinces and federally these older processes were replaced by a more modern approach referred to the **articles of incorporation** method. While the three methods are still used depending on the jurisdiction, the results are the same: the creation of a separate entity, the corporation.

The incorporating documents, in most provinces called articles of incorporation, are essentially the constitution of the company and are filed at the appropriate government office, along with a name search report and the payment of a fee. A certificate of incorporation is then issued. The articles of incorporation sets out such things as the name; the registered office; the share structure, which includes different classes of shares; the number and power of directors; and any restriction on the types of business that can be engaged in. In addition, each corporation creates by-laws (also called articles in British Columbia and Nova Scotia) setting out the normal operating rules of the company, such as the notice required and procedures for an annual shareholders' meeting, the responsibilities of directors and officers, and the management organization of the company. Note that it is at this initial stage of incorporation that shareholders will often enter into a shareholders' agreement. Such agreements can be extremely important and are described below.

Result is creation of separate legal person

A company incorporated in one province may register to do business in another

No matter what method of incorporation is used, the outcome is essentially the same: the creation of a corporation that is a separate legal entity from the members that make it up. This has developed into an extremely efficient method of doing business, both on a large and on a small scale. In all jurisdictions the basic structures, including rights and responsibilities of directors, officers, and shareholders and the methods of financing, are similar. Although incorporation in one jurisdiction allows the corporation to carry on business in others, a registration fee must be paid to do so. For this reason incorporation should take place in the jurisdiction where the business will be carried out, or federally, which allows the corporation to carry on business in any province. Note that in 2011 the *Quebec Business Corporation Act* was enacted, overcoming significant problems and bringing Quebec company law much more in tune with the rest of Canada.

## Structure

Broadly held corporations sell shares to public and are more regulated

Closely held corporations are smaller with fewer regulatory controls

Business corporations can be either **broadly held** or **closely held**. The primary difference is that the broadly held corporation will normally be selling shares to the public, usually on the stock exchange. Broadly held corporations are also referred to as reporting, public, or offering corporations. A closely held corporation is more like an incorporated partnership with only a few shareholders. Such a business is likely to be small. The directors, officers, shareholders, and managers are likely to be the same people, and the reporting and accounting requirements are much simpler and less stringent. It is in these smaller corporations where a shareholders' agreement becomes so important (much like a partnership agreement as discussed above). Closely held corporations also have restrictions placed on the free transferability of shares, which cannot be offered or sold to the public. Usually the number of shareholders will be restricted and they will have to sell the shares to current shareholders or get permission from the directors to sell them to someone else. These closely held corporations are not always small businesses. Even very large concerns, including companies with household names, are often owned and controlled by holding companies that are closely held. A minority shareholder in such a closely held corporation is in a vulnerable position since majority rules. The best way to protect such a shareholder is with a carefully worded shareholder's agreement as will be discussed below.

*Closely held corporations have restrictions on transfer of shares*

A broadly held corporation has many more regulations and controls that must be met. The rules relating to the protection of shareholders' rights, the responsibilities of directors, the requirements for annual meetings, and the reporting requirements are much more stringent. These larger corporations are generally traded on the stock market, which imposes even more regulations (see securities discussion in Chapter 5).

## Shareholders

The membership of the corporation is made up of **shareholders**. While they are separate from the corporation itself, they have very significant rights with respect to control of the corporation. Shareholders have the right to vote in shareholder meetings, and their vote controls what happens in the corporation. The supervision of the management and operation of the corporation is controlled by the **directors**, who are chosen by a vote of the shareholders, usually at an annual general meeting. The shareholders have a vote based on the number of shares that they have. For example, one shareholder holding 200 shares would outvote 10 other shareholders holding 10 shares each. The majority shareholder in a corporation has ultimate control, and the minority shareholder has very little say in the operation of the corporation. This is sometimes referred to as the tyranny of the majority and is one of the important differences between corporations and partnerships.

*Shareholders are separate from corporation*

*Shareholders control corporations through their votes*

*Majority rules*

In a corporation different classes of shareholders can be created, giving different rights and restrictions with respect to the shares. These usually take the form of preferred and common shares. **Common shares** normally give the right to exercise control of the corporation through voting and to share in **dividends** when they are declared. Dividends are the method used to dispense the profits of the corporation to the shareholders. If the directors choose to pay out these profits rather than use them for other company purposes, they make a declaration to that effect, and the shareholders receive a payment based on the number of shares they hold. The shareholders also have the right to see certain documents, including financial statements and the company's annual report, which must be made available at the company's registered office. It is also possible to create special shares with unique rights and restrictions that usually take the form of **preferred shares**. These usually do not convey voting rights, but have a commitment from the company to pay out a specific dividend payment each year. It should be noted that whether preferred or common shares are involved, there is no legal right to a dividend; the shareholder cannot sue if a dividend is not declared and paid. The best that the preferred shareholder can do is to demand to be paid the promised dividend before a dividend is paid to the common shareholders. If the promised dividend is not paid to the preferred shareholder that will typically trigger other rights such as giving the preferred shareholder a right to payment before subsequent dividends are paid to the common shareholder and the right to vote along with the common shareholders.

*Common shareholders have the right to vote and to dividends, once declared*

*Preferred shareholders have no right to vote but are promised a regular dividend*

*Shareholders have no legal right to a dividend*

*But where no dividend is paid, other rights can be acquired by the preferred shareholder*

## Separate Legal Person

A corporation is a separate legal person

The key to appreciating the nature of a corporation is to understand the consequences of it having a separate legal personality. A corporation has the same powers of a natural person to carry on business. It can employ others, it can be an agent, and it can even be a partner. Since it is an artificial creation without a body, everything it does is done through agents. Because of this, and the limited liability principle discussed below, it is important that those dealing with it understand they are dealing with an incorporated entity and those behind it have limited liability. Any contracts or other dealings should include a clear indication that those contracting are dealing with the corporation and not the person representing it. The corporate name must be clearly indicated and must include the designation that it is a limited company (such as "Ltd." or "Corp." set out at the end of the company name). Failure to do so can lead to the loss of that limited liability as indicated in the following case.

---

Case Summary 7.8 *Race-Way Construction & Management Ltd. v. Barker-Taylor*[16]

## Limited Liability Can Be Easily Lost

Race-Way Construction & Management Ltd. (Plaintiff/Respondent), Richard Barker-Taylor and Edwardo Tak Shinyei (Defendants/Appellants) in an action brought in the British Columbia Supreme Court and then appealed to the Court of Appeal.

Race-Way entered into a contract to renovate space in a mall with the "RBT Group of Companies." Payment was delayed and after some negotiation a different company, "345257 Ltd.," the lessee of the property where the work was done, issued a promissory note to it, which was also dishonoured. Race-Way was paid some funds from yet another company, but was still out $27 441 when it sued Mr. Barker-Taylor and Mr. Shinyei personally for the amount owing. They were the principals (directors and shareholders) behind 345257 Ltd. and the parties Race-Way had dealt with. In fact, RBT Group didn't exist, either as an entity or as an incorporated company. It was just a convenient "handle" given to a group of companies that were carrying on business under that umbrella.

The court found that the provision of the B.C. *Company Act* required that whenever an incorporated business operated it had to do so in its own name, indicating that it was a limited company.

. . . every company or extra-provincial company must display its name in legible characters . . . on all its contracts, business letters, and orders for goods, and on its invoices, statements of accounts, receipts and letters of credit.

The *Act* went on to impose personal liability on officers or directors who knowingly fail to do this. Based on this section the court determined that Mr. Barker-Taylor and Mr. Shinyei were personally liable for the amount still owing. The fact that Race-Way eventually accepted a promissory note from 345257 Ltd. didn't absolve them of that liability, since it took place after the original contract had been created and the work had been completed.

Although this case dealt with the application of a section of the B.C. *Company Act,* the same result would have been likely in any jurisdiction, since all require that, to obtain the protection of a limited liability corporation it must be made clear to those being dealt with that they are dealing with the corporation and that there is limited liability.

---

[16]2003 BC CA 163 (CanLII); 11 B.C.L.R. (4th) 304.

Normally there is no problem with a corporation having the capacity to contract, since in all jurisdictions they have now been given all of the capacity of a natural person to contract. A word of caution, however: in the case of special-act corporations (ones created by a special act of parliament, such as the CBC), it may be possible that they have restricted capacity. If you have dealings with such bodies and the transactions seem strange, it would be wise to check the legislation and make sure it has the capacity to do what its representative has proposed. The same caution should be exercised with banks, trust companies, trade unions, insurance companies, as well as government agencies and departments. Of course, since all dealings with a corporation are through agents, people should always ensure the agent has been given the appropriate authority to act.

*A corporation has the same powers and capacity of a natural person*

*Capacity may be limited with special act companies*

*Agents acting for corporations may have limited power*

## Limited Liability

Perhaps the most important consequence of the separate legal entity status of the corporation is limited liability. Since the corporation is a separate legal personality, any debts, liabilities, or other obligations of the corporation are those of the corporation itself, not the shareholders. This was established by a famous case, *Salomon v. Salomon & Co.*[17] Mr. Salomon operated a shoe business, which he subsequently incorporated with himself holding all but a few shares. He then sold the assets of the business to that corporation and became a secured creditor for the debt. The business ran into financial difficulties and the creditors turned to Salomon for payment. The court held that the debts were those of the corporation, not Mr. Salomon, and that only the corporation was responsible for payment. Thus, Mr. Salomon had limited liability. To make matters worse for those creditors, Salomon as a separate person could also be a creditor, and as a secured creditor, he had first claim on the remaining assets of the corporation ahead of those other creditors.

*Shareholders have limited liability*

Limited liability then means that the debts, liabilities, and other obligations of the corporation remain with the corporation. In normal circumstances they will not be imposed on the shareholders, directors, or other participants in the corporate business. But it is always important to remember that the **separate legal person** aspect of the corporation is a myth or fiction created for the convenience of doing business. As a result, in rare circumstances, the courts are willing to look behind the corporate structure (lift the corporate veil) and impose liability on the shareholders directly. This approach is usually restricted to situations where the corporation is being used by the shareholder to commit a crime, fraud, or some other wrong, including avoiding obligations of child support or division of assets in a matrimonial dispute. Exceptions are also included in legislation. For example, there is a temptation to create a number of smaller corporations rather than one big one to take advantage of lower tax rates for small businesses. But this is not permitted, and these corporations can be treated as one for taxation purposes. It should be noted that the position of the director is not always as protected as that of a shareholder. Because directors have a more direct involvement in decision-making, they have a significant duty of care to the corporation, and many statutes hold them directly responsible for the decisions made. Directors' liability will be discussed below.

*Shareholders are not liable for the debts and liabilities of the corporation*

*Court may lift corporate veil where there is crime or fraud*

*Several corporations may be treated as one for tax purposes*

*Directors do not have the same protection as shareholders*

---

[17][1897] A.C. 22 (H.L.).

## Case Summary 7.9 *Schreiber Foods Inc. v. Wepackit Inc.*[18]

# But the Corporate Veil Can Be Lifted

Schreiber Foods (Plaintiff), Wepackit Inc. and David Wiggins Defendants) in an action brought in the Ontario Superior Court of Justice.

Schreiber Foods Inc., a U.S. company, supplied Equipment to Wepackit Inc., an Ontario company, doing business supplying assembly packing equipment. When Wepackit failed to pay, Schreiber Foods obtained judgment against them, first in Wisconsin and then in Ontario. Wepackit lost an appeal of the Ontario judgment but failed to pay the judgment or the court ordered costs involved with respect to the trial and the appeal. Wepackit has no assets, and this action was brought against Wiggins, the sole shareholder, director, and officer of Wepackit in his personal capacity to enforce that judgment. At the time of the Appeal Court decision Mr. Wiggins had formed another company, Wepackit 2009 which took over the business and assets of Wepackit. To make matters more complicated another company owned by Mr. Wiggins, 116 Ontario Ltd. was the sole shareholder of both these companies. 116 Ontario Ltd was also the landlord of Wepackit and claimed to have seized the assets of Wepackit for failure to pay rent. With respect to all of these companies Wiggins was the director and officer and was the controlling mind.

The Court had no problem finding that this was an act of oppression designed to deny the creditors of Wepackit proper payment as ordered by the court and that Wiggins as director was personally liable. The Court also determined that this transfer of assets constituted a fraudulent conveyance by Wepackit, lifted the corporate veil and found that Mr. Wiggins as controlling mind was personally liable to pay the judgment and costs ordered against Wepackit in favour of Schreiber. This case not only illustrates the operation of the oppression remedy discussed below, but also shows when the courts will look behind the separate legal entity status of the corporation and impose liability on those controlling and directing that corporation.

---

Corporation does not die

**Continued Existence**   Another consequence of the corporation being a separate legal person is that it does not die. While the company can be dissolved voluntarily or by court order it cannot expire. As a result, many corporations have been in existence for hundreds of years and are still going strong. The Hudson's Bay Company (the Bay), established over 300 years ago, is an example, as is the Canadian National Railroad. Also, the corporation does not end when the shareholders die. The shares are merely assets held by the shareholders that are passed down to their heirs. The company carries on. Once issued, shares are assets that can be bought and sold without directly affecting the corporation. This characteristic of independence from the corporation makes shares such an attractive tool for investment. This has led to the creation of that venerable institution—the stock market.

The corporation does not end with deaths of shareholders

**Separate Management**   Another effect of the corporation being a separate legal person is the ability to have management that is separate from the owners or shareholders. In a partnership, the partners normally are the management, but in a corporation a separate management group can be hired to manage the corporation. The management can even be from the shareholders themselves. They can be hired as employees since, unlike a sole proprietor or a partnership, the shareholders are separate and independent from the corporation. Note that "owners" as used here is a little misleading. The shareholders do not technically own the corporation or its assets. The shares only give the shareholder control

---

[18]2013 ON SC 338 (CanLII).

of the corporation through voting. It is only upon dissolution of the corporation that the shareholder may have a claim to the assets of the company. Note, however, that there is a Supreme Court of Canada decision holding that the shareholder has a sufficient interest in the assets of a corporation to take out insurance and collect in the event of damage.[19]

The day-to-day operation and the responsibilities of the participants is determined by the articles of incorporation and the by-laws of the corporation. The parties in control are the shareholders, directors, and management team. This management team is hired by, and answerable to, the board of directors who are, in turn, answerable by election to the shareholders, who maintain ultimate control of the corporation but do not manage it.

Separate management can have a downside as well. In large corporations the management side is separate and apart and often develops different interests from the shareholders. As a result, it will sometimes act against the best interests of the shareholders to protect its own position or the corporation itself. For example, one corporation may attempt to take over another by offering a generous amount for outstanding shares. But the managers of the corporation to be taken over may see this as a threat to their jobs or not in the long-term interests of the corporation and do what they can to resist, even though the individual shareholders would be better off with the takeover. One defence tactic that has been developed when such a "raid" takes place is referred to as a "poison pill." This involves giving the directors power to issue more shares at a discount once one shareholder acquires more than a certain portion of outstanding shares (e.g. 35 percent). The effect is to dilute the value of the shares making it much more difficult for the raider to acquire a controlling interest. The idea is that just the presence of such an option will discourage such a take over attempt in the first place. These and other similar tactics can be an interference with shareholder rights and are regulated by statute in many jurisdictions.

## Shareholder Duties

An important result of the shareholders being separate from the company is that it allows the shareholders to carry on their own business activities without reference to the company. A partner has to be careful not to compete with the partnership and to always put the interests of the partnership ahead of his own, but a shareholder has no similar duty to the corporation. A shareholder is free to sell his or her shares, to compete, to be an employee of that corporation, to hold shares in other similar or competing businesses, to withhold information, and to pursue other business or personal interests that may even be detrimental to the corporation. Only where the shareholder becomes a director, officer, or other employee of the corporation may fiduciary or other duties be imposed. As explained in Chapter 5, where a shareholder holds enough shares to be classed as an insider or "significant shareholder" in a publicly traded company, there are also important limitations placed on his or her ability to purchase and sell those shares because of the privileged information the shareholder is presumed to possess. It has been suggested that because shareholders have such extensive rights and benefits with respect to the corporation, they ought to have greater responsibilities as well. This is inconsistent with the historical position of a shareholder and the reasons for the creation of corporation in the first place. Certainly at the time of writing the responsibilities of a shareholder remain minimal.

---

[19]*Kosmopoulos v. Constitution Insurance Co.*, [1987] 1 SCR 2 (SCC); 1987 CanLII 75 (SCC).

# Shareholders' Rights

Although there are very few duties imposed on a shareholder, there are several mechanisms built into the corporate structure designed to protect the interest of the shareholders and their investment. Shareholders have a right to vote and a right to a dividend if one is declared. They also have a right to a share of the assets of the corporation if it is wound up (dissolved). This right to vote and thus exercise ultimate control over the corporation is exercised at an annual shareholders meeting although other special meetings can be called where major decisions must be tabled. It is at this annual meeting that directors are elected and shareholders are given financial and other information upon which to base their decisions. The audited financial reports, shareholders' decisions in the form of resolutions, in addition to the articles and bylaws must be made available for inspection by the shareholders at the registered office of the corporation.

In closely-held corporations, where there are few shareholders who are also likely to be directors and officers the formal requirements are less stringent and often an annual shareholders' meeting does not actually take place. Nor are financial reports usually audited. Still a record of the decisions made must be kept and annual reports filed with the appropriate government office.

In broadly held corporations the shareholders will likely not actually attend the shareholders' meeting but will give representatives their right to vote, which is called a **proxy**. The exercise of the proxies allows a few individuals who have gained the confidence of the shareholders the power to control the meeting, choose the directors, and vote on the various proposals presented. Often the power of shareholders in a large corporation is more illusion than reality because of the dilution of their individual rights in such a huge body of shareholders. But holders of large blocks of shares where no one has a majority, can still have significant influence.

In addition to these rights, there are several mechanisms designed to protect shareholders from abuse. Sometimes the elected directors will make decisions that negatively affect the shareholders (usually a minority shareholder in particular). If the decision involves a major change for the good of the corporation that will have a negative impact on minority shareholders, the minority shareholders may have a right to **dissent** and have their shares purchased by the corporation at a "fair value."

Sometimes the directors representing the majority shareholders will make decisions that have a negative impact on both the corporation and the minority shareholders. Usually there has been a falling out and the majority shareholders are simply using their power to hurt the minority shareholders. Sometimes the majority shareholder, through the directors, may strip assets from the company for his own benefit or transfer, sell, or otherwise bestow a benefit onto another company at the expense of the corporation and the oppression of minority shareholders. When this happens, the minority shareholder can apply to the court seeking protection from such **oppression**. If the court agrees that the action of the directors or officers was oppressive or unduly prejudicial to the shareholders interests, there is considerable latitude as to what they can do. This includes stopping the offending conduct, compensating the victim, setting aside the offending contract or transaction, or altering its terms. It may also declare that new directors or a receiver be appointed, that terms in the articles or shareholders' agreement be changed, or that the corporation be wound up.[20] If

Shareholders have:

- Right to vote
- Right to dividend once declared
- Right to assets upon dissolution
- Right to inspect records

- Right to dissent
- Right to be free of oppression

---

[20]*Business Corporations Act*, R.S.O. 1990, c. B.16, s. 248.

the directors and officers can show that the decision made was reasonable and in the best interests of the corporation (the business judgment rule), there has been no oppression, even where the interests of the minority shareholder have been harmed. Note, as well, that the remedy of oppression is not limited to shareholders but can be brought by any "security holder, creditor, director or officer of the corporation."[21] For shareholders the representative or derivative action discussed below may be more appropriate depending on the circumstances.

---

### Case Summary 7.10 *Southpaw Credit Opportunity Master Fund LP v. Asian Coast Development (Canada) Ltd.*[22]

## Oppression Not Present Where Reasonable Business Decision

Southpaw Credit Opportunity Master Fund LP (Plaintiff), Asian Coast Development (Canada) Ltd. (ACDL) and its directors and officers (Defendants) in an oppression action brought in the British Columbia Supreme Court.

ACDL was incorporated to develop a massive casino project in Vietnam and arranged financing from Harbinger, Southpaw, and Bessemer in that order. To satisfy the Vietnamese government timetable it had to raise more capital. Unfortunately, because of the worldwide financial crisis in 2008 no such credit was available; thus, in order to keep going ACDL turned to its first investor Harbinger, which provided funds but on terms which had the effect of diluting the shareholdings of the other investors, Southpaw and Bessemer, by as much as 95 percent. This action was brought by Southpaw against ACDL, claiming oppression by the directors and officers of ACDL in that they failed in their duty to current shareholders to find more favourable financing.

Madam Justice Ross found that here was no oppression and therefore no wrongdoing. The parties knew

that investing in ACDL was risky and the economic downturn made matters worse. It was a reasonable business decision for the directors of ACDL to make these arrangements to obtain the financing needed. The judge found that ACDL had no alternative and so applying the "business judgment rule" the court dismissed the action. Not every decision taken by directors that has the effect of harming the position of a minority shareholder constitutes oppression. This decision was taken for the good of the company and the continuation of the project and so was a sound reasonable decision not oppressive to the shareholders. It should be noted that because of this decision, the project continued and the diluted investment of Southpaw was worth much more as a result than would be the case if they had an undiluted interest in a failed company. See the *Schreiber Foods Inc. v Wepackit* decision discussed above for an example of how inappropriate action by a director can constitute oppression.

---

Companies will often obtain new funding by issuing additional shares. This can have the effect of diluting the interest of other shareholders, especially those in a minority position, if a sufficient portion of those new shares are not offered to the minority shareholders. For example, suppose 10 000 shares have been issued and a minority shareholder holds 4000 of them. If 5000 more shares were issued but not offered to that minority shareholder, his or her share of the company would drop from a 40 percent interest to a 27 percent interest which could completely alter the control structure of the company. To overcome this problem **pre-emptive rights** will often be given to shareholders in closely-held companies which require that a portion of any newly issued shares must be offered

*Shareholder may have pre-emptive rights*

---

[21]Ibid. s. 207.

[22]2013 BC SC. 187 (CanLII).

first to the present shareholders sufficient to maintain their percentage control of the corporation. In this example, the minority shareholder having 40 percent of the outstanding shares would have to be offered 2000 of the newly issued shares to maintain his or her position. In those jurisdictions where such pre-emptive rights are not included in the statute, they are often built into the incorporating documents or into a shareholders' agreement.

Perhaps the most important right of the minority shareholder is the right to bring a **representative action** (sometimes called a **derivative action**). Where the corporation has been wronged and has the right to sue, the directors are the ones to make that decision and they may choose not to do so. It may be the directors themselves who have failed in their duty to the corporation and, not surprisingly, refuse to sue themselves. Or the majority shareholder may obtain some benefit from the decision not to sue, as would be the case where the majority shareholder has an interest in the company that might be sued. In these circumstances any shareholder has a right to bring an action on behalf of the corporation (a representative action) and pursue the claim. Note that it is still the company that is doing the suing, not the shareholder. The shareholder must first have the action certified by the court and the shareholder then proceeds with the action on behalf of the corporation, much like a parent would bring an action on behalf of an injured child. But the shareholder must be bringing the action in good faith to protect an interest of the company and not for some personal reason.

> **Shareholder has right to bring representative action**

---

## Case Summary 7.11 *Re Richardson Greenshields of Canada Ltd. and Kalmacoff et al.*[23]

## Derivative Action Used to Thwart Directors

Richardson Greenshields of Canada Limited (Applicant/Appellant), Russell Kalmacoff and others (Respondents/Respondents) in an application in the Ontario Supreme Court and appealed to the Court of Appeal.

Security Home Mortgage Investment Corporation had both common shares held privately and preferred shares sold to the public. A management company involving some directors and the CEO of Security Home ran the company. Dissatisfaction arose with the arrangement. A vote was held among the shareholders, including the preferred shareholders, and it was decided to terminate the services of the management company. The board complied, but then simply rehired all of the same people to manage Security Homes. Richardson Greenshields, which had been involved in the public offering of the preferred shares and the successful vote, protested. It stated that rehiring the managers went against the stated wishes of the shareholders. When the protest was ignored, it bought several preferred shares of Security Home and brought

this derivative (representative) action against the directors directly.

Was Richardson Greenshields an appropriate complainant with the right to bring such an action? The trial judge said it was not, since it had purchased the shares after the rehiring had taken place. But the Court of Appeal disagreed. It found that even though Richardson Greenshields had purchased shares after the action complained of had taken place, and with the express purpose of launching this derivative action, it was still entitled to do so and qualified as a proper complainant under the *Act*.

This case shows dramatically that any shareholder can bring such a derivative (representative) action on behalf of the company with the court's permission, as long as he or she was bringing the application in good faith and there was a legitimate issue to be tried. Here the court held that it was in the best interests of the company to determine whether the rights given to the shareholders had been "improperly extinguished or rendered meaningless by the directors."

---

[23](1995), 123 D.L.R. (4th) 628 (ON CA).

# Directors

LO 8

While shareholders owe no duty to the corporation, directors do. Directors approve all the important decisions with respect to the operation of the corporation. They are the ultimate decision-makers and essentially the alter ego of the corporation, and they are answerable to the shareholders only in the sense that they must face re-election. Directors must function at a high standard when performing their responsibilities and are liable to the corporation when their conduct falls below that standard and causes loss or damage. They are required to "exercise the care, diligence and skill that a reasonably prudent person would exercise in comparable circumstances."[24] It is important to note that this duty is owed to the corporation, not to the shareholders who can only sue the directors on behalf of the corporation through a representative action when they fail in their duty. But as was noted in the Wise case[25], this duty to act competently may extend to creditors as well. And directors will be liable in tort for their own conduct where it causes injury or loss to another even when that action was performed on behalf of the business.

*Directors must exercise skill of reasonably prudent person*

Directors must also "act honestly and in good faith with a view to the best interests of the corporation."[26] Thus, the director has a fiduciary duty, And the nature of this duty was clarified by the Supreme Court of Canada in the BCE case. There, the court made it clear that the fiduciary duty of the director is owed not to the shareholders but to the corporation and only the corporation. However, the court did point out that in determining what was in the best interest of the corporation the director could take into consideration the interests of all the stakeholders involved, including shareholders, employees, and creditors. As was the case in the discussion of partnership above and agency in Chapter 6, a fiduciary duty imposes an obligation on the directors to act in the best interests of the corporation, even to the point of putting the corporation's interests ahead of their own. Any information or business opportunities that come to a director because of his or her position in the corporation belong to the corporation, not the director. All such information must be disclosed to the corporation (the other directors), and any such business opportunity must be passed on to the corporation. Only where the board of directors rejects the opportunity and gives permission to the director to pursue it can he or she take advantage of the deal. And even then, if there is any danger that it might cause harm to the corporation it would be wise not to participate. Remember that a shareholder may be able to bring a representative action against the director in such circumstances. Secret profits, commissions, kickbacks from suppliers, or other under-the-table dealings are all violations of this fiduciary duty and may also constitute a criminal offence. If the director finds himself in a position where the corporation's interests conflict with his own, he must disclose that conflict and not participate in the discussion of the matter in question or influence the decision. For example, if the corporation of which he or she is a director is considering the purchase of land and he or she has an interest, is part owner, or would otherwise benefit by the purchase, he or she would have to disclose this conflict of interest and leave the room as the other directors discussed and voted on the purchase. When this fiduciary duty is breached the director is liable to the corporation, not the shareholders, for any losses suffered and must account for any profits received.

*Director's duty owed to corporation*

*Director must act in best interest of corporation*

*Directors owe duty of honesty and good faith*

*Business opportunities must be passed on to corporation*

*Information must be passed on to corporation*

*Hidden payments violate fiduciary duty*

*Conflict of interest must be disclosed*

*Where violation director must pay over any profit*

---

[24]*Business Corporations Act,* R.S.O. 1990, c. B.16, s. 134 (1)(a) & (b) and *Canada Business Corporations Act* R.S.C. 1985 c. C-44 s 122 (1)(a) & (b).

[25]*Peoples Department Stores Inc. (Trustee of) v. Wise* [2004] 3 S.C.R. 461; 2004 SCC 68 (CanLII).

[26]Ibid. s. 134 (1) (a).

## Case Summary 7.12 *UPM-Kymmene Corp. v. UPM-Kymmene Miramichi Inc. et al.*[27]

# A Director Breaches His Fiduciary Duty

UPM-Kymmene Corp. (Plaintiff), UPM-Kymmene Miramichi Inc. et al. (Defendant) in an action brought in the Superior Court of Justice, Ontario. The case was appealed but the Court of Appeal agreed with the trial court's findings and decision. (Note that UPM-Kymmene Miramichi Inc. amalgamated with Repap and in the process the name was changed; the events took place under the Repap name.)

Mr. Berg arranged through a company that he controlled to acquire majority control of Repap Enterprises Inc. This included the change of a number of old directors and the appointment of new ones under his control. As part of the process he had himself appointed as a director and senior executive officer of Repap. He then arranged for Repap to pay him an exorbitant compensation package, including a huge salary, stock options, bonuses, pension provisions, and a generous termination allowance.

Eventually the old shareholders regained control of the company, appointed new directors, terminated Mr. Berg's contract, and refused to pay the $27 million he claimed he was owed for those services.

This action is brought by the new directors for a declaration that Mr. Berg had breached his fiduciary duty to the corporation. In fact, he had not disclosed all the pertinent information to the new board members who had approved the compensation contract. There should have been an independent evaluation, which was not done. The company couldn't afford such an exorbitant amount for his salary and benefits, and Mr. Berg should have known it. This was a breach of his fiduciary duty and also amounted to oppression. The court set the contract aside, and Berg was deprived of any claim against the company under it.

---

**Directors liable to creditors for improper dividends**

In addition to these obligations owed to the company, there are other important duties and liabilities imposed on the directors by statute for the wrongdoings of the business. First, directors will be liable to creditors if they declare dividends when the company is insolvent. The capital of the corporation must be preserved and dividends can only be declared out of profits. They could also be liable to creditors if their conduct amounts to oppression as discussed above. Also, the corporation has an obligation to collect and forward HST or PST and GST taken from customers and the deductions from the wages of employees for income tax, employment insurance, and workers' compensation assessments. The directors have the responsibility to see that this is done. They are even responsible directly to the employees for several months' unpaid wages, the actual number of months varying with the jurisdiction. Directors can also be held liable for environmental damage caused by the corporation and for offences under the *Competition Act* and other federal and provincial legislation, as well as direct liability for fraud or criminal activity.

**Directors must forward taxes and deductions**

**Directors are responsible for unpaid wages**

**LO 10**

An important source of potential liability for directors relates to their responsibilities with respect to the issue and sale of shares and other forms of securities to the public. Securities regulation was discussed with respect to consumers in Chapter 5. Here we will look at the process from the perspective of directors and corporate governance. The key responsibility when a decision is made to sell shares to the public is to ensure that all information disclosed is accurate and in no way misleading. The principle document is a **prospectus** that must be filed with the relevant provincial Securities and Exchange Commission. It must not only disclose audited financial reports and all other relevant information with respect to the securities to be issued but must satisfy all other requirements of

---

[27]2002 CanLII 11098 (ON SC); (2002), 214 D.L.R. (4th) 496 (Ont. S.C.J.).

provincial securities law. The CEO and directors of the corporation must also certify the information contained in the prospectus as correct. If any incorrect or misleading information is included those officers will be subject to penalties under the provincial securities law but also to criminal prosecution. Each province has a *Securities Act* that in turn empowers a securities commission to regulate and otherwise enforce its provisions.

Once the shares have been issued the directors and officers must ensure that all information disclosed that might affect the value of shares is accurate and ensure that no insider with private information can take advantage of that information at the expense of other traders. Audited financial statements must be filed yearly with the commission and distributed to shareholders along with other relevant information that might affect the value of the shares. In addition, other financial reports and filings of information must take place periodically as events arise that may have a significant impact on share value. The idea is to get the information out to the public as quickly as possible to ensure that there is a level playing field for the sale and resale of all securities. Officers, directors, and shareholders, with large enough holdings to be classified as insiders, are not prohibited from trading, but they must file a report with respect to the trades they do make so that there can be a review later to see if they took advantage of **insider information**. If they do take advantage of such non-public information by using it themselves or disclose it to others, they are not only subject to penalties, that include imprisonment under the *Securities Acts* and *Criminal Code*, but in many jurisdiction other traders who have been harmed by the process can sue the offender for the profits made at their expense. Recent changes to securities legislation in the provinces has imposed more stringent obligations on public corporations. For example, requiring that all such companies form an audit committee composed of members, independent from management, to oversee the financial affairs of the company.

Further information must be filed where significant changes

Insider must file report of trades

It is because of this potential liability that we often see directors resign as a group from large corporations that have run into financial difficulty. Even the director's claims that he or she did not participate in a questionable decision or that he or she missed the meeting will not provide a sufficient excuse. Only where the directors can show that they exercised due diligence might they avoid such responsibility. In raising this defence, the director or officer charged must show that they have taken reasonable steps to ensure the violation did not take place or to comply with the regulations. This may require putting systems in place to ensure that the complained of event will not happen, for example, proper selection and training programs for employees and the establishing of policies and procedures that will avoid the problem.

Failure to establish adequate training for workers in the area concerned will likely destroy any due diligence defence.

A classic example of a director's liability for pollution involves a shoe manufacturing company that failed to store liquid waste properly. It was stored in barrels, which began to leak. Three executives were charged with environmental offences, but only one was able to raise due diligence as a defence and avoid responsibility. The plant manager made inadequate inspection of the site, and the director charged knew of the problem and failed to correct it. Only the president of the company was able to successfully claim due diligence on the basis of having established appropriate procedures to avoid the problem, and reasonably relying on the competence of those given the responsibility to implement those procedures.[28] Note that due diligence defences have been raised in many situations

Director responsible for pollution and other statutory offences

Director may use of due diligence defence

---

[28] *R. v. Bata Industries Ltd.* (1992), 9 O.R. (3d) 329 (Ont. Prov. Ct).

in addition to environmental legislation. These include failing to forward taxes and other funds collected on behalf of government; violations of the *Competition Act*, privacy legislation, and safety legislation for workers; *Food and Drug Act* violations; building code violations; and even parking ticket violations. Note, also, that under many of these statutes both the corporation and the directors themselves can be held responsible. Establishing due diligence on the part of the directors, who are the guiding minds of the corporation, or the manager or employee responsible for the area, will protect the corporation as well. To protect directors from this kind of exposure it is common to include in their contracts terms providing insurance and indemnification for losses they incur and legal expenses brought about by their involvement in these types of actions.

**Directors appoint and control managers**

An important responsibility of the directors is to appoint the various officers of the corporation that make up the management team. These are typically the chair of the board of directors, the president, vice-president, secretary, treasurer, general manager, and any others so designated that look after the day to day operation of the business. Their responsibilities are determined by the by-laws, but they bear a similar duty to the corporation as do directors—to perform their duties with the care, diligence, and skill of a reasonably prudent person, and to act honestly and in good faith in the best interests of the corporation. They also are usually included along with directors with respect to the liability imposed under the statutes discussed above. In a closely-held corporation it is common for these offices to be reduced to a minimum and held by the directors and shareholders. Note also that when a corporation is first formed, those promoting it have the same responsibilities to it as subsequent directors and officers, but they also have an obligation not to misrepresent or conceal information from future shareholders and not to sell property they hold to the corporation at an inflated price.

**Managers have similar duties as directors**

**Promoters also have a duty not to mislead**

---

## Case Summary 7.13 *Canada v Buckingham*[29]

## Director Responsible for GST/HST and Other Payments

Mr. Buckingham, Defendant in this action brought by the Crown in the Tax Court of Canada and Respondent when the Crown appealed to the Federal Court of Appeal.

Kevin Richard Buckingham was a director and major shareholder in Mosaic Technologies Corporation established in 1997 to provide educational services in various locations across Canada. The company had some success but generally lost money until it ceased operation in 2003. At the time the company ceased operation it had failed to remit income to the government with respect to GST/HST premiums and income tax, pension and employment insurance premiums that were required to be withhold from employees' pay. The company has no funds and so in this action the government is seeking to obtain those payments plus penalties and costs directly from the officer/

director of the company (Mr. Buckingham) as permitted under the *Estate Tax Act*, the *Income Tax Act*, the *Canada Pension Plan Act,* and the *Employment Insurance Act*.

Mr. Buckingham raises the defence of due diligence stating that he acted reasonably in the circumstances exercising proper business judgment and therefore is not liable. Before the company collapsed, Mr. Buckingham was trying to keep it afloat and had to use what funds it had to do so. He had tried to sell the business and had to keep the employees together and the firm as a going concern in order to get anything for it. In fact, one division was sold and some money was directed towards these government claims and to other creditors, but the total purchase price was never obtained and the company failed. This left considerable debt, including the outstanding claims with

---

[29]*Canada v. Buckingham*, 2011 FCA 142 (CanLII).

respect to GST/HST and employee deductions. This due diligence defence was accepted at the trial level but overturned on appeal.

The Court of Appeal found that with respect to these statutes the duty of the director was not to take reasonable steps to cure the failure to remit but to prevent it from happening in the first place. When the services were sold the GST/HST funds were paid by third parties. Those funds should have been remitted at that time not diverted to keep the company afloat. The same applied to the employee pay. When that pay was issued it included the amounts to be remitted to the government and the duty of the corporation was to remit those funds to the government not to divert them for other uses. Mr. Buckingham failed in this obligation and therefore was personally liable. He could not claim a due diligence defence even though it may have seemed like a sound business decision to divert these funds in order to keep the company afloat with the hope of curing the omission by selling off the company or portions of it later as a going concern.

The case illustrates that although most of these regulations provide for a due diligence defence, it is not enough to simply have a sound business reason that supports what has been done. In this case the provisions in the statutes were designed to discourage exactly what Mr. Buckingham did.

As illustrated here a corporation doesn't have a body and so everything it does has to be done through others. However, in some circumstances the corporation itself can be liable for the wrongs committed by its directors and other representatives. It is common for a corporation to be directly responsible in tort and contract law but it should also be noted that corporations can be held directly liable under several of the statutes discussed above where the directors and officers fail in their responsibilities. The *Criminal Code* was amended after the Westray Mine disaster in Nova Scotia, imposing increased accountability to those in charge of organizations, including partnerships and corporations and to the organizations themselves. Thus, the corporation itself can be criminally charged where a senior officer or others acting under authority negligently causes death or injury.

# FINANCING

LO 2/LO 9/LO 10

## Raising Funds

Perhaps the major advantage to incorporation after limited liability is the flexibility that structure allows with respect to raising funds. The company can obtain funds through **equity financing**, where investors purchase shares, and through **debt financing**, where money is loaned to the corporation by creditors (see Figure 7.4). When a company is first incorporated, it has an authorized share capital but normally only issues a portion of those shares to investors. This allows the company to issue more shares when additional funds are needed. In most jurisdictions no value is put on these shares when issued and the market determines their worth.

Corporations allow flexible financing

Equity financing involves the issuing of shares

Issued shares usually much less than authorized share capital

**Corporation**

$     $

**Equity financing**
- Preferred shares
- Common shares
- Other classes

**Debt financing**
- Bonds/debentures
- Unsecured loans
- Secured loans

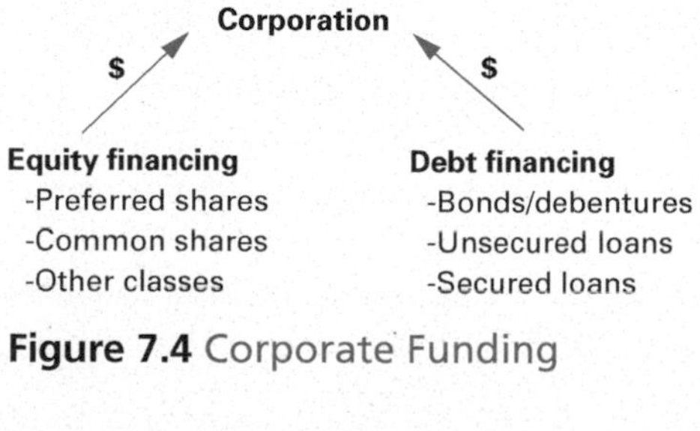

**Figure 7.4** Corporate Funding

**Common shares have no special rights or restrictions**

**Preferred shareholders are usually promised dividend but can't vote**

**Unpaid dividends can accumulate**

**Shareholders often loan funds to a corporation**

**Debt financing involves corporation borrowing money**

**Creditor usually takes security for loan**

**Personal guarantee defeats limited liability**

**Failure to pay usually gives creditor right to appoint receiver**

In a closely-held corporation, shares, whether common or preferred, are usually sold directly to the participants in the business, who are often employees, officers and directors, as well as shareholders. The formalities of reporting and communication of other information are less onerous, but the requirement of disclosure is still very stringent. As mentioned, common shares normally have all the rights associated with shares, including voting rights and earning dividends. However, preferred shares have restrictions. They usually have a specific dividend promised but have no right to vote, except where the dividend is not paid. But it must be emphasized that the actual rights associated with preferred shares can vary depending on the shares issued and that there is no actual right to a dividend whether the shares are common or preferred. If the expected dividend is not paid there is no right to sue although those unpaid dividends may accumulate and the failure may trigger the right to vote.

In a broadly held corporation, where shares are sold on a stock market, the controls imposed on the participants are much more stringent and formal. The idea is to keep the market at a level playing field by preventing any participant, including those associated with the corporation (called insiders), from having an advantage over those with less information. Thus, when shares are initially issued the corporation must issue a prospectus, which includes carefully drafted and regulated information that discloses to all potential investors the information that they need to decide to invest. If important information is withheld or is misleading, penalties, including criminal charges may be imposed on those responsible. (See Chapter 5 discussion of securities regulation.)

Since a corporation is a separate person in the eyes of the law, like anyone else, the corporation can borrow money. Thus, debt is another important method of financing the business. Often the shareholders will loan the corporation money to get it started. There is normally no advantage to purchase more shares, as that would only upset the control structure of the firm. The shareholder simply becomes a creditor for the amount of the loan and by taking a security against the assets of the business they can become a secured creditor much like Mr. Salomon did in the case noted above (see Footnote 17). Today, however, the shareholder even as a secured creditor may not be in as advantageous a position with respect to those others creditors as was Mr. Salomon.

Alternatively, the company can borrow from some other creditor such as a bank. Creditors will usually require some security that will ensure the repayment of the money advanced if the business fails. This is often difficult for a new business, even where there are significant assets, and so the creditor will usually insist that the shareholders, directors, or some other financially stable person sign a personal guarantee, usually in addition to other forms of security, to repay the loan. If the corporation fails and cannot repay the debt, the individual guarantor is personally responsible for that debt (see Table 7.1). By this single stroke the major advantage of incorporation, limited liability, is defeated. And, in fact, most new businesses are in this position, much to the dismay of the entrepreneurs starting them.

Where broadly held corporations are involved they will often turn to another form of debt financing involving the creation of a large debt obligation, either secured or unsecured, which a trustee is then named to manage. Small portions of this debt (called **bonds** or **debentures**) are issued to the public and then traded on the market much like shares.

No matter what form the debt financing takes, the creditor usually insists on a term in the contract giving them the right in the event of **default** to take over the business,

## Table 7.1 Liability Summary

|  | Nature of Business | Individual Liability |
|---|---|---|
|  | Sole proprietorship | Sole proprietor faces unlimited liability |
|  | Partnership | Partner faces unlimited liability for obligations of firm or other partners |
| When victim sues | Limited partnership | Limited partner faces loss of investment only (limited liability only) |
|  | Limited liability partnership | Only partner directly responsible faces unlimited liability |
|  | Corporation | Shareholders face the loss of investment only (limited liability only) |
|  | Corporation with personal guarantee | Guarantor liable for debt to creditor |

replacing the directors with a **receiver**. This is referred to as a corporation going into **receivership**.

Note that this is not the bankruptcy process discussed in Chapter 5, although it may trigger that process. Rather, this is simply the creditor exercising a right included in the financing agreement. Of course, the creditor will have any other rights included in the agreement, such as the right to seek payment from a guarantor or to take possession and sell whatever has been used to secure the loan. Note that, as discussed in Chapter 5, one of the options under the federal *Bankruptcy and Insolvency Act* is to make a proposal to the creditors. When this is done, the rights of the creditors are frozen, giving the debtor a limited period of time to reorganize the financial affairs of the company and solve the financial difficulties. Such a proposal would also prevent a receiver from taking over the management of the business until the expiration of the protection period. An application by large companies to the court under the federal *Companies' Creditors Arrangement Act* would have a similar delaying effect. Creditors can also sue for oppression.

Proposals delay actions by creditors

## The Shareholders' Agreement

LO 9

Throughout this discussion several references have been made to shareholders' agreements. These normally are involved with smaller businesses where the corporation is closely held. Usually, there are only a few shareholders and they want to set out rights and responsibilities with respect to each other that are not included in the incorporating documents. For example, three shareholders may get together to set up a restaurant: They may divide the shares equally but that structure may not reflect how they want to divide their responsibilities in the business. Their rights and obligations can be specified in a shareholders' agreement. The contract might designate one as the investor, and the other two as full-time employees (one chef and one manager) specifying the terms of that employment. The shareholders' agreement is much like a partnership agreement and can set out any unique provisions with respect to their business relationship that they want. For example, it might include terms that specify what wage the shareholders who are also employees are to be paid, under what circumstances that employment can be ended, and what then happens to

Position of shareholders can be further refined through shareholders' agreement

Shareholders' agreement can protect minority shareholder

their shares. Where the employment of one is terminated, the agreement might require the others to purchase that person's shares and the agreement would also likely include a method of valuation. A method for resolving disputes such an arbitration clause would also normally be included. Of course, there must be a consensus between them with respect to the contract and it must comply with any legislation in place.

Shareholders' agreements can ensure employment and restrict control

---

## Case Summary 7.14 *Wittenberg v. Merks Poultry Farms Ltd.*[30]

## Shareholders' Agreements Can Override Majority Rule in Corporations

Andrew Merks and others (Plaintiffs/Respondents), Richard Wittenberg and others (Defendants/Appellants) in an action brought before the Supreme Court of Nova Scotia and appealed to the Nova Scotia Court of Appeal.

In 2002, Richard Wittenberg and Andre Merks, two chicken farmers, agreed to form another corporation to supply feed for their various operations. Synergy Agri Group Inc. was formed and over the years more shareholders were added, making the total seven when a shareholders' agreement was entered into between them in 2006. Important terms of that agreement included that there were to be seven directors, one appointed by each shareholder, and that any changes to this arrangement would require a two-thirds majority vote. The percentages used to determine the eligible votes were to be based on the amount of feed purchased from the feedlot in the prior year. In 2007 relations deteriorated between the directors, and Mr. Merks resigned as president but remained as a director. His company's purchases for feed from Synergy also declined. In 2008, over his objections, on a vote of 6 to 1 he was voted out as director and the total number of directors reduced to six.

He brought this action for oppression based on the shareholders' agreement for a declaration that he was still a director and that there were still seven directors. The judge examined the percentages of votes and determined that the decision was not based on a 2/3 majority as required by the shareholders' agreement. He determined therefore that Mr. Merks was still a director and the decision to oust him and reduce the number of directors was void. The judge also noted that even if a 2/3 majority was not required for the decision, the shareholders' agreement still required that the number of the directors be seven and that they were to be appointed by each of the shareholders. The agreement also required complete agreement for any of the terms of the shareholders' agreement to be changed.

This case illustrates just how important the terms of a shareholders' agreement can be. Here the other shareholders were not able to force Mr. Merks out as director even by a majority vote because of that agreement. And it is yet another example of the importance of the right to sue for oppression.

---

## LO 11    Corporate Governance—Abuses and Responsibilities

Although this is an introductory text, a few words must be added about the responsibilities of those in control of these corporations, especially broadly held corporations traded on the stock exchange. In recent years there have been many examples of ineptitude, abuses, and even outright fraud and theft. The 2007 financial debacle in the United States and its aftermath created a worldwide crisis with the near collapse of the economy, including the failure of several banking and trading organizations and the failure of the mortgage giants of Federal Home Loan Mortgage Corporation (Freddie Mac) and Federal National Mortgage Association (Fannie Mae). These have led directly to huge downturns in the stock

---

[30]2009 NS CA 70 (CanLII).

and housing markets and are responsible for the global recession from which we are slowly recovering. The Enron scandal, which led to the failure of that company and brought down the accounting partnership of Arthur Andersen, was the direct result of the fraud of the principals of that corporation. WorldCom (another accounting fraud) and the prosecution of Conrad Black are more examples of criminality resulting in tremendous losses to ordinary people. The largest Ponzi scheme in history was perpetrated by Bernard Madoff, who was convicted and will be spending the rest of his life in prison. This fraud resulted in the suicide of his son and at least one suicide of an individual who had lost billions of dollars he invested in that scheme on behalf of his clients.

All of these failures and frauds have resulted in increased vigilance and tighter regulation, but no matter how tight these controls are there will always be clever people who can get around them. The separate legal entity nature of corporations doing business abroad, such as mining companies operating in the third world has led to an as yet unresolved problem. Usually a shell company is incorporated for this purpose with shares held by the parent company. Where human rights abuses take place, such as protesting workers who are beaten or murdered, the parent company bears no responsibility because of its separate legal entity status even though it may directly or indirectly benefit from the violence. The most we can do is ensure that ethical standards practiced in our own business endeavours remain high and that we take great care in selecting the people who will control companies. To encourage ethics in multinational corporations, the United Nations has established the **Global Compact**, a network of public and private institutions designed to advance ethical behaviour and to encourage all institutions and corporations to align their operations and strategies with the following ten principles, which constitute a basic ethical guide (see Table 7.2).[31]

Global compact encourages ethical behaviour

### Table 7.2 Ten Principles of the Global Compact

| | |
|---|---|
| Human Rights | 1. Support and respect the protection of internationally proclaimed human rights |
| | 2. Make sure that they are not complicit in human rights abuses |
| Labour Standards | 3. Uphold freedom of association and the effective recognition of the right to collective bargaining |
| | 4. Eliminate of all forms of forced and compulsory labour |
| | 5. Support the effective abolition of child labour |
| | 6. Eliminate discrimination in respect of employment and occupation |
| Environment | 7. Support a precautionary approach to environmental challenges |
| | 8. Undertake initiatives to promote greater environmental responsibility |
| | 9. Encourage the development and diffusion of environmentally friendly technologies |
| Anti-Corruption | 10. Work against all forms of corruption, including extortion and bribery |

---

[31]See an overview of the UN Global Compact at http://www.unglobalcompact.org

Most of the scandals mentioned above have involved attempts to manipulate the stock market through accounting or other frauds. Section 397 of the *Criminal Code of Canada* states that anyone who "destroys, mutilates, alters, falsifies, makes a false entry in or omits forms in a valuable security, book or document with an intent to defraud is guilty of an offence and liable to imprisonment for up to five years."[32] There are also many other specialized sections dealing with serious internal and external embezzlement and fraud.

**Fraud and embezzlement can constitute criminal offence**

In fact, the instances of such fraud are increasing, partly due to corporate downsizing, which weakens internal controls and creates employee uncertainty. These, in turn, affect loyalty. Mergers often lead to problems with integrating people from different organizations into a new one. Additional risks have been created by the communications revolution and the global economy. The combination of these things results in fewer mechanisms of detection and control, and more opportunity to defraud a business from within and without. It should not be surprising that long-term employees in positions of trust and control commit most internal fraud, since they have the opportunity to divert company funds or initiate actions that manipulate the market and are least likely to be suspected. Fraud increases when the ethical structure of a business weakens. Technology and globalization contribute to the risk due to increased opportunity. Opportunity is also increased by dealing with strangers and with people with a wide range of values and business ethics. Business practices that are illegal here are sometimes common in other cultures. Corporate bribery in association with carrying on business in foreign countries has historically been treated as simply an additional cost of carrying on business. Today such bribery is now a crime in Canada the US and the UK. And the enforcement is becoming more stringent with even the payment of "facilitation fees" to foreign government officials forbidden.

Another significant factor contributing to the increase in corporate crime is the increased role played by organized criminal organizations both in Canada and in other countries where Canadian corporations deal. These organizations are often involved in laundering funds from various criminal activities such as counterfeiting, forgery, drugs, prostitution and various forms of computer and internet fraud by transferring those funds to legitimate business activities or to offshore banks and financial institutions. Because this has become so prevalent, controls are now imposed requiring companies and institutions dealing in large sums of money especially when those funds are transferred abroad, to satisfy much stricter regulations.

**Loss-prevention team can reduce fraud**

A major objective of a business, and an area that is often neglected, should be the prevention and detection of corporate fraud. Management must take responsibility and institute appropriate measures. Often the appointment of a specific loss-prevention team will focus efforts in this area, enabling managers to buy into the loss-prevention process, even though it is unpleasant. A comprehensive system of audits, not only of financial matters but also inspecting other aspects of the business, including how computers and other company facilities are used, can also be very helpful. Management that is vigilant in assessing risk and develops proactive strategies for risk avoidance is vital. Having good ethical standards and a published and distributed statement of the company's policies and code of conduct, combined with appropriate accountability and training for employees and staff, may go some way to avoid internal fraud. It may also serve to establish a due diligence defence by showing that reasonable efforts were made on the part of a corporation to avoid

---

[32]*Criminal Code* sec. 397.

illegal activity. And whenever there is doubt, it is always a good principle to seek the advice of professionals such as accountants and lawyers.

## FLEXIBILITY

It is also important to point out that partnerships and corporations as set out above are the basic building blocks of modern business. Many different combinations of these structural elements can be arranged to satisfy the needs of various enterprises. For example, it is common for companies to engage in **joint ventures** with each other. These are contractual relationships where two or more businesses get together for some project, usually of limited duration usually giving rise to a duty of good faith between the participants. In fact, joint ventures can take many different forms. They can be no more than a contractual arrangement, but they can also involve partnership arrangements, corporations, corporations in partnership, holding companies, and the like. For example, two different oil companies might cooperate to develop a pipeline or combine their resources to open a particular gas field. They might incorporate a separate company to take on the project, each making a financial contribution as a shareholder in that new corporation and each appointing directors to run it. There would likely be a shareholders' agreement, and the money might well be put forward as a shareholders' loan. Or the two companies might enter into a partnership to carry on the project, again with particulars set out in a partnership agreement. Remember that although the partnership conveys unlimited liability, the partners themselves are corporations each with the advantage of limited liability for the shareholder.

Another common way these organizations are combined is with a holding company. One individual might have 51 percent of the shares in a company that, in turn, has 51 percent of the shares in another company that, in turn, has 51 percent of the shares in a third company. That individual, with only a fraction of the actual equity ownership of the third company, retains complete control of all of them.

Preferred shares, shareholders' loans, and shareholders' agreements can also be used in joint ventures and other business enterprises, giving the business person a very flexible canvas on which to create a structure to do business that is completely unique to his or her needs. As a result, there is no specific form these business ventures can take, and the liability of the participants will be based on agency, partnership, and corporation principles, depending on the vehicle chosen.

## FRANCHISE

Another common method of doing business today is through a **franchise**. A franchise is not a specific legal structure of carrying on business, but has become an important vehicle, especially for retail business in Canada. In a franchise arrangement one business enters into contract with another to sell its product exclusively with appropriate names, logos, and advertising exclusive to the chain. From the point of view of the franchisor, it is a very effective way to expand their business with little risk, and from the point of view of the franchisee, they become part of a successful business enterprise. It must be emphasized that the franchisee and the franchisor are two different corporations, and they are normally not considered to be in partnership with each other.

Typically the franchisor will sell the right to do business in a given area to a smaller corporation (the franchisee). The franchisor provides the product and other supplies and

*Corporations and partnership can be used in combination*

*Companies can come together in a joint venture*

*Holding companies ensure control*

*Franchise relationship based on contract*

equipment; advertising; a licence to use the name, trademark, and logos; any secret formulas; as well as training and careful supervision, including management help. They sometimes even provide financing to the franchisee. Usually a standardized accounting system is supplied, likely more to protect the franchisor than to assist the franchisee. The franchisee must comply with rules, standards, and specifications with respect to the preparation of products, prices, advertising, and accounting so that there is a commonality among the various franchisees and different locations. Often the franchisor will actually own the land and build the facility, leasing it as a going concern to the franchisee.

In addition to an initial investment of capital, the franchisee is normally required to pay a substantial franchise fee, as well as regular payments to the franchisor for supplies and services, and often a percentage of the profits. Common examples of franchises in Canada range from fast-food outlets like Tim Hortons, A & W, KFC, and Starbucks, to other forms of businesses, including Budget and other car rental agencies, computer stores, and the like. The franchisee, of course, gets exclusive access to the product, the advantage of the advertising, the right to use the trademarks, company logos, and other promotional materials, and to participate in promotions and other activities generated by the parent company.

**Danger of unequal bargaining position of franchisee**

One important drawback to these arrangements is the unequal bargaining position of the parties. Typically, the franchisor is a very large organization and the franchisee is a small entrepreneur who is not in a position to insist on favourable terms in any agreement. Standard form contracts are thus imposed on the franchisee, usually greatly favouring the parent franchisor with the inclusion of restrictive covenants and limited liability exemption clauses. Still, it is in the franchisor's interest to do all they can to ensure the success of the franchisee outlet, and so many of these arrangements have proved a very successful method of carrying on business.

**Statutes passed to control abuses**

This structure is open to abuse and there are many examples of such abuse, both by the franchisor and the franchisee. Because of this, several provinces (Ontario, Alberta, Manitoba, Prince Edward Island, and New Brunswick) have statutes regulating the franchise business. The idea is to create a more level playing field between the parties, much like consumer protection legislation. The main provisions of these acts are the obligation of fair dealing and good faith for both parties and the disclosure requirements imposed on the franchisor, as well as the remedies imposed for violations. Note also that because of broad wording in the statutes, franchise law is being extended to cover other contract based relationships, such as distributorship agreements for products or services where the parties never intended or imagined that they were in a franchise relationship. The following case is an example of what happens when those disclosure provisions are not followed.

---

Case Summary 7.15 *Salah v. Timothy's Coffees of the World Inc.*[33]

## Franchisee's Successful Claim for Breach of Contract and Breach of Good Faith

Abdulhamid Salah and his company (Plaintiffs/Respondents), Timothy's Coffees of the World Inc. (Defendant/Appellant) in an action brought in the Ontario Superior Court of Justice and appealed to the Court of Appeal.

Timothy's entered into a five-year lease of a premises on the third floor of a shopping mall operated by Bayshore Shopping Centre in Ottawa. Then they entered into a franchise agreement as franchisor with Mr. Salah as franchisee

---

[33]2009 CanLII 58066 (ON SC) trial and appeal 2010 ON CA 673 (CanLII).

and sublessee of that premises. At the time of the franchise agreement, the lease had four years remaining and because of Mr. Salah's concern about the short term remaining, a schedule "A" was added to the franchise agreement stating that if a new lease were entered into with Bayshore, the franchise agreement would be renewed with a new sublease for the same period. Prior to the expiration of the head lease for the third-floor location Timothy's negotiated for a new lease with Bayshore but at a different location on the second floor. It did not inform Mr. Salah about this and in fact went so far as to direct Bayshore to keep any information about the new lease from Mr. Salah. Bayshore entered into a different agreement with a new franchisee with respect to that new second floor location and simply let the third-floor lease expire, thinking that that would end their relationship with Mr. Salah.

Mr. Salah sued, seeking damages for breach of the franchise agreement and for the bad faith shown by Timothy's. Timothy's took the position that the franchise agreement applied only to the third-floor location, and since that lease had expired so had the agreement. But the trial judge determined that the terms of the franchise agreement, in particular schedule "A," made no reference to the third-floor location but in fact specifically referred to a new lease with Bayshore and that included anywhere in that Bayshore mall. In creating the new lease and not renewing the franchise agreement with Mr. Salah, Timothy's had breached the franchise agreement. Damages of $230 358 were awarded for the breach of the agreement. Further, their conduct in trying to keep the information from Mr. Salah amounted to bad faith and a further $50 000 damages were awarded for a breach of the duty of good faith owed and for mental distress. The Court of Appeal upheld this decision. Note that the damages for the breach of the duty of good faith was an application of the *Arthur Wishart Act*,[34] which is the Ontario act designed to protect franchisees.

This case illustrates how important it is for a franchisee to anticipate all important aspects of the transaction and ensure they are included in the franchise agreement. It also illustrates how many provinces are enacting legislation specifically intended to protect franchisees from this kind of abusive conduct.

There are many different variations of business arrangements, and likely many more will be developed by creative business people. The point is that the various methods of doing business as described in this chapter are only the basic organizations. They can be combined and varied to such an extent that most business needs can be accommodated.

*Many variations of organization accommodate business*

## Key Terms

**articles of incorporation** (p. 218)

**bonds** (p. 232)

**broadly held corporation** (p. 218)

**closely held corporation** (p. 218)

**common shares** (p. 219)

**conflict of interest** (p. 211)

**debentures** (p. 232)

**debt financing** (p. 231)

**default** (p. 232)

**derivative action** (p. 226)

**directors** (p. 219)

**dissent** (p. 224)

**dividends** (p. 219)

**equity financing** (p. 231)

**franchise** (p. 237)

**Global Compact** (p. 235)

**insider information** (p. 229)

**joint ventures** (p. 237)

**letters patent** (p. 218)

**limited liability** (p. 215)

**limited liability partnerships** (p. 210)

**oppression** (p. 224)

**partnership** (p. 206)

**partnership agreements** (p. 212)

**pre-emptive rights** (p. 225)

**preferred shares** (p. 219)

---

[34]*Arthur Wishart Act (Franchise Disclosure)*, 2000, S.O., c.3.

profit (p. 207)

prospectus (p. 228)

proxy (p. 224)

receiver (p. 233)

receivership (p. 233)

registration (p. 218)

representative action (p. 226)

separate legal person (p. 221)

shareholders (p. 219)

sole proprietor (p. 204)

unlimited liability (p. 204)

## Questions for Student Review

1. Why is it so important to take care in choosing the method used to carry on a business?

2. Explain the nature of a sole proprietorship and the liability of a sole proprietor. Why do professionals often do business in this way?

3. Describe the nature of a partnership, the purpose and effect of the *Partnership Act*, and the effect a partnership agreement can have on the relationship between the parties as set out in that statute.

4. What factors will indicate the existence of a partnership?

5. Explain the nature of the liability of partners and the effect of a partnership agreement on a partner's liability to outsiders. How will the retirement of a partner affect those obligations?

6. Explain how major decisions are made in a partnership and how partners are paid.

7. What is the nature of a partner's duty and to whom is that duty owed?

8. Explain what will bring a partnership to an end and how the assets of the partnership are to be distributed upon dissolution.

9. What is a limited partner? What is the extent of limited liability? What qualifications must be met for such a limited partnership to exist and how can it be lost? Distinguish such a limited partnership from a limited liability partnership.

10. What is the effect of incorporation and what is meant by the term "corporate myth"?

11. Distinguish between the articles of incorporation and the by-laws of a corporation.

12. Distinguish between broadly held and closely held corporations.

13. Explain the right of a shareholder with respect to control of the corporation, how that right is exercised, and what is meant by shareholders' limited liability.

14. Explain under what circumstances the courts may "lift the corporate veil," and the consequences of that happening.

15. Explain the consequences of a corporation being a separate legal entity and what happens to a corporation when all of the shareholders die.

16. Describe the advantages and disadvantages of having the ownership and management of a corporation separate.

17. What is meant by a shareholder's right to dissent, to be free from oppression, and pre-emptive rights with respect to the corporation?

18. Explain what is meant by a representative action, when it arises, and who can bring such an action.

19. What are the duties of a director and to whom are those duties owed? What standard of care is required of that director? What constitutes a director's duty of good faith?

20. What are the various ways a director can breach his or her fiduciary duty? Explain the consequences of such a breach.

21. Explain a director's liability for improperly declared dividends, failure to collect deductions from employees, and the consequences of such a failure. How does due diligence affect those obligations?

22. Describe effective strategies for a corporation to avoid being the victim of fraud and theft.

23. Distinguish between authorized and issued share capital, and common and preferred shares. Explain the rights of a preferred shareholder when they are not paid the dividend promised.

24. Distinguish between equity and debt financing. Explain the nature of bonds and how they differ from shares.

25. Explain what is meant by a company going into receivership. How does receivership differ from bankruptcy? Explain how a proposal under the *Bankruptcy and Insolvency Act* may affect the position of a creditor.

26. Describe the kind of corporations where a shareholders' agreement would likely be found and the effect it will likely have on the position of a minority shareholder.

27. Give examples of various ways that corporations can be abused and how those abuses can be avoided.

28. Explain what is meant by a joint venture, a holding company, and a franchise. Why are they attractive ways of doing business?

## Questions for Further Discussion

1. One of the great advantages of a corporation over a partnership is the limited liability of the shareholder investors. If the business runs into trouble, the debts are the corporation's rather than the shareholders', who can only lose what they have invested. This is one of the most important characteristics of a corporation and one of the significant limitations of a partnership. Discuss whether such limited liability is appropriate from a business point of view. Is it fair to all parties? What about creditors or others who have claims against the business because of poor decisions that have been made? Who should be responsible? In your response consider the movement toward creating limited liability partnerships and whether this is a forward or a backward step. Also consider the creation of the corporate myth, which is the basis for the limited liability of shareholders.

2. It is possible to be in partnership with someone else without knowing it, simply by getting into some sort of cooperative business venture. The burdens associated with partnership, especially unlimited liability for a partner's actions, can be very onerous. Discuss whether people should ever have partnership imposed on them or whether this relationship should be limited to those situations where there is a clear understanding between the parties to create such a partnership relationship.

3. A corporation is considered a legal entity, separate and apart from the shareholders who make it up. This is a myth or fiction and has no basis in reality. Most of the unique characteristics of corporations result from this separate legal entity status. Discuss whether this bit of make-believe in our legal system is justified, considering the result. In your answer consider the recent well-known events involving corporate crime, swindles, and other abuses such as Enron or WorldCom, the banking and subprime mortgage scandals, and the worldwide recession caused by the collapse of the financial sector. Do you think doing away with the corporate myth would make any difference?

4. While shareholders are isolated from liability for the careless actions of corporations, this protection is not always carried through to directors, who may be held criminally and civilly liable for the actions of the corporation, especially when they cause physical injury to others.

Directors, like partners, also owe a fiduciary duty to the corporation and can be personally sued when they violate that duty. Discuss the relative obligations of directors and partners to each other, to the business, and to outsiders. Consider whether the imposition of such liability goes too far or not far enough from a business and ethical point of view. In your discussion consider the nature of fiduciary duty and whether such an overwhelming obligation has any place in the business world.

## Cases for Discussion

1. *Atlantic Glass and Storefronts Ltd. v. Price,* (1974), 48 D.L.R. (3d) 471 (N.S. Co. Ct.)

   Mr. Price originally operated "Fins, Furs and Feathers" as a sole proprietor but neglected to register the change under the *Partnerships and Business Names Registration Act* when he incorporated the business as P.R. Enterprises Ltd. When the company failed to pay its supplier—Atlantic Glass and Storefronts Ltd.—the supplier sued Mr. Price directly instead of the company. Is Mr. Price personally liable? Explain the arguments on each side.

2. *Red Burrito Ltd. v. Hussain* 2007 BC SC 1277 (CanLII)

   Hussain and Hingora operated the Papaya Market and they entered into a "letter of understanding" with Red Burrito, the operator of several restaurants in the Vancouver area, to convert the market into another Red Burrito restaurant. A new company was to be incorporated, with Hussain and Red Burrito having equal shares. Red Burrito was to arrange and pay for remodelling and start-up costs and Hussain was to manage the business. Hussain was also responsible to arrange that the lease for the premises held by himself and Hingora would be assigned to the new company. The new company was never incorporated and the lease was never assigned. The remodelling was done and the business opened, but after a disagreement, Hussain locked the Red Burrito people out of the restaurant and continued running it himself. They sued claiming a share of the assets and lease. Explain the arguments on each side and what the court will likely do in these circumstances.

3. *Public Trustee v. Mortimer et al.* (1985), 16 D.L.R. (4th) 404 (Ont. H.C.J.)

   Mortimer was a partner in a law firm and acted as the executor for the estate of Mrs. Amy Cooper. When she died, he distributed the proceeds of the estate to a series of beneficiaries. He also stole over $200 000 of the estate, keeping it for himself. The problem here was whether the other partners were also liable for Mr. Mortimer's wrongful conduct. Discuss the arguments on both sides. What kind of information is needed to answer the question?

4. *Schmidt v. Peat Marwick Thorne* 1994 CanLII 453 (BC CA)

   Mr. Schmidt worked as a partner in the Abbotsford accounting firm of Peat Marwick Thorne, when he informed the partnership that he wanted to retire and help his sons on their farms. The partnership agreement notice period was reduced considerably and the firm agreed to pay out Mr. Schmidt over $125 000 for goodwill from a previous merger, $65 000 for work in progress, a $55 800 "disposition fee" payable over five years, and a two-year consulting contract to cover the transition. The agreement also included a term that if he did enter into practice again the "disposition fee would not be payable," but that there would be no other ramifications. In fact, he never did intend to retire but had arranged to join another accounting firm, Ernst and Young, and take his clients with him. He eventually took 65 clients with him and had actually been soliciting several other accountants of the firm to go with him during the time he had been negotiating the early retirement agreement. The firm learned of his plans just after he left and stopped payment on the cheques they had issued. Schmidt sued to enforce the contract, and Peat Marwick Thorne sued for the losses associated with the clients lost. Explain the arguments on both sides and the likely outcome.

5. *Rochwerg et al. v. Truster et al.*, 2002 CanLII 41715 (ON CA) ; [2002] O.J. No. 1230 (C.A.)

   Mr. Rochwerg was a partner in an accounting firm, and while he paid over some of the remuneration he received from serving as a director on two associated companies, he failed to disclose the fact that he was also entitled to stock options. When the other partners discovered the existence of the stock options, they demanded an accounting. Explain whether Rochwerg is or is not obligated to turn over these shares to the partnership.

6. *Lynch v. Segal*, 2006 CanLII 42240 (ON CA); (2006), 277 D.L.R. (4th) 36; (2006), 26 B.L.R. (4th) 14; (2006), 33 R.F.L. (6th) 279; (2006), 219 O.A.C. 1 (ON CA)

   Mr. Segal is a wealthy man, and among other properties is the sole beneficial owner of two corporations that own substantial land in Ontario. He and his wife divorced and as part of the proceeds she obtained a judgment that she was unable to collect on because all of Mr. Segal's assets were offshore or otherwise protected and shielded through a series of holding companies and nominal owners. His wife located two properties in Ontario owned by corporations controlled by Mr. Segal. The court found that although Mr. Segal was not the actual shareholder of those corporations, he was the beneficial owner through a chain of holdings and that the shares were held in trust for him. Explain the arguments for and against whether Mrs. Segal can enforce the judgments against the properties and the likely outcome of the action.

7. *Re S.C.I. Systems, Inc. and Gornitzki, Thompson & Little Co. et al.* (1997), 147 D.L.R. (4th) 300 (Ont. Gen. Div.)

   S.C.I. Systems was a creditor and held a promissory note against Gornitzki, Thompson & Little Co. Ltd. (G.T.L.). Instead of paying the note, the director and sole shareholder of G.T.L. had the company declare and pay dividends, pay down loans to themselves, and transfer funds to other related corporations so that there was no money left to pay S.C.I. Explain what options S.C.I. has in these circumstances and the likely outcome.

# Chapter 8
## Property

Andy Dean/Fotolia

## Learning Objectives

LO 1  Distinguish between real and personal property

LO 2  Identify the rights and responsibilities associated with possession of personal property, keeping in mind owners, finders, and bailees

LO 3  Recognize the rights of real property owners and the owners of lesser interests in land

LO 4  Distinguish between the different methods of owning property together

LO 5  Outline the process for transferring title to land in various jurisdictions

LO 6  Explain the nature and role of mortgages and the nature of the foreclosure process

LO 7  Describe the rights and responsibilities of landlords and tenants in commercial and residential tenancies

LO 8  Discuss the implications and regulations of environmental protection for property owners

LO 9  Note the role of insurance in risk avoidance

Some of the most important decisions that business people face relate to their investment in, acquisition, and use of property (see Table 8.1). The monetary amounts are significant, and mistakes can have a very serious negative impact on a business. **Real property** consists of land and the things permanently affixed to it such as buildings, bridges, dams, and other structures. The other major category of property is called **personal property**, which consists of tangible, movable things called **chattels** or **goods** and various forms of intangibles referred to as **choses in action**. Today we often hear reference to another type of property called **intellectual property**. In fact, intellectual property is another form of intangible personal property. Intellectual property has become extremely important for businesses and will be dealt with as a separate topic in Chapter 9. In this chapter we will briefly look at personal property and then do a more thorough examination of real property, including landlord–tenant relationships and mortgages. We will also examine some environmental issues, which are an increasingly important consideration when owning or acquiring land. No matter what form of property is involved, it is always important to reduce risk by anticipating damage to or loss of that property. A brief discussion of insurance has been included in this chapter with reference to that risk management objective.

*Real property consists of land and buildings*

*Personal property may be tangible or intangible*

**Table 8.1 Property**

| Real property | Land |
| | Things affixed to the land |
| Personal property | Chattels (tangible goods or movables) |
| | Choses in action (intangible claims) |
| | Intellectual property (ideas and information) |

## PERSONAL PROPERTY

The term *property* does not refer to the thing itself; rather, it refers to a person's rights in relation to that thing. For example, a person's property is not the house or car, but the property rights that person has in the house or the car. This allows us to separate the thing from the title or right to it, so that you can loan your car or rent your house and still be the owner. This is a vital concept to keep in mind as we discuss all forms of property in this and the next chapter.

Personal property includes both tangible and intangible personal items. Tangible personal property comprises movables called chattels or goods as opposed to real property or land, which by its nature is always fixed in one location. We have dealt with tangible personal property when we discussed its transfer under the *Sale of Goods Act* and its use as security in Chapter 5. In Chapter 4 we talked about negotiable instruments as an example of intangible personal property. Cheques, drafts, and promissory notes have no intrinsic value but represent claims or rights. We will examine some other aspects of personal property below.

Today because of the internet, and the gaming industry in particular, a new form of intangible virtual property has developed that is traded and often purchased and sold by the participants. This involves imaginary assets associated with the games such as weapons and ammunition and huge funds can be involved. This is an area which has not yet attracted the attention of lawmakers.

**LO 1/LO 2**

*Property relates to your rights to something rather than the thing itself*

*Tangible personal property is called chattels or goods*

| Table 8.2 Rightful Owner Depends on Where Goods Are Found | | |
|---|---|---|
| **Order of Priority** | **First Claim** | **Then** |
| Goods found on public property | Rightful owner | Finder |
| Goods found on public part of employer's property by non-employee | Rightful owner | Finder |
| Goods found by employee doing job on employer's property | Rightful owner | Employer |
| Goods found on private part of employer's property by non-employee | Rightful owner | Employer |

## WHO HAS THE RIGHT TO THE GOODS?

*Possession gives right to goods over all but someone with prior claim*

The basic principle is that the person in possession of the goods has the right to them over anyone else, except someone with a prior title that has not been extinguished (see Table 8.2). Thus, a person's right to the chattel will largely depend on how it was acquired. If it was purchased or received as a gift, title has been conveyed from the prior owner to the new owner. When we find an object, we have a right to it over everyone

*Rightful owner retains title*

else but the rightful owner, usually the person who lost it. If you find a watch or a camera in a public place in a mall, for instance, it is yours unless it is claimed by the rightful owner. Even where it is handed in to the police or the lost and found, if the rightful owner fails to claim it, it must be returned to the finder, who gets to keep it, not the police or the owners of the mall. Of course, if you are an employee of the mall or it is found in some private part of the mall, then the mall owners have a right to it, not you.

The same applies to money that is found. Of course, if it is established that the money came from an illegal drug transaction, or some other prohibited activity, those funds would go to the government.

---

### Case Summary 8.1 *Landmark Vehicle Leasing Corporation v. Theti Holdings Inc. and Big Dog Solutions Limited*[1]

## Rightful Owner Retrieves Goods from Landlord

Landmark Vehicle Leasing Corporation (Plaintiff), Theti Holdings Inc., and Big Dog Solutions Limited (Defendants) in an action brought in the Ontario Superior Court of Justice.

Landmark Vehicle Leasing Corporation (Landmark) leased 6 tractors and a trailer to Bittu Transportation Services (Bittu), a highway trucking company. The lease was properly registered under the *Personal Property Security Act*. Bittu stored them on the property of Theti Holdings Inc. (Theti). When Bittu ran into financial problems, both Landmark (as lessor and Theti) as landlord claimed the vehicles, as Bittu had failed in making payments to both. The court had

to determine which of the two creditors had priority. Theti as landlord had a right to seize Bittu's property for unpaid rents under the *Repair and Storage Liens Act* but the court determined that the vehicles were not the Property of Bittu. They were owned by the lessor Landmark and the security had been properly registered under the PPSA. The landlord had to look to Bittu for a remedy. This case deals with conflicting security claims that were discussed in Chapter 5. But the decision came down to who actually owned the vehicles. Landmark had a prior title to the vehicle, and Theti who had possession had to return them to the rightful owner.

---

[1]2010 ON SC 644 (CanLII).

Who the rightful owner is will depend on the history of the item in question. The rules with respect to transfer of title as set out in the *Sale of Goods Act* are discussed in Chapter 5. Any other contractual provisions that may affect who has claim to those goods, any other legislation that may affect those rights, such as the *Personal Property Security Act,* and whether the goods were stolen or wrongfully converted to another in the past, would all have an effect on who is ultimately entitled to them. The process and claims are not always straight forward. There are many examples of heirs claiming ownership of paintings, jewelry and other valuables that were taken from Jewish families during the wars in Europe and subsequently showing up in museums and private collections. The valuables have often gone through several hands before arriving in their current location, but if the original owners can prove their claims, they are being returned to them.

## Bailment

When goods are in the possession of one person but owned by another this is called a **bailment**, with the owner referred to as the **bailor** and the person in possession as the **bailee**. The important question is just how careful that bailee has to be in caring for those goods. When the bailment is voluntary, it depends on who benefits. The level of care needed is higher if the bailment is a **gratuitous bailment for the benefit of the bailee,** and lower where it is a **gratuitous bailment for the benefit of the bailor**. Also, the level of care will be greater if the item involved is valuable or more fragile. For example, if you borrow your neighbour's lawnmower to cut your lawn, the duty of care will be higher than if you simply agree to store that lawnmower while that neighbour is away on vacation. And, of course, the duty would be even greater if it was a violin that was being borrowed or stored. When someone simply leaves a coat or umbrella behind in a theatre, when the usher picks it up it becomes an **involuntary bailment** and the duty imposed is only the level expected of one looking after his or her own goods. In practice, the judge will impose the reasonable person test and take into consideration how the bailment arose and which party benefits from the bailment.

A **bailment for value** takes place where a business relationship is involved such as when storing a fur coat or a vehicle or leaving a watch for repair. Here the duty of care would be higher but because a contract is normally involved, the bailee usually limits his or her liability in the agreement, shifting the risk to the customer. Alternatively, the court, when applying a reasonable person test, will look to the normal standards practiced in the particular industry involved.

Where goods are leased or rented, the bailor also has an obligation to deliver goods that are fit for the purpose intended. If that equipment is inappropriate for the job or is defective and causes injury, the bailor can be liable on the basis of contract or tort with a relatively high standard of care imposed, depending on the circumstances. Again, limitation clauses included in the contract usually significantly lessen that duty or limit the liability of the bailor. From a risk management point of view, a wise business person will take steps to eliminate those situations involving care for the property of others; where that cannot be avoided, a sign or other notification should be posted that reduces liability. When a contract is involved, a carefully worded exculpatory clause should be included, limiting liability as much as possible.

Common carriers and innkeepers have a particularly high standard imposed on them to care for the goods of their customers. A common carrier is an airline, railroad, or trucking

Bailment involves one person holding goods of another

Duty higher where voluntary for bailee's benefit

Lower where voluntary for benefit of bailor

Where bailment for value, duty is determined by contract or industry standards

Duty of common carriers and innkeepers now determined by statute

company in the business of taking general goods from the public on a regular basis and shipping them to other locations for a fee. Innkeepers provide transient accommodation (food and lodging) to travelers. Under the common law they are responsible for any damage to property left in their care, even where there was no negligence involved. This liability would be imposed unless the problem was caused by some defect in the goods themselves or was the fault of the bailor. Today, legislation now places limits on such liability, either by reducing the standard imposed, or by allowing the bailee to limit the maximum amount that can be claimed. In Ontario, for instance, the innkeeper's liability is limited to $40 unless the loss is caused by the negligence of the innkeeper or an employee, or if the lost or damaged goods were actually left with the innkeeper for safekeeping.[2]

Where goods are left with the bailee for value, and the service such as repair or storage is not paid for that bailee has a right to keep the goods and eventually to sell them to recover his or her costs. This right is referred to as a lien against the goods, and today specific statutes extend or enhance these common law liens in specific businesses such as storage warehouses or repair services. This allows them to hold onto the goods if they are not paid for their service. Where goods are leased and not returned, the bailor also has a lien and a right to recover those goods from the bailee. In Case Summary 8.1, discussed above, the landlord was not able to enforce a right of lien because the lessor had a superior claim to the goods. Note that it is a criminal offence for a bailee not to surrender property to a sheriff or other official who is properly seizing it under a valid agreement (*Personal Property Security Act*) or court order. The *Criminal Code* also makes it a crime to possess stolen property and has created several offences relating to how personal property is used. These include firearms offences and possession of tools and paraphernalia for producing illegal drugs, forging credit cards, and breaking into houses.

Finally, it is important to distinguish between a bailment and a licence. If you park your car in a parking lot is it a bailment or a licence? The key is to determine if you have given up possession. If you left the keys with the attendant or gave them to a valet to park the car it would be a bailment, but if you simply parked the car on a lot and took the keys with you, you would have a licence to use the parking space but the vehicle would still be in your possession while in the parking lot. You have retained control of it. The same would apply to leaving your coat at a restaurant. If you gave it to a coat check person, it would be a bailment, but if you just left it on a hanger provided for that purpose, it would likely be a licence rather than a bailment. The determining factor seems to be just who retains control. The following case illustrates the principle.

*Unpaid storer or repairer has a lien on the goods left in his care.*

*Bailment requires control of goods left by bailee*

[2]*Innkeepers' Act*, R.S.O. 1990, c. I.7, s. 4.
[3]2009 SK PC 84 (CanLII).

## Case Summary 8.2 *Boire v. Eagle Lake Enterprises Ltd.*[3]

## Stored Goods Not a Bailment

Mrs. Boire (Plaintiff), Eagle Lake Enterprises Ltd. (Defendant) in an action brought in the Saskatchewan Provincial Court.

Mrs. Boire made arrangements with Eagle Lake Enterprises to store her household belongings in one of their storage units. She had to ask to be let into the facility, but she had a key to her individual unit and had complete control over it. After four years she sought to recover her goods, and, on inspection, discovered they had suffered considerable damage from seepage and from mice. She had made it clear when leasing the facility that moisture and rodent control were important to her, and the manager had assured her that temperature control and rodent control were not an issue. She sued, claiming breach of a bailment for reward. Because she retained control of the storage unit, the judge determined that there was no bailment. Rather this was a licence situation. Still, the judge determined that there was a duty of care that had been breached. He also determined that there was a contract of storage, which also had been breached, and so she was entitled to compensation for

the loss. It was also determined that Mrs. Boire should have inspected the goods periodically; her failure to do so amounted to either contributory negligence or failure to mitigate her losses under the contract, and her damages were reduced accordingly. Instead of damages of $20 000 (the maximum jurisdiction of the small claims court) the loss was split and she was awarded $10 000 plus $500 in costs.

The case illustrates the difference between bailment and licence but also shows that there still may be a legal obligation to look after another's property if the relationship warrants.

## REAL PROPERTY

LO 1/LO 2/ LO 3/LO 4

The acquisition and use of real property can be one of the most important problems facing businesses. Real property consists of the land and things permanently attached to it. This usually involves buildings, but may also include other types of structures such as dams, aqueducts, bridges, fences and the like. It can also include heavy-duty machinery that has to be affixed to the land for it to operate. Prior claims on such items can cause problems since they are personal property (movable) until attached. Special rules have been developed with respect to such **fixtures**.

Personal property can become part of real property when affixed to it

Another problem relates to just what the land includes. You own the space above your land and below the surface only as far as you can make use of it. Thus, you cannot sue the owner of an airplane that flies over your property for trespass. Still, there is a right not to have some other structure permanently intrude over the property. If your house is located next to a tall building and your neighbour puts up a sign that hangs over your property, it would constitute a trespass, and you could force your neighbour to remove it. The same applies to under-the-surface rights. A property owner only has a right to that part of the land beneath the property that can be used. Mines, caves, and other underground activities that do not interfere with the surface will not give rise to a complaint. When the right to land is acquired, normally the under-surface mineral rights, as well as oil and gas rights, are not conveyed with the title but are retained by the Crown. The owner of the land will not have the right to minerals and other valuables found under the land. As a result, the owner may have to tolerate prospectors looking for minerals and even have to submit to some interruption on the surface to accommodate a mine or oil well. As well, the owner will get little compensation when such valuables are discovered.

Real property above and below ground is limited to what the holder can reasonably use

Mineral rights usually withheld by Crown

## Fee Simple Estates

The law of real property is based on rules developed in feudal times and still incorporates some aspects of that ancient law. For example, in those days all land belonged to the king. Others had a right to hold it and use it—called an **estate** in the land—which was based on various types of services given to the king. An estate, then, is different from the land itself. It is a right to the land or a right to use the land. Today, we still technically do not "own" our homes or property; rather we have an interest in the land called a **fee simple estate**,

Fee simple estate equivalent to ownership today

| Table 8.3 Limitations on Fee Simple Ownership |
| :--- |
| • Extends only to reasonably useable distance above the surface |
| • Extends only to reasonably useable distance below the surface |
| • Mineral rights usually withheld |
| • Restrictions (covenants, building schemes) |
| • Government powers (building permits, taxation, expropriation) |

*Governments have power to control or acquire land*

which gives us the same kinds of rights as ownership, including the right to develop, use, sell, and will it to others. The difference is more theoretical than practical (see Table 8.3). But we should always be aware of the overriding power of government to control and restrict how we use land through licensing and zoning, even to the point of forcing its sale through expropriation.

*Life estate lasts for life and then reverts*

In some circumstances the fee simple estate in land is split. A beneficiary in a will, such as a spouse, may be given a life estate in a particular property to ensure that person is cared for during his or her remaining life. The estate will go to other heirs when that person dies. During their lifetime the beneficiaries are said to have a **life estate** in the property and the other heirs have a **remainder** interest, or a **reversion**, if the interest goes back to the estate as opposed to a specified individual (see Figure 8.1). Note that there is a restriction on the holder of the life estate to do nothing to hurt the property that might decrease its value, for example, having a forested property logged.

## Leasehold Estate

*Leasehold estates are for specified time but may also be periodic*

Another example where the fee simple holder gives up the right to exclusive possession is the leasehold estate. Here the tenant is given exclusive possession and right to use the land for a specified period. Lease arrangements are common to both commercial and residential properties. Most last for just a few years, although 99-year leases are not uncommon. It is also common for a lease to be periodic in nature, meaning it is from week to week, month to month, or year to year. In effect, it is for only that one period, for example one month, but is renewed automatically, unless notice is given by either party to end it. The landlord–tenant relationship will be discussed in more detail below.

## Lesser Interests in Land

It is sometimes necessary to allow a power, water, or sewer line to permanently cross over or under one property to service another or to allow one building to permanently overhang

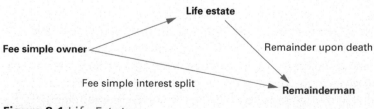

**Figure 8.1** Life Estate

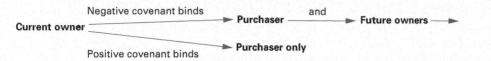

**Figure 8.2** Restrictive Covenants

another. When this is done, the legal arrangement made with the property owner is called an **easement**. When the intrusion is not permanent, but is simply the right for a vehicle or individual to cross over one property to get to another, it is called a **right of way**. Such easements are also an interest in the land, and the formalities associated with having an interest in land should be complied with. The portion of land benefited by the easement is called the **dominant tenement** and the one restricted the **servient tenement**. Where a sewer or power line merely crosses under or over the property serving the whole community, there is no nearby dominant tenement. This is usually referred to as a statutory easement.

Another right often incorporated into land transactions is a **restrictive covenant** (see Figure 8.2). When land is sold, the seller might put some sort of restriction on what the land can be used for or what can be built on it. For example, where a person subdivides her lot she might include a provision in the contract that the portion separated not be used for commercial purposes. So long as it was worded negatively and was properly registered, it would not only bind the purchaser but any subsequent owner. Such a negatively worded restrictive covenant is said to "run with the land" and bind all future owners. If the clause stipulated that a house had to be built on the property within one year, however, this would only bind the purchaser, any subsequent purchaser of the property would not be bound because this was worded as a positive rather than a negative covenant and privity of contract (that the contract provisions only bind the parties to it) would apply.

A **building scheme** is very similar. In this case all of the properties in a particular development have the same negatively worded restrictions put on them: all houses must be no more than three stories; or no style can be erected except Tudor; or no other roof can be used except shake or tile. As with easements, restrictive covenants will have one property that benefits (the dominant tenement) and one property that is restricted (the servient tenement). But with a building scheme all properties are benefited, and all are restricted. A building scheme accomplishes similar outcomes as municipal zoning. It binds all builders and subsequent owners except that it is done privately by the developer. Municipal zoning regulations are also very important to developers and users of property and usually specify not only what can be built on the property but the uses to which that property can be put such as commercial or residential.

Sometimes people are given the right to use or access property for some particular purpose. This is a **licence**, not an interest, in land. It is simply a contractual right to use the land for some limited purpose. Renting a hotel room where a maid will come in to clean it, or parking a car in a parking lot but keeping the keys are examples. A similar right called a **profit à prendre** gives a right to remove something such as gravel or trees from the land.

These restrictions can be very important especially with respect to commercial property. If you purchase land to be used as a manufacturing plant and find out later that it is

Easement gives others the right to use the land

Right of way is a type of easement, giving someone the right to cross property

Only negative restrictive covenants bind future owners

Building schemes are like restrictive covenants but bind whole subdivisions

A licence does not convey an interest in land

Purchasers of land should check for restrictions on how it can be used

not zoned for that purpose, or there is a restrictive covenant prohibiting such a use, or there is not sufficient access to the property the results can be disaster. Any competent lawyer who is informed of the use you wish to make of the property should be able to determine the physical dimensions and other aspects of the property and search the title and appropriate by-laws in place to ensure that such difficulties are avoided. But the same problem can be encountered with respect to residential property. For example, if you want to purchase a lot near a lake to build a cabin, you should find out if you have access to the lake from that location. Can you build what you want on the property given restrictive covenants and zoning? Is there proper sewer connection, or is the property large enough for a septic system if this is permitted at all? Is there adequate access to good water, or can you dig a producing well? If you are next to the lake can you build a dock? What about conservation rules? How close to the lake can you build your cabin? What about flooding? What happens to the ownership of the property between you and the lake if the lake subsides? Is there an easement, or right of way affecting the property? Can you subdivide the property? These are the types of questions you should be looking into before making such a purchase.

## LO 4    Owning Property Together

People wishing to share the ownership of property can accomplish it in two main ways. The **joint tenancy** arrangement is often used by families, especially spouses, to get around inheritance taxes and probate fees. Here, both tenants own the whole property, but neither can point to any portion of it as exclusively theirs. When one dies, the other still owns all of the property, only now he or she owns it exclusively. That person has taken complete title of the property by survivorship. The important point is that the property did not go through the estate. The survivor owned it all, together with the other joint tenant, and after death the survivor continued to own it all. Note that it is not only real property that can be owned in joint tenancy. Bank accounts, cars, boats, and other assets are often held jointly for the same reason. Such joint ownership is an important factor in estate planning.

> Joint tenancy includes right of survivorship

The other way to own property together is by **tenancy in common**. Here both parties have an undivided interest in the property. Again, neither party can point to any part of the property as his or hers alone. They both own an interest in every part of it, equal to their designated portion. But in this case, if one dies, the other still only owns his or her part interest. Either party can sell his or her portion of the property, use it as security, or otherwise deal with it during his or her lifetime. Upon death, the deceased person's interest will go to his or her heirs. Note that if people own property as joint tenants, and they don't want to continue as joint tenants, that joint tenancy can be severed. When that is done, the result is a tenancy in common. When one party sells or attempts to sell his or her interest, the joint tenancy will be severed. A creditor can also accomplish severance as is the situation in Case Summary 8.3, discussed below. Alternately, an application can be made to the court to have the joint tenancy partitioned, accomplishing the same result. But just expressing an intention to sever is usually not enough.

> Tenancy in common does not include the right of survivorship

> A joint tenancy can be changed to a tenancy-in-common

It is important to understand that this severance cannot be accomplished in a will. The will takes effect after death, and the right of survivorship in a joint tenancy will take effect with death. Hence, there is no interest left to will to your heirs, as the right of survivorship has already operated to give the survivor the whole interest in the land. Note as well that shared claims to property have also been created by statute. **Dower rights** and **homestead rights** have traditionally protected a spouse in the event of marriage breakdown. Today, modifications of these statutes and other family relations statutes in various forms are in place in all provinces giving a spouse (whether formally married or not) a claim to family assets even where they are not registered on the title.[4]

Dower and homestead rights protect spouse's claim to property

---

## Case Summary 8.3 *Royal & SunAlliance Insurance Company v. Muir*[5]

## Joint Tenancy Severed by Creditor's Action

Royal & SunAlliance Insurance Company (Applicants), John and Nancy Muir (Respondents) in this application in the Ontario Superior Court of Justice.

John Muir and Nancy Muir owned a condominium in joint tenancy. Royal obtained a judgment against John and took steps to enforce that judgment against John's interest in the condominium. That involved having a letter threatening to sell the property pursuant to the judgment debt sent to them from the appropriate government office and then advertising it for sale. The property didn't sell, and Royal did nothing more for several year.

Nancy had made a will in which she stated the condominium was owned in joint tenancy with John but also she stated that she bequeathed her half interest in the condominium to her son Michael. (This of course creates a problem, as she can't have it both ways.)

When Nancy died, Royal took the position that since John was a joint tenant he took the property by survivorship and it claimed it all pursuant to the judgment debt (then amounting to over $1 million). Michael claimed to be entitled to half of the Condominium as per the will.

The court held in favour of Michael, awarding him a half interest in the condominium. Royal was correct in that the right of survivorship took place at death and the will after death and so John should have taken it all by survivorship. However, that would apply only if it was still held as a joint tenancy at the time of Nancy's death. The court found that the actions of the creditor Royal in trying to sell the property had the effect of severing the joint tenancy at that time. Therefore, when Nancy died the condominium was no longer held in joint tenancy but was a tenancy in common, and Michael was entitled to a half interest pursuant to the will. This case illustrates the difference between a tenancy in common and a joint tenancy, as well as the fact that a joint tenancy can be severed by a creditor taking sufficient steps to seize and sell the property. The judge pointed out that simply obtaining the writ would not be enough but here the creditor actually tried to sell the condominium. Advertising it for sale was sufficient execution of the writ and severed the joint tenancy.

---

**Condominiums**    The growth of high density housing in cities has led to a unique statutory development in common ownership called the **condominium**. This allows people to own property that is separated vertically as well as horizontally. Condominium owners have a fee simple interest in their individual unit and share an interest in the common elements of the development. The units can be sold, mortgaged, or otherwise dealt with as any fee simple property. The sale or mortgage of one unit doesn't affect the other units in any way.

Statutes now allow fee simple to be separated vertically and horizontally: condominiums

---

[4]For example the *Homesteads Act*, 1989, S.S. 1989–90, c. H-5.1; *Family Relations Act* [R.S.B.C. 1996] c. 128; *Family Law Act*, R.S.O. 1990, c. F.3.

[5]2011 ON SC 2273 (CanLII).

## Case Summary 8.4 *The Owners, Strata Plan LMS 4255 v. Newell*[6]

# Court Orders Condominium Owner to Be Quiet

The Owners, Strata Plan LMS 4255 (Petitioners), Newell (Respondent) in an application for an injunction brought before the Supreme Court of British Columbia.

Steven Newell occupied the penthouse in a high-rise condominium tower in Yaletown, Vancouver. The penthouse had access to a deck and balcony that were common property but his was the only unit that had access. Mr. Newell equipped this space with a hot tub, barbeque, air conditioner and entertainment center with a big screen TV, amplifier and several large speakers. He played this system loudly and had loud parties into the morning hours leading his neighbours to complain. Note that the strata by-laws require a quiet time between 11: pm and 8:00 am and prohibit the alteration of the common space without permission. Permission for a hot tube was specifically refused, and the barbeque and entertainment system were also installed without permission. The strata in this application is asking for an injunction requiring the removal of the hot tub, air conditioner, and speakers (the barbeque

had already been removed) and that Newell be required to observe the rules with respect to quiet hours. This application was for an injunction because the normal remedy of fines issued for infractions was not effective. Mr. Newell merely treated such fines as a cost, promptly paying them and then continuing on with the infractions. The judge refused to issue an injunction with respect to the hot tub and the TV, determining that these were not an alteration of the common space. However, he did enjoin their use during the quiet hours.

The case shows some of the disadvantages of condominium living. Tenants must be considerate of their neighbours and obey the strata by-laws. The judge noted:

"Mr. Newell's attitude seems to be that his closest neighbours—Mr. Yu and Mr. Beilhartz—are killjoys and do not belong in Yaletown. But Yaletown living does not give Mr. Newell an excuse for ignoring the bylaws of his strata corporation."

---

Condominiums involve shared property and rules

The unique aspect of condominium ownership is the shared ownership attached to each unit with respect to common property such as hallways, foyers, and elevators, as well as fitness and recreational facilities, pools, lawns and gardens, and parking lots. The owners of each unit must pay a maintenance fee for the operation and upkeep of these common areas, including insurance on the common areas and the building as a whole. Those fees, as well as other rules and restrictions applicable to the use of the property—even including what can take place within each unit—are set by the **condominium corporation** (sometimes called the *strata corporation*). Each unit owner has a vote and can participate in elections to a condominium council which directs the affairs of the condominium corporation, sets the fees, makes the rules, and otherwise makes decisions with respect to the condominium as a whole. One of the dangers of such condominium ownership is that the owner of each unit is at the mercy of the others as far as fees and restrictions on what they can do as Mr. Newell discovered to his sorrow in Case Summary 8.4 above. Normally the fees set are reasonable, but when things go wrong, those fees can become excessive. Unlike normal ownership, condo owners are responsible for covering major expenses that occur with respect to the whole building or complex. Normal maintenance can be built into the regular fees and, if the condominium council shows wisdom, a contingency fee for unusual expenses should also be included. But there can be large unexpected expenses for such things as a leaky building, plumbing or electrical problems, a new roof, or the replacement of elevators. When such problems arise and the reserve

---

[6]2012 BC SC 1542 (CanLII).

fund is not sufficient, a special levy will be ordered, and each individual owner may be required to pay thousands of dollars per unit for the unexpected expense. Owners can be forced to sell if their fees are unpaid or they have committed sufficient violations of the rules. These potential expenses and unwanted rules and restrictions often discourage people from condominium ownership.

Special levy for unusual expenses

Older buildings are often converted to condominium ownership, and this poses another problem for potential owners. It may be a new unit to them, but if the building is 50 years old, it likely has a limited life expectancy. Certainly the maintenance and repair costs will be higher than with a new building, making them much less attractive investments. Any prospective purchaser should take steps to inspect the records and premises to determine not only the rules in place, any fees, and past levies paid, but any likely future expenses and whether funds have been set aside to cover them.

**Cooperatives** are similar in that the property is owned together but instead of each member owning a fee simple interest in a specific part, here the members own the whole property together and each share entitles them to occupy a specific apartment. Alternatively, the property is owned by a corporation and the members have shares in the corporation and lease their individual unit. They are like tenants in a building in which they are part owners. Cooperatives will normally be financed through a mortgage secured against the whole property with each member having to pay a share. As was the case with condominiums, members of a cooperative are required to live by the rules agreed upon by the members and failure to do so can lead to their eviction.

There are still other kinds of interests in land to consider. Sometimes when property is to be sold, an **option to purchase** will be arranged. As you will recall from the discussion of offer and acceptance in Chapter 3, an option is a subsidiary contract where, for a fee, the offeror commits to hold his offer open for a given period of time. Thus, the offeror is bound by its terms and cannot revoke the offer during that period. But the purchaser has no obligation beyond paying the normally small price paid for the option. Developers will often use this arrangement when they are trying to assemble a block of properties from several different owners. They will acquire an option on each property, usually for a small fee. When they have options on all of the properties they need, they exercise the options and purchase the properties. If they cannot persuade some key property owners to sell for a reasonable price, they can walk away from the transaction, losing only what they paid for the option agreements. Speculators will also purchase options and resell them as a method of flipping property, earning substantial returns for very little investment. Note that such options, like other interests in land, must be registered to protect their value.

Option to purchase holds offer to sell open for specified time

Options often used by developers and speculators

The common method of financing the purchase of property is through a **mortgage**. Here the purchaser conveys the title to the creditor (usually a bank or other financial institution), and the bank holds onto the title as security until the final payment is made. The bank then reconveys title to the former debtor. While the debt is outstanding, the creditor has title as security. Mortgages will be discussed in more detail below. When the seller is also providing the financing it is also possible to use an agreement for sale transaction. This involves a two stage sale of the property. When the agreement is made the purchaser obtains possession but not title, which the vendor retains until the final payment is made. The vendor then transfers title to the former debtor. If there is a default, the creditor can take steps to reclaim the property, but mortgages and agreements for sale must be registered to be effective against third parties.

# Requirement of Registration

As indicated in the discussion above, it is important to register any of these interests in land as notice to the public and for protection against outsiders who might deal with the property in question and otherwise defeat the unregistered interest. Without such a registration system, any business people dealing in property might have their position weakened by other competing claims for the property of which they are unaware. The registration systems were developed to ensure that does not happen. There are two different systems of land registry in place in Canada. The traditional **land registry** involves the creation of a depository or registry to keep copies of documents that affect the title of land (see Figure 8.3). The purchaser or lender has the assurance that only those documents registered in the land registry will affect them, but they have to search the documents themselves to determine just who the rightful owner is and what claims there are against the property. If you purchase a house, for example, one of the first things your lawyer will do is to go through those documents, checking the chain of ownership to make sure that the seller has the right to sell the house and that there are no other undisclosed interests such as judgments, easements, or mortgages registered against the property. Hence the expression "searching the title." Most unregistered claims will have no effect on subsequent purchasers. Note that the registry is simply a depository which provides no guarantee as to the content of the documents registered, only an indication as to the date and time of registration, which will determine priority between conflicting claims based on timing.

The other system of land registry used in Canada is the **land titles system**, first adopted in British Columbia and now used in most other provinces and districts. It has the singular advantage of guaranteeing title. When property is transferred, a form is filed with the land titles office, which generates a new "certificate of indefeasible title," certifying the purchaser as the registered owner of the property. The key to understanding the difference between the two systems is that the **certificate of indefeasible title** is guaranteed and is conclusive evidence of who has title to the property in any court. Note that any mortgages, **liens**, judgments, or other interests such as an easement or right of way are noted on the certificate form as a *charge* against the title. No other claims can affect subsequent purchasers. There is no need to search any other documents. Sometimes this can lead to problems when mistakes are made or titles are changed by fraud. Title fraud is becoming more common and places a considerable burden upon homeowners and other innocent parties as illustrated in the Rabi case discussed below. Note that some jurisdictions are transitioning from a land registry to a land titles system. Nova Scotia, for example, is in the process of modernizing and digitizing their system, providing a guarantee of ownership similar to the land titles system used in other provinces. Another important recent development in Canada is the use of title insurance to cover the risks associated with such transactions in both registration systems.

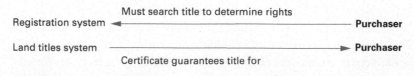

**Figure 8.3** Land Registry

## Case Summary 8.5 *Rabi v. Rosu*[7]

# Title Obtained by Fraud Is Void Even in a Land Titles Jurisdiction

Seyed Rabi and Shohreh Shafie (Applicants), Ion Rosu and the Toronto Dominion Bank (Respondents) in this application brought before the Superior Court of Justice, Ontario.

Rabi and Shafie were the owners of a condominium located in north Toronto and in 2004 were the victims of serious property fraud. Two individuals posing as owners fraudulently sold the property to a confederate, who registered the change of title and then arranged for a mortgage with TD Bank, which was registered against the title. The fraudsters then absconded with the funds. When the facts were revealed, the title to the property was returned to the proper owners, but TD Bank still insisted that they had a valid charge against the property and this action was brought to remove that charge. The court held that because TD Bank had dealt with the fraudsters and no title could be advanced by fraud, their charge was invalid and removed from the title. But what would have happened if the fraudsters had managed to sell the property to an innocent third party who then arranged for the bank mortgage?

In fact, that happened in *Reviczky v. Meleknia*.[8] In that case a fake power of attorney was used to convey the property from the legitimate owner, Paul Reviczky, to Pegman Meleknia, an innocent purchaser, who in turn arranged a mortgage against the property with the HSBC Bank. TD Bank advanced $300 000 to Meleknia, who in turn paid it to the fraudsters, and TD Bank registered the mortgage against the property. Meleknia, although innocent, did not obtain good title because title cannot be transferred through fraud.

TD Bank argued that they had not dealt with fraudsters since they had registered their mortgage and advanced the funds relying on the registered title and they dealt with an innocent party. Therefore, the mortgage should remain as a charge against the property owned by Reviczky.

But the court decided that because TD Bank had been negligent, it could not prevail against the completely innocent Reviczky. The power of attorney stated that it was valid until death or until Reviczky revoked it. Nobody checked to see if the power of attorney was still valid or whether Reviczky was still alive or had revoked the power of attorney before its use in these circumstances. The principle applied in both cases is that the burden of the loss is placed on the party that had the opportunity to avoid the fraud.

These cases illustrate the operation of the land titles system and some safeguards included to prevent abuse.

## Transferring Land

The traditional method of transferring land involves the use of a *grant*, often called a **deed of conveyance**. Note that the *Statute of Frauds* or its equivalent, as discussed in Chapter 3, applies to real estate transactions and so a verbal agreement itself will normally not be binding. Initially, a contract in the form of an **agreement of purchase and sale** is concluded between the parties. This may contain conditions that have to be met before the deal is finalized, such as the purchaser selling their own home first or arranging satisfactory financing. At the closing date a deed of conveyance under seal is executed, which accomplishes the actual transfer. Of course, the documents are then deposited in the registry to ensure protection against subsequent claimants. In a land titles jurisdiction a similar purchase and sale agreement is concluded, which establishes the rights of the parties, but the actual transfer is accomplished by completing and filing the appropriate transfer form with

**LO 5**

Transfer by deed in land registry jurisdiction

Mortgages on property and agreements for sale used to secure loan

Form submitted to transfer title in land titles jurisdiction

---

[7]2006 CanLII 36623 (ON SC); 277 D.L.R. (4th) 544.

[8]2007 CanLII 56494 (ON SC); 287 D.L.R. (4th) 193.

Criminal offence to falsify or conceal title documents

Obligation on vendor to disclose defects

the land titles office. That office then generates a new certificate of indefeasible title. The importance of preserving the authenticity of these documents is emphasized in the *Criminal Code*, which makes it a criminal offence to alter destroy or conceal such documents. There is also an obligation on the vendor to disclose any information about material defects that would likely be considered important to the purchaser. In all cases any misleading information will amount to misrepresentation, as was the situation in Case Summary 8.6 discussed below. Misrepresentation and the appropriate remedies was discussed in Chapter 4. Because of the great expenditures involved and the complexities of the process, this is one area where the services of a professional such as a lawyer should be used. They not only have the expertise but are insured if anything goes wrong. Involving a real estate agent and a home inspector is also advisable where residential transactions are involved. It may also be necessary especially with commercial properties to involve an engineer, and appraiser and do an environmental audit.

## Case Summary 8.6 *Guiseppe Iatomasi and Gabriella Iatomasi v. John Conciatori and Angela Conciatori*[9]

## Vendor Liable for Misrepresentation

Mr. and Mrs. Iatomasi (Plaintiffs), Mr. and Mrs. Conciatori (Defendants) in an action brought in the Ontario Superior Court of Justice.

Mr. and Mrs. Iatomasi purchased a home from Mr. and Mrs. Conciatori that had serious water leakage problems in its basement walls. Mr. Iatomasi had visited the property several times before purchase and noted the patches in the basement walls. He was assured they were there to support scaffolding during construction. When asked specifically about water leakage, the vendor replied that there had been no history of water leakage in the basement. After purchase the water leakage problems became apparent and the purchasers expended over $80 000 in repairs. The court determined that the Conciatoris as vendors had made material false representations with respect to the property and the purchasers had relied on those misrepresentations when entering into the contract of purchase. The vendors were liable to pay damages in the amount sought minus a small amount that the purchasers had overpaid in labour costs.

In this case there was an actionable misrepresentation that the purchasers had relied on to their detriment. But most jurisdictions today require a disclosure statement where any such defects must be disclosed to the purchaser whether they are the subject of questions or not.

Right to land may be obtained by adverse possession or prescription in land registry jurisdiction . . .

■ but normally not in a land titles jurisdiction

It is still possible, but only in land registry jurisdictions, to acquire rights to property through use alone. Where a person has occupied property openly without the actual owner taking steps to remove them for over 20 years, the "squatter" would have obtained a right to the land through **adverse possession**. Similarly, where people regularly cross over land without the owner taking any measures to stop them, after 20 years they have acquired the right to continue to cross over by **prescription**. This is specifically prohibited by statute in land titles jurisdictions where whatever is stated on the certificate of indefeasible title must prevail.[10] But note the following case.

---

[9]2011 ON SC 3819 (CanLII).
[10]*Land Title Act*, R.S.B.C. 1996, c. 250, s. 24; and *Limitation Act*, R.S.B.C. 1996, c. 266, s. 12.

## Case Summary 8.7 *Cantera v. Leah Eller*[11]

## Adverse Possession Still Works Despite Conversion to Land Titles

Laura Cantera (Plaintiff), Wendy Leah Eller and Paul Wright (Defendants) in this action brought before the Superior Court of Justice, Ontario.

Laura Cantera purchased her home in Toronto in 1997 from the Connollys, who had lived there since 1962. Her neighbours, Wendy Eller and Paul Wright, purchased in 2004. The dispute between them related to a narrow strip of land between the two properties. The problem was that Eller and Wright intended to demolish the old house and build; in the process they determined that the fence between the properties was located on their lot. They claimed the strip of land that was part of their lot located on the Cantera side of the fence and removed the fence. Cantera sued for trespass. The fence, first appearing on a 1952 survey, had been there for over 40 years, and the Connollys testified that they never knew the fence stood on the other lot. The result was that the lots were surveyed at 50 feet wide each, but with the fence in place the Cantera property was 52 feet wide and the other property 48 feet. Wright was afraid that this situation would affect his ability to get a building permit and so brought this action. In any case, he was willing to rebuild the fence but not where it was.

The court determined that this was a case where the strip of land had been acquired by the Cantera lot by adverse possession for a period of over 40 years. Thus, Cantera was entitled to the property and succeeded in her trespass action. Note that this is a land titles jurisdiction, and while the title is conclusive evidence of its contents, because this was an area involved in a transition from the land registry to the land titles jurisdiction, the *Act* contains a provision that nothing in the new *Act* will overrule title to land acquired through prescription or adverse possession before the *Act* came into force. This qualification was noted on the title of the lot purchased by Wright and Eller.

The case illustrates the operation of adverse possession. It also shows that in a jurisdiction that is going through a transition from a land registry to a land titles system adverse possession can still affect those titles if acquired before the transition to the new system.

It should also be noted that a major advancement that has taken place in the field of registration of interests in land is the adaptation to technological change. Now most data storage and even the transfer of interests in land takes place electronically.

## Mortgages

## LO 6

Most real property transactions involve financing, with the mortgage the most common form of security taken. In the following discussion, since the mortgage is a form of security given by the debtor, that debtor is called the **mortgagor**. The creditor or person in receipt of the security is called the **mortgagee**.

When land is used to secure debt, the title is transferred as security, but possession remains with the debtor. Since the title is returned upon repayment of the loan, it is a dead transfer, or a *mortgage*. Originally, if there was a default, the transfer of title allowed the creditor to take possession of the property, but the debt was still owed by the debtor. This unfairness was overcome by the Courts of Chancery recognizing a right in the debtor to redeem his or her property from the creditor even after default by paying what was owed. This **equity of redemption**, as it has become known, has a distinct value and is of central importance in today's law of mortgages (see Figure 8.4). If property is worth $500 000 and

*Mortgage involves transfer of title to creditor as security*

*Equity of redemption allows debtor to regain property even after default*

---

[11]2007 CanLII 17024 (Ont. S.C.), 56 R.P.R. (4th) 39; 157 A.C.W.S. (3d) 544.

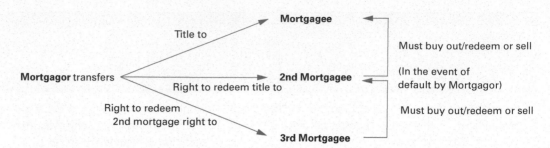

**Figure 8.4** Nature of Equity of Redemption

the debt secured by the mortgage is $200 000, the value of the equity of redemption would be $300 000. This term has been shortened to **equity** and is used commonly in all our financial dealings to describe the value of the interest we have in a possession after the amount owing on it has been deducted.

To avoid the property being tied up indefinitely with the threat of redemption, it was also necessary for the Court of Chancery to put a time limit on its operation. At the request of the creditor/mortgagee a time limit was imposed and at the expiration of that time limit, the debtor/mortgagor was foreclosed or prevented from exercising that equity of redemption. This describes the origin and the nature of the **foreclosure** process. The mortgage represents security by the transfer of title, and if the debt is paid, the title is retransferred. If there is a default, the foreclosure process takes place in two stages. First, the creditor/mortgagee asks the court to put a time limit on the exercise of the equity of redemption, for example, six months. After that period expires and payment is not made the creditor/mortgagee returns to the court and asks that the foreclosure be made absolute. During that redemption period efforts are usually made by the mortgagor to refinance or to sell the property.

Since the equity of redemption has value, it too can be transferred to another creditor as security. This is known as a **second mortgage**, and because it is the right to redeem that is being transferred rather than the title, there is more risk to the second mortgagee. If there is a default, the foreclosure process by the first mortgagee is aimed at ending that right to redeem, and so the second mortgagee has to be prepared to pay off the first mortgage or lose the security (see Figure 8.5). Hence, a higher interest rate is charged because

*Foreclosure puts a time limit on debtor's right to redeem*

*Final order ends equity of redemption*

*Equity of redemption can be used to secure further debt*

*Second mortgagee must be prepared to pay out first*

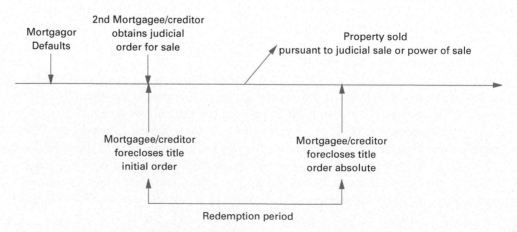

**Figure 8.5** When Mortgagor Defaults

of the higher risk. It is also possible to have a third or fourth mortgage, but these are rare because of the even higher risk for these creditors.

In jurisdictions using the land registry system, the process takes place as described above with the title actually transferring to the creditor. The second and subsequent mortgages are then referred to as *equitable mortgages*, because it is the equity of redemption that is being used as security, rather than the legal title to the property. In land titles jurisdictions the mortgagor remains the registered owner on the certificate of title and the first, second, and subsequent mortgages and other claims are simply listed as charges on that title document, with the priority among them established by the order of registration. The rights existing among the parties are essentially the same in both systems.

The possibility of foreclosure puts the second and subsequent mortgagees, as well as any other creditors that might have a claim against the property, at considerable risk. Consequently, during that redemption period the court gives these parties the right to try to sell the property. This is referred to as an order for judicial sale or an exercise of the power of sale, depending on the jurisdiction. In British Columbia, for instance, an application is brought before the court and the judge orders the property to be sold (a **judicial sale**). In Ontario the court simply endorses the exercise of the provision contained in the mortgage agreement to sell in the event of default (the **power of sale**), but the result is essentially the same. During that six-month period, referred to as the *redemption period*, these parties are given the right to find a buyer and sell the property. The process then is for the first mortgagee upon default to go to court and get an order of foreclosure setting the redemption period and for the second mortgagee and other claimants at that same hearing to apply for a court order (order of judicial sale or power of sale depending on jurisdiction) to sell the property immediately. The result is that the property might be sold in the next week even though the redemption period has several more months to run. The mortgagor/debtor often fails to understand this. They think they have six months to solve their problems, when in fact their home might be sold right away to satisfy the debt and keep additional costs and interest from accumulating. Note that the actual process of foreclosure may vary to some extent between jurisdictions. In some provinces there must be an attempt to sell the property first, and in Nova Scotia the remedy is for a court order for the sale of the property (referred to as foreclosure and sale).

If the property is sold pursuant to a court order and, as is often the case, there is not enough to pay off the second mortgage and other claimants completely, the debtor may still be required to pay the shortfall, depending on the jurisdiction. If a property sells for $160 000, a first mortgage claim of $125 000 might increase to $140 000 because of the added interest and legal costs. Similarly, a second mortgage of $30 000 might become $40 000, with the result that after the first mortgage claim is paid, there is only $20 000 left, leaving a shortfall of $20 000 still owed to the second mortgagee. Thus, the debtor/mortgagor not only loses their property, but still must pay a substantial sum to the second mortgagee. Typically, a mortgage agreement will also give the mortgagee the right to take possession of the property in the event of a default, but this is seldom pursued unless the property has been abandoned.

Remember that a mortgage involves a contractual agreement as well as a real property transaction and many of the rights of the parties are established either in that contract or by provincial legislation. For example, the contract will establish the amortization period upon which repayment is to be calculated, say 30 years. In addition, the contract will set out the interest rate payable over the term of the mortgage. The mortgage term is a period

The exercise of the power of sale/judicial sale shortens the redemption period

A less common remedy involves taking possession of the property

Mortgage term sets interest rate and requires repayment after a few years

of time, say five years, at the expiration of which the entire amount of the mortgage becomes due and the parties must renegotiate the terms, usually involving setting a new interest rate. As with all contracts there are many variations, including variable rate mortgages, where the interest rate is not fixed, and reverse mortgages, where payments are made to the mortgagor with the debt accumulating to be repaid upon the sale of the property or the death of the mortgagor.

*Note contract variations*

### Case Summary 8.8 *Meridian Credit Union Limited v. Hancock*[12]

## Mortgagee Is Responsible for Shortfall When in Default

Meridian Credit Union Limited (Plaintiff), Dave and Heather Hancock (Defendants) in this action before the Superior Court of Justice, Ontario.

Dave and Heather Hancock defaulted on their mortgage with Meridian Credit Union Limited, owing $236 193.04. The credit union exercised their power of sale and listed the property for sale after obtaining a property valuation of $225 000. They listed the property for sale for nine days and an offer was made to purchase for $226 000, which was accepted. When interest and costs were included, this left a shortfall of $24 473.80, which is the subject of this action. The Hancocks claimed that the market value of the property was between $235 000 and $250 000, and that the credit union had not listed the property long enough to obtain an adequate price. The Hancocks claimed improvident sale, which would relieve them of the obligation to pay the shortfall.

The court found that the sale was proper and that the Hancocks, therefore, were liable for the shortfall on the sale. Note that Mr. Hancock had listed the property for some time prior to the exercise of the power of sale, lowering the price in successive steps before finally listing it for $255 000, at which price he was still unable to sell it. The court found, therefore, that the length of time listed by the credit union was not too short and the sale was as good as could be expected in the market and above the appraised value. It is interesting to note that Hancock had received offers of considerably more than the sale price, but had refused them, and that the house was insured for considerably more.

The case nicely illustrates the obligation of the debtor to pay any shortfall when the property is sold. It also shows the arguments that can be raised (in this case unsuccessfully) when the sale by the creditor is improvident. Note also that the procedures involved vary but the result will be the same in most jurisdictions.

## LO 7   LEASEHOLD ESTATES

*A lease conveys possession of property for a specified period*

*Periodic leases involve automatic renewal until notice*

A **leasehold estate** is both an estate in land and a specialized contract and provides the tenant with a right to exclusive possession and use of the premises for a specified period of time. Such leases may be of short duration such as a month, or for much longer periods, even 99 years. A **periodic lease**, also common, is where the lease is only for one month but then is automatically renewed every month until notice is given to terminate. Any period may be specified, but a month-to-month period is the most common, with week-to-week and year-to-year also used. A tenancy at sufferance takes place where the tenant stays after the expiration of the lease without the landlord's permission, and a tenancy at will takes place when the landlord has given permission. This discussion must distinguish between commercial lease and residential lease arrangements. Both may be governed by statute, but the commercial tenancy statutes make fewer changes to the common law and allow the parties much more scope to alter their rights and obligations by agreement in

---

[12]2009 CanLII 60093 (ON SC); [2009] O.J. No. 4609.

the lease itself. Residential tenancy acts (or their equivalent in place in all provinces) are more like a form of consumer protection legislation, imposing many obligations on the parties that cannot be modified by agreement. The following general discussion relates primarily to commercial tenancies. Remember, however, that the principles discussed here also apply to residential tenancies, except where they have been changed by statute. These statutory modifications for residential tenancies will be discussed separately below.

*Agreement determines obligations in commercial tenancy*

## Commercial Tenancies

One of the requirements of the *Statute of Frauds* or its equivalent is that any interest in land, including a lease, must be evidenced in writing to be enforceable. Most jurisdictions modify this, so leases for three years or less, whether residential or commercial, are still enforceable even without writing. Similarly, the lease must be registered in order to be enforceable against third parties such as subsequent purchasers—again with this three year exception. The doctrine of frustration does not apply to leases under common law. So if leased premises were to burn down through no fault of either party, the tenant would still have to pay rent unless, of course, the parties have specified otherwise in the lease agreement. In many jurisdictions, the doctrine of frustration is made applicable to residential leases by statute, with the result that the tenant's obligation to pay rent would be ended in the event of such a fire. In British Columbia the doctrine of frustration has also been applied to commercial tenancies.[13] Even where frustration has not been imposed by statute, if the lease relates to an office in a high-rise and the building is destroyed, the obligation to pay rent would likely end, since you can't lease something that doesn't exist.

*Statute of Frauds requires longer leases to be evidenced in writing*

*Leases are binding on a subsequent purchaser if registered*

*Frustration applies to leases in some jurisdictions by statute*

---

### Case Summary 8.9 *Fitkid (York) Inc. v. 1277633 Ontario Ltd.*[14]

## Accepting Rent Overrides Notice to Vacate

Fitkid (York) Ltd. (Plaintiff), 1277633 Ontario Ltd. (Defendant) in this trial before the Superior Court of Justice, Ontario.

In this case the commercial lease was to run to 2006, but in 1999 a disagreement arose between the landlord and the tenant, Fitkid, over the amount of rent to be paid and repairs to the roof. For several months Fitkid withheld rent and then paid after a default notice. When a rent increase came into effect, the tenant paid rent at the lower rate, not the increased one. Finally, in April 1999, after again accepting rent at the lower rate, the landlord changed the locks and evicted the tenant. Fitkid could not find other premises and went out of business. In this action Fitkid sought damages from the landlord for wrongful termination of the lease.

The court had to determine whether the landlord had the right to terminate the lease in these circumstances. The court held that the failure to pay the proper rent would have been grounds for evicting the tenant, but when the landlord took the lower payment in April before changing the locks, he reinstated the lease and lost the right to evict. Accepting the rent payment was inconsistent with the termination of the landlord-and-tenant relationship. As a result, Fitkid was awarded $198 201 in damages. Note that seizing the tenant's property before termination has the same effect, and landlords should seek legal advice before resorting to such action.

---

[13]*Commercial Tenancy Act, R.S.B.C. 1996, c 57.*
[14]2002 CanLII 9520 (ON SC).

Although lease agreements can modify obligations between the parties, there are some basic obligations that are normally in place in all tenancies. For example, the landlord has an obligation to deliver **vacant possession** of the property. This means that he has to make sure that any prior tenants are gone before the scheduled time for the new tenants to occupy the premises. The landlord also has to provide **quiet enjoyment**, which means the tenant has to be able to use the premises for the purpose for which they were let. For example, blasting going on nearby that interferes with the tenant's work or sleep, construction that interferes with the tenant's access to the office, or even a major leak so that the premises are no longer fit for human habitation, all would constitute breaches of the tenant's right to quiet enjoyment.

The question of who has the obligation to make repairs is normally an obligation that is specified in a commercial agreement. Usually neither party has an obligation to make repairs where normal wear and tear is involved. The tenant takes the premises in the condition let and returns them in the same condition, except for normal wear and tear. Where major repairs are needed, the tenant must notify the landlord of the problem. If the landlord then fails to make appropriate repairs as required in the lease, the tenant can seek a court order whereby he will be allowed to pay less rent (**abatement**), using the excess to make the required repairs.

If the tenant causes damage beyond normal wear and tear, either willfully or through neglect, he or she will be responsible to repair it. Sometimes the tenant causes more damage than expected by using the premises in a way different from what was intended when it was originally let. For example, if the premises were let as an office but were used for heavy manufacturing, the tenant would be responsible for any excess damage caused by this non-approved use. As mentioned above, if there is unusual damage that causes the premises to be unusable and is not caused by the tenant, such as a major leak or fire that interferes with the tenant's right to quiet enjoyment, the landlord has an obligation to make the repairs. Whether tenant or landlord, all of these problems can and should be anticipated in the lease agreement so that there are no surprises and so that unexpected expense can be avoided, or at least the risk be brought into the rent calculations.

A problem often arises with respect to the termination of the tenancy. Of course, if the lease is for a set time, such as two years, the tenant will have to be out at the expiration of that term. Sometimes the tenant, either with or without the agreement of the landlord, stays after the expiration of the lease. If the landlord wants the tenant out, he can take steps to have the tenant removed and is entitled to compensation from the over-holding tenant. But if rent is paid and accepted, normally a month-to-month periodic tenancy is created. Where a periodic tenancy is involved, it can be terminated by either party giving one clear rental period notice. Thus, in a month-to-month tenancy where the tenant wants to move at the end of May, that tenant must give notice at the end of April to be effective at the end of May. If the rent is due on the first day of the month, the notice must be given the day before (April 30 in this case) to be effective the last day of the next month (May 31). Unsophisticated landlords and tenants often make the mistake of giving notice on the same day the rent is paid, expecting it to be effective at the end of that month. This is improper notice and will be ineffective, unless the other party agrees to accept it. The amount of notice required and when it must be given is usually one of the changes imposed in residential tenancy legislation.

Landlord must deliver vacant possession and quiet enjoyment

Responsibility for repairs is subject to agreement

Normally neither party is required to pay for normal wear and tear

Court may authorize tenant to pay less rent to pay for repairs

Tenant must use premises as agreed

Commercial lease terminated at end of specified lease period

Where a periodic lease is involved, one clear rental period notice is required

The obligations of the tenant consist of paying rent, using the property only as agreed, and otherwise living up to the terms of the lease agreement, which may include other obligations such as paying taxes, insurance, and utilities. If the tenant fails to pay rent, the landlord must make a choice. In a commercial tenancy he can terminate the tenancy by removing the tenant, or he can distrain for rent. Terminating the tenancy, even by simply changing the locks, is called **forfeiture** and no court order is needed. Note that an important right of the tenant in these circumstances is to ask the court to order **relief against forfeiture**, which would allow the tenant to reinstate the lease by paying the back rent due. **Distraint** involves seizing the tenant's goods for the rent owing. This is inconsistent with termination of the tenancy, since the rent is being paid by the seized property. Since there is no longer a breach of the lease, the tenancy continues. Where the tenant abandons the premises before the lease period is up, the landlord can sue for the rent for the remaining term of the lease. The landlord is not required to find another tenant or otherwise mitigate his losses. But if he does take over the premises or leases them to someone else, the landlord has accepted the tenant's surrender of the premises, and the tenant's only obligation would to be to pay any arrears in rent owing at the time of surrender. If the tenant goes bankrupt, the landlord has a priority claim over other creditors for three months unpaid rent. Other remedies, such as monetary compensation (damages) for damage to the premises, or an injunction to stop certain practices inconsistent with the lease terms, may also be available. The tenant may also have an action for damages or obtain an injunction where the landlord has breached important terms of the lease.

In addition to who will be responsible for repairs, a commercial lease will often include a right for the tenant to renew the lease and an option for the tenant to purchase the property at the expiration of the lease period. These terms must be specific and clearly state the amounts to be paid, or how the funds involved can be calculated in order to be binding on the parties. And when such a renewal or the exercise of the option is desired, the tenant must be careful to comply exactly as required by the lease. If 12 months' notice is required in a specific form, the notice must be given in just that form. It may well be that a technical flaw in giving the notice or exercising the option may allow the landlord to allow the lease to expire so that the property can then be let out at a higher rent to the next tenant, which might be desirable because of changing economic conditions.

The tenant is also generally permitted to sublease the premises or to assign them to someone else, although in both situations they remain primarily responsible on the lease. This right is usually restricted in the lease agreement, which normally requires the landlord's consent before the assignment or sublease can take place. The landlord cannot unreasonably withhold this consent. Note that there is often another provision giving the landlord the option to terminate the lease upon receiving the request to assign or sublet.

Another problem which often arises when tenants leave regards just what they can take with them. A fixture is something that has been permanently attached to the property, such as a building or foundation, and it becomes part of the real property. But tenants often attach items onto the property to use in their business that they have no intention of leaving with the property. The general rule is that tenants can detach such items and take them with them, providing they do no serious harm to the property in the process. For example, tools in a workshop often have to be attached to the floor or walls to operate, and these would normally be tenants' fixtures that could be taken with them at the end of the lease period.

Tenant must comply with agreement and may be required to pay utilities and taxes

In the event of default, the landlord can evict tenant or distrain for rent

In the event of default, landlord can seize tenant's goods

If tenant defaults, landlord can sue for rent for remaining term

Landlord has no obligation to mitigate

Injured party can seek damages or injunction

Lease also may provide right for tenant to renew, or an option to purchase

Tenant can sublease or assign with landlord's permission

Tenant's fixtures can be taken with them when they go, if they've caused no damage

Commercial tenancy statutes normally allow parties to determine lease obligations

Where legislation is in place with respect to commercial tenancies, the statutes only make minor changes to the common law. Normally the parties are allowed to make whatever kind of arrangement they want by setting it out in the lease agreement. Both landlord and tenant must exercise great care in determining the terms of that lease contract. They should use tried and tested standard forms and make such modifications as needed, as dictated by their unique needs. They must also anticipate changing needs and provide for the possibility of things going wrong, as well as options, such as the right to renew the lease, end it earlier, or sublet. Ideally, the services of a lawyer should be used to prepare the lease. The same is not true for residential tenancies. Here important statutes are in place that impose obligations on both parties and make substantial changes to the common law.

It should also be noted that whether the lease is for commercial or residential premises, a lease longer than three years must be registered in the land registry to be effective against any subsequent owner. This applies whether the land is sold or even claimed by a mortgagee or other creditor, as in the following case.

## Case Summary 8.10 *Canada Mortgage and Housing Corporation v. Seetarram*[15]

## Mortgage Prevails Over Unregistered Lease

Canada Mortgage and Housing Corporation (Applicant), Jasmin Seetarram (Respondent) in an application brought in the Superior Court of Justice, Ontario.

Jasmin Seetarram was a tenant in a home in Mississauga and the owner of the home defaulted on the mortgage taken out with the Royal Bank of Canada. The Canada Mortgage and Housing Corporation(CMHC) as insurer for the RBC mortgage has taken over their position and foreclosed, taking possession of the house. This action is brought by CMHC for a declaration that the mortgage interest will prevail over the lease. The lease was for five years and was not registered. In an application before the Landlord & Tenant Board the lease was found to be valid, but under the *Land Titles Act* a lease for longer than three years has to be registered. Since this lease was for five years and was not registered, the Royal Bank had no notice of it and was not affected by it.

The court, therefore, declared the lease was not enforceable against the mortgage and the tenant had to vacate the premises. Even when dealing with leasehold interests, it is vitally important to properly register a lease. The interest will then run with the land and any new owner, or in this case a mortgagee taking possession on a defaulted mortgage, will have to take subject to that lease.

## LO 7  Residential Tenancies

Legislation creates protection for residential tenants

Under the common law there is very little distinction made between commercial and residential tenancies. However, all jurisdictions have passed legislation that considerably modifies the common law and essentially creates a consumer protection scheme, designed primarily to protect tenants. There are considerable differences among jurisdictions, and so no comprehensive attempt will be made to cover the subject. In the discussion below we will look at the main areas where changes have been made by the various residential tenancies acts. These areas of change deal primarily with rent increases, security deposits, termination requirements, repairs, privacy, and services.

---

[15]2008 CanLII 10379 (Ont. SC); [2008] O.J. No. 965.

**Form**    Several jurisdictions require the tenancy agreement creating the lease to follow a standard form, and all require a copy to be in writing and delivered to the tenant within a few weeks of its creation. Most permit some terms to be added if they are reasonable, but *acceleration clauses*, requiring all payments to become due if any default, are generally prohibited.

Standard form leases often required

**Repairs**    Consistent across jurisdictions is an obligation on the landlord to make general and emergency repairs to the premises and to maintain minimum health and safety standards. That means that the premises must be reasonably fit for human habitation, satisfying the local municipal by-laws with respect to health safety and sanitation. There is a corresponding obligation placed on the tenant to maintain the premises to a minimum standard of cleanliness. Note that the tenant is normally responsible as occupier for injuries that occur on the property because of disrepair or dangerous conditions under the *Occupiers Liability Act*, but the landlord would also be liable if his failure to meet his obligation to keep the property in safe and in good repair contributed to the injury. The tenant is also responsible for any damage to the premises caused by his or her own willful or negligent conduct or that of a guest. But the tenant is not responsible for the normal wear and tear that takes place on the premises, nor is the landlord, unless it expands into other damage that interferes with the tenant's use and enjoyment of the premises. Thus, if a leak developed in the roof and the landlord did not bother to repair it, that leak could expand, eventually destroying that part of the roof and making the premises uninhabitable.

Landlord obligated to make general and emergency repairs

Tenants are obligated to pay for damages they cause

Neither party required to repair normal wear and tear

**Privacy**    One consistent provision in all of these statutes is a restriction placed on the landlord from entering into the premises once rented. In general, the landlord has a right to inspect or to enter to make repairs, but only upon giving the tenant notice and only during the day. This right expands slightly once notice of termination has been given and it becomes necessary to show the premises to potential tenants. In the same vein, neither the landlord nor the tenant can change the locks or re-key them without the agreement of the other party. Tenants also generally have the right to sublet or assign the leased premises. This means they can find someone to replace them for a portion or the duration of the lease. Although they must obtain permission from the landlord to do this, the statutes state that such permission shall not be unreasonably withheld.

Landlord restricted from entering premises

**Security Deposits**    In most jurisdictions the practice has developed of landlords taking a **security deposit** to cover any damage done or rent not paid. This practice is controlled in all provinces with most restricting the amount to one month or one-half of one month's rent. In most provinces the security deposit is to cover damages to the premises, but with the agreement of the tenant, it can also be used to help cover the last month's rent. Ontario allows one month's rent to be taken as security deposit, which can only be used against unpaid rent, not damage. In all cases the landlord is required to hold the funds in trust and to pay the tenant a specified rate of interest on those funds within a short time after termination. In some jurisdictions, the landlord is also permitted to take a pet damage deposit where pets are allowed.

Amount and purpose of security deposits restricted and must be returned with interest

Case Summary 8.11 *Cote v. Armsworthy*[16]

## Tenants Get All Money Back for Illegal Suite

Sophia and other students (Appellants), Allan Armsworthy (Respondent) in an appeal from a decision in the Nova Scotia Small Claims Court overturning the order of the director of residential tenancies.

Several students leased a basement suite from Armsworthy from the period of August 1 2008 to May 30, 2009. The suite was illegal in that there was no occupancy permit and, upon inspection, several deficiencies were noted; including lack of fire protection, proper headroom and the presence of mould. The tenants vacated the premises at the end of January 2009 and refused to pay any further rent because of the presence of mould. The tenants applied to the director of the *Residential Tenancies Act* who excused them from any further rent obligations and ordered the return of any rents already paid. This was appealed to an adjudicator in the small claims court who overturned the award, allowing the landlord to keep rent paid but excusing the students from any further payment. The case was further appealed to the Nova Scotia Supreme Court. In this decision the court found that the mould and other deficiencies made the suite unsafe and unfit for human habitation, which made the lease void and illegal. The Court found that there was a failure to meet the standards required in the *Residential Tenancy Act* and so no further rents were payable and any rent already paid had to be returned. Note that the Court did allow an amount to be withheld to cover the costs the landlord incurred in extra heat and light.

This case shows the rights of the tenant and how they are enforced. It also illustrates the dangers of ignoring the legal requirements of local legislation, including the *Residential Tenancy Act*.

---

**Rent increases normally limited to one per year with substantial notice**

**Rent increases**   Most jurisdictions limit how often the rent can be increased (usually once per year) and some limit the amount it can be increased, or require the landlord to justify the increase. Notice of the increase must be given to the tenant several months in advance (at least 90 days in Ontario).

**Notice period for landlord to terminate lease is extended**

**Termination**   There are also special rules with respect to the termination of the tenancy. Notice must be given at least one clear month before termination of a month-to-month tenancy under common law, but most jurisdictions have expanded this with respect to notice to terminate by the landlord. In Ontario, 60 days' notice of termination must be given and this even applies where the lease is for a fixed term. Even more notice may be required where the premises are to be converted to ownership units or are to be used by the landlord's family. The tenant is only required to give one month's notice; and in several jurisdictions this is even shorter, to allow the tenant to give notice of termination on the same day he or she pays rent. In Ontario the tenants, like the landlord, must give 60 days notice of termination.

**Tenant can give notice at the time rent is paid in some jurisdictions**

**Landlord must maintain services**

**Services**   In addition to these specific requirements, landlords are generally prohibited from making changes or charging more for the services provided. For example, where parking is included or laundry facilities are provided, withdrawing the service or charging a higher fee for them would be an indirect rent increase and so is prohibited.

**Landlord may give reduced notice where tenant is in default**

**Remedies**   Where the tenant breaches the lease, for example by not paying the rent or using the unit for an inappropriate purpose, the landlord may be able to give the tenant reduced notice to vacate. Usually the landlord will turn to a tribunal, where disputes can be arbitrated or the officer can make an order requiring the breach to stop or even require

---

[16]2012 NS SC 15 (CanLII).

the tenant to vacate the premises. If the order is not obeyed, there is normally provision for an application to the court to enforce the order and evict the tenant. In most jurisdictions the remedy of distress, where the landlord seizes the tenant's property for failure to pay rent, has been abolished with respect to residential tenancies. Also, when the tenant abandons the premises, the landlord is now required to mitigate the damages by re-renting the premises to another tenant.

Landlord cannot seize tenant's property and must mitigate loses

The tenant can also bring complaints to the tribunal. The officers have considerable power to award remedies that will overcome problems, ranging from ordering the landlord to stay out of the premises, to reducing the rent to pay for repairs or in recognition of reduced services, to even ordering the landlord to restore services that have been discontinued. It should also be noted that the doctrine of frustration does apply to residential tenancies.

Statutes establish tribunals to hear complaints

Frustration applies to residential tenancies

The statutes also usually contain special provision for dealing with unique situations such as mobile homes. In that case only the pad is rented, but it is extremely difficult for the tenant to vacate, which would involve moving the mobile home. Some acts, including Ontario's *Residential Tenancies Act*, contain provisions with respect to special care homes for disabled tenants.

The various human rights statutes in place also apply to the provision of rental accommodation, and complaints with respect to discrimination in providing this service can be brought to the appropriate officer or board empowered to enforce the statute. Landlords also have to be aware of and comply with other regulatory statutes, including building and fire code requirements and municipal licensing requirements and restrictions.

When disputes do arise both landlord and tenant should takes care to determine what they can and can't do before acting. In most jurisdictions there is a Landlord and Tenant office that will advise the parties and provide them with sufficient information to help in that process.

Finally, it should be noted that under the *Criminal Code* several types of property use are prohibited and the landlord may be charged as well as the tenant. For example, using premises for unauthorized gambling or for prostitution and even for an immoral theatre production are prohibited.

Property owners and occupiers responsible for immoral acts on property

# REGULATION OF THE ENVIRONMENT

## LO 8

Increasing environmental regulation has become important concern of business

A discussion of property law would not be complete without an examination of environmental regulation, and the responsibilities imposed on landowners and businesses that use land in a way that encroaches on the environment. Environmental protection has become an increasingly important concern of the public and governments at all levels. There has always been the recognition of an individual's right to protect his or her immediate environment from pollution and degradation by others under the common law. The large-scale expansion of mining, forestry, coal, oil, hydroelectric, and nuclear generating plants has put an increasing strain on the environment. There has been a general recognition of the deterioration of the environment and the need for greater controls, not only to prevent further damage, but also to correct the damage that has already occurred. Statutory intervention at the federal, provincial, territorial, and municipal levels has become an important consideration in doing business, especially when a new venture is undertaken or where the purchase or sale of potentially contaminated property is involved.

# The Common Law

Riparian rights are the right to continued quality and quantity of water flow

The main area where common law provides protection is with riparian rights, which give people living on a river or stream (except for normal domestic depletion) the right to have the water continue to flow to them with undiminished quantity or quality. This basic right continues but is often overridden by a government's statutory power when it issues water-use permits to industries and municipalities. Thus, if the government grants a permit to a pulp mill to dump pollutants into a river, the downstream users cannot complain, as their riparian rights have been overridden by the exercise of a statutory power.

Riparian rights are often overridden by statute

The tort of private nuisance can be used to seek a remedy when a neighbour interferes with a person's enjoyment of his or her property, through the escape of water, noise, smoke, odours, etc. The injured party can bring an action seeking damages or an injunction. Even negligence or the principle of strict liability, as discussed in Chapter 2, can be relied on when dangerous things escape from one property, causing damage or injury to neighbours or their property. In rare circumstances, where there is actual physical interference with a property, the law of trespass can be used to obtain a remedy. But all of these common law provisions have one thing in common. They require an individual to go to the expense and take the time to sue. The polluting activity is treated as a private matter between the person injured and the offender. Someone who is not directly injured has no right to bring an action. There is generally no community right to action, and except in the most serious of cases, most individuals will not go to the trouble or expense to sue. These factors make the common law an ineffective tool to control pollution or protect the environment in any comprehensive way. It should be noted that the private right to sue for private nuisance was given a significant boost with the Supreme Court of Canada decision in *St. Lawrence Cement Inc. v. Barrette.*[17] This was a Quebec case involving a class action brought by the residents of the greater Quebec City area against St. Lawrence Cement Inc. for the noise, dust, and smoke pollution caused by the plant. Although this case involved the application of the Quebec *law* it is helpful to the rest of Canada because the Court found the cement company liable and stated that the common law doctrine of nuisance would have led to the same result in other parts of Canada. The Court also gave a broader definition of *neighbour*, giving all of the people affected a right of action. It is also important to note that this action went forward as a class action, allowing the burden of bringing the action to be spread much more widely, making private nuisance a more effective tool.

Common law is generally not efficient in protecting the environment

Nuisance can be used to stop pollution

Class action available for nuisance

---

## Case Summary 8.12 *Scarborough Golf & Country Club v. Scarborough (City)*[18]

## Golf Course Has Riparian Rights

Scarborough Golf and Country Club (Plaintiff), the City of Scarborough (Defendant) in this trial before the Ontario Supreme Court.

As the City of Scarborough expanded, more and more rain runoff was diverted into a particular stream, eventually causing considerable damage to a golf course. The golf course sued the city, claiming nuisance and a violation of their riparian rights (the right to have water continue to flow in undiminished quantity and quality).

---

[17][2008] S.C.J. No. 65. 2008 SCC 64 (CanLII); 299 D.L.R. (4th) 385).
[18]1988 CanLII 4829 (ON CA); (1988), 54 D.L.R. (4th) 1.

The city had the right to natural drainage through the stream but it had diverted water into it, causing the damage. The court had to determine whether the city was in violation of the riparian rights of the golf course.

The court found that the riparian rights of the golf course were infringed and the city had to pay compensation. The court also based the award of damages on private nuisance.

# Federal Legislation

This is an area where both the federal (including territorial) and provincial governments have the power to pass legislation. A business may find itself dealing with provincial or federal regulatory bodies, and sometimes both, depending on the nature of their business. The federal jurisdiction applies to all areas where a business is involved in a matter given specifically to the federal government under the *Constitution Act (1867)*. This includes such areas as navigable waters, fish-bearing waterways, inter-provincial or international undertakings, railways, ferry services, banks, broadcasting, and air transportation. Note that almost every stream and river is fish-bearing, giving the federal government power to regulate in almost all areas involving natural resources, where there is some discharge of polluting material into a water course. Historically the federal *Fisheries Act*[19] has been the most effective environmental protection legislation, allowing criminal charges to be leveled at anyone discharging any effluent into a fish-bearing watercourse. Section 36 (3) states:

> Subject to subsection 4, no person shall deposit or permit the deposit of a deleterious substance of any type in water frequented by fish or in any place under any conditions where the deleterious substance or any other deleterious substance that results from the deposit of the deleterious substance may enter any such water.

Beyond this, the federal regulations can also apply to all businesses providing services to the federal government, federal agencies, or federally supported activities, including all projects that receive federal funding. This creates considerable overlap, and businesses often find themselves dealing with federal, provincial, territorial, and even municipal environmental regulations, especially on larger projects.

**Canadian Environmental Protection Act**   The main federal statute in this area is the *Canadian Environmental Protection Act*.[20] This legislation provides for the establishment of a government department charged with preventing pollution and protecting the environment and human health, while contributing to sustainable development. In brief, the *Act* provides for research—the gathering, compilation, storage, evaluation, and publication of information and data; the setting of standards, guidelines, and codes of conduct; monitoring and inspection; the identification of prohibited and controlled activities; and the enforcement, remediation, and imposition of penalties when offences and violations take place.

Under the *Act*, where environmentally sensitive activities are involved, an individual or business can be required to develop and implement pollution prevention plans. Lists of toxic substances are specified, and their importation, export, and use in Canada are

*Environmental regulation comes from all levels of government*

*Federal environmental regulation may apply even to local projects*

*Statute authorizes government department*

*Spills must be reported and remedied*

[19]R.S.C. 1985, c. F-14.
[20]S.C. 1999, c. 33.

**Controls imposed and whistle blowers protected**

prohibited or controlled. Individuals are required to report the escape of such materials, and employees who do so (whistle blowers) are protected from reprisals.[21]

There are also restrictions on the disposal of waste at sea without special permits and on the use of unregulated fuels in Canada.

**Enforcement officers given significant powers of inspection and enforcement**

Enforcement officers have significant power under the *Act*. They can enter and inspect premises, stop and inspect conveyances to take samples, detain vehicles and material to make tests, and examine records and computers. They can issue environmental compliance orders, which may involve, among other things, the requirement that a person refrain from or stop doing something in contravention of the *Act*. Finally, they can charge individuals with offences where violations do occur, and penalties under the *Act* are significant. Note that these orders can be appealed to review officers and then to the Federal Court, if necessary.

**If a company fails to act, costs can be imposed on the violator**

When an unauthorized release of toxic substances or pollution does take place, and the property owner fails to report the release and warn the public, the enforcement officer can take the necessary action to remedy the situation and charge the costs back to the violator. Directors, managers, and agents of corporations can be held directly responsible unless they can show that they acted with due diligence. Due diligence requires officers to show that they have set up systems to ensure that the *Act* will be followed, including training employees and establishing policies to ensure compliance.

**Significant penalties are imposed on company and its directors but note due diligence defence**

**Limited civil remedies are provided**

Note that the *Act* also provides for civil remedies allowing an injured individual to bring an application in court for an injunction to stop an activity prohibited by the statute, or for monetary compensation where damages have been sustained.

This brief summary of the *Act* just touches the surface, and we have not looked at the great volume of regulations authorized under the *Act* to accomplish its objectives.

**Canadian Environmental Assessment Act**    Another important federal act is the *Canadian Environmental Assessment Act*,[22] 2012, replacing an earlier statute by the same name. The new act simplifies the assessment process applying it only to major projects that the federal government has control over (through granting permits licences funding and the like) to go though an environmental assessment process. This assessment process can take several different forms, depending on the potential risks involved and the size of the project. It should also be noted as a practical matter that these federal agencies often show considerable flexibility in their enforcement regime to encourage voluntary compliance and to foster economic development. Other federal statutes can have environmental implications. For example, the *Criminal Code* imposes serious penalties where the release of such pollution causes injury or death.

**Act imposes environmental assessment process**

## Provincial Legislation

**Provinces also require environmental assessment process**

While the legislation in place varies considerably from province to province and the territories, all have acts similar to the *Canadian Environmental Protection Act* designed to create general standards and monitoring and enforcement mechanisms to deal with environmental concerns in the areas of provincial jurisdiction. With the federal statutes as the examples, no attempt will be made here to do any kind of comprehensive review, but a few points should be noted. These statutes regulate the transport and disposal of waste,

---

[21]*Canadian Environmental Protection Act*, S.C. 1999, c. 33, s.16(4).

[22]S.C. 2012, c. 19, s. 52.

the use and transportation of hazardous materials, the cleanup of contaminated sites, the treatment of sewage, motor vehicle emission discharges, and the disposal of by-products from manufacturing, mining, and other activities. The statutes also control what happens at specific locations by limiting industrial, commercial, and residential uses. Most provinces, like the federal government, have an environmental review process that must be complied with before environmentally sensitive projects can go forward.

---

### Case Summary 8.13 *Podolsky v. Cadillac Fairview Corp.*[23]

## Private Prosecution for Environmental Interference

Ms. Podolsky, (Plaintiff), Cadillac Fairview Corporation (Defendant) in a private prosecution before the Ontario Superior Court of Justice.

Cadillac Fairview operated a property consisting of three buildings in a low rise complex called the Yonge Corporate Centre. These were low rise buildings with large areas of reflective glass which migratory birds hit on a regular basis, and the birds were then injured or killed. This action was brought as a private prosecution under the *Ontario Society for the Prevention of Cruelty to Animals Act, Ontario's Environmental Protection Act*) and the federal *Species at Risk Act (SARA)*. In a private prosecution the person prosecuting must prove that the conduct of the accused amounted to the prohibited action. This is known as the *actus reus*. Essentially, the prosecution must prove that the accused did what he or she was accused of and that amounted to an offense under the act. Here they were accused of erecting a building that interfered with migrating birds and was a threat to species at risk. It was clear that the reflective glass did cause confusion to the birds, resulting in many collisions. The reflective light qualified as the discharging of a contaminant,

(light) that caused the death and injury of the birds, which satisfied the EPA offense, and that the act of erecting the building with reflective glass satisfied the offense of killing or harassing a species at risk under the *SARA*.

The manager of this location had made considerable effort to work with an environmental group (Fatal Light Awareness Program) to help assess the injury to birds and to find ways to overcome the problem. But the environmental group was not content with those efforts and brought this action through its manager Ms. Podolsky. These offences are strict liability offenses in the sense that there is no need to prove a guilty mind (*mens rea*). It is therefore no defense to establish that there was no intention to do harm. Still the defense of due diligence, as discussed in Chapter 7, can be used— and in this case the court found that the efforts of the manager in helping the environmental group to acquire the statistics and to find a way to ameliorate the problem satisfied the requirement of due diligence. Thus, Cadillac Fairview was found not guilty on all charges. The case emphasizes the effectiveness of provincial legislation, the use of a private prosecution, and the use of the due diligence defense in such actions.

---

Government departments have been created to implement these policies. They establish codes of conduct and regulations to follow. To keep degradation of the environment to a minimum, government departments grant permits with restrictions and requirements, and supervise the discharging and storing of waste. There is an enforcement arm that is charged with enforcing those standards through inspection, investigation, the holding of hearings, and the levying of fines and other penalties. In fact, most of the litigation involving environmental matters takes place at the provincial level and involves provincial legislation. Often alternative remedies are provided that allow for negotiation, mediation, and agreements that facilitate working with the business to help them obtain compliance.

Provincial departments enforce environmental protection provisions

[23]2013 ON CJ 65 (CanLII); 112 OR (3d) 22 (ON CJ).

Municipalities also have power to impose controls on business

It is important to understand that even municipalities have extensive powers to deal with the environment. A business will often have to comply with municipal by-laws with respect to where a business is to locate. Nuisance, noise, odours, vibration, illumination, and dust emanating from the business, the discharge of sewage, and what can be discharged into the municipal drain system are also municipal concerns.

Overlap of regulation poses a serious problem for business

This illustrates the major problem of overlap and duplication of environmental regulation at the various levels of government, especially where the granting of permits is concerned. For example, a permit under the provincial regulations may be granted for a pollution-causing activity, and yet it may still be in violation of federal statutes and punishable. Several provinces have taken steps to reform their environmental regulatory regime to make them more business friendly and eliminate red tape. For example, Nova Scotia has amalgamated several enactments into one statute. But the problem of complying with these various regulatory requirements at all levels of government remains and presents a serious problem for business.

An important consideration from a business point of view is the problem of just who will pay for pollution when it does take place. In general, the polluter will pay, but this is not always the case. "Brownfields" legislation, dealing with the cleanup of contaminated commercial sites, will often impose cleanup obligations on whoever owns the land. Often the legislation involved will require that the current and former owners and the actual user who contaminated the property in the first place share clean-up responsibilities, but even this partial responsibility can be a significant expense. Still, it is in the best interests of governments at all levels to have these sites cleaned up and developed; and rather than take a punitive approach, often the various levels of government regulatory bodies and involved parties will work together to reach a mutually advantageous result. These factors must all be taken into consideration before purchasing or even getting involved in these potentially contaminated sites, making it extremely difficult to place a value on them for business purposes. Note that this type of environmental concern is yet another area where the business risks involved can be reduced by acquiring adequate insurance coverage.

## LO 9 INSURANCE

Insurance involves paying a premium to spread the risk

The main principle involved with insurance is the spreading of risk. Each participant pays a relatively small sum called a **premium** to cover a specified type of risk such as fire damage, theft, or lost property, and since only a few will have to be compensated, the risk of loss is thus spread among the many premium payers. In fact, huge sums are involved and large companies provide the insurance service, covering most of the various types of risk that may be encountered personally or in business. These companies will then often turn to even larger companies to insure themselves against unusual losses caused by unexpected circumstances such as the ice storm in Ontario and Quebec or the forest fires in British Columbia. This practice is called **reinsurance**. Because of

Insurance companies will often reinsure to cover their risk

the potential for abuse these companies are highly regulated, as are the insurance agents who sell the insurance coverage to businesses and the general public. Note that sometimes this insurance is obtained through an insurance broker rather than through an agent. The difference is that the **broker** represents the insured and arranges insurance for him or her with the companies, whereas the **insurance agent** represents the insurance company itself, either as an employee or an independent agent (see Figure 8.6).

Insurance agents represent the company whereas insurance brokers represent the insured

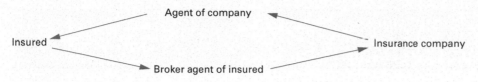

**Figure 8.6** Insurance

Note that for the purposes of vicarious liability and authority to contract, the broker can still be considered the agent of the insurer when it appears to the insured that he or she is representing the company. Note also that these brokers and agents have a duty of care toward the clients in their own right and, for example, can be liable for a failure to explain exclusions in the policy or bring attention to availability of extended coverage. Today, acquiring insurance to cover many of the variables in business has become a vital aspect of carrying on business.

The contracts involved, called **insurance policies**, usually take the form of a standard form contract dictated by regulation. Often a **rider**, which provides added coverage related to the unique needs of the particular customer, will be attached. The policies may be renewed each year with the premium changing to reflect changes in the market, higher costs of meeting the risks, or changes to the circumstances of the insured. When modifications to an existing policy are needed, an **endorsement** outlining the specific change is added.

> Insurance policies may include riders or endorsements that modify or add to the original terms

## Property Insurance

A major area of insurance coverage deals with damage or loss of property, both personal and real. It is traditional in the insurance field to acquire specific coverage for different types of risk. Losses through fire, flood, accident, and theft must be specified. It is vital, therefore, that you exercise great care in determining the extent of the insurance coverage obtained. Today this problem is overcome with the more comprehensive, all-risk policies. However, there will still be exclusions and so care is still needed when acquiring any form of insurance.

> Take care to read the contract, especially the fine print

Insurance, like a wager, returns a large payoff in return for a small payment if a certain event takes place. To avoid the contract being void as a wager there must be an insurable interest in the thing insured. This means that the insured must suffer a loss if the event insured against takes place so that the payout only compensates for that loss and is not a windfall. If you took out insurance on your neighbour's house and it burned down you would likely get nothing since you had no interest in the house and lost nothing. But if you took out insurance on your own house and it burned down you would be compensated for your loss. Shareholders in small closely held corporations often fail to distinguish between the property of the corporation and their own property. And when the corporation is incorporated they don't think to change over the insurance policies into the name of the company. In the past this was a problem but the Supreme Court of Canada has made it clear that shareholders do have a sufficient, although indirect, interest in the assets of a corporation to take out insurance on them and receive compensation if they are damaged or destroyed.[24]

> An insured must have an insurable interest to recover for a loss

> Shareholders now have an insurable interest in a company's assets

---

[24]*Kosmopoulos v. Constitution Insurance Co. of Canada Ltd.*, [1987] 1 SCR 2; 1987 CanLII 75 (SCC).

## Case Summary 8.14 *Paul v. CUMIS Insurance Company*[25]

# No Insurable Interest in Dead Spouse

CUMIS Life Insurance Company (Appellant), Mrs. Paul (Respondent) in this appeal of a decision of the Supreme Court of British Columbia in the British Columbia Court of Appeal.

Mr. and Mrs. Paul purchased a home and arranged for a mortgage with the North Shore Credit Union(NSCU). The house was in Mrs. Paul's name, but Mr. Paul arranged for life and disability insurance coverage through NSCU with CUMIS on the mortgage. After some time Mr. and Mrs. Paul separated, but Mr. Paul continued the insurance premiums until August 2008 when he let them lapse. Mrs. Paul was not aware of the lapse until after he died. When she discovered the problem, she contacted NSCU and CUMIS and arranged to reinstate the policy paying the arrears and making further monthly payments. She eventually made a claim on the basis of the death of

Mr. Paul, but CUMIS refused to pay claiming that the reinstatement had taken place through a mistake. At trial the judge found that because of the conduct of their agents and the fact that they took her money, CUMIS was estopped (could not deny) that they reinstated the policy. This was appealed and on appeal that decision was reversed. The appeal court found that because Mr. Paul was deceased at the time of the purported reinstatement of the life insurance, Mrs. Paul had no insurable interest in Mr. Paul. There was no life to insure and therefore the reinstatement had no effect.

This is a good case to illustrate the nature of an insurable interest. In order to insure something, including a life, you must demonstrate that you have an interest in that thing, that there is a risk to insure against. Here with the death of Mr. Paul that insurable interest ended.

---

**Be careful not to overinsure**

It is also important with property insurance to take out the right amount of insurance. Too much and you are overpaying the premiums because you can only collect what you have lost. Too little and you won't be fully covered for a total loss and, to make matters worse, you will be considered a **co-insurer**. Even if you suffer a small loss, you will collect only a portion of it since you are now sharing the risk with the insurer. For example, if your property is worth $500 000, you will be required to insure it for a percentage of that total (usually 80 percent). If you insure it for only $200 000 and you have a fire and suffer a $50 000 loss you won't be fully covered. You should have had $400 000 coverage (80 percent of $500 000) and paid premiums at that rate. Since you had only $200 000 coverage you are a co-insured and bear $200 000/400 000, or half the risk. For that small $50 000 loss you will only get a $25 000 payout minus your deductible.

**Be careful not to underinsure**

**Insurer has the right to salvage what he or she can from the loss**

The insurance company usually maintains the option to pay for, repair, or replace the property involved. It also has the right to **salvage** whatever value it can from the damaged or replaced parts. Also, the insurance company will be **subrogated** to the rights of the insured. This means that once they have paid, they take over the rights of the insured to sue whoever caused the loss in the first place.

**Once paid, insurer assumes insured's right to sue**

**Insurance is also available to cover business downtime**

But property insurance will not provide compensation for lost business while repairs are being made. For this it is quite common and quite prudent as a risk avoidance strategy for business people to obtain **business interruption insurance**, which provides an income during this downtime.

**Liability insurance covers injury or loss caused to others**

**Liability Insurance**   **Liability insurance** is available to cover such things as injury to other people or their property caused by the personal conduct of an individual, an

---

[25]2012 BC CA 35 (CanLII).

employee, or through the operation of the business. Examples would be people injured while on business premises or in accidents involving vehicles owned by the company or driven by employees, as well as the malpractice of professionals. Normally, such liability insurance will not only provide coverage for the loss but also will provide legal representation when the insured is being sued. This is in the insurance company's best interest, since it will ultimately have to pay if the insured is found liable for the loss or damage claimed.

As a rule, insurance will only cover negligence in these situations, not the willful actions of the insured or their employees. Also, as a matter of public policy, a beneficiary will not be able to collect a payment resulting from his or her own wrongdoing. For example, if a husband killed his wife he would not be able to collect as beneficiary of her insurance policy. **Bonding** is similar to insurance and involves the business purchasing a **fidelity bond** to cover wrongful conduct by employees. If an employee steals or cheats clients, the bonding company will provide compensation, but retains the right to go after the employee to recover what it has had to pay out. Sometimes a construction company will be required to put up a bond to ensure it will perform as required in a contract. This is a **surety bond** and guarantees performance of a contract rather than compensation for wrongful conduct.

Bonding is available to cover wrongful acts of employees . . .

## Case Summary 8.15 *Ouimet Estate v. Co-operators Life Insurance Co.*[26]

# Insurance Claim Denied Because of Misrepresentation

The Ouimet estate (Plaintiff/Respondent), the Co-operators Life Insurance Company (Defendant/Appellant) in this appeal before the Court of Appeal for British Columbia.

Bonnie Ouimet took out travel insurance from Co-operators Life Insurance before going on a trip to Denver, Colorado. While there she suffered an infection, and after eight days of hospitalization she died. The cost of hospitalization was $115 000, and the estate claimed this amount from the insurance company. The claim was denied on the basis that Ouimet had misrepresented her state of health when she declared on the application form that she was "in good health and [knew] of no reason to seek medical attention." In fact she had a serious problem with alcohol and the night before making the declaration she "was found unconscious in her home in a state of respiratory distress induced by her having taken a prescription narcotic while in a state of gross intoxication sufficient to give rise to mental confusion and disorientation. She was taken to a hospital where she was revived." The estate claimed this was a single incident and did not affect the validity of the declaration that she was in good health.

The court agreed but this decision was overturned on appeal. The declaration was of utmost importance because it determined the risk and the amount of premium that would be paid. Ouimet had a duty of good faith to the insurance company, and the court agreed that at the time of the declaration she could not have said she was in good health. The argument between the parties turned on the meaning of "In good health" and "to seek medical attention." The Ouimet estate claimed this should be taken to mean "non-routine or emergency medical attention," while the insurer put a broader interpretation, taking the declaration to include routine non-emergency medical attention. The court of appeal held that the plain meaning should prevail and that because of the previous hospitalization and her condition she had misrepresented the state of her health and thus the insurance company was required to pay nothing.

This case shows the importance of disclosing all relevant information to the insurer and that the benefit of insurance can be lost by failing to make a proper disclosure and withholding relevant information. It also emphasizes the utmost good-faith relationship involved.

---

[26] 2007 BC CA 163 (CanLII), [2007] 6 WWR 68; 65 B.C.L.R. (4th) 340.

Life insurance pays beneficiary when insured dies

There are many other types of insurance that are commonly available. **Life insurance**, for example, provides compensation to named beneficiaries when the insured dies. **Term insurance** involves a premium paid strictly to insure against the death of the insured. **Whole life insurance** involves a certain investment aspect as well as the insurance coverage, so that the insured will receive a return on that investment to assist in his or her retirement. There are many different combinations of these various schemes, some of which have important income tax implications.

Businesses often obtain life insurance on key personnel

From a business point of view, partners will often take out life insurance on their partners to sustain the business if one dies. Larger businesses will also take out life insurance on key personnel for the same reasons. Today, businesses also often supply health and disability insurance for their employees, providing extended coverage for such things as dental care and prescription drugs over and above the basic provincial coverage provided in all jurisdictions in Canada. **Disability insurance** provides an income to the insured when, because of accident or sickness, they can no longer work. For those who are professionals, self-employed, or in a business where such extended coverage is not provided, it can be obtained by paying a separate premium, often at higher rates, to an insurer on an individual basis. To have a separate policy and pay a separate premium for each of these various types of risk is not only a nuisance but would very likely result in gaps in the coverage. Today it is common to obtain comprehensive policies that will provide coverage for all or most of these various forms of risk in one policy, without the requirement that each type of risk covered be specified. The cost may be a little higher, but the advantages usually outweigh the disadvantages. In today's business world an important component of business strategy is to reduce the risks faced by that business as much as possible. As can be seen from this discussion, acquiring appropriate insurance coverage is a vital aspect of realizing that goal of risk reduction. The downside, however, is that the cost of insurance now in some cases is exorbitant and even large businesses have trouble justifying the premiums that must be paid.

A comprehensive policy covering all or many risks may be the best solution

Insurance involves a good faith relationship

Insurance involves a **good-faith relationship** between the insured and the insurance provider. That means that there is an obligation on the part of the insured to provide full disclosure of any condition or circumstance that might affect the creation of the policy or the cost of the premium. For example, with real property there is an obligation to inform the insurer if the premises are to be left vacant for any extended period of time or to be used in a way that exposes them to extra risk, for instance, storing fireworks, or changing its use from an office to some other function such as furniture manufacturing. With life or disability insurance there is an obligation to inform the insurance company of any pre-existing condition or disease that would put the insured at greater risk. When this kind of information is intentionally withheld from the insurance company, it constitutes misrepresentation and may void the policy. A good example of this is found in a Quebec case[27] where the beneficiary of a smoker was denied the benefits of a life insurance policy, even though he was killed in a car accident. He had lied on his insurance application claiming he no longer smoked, and as a result he obtained insurance coverage at a reduced premium. This was sufficient for the insurance company to avoid payment of the benefit, even though the cause of death had nothing to do with his smoking. It should also be noted that this duty of good faith works both ways as illustrated by the following case.

Health and disability insurance are also common

---

[27]*Ouellet v. L'Industrielle compagnie d'assurance sur la vie*, Que. C.A., 1993, as reported in *Lawyers Weekly*, Vol. 12 No. 44 (March 26, 1993).

## Case Summary 8.16 *Whiten v. Pilot Insurance Co.*[28]

# Punitive Damages Upheld for Insurance Company Abuse

Whiten (Plaintiff/Appellant), Pilot Insurance Co. (Defendant/Respondent) in this appeal before the Supreme Court of Canada.

The Whitens experienced a total loss of their home to fire on a winter night in 1994. The husband, wife, and daughter had to take refuge outside in sub-zero cold. Mr. Whiten suffered serious frostbite to his feet as a result. The insurance company initially made a payment of $5000 for living expenses, which only covered expenses for a few months. It then cut off payment, leaving the family in very difficult financial circumstances. The company refused to pay any more, claiming the family had set fire to their own home. This resulted in lengthy litigation and trial, with the insurance company dragging its feet and adopting a confrontational style through the whole process. Finally, at trial the lawyer for the insurance company, in the face of strong evidence from the fire chief and even from its own expert witness, was compelled to admit there was no basis for the claim of arson and no basis for the refusal of payment of the benefits of the insurance policy.

The Supreme Court had to decide not only whether the plaintiff was entitled to the claimed compensation for the loss but also whether the award of $1 million punitive damages should be reinstated. Madam Chief Justice McLachlin characterized the conduct of the insurance company as exceptionally reprehensible. It was planned and deliberate, taking place over a two-year period. It not only denied the Whitens compensation for their loss and the extra costs of finding new accommodation, but also imposed considerable unnecessary legal costs as well. An incensed jury not only awarded $345 000 for the insurance claim and $320 000 for legal costs in compensation but also $1 million in punitive damages. This was reduced on appeal but reinstated by the Supreme Court of Canada in this very important decision.

This case illustrates the special relationship of trust between an insurance company and its clients. It also indicates the powerful impact of punitive damages as a method of controlling abuses of such good-faith relationships.

## Key Terms

abatement (p. 264)

adverse possession (p. 258)

agreement of purchase and sale (p. 257)

bailee (p. 247)

bailment (p. 247)

bailment for value (p. 247)

bailor (p. 247)

bonding (p. 277)

broker (p. 274)

building scheme (p. 251)

business interruption insurance (p. 276)

certificate of indefeasible title (p. 256)

chattels (p. 245)

chose in action (p. 245)

co-insurer (p. 276)

condominium (p. 253)

condominium corporation (p. 254)

cooperatives (p. 255)

deed of conveyance (p. 257)

disability insurance (p. 278)

distraint (p. 265)

dominant tenement (p. 251)

dower rights (p. 253)

easement (p. 251)

endorsement (p. 275)

equity (p. 260)

equity of redemption (p. 259)

estate (p. 249)

[28][2002] 1 SCR 595; 2002 SCC 18 (CanLII).

fee simple estate (p. 249)

fidelity bond (p. 277)

fixture (p. 249)

foreclosure (p. 260)

forfeiture (p. 265)

good-faith relationship (p. 278)

goods (p. 245)

gratuitous bailment for the benefit of the bailee (p. 247)

gratuitous bailment for the benefit of the bailor (p. 247)

homestead rights (p. 253)

insurance agent (p. 274)

insurance policies (p. 275)

intellectual property (p. 245)

involuntary bailment (p. 247)

joint tenancy (p. 252)

judicial sale (p. 261)

land registry (p. 256)

land titles system (p. 256)

leasehold estate (p. 262)

liability insurance (p. 276)

licence (p. 251)

liens (p. 256)

life estate (p. 250)

life insurance (p. 278)

mortgage (p. 255)

mortgagee (p. 259)

mortgagor (p. 259)

option to purchase (p. 255)

periodic lease (p. 262)

personal property (p. 245)

power of sale (p. 261)

premium (p. 274)

prescription (p. 258)

profit à prendre (p. 251)

quiet enjoyment (p. 264)

real property (p. 245)

reinsurance (p. 274)

relief against forfeiture (p. 265)

remainder (p. 250)

restrictive covenant (p. 251)

reversion (p. 250)

rider (p. 275)

right of way (p. 251)

salvage (p. 276)

second mortgage (p. 260)

security deposit (p. 267)

servient tenement (p. 251)

subrogated (p. 276)

surety bond (p. 277)

tenancy in common (p. 252)

term insurance (p. 278)

vacant possession (p. 264)

whole life insurance (p. 278)

## Questions for Student Review

1. Distinguish between real property, personal property, and intellectual property. Distinguish between a chattel and a chose in action. Explain how personal property can be used to secure a loan.

2. Explain how the expression "finders keepers" relates to property law. Explain who is entitled to goods found in the public or private part of a building.

3. Explain bailment and how the obligations of the bailee varies when it is a gratuitous bailment for the benefit of the bailee or for the benefit of the bailor. What if the bailee is an innkeeper or common carrier?

4. Explain what is meant by a fee simple estate in land and what limitations there are to a person's right to that land. How can personal property become real property?

5. What is the nature of a life estate? Who is entitled to the reversion and what obligations are imposed on the holder?

6. Distinguish between an easement, a right of way, a restrictive covenant, and a building scheme.

7. Compare a joint tenancy and a tenancy in common, and explain severance and its effect on such tenancies.

8. Explain the nature of a mortgage and how it is used to secure a loan. Identify the parties to the mortgage.

9. Distinguish between the effects of a registration in a land registry and a land titles jurisdiction, and explain why registration of interests in land is important. How does a mortgage affect the title in these jurisdictions?

10. Explain what is meant by adverse possession and prescription, and the role these principles play in land titles and land registry jurisdictions.

11. Describe an equity of redemption, foreclosure, and the redemption period. Why are they important to mortgage transactions?

12. Explain what is meant by a lease and distinguish the lease from other types of interests in land. What is meant by a periodic lease and how is it ended?

13. Summarize the landlord's and tenant's obligations with respect to commercial tenancies and the effect of the lease terms on those obligations. Indicate the amount of notice that normally must be given by the parties to terminate the tenancy or to increase the rent.

14. How do most residential tenancy statutes modify the obligations of the parties to make repairs to the premises? Explain how the rights of the landlord to enter residential premises have been restricted.

15. Explain the nature of a security deposit and any restrictions on the landlord's right to retain all or some portion of the security deposit.

16. Explain the landlord's obligations with respect to services provided during the term of the tenancy. What can a landlord do when a tenant defaults in a residential tenancy?

17. How does federal legislation with respect to the environment become important to landowners and business people?

18. Explain the role of the *Canadian Environmental Protection Act* and how its objectives are realized.

19. Explain the role of enforcement officers appointed under the *Canadian Environmental Protection Act* and how they can interact with business.

20. Who can be charged with an offence under the *Canadian Environmental Protection Act*?

21. Explain what is meant by an insurable interest, and distinguish between an insurance agent and a broker.

22. Explain the nature of the insurance policy, a rider, an endorsement, and reinsurance. Summarize the different types of insurance that are available to businesses.

23. Distinguish between liability, property, and life insurance. Explain the difference between whole life and term insurance, indicating why life insurance might be important for a business or for professionals to acquire.

24. Distinguish between bonding and insurance. Explain the difference between a fidelity bond and a surety bond.

## Questions for Further Discussion

1. There is a considerable difference between the laws with respect to residential and commercial tenancies. Most of the statutory changes favour the tenant and have led to much complaining by landlords about the difficult position they find themselves in. Do you feel that the changes introduced by statute have unfairly interfered with what should be a relatively simple commercial relationship? Is this another instance of government imposing inappropriate regulation that unfairly restricts a landlord's right to manage his or her property? Consider this as a form of consumer protection legislation and ask what problem it was intended to solve, whether an adequate solution has been arrived at, and whether the solution creates more problems than it solves.

2. Bailment involves one person putting his or her personal property into the care of another. The responsibility to look after that property is often limited in the contract creating that relationship. Do you think that a party agreeing to be responsible to look after another's property, either in the process of repair, storage, or otherwise, ought to be able to contract out of their responsibilities with an exemption clause? This question really is much broader. This is because, whenever an exemption clause is included in any contract, one party is severely disadvantaged. Should the parties to contracts, especially where the bailment of goods is involved, be able to contract out of such basic responsibilities? In your discussion, consider the often unequal bargaining power of the parties, the consideration between the parties, and standard form contracts.

3. Consider the laws that have been imposed on individuals and businesses to control pollution and reduce waste. Is this a reasonable demand? Consider how these policies might affect Canadian who move their businesses abroad, perhaps to evade these costly requirements. Who should pay for the damage caused by pollution and the costs of cleanup, including "brownfield" sites?

4. A serious problem that often arises for an insured claiming on an insurance policy is the requirement that all information be accurate or that any changes in circumstances be communicated to the insurance company. Benefits have been denied when the loss takes place when the premises were left vacant, where the use of the premises has changed, or where the information on the application is accidentally or knowingly incorrect—even if the information has nothing to do with the event giving rise to the claim. Discuss whether such an approach is too harsh and gives too much advantage to the insurance companies and whether consumers are adequately protected from abuse.

## Cases for Discussion

1. *Backmirzie v. 1500569 Ontario Ltd.*, 2006 CanLII 40669 (ON SC); [2006] O.J. No. 4831

   Parvanh Backmirzie left two valuable Persian rugs with La Moquette Fine Rugs and Furnishings to be sold on consignment. However, the rugs were not sold; and while held at the store to be picked up by Backmirzie, they were stolen during a break-in. This action is brought by Backmirzie against the company owner of the store in a demand for compensation for the loss. Explain the basis of this action, the arguments that could be advanced by both parties, and the likely outcome. Would your answer be affected by the additional information that several days before the break-in the proprietor of the store phoned Backmirzie saying she should pick up the rugs as she had observed two men in the store looking at them. They appeared to be "casing" the store, and the proprietor feared a break-in. But Backmirzie delayed picking the rugs up and they were stolen.

2. *Lawrence v. Maple Trust Company*; 2007 ON CA 74 (CanLII); (2007), 84 O.R. (3d) 94; (2007), 278 D.L.R. (4th) 698; (2007), 220 O.A.C. 19

Susan Lawrence owned a home in Toronto. A person, posing as Ms. Lawrence, went to a lawyer with a forged agreement to purchase and had the property transferred to another person who called himself Thomas Wright. Wright obtained a mortgage for $291 924 from Maple Trust Company, which was duly registered against the property. An existing mortgage on the property in favour of the TD Bank was paid off and the imposters took the remainder. Maple Trust had no knowledge of the fraud and had in fact lived up to its due diligence requirements with respect to the transaction. Ms. Lawrence was also innocent, having no idea of what had happened. This happened in a land titles jurisdiction. Who should bear the loss in this situation? Explain the arguments on both sides and the likely outcome.

3. *Flying Saucer Restaurant Ltd. v. Lick's Leasing et al*, 2011 ON SC 718 (CanLII)

The Flying Saucer Restaurant leased their premises to Lick's Leasing Ltd., who in turn sublet to a tenant who left without paying. The plaintiff then looked to Lick's Leasing for compensation as per the lease, but Lick's had no assets and paid nothing. In this action the Flying Saucer Restaurant is seeking the rent owed from the principal of Lick's leasing, Mrs. Meehan, as well as from several related companies. Explain the arguments for each party. Would it affect you answer if Mrs. Meehan had made a personal guaranty for the rent? What if that guaranty was verbal? What if she had made a misrepresentation? What if the other related corporations were successful, had funds, and were owned by the same people?

4. *R. v. Petro-Canada* 2003 CanLII 52128 (ON CA); (2002), 222 D.L.R. (4th) 601

Petro-Canada was charged with "discharging a contaminant into the environment," an offence under the *Ontario Environmental Protection Act*. In fact, a pipe had failed and leaked gasoline, but Petro-Canada responded quickly. It was also established that there were a number of safety systems and procedures in place. Petro-Canada claimed due diligence as a defence. Explain what must be established to succeed in a due diligence defence and on which side the onus of proof resides. How would it affect your deliberations to know Petro-Canada had used piping "not up to industry standards?"

5. *Dhingra v Dhingra* 2012 ON CA 261 (CanLII)

Mr. Dhingra had a substantial life insurance policy when his wife, who was the beneficiary of the policy, murdered him. Do you think she should be allowed to collect? What if she was found not criminally responsible on the basis of her own mental disorder?

6. *Clemmer Steelcraft Technologies Inc. v. Bangor Metals Corp.*, 2009 ON CA 534 (CanLII); 55 C.B.R. (5th) 177; 169 A.C.W.S. (3d) 671

Brute Manufacturing Ltd. operated a manufacturing business and was under the supervision of the *Companies' Creditors Arrangement Act*. With the court's approval it sold certain heavy equipment to Steelcraft, including a large spray booth used in the process of painting large equipment. But Brute was also a tenant of Bangors Metal Corp. at the time of the sale, and Bangor claimed it was entitled to the spray booth as a permanent fixture. Explain the arguments for both sides and who would likely be ultimately entitled to the spray booth. Would it affect your answer to know that the spray booth was very large, was fastened to the floor and roof, and connected to the electrical and natural gas supply? What if the terms of the lease provided it could not be removed without the permission of the landlord?

# Chapter 9
## Ideas and Information

Olly/Fotolia

## Learning Objectives

LO 1  Distinguish between intellectual property and other kinds of property

LO 2  List and describe what is protected under copyright law

LO 3  Summarize the recent changes in copyright law that have an impact on digital recordings

LO 4  Explain what a patent protects and how patent protection is obtained

LO 5  Outline the protections afforded by the *Industrial Design Act*

LO 6  Describe what is protected by the *Trade-marks Act*

LO 7  Describe confidential information and the ways it can be protected

LO 8  Consider the role of privacy acts and describe how they protect a business from disclosure of confidential information

An information revolution has taken place over the past 40 years, fuelled primarily by the use of computers. This chapter discusses the intersection between law, business, and information technology. It includes an examination of intellectual property, including copyright, patents, and trademarks, as well as a review of the legal issues associated with securing information and protecting personal privacy. The following chapter is devoted to examining the legal issues associated with electronic commerce and international trade, and includes a discussion of doing business over the internet. Technology changes so fast it is difficult to keep abreast of the social impact of these advances, not to mention the laws that are developed try to regulate them. Just one example of such development is a new category of legal practice called Applaw. The apps available for downloading on mobile devices are affected by all the topics covered in this chapter, including copyright, patent, and trademark. Enforcing such rights can be a costly and time-consuming exercise and has caused a new specialization in the legal industry. Failure of a business to keep up with the changes can expose them to unexpected liability, but more importantly, can shut them out of important business opportunities and leave valuable intellectual property resources unprotected. In this chapter we will look at the nature of these resources, outline the problems associated with them, and examine the directions in which our lawmakers seem to be going.

*Great changes caused by computers and internet*

## INTELLECTUAL PROPERTY

**LO 1/LO 2/LO 3**

We identified the forms of property in the last chapter, dividing personal property into chattels (tangible, movable goods), and choses in action (intangible personal property). Intellectual property is a special type of intangible personal property. Copyright does not refer to a particular book, song, software program, or painting, but to the right to control its reproduction. In the same sense patents, trademarks, industrial designs and the structure of integrated circuits do not refer to actual things produced, but to the protection of the idea, mark, or design associated with a product.

*Intellectual property is intangible personal property*

Intellectual property is a valuable business asset that can be stolen or damaged. Unauthorized exploitation may deprive the copyright holder of income or damage the goodwill associated with a trademark. Patented inventions can be misappropriated, and confidential information can be misused. Intellectual property is often underdeveloped, undervalued, and underprotected by business people. This seems to be a particular problem in Canada. A business may be so focused on marketing that it fails to realize the potential of a production process or software that has been developed for its own purposes. Even if a business does sell or licence the process or software, there may be a failure to properly account for royalties or enforce the contract.

*Businesses often undervalue and fail to protect intellectual property*

Intellectual property law usually requires that active steps be taken to protect an asset. The federal government has enacted legislation dealing with intellectual property, including copyrights, patents, and trademarks. Thus, most disputes dealing with intellectual property matters are heard by the Federal Court. However, this is one area where federal and provincial courts both have jurisdiction, and so these matters may be dealt with by provincial superior courts as well. But as in other areas of business, having to resort to litigation to resolve property disputes will likely indicate a weakness rather than a strength.

*Federal and provincial courts often have concurrent jurisdiction with respect to intellectual property*

# Copyright

We are living through a period of revolutionary change. It has been stated that the information age brought about by computers and the internet has brought about world change as significant as that initiated by the invention of the printing press in the 15th century. The focus of that change is twofold: first, the access we have to the vast amount of information that is stored and transmitted digitally, and second, the ease with which that information can be copied, communicated, and otherwise manipulated. With respect to law, the impact of these changes has its greatest influence in the field of copyright. The federal *Copyright Modernization Act*[1] passed in 2012 updates and expands the former *Copyright Act*.[2] It protects books, photos, music, and other artistic works. Keep in mind that it is only the expression of the idea that is protected, not the idea itself. If someone photocopies the text that you are now reading, she will be in breach of the author's copyright, but if she writes another book expressing the same ideas in a different way, she has a right to do that. **Copyright** protection is extended to authors and artists for 50 years after the death of the creator of the work. In effect, the owner of the copyright controls the reproduction of the work during that period, after which the work becomes part of the public domain and no longer subject to anyone's control. The idea is to give the creator of the intellectual property the exclusive right to profit from and otherwise control his creation for a specified period of time. This period is reduced to just 50 years when a corporation is involved, the author is not known, or the work involves such things as movies, photographs, performances or sound recordings Note that there are important exceptions that will be discussed below. For example, the new *Act* has an expanded fair dealing clause which allows for more liberal copying of material that is to be used for educational purposes, but also requires institutions to be more accountable for the amount of material that it photocopies.

It is common for a publishing company to produce and market the work and for the author, artist, or composer to receive royalties from the sales. **Royalties** consist of a percentage payment (for example, 10 percent), based on the net proceeds the publisher receives from each item sold. The copyright is then assigned to the publishing company. Of course, creators can publish their own material, retaining for themselves complete control over the copying, reproduction, or performance of their work, but marketing the work on any large scale usually requires different skills that are provided by an expert in the field, the publisher.

**Copyright protects the expression of the idea, not the idea itself**

**Copyright lasts for the life of author plus 50 years**

---

**Case Summary 9.1** *Society of Composers, Authors and Music Publishers of Canada v. Bell Canada*[3]

## Previews Not Subject to Royalties

This is an application by SOCAN (Society of Composers, Authors and Music Publishers of Canada) for judicial review of a Copyright Board decision taken first to the Federal Court of Appeal and then to the Supreme Court of Canada.

SOCAN is, a body set up to collect royalties for musicians and publishers whenever their music is used. There is no question that royalties are payable when music is downloaded over the internet, but potential buyers through iTunes and other music services typically listen to

---

[1]*Copyright Modernization Act*, S.C. 2012, c. 20.
[2]*Copyright Act*, R.S.C. 1985, c. C-42.
[3]2012 SCC 36 (CanLII), [2012] 2 SCR 326 (SCC).

a preview before deciding to purchase. This consists of listening to a 30 to 90 second segment of the music under consideration. Here SOCAN was attempting to impose a royalty payment every time such a preview takes place and followed the appropriate process filing proposed tariffs with the Copyright Board.

The Board agreed that SOCAN was entitled to royalties for downloaded music generally but not for previews. They determined that listening to a preview was essentially "fair dealing" under the research and private study exception under Section 29 of the *Copyright Act* and therefore not subject to the payment of royalties. SOCAN applied to the Federal Court of Appeal for judicial review of the Board's decision, but when the Court dismissed their application they took the matter to the Supreme Court of Canada. To determine whether previewing qualified as "fair dealing" required a two-staged approach. First, the Court had to determine whether previewing in this way was research. SOCAN argued that research required some element of creativity, not simply determining whether or not to purchase. But the Supreme Court took the broader approach and agreed that previewing in this sense qualified as research under the *Act*. The second part of the test was whether previewing before purchase was "fair." The Supreme Court noted that in determining whether the use was fair it was appropriate to consider such matters as the "purpose, character, and amount of the dealing; the existence of any alternatives to the dealing; the nature of the work; and the effect of the dealing on the work."

The Supreme Court agreed with the Copyright Board and the Court of Appeal that the use qualified as research and the use was fair. Thus, previewing qualified under the "fair dealing" exception and no royalties were payable.

Even where the copyright has been assigned to a publisher or some other party, the author retains some significant rights. **Moral rights** consist primarily of the author having the right to continue to have his or her name associated with the work as creator, and to have the integrity of the work preserved. This means that the work cannot be modified, distorted, or defaced without the author's permission, even after it has been sold. If an author assigned the copyright of a book to a publisher, who then decided to publish it using the name of a different author, that would violate the original author's moral rights. Another example of the protection of moral rights involved a sculpture of Canadian geese in a shopping mall. A retailer decided to hang red ribbons on it for Christmas. The sculptor protested, and the court agreed that the added decoration interfered with the artist's moral rights not to have his work degraded and ordered the mall to remove the ribbons.[4] Moral rights also relate to association. Thus, an artist would be entitled to prevent a political party or candidate that they did not support from using their music for a theme song. Keep in mind that these moral rights are limited to Canada, although similar rights are recognized by many other jurisdictions. The United States does not recognize moral rights.

*Copyright can be assigned, but authors retain moral rights*

It is not always the creator of the work who is entitled to copyright. When an author is working as an employee, the work created will belong to the employer, unless the employment contract states otherwise. Also, when consultants write an instruction manual for a software producer, for example, the contract may state that copyright will be held by the software company. Here again we see the importance of a separate contract setting out the expectations and rights of the parties, including what work is to be created and the consideration to be paid, but also which party will acquire copyright. Think about the implications this might have for the distribution and use of an app that you have downloaded onto your mobile.

*Employers entitled to copyright unless agreement otherwise*

---

[4]*Snow v. Eaton Centre Ltd.* (1982), 70 C.P.R. (2d) 105 (Ont. H.C.J.).

## Case Summary 9.2 *Boudreau v. Lin et al.*[5]

## Students Own Copyright in Papers Written for Professors

Boudreau (Plaintiff), Lin (Defendant) in this trial in the Superior Court of Justice, Ontario.

Boudreau was an MBA student attending university under the supervision of the defendant Lin. As part of the requirements, he prepared a paper and submitted it to Lin. Lin later published it along with another professor as contributor with only minor revisions and without acknowledging the role Boudreau played in its preparation. The paper was later included in a casebook, which was used in other classes at the university. When Boudreau discovered his paper in the casebook, he brought this action against both the university and Lin. The court had to determine who had copyright in the paper.

The court found that Lin "was neither the originator nor the developer of any substantive ideas or concepts. His contributions consisted of general comments that were directed to polishing the paper and were those that one expects from a professor who is editing and discussing a paper written by a student. None of the changes he proposed affected the substance of the paper." He could not even be called a co-author.

The Court found that Lin, and the University as his employer, were liable for breaching Boudreau's copyright with respect to the paper in question. Note as well that the Court determined that Boudreau's moral rights in the paper had also been breached by the changes made, which affected the integrity of the work, and by the removal of his name as author. The judge characterized this as an example of plagiarism and academic dishonesty, which "most certainly should not be tolerated from the professors who should be sterling examples of intellectual rigour and honesty." The actual award of $7500 in general damage didn't reflect his loss, which was difficult to calculate, rather the amount was in recognition of his indignation and the wrong committed against him. The Court also issued an injunction to refrain the defendants from interfering with Boudreau's copyright in the paper.

---

**Computer software is now protected by copyright**

In addition to the creative products mentioned above, there are several less obvious areas that are covered by the *Copyright Act*. Copyright can extend to "every original literary, dramatic, musical, and artistic work" produced in Canada as well as a "performer's performance, sound recording, and communication signals." Past confusion about whether computer programs and software were better protected under patent or copyright legislation resulted in amendments to the *Copyright Act*[6] to protect computer programs as literary work. Table 9.1 lists examples of what is included in these various categories. Note that there can be considerable overlap among them.

**Copyright protection in Canada can give protection in other jurisdictions**

Other nations have similar laws, and there are treaties between nations giving copyright protection in one nation to works created in another. So long as the originator is a citizen or resident of Canada, or of a country that is a signatory to the Universal Copyright Convention, the Bern Convention, the Rome Convention, or is a member of the World Trade Organization, that work has copyright protection in Canada and those other countries.

**Copyright protection is automatic in Canada but registration provides additional benefits**

It is also important to note that no special steps need be taken in Canada to create copyright. Registration is not required, since the mere production of the work creates the copyright. Still, registration is permitted under the *Act*[7]; this is often done to establish

---

[5](1997), 150 D.L.R. (4th) 324 (Ont. Gen. Div.); *Aubry v. Duclos et al.*; *Canadian Broadcasting Corp.*, *Intervener* (1997), 157 D.L.R. (4th) 577 (SCC).

[6]*Copyright Act*, R.S.C. 1985 c C-42.

[7]*Copyright Act*, R.S.C. 1985, c. C-42, s. 54.

## Table 9.1 The Scope of Copyright

| Category | Examples |
| --- | --- |
| Literary works | Books, pamphlets, manuals, computer programs, and translations |
| Dramatic work | Plays, recitations, mime, movies (including the scenery) |
| Musical work | Musical compositions and arrangements |
| Artistic work | Paintings, drawings, maps, charts, plans, photographs, engravings, and sculptures |
| Performances | Dancing, singing, instrumentals, acrobatics, and acting |
| Sound recording | Tape recordings, records, computer memory, compact disks, memory cards, and DVDs |
| Communication signals | Radio, television, cable, and internet broadcasts |

when the work was created and who created it, or to ensure that the work has copyright protection in other nations that require such registration. Registration can take place by making an application to the copyright office at the Canadian Intellectual Property Office (CIPO). That office will issue a certificate of registration and maintains an official registry of copyrights that can be accessed and used for legal purposes. Copyright is indicated by the symbol © accompanied by the year of publication and the name of the copyright holder.

To qualify for copyright protection, the work must be original. This does not mean it has to satisfy some critical standard, but it must originate with the author. Facts, numbers, images, or material copied from other sources are not protected by copyright, only the part that originates with the author or artist is protected. The protected work must also be fixed in some permanent form as in the recording of a song in digital format or capturing of an image on film. It could also include a written choreography, a stage play, or a manuscript stored on computer.

For copyright protection work must be original and fixed in a permanent form

---

### Case Summary 9.3 *Entertainment Software Association v. Society of Composers, Authors and Music Publishers of Canada*[8]

## Music in Downloaded Video Games Not Subject to Royalties

This is an application for judicial review of a Copyright Board decision taken first to the Federal Court and Federal Court of Appeal and then to the Supreme Court of Canada by EMS.

This case also involves SOCAN attempting to impose royalties for music downloaded through the internet, but in this case the music involved was imbedded in video games. When video games are sold in the stores

the royalties are negotiated and paid to the music provider at the time of production. They are set before the game is sold and no further royalties are payable at the point of sale. But SOCAN took the position that since it is charged with collecting royalties when music is downloaded over the internet, a further royalty should be imposed at the point of downloading. In effect, royalties would be paid twice. The Copyright Board and the Federal

---

[8]2012 SCC 34 (CanLII), [2012] 2 SCR 231,(SCC).

Court of Appeal agreed. But the Supreme Court of Canada disagreed and allowed the appeal. It found that imposing the second royalty payment violated the principle of technological neutrality, which required that the *Act* work equally when different forms of media are used. The traditional method of distribution is through sale in a store or by mail, requiring no further royalty payment. Using the internet is simply a different more efficient form of delivery of exactly the same product and technological neutrality requires that the different delivery methods be treated equally with no additional royalty imposed. "The principle of technological neutrality requires that, absent evidence of Parliamentary intent to the contrary, we interpret the *Copyright Act* in a way that avoids imposing an additional layer of protections and fees based solely on the *method of*

*delivery* of the work to the end user. To do otherwise would effectively impose a gratuitous cost for the use of more efficient, Internet-based technologies."

SOCAN argued that it was entitled to impose a royalty when musical works were "communicated" using the internet. The Supreme Court agreed but observed that historically "communicate" in this sense was always associated with the performance of the work. In this case the internet was simply being used as a vehicle to deliver the work like mail delivery and was not "communication" within the meaning of the *Act*. Using this narrower definition the right to impose a further royalty did not apply. The appeal was allowed.

This case further refines what downloaded material is subject to royalties.

**Limited copying is permitted**

It is only when substantial portions of the work are copied that there is an infringement of the copyright. Photocopying a few pages of a textbook for personal use might not violate copyright but copying several chapters or even a few lines of a vital portion clearly would. Use of small portions of a work for research or for private study is permitted, and there is no infringement when portions of a work are reproduced for review, criticism, or news reporting (this is called "fair dealing"). Educational institutions, as well as libraries, museums, and archives have additional rights to use portions of such works for educational and research purposes. Note that the changes in fair dealing allowed by the new *Act* and the way the courts have dealt with these questions is discussed in more detail below.

**Fees paid to Access Copyright and SOCAN**

Where there is a question as to the right to use copyrighted material it is best to get a licence from Access Copyright, which is the nonprofit body set up to represent authors in these matters. Access Copyright collects a fee and distributes it to the author, legitimizing a reasonable amount of photocopying. SOCAN provides the same service for musicians and composers of recorded music. The Copyright Board, a government regulatory body established under the *Copyright Act*, sets the royalty fees charged by these bodies and other matters, including the arbitration of some disputes with respect to copyright. Under their direction, a tariff has been levied against all recordable media (so far limited to CDs, DVDs and tapes). This allows the private copying of music and other material for noncommercial use without violating copyright.

**Canadian copyright law under attack**

Bill C-11 The *Copyright Modernization Act* was passed in November 2012 after a decade of wrangling among judges, lawyers, legislators and users. The amendments to the copyright law are designed to address the major concerns with the previous legislation.

The law needed first of all to be brought in line with the international treaties that have been in place since 1996. The World Intellectual Property Organization ("WIPO") and the WIPO Performances and Phonograms Treaty ("WPPT"). The courts have been active in updating the law and the legislators have made an effort to reconcile the *Act* with many of those judicial decisions, especially those that made their way to the Supreme Court of Canada.[9,10] Some important changes are set out below.

**Compensation**   Performers will continue to receive compensation through organizations such as SOCAN when others use their works but the Copyright Board will now establish the tariffs to be paid, including the tariffs with respect to the use of these works in other countries (called "neighbouring rights").

**Photography**   The amended *Act* has a new protection for photographers treating the photographer as the author and owner of the photograph rather than the person who commissioned it. The individual who commissioned the work can use it according to the agreement with the photographer; otherwise, the use is limited to private or non-commercial purposes.

**Fair Dealing**   The Supreme Court of Canada established a standard for 'fair dealing' exception to copyright protection in *CCH Canadian Ltd. v. Law Society of Upper Canada*, 2004 SCC 13. The new act expands the right to use copyrighted work under certain conditions. If a copyrighted work is used for the purposes of education, satire and parody in addition to the allowable circumstances set out in the original act (research, private study, news reporting, criticism, and review) there is no infringement of copyright providing the use also meets the 'fairness factors' established by the Court that take into account, the purpose, nature, amount, the alternatives, and the effect of the dealing in the work. Significantly, the amended *Act* provides new exceptions that allow the use of internet materials in education. Educational institutions may now reproduce, display and distribute protected works in any form of media. Generally, the exceptions require that students receiving such materials destroy them within a certain period after the course is finished.

---

[9] A summary of the new Act can be found at http://www.ic.gc.ca/eic/site/crp-prda.nsf/eng/h_rp01153.html#amend

[10] The following cases decided by the Supreme Court of Canada in the past decade contributed to the amendments in the *Copyright Modernization Act* with respect to fair dealing:

> *Théberge v. Galerie d'Art du Petit Champlain Inc.*, [2002] 2 SCR 336, 2002 SCC 34 (CanLII)
>
> *CCH Canadian Ltd. v. Law Society of Upper Canada*, [2004] 1 SCR 339, 2004 SCC 13 (CanLII)
>
> *Society of Composers, Authors and Music Publishers of Canada v. Canadian Assn. of Internet Providers*, [2004] 2 SCR 427, 2004 SCC 45 (CanLII)
>
> *Robertson v. Thomson Corp.*, [2006] 2 SCR 363, 2006 SCC 43 (CanLII)
>
> *Euro-Excellence Inc. v. Kraft Canada Inc.*, [2007] 3 SCR 20, 2007 SCC 37 (CanLII)
>
> *Entertainment Software Association v. Society of Composers, Authors and Music Publishers of Canada*, [2012] 2 SCR 231, 2012 SCC 34 (CanLII)
>
> *Rogers Communications Inc. v. Society of Composers, Authors and Music Publishers of Canada*, [2012] 2 SCR 283, 2012 SCC 35 (CanLII)
>
> *Society of Composers, Authors and Music Publishers of Canada v. Bell Canada*, [2012] 2 SCR 326, 2012 SCC 36 (CanLII)
>
> *Alberta (Education) v. Canadian Copyright Licensing Agency (Access Copyright)*, 201 [2012] 2 SCR 345, 2012 SCC 37 (CanLII)
>
> 37 Re:Sound v. Motion Picture Theatre Associations of Canada, [2012] 2 SCR 376, 2012 SCC 38 (CanLII)

**Personal Use**   The amended copyright act now allows time shifting and format shifting. This permits people to record television programs and copy music to view or listen to at a more convenient time. But the copies can't be given to others. "Mashups" are also now permitted with limitations. This involves an individual taking portions of other publicly available works and incorporating them into their own creation.

**Digital Locks**   The amended Act also allows music and movie producers to incorporate digital locks into their products preventing the copying of that work. It is illegal to break or circumvent a digital lock.

The *Act* permits internet service providers (ISPs) limited copying rights to provide search engines and cloud computing services but also imposes a new "notice and notice" requirement. This requires an ISP when notified of infringement to notify the subscriber as soon as possible of the infringement and provide the infringing subscriber's information, including identity, to the copyright holder claiming infringement. ISPs also face greater liability where their services are involved in such activities as hosting websites facilitating the illegal sharing of copyrighted material such as music and movies.

*Copyright Act amended*

It should also be noted that the *Act* reduces the statutory damages that are available. These are discretionary damages that a judge can award without specific proof of any loss. Now statutory damages are limited to $100 - $5 000 and are available only where a non-commercial use is involved, and no matter how many infringements are involved in that particular case.

## LO 4   Patents

Patent protection continues for 20 years but requires disclosure

Corresponding to the revolution in information and its availability is a similar exponential expansion of innovation and development in the biological/technical area. With respect to law this area has its primary impact in the field of patent law. A **patent** is a form of monopoly that gives an inventor the exclusive right to produce and profit from his or her invention for a period of 20 years. A government regulatory body was created to deal with applications. This is the Patent Office, which is part of CIPO. The inventor must disclose in the form of drawings, plans, and text material enough information so that someone else could reproduce the invention. Inventors are encouraged to share their invention with others who will then benefit by the knowledge and be inspired to further innovation and invention. There is no obligation to disclose this information by getting a patent, but when it is kept secret, there is the danger that someone else will independently produce the same item. In such a case the first inventor will have no protection. If the second inventor is granted a patent, the original inventor will be prohibited from using his or her own invention. Deciding to disclose through a patent or to keep the invention a trade secret is an important and usually a difficult decision, often based on the likely duration of the usefulness of the invention and how likely it could be discovered by reverse engineering. The source of patent rights in Canada is the federal *Patent Act*.[11]

---

[11]R.S.C. 1985, c. P-4.

## Case Summary 9.4 *Excelsior Medical Corporation v. Canada (Attorney General)*[12]

# Procedures Must Be Carefully Followed to Preserve Patent Application

Excelsior Medical Corporation (Appellant), Canada (Attorney General) the respondent in this appeal before the Federal Court of Appeal.

Under the *Patent Act* maintenance fees must be paid in order to preserve an application for a patent. The party applying for the patent is required to deal with the Patent Office through a designated agent (Authorized Correspondent). In this case the appropriate documents were not filed and the Patent Office was not advised when a change in the authorized correspondent was made. A new agent submitted the payment that was inadvertently accepted and the patent application was reinstated. When the mistake was discovered, a letter was sent to the new, would be, agent nullifying the reinstatement and indicating that the patent application was dead. The agent was invited to send a request for a refund of the amounts paid. The new agent brought this

action applying for judicial review of the Patent Office decision.

The Federal Court dismissed the application and the matter was appealed to the Federal Court of Appeal, which also dismissed the application.

It was clear from the Act that the Patent Office could only deal through an Authorized Correspondent, and since the fee was submitted by an unauthorized agent it could not be accepted. Since the maintenance fee was not paid by the authorized correspondent within the grace period required, the patent application was dead and could not be revived. It was appropriate to refund the fee but the patent application remained dead.

This case illustrates just how important it is to follow the strict requirements of the legislation when dealing with government agencies such as the Patent Office.

---

Unlike copyright, it is the idea that is protected in a patent, not the expression of the idea. Thus, if someone produces another product that is quite dissimilar to a patented invention, but incorporates the same principles or ideas, it would still be an infringement of the patent associated with that invention. The *Act* defines an **invention** as "... any new and useful art, process, machine, manufacture or composition of matter, or any new and useful improvement in any art, process, machine, manufacture or composition of matter."[13] To be patentable the invention must be useful in the sense that it is functional or can do what it claims and contributes in some way to improving our society by making some aspect of production more efficient or our lives more enjoyable. It also must be new. A patent will not be granted to someone who simply finds some process or machine that is in use but has not been patented. A patent will be denied if the invention has been the subject of prior publication more than a year before the application. It will also not succeed if the invention is embodied in some product that has been sold prior to the application or if the nature of the invention can be discovered by examination of the product, known as **reverse engineering**.

*Patent protects the idea, not the work itself*

*Invention must be new and useful*

---

[12]2011 FCA 303 (CanLII).

[13]*Patent Act*, R.S.C. 1985, c. P-4 s. 2.

## Case Summary 9.5 *Canwell Enviro-Industries Ltd. v. Baker Petrolite Corp.*[14]

# Pre-disclosure Invalidates Patent

Baker Petrolite (Plaintiff/Respondent), Canwell Enviro-Industries (Defendant/Appellant) in this appeal before the Federal Court of Appeal.

Baker Petrolite developed a product to remove the offensive odour from sour gas. But its patent was challenged on the grounds that it had been disclosed to the public more than a year before the patent had been applied for. In fact, Petrolite had started to sell the product more than a year before applying for patent protection in either the United States or Canada, and the court had to determine whether this was sufficient predisclosure of the process to disqualify the patent.

The court held that this amounted to such disclosure and refused the patent. Although they didn't actually disclose how the product could be made, it was a simple matter of reverse engineering for an expert in the field to take the product, analyze it, and reproduce the effect. The patent was invalid. Note the dilemma of the manufacturer, who is often pressured to get the product to market as fast as possible but also to delay long enough to get patent protection.

---

**No patent is granted for obvious improvement, scientific principle, or higher life form**

Nor will a patent be granted for some improvement to an existing machine or process that would have been obvious to someone with similar knowledge and training. The *Act* also makes it clear that, "No patent shall be granted for any mere scientific principle or abstract theorem."[15] Thus Einstein's famous formula, $E = mc^2$, could not be the subject of a patent.

Also, higher life forms such as modified animals are not patentable in Canada.[16] But the Supreme Court has made it clear that a modified gene can be patented. To protect that gene, the court will also protect the animal or plant produced by that modified gene, thus arguably accomplishing the patenting of modified animals indirectly.[17]

**Business practices less likely to be patented in Canada**

It has become common practice in the United States to patent unique methods of carrying on business, but such **business patents** were thought not to be available in Canada. In recent years, however, this has changed and business patents have been granted in Canada, albeit not on the same scale as in the United States. It was also thought that computer software was not patentable in Canada but this has also changed, especially where some physical component or technological device is associated with the software program. Still, the *Copyright Act* specifically includes computer programs as protected by copyright law.

Special provisions are in place with respect to the production of patent medicines in Canada. These are designed to consider the interests of consumers and protect them from excessive pricing, while providing sufficient protection and income to the patent holder. Historically, Canada forced international companies to grant licences at low cost to Canadian companies so that they could produce cheaper generic drugs for this country. That was changed in 1993. Drug manufacturers gained greater patent protection with the cost of patented drugs going up as a result. This has been balanced by introducing the requirement that the prices at which patent-protected drugs are sold must be justified

---

[14][2003] 1 FCR 49, 2002 FCA 158 (CanLII).

[15]*Patent Act*, R.S.C. 1985, C. P-4 s.27(8).

[16]*Harvard College v. Canada (Commissioner of Patents)*, [2002] 4 SCR 45, 2002 SCC 76 (CanLII).

[17]*Monsanto Canada Inc. v. Schmeiser*, [2004] 1 SCR 902, 2004 SCC 34 (CanLII).

before a Patented Medicine Prices Review Board (PMPRB). The result has been a significant increase in the price of patent-protected drugs in this country. To make matters worse, practices such as "**evergreening**" have been introduced to further increase the length of patent protection. This involves developing some small change in the already successful drug so that it can be treated as a new drug with another 20-year span of patent protection.

Note that the problem is much worse for developing countries that simply cannot afford the costs of modern drugs. The World Trade Organization (WTO) now permits the creation of generic drugs, under licence, for export to developing countries, and this has gone some distance toward responding to the battle against AIDS, especially in Africa. Historically, it was up to the generosity of drug producers, the patent holders, to supply such drugs to meet developing country requirements. Now that licences are granted to other producers, cheaper drugs are available, but there is also a growing problem with the cheaper drugs getting back into Western countries at the lower costs.

Unlike copyright, in Canada patent protection does not come automatically, but must be applied for. The process of applying for a patent is complex and expensive, and is best left to experts who are registered patent agents. They, typically, will make a search of the patent registries of Canada at the Patent Office and similar registries in other countries to see if a similar patent has been granted. Then they will submit an application in which they set out full disclosure with respect to the invention. The documentation must also describe what is new and innovative about the invention. The application must be provided in a specified form, along with accompanying documents and a fee to the Patent Office. The documents are examined to determine if the invention qualifies as something new. If it is indeed new, and the requisite fees are paid, the commissioner for patents grants approval for the patent. The payment of an annual maintenance fee is also required to maintain the patent protection over its 20-year life.

*Patent must be applied for and fee paid*

Once a patent has been obtained the invention must be used. Inventors cannot simply sit on their invention, using their patent rights to prevent others from using them. Upon application to the patent board, an individual can require a patent holder to grant a licence to use the invention, thus ensuring that the public benefits from it.

*Where patent not used, the patent holder can be forced to grant a licence*

Although a patent granted in Canada provides patent protection in this country only, once a patent has been granted here, protection can be obtained in other countries that are signatories to applicable treaties. The Paris Convention for the Protection of Industrial Property, and the Patent Cooperation Treaty on Intellectual Property are the most important of these treaties and apply to all nations that are signatories to them. The treaties do not grant patents in those other countries, rather they establish priority so that once the patent is filed in Canada the inventor then has a specific period of time (usually one year) to file a patent application in those other countries. The general rule is that the first to apply is the one entitled to the patent. But under these treaties this priority is established with the original application in Canada, not the later date of application in another country. The reverse is also true, of course, giving patents obtained in other countries priority in Canada as well. Foreign patents are vitally important for Canadian businesses involved in significant international trade. Note that filing a patent application in the European Patent Office pursuant to the European Patent Convention (EPC) is an application for patent protection in all of those European countries that are signatories to the EPC. It is not necessary to file additional application in each separate country.

*Canadian patent establishes right to patent in other jurisdictions*

**Employee has right to patent unless agreement otherwise**

As was the case with copyright, it is important to include provisions that clearly state who is entitled to any patent arising from work done under the contract or pursuant to the employment in contracts with consultants, employees, and independent contractors. Note that when an employee creates copyrightable material, there is an assumption that the copyright vests in the employer, but the same is not true with a patent. In that case, without a contract stating otherwise, the employee inventor is entitled to the patent even if created during working hours unless inventing was the purpose of his employment.[18] As was the case with copyright, patents can be assigned to third parties and can be used as security for a corporation's financing arrangements.

**Federal and provincial courts can hear patent infringement case**

Decisions to grant or not grant a patent or decisions about patent infringements may be challenged in the Federal Court. Where an infringement has taken place, the *Patent Act* gives both the federal and provincial courts concurrent jurisdiction to deal with that infringement and to provide appropriate remedies.

## LO 5  Industrial Design and Circuit Topography

*Industrial Design Act* protects distinctive design or shape

Two other acts providing similar protection are the *Industrial Design Act* and the *Integrated Circuit Topography Act*.[19] These federal statutes are relatively unknown but can provide significant protection in the right circumstance. The *Industrial Design Act*[20] protects distinctive designs, shapes, or patterns associated with an article (anything made by hand, tool, or machine and usually mass produced) that has no useful function, but simply adds to the appeal. An industrial design protected by the *Act* is defined as "features of shape, configuration, pattern or ornament and any combination of those features that, in a finished article, appeal to and are judged solely by the eye." The distinctive shapes of a utensil, a chair, or even the unique icons found on computer screens are examples. Protection of such designs is acquired by registration lasting for 10 years with the payment of the appropriate fees, including maintenance fees to be paid over the 10-year period. Registration takes place by making an application to the Office of the Commissioner of Patents, through the Industrial Design Division of CIPO. The item registered must be new and unique and the registration must take place within one year of its publication. Any design that makes clothing, automobiles, appliances, or other manufactured goods attractive can be covered. The *Act* provides penalties against persons that "make, import for the purpose of trade or business, or sell, rent, or offer or expose for sale or rent, any article in respect of which the design is registered."[21] As was the case with patents, once such protection is obtained by registration in one country that protection extends to other countries that are also a party to the treaty, but it must be registered in that country within a short period of time. Note that since the design of a manufactured product includes both the expression of an idea and a physical manifestation of it, overlapping protection may be available under copyright and trademark and in rare instances under patent. Note also that while the registration of an industrial design might protect it from being copied and sold without permission, it would provide no protection from it being depicted in a

---

[18]*Comstock Canada v. Electec Ltd.*, (1991) 38 C.P.R. (3d) 29, 45 F.T.R. 241 (FCTD).

[19]*Industrial Design Act*, R.S.C. 1985, c. I-9; *Integrated Circuit Topography Act* S.C. 1990, c.37.

[20]R.S.C. 1985, c. I-9. s.2.

[21]*Industrial Design Act*, R.S.C. 1985, c. I-9, s.11,(1) a.

photograph movie or video game, although such protection may be available under trademark legislation.

The *Integrated Circuit Topography Act*[22] is legislation intended to protect the unique design of the integrated circuits that are the heart of the modern computer revolution. The various components that make radios, televisions, computers, automobiles, watches, and most other modern products work are now miniaturized onto semiconductor material. They form the *integrated circuits* protected by this *Act*. To obtain this protection the design must be registered within two years of its first commercial use, and the protection also continues for a 10-year period. This registration takes place through the Office of the Registrar of Topographies, which is part of CIPO. As with the other types of protection, registering in Canada provides protection in other countries as well, providing those countries are party to the appropriate treaties. Copies made for commercial purposes are prohibited, but if they are used for research or nonprofit purposes there is no infringement of the *Act*. The *Act* provides broad remedies for infringement, including ordering injunctions, the payment of royalties, the payment of damages or profits (including punitive damages), and the seizure and destruction of offending items.

*Integrated Circuit Topography Act* protects computer chip design

## Trademarks

## LO 6

**Trademarks** are names, symbols, logos, or other distinctive marks that are associated with a business. A valuable business asset is its good relationships with customers, suppliers, and the public. This is referred to as **goodwill** and is often associated with the business name or some distinctive mark, such as McDonald's golden arches, Apple's depiction of an apple with a bite taken out, or the shell symbol appearing on all of Shell's service stations and other operations. The federal *Trade-marks Act*[23] provides a mechanism for trademarks to become registered and protected in a formal way. This registration takes place through the Office of the Registrar of Trade-marks that is part of CIPO. This protection gives the owner of the trademark the exclusive right to use it throughout Canada with respect to the particular type of business, or similar products or services as indicated on the application. This protection lasts for a period of 15 years and is renewable, but it must be used during that time or it will be considered abandoned. Note that at the time of writing there is a proposed amendment to the *Trademark Act* reducing this period of protection to 10 years. A trademark registered in Canada will provide proof of ownership for registration in another country. The converse is also true; registration in another country will provide proof of ownership in Canada.

*Trade-marks Act* protects distinctive names and logos

Trademark protection is obtained by registration and currently lasts for 15 years

If another business uses a similar symbol so as to cause confusion, making its customers think they are dealing with the actual owner of the trademark, an infringement has taken place. Intentional copying of a registered trademark is not the only way an infringement can take place. Any use of a similar mark that devalues the goodwill or reputation of the business can qualify as an infringement, whether intentional or not.

Infringement involves others using the mark, confusing the public or devaluing the business

[22]S.C. 1990, c. 37.
[23]R.S.C. 1985, c. T-13.

## Case Summary 9.6 *Mattel, Inc. v. 3894207 Canada Inc.*[24]

# What's in a Name?

Mattel Inc. (Plaintiff/Appellant), 3894207 Canada Inc. (Defendant/Respondent) in this appeal before the Federal Court of Appeal.

A numbered Ontario company was doing business as "Barbie's Restaurants" in several locations in Montreal. When it attempted to register a trademark to that effect, it was opposed by the Mattel company, claiming that it infringed on their registered trademark for their "Barbie" doll, a very successful toy doll marketed by that company. The issue was whether the restaurant names infringed the Mattel trademark. The restaurant chain countered that the use of the name was with reference to the term Bar-B-Q as in "Throw some ribs on the barbie" and that it was so different that it would not cause confusion among the public. The Trade-marks Opposition Board agreed, allowing registration of the "Barbie" trademark for the Montreal restaurant chain.

This was appealed by the Mattel organization all the way to the Supreme Court of Canada, with each court agreeing with the board and allowing registration of the restaurant's "Barbie" name. The Court upheld the original decision, finding that there was little likelihood of confusing the "Barbie" doll with the restaurant chain. "Barbie's" fame was tied to dolls, not restaurants, and so there was no confusion created.

A similar result took place when Toyota challenged a food company for using the name "Lexus foods"[25] and when the producers of Cliquot Champagne tried to prevent a chain of small women's clothing stores from using the "Cliquot" name for their stores.[26] These cases show that similar trademarks can sometimes exist side by side if they are for different products and don't cause confusion in the marketplace.

When an infringement takes place, the owner of the trademark may seek a remedy in either the Federal Court or the superior courts of the provinces. The advantage of going to the Federal Court is that the judgment can be enforced throughout Canada.

**Trademarks can be words, symbols, or both in combination**

Trademarks can consist of words, expressions, trade names, symbols, logos, designs, or combinations of them. The apple logo associated with the word "Apple" on that company's computers is an example of such a combination. Trademarks include the specialized marks associated with quality or standards such as the CSA (Canadian Standards Association) approval found on electrical and other appliances. These are called **certification marks** and have the same protection in Canada as other forms of trademarks. Organizations associated with the government such as Canada Post and the Red Cross can also register "**official marks**." These are actually stronger than trademarks since the owner does not have to be concerned about similar pre-existing marks. Official marks prohibit all others from using marks that might be confused with them, pre-existing or otherwise. Good examples of this are the official marks that were registered with respect to the 2010 Olympics. The organization responsible for the Olympics registered many names and symbols associated with the games, including symbols such as the name Olympics, the interlocking rings, and even the term "Gold medal" as official marks that prohibited others from using any marks that even resembled them.

**Certification marks and official marks are also covered by the *Trade-marks Act***

It is also possible to register the distinctive shape of a product or its container, such as the unique Coca-Cola bottle shape. This is called a **distinguishing guise** and registration

---

[24][2006] 1 SCR 772, 2006 SCC 22 (CanLII); 2006), 268 D.L.R. (4th) 424.

[25]*Toyota Jidosha Kabushiki Kaisha v. Lexus Foods Inc.*, [2001] 2 F.C. 15; (2000), 194 D.L.R. (4th) 491; (2000), 9 C.P.R. (4th) 297; [2001] 2 FCR 15, 2000 CanLII 16447 (FCA).

[26]*Veuve Cliquot Ponsardin v. Boutiques Cliquot Ltée*, [2006] 1 SCR 824, 2006 SCC 23 (CanLII); (2006), 270 D.L.R. (4th) 1 (SCC).

also provides trademark protection. But if that unique shape is functional in the sense that it is part of what makes the object do what it is supposed to do, it will not constitute a trademark. For example, Lego argued that their unique system of eight knobs on the top of their blocks constitutes such a mark, but the Supreme Court of Canada refused to recognize this because those knobs were functional in that they were an essential aspect of the design that caused the blocks to join together.[27] This same limitation applied to industrial designs, as discussed above.

Under the *Trade-marks Act* an application can be made not only for a mark presently used in association with a product or service but also can be made for a **proposed trademark**, where the mark has not yet been used and is not known to the public but will be used in the future.

The recent innovation of 3D printing is one more example of technological advances out-stripping the law. 3D printing poses challenges with respect to trademarks as well as copyright and patent, especially where people use 3D printing for personal use. Now many items that could only be obtained by purchase after being commercially manufactured can be made by any individual working in his home using a basically simple printing device. At the present time like copyright there appears to be no prohibition in the trademarks act against recreating goods even with distinctive marks for personal, non commercial purposes.

The process of applying for and registering trademarks in Canada is a complex one, usually requiring the services of experts called *trademark agents*. Searches of indexes and registries must be made in Canada (a database is maintained for this purpose at the CIPO offices) and usually in other countries—especially the United States—to determine if the mark has already been granted or is in use here or elsewhere. Then the agent makes the application to the Registrar of Trade-marks, setting out a description of the mark, the wares or services it is to be used with, and the names and addresses of the agent and owner of the trademark along, with the appropriate fee.

There are several restrictions on what can be used as a trademark. For example, anything associated with royalty, national flags, institutions such as the Red Cross or RCMP, or provincial or national coats of arms cannot be used without permission. Of course, anything obscene or illicit is also prohibited. Normally, a simple surname of a living or recently deceased individual will not be accepted. But there are exceptions if the name has already become associated with the product or business. Also, a term that is simply descriptive of the product, the nature of the service, the location, or one that is misleading in any way will be rejected. And of course, no trademark can be used that can be confused with the registered or unregistered mark of another similar business or one selling similar products or services. Note that at present unique sounds cannot be registered as trade marks because of the difficulty in describing them. Also, the trademark in a name or symbol can be lost when it is no longer unique in that it no longer identifies a particular business, but is used generally to describe any number of similar products. For example, the terms *nylon* and *escalator* have lost their trademark value for the companies that originated the term due to their common use. Google, the internet search provider, has sent off notifications to media and other users to stop using their name as a verb in order to avoid the same consequence for that term.

Distinctive shapes and proposed trademarks may also be the subject of protection.

Trademark protection requires registration and the payment of a fee

Trademark must be distinctive, socially acceptable, and not associated with prohibited institutions

Trademark may be lost when it comes into common use

---

[27]*Kirkbi AG v. Ritvik Holdings Inc.*, [2005] 3 SCR 302, 2005 SCC 65 (CanLII); (2005), 259 D.L.R. (4th) 577; (SCC).

Trademarks can now be licensed for use by others

Disputes with respect to the registration of trademarks are handled by the Registrar of Trademarks and the Trademarks Opposition Board, with appeals going to the Federal Court. An application can be brought to have a trademark expunged where there has been misrepresentation with respect to the application or for some other reason the mark doesn't qualify for registration, and this challenge can be brought even years after the trademark has been registered. It is appropriate, although not required, to indicate the presence of a trademark by the symbols ® where the trademark is registered or ™ when unregistered. Trademarks can be challenged up to five years after registration. It should also be noted that such trademarks as well as the licences associated with them can be assigned to other companies.

---

## Case Summary 9.7 *Reynolds Presto Products Inc. v. P.R.S. Mediterranean Ltd.*[28]

## Trademarks Must Not Be Confusing

Reynolds Presto (Appellant), P.R.S. Mediterranean (Respondent) in this appeal before the Federal Court of Appeal.

Both Reynolds Presto Products and P.R.S. Mediterranean were involved in producing cellular confinement systems designed to prevent erosion and stabilize ground. Strips of material were combined to create a honeycomb shaped product used for that purpose. Presto registered their trademark GEOWEB and licenced P.R.S. Mediterranean to use it. When the licence ran out P.R.S. continued to use the process and registered their own trademark NEOWEB to describe an essentially identical system. This application is brought by Reynolds Presto to have that mark struck from the trademark registry on the grounds that it caused confusion with their own mark GEOWEB describing their similar process. The application was rejected at the Federal court level but Reynolds Presto was successful at the Federal Court of appeal level and their appeal was allowed.

The Court of Appeal found that the marks were similar enough to cause confusion with only the first letter different. It was likely that the similarity in sound and the use of the N substituted for the G would make consumers think that NEOWEB was simply a newer version of GEOWEB. Because the products were similar and the companies were in the same business, this caused sufficient confusion to invalidate the trademark and the mark NEOWEB was struck out of the trademark registry as requested.

Trademarks that are likely to cause confusion with other trademarks in similar businesses in the same market can be challenged even after they have been successfully registered.

---

**Passing-Off**    The *Trade-marks Act* provides statutory protection for registered trademarks, but even unregistered marks and names are protected under the common law tort of passing-off. Any person or business that advertises their service or product in such a way as to lead others to believe they are being supplied by or associated with another business, when they are not, is liable to be sued for the tort of passing-off. Counterfeit Rolex watches and Hermès handbags are examples. With the use of the internet and private website marketing, the problem of counterfeit and pirated goods being sold in Canada has greatly increased.

A business that passes itself off as another may be liable

Sometimes a business will use a similar name, which might lead customers to believe they are associated with another business when they are not. This too may qualify as passing-off. For example, the British Columbia Supreme Court issued an injunction restraining a newly formed real estate company from using the name Greystone Properties Ltd. on

---

[28]2013 FCA 119 (CanLII).

## Table 9.2 Intellectual Property Legislation

| Statute | What Is Protected | Requirements | Protection Period |
|---|---|---|---|
| *Copyright Act* | Original books, photos, music, software, and other artistic works (the expression) | Mere production | Death of author of work plus 50 years, or in some cases only 50 years |
| *Patent Act* | Original invention or innovation (the idea) | Application and registration | 20 years from filing |
| *Industrial Design Act* | A product's distinctive design, shape, or pattern | Registration | 10 years from registration |
| *Integrated Circuit Topography Act* | Design of integrated circuits | Registration | 10 years from filing or use |
| *Trade-marks Act* | Trade names, symbols, and logos associated with a business | Registration* | 15 years renewable (but note pending amendment to reduce to 10 years) |

*Note that some trademarks receive unregistered protection through passing-off action.

the basis that it caused the public and the customers of the already-established Greystone Capital Management Inc. to be confused. Their use of the name devalued the goodwill of that company, even though the plaintiff company was based in Saskatchewan. It had no office in British Columbia, but did some business with the real estate and pension fund investment community in that province. The court found that 1) the plaintiff had a reputation of goodwill in British Columbia that could be injured; 2) the businesses were similar enough to cause confusion by the action complained of; and 3) the value of the goodwill or reputation was injured. These are the necessary elements to establish a passing-off action.[29] In effect, the ability to bring a passing-off action prevents other businesses from trading on the reputation and goodwill of another business through intentional or accidental misrepresentation and in the process injuring the value of that reputation and goodwill. A passing-off action will be available to an injured party whether or not their trademark is registered under the *Trade-marks Act*. Table 9.2 provides a summary of the legislation protecting intellectual property in Canada.

*A registered trademark not required for a passing-off action*

## Case Summary 9.8 *Walt Disney Productions v. Triple Five Corp.*[30]

# The Danger of Using Similar Names

Walt Disney Productions (Plaintiff/Respondent), Triple Five Corp. (Defendant/Appellant) in this appeal before the Alberta Court of Appeal.

When in 1983 the Edmonton Mall used the name "Fantasy Land" for their new amusement park, the Walt Disney Corporation, which had used that name in association with their amusement park for decades, sued them for passing-off. The issue was whether the use of "Fantasy Land" in Edmonton could cause confusion in the public mind with the Disney Fantasy Land in California.

---

[29]*Greystone Capital Management Inc. v. Greystone Properties Ltd.* (1999), 82 C.P.R. (3d) 501; 46 BLR (2d) 45 (BC SC).

[30](1994), 113 D.L.R. (4th) 229; 1994 ABCA 120 (CanLII) (AB CA).

The court agreed that the use of the similar name would cause confusion in the minds of the public and issued an injunction against the Alberta corporation that prevented the continued use of the name. Even though Walt Disney Corporation didn't carry on business in Alberta, they did advertise there, and the goodwill developed by that promotion had been damaged. The fact that there was no intention to mislead did not take away from the damage caused, and an injunction was the appropriate remedy.

## Remedies

*Interim injunction requires the balance of convenience to favour the applicant*

The remedies available to the court when intellectual property rights are infringed are similar in all cases (see Table 9.3). Damages are available, but only at trial and after a lengthy delay. As mentioned above even though legislation with respect to intellectual property is federal, this is one area where both the Federal Court and superior courts of the provinces have concurrent jurisdiction and an action can be brought in either court. The needs of the parties in intellectual property disputes are usually urgent, requiring a more immediate remedy to prevent further losses. Often when an infringement is discovered, the offended party will make an immediate application to the court for an injunction to stop the offending practice until the court can deal with the matter at trial. An interim injunction will only be granted when the applicant can show a strong case, indicating a likelihood of success at trial and also that the **balance of convenience** is in the applicant's favour. This means that the court has to be convinced that more damage will be suffered by the applicant if the injunction is not granted than would be suffered by the offending party if the injunction were issued. As with other equitable remedies it must also be shown that an award of damages at trial will not provide a sufficient remedy. Often where contracts and licenses are involved it is advisable to include

### Table 9.3 Remedies for Interference with Intellectual Property

| Remedy | Nature of Order | When Available |
|---|---|---|
| Damages | Statutory damages | Awarded at the discretion of judge under *Copyright Act* |
| | Monetary damages | Common law remedy awarded at discretion of the judge where available at trial |
| Injunction | Order to stop offending conduct | Interim injunction available before trial |
| | | Permanent injunction available at trial |
| Anton Piller order | Order to seize documents or other material before it can be destroyed or moved | Before trial and without notice to the other party |
| Accounting | Disclosure and payment to the plaintiff of improper profits made from offending conduct | At trial |
| Criminal | Imposition of fine and/or imprisonment | If provided in statute, ordered at trial |

restrictive covenants and provisions that acknowledge that if a breach does take place immediate and irreparable harm will occur for which damages will not provide adequate compensation. This will strengthen the argument in support of an injunction if the breach does take place. Another effective interim order is an **Anton Piller order**. Here the court orders that offending products or records be seized before they can be destroyed or removed. This involves authorizing a search of premises to find the material described in the order. This remedy is often referred to as a civil search warrant. To be effective this must be done without notice to the offending party. Such an order will only be granted where the applicant can demonstrate: 1) there is a strong *prima facie* case; 2) there is danger of considerable further damage to the applicant; and 3) it is clear that the offending party has the documents or products in its possession and is likely to destroy or otherwise dispose of them before any hearing or trial. Anton Piller orders are sometimes abused where they are used to support a "fishing expedition" or as a tactic to interfere with a competitor's business. Because of this courts are reluctant to grant such remedies except in the most extreme cases.

Anton Piller order provides for seizing of offending documents or products without notice

Any other remedy must wait until trial, but often, given the fast pace of intellectual property disputes, once an interim injunction is or is not granted, there is no sense in taking the matter further. If the dispute does go to trial, the object is usually to make the injunction permanent or to obtain damages. But the actual value of intellectual property involved and the damages suffered are often difficult to determine. Often, it is more appropriate to seek an order for an accounting. As explained in Chapter 1, with this remedy the court determines any improper profits made by the defendants through their offending conduct and orders these profits to be paid to the plaintiff, or a reasonable royalty (in the case of patents) is calculated based on those profits and that royalty must then be paid over to the victim of the infringement. Of course, if there are no such profits, damages are a more appropriate remedy. The court may also order that the offending product or documents be surrendered to the plaintiff, which then can be destroyed, but an award of damages or an injunction are still the primary remedies when intellectual property rights are infringed.

Accounting requires improper profits to be paid to victim

Because of the difficulty often encountered in assessing the actual losses to be compensated, there is an increasing tendency to award punitive damages in these cases. Because of these problems the *Copyright Act* allows the victim of an infringement (by an individual for non commercial purposes) to elect an award of **statutory damages** without the necessity of actually proving the actual loss. The election for statutory damages can be made anywhere in the process and the award, which was reduced by recent amendment, will be between $100 and $5 000 at the discretion of the judge.

In addition to the civil remedies available for copyright and patent infringement, both the *Copyright Act* and the *Patent Act* contain specific provisions that make some forms of infringement a criminal offence. Under the *Copyright Act*, the penalties when the prosecution is by indictment can be as high as five years in jail and a million dollar fine. The penalties for a *Patent Act* infringement are considerably less, even when treated as an indictable offence. The maximum penalty for pricing offences with respect to patented medicines can be as high as $25 000 ($100 000 for a corporation) and six months in jail. Note, however, that with some specific forms of infringement, each day the infringement continues can be treated as a separate offence with the penalties accumulating. When patent infringements that do not involve patent medicines are involved, the penalties are much less.

Criminal penalties exist in *Copyright Act, Patent Act,* and *Criminal Code*

## Case Summary 9.9 *Lari v. Canadian Copyright Licensing Agency*[31]

### Abuse of Photocopying Is Not Tolerated by the Courts

Riaz Lari (Defendant/Appellant), Canadian Copyright Licensing Agency (Plaintiff/Respondent) in this contempt of court proceeding before the Federal Court of Appeal.

Mr. Lari carried on businesses as U Computer Copy Shop in Montreal and persisted in photocopying textbooks for students at the local university. Actions had been brought against him in the past with the award of a permanent injunction to stop the practice. He ignored the injunction and continued to photocopy the texts. He had been fined in the past, and in a civil action was ordered to pay $500 000 damages and a further $100 000 as punitive damages. This didn't stop him. Access Copyright (the Canadian Copyright Licensing Agency—formerly known as CanCopy, an organization representing authors)

learned he was again photocopying and successfully obtained an Anton Piller order forcing the surrender of the offending copies as well as another injunction.

Lari had been found in contempt in the past and on this occasion the court imposed a six-month jail term for his continued contempt. The jail term was suspended, but there was also an order that he perform 400 hours of community service and an order that if he violated the injunction again the plaintiff could apply *ex parte* for a committal order. The ruling was appealed to the Federal Court of Appeal, which upheld the lower court decision.

This is a very serious case, which indicates that the courts take such infringement seriously and are willing to enforce their orders when necessary.

---

The *Trade-marks Act* itself contains no criminal penalties, but there are specific offences found in the *Criminal Code* relating to trademark infringement. In addition, other general remedies associated with fraud and theft—sections 406 to 412—make it an indictable offence to forge, alter, deface, conceal, or remove a trademark or even to refill a bottle with someone else's trademark to deceive or defraud. Also, passing-off, as well as the practice of reselling goods without disclosing them to be used or reconditioned are also indictable offences. The potential punishment is two years in jail if treated as an indictable offence. Note that one area of conflict with respect to trademarks relates to the registration of domain names for the internet. There are specific processes available for dealing with disputes in this area and they will be discussed in the following chapter.

Undervaluing and failure to keep track of intellectual property resources and to account for licensing fees and royalties is a major problem when dealing with this type of asset. Where circumstances permit, businesses and individuals should take steps to keep track of and protect these resources. Regular audits and online monitoring should take place and when such an infringement is detected, usually speedy intervention is required to prevent significant damage.

## LO 7/LO 8 PRIVACY, SECURITY, AND CONFIDENTIAL INFORMATION

Personal privacy has also been greatly affected by technological change. Mobile phones have become smartphones providing photographic, video and sound recording services as many celebrities and public officials, including police officers have learned to their

---

[31]2007 FCA 127 (CanLII) (2007), 56 C.P.R. (4th) 177.

detriment. Also, many people who use social media services such as Facebook are finding that what they thought was a private communication has become very public, to their embarrassment.

Businesses face similar problems. Almost all businesses have some sort of confidential information that they want to keep away from competitors, customers, shareholders, or the public. This might be in the form of trade secrets, customer lists, or negative information about the company, the executives, or other key employees. Much of the intellectual property of a company is stored in databases that summarize information about its customers and their buying habits, future production plans, or even secret strategies, processes, or techniques. The common thread is that the information is not generally known, and its disclosure will cause harm to the business. When secret processes, recipes, or formulas are involved, they are known as trade secrets and are often not protected by patent, copyright, or trademark. While not property in the strict sense, so long as it remains confidential such information constitutes a valuable asset of the business and must be safeguarded.

## Confidential Information

There are no federal or provincial statutes designed to protect such **confidential information**, but as a rule, employees, suppliers, and contractors have a common law obligation not to disclose this information to others. This may be based on a fiduciary relationship of trust or simply as part of the contractual obligations between the parties. A fiduciary duty arises where one party places trust in another and is vulnerable to harm if that trust is abused and that other party either expressly or by implication undertakes a duty of loyalty to the vulnerable party. Examples of such fiduciaries are partners, senior employees, agents, and professionals employed by the business such as lawyers and accountants. This duty can best be described as an obligation to act in the best interest of the party to whom the fiduciary duty is owed. An important aspect of that duty is the obligation to keep confidences. Even without a fiduciary duty, there can be a legal obligation not to disclose such information or to use it for your own purposes where the information was given in confidence.

Such an obligation can also be imposed by contract, either expressed or implied. When businesses work together, or when a consultant or contractor does work for a business, it is good practice to include a non-disclosure provision in the contract. An employer will often include a restrictive covenant in the initial employment contract, requiring an employee not to work in the same industry or for a competitor while employed and for a specified period after that employment ends. Restrictive covenants can also be useful in specifically prohibiting employees from conveying confidential information to others. This protects the employer, not only from having customers follow the terminated employee, but also prevents that employee from disclosing customer lists, production plans, and even manufacturing methods to a competitor. Even without such a contract, the courts have no hesitation in finding that employees have breached an important obligation when they solicit clients in the last few days of their employment with the idea of taking them with them when they leave. But even an honest employee can inadvertently disclose confidential information, if he or she does not know that it is confidential. It is, therefore, vital to make sure employees understand what is confidential and what is not.

*Common law requires confidential information not to be disclosed or used by the confidant*

*It is a good policy to include non-disclosure provisions in employment and consulting contracts*

*Important to inform employees of what is confidential*

**Interim injunction common where need for remedy is urgent in intellectual property disputes**

**Injunction is often more effective as a remedy than damages or accounting**

**Inducing breach of contract can sometimes be claimed when an employee moves to a competitor**

The most common remedies associated with abuse of confidential information are the award of damages, injunction, and in some cases where improper profits have been made, an accounting. Damages, as well as an accounting, are only obtained after the loss has been suffered. Often the most effective weapon to keep the confidential information from being disclosed is to obtain an **interim injunction** where the employee, contractor, and so forth is ordered not to work for the competitor or not to disclose the information. Sometimes a competing employer will attempt to hire away a key employee, primarily to get access to this kind of confidential information or better access to the competitor's customers. Where the competitor has encouraged the employee to leave and to breach his or her duty of confidentiality or contract of employment, it may be possible to seek redress from that competitor in the form of damages for inducing a breach of contract. This would also be an appropriate situation for the remedy of an accounting, which requires the competitor to disclose any profits earned by his or her abuse and to surrender them to the injured employer.

---

## Case Summary 9.10 *Imperial Sheet Metal Ltd. et al. v. Landry and Gray Metal Products Inc.*[32]

## Post-Employment Obligations Minimal to Former Employer

Imperial Sheet Metals Ltd. (Plaintiff/Appellant), Landry and Gray Metal Products Inc. (Defendant/Respondent) in this appeal before the Court of Appeal of New Brunswick.

Joseph Landry was employed by Imperial for 19 years, working his way up to vice president (although the nature of those responsibilities are in dispute) before that employment was terminated. Shortly afterwards he gained employment with Gray Metal, a competitor of Imperial. This action was brought by Imperial claiming that Landry was in violation of a fiduciary duty and using confidential information in undercutting prices and taking customers away from Imperial.

This application was for an interlocutory injunction before trial prohibiting him from using this information against the interests of and in competition with Imperial. To succeed Imperial had to show 1) that there was a serious issue to be tried; 2) that Imperial would suffer irreparable harm if the injunction were not granted; and 3) that the balance of convenience favoured Imperial.

Although the court determined that there was a serious issue to try, Imperial was not able to show that Landry had used any of the information that it considered

confidential in his dealings as an employee of Gray. In fact, only one customer had been persuaded to leave Imperial and go to Gray. Thus, no irreparable harm had taken place. Finally, if the injunction were granted it was unlikely that Landry could continue his employment with Gray, whereas Imperial would suffer no more than minimal damage. The balance of convenience therefore favoured Landry, and the injunction was refused.

The judge observed that when a non-fiduciary employee was terminated, he was then free to compete with his former employer using skill and knowledge gained in that former employment providing there was no misuse of confidential information. This right to compete includes the right to solicit customers of that former employer. The judge also made it clear that low-level employees do not face the same fiduciary obligations as executives and senior management.

Although this case was an application for an interlocutory injunction, it is instructive in several ways. It not only shows the three requirements for obtaining such an interlocutory injunction, but also illustrates the dilemma associated with employees leaving and competing with their former employers.

---

[32]2007 NBCA 51 (CanLII), 315 N.B.R. (2d) 328 (NB CA).

# Privacy

Closely related to confidential information is the topic of privacy. There is no separate privacy protection under common law. In most provinces it is only where the conduct constitutes some other tort, such as defamation or trespass, or where a contract or fiduciary duty has been breached, that it will be actionable under common law. Several provinces have statutes making breaches of privacy actionable torts.[33] These acts leave it to the court to determine what constitutes a violation of privacy, but they also state that privacy may be violated by eavesdropping, surveillance, or by the unauthorized use of a name or portrait. The technological advances in data compilation and email communications have led to a number of statutes, both at the federal and provincial levels, being enacted to protect personal information. The federal government, in response to international pressure and the threat of lost business, enacted two statutes. The *Privacy Act*[34] protects personal information in the hands of federal government institutions, limits its collection, and provides for limited access where appropriate. It also establishes the office of the Privacy Commissioner. It is the second *Act* that is more important for business. This *Act*, referred to as the *Personal Information Protection and Electronic Documents Act (PIPEDA)*,[35] is unique in that it is declared to be the law in areas of federal jurisdiction and in all provinces unless a province enacts a "substantially similar" act. Several provinces, including Quebec, Alberta, Manitoba and British Columbia, have enacted their own legislation, and still others, including Ontario, New Brunswick, Nova Scotia, and Newfoundland and Labrador, have enacted legislation restricted specifically to health related information. Note that Nova Scotia has gone further and enacted legislation intended to ensure that personal information in the control of public bodies is protected from disclosure from international threats such as the operation of the U.S. *Patriot Act*.[36]

Other provinces, including the territories, have simply adopted the federal *Act* by not passing a similar statute. These acts are meant to control the collection, use, disclosure, and disposal of personal information. As of 1 January 2004 the federal *Act* applies to all organizations in Canada involved in the collection, use, and disclosure of personal information in connection with a commercial activity. The only exceptions are companies already subject to "substantially similar" provincial legislation. Note that this applies to both personal and business related information about individuals with whom it does business. These may include any medical conditions, treatments, and prescriptions, but also purchasing habits, credit ratings and entertainment preferences, information gathered from surfing websites, subscriptions to magazines and internet services or any other personal information that a company has in its possession that relates to identifiable individuals. It applies not only to the personal information of customers and clients, but also to anyone about whom the business compiles personal information, including—to a limited extent—their employees. The provincial acts impose much more stringent standards with respect to an employer's compilation, use, and disclosure of personal information, especially the health information of employees.

Several provinces have made breach of privacy an actionable tort

Federal *Privacy Act* protects personal information in federal government institutions

Federal *PIPEDA* applies in all provinces that don't have a substantially similar statute

These acts impose restrictions and obligations on all companies that have personal information in their control

[33]For example, *Privacy Act*, RSBC. 1996, c. 373; *Privacy Act*, R.S.S. 1978, c. P-24; *The Privacy Act*, C.C.S.M. c. P125; and *Privacy Act*, R.S.N.L. 1990, c. P-22.
[34]R.S.C. 1985, c. P-21.
[35]S.C. 2000, c. 5.
[36]*Personal Information International Disclosure Protection Act*, S.N.S. 2006, c. 3.

Case Summary 9.11 *Canada Safeway Limited v. Shineton*[37]

# Sharing Private Information May Violate Privacy Rights

Mrs. Shineton (Applicant), Canada Safeway Ltd. (Respondent) in this judicial review of the decision of the Information and Privacy Commissioner of Alberta.

Mrs. Shineton was a customer at a Safeway store and was detained by security after she left the store. She had paid for only some of the goods she had taken. The police were called but they declined to lay charges and after the unpaid goods were returned she was allowed to leave. She was employed by Calgary Co-op and was wearing her Co-op uniform at the time of the incident. Safeway, without her consent, notified her employer of this alleged theft and she was then terminated from that employment. In this action she has laid a complaint with the Information and Privacy Commission of Alberta claiming that the disclosure violated her right to privacy by "wrongfully disclosing her personal information without her consent" contrary to s. 7(1)(d) of the Alberta *Personal Information Protection Act*.[38] The decision of the officer held that her privacy rights were violated by the Safeway disclosure. Safeway then asked that the decision be reviewed by the Commissioner, claiming that its *Charter* right to freedom of expression had been breached.

This was rejected on the basis that a balance was to be struck between the right to free expression and the right to privacy. The protection provided by the *Act* recognized that balance and did not violate Safeway's freedom of expression. Safeway also claimed they had the right to disclose the information because it was done in the process of furthering an investigation. This argument was also rejected on the basis that the disclosure to the employer had nothing to do with the Safeway investigation. This action is brought by Safeway for judicial review of that decision.

The court first determined that the *Charter* argument advanced by Safeway failed. The court found that this was not the kind of expression the *Charter* was meant to protect. The judge went on to find that even if it was, the protection provided by the *Personal Information Protection Act* was a reasonable limit to that freedom of expression as found in section 2(b) of the *Charter*. With respect to the argument that the disclosure was made pursuant to an investigation, the court refused to interfere with the commission's determining that it was not, finding that the decision was reasonable given the facts and the law.

The case is instructive as it shows the power of these statutes to protect the disclosure of personal information. It is also interesting to note that in Alberta the power to make this determination is given to the same officer who deals with human rights violations. It also shows the deference the courts give to the decisions made by those regulatory bodies.

---

The federal *Act* requires the business or organization to develop a privacy policy that will protect such private information from being disclosed to others. A model policy is included in Schedule 1 of the *PIPEDA*. Each organization is required to develop and implement policies and procedures to protect personal information, to handle complaints and inquiries, and to train staff about the policies developed. Each business must develop its own policies and procedures, but they must satisfy the following:

- make business accountable for information
- obtain consent to use information
- place limits on information collection, use, retention, and disclosure
- ensure accuracy and safeguard information
- provide access and a process for challenging the information's accuracy

■ The organization must be accountable for the information collected.

■ Consent must be obtained from those whose information is used (although in some circumstances this can be implied).

■ Reasonable limits must be placed on the collection, use, retention, and disclosure of the information.

■ Provisions must be in place for maintaining the accuracy and safeguarding of personal information, including safeguarding from abuses by the employees of that organization.

---

[37]2007 ABQB 773 (CanLII), 444 A.R. 131; [2008] 6 W.W.R. 702 (AB QB).
[38]S.A. 2003 c.P-6.5.

■ Individuals must have access to the collected information to determine its accuracy and challenge the information collected where appropriate.

An individual in the organization should be appointed to be responsible for implementing these policies and for the organization's compliance, even when that information is conveyed to third parties.

The obligations associated with a company's collection and use of such personal information have become a significant aspect of doing business; something as commonplace as selling a customer or subscription list can run afoul of these statutes. While current enforcement of these provisions may be somewhat haphazard, the intense concern about the misuse of personal information compiled in various databases associated with the internet and the ease of accessing that information makes it likely that this will be an area of intense regulation in the future.

The *PIPEDA* also contains serious penalties for infractions. Failure to provide requested information, obstructing the process, or dismissing or otherwise disciplining an employee for acting as required under the *Act* constitutes an indictable offence, punishable by fine up to $100 000. Also section 184 of the *Criminal Code* makes it an indictable offense to electronically intercept private communications.

## Security

Whether a business is concerned with protecting the private information of others or their own confidential information, keeping such information secure has become a great concern. The problems associated with security relate to preserving information, protecting it from corruption, and preventing its interception and disclosure to others. These are not areas where government regulation will likely be of much help.

When information was stored on paper, filing vast quantities of it posed a considerable problem. Today, whole libraries can be stored on one small disc or memory card, and while this eliminates one problem, it raises another. Discs and memory cards are easily lost, stolen, or destroyed. The decision to dispose of information may be made consciously, but when it is erased unintentionally, the results can be disastrous. Even the crash of a hard drive or the loss or destruction of a memory card or DVD can cause the loss of volumes of irreplaceable information.

The solution, of course, is to make regular backups of all important information and to store them in a different location. But it is surprising how many individuals and businesses fail to follow such a fundamental requirement. It is certain that the days of great paper archives of information and libraries full of books and collections of periodicals and government publications are ending. Information is now stored digitally, but mechanisms must be in place to preserve the information so that it is accessible by both old and new technologies. Information must be protected from inadvertent or intentional destruction. Data storage in clouds is now commonplace where much concern has been placed on the security of the data. How this process and the policies that govern it will evolve merits a business person's close attention.

When using these services it is important to keep backups. It is also important to remember that when third parties or the "cloud" are used the exposure of information is usually international and it is likely not to be as well protected as it would be in your own organization.

An equally important problem for business is to protect confidential information from interception or accidental disclosure. Simple mistakes can allow the information to be misdirected inadvertently by typing in the wrong email address or by returning a message to a group rather than to an individual. Email communication is not secure; it is more like a postcard than a sealed letter. It is now common for email communications to be systematically scanned by hackers or even government agencies that use sophisticated programs to look for key words and phrases. Passwords may help, but the way most of us use them they are easily compromised. The best way to ensure the privacy of electronic communications is through high level **encryption**. Email has been judicially recognized as not secure and a business may soon be required to use encryption of email communication and other stored personal information to meet their obligations under the federal *PIPEDA* or equivalent provincial privacy legislation discussed above.

*Encryption is important to keep information secure, especially for electronic communications*

The threat to a business's computer system is not always associated with the internet or the direct accessing of a company's computers on their premises. When a business uses a wireless network, communications can be accessed by computers outside or in another part of the building. There are security programs available to protect businesses from this kind of violation.

*Wireless networks can be easily compromised*

**In House Security Issues**    Dishonest or careless employees can pose a threat to a business. Aside from theft, fraud, and other forms of white-collar crime, employees may cause harm through inadvertent conduct. They may disclose confidential information unwittingly or cause damage and loss though misuse of the business computer and communication system. Beyond simple waste of resources, where the computers are used for personal purposes such as playing games or using the internet for personal entertainment, employees may expose the company to embarrassment and liability when they use company equipment or company email accounts for illegal or otherwise inappropriate purposes. This may include accessing a customer or client's private information; downloading inappropriate material such as pornography; gambling; or distributing defamatory, sexually explicit, harassing, or hateful material. The remedy is for the company to have mechanisms in place to monitor the employees' use of the computers and other company resources. If this is done surreptitiously, however, it may violate the employees' right to privacy and subject the business to fines or other punishment. The best option is to inform employees at the outset that their phone calls, computer use, and other employment-related activities are subject to monitoring. This not only avoids the problem of being accused of violating employees' privacy, it also informs them of what they can and cannot do with respect to company resources.

*Employers may be liable for employees' abuses*

*Solution is to monitor employees' use of computers and other resources*

*Important to inform employees of surveillance*

Of course, there is always the danger of an employee being persuaded by a competitor to convey confidential information or trade secrets such as the company's new line of products or customer lists to the competitor. It is difficult to prevent this problem other than by being extremely careful when hiring. But the risk may be contained to some extent by making sure that this kind of confidential information is given only to those that require it as part of their jobs. Passwords to computers should be given only to those who need them. Different levels of password protection can be arranged so that even on the same computer information is only given out according to the level of the password used. Blocking software can also be used to prevent employees from accessing inappropriate websites. In all cases the best protection against improper conduct of employees is the development and communication in writing of clear policies and procedures with respect to the use of

*Confidential information should be contained, and employees should be told what information is confidential*

company resources; careful hiring practices, including criminal and credit record checks; thorough training; and appropriate accountability, including surveillance and monitoring.

Careful hiring practices are the best safeguard

As can be seen from this discussion, while there has been some attempt to regulate privacy and confidential information, effective protection falls largely on the shoulders of the individual or corporation. In addition to the general provisions relating to fraud, gambling, obscene material, and the like, the *Criminal Code* contains specific provisions relating to computer and internet offences. Section 184 makes it an indictable offence to intercept private communications and is punishable with up to five years in prison. Section 342.1 specifically prohibits the fraudulent obtaining of computer and internet services, whether directly or indirectly, including the possession of passwords and various forms of equipment to accomplish that purpose. This is an indictable offence, punishable with up to 10 years in prison. Section 430 prohibits the commission of mischief and includes a special section prohibiting the destruction of or interference with computer data or with someone's authorized use of that data. This would cover hackers as well as computer viruses that wreak havoc on computer information and operations. Mischief, with respect to data, can also be treated as an indictable offence, punishable with up to five years in prison.

Computer viruses and the conduct of hackers in all forms have become known as cyber-crimes and the effect can be devastating. The above sections of the *Criminal Code* can be effective, but often hackers and virus creators reside offshore or are underage and are subject to the less rigorous penalties included in the *Youth Criminal Justice Act*.[39] It is generally accepted that only the amateurs get caught. Most sophisticated hackers are also effective in covering their tracks. Hackers often consider themselves to be crusaders fighting big business domination of the internet and computers generally, and some claim to be advocates of reforming computer services. Many, however, are simply mercenaries profiting from the information they manage to steal or the destruction they cause. Whatever the motivation, the effects are extremely costly to business.

The only sure way for businesses to protect themselves is to take their own defensive measures. Like the ongoing battle between the creators of viruses and virus protection programs, a business must take steps to protect itself from the threats posed by the internet and quickly changing computer technology.

Business must take defensive measures

Note that the problems associated with identity theft can also cause serious problems to business. Identity theft and identity fraud are criminal offenses contained in sections 402 and 403 of the Criminal code which strengthens several other criminal code offenses.[40] The penalty imposed can be up to 10 years imprisonment.

## Key Terms

**Anton Piller order** (p. 303)

**balance of convenience** (p. 302)

**business patents** (p. 294)

**certification marks** (p. 298)

**confidential information** (p. 305)

**copyright** (p. 286)

**distinguishing guise** (p. 298)

**encryption** (p. 310)

**evergreening** (p. 295)

**goodwill** (p. 297)

**interim injunction** (p. 306)

**invention** (p. 293)

**moral rights** (p. 287)

**official marks** (p. 298)

---

[39]S.C. 2002, c.1.

[40]Criminal Code, RSC 1985, c C-48.

**patent** (p. 292)

**proposed trademark** (p. 299)

**reverse engineering** (p. 293)

**royalties** (p. 286)

**statutory damages** (p. 303)

**trademarks** (p. 297)

## Questions for Student Review

1. Distinguish between intellectual property and other kinds of property, and explain which courts have jurisdiction with respect to intellectual property disputes.

2. What is protected under copyright law? How is that protection obtained and how long does it last? Include a discussion of the recent amendments to the *Copyright Act.*

3. Who is entitled to patent and copyright protection when an employee or consultant develops the material?

4. What federal statute protects computer software?

5. What qualifications must be met for a work to qualify for copyright protection?

6. Explain what a patent protects, how patent protection is obtained, and how long that patent protection lasts.

7. What qualifications must an invention meet to qualify for patent protection? What will not qualify?

8. What do the *Industrial Design Act* and the *Integrated Circuit Topography Act* protect?

9. Distinguish between a certification mark, a trademark, and a distinguishing guise.

10. Explain the distinction between a trademark infringement action and a passing-off action, and indicate when one would be chosen over the other.

11. Explain what the *Trade-marks Act* protects; how that protection is obtained, and how long it lasts.

12. What harm does a trademark infringement cause a business?

13. What will cause an application for trademark to be refused?

14. Distinguish between an injunction, an Anton Piller order, damages, and an accounting. Explain where one would be preferred over the others.

15. Explain the common law obligations with respect to people who are given confidential information.

16. What steps should be taken by a business to ensure their employees do not divulge confidential information?

17. Explain the importance of provincial privacy acts, the federal *Privacy Act,* and the federal *Personal Information Protection and Electronic Documents Act* and how they interrelate.

18. Explain why the *Personal Information Protection and Electronic Documents Act* is in force in some provinces and not in others.

19. What must be included when a business develops policies and procedures under the *Personal Information Protection and Electronic Documents Act*?

20. Explain why digitally stored information is particularly vulnerable to loss or disclosure. How can that information best be secured from intentional or inadvertent loss?

21. How can a business best protect their communicated information from inadvertent disclosure or intentional interception?

22. Explain how a business can ensure that their employees are not involved in any illegal or other inappropriate activity with respect to computers, the internet, and voice mail.

23. What steps should be taken to ensure that the employees don't become involved in such inappropriate activities in the first place?

## Questions for Further Discussion

1. There are two ways of looking at the problems associated with intellectual property. As with any form of property law, the rules restrict and protect that property for the use of one individual or group and exclude others. But intellectual property is the vehicle for commercial and economic progress and is not restricted by international boundaries. Also, because it is intangible, the use by one group does not deny it to another, as would be the case with a stolen car, for example. Developing countries, even emerging economic giants like China and India, often look at such intellectual property laws as a way to restrict their advancement and further the profits of Western capitalistic nations and corporations at their expense. The same kind of debate happens at home between those who copy music over the internet and those large record companies and artists that feel that such activities are akin to theft. Consider these positions and discuss the relative merits of both sides. Is there any way to accommodate these conflicting interests? In your answer consider the recent amendments to the *Copyright Act* discussed in the text.

2. The AIDS epidemic is just one of the catastrophic health problems that illustrate the disparity between medical advances and the costs that make them inaccessible to those who need them. Today, steps are being taken to provide low-cost drugs to developing countries, but the general problem remains, and it surrounds the patent protection provided to the companies that develop the drugs. Consider the balance now struck between guaranteeing profits of pharmaceutical giants that developed these drugs and the need for inexpensive variants to preserve life. Discuss the negative impact of our patent protection policies in these areas and consider what can be done to overcome the problem.

3. Consider the introduction of privacy laws at both the federal and provincial levels and the restrictions and controls this imposes on business. Does this place an unreasonable burden on business? How would you suggest that these provisions be expanded, reduced, or otherwise altered?

## Cases for Discussion

1. *Parker v. Key Porter Books Ltd.* 2005 CanLII 18294 (ON SC)

   Tonya Maracle was a Mohawk artist who produced several small, unique wood pieces called dream catchers (a striking circular piece constructed of interwoven twigs and other material). A representative of Key Porter Books Limited approached Ms. Maracle and expressed an interest in publishing photographs of them. To that end she gave her permission, so long as they would be used only in a children's book and that Soaring Eagle, the business she owned with her sister, would get the credit. This was agreed and after several of the dream catchers were taken, she heard nothing more for several weeks. Finally, she received a letter returning them but with no explanation. She simply assumed that Key Porter had changed its mind. But her sister discovered a book published by Key Porter Books, *Dreamcatchers: Myths and History*, which contained 21 photographs of Ms. Maracle's dream catchers, including a picture on the cover. A total of 9550 copies of the book had been published. What is the basis of her complaint if any, and what would be the appropriate remedy in the circumstances?

2. *Robertson v. Thomson Corp.* 2006, 274 D.L.R. (4th) 138; [2006] 2 SCR 363; 2006 SCC 43 (CanLII)

   In 1995 Heather Robinson, a freelance journalist, wrote two articles for the *Globe and Mail*. The *Globe and Mail* republished the articles, including them on CD-ROMs as essentially an archived record of the newspaper. They also made the articles available through an online database. She brought this action for breach of her copyright in those articles.

She challenged both the inclusion of the newspaper in the CD-Rom as well as well as the making available of the articles in the online database as unauthorized reproductions of her work without compensation. She sued, claiming a violation of her copyright. Explain the arguments on both sides and the likely outcome.

3.  *Halford v. Sea Hawk Inc.*, 2006 FCA 275 (CanLII); 275 D.L.R. (4th) 556; 54 C.P.R. (4th) 130 (FCA)

    James Halford was a university-trained farmer who invented a device for putting seeds and fertilizer into the ground in one operation. It was a relatively simple device, but he was granted a patent for it. Norbert Beaujot, an engineer and part-time farmer, developed a similar device and incorporated a company to commercially exploit it. Halford sued. Beaujot had seen the Halford device in operation before he developed his own, but the machine he developed was quite different although it accomplished the same thing. What is the nature of Halford's complaint? Explain the arguments for both sides and the likely outcome. What is the appropriate remedy if Halford is successful?

4.  *Hermès Canada Inc. v. Henry High Class Kelly Retail Store*, 2004 BCSC 1694 (CanLII); (2004) 37 C.P.R. (4th) 244

    The defendants operated a store in the Vancouver area that carried a line of handbags and other products, all of which were copies of the famous Hermès brand. The term Hermès didn't appear on any of the products and on very close inspection "HENRY HIGH CLASS KELLY" (the name of the store) was imprinted on the handbags and other products in question. Hermès brought this action to stop the sales of these products. On what basis should Hermès base their complaint and what remedy would be appropriate? Would it affect your answer to know that there is no registered trademark or other protection in the design of the bags themselves, just the Hermès name?

5.  *General Motors of Canada v. Décarie Motors Inc.*, [2001] 1 FCR 665; 2000 CanLII 16083 (FCA)

    Décarie Motors Inc. operated a business selling automobiles on or near Décarie Boulevard in the City of Montreal. It applied for and obtained the registration of the trademark "Décarie Motors" in 1993 and the term "Décarie" in 1995. This appeal deals with an application brought by GM to have that trademark registration of "Décarie" expunged. Note that "Décarie" was a surname, but had been in use in that business since 1972. It was also the name of a specific geographical location. Do you think that the trademark should have been registered in the first place? Would it make any difference to your answer to know that the name was used in association with several other businesses?

6.  *York University v. Bell Canada Enterprises*, 2009 CanLII 46447 (ON SC)

    York University claimed that several anonymous authors had published a number of libelous emails and web postings. This action was brought against Bell and Rogers for an order requiring them to disclose the identity of these people so that York University could bring a libel action against them (this is called a "Norwich" order). The emails in question accused the President of academic fraud and alleged that a newly appointed dean did not have the academic credentials claimed. These were purportedly published by a group of concerned York students. Should such an order be made? Explain the arguments (both legal and social) on each side.

# Chapter 10

## Electronic Commerce and International Trade

Karin & Uwe Annas/Fotolia

## Learning Objectives

LO 1 Describe the nature of electronic commerce and its impact on business relationships

LO 2 Outline the jurisdictional issues that complicate online transactions

LO 3 Recognize specific kinds of tortious conduct that are pervasive on the internet

LO 4 Describe the concerns electronic and global business transactions have in common

LO 5 Analyse how to avoid the difficulties in pursuing international contracts

LO 6 Describe how contractual problems are best resolved in the global environment

LO 7 Outline how international commerce is regulated

LO 8 Evaluate jurisdictional issues and their impact on the enforcement of judicial decisions

For most of us the internet has changed the way we conduct our lives. We shop online, ordering everything from groceries to cars. Using the internet we don't have to deal with salespeople, agents, or manufacturers. We can have an item shipped from anywhere in the world without leaving our home or office. Whether we are functioning as an individual consumer, a small business, or a large corporation, it is inevitable that a considerable portion of what we do will be done over the internet and probably across borders. It is vital that anyone conducting businesses online or across borders knows the basic rules that govern those relations and understands that there is ongoing legislation that frequently changes the rules. It is also important to recognize the efforts made by various branches of government to make the rules more transparent, and to facilitate their application and enforcement. While international trade has always been an important source of business relationships, the internet has facilitated the trading process in ways that could not have been imagined two decades ago. It is important to look at some of the laws affecting these two areas and consider how they are applied in both electronic and global commerce. As well, the need for and the impact of government regulation in both these areas should be examined. They share some commonalities that will be discussed in this chapter, including jurisdictional issues, contractual processes, and the resolution of disputes. But this short chapter cannot hope to cover all of the regulations that affect the internet and doing business in foreign jurisdictions. This introduction can only try to make business people more alert to potential problems.

## LO 1/LO 2/LO 3    BUSINESS AND THE INTERNET

Internet facilitates business and education

The enormous expansion of the internet has brought about significant and basic changes to our economy and society. Communication of information has never been so easy and so seamless. The internet is much broader than just a business tool. It also provides education, entertainment, and social interaction. It has, to a large extent through electronic mail services, supplanted paper correspondence.

Normal civil and criminal remedies apply to internet

Electronic commerce facilitates the purchase and sale of goods and services at the retail level and also between businesses of all sizes. Even the most complicated forms of business transactions are now largely completed over the internet or involve other forms of electronic communication. It is also important to remember that all of these transactions normally involve third parties that facilitate the deals. In retail sales, service providers such as eBay and PayPal advertise the products and facilitate payment, collection and in some cases dispute resolution. Less obvious are the usually invisible streaming services supplied by the internet service providers. The development of the internet and electronic commerce has moved forward at an astounding rate and has created a free and open wild west–style online environment, which has been relatively free of government regulation and legal restrictions. Now we can enjoy the benefits of Web 2.0, which enables the more interactive modes, such as texting, blogging, tweeting, wikis, Facebook, and ever more varieties of online communication. These additional layers of complexity make it that much more difficult for government controls to be effective. In fact, most users feel that government interference in online communication of any sort is unacceptable. But it should be understood that the various forms of law, including civil remedies for fraud, breach of contract, and tort, as well as most forms of criminal law and federal and provincial regulation, apply to transactions and activities conducted online. Recognizing the gap between e-business growth and the law, federal and provincial governments have been moving forward with extensive amendments to existing law to try to address the issues related to electronic business activities. In addition, government websites now facilitates the administration and enforcement of what laws there are to regulate electronic business. Now the courts and legal professionals are contemplating or conducting e-trials, experimenting with paperless law-offices, referencing digital law libraries and allowing the use of electronic graphics and videos in the courtroom to provide non-textual evidence that heretofore relied solely on expert witnesses. While the transition to the full use of such resources can be costly, the time and expenses usually expended to resolve business disputes can be dramatically reduced.

Legislators and the courts are addressing e-business issues and doing it online.

## Jurisdiction and the Internet

An important feature of the internet is that it is not restricted to one country or state. It does not recognize borders, either within Canada or internationally. Nevertheless, valid laws do apply, and a range of enforcement processes can be imposed on those who ignore or defy them. The problem for business people is to determine what, where and when the laws apply. The requirement that every advertisement or online service conform to the local laws of each nation, state, or province in which it appears would be impossible to comply with and if imposed would completely destroy the freedom of internet communication. In the Bodog.com case in 2012, prosecutors in the United States obtained a warrant ordering a dot-com domain name registry to redirect people clicking on a Canadian sports gambling website to a page indicating that the website had been seized by the U.S. Department of Homeland Security. Although the site did not infringe on any Canadian law and U.S. gamblers were not allowed to participate, the U.S. prosecutors assumed jurisdiction. As such it appears that the United States has claimed a form of "super-jurisdiction' over internet activities—an assumption that has been broadly criticized as unduly restricting online activity. A major basis for the issuing of the warrant was the finding that by using a dot.com domain name the accused had opted into the jurisdiction of U.S. courts and U.S. law applied.[1] Note that U.S. officials also claim jurisdiction over domain names such as dot net, dot org and dot biz as well. This case involves a prosecution for a criminal offence. It remains to be seen whether the same approach will be taken with respect to jurisdiction when such dot.com companies are involved in civil disputes.

People who call themselves 'whistleblowers' often post private information that they consider to be in the public interest on websites such as wikileaks, suggesting that they are exposing abuses, corruption and governmental practices that infringe on personal privacy. But one person's whistleblower is another's purveyor of confidential information, government secrets, or even a traitor. Governments anxious to suppress such exposure may try to prohibit and punish such online activities by extending current laws or by creating new criminal prohibitions. Often these attempts are met with widespread opposition for fear of the inhibiting effects this might have on the freedom of the internet and corresponding human rights. Still, it would be prudent from a business point of view to take care to determine if the online activity you are engaged in is prohibited in any jurisdiction, ensure that your business is not associated with that jurisdiction in any way.

Some nations assume jurisdiction even when online activity is directed away from that nation

---

[1]Michael Geist.ca March 6, 2012.

A major problem is determining where an action should be brought

Jurisdiction is also a problem when disputes arise with an online offender. It is often unclear who to sue or prosecute, or where to bring the legal action. One advantage of the internet is that a company or individual can work anywhere in the world, and the place of origin of the material will not always be apparent to the users. Kazaa, for example, was a popular music-downloading service on the internet. The program was developed for a company in the Netherlands, which then sold it to another company operating from a small Pacific island, whose executives and principals work out of Australia. Which jurisdiction is appropriate for an action to be brought against them? Would it be Canada, Europe, or the United States, where the data was downloaded? Could people bring an action in the Netherlands or Australia, or are they limited to launching a complaint in that small island nation where the laws are likely to be more friendly to the providers of the service? The problem is made worse when fraud is involved and the perpetrator intentionally hides or chooses a jurisdiction where pursuing the matter is especially awkward and difficult.

Businesses providing services over the internet may be subject to different laws in many jurisdictions

The general rule is that a particular location can exercise jurisdiction if the person being sued is resident in that jurisdiction or if that is where the complained-of action took place. The problem is that most offensive content does not target a particular victim in a particular place, but is directed at anyone with a computer. Many jurisdictions have passed **long-arm statutes**, allowing them to take jurisdiction even when no resident is directly involved, with the result that business people providing an internet service from one area where the activity is completely legal will find themselves being sued or prosecuted in jurisdictions they were not aware of, and where they had no idea they were breaking the local law. The Bodog.com case cited above is a good example. In that case the service provider took great pains to ensure that it was not doing business with anyone in that jurisdiction, but still ended up being prosecuted. A better approach now generally adopted in Canada is to allow a judicial action only where there is a close connection between the jurisdiction and the act complained of. Thus, if an internet site offered pornographic materials or gambling services, and an internet user in a particular state or province subscribed or placed a bet, that would be enough of a connection to establish the jurisdiction and have an action brought there. But even this limited interference with the operation of the internet goes too far for many.

Canada requires a real and close connection for action to be brought

Passive internet messages are more likely to be exempt from action

Internet offer or service should state limitations of availability

To avoid such unwanted prosecution, an attempt should be made to keep the internet message passive; that is if there was no interaction in that jurisdiction, no bets taken, and no orders or subscriptions sent, there would be less likelihood that an action could be brought against that business in the courts of that state or province. But it is often difficult to selectively do business in that way. It may help to state within the contract for the service or goods that the law of a particular jurisdiction, such as Ontario or British Columbia, will govern the transaction. It could also be stated in the website or internet pop-up advertisement that the offer is not extended to specific provinces or states where the activity is prohibited. But even these steps are no guarantee that such a business will not find itself sued or prosecuted in another jurisdiction, as the Bodog.com case illustrates.

Another example is the operation of the Ontario *Consumer Protection Act*[2] which specifically provides that the rights set out in it apply to all consumer transactions where the consumer or the other party is located in that province at the time of the transaction[3]

---

[2]S.O. 2002, c. 30, Sch. A.
[3]Ibid., s. 2.

and that the rights set out in the *Act* apply despite any agreement to the contrary.[4] The *Act* even has a provision stating that any clause requiring arbitration in a consumer contract is invalid where it attempts to limit the consumer's right to bring an action in the Ontario Superior Court.[5]

---

## Case Summary 10.1 *Dow Jones v. Gutnick*[6]

### What Court Has Jurisdiction for Internet Defamation?

Gutnick (Plaintiff/Respondent), Dow Jones (Defendant/Appellant) in this appeal before the High Court of Australia.

In this case an article by an American company published on the internet defamed an Australian resident. The issue was whether Australia was an appropriate jurisdiction to bring a defamation action. The Australian court found that the harm done was in Australia, thus creating a sufficient connection between the defamation and that country for the case to be heard in an Australian court. The American company, Dow Jones, pointed out that this would require it to know and comply with the laws of every country, "from Afghanistan to Zimbabwe."

In a similar case brought in Ontario[7] an article published on the website of the *Washington Post* stated that the United Nations, after several investigations, failed to renew Bangoura's contract because of "misconduct and mismanagement." In fact, Bangoura was not an Ontario resident at the time of the conduct complained of, but only moved there later and initiated the action in that province. The *Washington Post* brought an application to have the action dismissed, claiming that the most convenient jurisdiction was the District of Columbia. Note that the libel laws in the United States are much friendlier to media than in Canada, and require proof of actual malice when public figures are defamed.

At the trial court level the judge dismissed the application, but on appeal the Ontario court held that since the plaintiff did not reside in the province at the time of the alleged liable, and there was little other connection between Ontario and the libel action (there were only eight subscribers to the *Washington Post* in the province at the time), the application of the *Washington Post* to stay the Ontario action was granted. In the Australian case the plaintiff lived in Australia and the harm done was in that country. In the Canadian case there was little connection to that province, and the courts refused to hear the matter. These cases illustrate the general approach used when determining whether a court has jurisdiction to hear a case or not.

---

When a judgment is obtained in a foreign court, the Canadian defendant sometimes assumes he or she is insulated from that judgment and ignore it. This is a dangerous assumption because such foreign judgments are usually enforceable in this country pursuant to various reciprocal treaties. The enforcement of foreign judgments will be discussed in more detail below under the heading Litigation and Jurisdiction.

*Dangerous to ignore foreign actions since judgments can be enforced at home*

## Domain Names

Many businesses did not anticipate the growing significance and potential of the internet and failed to take the steps necessary to protect their valuable assets by registering their business and brand names. When they eventually tried to do so, they often discovered someone else had appropriated their name or phrase by registering it first. It is not surprising, therefore, that conflicts have arisen over **domain names**. Such conflicts may arise legitimately because of the

---

[4]Ibid., s. 7.1.

[5]Ibid., s. 7.2.

[6][2002] H.C.A. 56 (Aust.).

[7]*Bangoura v. Washington Post* 2005 CanLII 32906 (ON CA) (2005), 258 D.L.R. (4th) 341; (2005), 202 O.A.C. 76.

global nature of the internet, where two similar businesses in different locations try to register the same name, or two dissimilar businesses have similar names. Registering a trademark or a copyright, even when done in more than one jurisdiction, will not normally be sufficient to give that registrant a sure claim to a corresponding domain name. The problem is that each domain address is unique and not limited to the geographical location where the business is active or to one type of business as opposed to another. Only one of them can have that domain name. Conflicts also arise when less well-intentioned individuals register the names first and then, in effect, hold the names for ransom. This is called **cybersquatting**, and even when there are methods for dealing with such practices, it is often cheaper for a business to simply purchase the address, name, or phrase from the cybersquatter who has managed to register it first. Sometimes similar names are registered so that visitors making slight but expected mistakes are intercepted and redirected to a competing business.

*Businesses failing to register domain names may have to address conflicting claims*

---

## Case Summary 10.2 *Tucows.com Co. v. Lojas Renner S.A.*[8]

# Domain Names are Intangible Personal Property

Tucows.com Co.(Plaintiff /Appellant), Sojas Renner S.A. (Defendant/Respondent) in an application before the Court of Appeal for Ontario to determine if it had jurisdiction.

Tucows.com Co. was a registrant of domain names in Ontario. It had registered 'renner.ca.' A Brazilian company, Renner S.A., claimed the right to the domain name having registered "RENNER" as a trademark in that country. Renner S.A. brought an application before WIPO (Arbitration and Mediation Center) to arbitrate the dispute, but its attempt to resolve the dispute was discontinued when Tucows initiated the Ontario action. Note that the arbitration service offered by the World Intellectual Property Organization (WIPO) does not replace the right to litigate but is simply a cheaper, faster alternative if the parties choose to use it. The dispute revolved around whether the Ontario Court had jurisdiction to hear the dispute and whether Tucows had the right to serve notice on the Brazilian company requiring it to submit to the Ontario Court. The legal arguments are quite involved but for our purposes the important question is whether the domain name in question was intangible personal property. If it was, then there was a substantial connection to Ontario and the Ontario courts would have jurisdiction. The lower court determined that the domain name was not intangible personal property, but that decision was overturned by the Court of Appeal for Ontario. Following analysis of international jurisprudence and academic commentary, the Court decided that "the dominant view. . . appears to be that domain names are a new type of intangible property." And following a survey of Canadian law over what constitutes property, including the observation that domain names are treated as assets which can be purchased and sold, it concluded that the bundle of rights associated with a domain name were sufficient to make it personal property. As such, Tucows' claim was allowed.

Note that no decision was made with respect the merits of the case, only that the Ontario court had the right to hear the matter and that Tucows had the right to serve notice out of province on the Brazilian company. The matter then went back to the trial court for a hearing and decision. For our purposes, the decision is important because it designated domain names as a new form of intangible personal property. We also learn that the arbitration service offered under WIPO does not displace litigation but is simply an alternative to it if the parties wish to take advantage of that service.

---

Some of the current problems with conflicting domain names may be resolved with the expansion of the range of gTLD's (generic Top Level Domain Names) by ICANN (the Internet Corporation for Assigned Names and Numbers). Applicants can now try to

---

[8]2011 ONCA 548 (CanLII).

register their domain names under a much wider variety of suffixes, i.e. *.auto* for car dealerships or *.yates* for personal use. They may now have addresses that are more personalized or customized to their country or industry. Hopefully, this will mediate some of the contests over who owns a domain name.

Until then, arbitration processes established to deal with disputes over the entitlement to domain names, have attempted to reduce the problem. The bodies responsible for the registration of domain names, for example, the Canadian Internet Registration Authority (CIRA), have established a policy for the arbitration of bad-faith domain-name registration disputes, which gives preference to the businesses with the more legitimate claim. In Canada, for *.ca* designation domain names, bodies such as the British Columbia International Commercial Arbitration Centre (BCICAC) and Resolution Canada Inc. have been authorized to provide arbitration services in such disputes. The largest organization providing domain-name dispute arbitration services is the World Intellectual Property Organization (WIPO). Disputes involving legitimate conflicting interests can often be handled through traditional trademark or passing-off litigation. As with most disputes, it is much better to take steps to avoid the problem in the first place.

> Arbitration and litigation is possible, but it is often cheaper just to buy the name

> It is important to take steps to avoid name infringement problems

## Torts

The most common type of tort on the internet is defamation, but the approach will likely be the same where passing-off, fraud, or other forms of tort are involved. Widespread distribution and uncertain jurisdiction are the factors that make internet cases unique. As with written communications, online defamation can take many different forms, ranging from a remark made in a private email message, to chat room conversations, to postings on social network sites, tweets and blogs, or to an article posted on a business' website that says disparaging things about a supplier, customer or competitor. Newspapers and magazines also run into problems when they place their material on the internet.

> Ease of distribution makes internet defamation a particular problem

A passing off-action is another form of tort that often arises over the use of domain names and trademarks. To succeed in an action the plaintiff must establish that there is goodwill in the domain name in question the loss of which would cause harm to the business. Also, the plaintiff must establish that there has been misrepresentation, deception and that substantial damages have been suffered. Note that this tort, like negligence, does not require intention of malice.

---

### Case Summary 10.3 *Manson v. John Doe*[9]

## Defamation Involving an Anonymous Defendant

Tycho Manson (Plaintiff), John Doe (Unknown parties) (Defendants) in this action for defamation in the Ontario Superior Court of Justice.

The defendant engaged in what the court described as "an anonymous electronic campaign of libel" against the plaintiff. The 'defendant' remains anonymous, and it is unclear whether there is one defendant or multiple defendants or where he, she, or they are located. The campaign of defamation included multiple defamatory posts on multiple blogs hosted by various service providers, and even an email sent to the plaintiff's work colleagues and superiors from a gmail account which contained links to the offending posts.

---

[9](2013) ONSC 628 (CanLII).

Despite efforts to identify the defendant(s), including court orders to compel the online service providers to disclose the contact details of the individual(s) who had created the accounts, and additional court orders requiring the defendant(s) to identify themselves, the plaintiff and his lawyer were unable to do so. That inability proved somewhat daunting when it came to serving notice of the court action on the defendant, but the plaintiff was able to get the court to validate service via email.[10]

The case is a guide for how to proceed against anonymous online defamation: (1) get the ISPs to remove the content; (2) get the ISPs to provide information to identify the defendant; (3) attempt service of process via email (which needs to be validated by the court); (4) bring actions against the anonymous defendant and continue the process until you have obtained judgment.

The court awarded damages as follows:

- general damages (for harm to reputation) - $100 000
- aggravated damages (the defendant never apologized for or retracted the statements, continued to make defamatory statements even after the initial

filing of the statement of claim and actively forwarded the links to the plaintiff's co-workers) - $50 000
- punitive damages - $50 000

Thus, for a campaign of defamation involving "shocking, disgusting, outrageous, racist and provocative" statements, a total of $200 000 in damages was awarded. (The court also ordered the defendant to pay the plaintiff's legal costs in the amount of $49 965.89.) It is also worth noting that the court made explicit mention of the fact that the plaintiff was a lawyer in awarding general damages, citing the Supreme Court of Canada decision in *Hill v. Church of Scientology*,[11] where the court observed that "for all lawyers their reputation is of paramount importance"—the implication being that a plaintiff who was not a member of the bar or in a similarly vulnerable occupation might not be able to avail themselves of such extensive damages. Of course, this judgment may be hollow if the defendant(s) cannot be identified; and, from a business point of view, it would normally be treated as a situation of throwing good money after bad. Still, in this case the decision stands as a vindication of the plaintiff, going some distance to rehabilitate his damaged reputation.

Note that the danger of liability extends to the employer or business providing access to the internet

There are dangers for businesses that are not careful about their internet and email communications. Note that not only will the person making the defamatory statement be liable, but the business that employs him or her may be liable as well, especially if company email services or websites are used to publish the offending statements. When a business provides access to its website for chat rooms or for discussion forums, there is also the danger it too could be held responsible for any defamatory or otherwise offensive statements that are made. It is unlikely that the actual ISP will be liable, unless it fails to remove or block the offending messages once required to do so by a court. A major area of controversy now is whether ISPs should be obligated to disclose the identity of users accused of defamation or other internet offences. It is likely that those businesses providing their employees with access to the internet will also be responsible where criminal law or other government regulations are infringed, depending on the degree of control they had or should have exercised over the offending communications.

## Case Summary 10.4 *Mosher v. Coast Publishing Ltd.*[12]

## Must Service Providers Disclose Identity of Users?

Mosher and Thurber (Plaintiffs), Coast Publishing Ltd. and Google Inc. (Defendants) in this application before the Supreme Court of Nova Scotia.

An article was published in a Halifax weekly newspaper *The Coast* about racism in the fire department. *The Coast* also provided a website where comments could be

---

[10]*Manson v. John Doe No. 1*, [2011] O.J. No. 3572, 2011 ONSC 4663 (Sup.Ct.) (CanLII).

[11][1995] 2 SCR 1130, 1995 CanLII 59 (SCC).

[12]2010 NSSC 153 (CanLII), [2010] N.S.J. No. 211. (NS SC).

made, and several anonymous, offensive, and likely defamatory comments were posted on that website in response to the article. Similar comments were published anonymously through a gmail account. This action is brought by the fire chief and deputy fire chief, who were the subjects of the offensive comments, asking for an order that *The Coast* and Google be ordered to disclose the identity of the offenders so that an action for defamation could be brought against them. The order was granted. The judge commented:

> "Because the court does not condone the conduct of anonymous internet users who make defamatory comments and they like other people have to be accountable for their actions. So, this is an

appropriate circumstance where your clients should have the right to seek the identity of those persons so you can take the appropriate action with respect to the alleged defamatory acts."

This case illustrates not only how defamation on the internet is actionable but also the fact that some courts are willing to assist the injured party by ordering ISPs and those operating bulletin boards and websites to disclose the identity of individuals who use their services for inappropriate purposes. It is interesting that neither of these defendants opposed the application, and in fact Google cooperated in the wording of the application. This action resulted in the identification of the offending parties making it possible to sue them.

## Online Contracts

Whether a company is involved in direct retailing of products, software, or services to consumers over the internet or is simply contracting with other companies through email or on a website, it is transacting business and creating new legal relationships. The common thread with respect to all of these internet transactions is that their legal status is determined by contract law.

*Traditional contract rules apply to internet transactions*

**Consensus and Writing**   Written evidence of a contract, while not generally required, is a sensible thing to have. It is a permanent record that can be referred to later and constitutes evidence if any disagreement arises. In some cases, under the *Statute of Frauds* or equivalent legislation, such writing and signatures are required for the transaction to be legally enforceable. Most jurisdictions now recognize digital signatures and scanned documents, but are aware how easily they can be altered.

*Good idea to keep written copies of transactions*

Under the direction of the federal government, a working group following international recommendations produced the *Uniform Electronic Commerce Act (UECA)*.[13] This document has no legal standing, but served as a model for provincial statutes. The object of the provincial legislation is to make electronic documents and signatures as binding on the parties as written ones. In general, the *UECA* and provincial acts do not change the law with respect to the requirement of written documents and signatures. Rather, they recognize electronic or digitally stored documents and signatures, or their equivalent, as satisfying those requirements. A signature equivalent might be a password or some other form of encryption, which is controlled by the author of the document (and possibly verified by a trusted third party). The password or encryption would authenticate the document and give it the same status as one that was written and signed. Note that this doesn't apply in all cases and some types of documents, such as wills, still have to be in writing and signed to be valid. Note, as well, that there are important variations between provinces and that some provinces now allow many forms of government documentation, including court registry filings and land registry transactions, to take place electronically. Many

*Provinces have adopted guidelines set out in* Uniform Electronic Commerce Act

*Statutes recognize electronic equivalent of written documents and signatures*

---

[13]http://www.ulcc.ca/.

jurisdictions also allow the use of electronic documents relating to proxies, prospectuses, and other documentation related to the purchase and sale of securities.

In online commercial transactions the concerns over consensus are normally addressed by the understanding that hitting an "I accept" button on a website is the equivalent of removing the shrink-wrap on a package or downloading software. It entitles the purchaser to limited use of the product. The "I Accept" button indicates to the seller that the buyer has read and agreed to the terms of the contract. It achieves the consensus element of a contract. The seller then confirms that the order has been received. It is now generally accepted that where such instantaneous methods of communication are involved, the post-box rule should not apply. Also, although internet communication involves intermediaries located in other jurisdictions, the *UECA* recommendations make the location of these intermediaries irrelevant in determining the validity of the contract and the legal obligations between the parties. Thus, such contracts are formed not where the customer hits the "I Accept " button but where the offeror's computer receives notification, typically where the sellor's offices are located. As you will recall, an offer ends when a revocation is received and, where implemented, these *UECA* recommendations determine when that takes place and can have a direct impact on that pre-contract negotiation process.

But what happens when a ongoing service relationship is involved and the provider unilaterally makes changes to the terms of the contract on its website? In an Ontario case, *Kanitz v. Rogers Cable*,[14] the court was asked to determine what happens in such circumstances. The court decided that as long as that possibility was stipulated on the website in the first place, it was sufficient notification that the terms of the contract were being altered. It is important that both sellers and purchasers be aware of such a condition in the electronic contract. As with contracts generally, when exemption clauses are included, these must be brought to the attention of the person accepting. This is effectively done in most cases by forcing the consumer to indicate they have read and accepted all of the terms before they can click the acceptance button completing the contract. Of course, local legislation will protect consumers where standard-form contracts include disadvantageous terms, but the problem remains to determine the law of what jurisdiction will apply to the transaction.

**Capacity**   It is difficult to determine in an online transaction whether the parties actually have the capacity to enter into a contract. A person's age, mental capacity, or even whether a business has or has not been incorporated is difficult to verify online. Parties should if possible take care to find out as much as they can about the company or individual, relying on more than the webpage to gain that information. The question of authenticating someone's identity may also present a challenge, as trust is a diminishing quantity in the online environment. **Electronic signatures** are most effective in identifying people if used in conjunction with trusted third parties who provide a digital certificate that authenticates the identity of a party to the contract. The federal government has provided guidelines for the development, implementation, and use of authentication products and services in Canada.[15]

Clicking a button will bind party to terms

Post-box rule does not apply to internet transactions

Watch for conditions and exemption clauses in online contracts

Care should be taken to authenticate identity and capacity of contracting parties

---

[14]2002 CanLII 49415 (ON SC).

[15]Industry Canada, *Principles for Electronic Authentication*, May 2004, http://www.ic.gc.ca/epic/site/ecic-ceac.nsf/en/h_gv00240e.html.

**Legality**    The legality of the activity that is at the heart of the contract is also a concern, and it is important to note that illegal activity is rife on the internet. Of course, such illegal contracts are void, but that usually is not much help. The potential to remain anonymous and avoid regulation and policing of one's activities have provided an opportunity for every sort of real world criminal activity such as gambling pornography and fraud to move into the virtual world of the internet. While the sales of goods acts and consumer protection legislation theoretically apply to online transactions, it is extremely important that buyers be careful, as fraudulent scams are commonplace in this medium. The law cannot keep up with the creative schemes of people who take advantage of the opportunities to disguise their intentions in online communications. One means of avoiding the rules in a given jurisdiction is to simply move the illegal operation outside of the countries where the activity is deemed illegal, thus avoiding liability when dealing with clients. Victims of such scams usually find it extremely difficult to seek redress when the perpetrator is in another country or on another continent.

*Internet a haven for illegal activities*

**Payment Online**    Even when the goods are being legitimately bought and sold, payment for products purchased also becomes a problem. Many services have been created, such as PayPal and credit cards services, to insure that the customer gets what he has paid for or to provide a remedy if a dispute arises. The problem is that, while these methods seem foolproof, there is a constant cohort of scam artists developing ways to overcome them and separate people from their money.

*Securing the exchange of money online is a challenge*

Where significant transactions between large businesses are involved it is common to have a third party such as a bank hold the funds and advance them to the other contracting party only when they have satisfied some aspect of the contract and upon receiving a release from the payer. Even before the advent of ecommerce this was accomplished by issuing a bill of exchange or a draft drawn on a bank (usually chosen by the payee) so they could be assured the funds were available before delivering the product.

## Online Dispute Resolution

Whenever there is an agreement, one should anticipate the possibility of a dispute, whether the contract is negotiated in a real or digital place. In either case there may be advantages to resolving the dispute using electronic technologies rather than high-priced lawyers and courtrooms. Financial transaction sites such as eBay and PayPal deal with upwards of 60 million disputes among buyers and sellers annually.[16] A variety of organizations and websites have been developed to address these online disputes.[17] Provisions for the online resolution of disputes ought to be included in retail purchases, but also in transactions between businesses of any size. Note, however, that there may well be consumer protection legislation in place making any term that provides for mandatory arbitration rather than recourse to the courts invalid. (See the Ontario *Consumer Protection Act* discussed above.) It is also important to keep in mind that these alternate dispute resolution processes are often designed to facilitate the on-going business interests of the business

*Many organizations facilitate arbitration of disputes*

[16]Darrin Thompson, Nexsyslegal http://nexsyslegal.tumblr.com.

[17]For more information click on www.odr.info or to deal with a consumer issue, try www.consumerprotectionbc.ca for a pilot project assisting buyers to deal with their complaints against a manufacturer.

against which the complaint is being launched. Still, a simplified, less costly process may be attractive to both sides.

## Regulating the Internet

Governments have been alert to the development of online business, and while there is considerable reluctance to introduce legislation and regulations to control illegal activity that would require enormous effort and expense to enforce. However, they are somewhat more anxious to regulate the collection of taxes even though it remains a challenge to discover tax goods and services that can be downloaded on private computers. Some companies seek to avoid the imposition of taxes on their products by selling their products from other jurisdictions. Attempts to insure that tax laws are properly enforced have had mixed results. One angle where control has been attempted is by holding the ISPs responsible to control illegal online activity, but this also has had limited success. In a federal Court of Appeal case the court refused to order ISPs to disclose identity of customers.[18] Note that with respect to copyright violation the recently passed Bill C-11 requires that the ISP once notified of a violation must in turn notify the customer of the illegal activity and disclose the appropriate identifying information and details to the complainant.

The Canadian government was successful in forcing the Canadian arm of eBay to disclose to Revenue Canada, its financial records on certain "power sellers" even though records of such transactions are kept at their California offices. This was done to ensure that required taxes were paid on their successful business activities.[19] One significant problem that arises is the threat to personal privacy. If the Canadian government can force businesses to disclose such information, there is nothing to protect them from similar access by foreign governments.

Legislative attempts to limit internet abuses

In 2013 Canada passed Bill C-28 commonly known as the Anti Spam Act (CASL).[20] The intent of the *Act* is to prohibit unsolicited commercial email, prohibit false and misleading representations, prohibit the collection of personal information, impose liability for abuses, and control other abusive practices such as identity theft, phishing, and spyware. The CRTC, the Privacy Commissioner, and the Competition Bureau have been given additional powers under the *Act* to investigate, regulate, and provide remedies. It is clear that the *Act* goes further than the simple control of "spam," but it remains to be seen just how effective this type of regulation will be. Note as well that the Canadian Bar Association has argued that the *Act* goes too far in interfering with the *Charter* protection of free speech.

After years of consultation, Bill C-11 was finally passed in June, 2012.[21] This is an amendment to the *Copyright Act*, intended to control downloading of music, games, movies, and other forms of information and data. This statute has significant impact on all those involved in the internet and was discussed in some detail in Chapter 9.

Of course, laws in both provincial and federal jurisdictions are being applied to internet transactions where appropriate as the following case illustrates.

---

[18]BMG *Canada Inc. v. Doe*, 2005 FCA 193 (CanLII); [2005] 4 C.F. 81; (2005), 252 D.L.R. (4th) 342 (FCA).
[19]*eBay Canada Ltd. v. Canada (National Revenue)*, 2008 FCA 348 (CanLII).
[20](Anti Spam Act) S.C. 2013, c.23.
[21]Bill C-11 *Copyright Modernization Act* S.C. 2012, c.20.

## Case Summary 10.5 *Ontario College of Pharmacists v. 1724665 Ontario Inc.*
### *(Global Pharmacy Canada)*[22]

# College of Pharmacists Exercises Control Over Online Sale of Pharmaceuticals

Application for an injunction by the Ontario College of Pharmacists (Applicant/Respondent), 1724665 Ontario Inc. and RX Processing Services Inc. (Respondent/Appellant). An appeal from the Ontario Superior Court of Justice to the Court of Appeal for Ontario.

In this case an Ontario call centre was set up to handle the sale of generic prescription drugs to American consumers. Considerable corporate restructuring, designed to make sure the College did not have jurisdiction, took place when the Ontario College of Pharmacists started to investigate, but these attempts were unsuccessful. In the end, Global Pharmacy Canada operated the website and RXP operated the call centre, with both operations located in Ontario on behalf of a Belize company, taking orders and processing payment for sales made by the company in Belize to American customers. Note that RXP and Global Pharmacy Canada, although separate corporations, had the same controlling minds (major shareholders and officers). Once the order had been placed, RXP gave the order to the Belize company which then arranged it to be filled by suppliers in India who sent the prescription drugs directly to the American customers.

The Global website indicated that the service was being offered by Global Pharmacy Canada, and a maple leaf was also placed prominently on the web site. In fact, the Ontario call centre took the orders and payment, primarily by credit card, but payments by money order or cheque were also taken which were cashed in a Canadian bank. Payments were then forwarded to offices in Belize.

Canadian access to the website was blocked and no orders from Canadians were accepted.

The College was applying for an injunction to prevent Global and RXP from selling any drugs in Canada and from using the word "pharmacist" or any related term in their advertising and operation. The question was where the sale took place and whether the College had any jurisdiction to regulate the business. The court held, on appeal, that it did. The lower court found that the sale actually took place in Canada, and the Court of Appeal agreed. The court found that considering the overriding purpose of the legislation it was the substance rather than the form of the transaction that should be looked at to determine where the sale took place. Here the court had no problem determining that since the transaction took place through an Ontario company, the sale took place in Ontario; therefore, the Ontario College had jurisdiction, even though the products were not sold to Canadians. The regulatory authority related to the conduct of the parties, not to whom those products or services were offered or provided. And that conduct, the sale, took place in Canada.

Who can regulate these offshore call centres selling products to Americans is a thorny issue. In this case the courts had no problem determining that since the customers were led to believe they were dealing with a Canadian company, and since that company was sufficiently involved in the sale process, the sale could be said to have taken place in Canada for the purposes of the legislation. The Ontario College of Pharmacists had power to investigate and regulate the process and an injunction was ordered.

# INTERNATIONAL BUSINESS TRANSACTIONS                LO 4/LO 5/LO 6

Because of the borderless nature of the internet, much of what has been covered in the first part of this chapter applies to the international aspects of business law as well. What follows are issues and information relating specifically to doing business in other jurisdictions. Industry Canada is working to facilitate international business transactions and helpful information can be found on their website at www.ic.gc.ca. In addition

[22]2013 ONCA 381 (CanLII).

Import and export of goods most common

to electronic commerce, Canadian businesses can become involved in other countries in many different ways, but perhaps the most common is the import and export of goods. Strong exports indicate a strong economy; importing of goods helps to maintain positive relations with other nations. Foreign trade often requires that companies maintain a presence in the countries of trading partners and so an awareness of the laws affecting trade relationships is important for the business person. International organizations and agreements, such as the World Trade Organization (WTO) and the General Agreement on Tariffs and Trade (GATT), attempt to streamline the process, but disputes that cannot be resolved through online or personal communication will have to be resolved by the local or national courts of the jurisdiction in which the conflict arises. Businesspeople should also be aware of bilateral agreements between countries that encourage and facilitate business transactions.

A corporation's presence on foreign soil will also usually involve its intellectual property, including copyrights, patents, and trademarks. Disputes often arise where such intellectual property interests are not recognized and patents or copyrighted material is wrongfully reproduced without respect for the rights of their creator. A related offence is the practice of selling **grey market** products, which involves importing materials from another jurisdiction in violation of a local distributor's exclusive right to distribute the product. Brand-name electronic goods, watches, and fashion accessories brought in from another jurisdiction where they sell for less are examples. Often the laws in place in that foreign jurisdiction are different from ours and they either don't recognize our intellectual property interests or don't provide adequate enforcement measures. Knowing and complying with both local and Canadian policies and laws is an important consideration for international business transactions. This will include arrangements for financing, ensuring that contractual terms that limit liability are included in agreements, that adequate insurance coverage is acquired, and that a process for arbitrating disputes is clearly set out.

Protection of intellectual property serious problem

In addition to the selling and licensing of physical and intellectual products in other countries, Canadian businesses will often become involved in providing or acquiring services from other jurisdictions. This may involve call centres for banking, credit card, telephone, and other services, but may also include warehouse distribution and data storage centres, which are increasingly being located offshore. They will also become involved in activities in those other countries such as mining and resource exploration development and management. This can involve joint ventures with a business in that foreign country or setting up branch plants, local offices, or distribution facilities. Whatever forms the international business activities take, there are some common legal considerations that must be kept in mind. First, properly drawn contracts, controlling as many variables as possible that might arise when dealings between jurisdictions are involved, are a vital aspect of doing business abroad. It is vital to acquire the services of an expert in the local law as the effect of such agreements may vary between jurisdictions. Second, the parties must carefully comply with government regulations both in Canada and in the foreign jurisdiction. Expert guidance is necessary here as well. Keeping careful records, being aware of a changing political climate, and being vigilant with respect to export permits and tariff requirements are a few examples.

Governments will often become involved when the project is big enough, entering into BITs (bilateral investment treaties) and FIPAs (foreign investment and promotion agreements) designed to stabilize the investment environment for corporations doing business abroad, especially for those involved in mining and natural resources extraction in countries where the political climate is unstable. Insurance is also available from the Export Development Bank and various private companies that insure against political risks such as expropriation, government contracts that are breached, and political violence. Although expensive, such insurance may be especially attractive for smaller companies doing business abroad in unstable countries.

Bribing officials in foreign countries has become common place, and is often considered a necessary evil to help gain a more favourable status when bidding on contracts or conducting day-to-day operations in developing countries. It has landed more than one big company in serious trouble. Both Canada and the United States have been actively drawing attention to their tough anti-bribery legislation to discourage this practice. Because of investigations into the practices of such companies as the SNC Lavalin Group and accusations of bribery with respect to the building of a bridge in Bangladesh, Canadian corporations are paying more attention to the terms of COFPA (*Corruption of Foreign Public Officials Act*[23]). Under the *Act* Canada will assume jurisdiction when there is evidence of bribery committed in a foreign nation by a Canadian company. To avoid the risk of such a charge, the directors of Canadian corporations should develop an awareness of the terms of COFPA and make known to their employees and agents clear policies that reduce the possibility of infractions. Careful accounting and record keeping that would detect instances of bribery should be implemented, keeping in mind that the corporation can be held vicariously responsible for the conduct of all parties associated with its ventures abroad. Directors might also conduct periodic risk assessments especially in areas where there are higher rates of corruption.[24]

---

## Case Summary 10.6 *Her Majesty the Queen and Griffiths Energy International Inc. Court of Queen's Bench of Alberta*[25]

## Canadian Courts Enforce Anti-Corruption Legislation

In 2011 Griffith's International (GEI) pleaded guilty to charges laid under COFPA and was fined in the order of $10 million for the offenses committed during the course of developing oil and gas operations in the African Country of Chad. Officers of the company made regular contact with the Chadian Ambassador to Canada, who was located in Washington, D.C. where he also functioned as Ambassador to the U.S. and several other countries. After considerable negotiation and the development of a memorandum of understanding, the company agreed to pay the Ambassador and a number of his associates a signing bonus that grew over time from two million to $40 million. By 2011 the firm had paid out $2 million when the CEO was killed in a boating accident and new directors took over the corporation and prepared it for public offering. When they reviewed company records and became aware of the compromising transactions, a full investigation was launched that included an RCMP investigation and the pursuant charges. GEI cooperated fully in the investigation and pleaded guilty to the charges, and the penalties imposed were commensurate with the costs incurred due to the offense.

This is just one of the recent cases involving a more vigorous enforcement of the *Corruption of Foreign Public Officials Act* discussed above.

---

[23]S.C.1998, c.34.

[24]*Lawyers Weekly*, October 2011 Christine Mingie Duhaime "10 Tips on Complying with Anti-corruption Laws."

[25]www.cba.org/CBA/advocacy/PDF/Griffiths_Amended_Statement_of_Facts.pdf).

# Contracts

Contract governs all international transactions

Important to know who you are dealing with

Expert help needed to draw up agreements

Before even contemplating the terms of a contract, the importance of knowing whom you are dealing with can't be overemphasized. No amount of precision in the language in a contract can replace careful research into the reliability and reputation of the people you are dealing with, whether in Canada or in a different jurisdiction. Disputes can still arise, but at least you can be somewhat assured that you are dealing with honourable and reputable people.

Just as with any business contract, the parties must be careful to set out all the obligations and expectations of both parties. Any assumptions that these obligations are based on should be set out as well, eliminating all ambiguous language. At the outset it must be emphasized that any contract to be applied in a foreign jurisdiction must take into consideration the specialized rules or practices in that jurisdiction. For example, when dealing with a civil law jurisdiction or even some other common law jurisdictions, and especially when dealing with less sophisticated countries, the very terminology used may have different meanings. The only way to safely deal with this kind of problem is to acquire the services of a professional specializing in the law of that jurisdiction.

**Financial Reporting**    Another important provision to include in such contracts is a method to account for profits or royalties (depending on the nature of the transaction). This usually includes specifying what records must be kept by that foreign partner or customer and the method of providing access to them for your accounting department or for a specified accounting firm mutually agreed on by the parties.

**Foreign Ownership**    Where the business activity contemplated involves actually setting up a branch operation in that foreign country, incorporation in that jurisdiction is likely. Often these countries have legislation in place restricting foreign ownership of land, as well as shares or directorships in such corporations. This will likely require contractual relationships to be established with local residents who will own the land and the majority of shares and function as directors, causing more complication and risk. Of course, operating a branch business in a foreign country subjects the Canadian business to all of the laws in place in that jurisdiction and all must be complied with whether they govern the workforce, prices charged and paid, marketing practices, or environmental restrictions.

Supplementary standard-form contracts:

- Bills of lading
- Letters of credit
- Insurance

**Specialty Contracts**    Depending on the nature of the transactions, additional specialized contracts may also be involved. Examples are a bill of lading, to establish the rights and obligations of the parties and the carrier when goods are shipped through a third-party carrier; a letter of credit or other financing instrument, to ensure that the selling party is paid when the purchasing party is satisfied; and insurance, to cover the risks of the transaction. Note also that whenever common documents such as these are involved, there are standard-form contracts in place using tested terminology that are generally accepted by all parties and used exclusively. In addition, the governments of both parties often require customs declarations and invoices and other information relating to the transaction.

# Dispute Resolution

It is particularly important to include provisions in the contract setting out what will happen if things go wrong. A dispute mechanism other than the courts is usually vital and can avoid much hardship, as can clauses setting out the law of what jurisdiction is to govern the transaction and be applied in the event of a dispute. Note that the declared law does not have to be the local law of either party, but may be that of some third jurisdiction, usually chosen because it better deals with the types of transactions involved. Using the phrase "the agreement will be interpreted under the laws of Ontario" will normally determine what law will govern the transaction, and that Ontario courts would have jurisdiction to hear any dispute arising from it. Even then, that choice may be overridden by local rules or circumstances. For example, the designated court may determine that they are not the appropriate court to deal with the matter because of where parties live, where the witnesses reside, where the contract was negotiated, or where the alleged breach took place and will acquiesce to the jurisdiction of a different court in another jurisdiction. And there may be legislation in place in that other jurisdiction that simply prevents the ousting of the jurisdiction of the local court. For example, the Ontario *Consumer Protection Act* makes any attempt to limit the jurisdiction of the Ontario court in such transactions "invalid."

When a binding arbitration clause is included, the clause will require that all disputes be determined by arbitration and set out how the arbitrator is to be chosen, as well as the powers and procedures to be used. But even these clauses can be overridden where the local rules or circumstances require.

Alternate dispute resolution was discussed in Chapter 1 and online dispute resolution earlier in this chapter, but it is reviewed here because of its profound value in international transactions. All of its advantages, especially over litigation, apply to international transactions because of the lack of any court of international jurisdiction to deal with private disputes, and because of the uncertainty and risks associated with submitting to a court in a foreign jurisdiction.

Alternate dispute resolution can consist of negotiation, mediation, and arbitration. Negotiation and mediation are, of course, just as valuable in international dealings as in domestic relationships, but it is arbitration that is particularly appropriate when dealing with international disputes. The risks and potential expense and delay associated with the litigation process are amplified significantly when dealing with foreign courts. The idea, of course, is for the parties to include a provision in their contract to submit any dispute arising from the transaction to an arbitrator chosen by them, and also setting out any limits on what that arbitrator can decide and what kind of decisions and remedies can be imposed. In effect the parties create a private court designating the judge and the power of the court to resolve disputes arising between them, and local courts will usually honour such contract provisions; refusing to hear a case that should have been arbitrated. The parties then exert some control over the dispute and reduce the uncertainties, costs, and delays associated with the litigation process.

When the parties include an arbitration clause in their contract, they can determine who shall arbitrate any disputes between them. This normally makes both parties more satisfied with the outcome, no matter which side it favours. Also, they can specify an arbitrator with particular expertise in the industry or business that the transaction involves,

Important to declare what law applies

Arbitration clause can avoid litigation

Parties can control who arbitrates and arbitration process

which provides more confidence in a proper outcome. The decision may be made in a more expeditious and efficient manner when the arbitrator already has knowledge of the business or industry, and the formalities involved in a trial are avoided. Alternatively, the contract can specify that the arbitrator be chosen by the body selected to do the arbitrating; for example, the London Court of International Arbitration. Such arbitration clauses work best when the parties are essentially equal. Where one party is dominant, dictating the terms of the agreement as in consumer transactions, the inclusion of such an arbitration clause can seriously disadvantage the weaker party. The result may be to prevent litigation of a dispute and force arbitration in a jurisdiction where the rules are more favourable to the stronger party and more inconvenient to the weaker party. A customer in Alberta is not likely to dispute a problem with a purchased product where the laws of Texas apply and the arbitration must be done through a designated arbitrator in that State. The Dell Computer case discussed below is a good example.

The main advantages of arbitration are reducing risk, respecting mutual obligations and rights, and minimizing costs. Any delays can be kept to a minimum and the dispute can be less confrontational and remain confidential, all of which are valuable where the relationship will continue. There are a number of international bodies mandated to arbitrate private disputes between trading partners in different jurisdictions. The London Court of International Arbitration, the American Arbitration Association, and the International Chamber of Commerce are examples. It should be noted that the United Nations Commission on International Trade Law (UNCITRAL) has provided rules to guide such arbitrations and these bodies have adopted those rules. The British Columbia International Commercial Arbitration Centre has been operating since 1986. For information about its functions see www.BCICA.ca.

Case Summary 10.7 *Dell Computer Corp. v. Union des consommaterus*[26]

## Can Arbitration Clause Prevent Consumers' Action?

Dell computers (Respondent/Appellant), Union des consommaterus (Applicant/Respondent) in this appeal before the Supreme Court of Canada. The issue was whether the parties were restricted to arbitration of the dispute as set out in the contract.

Dell computers had a head office in Toronto and a facility in Montreal. On 4 April 2003, an error was made on their internet ordering site that stated the price of two models of handheld computers to be substantially lower than they should have been. When the error was discovered, Dell blocked orders on the site, issued a correction, and announced that they would not process any orders at the lower prices. When Olivier Dumoulin learned of the low price, he found the site blocked and used a "deep link" to get around the block and place an order. When Dell refused to honour that order he, along with a Quebec consumer group, brought this application to commence a class action against Dell. Dell opposed the application and submitted that the parties be directed to use an arbitration process as required in the order of sale contract. The contract required that all such disputes "SHALL BE RESOLVED EXCLUSIVELY AND FINALLY BY BINDING ARBITRATION ADMINISTERED BY THE NATIONAL ARBITRATION FORUM ("NAF") under its Code of Procedure. . ." located in Minneapolis, Minnesota. Despite a provision in the Quebec *Civil Code* stating that in consumer transactions the Quebec courts will have jurisdiction to hear a dispute despite an arbitration

---

[26]2007 SCC 34 (CanLII), (2007), 284 D.L.R. (4th) 577.

clause to the contrary, the Supreme Court of Canada held that the arbitration clause prevailed, the class action application should be dismissed, and the matter should be referred to arbitration.

This was done despite the inconvenience of the American process of arbitration specified in the contract. The court held that the contract did not require the dispute to be submitted to a foreign authority, but that the arbitration clause was a private agreement between the parties and the private aspect of the contract was being enforced. Note that a similar case for class action proceedings against

Dell in Ontario was successful using different legislation, and so it is not clear whether Dell will be able to hide behind this arbitration clause in their standard contract in the future.[27]

Dell's preference for its arbitration clause is easily understood when you realize that Dell is much better off if it can stop any class action suits against it and force individuals to submit their complaints to arbitration. Such actions will probably not proceed, given the minimal amount of money involved and the difficulty of dealing with a U.S. jurisdiction.

The main disadvantage to arbitration used to be the difficulty in enforcing the award. This is less of a problem today, with Canadian courts showing considerable deference to the awards of an arbitrator, whether domestic or international. Examples of several bodies specializing in the arbitration of private disputes arising within the North American Free Trade Association (NAFTA) region are the International Commercial Arbitration Centre, the Canadian Commercial Arbitration Centre (formerly the Quebec National and International Commercial Arbitration Centre), the Mediation and Arbitration Center of the Mexico City National Chamber of Commerce (CANACO), and the American Arbitration Association.

Additionally, provincial and federal legislation provide for the enforcement of such international arbitration awards pursuant to international treaties and conventions signed by Canada and many other nations. Pursuant to these agreements, arbitration awards can be submitted to the courts and will be enforced as a term of the contract using the court's enforcement facilities. It is interesting to note that in fact such international arbitration awards are now more likely to be enforceable in our courts than are the foreign judgments as discussed below. The New York Convention (the Convention on the Recognition and Enforcement of Foreign Arbitral Awards) provides for enforcement of arbitration awards in the 148 nations that are signatories. Of course, many problems can be avoided altogether by simply arranging for adequate insurance coverage to support the transactions.

*Arbitration awards enforceable in courts*

## Litigation and Jurisdiction

The principles discussed above under the heading "Jurisdiction and the Internet" relate generally to all business transactions across borders. There is no international court that has jurisdiction over private disputes between individuals or businesses. When the matter disputed involves interests in more than one country, the problem arises as to where to launch a lawsuit. Typically, the plaintiff will bring an action in his or her jurisdiction and an application will then be brought by the defendant to have that court declare that it does not have the jurisdiction to deal with it. This is referred to as an application for an

*Right of a court to hear action may be challenged*

---

[27]*Griffin v. Dell Canada Inc.*, 2009 CanLII 3557 (ON SC).

| **Table 10.1** Factors Determining Jurisdiction |
| :--- |
| 1. Where was the contract formed? |
| 2. Where was it to be performed? |
| 3. Where do the parties (and witnesses) reside? |
| 4. Where did the problem occur? |
| 5. Where are the goods or property located? |
| 6. Does the choice by either party benefit the stronger? |
| 7. Which jurisdiction is most closely connected? |

order of *forum non conveniens* but a court is often reluctant to surrender jurisdiction in such matters. Note that the stated choice of law or jurisdiction in the contract is most likely to be overruled where it is clear that one party is stronger than the other and the choice of law benefits one at the expense of the other. Such abuse is most often found in consumer transactions. Table 10.1 lists the questions the court will consider before determining whether it has jurisdiction.

Many jurisdictions are tackling these problems through statutory enactment. For instance, British Columbia has passed legislation stating how the jurisdiction of British Columbia courts is to be determined.[28] Basically, the legislation follows a Supreme Court of Canada decision and recommendations by the Uniform Law Conference of Canada to simplify the process of determining when the local courts have jurisdiction.[29] The test is "**territorial competence**," the term replacing more involved and vague terminology found in the common law.

*Legislation replaces common law in determining jurisdiction of court*

Essentially, British Columbia courts will have territorial competence or jurisdiction where there is a close connection between the province and the facts giving rise to the case or where 1) a party being sued has agreed that the court will have jurisdiction; 2) the party has attorned (submitted) to that jurisdiction; or 3) he or she is ordinarily resident in British Columbia. Ordinary residence for a corporation may include having an office or other place of business in British Columbia or managing its business from a location in that province. Note that the court will have territorial competence if one of these factors is present regardless of what the parties have agreed. In a tort action the British Columbia court has jurisdiction when the tort was committed in British Columbia or when the defendant resides in that province. Several other provinces, including Saskatchewan and Nova Scotia, have passed similar legislation. Given the Supreme Court of Canada decision referred to above, this indicates the most likely future direction for all provinces. An important feature of the *Act* allows the court to transfer an action started in British Columbia to a court in another jurisdiction where it is convenient to do so, thus eliminating the problem of the plaintiff having to start all over again.

*Legislation allows transfer of the action*

---

[28]*Court Jurisdiction and Proceedings Transfer Act*, S.B.C. 2003, c. 28.
[29]*Morguard Investments Ltd. v. De Savoye*, [1990] 3 SCR 1077, 1990 CanLII 29 (SCC).

# When Will a Canadian Court Take Jurisdiction?

Van Breda (Plaintiff), Club Resorts (Defendant) at the Court of Appeal for Ontario. Club Resorts appealed that decision to the Supreme Court of Canada.

The court in Van Breda ruled on two unrelated actions involving lawsuits that stemmed from incidents in Cuba involving tourists who booked their travel packages in Ontario.

Morgan Van Breda suffered injuries while on vacation in Cuba in 2003 that rendered her a paraplegic. Claude Charron drowned while scuba diving during a 2002 vacation in Cuba. In both cases, Club Resorts Ltd., which is incorporated in the Cayman Islands, managed the hotels where the accidents occurred.

Club Resorts argued that Ontario courts lacked jurisdiction and that a court in Cuba would be a more appropriate forum. The Supreme Court upheld the decision of the Court of Appeal for Ontario that both cases should proceed in Ontario. Justice Louis LeBel wrote:

"These appeals raise broad issues about the fundamental principles of the conflict of laws as this branch of the law has traditionally been known in the common law, or 'private international law,' as it is often called now."

For a trial court to assume jurisdiction, some of the determining factors include whether a defendant is a resident or carries on a business in the province, whether the tort was committed in the province, or whether a contract connected with the dispute was made in the province. In both of these cases the Ontario Court had jurisdiction on the basis that the contracts were entered into in Ontario and the defendant carried on business in that province.

Still, the Ontario Court can surrender its jurisdiction if it appropriate to do so on the basis of *forum non conveniens*. Here the burden was on the defendants to show that Cuba was a more appropriate place to hear the action and they failed to do so. It was clear that a trial in Cuba would present serious difficulties to the plaintiffs and it would be a far greater burden on them to bring an action there.

This principal was applied in *Colavecchia v. The Berkeley Hotel*.[31] Sandro Colavecchia and Christene De Gasperis arranged their vacation in the United Kingdom. They made reservations online to stay at the Berkley hotel, and Christene arranged payment through her Toronto Dominion Bank Visa card reward points program. The day after their arrival Sandro slipped in the bathroom and was seriously injured causing them to return to Ontario the next day. This action was brought in Ontario seeking damages from the Berkley Hotel for the injuries and resulting loss of income. The hotel challenged the jurisdiction of the Ontario court which agreed that this was an inappropriate jurisdiction to hear the matter and refused to consider the claim. Here there was no jurisdiction in the first place. The contract was made when the plaintiffs checked into the hotel in London, the tort took place in London, the defendant did no business in Ontario and did not reside there. The only connection with Ontario was that was where the plaintiffs resided and where treatment was obtained, neither of which establish a sufficient connection with the province to create jurisdiction. The court also observed that had jurisdiction been established the action still would have been dismissed on the basis of *forum non conveniens*; the United Kingdom being a more appropriate location to bring the action.

**Enforcement**    Once the judgment has been obtained, there remains the problem of enforcing it. That is not a serious difficulty where the losing party has assets in the jurisdiction where the judgment was rendered. The judgment can be enforced against those assets like any other judgment. The problem arises when the party obtaining the judgment from a court in one jurisdiction wants to enforce it in another. At the outset, a court in one jurisdiction simply does not have the power to make an order enforceable in

---

[30][2012] 1 SCR 572, 2012 SCC 17 (CanLII).

[31]2012 ONSC 4747 (CanLII).

**Foreign courts will enforce a judgment if reciprocal enforcement agreement in place**

another. The result is that such an order will only be effective in that other jurisdiction if a court in that jurisdiction adopts it. This is true even between provinces, and a receivership order from an Ontario court, for example, will have no effect in Alberta. To seize assets in Alberta, the Alberta court must adopt the Ontario order. While this is commonly done in common law jurisdictions, it is often a serious problem when dealing with foreign jurisdictions, especially in developing countries. Again, there are conventions between nations, provinces, and states to solve this problem, and most provinces and many states in the United States and countries such as Australia have reciprocating enforcement statutes allowing the judgment or order of one jurisdiction to be enforced in another as if it were an order of that court. If there is no such reciprocating enforcement agreement in place, the person wanting to enforce the order in another jurisdiction will have to start all over, suing on the judgment in that other state to get at the assets of the debtor. These orders are normally restricted to defined monetary claims, although there is a growing willingness for Canadian courts to enforce non-monetary orders such as injunctions.

---

## Case Summary 10.9 *Disney Enterprises Inc. v. Click Enterprises Inc.*[32]

## Can Canadian Court Enforce U.S. Judgment?

Disney Enterprises (Applicant), Click Enterprises and Phillip Evans (Respondents) in this application to enforce a New York court judgment brought in the Ontario Superior Court of Justice.

Phillip Evans, through Click Enterprises, operated a software and internet business in Ontario to facilitate the illegal copying and downloading of movies. Disney Enterprises Ltd., a movie producer, brought an action against Click in New York State. After being personally served, Evans and Click did not defend the action and in a default judgment were found to be acting illegally and ordered to pay damages of US$468 442.17. It is this judgment that the Ontario court is being asked to enforce against Click and Evans personally. As a matter of policy the Ontario

court will enforce a New York judgment if that court had the jurisdiction to hear the matter in the first place. That question of jurisdiction is determined on the basis of whether there was a real and substantial connection between the conduct complained of and the state. In this case the services were provided to residents in New York State and payments were made to the defendants. Click's involvement in the United States was not passive, but consisted of tendering its products and selling directly to residents in that state, making a profit and being paid for its services in the United States. This created sufficient connection with that state and the Ontario court ordered the enforcement of the New York judgment.

---

**Difficult to enforce a court order in another jurisdiction**

Most foreign jurisdictions will recognize the validity of a judgment of a Canadian court, but the process of suing on that judgment is more involved, with many more pitfalls and greater expense than simply registering that judgment and enforcing it as is done in a reciprocating state. Proof that the debtor has actually been properly served in such an action is often a problem and it is common practice for an absconding debtor who is trying to escape his obligations to move to a jurisdiction where there is no reciprocating enforcement agreement and then avoid being served. Such tactics can be overcome, but the process is delayed and made more expensive and often is just not worth the trouble.

---

[32]2006 Can LII 10213 (ON SC); 2006, 267D.L.R. (4th) 291.

Finally, it should also be noted that the awards of internationally recognized arbitrators can also be enforced by filing them with a local court in the same way as a foreign judgment. In fact, as discussed above, they are often easier to enforce because there are more comprehensive agreements and conventions between nations in place allowing for such enforcement.

*Courts more likely to enforce arbitration award*

**Defences**    When suing on a foreign judgment there are many defences that can be raised to prevent its enforcement. A problem with process, such as improper service or a failure to allow a party to give evidence, may be fatal to the action. When laws are different in the foreign jurisdiction where you wish to enforce the judgment, it can also pose an insurmountable difficulty. That country may not enforce a judgment based on a legal principle that it does not recognize. For instance, if a judgment is based on the breach of a non-competition clause in a contract for the sale of a business, and that country does not allow such a restriction on competition, it is not likely to enforce the judgment or order.

*Judgment difficult to enforce where laws are different*

---

## Case Summary 10.10 *Yugraneft Corp. v. Rexx Management Corp.*[33]

## Does Alberta *Limitation Act* Apply to a Foreign Arbitration Award?

Yugraneft Corp. (Plaintiff/Appellant), Rexx Management Corp. (Defendant/Respondent) in this appeal in the Supreme Court of Canada. (There were also a number of groups specifically concerned with ADR that were interveners.)

The defendant contracted with the plaintiff, a Russian company, to supply certain oil production equipment, but a dispute arose that was arbitrated by a Russian arbitration tribunal as provided in the contract (the International Commercial Arbitration Court at the Chamber of Commerce and Industry of the Russian Federation). That arbitrator found against the Alberta company and ordered it to pay the Russian company US$952 614.43. This arbitration award was presented before the Alberta court for its enforcement against the defendant. Nothing in the arbitration award nor in any of the treaties or agreements involved stated that the Alberta *Limitation Act*[34] or any other limitation provision applied, and the issue before the court was to determine whether in this case the provisions of the Alberta *Act* applied to the arbitration award.

The Supreme Court of Canada in this decision has made it clear that the treaties and rules involved require that the award be enforced "in accordance with the rules of procedure of the territory where the award is relied upon." As a result the Court decided, "Alberta need only provide foreign awards with treatment as generous as that provided to domestic awards rendered in Alberta." Any local arbitration award would be subject to a two-year limitation period after which it could not be enforced. This Russian award was subject to the same limitation, and since it was beyond that time limit, it could not be enforced.

The case illustrates the flexibility of such arbitration awards and how they can be enforced in most jurisdictions in the world, as well as the operation of the special treaties and rules in place that apply to them. But it also illustrates that local rules may still apply and is a reminder of the operation of the limitation rules in place in all jurisdictions, which in this case made the enforcement of the award impossible where the time limitation had run out.

---

[33]2010 SCC 19, [2010] 1 SCR 649, 2010 SCC 19 (CanLII).
[34]*Limitations Act*, R.S.A. 2000, c L-12.

## LO 7/LO 8  GOVERNMENT REGULATIONS AND TREATIES

### International Treaties

From the above discussion and from prior chapters it should be clear that there are a number of international treaties and conventions that Canada is party to that either directly or indirectly affect the transactions carried on between business people in different countries. For example, as noted in Chapter 9, Canada has adopted the World Trade Organization (WTO) copyright protections and the Bern and Rome conventions with respect to copyright, with the result that rights of copyright holders in other countries that are signatories to those conventions are recognized here, and in turn Canadian copyright holders have rights to protection in those countries as well. Canada also has accepted the United Nations Convention on Contracts for the International Sale of Goods, and statutes have been implemented at both the federal and provincial levels[35] declaring the convention to be law in those jurisdictions. This requires that each province pass its own version of the *International Sale of Goods Contracts Convention Act*, and like the regular sale of goods acts discussed in Chapter 5, the provincial acts supply missing terms into contracts between businesses for the sale of goods across borders. Again, like the normal sale of goods acts, when the parties include terms in their agreements that are inconsistent with the terms of the provincial act, the contract terms will override the provisions of the provincial act.

*Provinces have enacted versions of the international sale of goods act*

These acts apply to consumer goods, to goods sold by auction, to securities, to ships and aircraft, and even to electricity sold across boarders. The *International Sale of Goods Contracts Convention Act* sets out how and when the contract is formed, who bears the risk and when it is transferred, and the remedies available in the event of breach. To facilitate this *Act* and the transactions taking place that are covered by it, standardized definitions and rules of interpretation have been developed to make the interpretation of such contracts clearer and thus avoid disputes. When disputes do arise, these rules make their resolution much simpler. The definitions and rules are called Incoterms® (International Commercial Terms) and are used worldwide in contracts for the sale of goods. Recently they have been extended (where applicable) to domestic contracts as well.

Perhaps the most important consequence of international treaties is the encouragement of free trade between nations. These agreements reduce or eliminate tariffs and duties that are usually imposed by a nation to protect their own industries. Canada was an early signatory to GATT(General Agreement on Tariffs and Trade), which was designed to promote fair trade, encourage balanced competition, and prohibit or control abusive practices.

*GATT reduces trade barriers*

GATT required that a member grant all other members the same tariff advantage as the lowest tariff they charged on similar goods from any nations. This was called **most favoured nation status**. The agreement also required that goods that were imported into the country from a member state had to be treated the same as domestic goods, with no special requirements or restrictions.

*WTO expands on GATT*

GATT has been incorporated into the WTO (World Trade Organization), whose objectives are the same: to reduce trade barriers, thus encouraging international trade; to

---

[35]United Nations, "United Nations Convention on Contracts for the International Sale of Goods (1980)"; *International Sale of Goods Contracts Convention Act*, S.C. 1991, c. 13, and for example *International Sale of Goods Act*, RSBC 1996, c 236.

foster cooperation; and to contribute to the process of globalization generally. The WTO goes further than GATT in that it is an organization of countries rather than just an agreement between them. It adds a dispute resolution process, and while GATT was limited to the trade of goods, the WTO covers subjects beyond goods, including financial and other services and intellectual property. GATT started as a negotiated agreement between 23 contracting parties, but the WTO is an organization now consisting of 160 member countries as of June 2014.

**Continental Treaties**    In addition to these world organizations, Canada is also a participant in more localized trade treaties, such as NAFTA (North American Free Trade Agreement). NAFTA is an agreement between Canada, the United States, and Mexico, and is designed to promote easier trade relations between the three countries. It eliminates trade barriers in the form of tariffs and duties as much as possible, and promotes free trade between the three countries. The agreement expands on the WTO agreement between these three countries, and most duties and tariffs have been or are being removed on goods and services traded between them. This free trade is extended to allow some professionals greater access to the other nations as well, allowing them to move more freely and practice their profession in the three countries. There are also environmental protection provisions and labour standards included in the agreement. NAFTA also provides for a dispute resolution mechanism. There is a movement to admit other countries into NAFTA, and so we are likely to see something like a North and South American free trade agreement in the not-too-distant future.

NAFTA creates free trade zone between Canada, the United States, and Mexico

NAFTA includes dispute resolution mechanism

Note that these agreements are very complex and this discussion only indicates the basic features; in no way is it an attempt at a comprehensive summary or critical analysis. When dealing with NAFTA, the WTO, or any other of the many treaties and conventions that may affect your business transaction, there is no substitute for specific advice from a professional such as the advisors at Industry Canada, or the Canadian Border Services Agency, as well as private services such as customs brokers and freight forwarders. The Canadian government provides information on the treaties to which Canada is a signatory at www.treaty-accord.gc.ca.

Sometimes regulations in place in other countries, especially the United States, will have an impact in this country. For example, ever-evolving global warming initiatives designed to reduce harmful emissions are being set out in international protocols, and the resulting national regulations need to be taken into consideration when operating a business abroad. There is also a growing movement to impose liability on domestic companies and individuals for human rights violations that take place in their operations abroad. For example, an action was brought in Ontario against Copper Masa and its directors and the Toronto Stock Exchange for human rights abuses that the company allegedly committed against workers at their copper mining operation in Ecuador. (The action was dismissed as not disclosing a valid cause of action and that decision was upheld by the Court of Appeal for Ontario.)[36] There is considerable pressure on governments to bring in legislation to control such abuses and on security regulators to impose audit and reporting requirements on companies with respect to their foreign operations.

---

[36]*Piedra v. Copper Mesa Mining Corporation*, 2011 ONCA 191 (CanLII).

# Canadian Regulations

World trade negotiations generally deal with such concerns as free trade between countries, eliminating trade barriers, prohibiting dumping of goods, protecting lower-income economies, allowing for sustainable use of natural resources, and protecting the environment. When Canada subscribes to such international agreements, they commit to the regulations imposed by trading partners and expect that other countries will do the same.

The Government of Canada has imposed a considerable body of regulations that must be adhered to when doing business between countries. In this final section of the text we will look at a few of the statutes in place in this country designed to regulate businesses carrying on their business across borders.

Canada imposes few restrictions on exports

**Exports**    There are only a few federal statutes that affect the export of Canadian products to other countries. There are controls in place that are mainly concerned with security and anti-terrorism measures, the laundering of money, and the avoidance of taxes. In addition, the *Export and Import Permits Act*[37] empowers the federal government to restrict certain exports to specific countries. The government department involved (Foreign Affairs and International Trade Canada now called Foreign Affairs, Trade and Development Canada) manages several lists that set out certain countries to which some exports are restricted. If the specified goods are to be exported to one of these designated countries, a permit must be obtained from that body. There are restrictions on the export of certain strategic materials such as weapons and sophisticated computer technology, as well as on the trade of exotic and threatened species, but these are relatively insignificant restrictions on exports.

There are also a number of statutes regulating specific goods or practices, such as the *Softwood Lumber Products Export Charge Act (2006)*,[38] the *Export and Import of Rough Diamonds Act*,[39] the *Cultural Property Export and Import Act*,[40] and the *Corruption of Foreign Public Officials Act*.[41]

The main problem for Canadian businesses involved in exporting is to overcome the restrictions imposed on them by the importing nation, including significant tariffs and duties. Canada is essentially an exporting nation, which is why international trade conventions and organizations like NAFTA and the WTO are so important to us. They are very helpful in removing the roadblocks that have historically restricted the export of our goods into other countries. One of the main functions of the various government agencies operating at home and abroad is to support Canadian businesses, helping them to develop markets, to expand their businesses, and to otherwise smooth the road for companies doing business in foreign countries. This involves everything from arranging trade missions by government officials and business leaders to helping to resolve individual problems by direct intervention with foreign officials. Export Development Canada (EDC.ca) also assists and encourages foreign trade by offering a wide range of protective services to reduce many of the risks associated with foreign business transactions. In addition, the

---

[37]R.S.C. 1985, c. E-19.
[38]S.C. 2006, c. 13.
[39]S.C. 2002, c. 25.
[40]R.S.C. 1985, c. C-51.
[41]S.C. 1998, c. 34.

federal government departments of Foreign Affairs, Trade and Development Canada, as well as Industry Canada, offer services that assist corporations doing business in Canada and abroad. These services range from advice on what regulations apply to various activities in Canada and to best practices for Canadians doing business in foreign countries. The services offered by these bodies are invaluable to any business and it is recommended that you familiarize yourself with them and the services they offer. The website for Industry Canada is www.ic.gc.ca and for Foreign Affairs, Trade and Development Canada is www.international.gc.ca.

Of course, a good understanding and careful compliance with labeling, content, and other product requirements in the destination jurisdiction is also necessary. For example, the European Union has imposed important new regulations with respect to the importation of chemicals, requiring registration and further information under REACH (Registration, Evaluation, Authorization, and Restriction of Chemicals) that exporters must now comply with. It is also important to note that the growing practice of laundering money through international trade (money that was obtained in various criminal enterprises) has forced governments to expand their investigation activities to this area. Such money laundering can take place by over- or undercharging for the services or goods supplied, by issuing multiple invoices for those services, or by falsely describing the goods or services that are supplied.

**Imports**   Import of goods is regulated in Canada primarily by the *Customs Act*.[42] The *Customs Act* empowers customs officials (the Canadian Border Services Agency, CBSA) to enforce various regulations that restrict what can be imported or to impose duties of varying amounts on those goods. CBSA officials have significant enforcement powers that may lead to confiscated goods and the imposition of penalties for failure to properly comply with the declaration permit and duty regulations. Canada, the United States, and other developed countries all have statutes in place preventing the sale of products manufactured in other countries that unfairly compete with products manufactured in their own, either because of subsidies, unusually low wages, or simply because the foreign manufacturer is selling below cost to get rid of excess production. This is called **dumping**, and in Canada extra duties are imposed under the *Special Import Measures Act*[43] to overcome the unfair advantage. In addition, the *Excise Act (2001)*[44] creates special procedures requiring licensing, permits, and duties for the import of beer, wine, and spirits.

As mentioned above, the WTO and NAFTA give goods imported from nations associated with these treaties special status, with generally lower or no tariffs imposed, but the application of the regulations to actual imports can be very complex. These agreements have force in Canada under the *North American Free Trade Agreement Implementation Act*[45] and the *World Trade Organization Agreement Implementation Act*.[46] There are also a number of special bilateral agreements that Canada has implemented giving certain developing nations, such as Costa Rica, favoured trading status.

Canadian government agencies assist export process

CBSA officials have extensive powers

Practice of dumping controlled

NAFTA and free trade reduces regulation of imports

[42]R.S.C. 1985, c. 1 (2nd Supp).
[43]R.S.C. 1985, c. S-15.
[44]S.C. 2002, c. 22.
[45]S.C. 1993, c. 44.
[46]S.C. 1994, c. 47.

Restrictions on the import of
dangerous, hazardous, and
environmentally sensitive goods

As mentioned above, under the *Export and Import Permits Act*,[47] certain countries are put on a list to which exports are restricted. The *Act* also restricts imports coming from these listed countries. There are also restrictions on the import of hazardous products and those posing a health risk, as well as products that are generally prohibited, such as certain types of weapons, exotic and threatened animals or products made from these animals, and products from other threatened species such as exotic plants and wood products. The point is that there is a veritable forest of regulations potentially affecting any business that imports products or services into this country, and a business doing so must determine ahead of time just what duties and permits are necessary given the foreign country involved and the product to be imported. When exporting goods or services or when developing resources outside of Canada it would be wise to first go to the Foreign Affairs and International Trade Canada website discussed above and access its very extensive services and information.

Finally, it should be noted that Canada has recently amended the *Competition Act* so that it now has the world's most comprehensive restrictions on the creation and operation of cartels. Where a person is found guilty of agreeing to fix prices, control markets, or restrict output, he or she can be imprisoned for up to 14 years and/or face fines of up to $25 million.[48]

## Extraterritorial Reach

Some foreign governments attempt
to apply their regulations beyond
their borders

Some counties, particularly the United States, have enacted laws that attempt to work extraterritorially. An important example of U.S. legislation that has an effect extraterritorially is the *Patriot Act*,[49] along with sections of the *Homeland Security Act*.[50] passed in reaction to the 9/11 terrorist attack. The *Foreign Extraterritorial Measures Act*[51] is designed to thwart the operation of U.S. laws that attempt to punish Canadian businesses dealing with countries such as Cuba. Such trade is prohibited by the U.S. but permitted by Canada. Other examples of retaliatory legislation have been passed in Canada, but these are generally ineffective because Canada is primarily an exporting nation and these retaliatory measures generally have to be imposed on imports. Unfortunately, retaliatory measures often simply encourage more restrictions on our exports in turn. Note that Nova Scotia has enacted legislation to ensure that the extraterritorial reach of the U.S. *Patriot Act* doesn't interfere with the privacy rights and personal information of Nova Scotians.[52] The United States is not the only country passing laws with extraterritorial reach, but we are particularly vulnerable to their laws because the United States is our biggest trading partner.

Finally, it should be mentioned that sometimes conduct in Canada by Canadians that affects others in another jurisdiction can lead to liability in that other jurisdiction, as the following case illustrates.

---

[47]R.S.C. 1985, c. E-19.

[48]*Competition Act*, R.S.C. 1985, c. C-34.

[49]*Uniting and Strengthening America by Providing Appropriate Tools Required to Intercept and Obstruct Terrorism Act, 2001* (USA PATRIOT Act) Public Law 107-56, U.S. Congress.

[50]*Homeland Security Act* (HSA) (Pub.L. 107–296; 116 Stat. 2135.

[51]R.S.C. 1985, c. F-29.

[52]*Personal Information International Disclosure Protection Act*, S.N.S. 2006, c. 3.

## Case Summary 10.11 *Pakootas v. Teck Cominco Metals, Ltd.*[53]

# Does Discharge of Waste in Canada Violate U.S. Statute?

Pakootas (Plaintiff/Respondent), Teck Cominco Metals (Defendant/Appellant) in this U.S. action in the United States Court of Appeals, 9th Circuit 2006.

The Canadian company operating a smelter at Trail, British Columbia, accidentally released a large discharge of tailing material into the Columbia River, causing damage on the American side of the border. This action was brought in an American Federal Court (the 9th Circuit) claiming violation of the *Comprehensive Environmental Response Compensation and Liability Act* (CERCLA). The action was resisted by Tecko Cominco, that claimed that the *Act* should not have extraterritorial application. The action was taken to the U.S. Supreme Court, which refused to hear the matter, pointing out that this was not an extraterritorial application of the *Act* since the toxic material had been discharged into the United States and caused damage in that country. Under the *Act* the plaintiffs could seek civil penalties, and the matter was sent back to the Washington trial level court for determination. This case illustrates how careful a business, especially a mining operation, has to be not to cause pollution that escapes across a border. Not only will it be subject to Canadian law, but it will likely run afoul of American law as well.

It is interesting to note that the reverse is also true. In 2007 the American company Detroit Edison (DTE Energy Company) was charged with violating the federal *Fisheries Act* because of a practice of releasing 2000 pounds of mercury per year into the St. Clair River (*Edwards v. DTE Energy Company*). The discharge took place in the United States, but the river flows into Canada so that the damage took place in this country.

The Teck Cominco case was followed as a precedent in the Detroit Edison case and the process was allowed to be served on the American company. But before the matter could proceed further, several actions were taken to clean up the St. Clair River and the charges were withdrawn. Note that in both cases environmental activists brought the private actions as permitted by the statutes in question.

## Key Terms

**cybersquatting** (p. 320)

**domain names** (p. 319)

**dumping** (p. 341)

**electronic signatures** (p. 324)

*forum non conveniens* (p. 334)

**grey market** (p. 328)

**long-arm statutes** (p. 318)

**most favoured nation status** (p. 338)

**territorial competence** (p. 334)

## Questions for Student Review

1. How has the internet changed the nature of doing business?

2. Explain the problems with jurisdiction that arise in internet business transactions.

3. What must be demonstrated for a Canadian court to hear an action in a dispute involving an online transaction?

4. What is the danger of ignoring an action brought in a foreign jurisdiction?

5. Explain why internet defamation has become a greater potential problem compared to ordinary written or spoken defamation. What other torts can be committed on the internet?

---

[53]452 F.3d 1066 (9th Cir. 2006).

6. What sorts of opportunities does the internet provide for losing control over personal information?

7. Explain the unique problems associated with the formation of contracts over the internet and what federal and provincial governments have done to respond to these issues.

8. Explain the role played by the federal *Uniform Electronic Commerce Act* and how it relates to provincial legislation.

9. What is cybersquatting and what attempts have been made to control it?

10. What is the most appropriate means of resolving disputes over online transactions?

11. What steps should a business take to ensure that employees don't engage in inappropriate online activities while in the workplace?

12. Explain the reluctance of governments to regulate the internet's business or even criminal activities.

13. Describe some of the overlapping concerns of electronic and global commercial transactions.

14. What are some things a business person who is contracting with someone in a foreign jurisdiction should consider?

15. Outline the basic provisions that should be included in a cross-border contract.

16. What provisions should be made for dispute resolution?

17. What is the likelihood of successfully pursuing a judicial action in a foreign jurisdiction?

18. What international organizations are set up to assist in the resolution of disputes?

19. What questions will a court ask to determine whether or not to hear a matter related to an international contract dispute?

20. Explain the problems associated with enforcing a judgment in a foreign country.

21. How effective are international treaties in place to assist contracting parties?

22. Explain what statutes and organizations are in place in Canada to support international trade.

## Questions for Further Discussion

1. One of the great advantages of the internet, and one of the reasons for its tremendous growth in recent years, has been its freedom from controls and regulation. It has been a little like the Wild West, with entrepreneurs, artists, and anyone with a desire to communicate free to do so, and limited only by his or her imagination. This has led to invention and creativity, but also to abuses. The debate today relates to control and regulation of the internet and the question for discussion is whether you think that this beast should be tamed. Consider the arguments pro and con, and discuss the various ways that such controls could be imposed. Look at the jurisdictional problems, but consider also how to maintain the freewheeling nature of the internet that has contributed to so much creativity.

2. A business person who is focused on the bottom line may overlook the social impact his or her business activities have on people, particularly if they occur in a foreign country. When financial interests are put ahead of public good, the results can be devastating. What concerns should an ethical business manager have in mind when contracting with or opening a plant in a developing country? Keep in mind economic, ecological, and social impacts. How can ignorance or dismissal of these factors negatively affect the business climate in Canada? Consider some examples from recent times where highly industrialized countries have exploited the people and resources of developing countries.

3. There is always pressure on the various governments involved to renegotiate NAFTA with an eye to protecting their own interests, such as by insulating local industries from outside competition. What are the implications for Canada if we do it or if they do it? How will it affect our trading relationships? Think about the problem of dumping. Should Canada make more of an effort to protect our manufacturing and commodities interests? In your answer, consider the way the softwood lumber dispute was handled.

4. Can we depend on international treaties to regulate and control electronic and global commerce? What role should world trade organizations play in encouraging and regulating international transactions? Is this a forum in which the United Nations can play a positive role? How can economic powers be balanced between trading partners? Who should be responsible for protecting lesser powers?

5. Try drafting your own standard-form contract for a business selling a product over the internet. Think about the elements that must be present for such a contract to be binding, including how the process of offer and acceptance will be accomplished. What kind of exemption clauses would you like to include? How would you solve the jurisdiction problem? How do you think a customer might react to these provisions?

## Cases for Discussion

1. *Dentec Safety Specialists Inc. v. Degil Safety Products Inc.*, 2012 ONSC 4721 (CanLII)

Two alienated brothers operated independent businesses dealing with safety products. One (Brother A) operated through Dentec Safety Specialists Inc. and used a domain name web site Dentecsafety.com. His brother (Brother B) knowing this, intentionally registered the name Dentecsafety.ca and at that web site redirected customers to his own website degilsafety.com. This action is brought by Dentic Safety Specialists operated by the first brother (Brother A). In it he claims the actions of Degil Safety products amounted to a passing off and seeks general damages and punitive damages. Explain the arguments for both parties, what has to be established in a passing off action and the likely outcome.

2. *Easthaven, Ltd. v. Nutrisystem.com Inc.* 2001 CanLII 27992 (ON SC); (2002), 55 O.R. (3d) 334; 202 D.L.R. (4th) 560 (Ont. S.C.J.)

Easthaven, Ltd. was a company registered in Barbados with a head office in that country. It registered the domain name of "sweetsuccess.com" to further an internet sports-related business. The domain name was registered with Tucows Inc., a company incorporated in Delaware but with a head office in Toronto. Nutrisystem.com Inc. was incorporated in Pennsylvania with a head office in that state as a weight loss business with products and trademarks based on the name "Sweet Success." When they approached Easthaven about the domain name, Easthaven offered to sell it to them for US$146 250. They brought a successful action in Pennsylvania asking that court to order that the domain name "sweetsuccess.com" be transferred to them. The Pennsylvania court sent an order to Tucows to transfer the name to Nutrisystem. In the meantime, Easthaven brought this action in the Ontario court for damages against Nutrisystem and an order against Tucows to prevent the transfer of the domain name to Nutrisystem. Do you think the Ontario court should become involved? How could the matter best be handled? How would your answer be affected by the added information that before the action went to trial in Ontario, Tucows reversed their decision to transfer the domain name to Nutrisystem and put it on "Registrar Hold," meaning it could not be used by either party? In response to this, Easthaven withdrew their action against Tucows. This left Nutrisystem the sole defendant in the Ontario action.

3.  *Corlett v. Hoelker*, 2012 BCCA 355 (CanLII)

    Martha Corlett was a citizen of Canada and William Hoelker a citizen of the U.S. Before they were married the parties purchased a condominium in Vancouver. During their relationship they resided in Arizona and in Washington. The condominium was purchased with the husband's money but it was registered in both their names. After the parties separated, the wife moved into the condominium. Both parties are claiming possession of the condominium. What law should apply to the dispute and where should the action be brought?

    How would it affect your answer to know that the husband commenced an action in the U.S. for divorce and possession of the condominium and that the wife fought and participated in the action that continued for 5 years? She never challenged the jurisdiction of that court, nor claimed that B.C law should apply. Only after she lost did she bring an action in British Columbia asking that the British Columbia court apply the more friendly *Family Relations Act* and not enforce the Washington decision.

4.  *Znamensky Selekcionno-Gibridny Center LLC v. Donaldson International Livestock Ltd.*, 2010 ONCA 303 (CanLII)

    The Russian applicant agreed to purchase 8500 pigs from Donaldson, but a dispute arose with respect to the health of the pigs and the matter went to arbitration in Russia as per the contract provisions. The Canadian company refused to go to Russia and participate in the arbitration because of alleged death threats received from the Russians. The Russian arbitrator decided against Donaldson and in this application the Russian purchaser is applying to have the $1 million plus award enforced in Ontario against Donaldson. Donaldson claims that the Russian arbitration should be set aside because of the death threats and is asking that the matter be set down for trial in the Ontario court. What do you think? Was the appropriate place to bring up this argument at the Russian arbitration centre or here, in Canada?

5.  *Crookes v. Wikimedia Foundation Inc.*, [2008] B.C.J. No. 2012; *Crookes v. Newton*, 2009 BCCA 392 (CanLII); *Crookes v. Yahoo*, 2008 BCCA 165 (CanLII); see also *Crookes v. Newton*, [2011] 3 SCR 269, 2011 SCC 47 (CanLII)

    Wayne Crookes is a business person from British Columbia who is claiming he was defamed on the internet. He has named several specific individuals who were the actual defamers but also is suing Yahoo, MySpace, Wikipedia, and other intermediaries, claiming that they are responsible for the defamation because they failed to monitor their sites properly to ensure that such defamatory articles were promptly removed. For example, he claimed Yahoo refused to take down an offending site (chat room), and MySpace failed to take down a personal page containing defamatory material and allowed a link to another site containing defamatory material. How far should the liability for defamation go? Should these intermediaries also be responsible? What if they fail to take the offending item down when asked? Are there any situations where an intermediary should also be responsible for defamation?

# Glossary

## A

**abatement** a court order to reduce the rent to be paid to compensate for breach of lease by landlord

**aboriginal rights** the rights of First Nations people to special status despite the *Charter of Rights and Freedoms*

**absolute privilege** exemption from liability for defamatory statements made in some settings (such as legislatures and courts), without reference to the speaker's motives or the truth of the statement

**accord and satisfaction** an agreement to end a contractual obligation where the person benefiting provides extra consideration to satisfy the claims of the other party

**accounting** court-ordered remedy where any profits made from wrongdoing must be paid over to victim. Also, where court orders agent to pay to the principal any money or property collected on behalf of that principal

**act** parliamentary enactments (federal or provincial) having the status of law, *see* **statute** and **legislation**

**actual authority** authority given to agent expressly or by implication

**adverse possession** a right to actual possession can be acquired by non-contested use of the land over a long period of time

**affidavits** written documents containing statements of witnesses made under oath

**agency** the service an agent performs on behalf of a principal

**agent** a person representing a principal in dealings with a third party

**aggravated damages** damages awarded in a tort action where the conduct of the defendant has been exceptionally offensive; often causing unusual mental distress

**agreement of purchase and sale** a contract between parties for the purchase of real property

**anticipatory breach** repudiation of contract before performance is due

**Anton Piller order** court order to seize offending material before trial

**apparent authority** conduct of principal suggests to third party that agent has authority to act on the principal's behalf

**appearance** document filed by the defendant indicating that the action will be disputed

**appellant** the party to an action that initiates an appeal to a higher court

**arbitration** where the parties to a dispute employ the services of a third party to reach a binding decision resolving the dispute

**arrest warrant** document issued by judicial official authorizing police to arrest offender

**articles of association** sets out the procedures for governing a corporation in Nova Scotia and must be filed along with memorandum of association

**articles of incorporation** the constitution of a corporation that must be filed as part of the process of incorporation in most jurisdictions in Canada

**assault** an action that makes a person think he or she is about to be struck

**assignment** where one person transfers their rights under a contract to a third party

**assignment in bankruptcy** a voluntary transfer of assets to a trustee in bankruptcy

**assignment of book accounts** merchants temporarily transfer to a creditor the right to collect money owed to the merchant by customers as security for a loan

**attachment** under the *Personal Property Security Act* where value has been given pursuant to contract and the creditor now has a claim against assets used as security

## B

**bailee** person acquiring possession of a chattel in a bailment

**bailment** when one person takes temporary possession of chattels owned by another

**bailment for value** where possession of a chattel is temporarily transferred to another with the exchange of some consideration

**bailor** the owner giving up possession of the chattel in a bailment

**bait and switch** where a product is advertised at a low price and the purchaser is persuaded to purchase a higher priced product when the lower priced one is not available

**balance of convenience** the test used by the court in an injunction application to determine which party will be most harmed by the issuance of the injunction

**bankruptcy** process by which an insolvent person voluntarily or involuntarily transfers assets to a trustee for distribution to creditors

**bankruptcy offence** punishable wrongdoing associated with bankruptcy such as withholding information or wrongfully transferring assets

**battery** unwanted physical contact

**bid rigging** where competitors bidding on a project coordinate to determine the winning bid

**bill** proposed enactment submitted to the legislature, which once approved becomes a statute

**bill of exchange** negotiable instrument where drawer directs the drawee to payout money to a payee; drawee need not be a bank, and the instrument may be made payable in the future

**bill of lading** a receipt for goods in the care of the shipper

**bonding** a fee is paid for a bonding company to pay compensation to a third party harmed by the wrongful conduct of an employee or the failure of the company to properly perform some contractual obligation

**bonds** a share interest in the indebtedness of a corporation

**breach of contract** failure to properly perform the obligations agreed to in a contract

**broadly-held corporation** a corporation that has many shareholders and is usually publicly traded on the stock market; also called a distributing corporation in some jurisdictions

**broker** agent retained by the insured to ascertain their insurance needs and secure the necessary coverage

**building scheme** restrictions placed on all the properties in a large development

**business interruption insurance** a form of insurance to protect the insured if business is interrupted

**business patent** a new process or method of carrying on business unique enough to be considered an invention and to be patented

## C

**capacity** Necessary ingredient for a contract. The legal standing to enter into a contract which is sometimes limited due to insanity, infancy, etc.

**causation** that the injury suffered was the direct result of the conduct complained of

**cause of action** the legally recognized wrong that forms the basis for the right to sue

**certificate of indefeasible title** a certificate generated by government agency that is conclusive evidence in any court as to who owns the property as well as other interests in it

**certification** government authorization of a union to bargain collectively with an employer

**certification mark** a special mark protected under the *Trade-marks Act;* used by official agencies to indicate the quality and standard of the certified product

**charge or encumbrance** an interest in property giving a creditor a prior claim to that property, often called a lien

**chattel mortgages** where title to a chattel is transferred to a creditor as security for a debt

**chattel** tangible moveable personal property or goods

**check-off provision** employees agree to have employer deduct union dues from payroll

**cheque** a negotiable instrument; a special form of bill of exchange drawn on a bank, payable on demand

**chose in action** the thing or benefit that is transferred in an assignment; intangible personal property, such as a claim or the right to sue

**CIF** a contract term placing the responsibility for arranging and paying for the insurance and freight for goods being transported from seller to purchaser

*Civil Code* the legal system used in most of Europe based on a central code, which is a list of rules stated as broad principles of law that judges apply to the cases that come before them

**civil law** the rules that govern our personal, social, and business relations, which are enforced by one person suing another in a private or civil action. Civil law is also used to refer to the legal systems based on the civil code used in France and other countries

**class action suit** a court certifies that one action can be brought on behalf of a number of different parties who have all suffered essentially the same kind of loss arising from the same complaint

**closed shop** only workers who are already members of the union can be hired

**closely-held corporation** a corporation in which there are relatively few shareholders with restrictions on the transferability of their shares; referred to as "non-distributing corporations" in some jurisdictions

**COD** a contractual term where goods that are sold are paid for upon receipt

**co-insurer** person who pays for only partial insurance coverage, and thus is only partially compensated for any loss that takes place

**common law** the legal system developed in Great Britain based on the practice of judges following precedent embodied in prior judicial decisions

**common shares** shares in a company to which no special rights or privileges attach

**conciliation** more commonly referred to as mediation, the process where a third party acts as a go-between by making non-binding recommendations to help the parties resolve a dispute

**condition precedent** conditions under which the contractual obligations will begin; also called "subject to" clauses

**condition subsequent** conditions under which the contractual obligations will end

**conditional discharge** a bankrupt is discharged but still required to pay a specified amount to creditors, as opposed to an absolute discharge where no such conditions are imposed

**conditional sales** the seller provides credit to the purchaser, holding title until the goods are paid for

**conditions** major terms of a contract

**condominium** an arrangement for owning real property separated vertically, as with an apartment in a high rise development

**condominium corporation** a vehicle for operating a condominium development, to charge fees and administer common areas controlled by individual condominium owners

**confidential information** secret information and data with restricted access, the disclosure of which can cause harm to the business

**conflict of interest** where a decision that would benefit the individual is not in the best interests of the organization as a whole

**consensus** necessary ingredient for a contract. The terms must be clear and both parties should have a shared understanding of them. Note that the test is objective.

**consent** where the person being assaulted has previously agreed to that treatment as with surgery

**consideration** Necessary ingredient for a contract. The exchange of commitments between parties to a contract often stated as the price one is willing to pay for the promise of another

**conspiracy** where two or more individuals act together to accomplish an illegal purpose

**consumer** an individual purchasing goods or services not for resale or to be used in a business

**consumer protection** legislation designed to ensure that consumers are treated fairly in the marketplace

**contempt of court** where a person has disobeyed the rules of the court or a court order, the judge can impose punishment in the form of a fine or imprisonment

**contract** a voluntary exchange of promises or commitments between parties that are legally enforceable in our courts

**contributory negligence** a claim that the plaintiff to an action has also been negligent and contributed to his own loss

**control test** employment relationship determined by employer's power to give instructions to employee of how to do the job

**conversion** a tort where a person takes property belonging to another and uses it as his/her own (corresponds to theft in criminal law)

**cooperative** a system of property ownership where the "owners" have a shared claim in the whole building but no specific estate interest to the suite they occupy

**copyright** an author's right to control the reproduction and use of his creation

**counterclaim** a statement of claim by the defendant alleging that the plaintiff is responsible for the losses suffered and claiming for those losses

**counter-offer** a response made by an offeree making a new offer with different terms from the original offer with the effect of ending that offer

**Courts of Chancery** the separate court that developed the law of equity

**cross-examination** the practice of one party putting questions to a witness produced by the other party to a litigation. Generally more latitude is allowed in such questioning compared to direct examination

**crowd funding** an informal way for a business or other project to obtain funding from the public often pursuant to an internet plea

**cybersquatting** the practice of quickly registering a domain name so that it can be sold later to a more legitimate claimant

**D**

**damages** an amount of money that the court orders one party to pay the other in civil litigation paid by the defendant; damages usually compensate the injured party but may be punitive as well

**debentures** a share interest in the indebtedness of a corporation similar to bonds

debt financing raising funds through the borrowing of money by selling bonds or debentures or though direct loans

deceit intentional misrepresentation where one party gains an advantage over another

deed of conveyance document transferring an interest in property

defamation a published false statement to a person's detriment

default the failure to pay a financial obligation when it comes due

default judgment judgment for the plaintiff awarded by the court when the defendant fails to defend the action

defendant the party being sued by the plaintiff

democratic rights rights set out in sections 3–5 of the *Charter of Rights and Freedoms* protecting rights to vote, hold elections, and run in those elections

dependent contractor a dependent contractor, like an independent contractor, operates a separate business but provides service more like an employee of one customer and is an essential part of that customer's operations

deposit money prepaid with the provision that the funds are to be forfeited in the event of a breach

derivative action *see* representative action

description where goods are purchased on the basis of a description set out in an advertisement or on packaged materials, including all manufactured goods

direct examination the practice of a party to litigation putting questions to a witness they have produced. Generally less latitude is allowed in such questioning compared to cross-examination

directors officers voted in by shareholders to control a corporation

disability insurance insurance arrangement whereby an insurer, for a premium, provides compensation when an insured, through sickness or accident, is no longer able to work and earn an income

discharge where the bankrupt is relieved of his debts, and his assets are no longer under the control of the trustee

discharge by agreement agreement by parties to end or modify a contract

discharge by performance where a party is relieved of further obligations by properly performing their contractual obligations

dissent the right of a shareholder in some jurisdictions to have their shares purchased where decisions are made that negatively affect their position

distinguishing cases the process judges use to decide which case is the binding precedent

distinguishing guise the unique shape of a product, which can also be registered under the *Trade-marks Act*

distraint a landlord's right to seize the property of tenant for failure to pay rent

dividends payments to shareholders out of company profits

division one proposal an alternative to bankruptcy under the *Bankruptcy and Insolvency Act* giving corporations and debtors with significant debt the right to make a proposal to creditors, which if accepted and performed, will avoid bankruptcy

division two proposal an alternative to bankruptcy under the *Bankruptcy and Insolvency Act* giving individual debtors involving lesser indebtedness the right to make a proposal to creditors, which if accepted and performed will avoid bankruptcy

domain name the registered name of a website used to access that address over the internet

dominant tenement the property enjoying the benefit of the restrictive covenant imposed on another property

double ticketing this involves the practice of placing two prices on an item and the merchant charging the higher of the two

dower rights statutory protection of a spouse's interest in property

down payment an initial payment under a contract that must be returned to the purchaser in the event of a breach

due diligence doing everything reasonable to avoid the problem leading to legal liability

dumping the practice of selling goods produced in one country in another, below the cost of producing them

duress force or threat to enter into a contract

duty of care an obligation to take steps to avoid foreseeable harm; an essential element for establishing liability in the tort of negligence

duty of good faith a fiduciary duty where an agent has a duty to act in the best interests of a principal

**E**

easement the right of a person other than the owner to use a portion of private property

economic duress threat to harm an economic interest used to pressure into a contract

electronic signature any online mechanism that indicates that the person adopts or is committed to the contents of the electronic message being responded to

employee a person working for another who is told what to do and how to do it

employment insurance a government-sponsored program designed to provide a limited number of payments to an individual after his or her employment has ended

*Employment Standards Act* legislation in place in most jurisdictions setting out a number of standards and obligations that employers must provide for their employees

encryption technological mechanisms designed to protect data and information, usually involving some form of encoding so the use of a key is necessary to retrieve it

endorsement the signature on the back of a cheque of the person assuming the obligation to pay if the drawee or maker defaults; a term added to an insurance policy at some later date modifying some aspect of that policy

equality rights among the basic rights provisions in the *Canadian Charter of Rights and Freedoms*; include the right not to be discriminated against on the grounds of gender, age, religion, race, or colour, and the guarantee of equality before the law

equitable remedies remedies developed by the Courts of Chancery, including the right to an accounting, injunction, and specific performance

equity value left in an asset after subtracting what the owner owes; mortgagor retains an interest in land even after default

equity financing raising funds through the issue of additional shares

equity of redemption mortgagor retains an interest in land even after default

estate a person's right to exclusive possession of land

estoppel when a person leads another to believe a certain fact is true, for example that "A" is my agent, he cannot later deny the truthfulness of that fact

evergreening the practice of changing some component or other aspect of a patented product so that a new patent can be applied for, thus extending the protection period

executory contracts when an agreement has been made, but before there has been any performance

exemption clause a term of a contract where one party tries to limit or eliminate obligations that would otherwise be present

expressed authority the authority that the agent has been given that has been directly communicated to him by the principal

## F

**fair comment** defence available when defamatory statements are made about public figures or work put before the public

**fair hearing** a person to be affected by a decision is given an opportunity to present their side in a process where all of the rules of procedural fairness are followed including adequate notice, an opportunity to be heard, and no bias on the part of the decision-maker

**false imprisonment** holding people against their will and without lawful authority

**fee simple estate** the highest interest in land that a person can have; equivalent to ownership

**fidelity bond** insurance against an employee's wrongful conduct

**fiduciary duty** a duty to act in the best interests of others such as partners, principals, and in some circumstances employers

**fitness and quality** a requirement of the *Sale of Goods Act* imposing an obligation on the seller to ensure a certain standard of fitness and quality on the goods they sell

**fixture** something attached or affixed to the land or building becoming part of the real property

**FOB** (free on board) a term designating the point that title and responsibility for goods sold transfers to the purchaser

**foreclosure** court process ending the mortgagor's right to redeem

**forfeiture** when lease is breached, the landlord may terminate the lease and require the tenant to vacate the property

*forum non conveniens* an application to the court asking it to surrender its right to hear a matter to another more appropriate jurisdiction

**franchise** arrangements based on contracts where a smaller party (usually a corporation) exclusively agrees to provide goods or services supplied by a larger corporation to consumers

**fraud** intentional misrepresentation where one party gains an advantage over another

**fraudulent misrepresentation** where the person making the misleading statement does not believe it to be true

**frustration** some outside, unforeseen event makes the performance of the contract impossible or fundamentally different

**fundamental freedoms** the basic rights in the *Canadian Charter of Rights and Freedoms* including freedom of conscience and religion, of thought and belief, of opinion and expression, and of assembly and association

## G

**general damages** an amount of money ordered by the court to compensate for losses that are not capable of direct calculation, such as pain and suffering or loss of future earnings

**Global Compact** a United Nations–sponsored group of private and public organizations committed to the advancement of global ethical behaviour

**good title** an obligation on the seller under the *Sale of Goods Act* to convey ownership in the goods being sold.

**good-faith relationship** the obligation to act honestly in the best interests of the other party with full disclosure of all relevant information

**goods** tangible, movable personal property that can be measured and weighed; also known as chattels

**goodwill** that part of the value assigned to a business based on its reputation and continuing relationship with customers

**gratuitous bailment for the benefit of the bailee** an individual (the bailee) borrows another's property for their own use without giving consideration

**gratuitous bailment for the benefit of the bailor** an individual (the bailee) voluntarily looks after another's goods

**gratuitous promise** a one-sided promise given without any reciprocating promise in return and is not binding on the promisor

**grey market** goods imported from other countries to circumvent exclusive marketing and distribution agreements between the manufacturer and a Canadian distributor

**guarantee** a written commitment whereby a guarantor agrees to pay a debt if the debtor doesn't

## H

**holdback** person owing funds under a construction contract must retain a specified percentage to be paid at a later time

**holder in due course** an innocent third party entitled to collect on a negotiable instrument in spite of any claims of the original parties

**homestead rights** statutory protection of a spouse's interest in property

**human rights legislation** provincial and federal statutes designed to protect people from racism, sexism, and similar wrongs committed by others

## I

**implied authority** the authority of the agent that has not been directly communicated by the principal but that can be implied from the principal's conduct or statements

**independent contractor** a person working for himself who contracts to provide specific services to another

**indictable offence** serious criminal offence with a more involved procedure and more serious penalties as compared to summary conviction offences

**inducing breach of contract** encouraging someone to break his or her contract with another

**injunction** court order to stop offending conduct

**injurious falsehood** defamation with respect to another's product or business; also known as product defamation and trade slander

**innocent misrepresentation** where the person making the misleading statement believes it to be true and is not negligent in that belief

**innuendo** an implied statement that is detrimental to another

**insider information** information that can affect the value of the shares of that company that is known to directors, shareholders, and others but not generally known to the public

**insolvent** where a person is unable to pay his or her debts as they become due

**insurable interest** a real and substantial interest in specific property

**insurance agents** the agents for insurance companies who sell policies to customers

**insurance policies** contracts with insurers to provide compensation for covered losses

**intellectual property** intangible personal property in the form of ideas and creative work

**intention** Necessary ingredient for a contract. The parties should be serious and expect that legal consequences should flow from their agreement. Note that this is an objective test.

**interest dispute** disagreement about the terms to be included in a new collective agreement

**interim injunction** temporary injunction obtained before the actual trial

**invention** a new and unique machine, process, or composition of matter that is useful and can be reproduced

**invitation to treat** invitations (often advertisement) to engage in the bargaining process leading to a contract

**involuntary bailment** where someone acquires possession of the property of another unintentionally as where it is left on their property or is found

## J

**joint tenancy** shared ownership with right of survivorship

**joint ventures** two or more corporations joining together to accomplish a major project

**judgment creditor** the winner of an award of damages in a civil action

**judgment debtor** the loser in a civil action who has been ordered to pay an award of damages

**judicial sale** court ordered and supervised sale of real property, usually resulting from default

**jurisdictional dispute** a disagreement over who has authority; in the labour context, a dispute between two unions over which one should represent a group of employees, or over which union members ought to do a particular job

**just cause** valid reason to dismiss an employee without notice

**justification** defamation defence that the statement is substantially true

## L

**land registry** a system requiring all documents affecting the title of real property be kept in a land registry office available for the inspection of interested parties

**land titles system** registration system that guarantees title to real property

**law** the definition of law used in this text is the rules enforceable in court or by other government agencies

**law of equity** legal principles developed in Courts of Chancery to relieve the harshness of the common law

**leasehold estate** an interest in land giving the tenant the right to exclusive possession for a limited specified time

**legal rights** among the basic rights provisions in the *Canadian Charter of Rights and Freedoms* (sections 7–14); includes rights such as the right to life, liberty, and security of

the person and security against unreasonable search and seizure and arbitrary imprisonment and detention

**legality** necessary ingredient for a contract. Both the consideration and the object of the contract should not be prohibited by law and not be against public policy

**legislation** parliamentary enactments (federal or provincial) having the status of law, *see* **statute** and **act**

**letters patent** method of incorporating granted by government when a company is set up in some jurisdictions in Canada

**liability** where one party to an action bears an obligation to provide some remedy to another

**liability insurance** provides coverage for wrongs committed by self or employees

**libel** the written form of a defamatory statement

**licence** a non-exclusive right to use property; permission to use another's land that can be revoked

**liens** interests in property giving a creditor a prior claim to that property, often called a charge

**lienfund** where a person owing funds under a construction contract must retain a specified percentage to be paid at a later time

**life estate** an interest in land ending at death

**life insurance** coverage providing compensation upon the death of the insured party

**limited liability** where a person is liable to lose only what he or she has invested in the business and is not responsible for other debts or obligations of the business

**limited liability partnership** a new and unique form of partnership where each individual "limited liability partner" faces unlimited liability only for his own wrongful acts and not for the wrongful acts of his partners

**liquidated damages** a contractual provision requiring party

responsible for a breach to pay a stated amount

**lockout** employer prevents employees from working

**long-arm statutes** where a jurisdiction has passed legislation giving them the right to take action against offending conduct taking place outside of that state or province

## M

**manufacturer's warranty** a term of the sales contract limiting a seller's or manufacturer's obligations with respect to a product beyond what they would otherwise be under the *Sale of Goods Act*

**mediation** sometimes referred to as conciliation, the process where a third party acts as a go-between by making non-binding recommendations to help the parties resolve a dispute

**memorandum of association** constitution of a corporation in a registration jurisdiction that is filed as part of the incorporation process; now only used in Nova Scotia

**minority language education rights** the right to have English or French, as the case may be, taught in the schools or made available to speakers of those languages set out in the *Charter of Rights and Freedoms*

**mistake** a misunderstanding about the nature or subject matter of an agreement that destroys consensus

**misunderstanding** when two parties to a contract have a different understanding as to the meaning of a specific provision

**mitigation** victims of a breach must make an effort to lessen the loss

**mobility rights** the right of all citizens of Canada to reside in or work in all parts of Canada as guaranteed by section 6 of the *Charter of Rights and Freedoms*

**moral rights** author's right to prohibit the copyright owner

from changing or degrading the original work

**mortgage** means of securing loans; title of property is held by the money-lender as security in some jurisdictions; in other jurisdictions, a mortgage is simply a charge against title

**mortgagee** the creditor who takes the title to the property as security

**mortgagor** the debtor who grants the mortgage on his or her property as security for a loan

**most favoured nation status** the practice of treating goods imported from such a designated country in a no-less favourable way than the most advantaged trading partner

## N

**negligence** inadvertent conduct falling below the reasonable person standard and causing injury or damage to another

**negligent misrepresentation** where the person making the misleading statement believes it to be true but has been careless in that belief

**negotiable instruments** substitutes for money or instruments of credit that bestow unique benefits; vehicles for conveniently transferring funds or advancing credit

**negotiation** the parties to the dispute directly or indirectly communicating with the object of settling that dispute

*non est factum* "It is not my act." Where a party is not bound by terms of a document because he didn't understand the nature of the document signed

**notice** the requirement that a union give a required period of advance warning to the employer of an impending strike

**notice of action** the document used in some provinces (such as Ontario) to commence a civil action

**novation** when a new contract is created by substituting a new party for one of the original parties to the original contract

## O

**offer** a tentative promise to do something if another party fulfills what the first party requests

**offer and acceptance** the party receiving an offer agrees to be bound by the terms set out in the offer

**official mark** a special mark protected under the *Trade-marks Act* to indicate an official organization has special status

**one-sided mistake** where only one of the parties makes a mistake with respect to the nature or effect of a contract; without misrepresentation, the contract will normally continue to be binding

**oppression** action brought against the directors or shareholders who have offended the rights of creditors or other shareholders

**option agreement** a subsidiary contract where some additional consideration is given to hold an offer open for later acceptance

**option to purchase** a subsidiary contract where some additional consideration is given to hold an offer open for later acceptance

**organization test** determines whether employment exists on the basis of the extent of a person's involvement in the employer's organization

## P

**paramountcy** when a matter is covered by both federal and provincial legislation and there is a conflict, the federal legislation takes precedence

**parliamentary supremacy** the primary law-making body is Parliament or the provincial legislatures in their respective jurisdictions, and statutes take priority over the common law

**parol evidence rule** court will not hear outside evidence to contradict clear contract wording

**partnership** two or more people carrying on business together with a view toward profit and without incorporation

**partnership agreement** a contract between partners setting out specific obligations and benefits between them, usually modifying certain provisions of the *Partnership Act*

**passing-off** a tort action available to prevent someone from misleading the public into thinking it is dealing with some other business or product when it is not

**past consideration** some benefit conveyed before an agreement is made; it is not valid consideration

**patent** government-granted protection giving an inventor exclusive right to profit from that invention for a specified period of time

**payment into court** the defendant estimates the true value of the claim and deposits it with the court; if the decision is for less than the deposit the plaintiff will be penalized through payment of additional costs

**perfection** registering a security or taking possession of the collateral used to secure a debt under the *Personal Property Security Act*

**periodic lease** automatically renewing tenancy; usually monthly with no specific termination date

**personal property** also known as personalty, chattels (tangible, movable things), and intangible rights called choses in action

**picketing** job action during a legal strike when employees circulate at the periphery of the jobsite to persuade people not to deal with that employer

**plaintiff** the party who initiates a civil action

**plea-bargaining** the process whereby the accused and prosecutor negotiate, usually resulting in a lesser charge being imposed in exchange for a guilty plea avoiding a trial

**pleadings** the exchange of documents (statement of claim, statement of defence, counterclaim) between plaintiff and defendant at the early stage of a civil action

**Ponzi scheme** a fraudulent investment scheme where funds invested by later investors are used to pay off earlier investors, creating a false sense of success

**post-box rule** the rule that an acceptance is effective when posted when that method of response is appropriate

**power of attorney** written authority by a principal giving an agent power to act on his behalf

**power of sale** a normal term in a mortgage agreement giving the creditor/mortgagee the power to have the property sold in the event of a default

**precedent** a prior decision made by a court of higher jurisdiction that a lower court must follow in our common law system

**predatory pricing** where a product is sold below cost to drive a competitor out of the market

**pre-emptive rights** a right given to a shareholder ensuring that in the event of a new offering of shares that shareholder will be given first refusal on enough of those shares to maintain his portion of control of the corporation

**preferred creditors** creditors that are secured so that they have a priority with respect to their claims against the debtor

**preferred shares** special shares structured to give the preferred shareholder a claim to a specified dividend each year. Normally they cannot vote unless that dividend is not paid

**premium** an amount paid by the insured to secure insurance coverage

**prescription** a right to access property acquired by non-contested use of the land over a long period of time

**presumption** a condition or set of facts assumed to be true in the absence of any evidence to the contrary

**price fixing** where competitors agree on a fixed price for selling their services or merchandise thus keeping prices high and defeating competition

**private law** the rules that govern our personal, social, and business relations, which are enforced by one person suing another in a private or civil action

**private nuisance** a tort action protecting against the use of property in such a way that it interferes with a neighbour's enjoyment of theirs

**privative clause** terms in a statute that attempt to restrict the right of judicial review

**privity of contract** contract terms apply only to the actual parties to the contract

**procedural law** determines how the substantive laws will be enforced; the rules governing arrest and criminal investigation, pre-trial and court processes in both criminal and civil cases are examples; law can also be distinguished by its public or private function

**product defamation** false statement with respect to another's product or business; also known as injurious falsehood and trade slander

**professional liability** a person who puts himself forward as an expert must live up to the standard expected of a reasonable expert

**profit** the net proceeds of the business after expenses have been deducted

**profit à prendre** contracts to take resources off the land

**progressive discipline** the process using escalating measures to record failings and encourage, help, reprimand, and discipline that employee, eventually leading to rehabilitation or termination

**promissory estoppel** when a gratuitous promise to do something in the future causes a person to incur an expense, the promissor may be prevented from acting in a way inconsistent with that promise; also known as equitable estoppel

**promissory note** a type of negotiable instrument where a maker promises to pay the amount stated on the instrument to a payee

**proposed trademark** the *Trademarks Act* permits an application to register a trademark that has not been used yet but will be in the future

**prospectus** a document issued by a corporation disclosing information to the public with respect to its financial position and prospects

**provincial offence** offenses under provincial statutes or regulations that impose penalties but do not qualify as criminal law

**proxy** where one shareholder gives authority to someone else to vote that share on their behalf

**public law** rules with respect to government (constitutional law) and our relations with government, including criminal law, human rights, and regulation

**punitive damages** monetary payment ordered by the court designed to punish the wrongdoer rather than compensate the victim; also known as exemplary damages

## Q

**qualified privilege** exemption from liability for defamatory statements made pursuant to a duty or special interest, so long as the statement was made honestly, without malice, and circulated only to those having a right to know

*quantum meruit* (as much as is deserved) reasonable price paid for requested services where there is no actual contractual obligation; sometimes called a quasi-contract

**quasi-criminal offences** offences under provincial legislation or federal regulatory statutes that impose penalties but do not qualify as criminal law

**questions of fact** just what happened, including events, injuries, damage, and consequences

**questions of law** what legal rules are applied to the situation

**quiet enjoyment** landlord must ensure that nothing interferes with tenant's normal use of the property

**quiet possession** goods must be usable by the purchaser in the way normally intended

## R

**Rand Formula** option in collective agreement enabling employees to retain the right not to join the union, but they are still required to pay union dues

**ratification** majority agrees with terms of collective bargain; principal confirms a contract entered into by his agent

**real property** land, buildings, and fixtures attached to land or buildings

**reasonable foreseeability test** what a prudent and careful person would be expected to anticipate in the same circumstances as the defendant

**reasonable notice** the amount of notice that must be given in terminating an employment contract, taking into consideration the position of the employee and time served

**reasonable person test** the standard of conduct that would be expected of a careful and prudent person in the same circumstances as the defendant in a negligence action

**receiver** a person or organization appointed to take over the management of a corporation defaulting on its obligations to a creditor

**receivership** proceeding in which a receiver is appointed for a corporation that has defaulted on its obligations to a creditor to protect its assets for the creditors

**receiving order** court ordering the transfer of debtor's assets to a trustee as part of the bankruptcy process

**recognition dispute** dispute arising between unions and employers while union is being organized

**rectify** court corrects the written wording of a shared mistake in the contract

**references** an application in the form of a question posed directly to the Supreme Court by the Prime Minister as opposed to a decision of a court being appealed to the Supreme Court

**registration** a legislated requirement for incorporating a company in some jurisdictions in Canada; also the process of filing a form to perfect a security under the *Personal Property Security Act*

**regulations** supplementary rules passed under the authority of a statute and having the status of law

**reinsurance** where an insurance company takes out insurance with another company to cover the risk they face if they are called upon to pay out on the insurance coverage they have issued

**relief against forfeiture** when a landlord retakes a property for failure to pay rent prior to the end of the lease term, the tenant can pay the arrears and apply in the court to have the lease reinstated

**remainder** third party with the right to the title of real property (fee simple) after the death of a life tenant

**remote** where the damages are too far removed from the original negligent act; in contract, where the damages could not have been reasonably foreseen by the breaching party when the agreement was made

**representative action** the right of shareholders to sue the directors on behalf of an injured corporation; sometimes called a derivative action

**repudiation** one party indicates to the other that they will not perform their contractual obligations

**rescission** returning the parties to the position they were in before the contract

**respondent** the party who responds to the appeal launched by the appellant

**restrictive covenant** seller imposes restrictions on what the purchaser can use the land for; in employment law, it is a commitment not to work in a certain industry or geographical area for a designated period of time

**reverse engineering** the process of analyzing a completed product and from that determining the process by which it was created

**reversion** upon death of life tenant, the title to real property reverts to original owner

**revocation** withdrawal of an offer before acceptance (must be communicated to the offeree)

**rider** a term added to a standard-form insurance contract usually arranging for extra or specialized coverage

**right of way** type of easement that allows the crossing of another's land

**rights dispute** disagreement about the meaning of a term or the enforcement of a collective agreement

**royalties** the payment publishers pay authors for the use and sale of their creations

**rule of law** the requirement that everyone in Canada is subject to the law and must obey it; government officials must be able to point to some law authorizing them to make the decision they have made affecting the rights of others

## S

**salvage** that portion of goods or property which has been saved or remains after a casualty such as fire or other loss

**sample** a chattel used to indicate to a purchaser the nature of similar goods usually to be delivered in the future; those goods must match the sample

**seal** formal mark on a document (usually an impression or wafer), which eliminates the need for consideration in contract law

second mortgage where the equity of redemption retained after title is transferred to the first mortgagee is also used as security for a loan from a second mortgagee

secured creditors creditors who have taken steps to ensure that they will be paid, usually by acquiring first claim to some property that ensures payment over other creditors

secured transactions collateral right to debt giving the creditor the right to take back the goods or intercept the debt owing used as security in the event of a default

security deposit an amount of money taken by the landlord at the outset of a tenancy to cover damages or failure to pay rent

self-defence a person can respond to an assault with as much force as is reasonable in the circumstances

separate legal person the term used to describe a corporate entity that has a legally recognized existence separate and apart from those that make it up

servient tenement the property upon which the restrictive covenant is imposed

shared mistake both parties make the same mistake, sometimes called common mistake

shareholder the investment interest or equity of a corporation is divided into units referred to as shares which are held by shareholders

slander spoken defamation

sole proprietor one person carrying on business alone, without incorporation

special damages an amount of money ordered by the court to compensate for expenses capable of actual calculation

specific performance court orders a breaching party to live up to the terms of the agreement

standard of care the test used to determine whether a person has exercised sufficient care in dealings with others to avoid being liable for the tort of negligence. The degree of care required is usually that of a reasonable person in the circumstances

standard-form contract contract where one party uses a form of contract that is the same for each transaction and not subject to negotiation

*stare decisis* a principle by which judges are required to follow the decision made in a similar case in a higher court

statement of claim the document setting out the nature of the complaint and alleged facts, which form the basis of the action served on the defendant at the beginning of the litigation process

statement of defence response to a statement of claim by the defendant setting out the alleged facts by the plaintiff and the contrary facts alleged by the defendant

statute parliamentary enactments (federal or provincial) having the status of law, *see* **legislation** and **act**

*Statute of Frauds* old English statute, a version of which is in place in most common law jurisdictions setting out the types of agreements that must be evidenced in writing to be enforceable

statutory assignment an assignment of contractual rights and benefits that meets certain specified qualifications; assignee can enforce a claim directly without involving the assignor

statutory damages a special monetary award authorized in the *Copyright Act* to compensate the victim of copyright infringement

stoppage in *transitu* seller retains the right to stop the shipment in event of default

strict liability offences regulatory offences at the provincial or federal level where the accused can be found liable even though no fault is demonstrated; where liability is imposed without any demonstration of fault (intention or falling below a standard of care)

strike unionized employees withdrawing their services from the employer

subrogated the right of insurer, upon payment, to take over the rights of the insured in relation to whoever caused the injury

substantial performance the parties have performed all but a minor aspect of the contract

substantive law establishes both the rights individuals have in society and also the limits on their conduct

summary conviction offence minor criminal offence involving a simplified procedure with less significant penalties imposed as compared to indictable offences

surety bond a commitment by a third party, such as an insurance company, to pay compensation if the company or individual on whose behalf the bond is issued fails to properly perform their contractual obligations

**T**

tenancy in common shared ownership but without the right of survivorship

tender of performance one of parties attempts to perform their contractual obligations, and where they are prevented by the other party, they are considered to have properly performed

term insurance life insurance that provides coverage for only a specific period of time and has no investment component

territorial competence the test used by the B.C. courts to determine whether they have the jurisdiction to deal with a matter brought before them that may also involve issues in another province or state

trademark a name, mark, or symbol associated with a business or product which helps to distinguish it from other businesses or products

trespass to chattels direct intentional interference causing damage to the goods of another

trespass to land entering upon another's land without permission or authority

trustee in bankruptcy licensed professionals who, for a fee, assist the debtor and creditors in the bankruptcy process, holding and otherwise dealing with that bankrupt's property for the benefit of the creditors

**U**

unconscionability when one of the parties to a transaction is under extreme disadvantage; merchants take advantage of disadvantaged customers

undisclosed principal where the identity or existence of the principal is not disclosed by the agent to the third party

undue influence a special relationship that induces a person to enter a contract to his disadvantage

unenforceable a binding contract or other obligation that the courts will not enforce, such as a contract that does not satisfy the *Statute of Frauds*

unfair labour practices practices by management or by employees in the collective bargaining process that are prohibited, such as intimidation or firing employees for their union activity

unilateral contract where an offer is made in such a way that to accept, the offeree must actually perform the act required as consideration

union shop new employees must join the union

unlimited liability where a person is liable for all of the debts and obligations of a business even to the extent of losing all personal assets

unsecured creditors (or general creditors); there is only a contract requiring a debt to be repaid, but no collateral contract giving that creditor priority with respect to some property in the event of default

## V

**vacant possession** owner has obligation to provide premises that are empty and ready for occupancy

**vicarious liability** employer is liable for the injuries caused by employees during the course of their employment

**void** not a legally binding agreement because an essential ingredient is missing; there is no contract

**voidable** there is a contract but one of the parties has the option to end it

**voluntary assumption of risk** the defence to a negligence action where the plaintiff has voluntarily put himself in harms way

## W

**warranties** minor terms of a contract

**whole life insurance** life insurance that provides ongoing coverage and includes a significant investment component

**workers' compensation** a government system set up to provide monetary compensation for someone who becomes sick or injured because of their employment

**World Intellectual Property Organization (WIPO)** an international organization set up to arbitrate disputes over the use of domain names on the internet

**writ of summons** a judicial order used to start a civil action in some jurisdictions

# Table of Statutes

*Note:* The page numbers given in parentheses at the end of each entry refer to pages in this book.

# Table of Cases

# Index